TYPES OF CONTEMPORARY DRAMA

CONTINENTAL PLAYS

VOLUME ONE

SELECTED AND EDITED BY

THOMAS H. DICKINSON

Editor, Chief Contemporary Dramatists, First, Second, and Third Series, etc.
Author, An Outline of Contemporary Drama, Contemporary Drama
of England, The Case of American Drama, etc.

HOUGHTON MIFFLIN COMPANY

BOSTON · NEW YORK · CHICAGO

DALLAS · ATLANTA · SAN FRANCISCO

The Riverside Press Cambridge

The Riverside Press

CAMBRIDGE · MASSACHUSETTS

PRINTED IN THE U.S.A.

CONTENTS

PREFACE — TYPES OF CONTEMPORARY DRAMA . . v

INTRODUCTION vii

THE POWER OF DARKNESS . . . *Leo N. Tolstoy* 1

PELLÉAS AND MÉLISANDE. . . *Maurice Maeterlinck* 83

THE WEAVERS . . . . . *Gerhart Hauptmann* 131

LIGHT-O'-LOVE . . . . . *Arthur Schnitzler* 215

FRANCESCA DA RIMINI . . . *Gabriele D'Annunzio* 267

THE CHERRY ORCHARD . . . . *Anton Chekhov* 409

A BRIGHT MORNING . . *Brothers Álvarez Quintero* 467

LILIOM . . . . *Ferenc Molnar* 483

THE TIDINGS BROUGHT TO MARY. . *Paul Claudel* 559

R. U. R. . . . . *Karel Čapek* 663

BIBLIOGRAPHIES AND PLAY LISTS 731

TYPES OF
CONTEMPORARY DRAMA

THIS is the first volume in a series of contemporary drama which differs from preceding collections in several important respects. Apart from their handy size and great economy, which are matters of book-making, the volumes in this series offer an entirely new approach in the critical principles governing the inclusion of plays.

In previous collections plays have been included for two principal reasons: (1) they were the outstanding plays of the period judged by merit and historical significance; (2) they were plays that served well in the classroom. These two principles must still operate in any collection of plays, and they have been kept in mind in the present series. But there are other principles of selection, not heretofore employed, which should no longer be ignored.

These principles derive from the fact that contemporary plays are by no means all alike, that they differ widely in *form*, that they are of various *types*. If we are to understand contemporary drama, we must not consider it by content alone. We must consider it in its wide variety of forms. As we learn in the General Introduction to this series, many of these forms go back to the earliest history of drama. Only by considering the content of the play in the light of its form can the real significance of the author's work be grasped.

It is the purpose of this series to present the great representative plays of the period in their significant variety of forms. Each volume will be complete in itself, and each volume will contain the widest possible variety of play forms.

To find place in this series, each play has had to satisfy three standards of judgment: (1) it must be an outstanding play of the period by merit and historical significance; (2) it must satisfy the classroom demands of teachers throughout the United States; (3) finally, it must be a typical example of one of the many important *forms* or *types* in which contemporary drama has been composed.

THE EDITOR

INTRODUCTION

DISTINGUISHING MARKS OF THE CONTEMPORARY DRAMATIC ERA

THE contemporary period of drama has often been compared with previous great periods of theatrical history — with the period of the Greek tragedians, the Elizabethan and Restoration periods in England, the neo-classic period in France, for example. There is indeed a certain validity in these comparisons. Deeper study reveals, however, that the present dramatic era is quite unlike any era that has gone before. If we are to understand the present era, it is important that we recognize not only the manner in which the present era resembles previous eras of theatrical history, but also the manners in which it differs from these eras.

In at least two respects what we know as the contemporary period of dramatic art is to be distinguished from all preceding periods. The first has to do with the great diversity in the forms of plays written during the contemporary era. The second has to do with the wide geographic range of creative activity of the period. While the great theatrical eras of the past have as a rule been characterized by a single type of play, dominated frequently by one or two personalities, and usually centered in a single capital, the contemporary period has been characterized by a lavish variety of forms, has been served by a multitude of great craftsmen but dominated for long by none, and has extended its field of operation over two continents.

If we are to understand contemporary drama, we must study it in its wide variety of forms, and seek its great works in the centers in which they appeared. Among other uses it is the purpose of these books to serve these ends. They seek to present contemporary drama in its great but representative variety of forms. And they seek to represent it as the product, not of one or two centers of activity, but of the wide-ranging imagination of the Western world as it expresses itself through the agencies of theatrical art.

TYPES OF DRAMA

Many attempts have been made to classify the forms of drama according to abstract differences. Few of these have been successful. For our purposes such efforts are unnecessary. It is our purpose to study the play itself as a living agency of the imagination, rather than through the medium of any abstract rules by which it may be judged. Nevertheless, reflection convinces us that plays differ widely among themselves, and while any hard-and-fast standards of judgment are certain to fail in application, there are some simple differentiations that possess not only the qualities of suggestiveness but also of validity.

THE NATURALISTIC PLAY

The most characteristic stage art of our time is that of naturalism. That does not mean that even a half of the great plays of our era are naturalistic in the strict sense of the term. It means simply that naturalism provides for our times the most useful standard by which plays of all types may be considered. While the naturalistic form is considered to be essentially modern, in fact it goes back a long way in history. There are qualities of naturalism in the early drama of almost all nations. But perhaps it would be suggestive to say that the naturalistic play as we know it today appeared sporadically in England, Germany, and France around two hundred years ago, and that the highest development of naturalism began about fifty years ago, that is, about the beginning of our era. Without seeking to find a strict definition of naturalism, which would perhaps be difficult, two comments upon it are appropriate: The first is that absolutely pure naturalism is never achieved and is perhaps impossible. The second is the fact that within the limits of naturalistic structure there is perhaps as great a variety of forms as is found in any type of play.

PURPOSE IN DRAMA

A quality which, next to that of naturalism, is highly typical of many contemporary plays is the quality of purpose. Because this quality frequently accompanies the naturalistic form, it is sometimes thought that the naturalistic play is invariably written to accomplish a purpose. This is not the case. Indeed the pure naturalistic play would probably be as purposeless as events themselves appear to be. On the other hand, as will be seen in these books, the element of purpose can be, and is, injected into all forms of drama including the romantic play, the play of artifice, and the modern morality or mystery play. In Germany the purpose drama is frequently called the *Tendenzdrama* or *Gegenwartsdrama*; in France the *pièce à thèse*.

ROMANTIC DRAMA

A certain strain of romanticism is very likely to appear in all plays, even those severely naturalistic plays which are presumed to be anti-romantic. Nevertheless, the romantic play stands in a class by itself, and can usually be distinguished from other forms by the possession of certain attributes. Perhaps the simplest test by which the romantic play is to be recognized is its literary quality. It is a type of play which is chiefly dependent on language for its movement, and this is often of an elaborate order, sometimes prose, often verse. It is written for reading as well as representation; it is produced by elocution rather than by action. This form of play has great repute in all countries as it was the form in which Shakespeare, Schiller, and Victor Hugo wrote. The romantic play is often contrasted with the classical play, but it is to be noticed that in many essential points they are very much alike. Both are literary forms. In both the movement subsists upon words rather than upon action. In both the speech itself is fashioned according to a standard of poetic beauty rather than of observation of common usage. In recent years there has been a tendency in some countries, notably Germany and Italy, to reintroduce the classical form of literary drama.

THE PLAY OF ARTIFICE

We come now to the most typical, and certainly the most widespread, of all forms of dramatic composition. Primarily the art of the theater is an art of artifice. In a short survey it is manifestly impossible to indicate the various kinds of artifice employed. It may be remarked, however, that as one of the oldest forms of art the theater has an artifice all its own. Plays of all kinds succeed or fail according as they possess this essential quality of the theatrical.

This quality is always present in the folk theater. It is also conspicuous in the great popular theater of sophisticated peoples. It is not lacking in many of the so-called artistic or literary types of plays, the poetic and the severely naturalistic, which may seek to conceal artifice.

Normally the play of artifice does not find its way into books of this kind at all, for the reason that its effects are of the moment and leave no records that can be perpetuated. And many such plays are not worth perpetuating. Among plays of artifice there are some forms which, though essentially of the theater, and therefore of the moment, have reached such standards of technical skill that they take a place as art of the highest class. Of all forms of the play of artifice, the *Commedia del'Arte* takes the highest rank. Under plays of artifice belong also comedies, farces, melodramas, and the various types of the *pièce bien faite*, or well-made play. It is worthy of note that while our period is as rich in plays of artifice as any other period, it is difficult to give this form of play adequate representation for the reason that its written and printed record misrepresents its real character. Aside from the artifice of the primitive theater, which is distributed broadly through all forms of folk amusement, the strongest influence in establishing the artifice of the modern theater is that of the French playwright Scribe and his followers, the creators of the "well-made" play.

THE SYMBOLIC PLAY

Every play has a specific central action incorporated in a plot. It usually happens that the real significance of the play is not limited to the action itself, but lies in what the action implies. In some cases the action itself is unimportant and negligible beside its larger meaning. The number of different types of plays of this kind is very great. Some of these go back to the most primitive society and represent the rituals of ceremonial and worship. The greater number of plays of this kind derive from the Middle Ages. Though there are many varieties of the symbolic play, two historic types are to be noted. In the morality type abstract qualities are endowed with personality and are involved in an action whose purpose it is to point a moral. In the miracle and mystery type an old and well-known legend, usually religious, is recounted in order to demonstrate spiritual truth. The so-called symbolical plays, mystical plays, and allegorical plays, well known in our time, are modern forms of drama in which what the play implies is of greater moment than what it does and says.

DRAMATIC ART DOES NOT STAND STILL

All of these types of plays, drawing their sources from the most distant times and places, are found in contemporary drama. Many of these types are represented in these books. We see now why contemporary drama is called the most eclectic of all dramas. Let us now notice an interesting fact about dramatic art. This is the fact that the values of dramatic art do not stand still. In form dramatic art must be forever moving. This does not mean that it is forever perfecting itself. Many of its changes are but returns to old forms. Various impulses urge the artist to change styles of playwriting. Among these perhaps one of the strongest is the sudden distaste for current modes which urges him to seek other modes of a dissimilar nature. Other incentives to change are the desire to perfect the medium, to extend its powers in the representation of truth or reality, to seek old mediums urged by nostalgia and maladjustment, and finally the freeing of the artist's hands to the pleasures of experiment. As the plays in these volumes are studied, it will be found that many of them are the products of one or another of these incentives to change.

REACTION AND REVOLT

From this it is apparent that one of the strongest impulses in the drama of our time has been revolt. Unfortunately this term is itself too vague to have a very definite critical meaning. Much so-called revolt in drama has been merely political or doctrinal, and has been constrained within the regular forms of drama enumerated above. But the most interesting revolt is that which has moved the playwright to turn away from the conventional forms and seek outlet beyond their restraints. Within the contemporary period there have been revolts against the literary drama, against romantic drama, against artifice in the theater, against naturalism, against sociological motivation, against the constraints of reason and observation, and against the limitations of a detheatricalized theater, as well as various social and political revolts activated by the drama.

PERFECTING THE MEDIUM

An active incentive in our time, which does not carry the playwright very far from his models, is that of perfecting the medium. This incentive has been particularly active in the case of naturalism. In the desire to refine the spiritual substance of the play, and to achieve an even greater accuracy in observation, and objectivity in method, naturalistic playwrights have carried this form to new heights. Laudable as is the endeavor, it frequently occurs that success is gained at the expense of vigor.

FREEING THE FANCY

Perhaps no subject is more discussed among artists than that of the "constraint of convention." In our day and in some quarters there has been a particularly strong urge to relieve the artist of all restraints. Some of this has indeed moved toward the widening of the boundaries of dramatic art. Much of it has moved toward anarchy. The later years of our era have been busily engaged in experiments into new forms. Among the impulses that may be isolated are the effort to adapt the play form to the new theories of psychology, and the effort to extend the action beyond a three-dimensional world. Incident to these efforts various words have gained currency, among these being Futurism, Expressionism, the Theater of Grotesques, and Monodrama. Although these various forms have been freely discussed it does not appear that they have done much to enrich the theater.

THE POWER OF DARKNESS

OR

IF A CLAW IS CAUGHT THE BIRD IS LOST

BY LEO TOLSTOY

LEO NIKOLAIEVITCH TOLSTOY

THE great mystic, poet, novelist, reformer, dramatist, Leo Tolstoy, was born August 28 (old style), 1828, at Yásnaya Poliána, Tula, Russia. He was educated at Moscow and at Kazan University, 1843–46; was with the Army of the Caucasus, 1851–55. He returned from the army to the brilliant life of society, from which he later turned to reformatory and educational efforts. He began writing in the Caucasus. *War and Peace* appeared, 1865–68; *Anna Karenina*, 1875–78. In later life his work became highly didactic. He dedicated his life to the practice of the ideals of poverty and service. While his plays take a minor place in his work, they made their impress upon the theater of Europe. Tolstoy died November 20, 1910, from exposure, having left his home to die in seclusion.

THE POWER OF DARKNESS

HISTORICALLY this is one of the most important plays in the entire range of contemporary drama. It is not only one of the earlier and still outstanding examples of naturalism in form, and strong social and moral purpose. It was one of the most influential plays in establishing the standards of the theater movement of the end of the last century. Written in 1886, *The Power of Darkness* was based upon a case which had come before the Tula law courts. First prohibited by the dramatic censor, it was privately performed in 1887. Its first public production was in the first season of Antoine's Théâtre Libre at Paris, as *La Puissance de Ténèbres*, translated by Paslovsky and Méténier, February 10, 1888. Thereafter it was done in three Paris theaters. Presented by the Freie Bühne in Berlin, it influenced Hauptmann in the composition of *Before Dawn*. Its first public performance in Russia was at the Souvórinsky Theater, St. Petersburg, October 16, 1895; later it was produced at the Little Theater, Moscow. It was first translated into English as *The Dominion of Darkness*, Chicago, 1890. The *Power of Darkness* is perhaps the supreme example of that early form of Naturalism which identified itself with pathological and debased strains in human life and conduct, and addressed itself directly to the righting of social wrongs. It is to be noted, however, that Tolstoy did not seek for the regeneration of society through a reform of its machinery. His appeal was always to the moral sense in men.

CHARACTERS

PETER IGNÁTITCH, *a well-to-do peasant, forty-two years old, married for the second time, and sickly.*

ANÍSYA, *his wife, thirty-two years old, fond of dress.*

AKOULÍNA, *Peter's daughter by his first marriage, sixteen years old, hard of hearing, mentally undeveloped.*

NAN (ANNA PETRÓVNA), *his daughter by his second marriage, ten years old.*

NIKÍTA, *their laborer, twenty-five years old, fond of dress.*

AKÍM, *Nikíta's father, fifty years old, a plain-looking, God-fearing peasant.*

MATRYÓNA, *his wife and Nikíta's mother, fifty years old.*

MARÍNA, *an orphan girl, twenty-two years old.*

MARTHA, *Peter's sister.*

MÍTRITCH, *an old laborer, ex-soldier.*

SIMON, *Marína's husband.*

BRIDEGROOM, *engaged to Akoulína.*

IVÁN, *his father.*

A NEIGHBOR.

FIRST GIRL.

SECOND GIRL.

POLICE OFFICER.

DRIVER.

BEST MAN.

MATCHMAKER.

VILLAGE ELDER.

VISITORS, WOMEN, GIRLS, AND PEOPLE *come to see the wedding.*

N.B.— The "oven" mentioned is the usual large, brick, Russian baking-oven. The top of it outside is flat, so that more than one person can lie on it.

ACT I

The Act takes place in autumn in a large village. The Scene represents PETER'S *roomy hut.* PETER *is sitting on a wooden bench, mending a horse-collar.* ANÍSYA *and* AKOULÍNA *are spinning, and singing a part-song.*

PETER (*looking out of the window*). The horses have got loose again. If we don't look out they'll be killing the colt. Nikíta! Hey, Nikíta! Is the fellow deaf? (*Listens. To the women.*) Shut up, one can't hear anything.

NIKÍTA (*from outside*). What?

PETER. Drive the horses in.

NIKÍTA. We'll drive 'em in. All in good time.

PETER (*shaking his head*). Ah, these laborers! If I were well, I'd not keep one on no account. There's nothing but bother with 'em. (*Rises and sits down again.*) Nikíta!... It's no good shouting. One of you'd better go. Go, Akoúl, drive 'em in.

AKOULÍNA. What? The horses?

PETER. What else?

AKOULÍNA. All right. (*Exit.*)

PETER. Ah, but he's a loafer, that lad... no good at all. Won't stir a finger if he can help it.

ANÍSYA. You're so mighty brisk yourself. When you're not sprawling on the top of the oven you're squatting on the bench. To goad others to work is all you're fit for.

PETER. If one weren't to goad you on a bit, one'd have no roof left over one's head before the year's out. Oh, what people!

ANÍSYA. You go shoving a dozen jobs on to one's shoulders, and then do nothing but scold. It's easy to lie on the oven and give orders.

PETER (*sighing*). Oh, if 'twere not for this sickness that's got hold of me, I'd not keep him on another day.

AKOULÍNA (*off the scene*). Gee up, gee, woo.

(*A colt neighs, the stamping of horses' feet and the creaking of the gate are heard.*)

PETER. Bragging, that's what he's good at. I'd like to sack him, I would indeed.

ANÍSYA (*mimicking him*). "Like to sack him." You buckle to yourself, and then talk.

AKOULÍNA (*enters*). It's all I could do to drive 'em in. That piebald always will...

PETER. And where's Nikíta?

AKOULÍNA. Where's Nikíta? Why, standing out there in the street.

PETER. What's he standing there for?

AKOULÍNA. What's he standing there for? He stands there jabbering.

PETER. One can't get any sense out of her! Who's he jabbering with?

AKOULÍNA (*does not hear*). Eh, what?

(PETER *waves her off. She sits down to her spinning.*)

NAN (*running in to her mother*). Nikíta's father and mother have come. They're going to take him away. It's true!

ANÍSYA. Nonsense!

NAN. Yes. Blest if they're not! (*Laughing.*) I was just going by, and Nikíta, he says, "Good-bye, Anna Petróvna," he says, "you must come and dance at my wedding. I'm leaving you," he says, and laughs.

ANÍSYA (*to her husband*). There now. Much he cares. You see, he wants to leave of himself. "Sack him" indeed!

PETER. Well, let him go. Just as if I couldn't find somebody else.

ANÍSYA. And what about the money he's had in advance?

(NAN *stands listening at the door for a while, and then exit.*)

PETER (*frowning*). The money? Well, he can work it off in summer, anyhow.

ANÍSYA. Well, of course you'll be glad if he goes and you've not got to feed him. It's only me as'll have to work like a horse all the winter. That lass of yours isn't over fond of work either. And you'll be lying up on the oven. I know you.

PETER. What's the good of wearing out one's tongue before one has the hang of the matter?

ANÍSYA. The yard's full of cattle. You've not sold the cow, and have kept all the sheep for the winter: feeding and watering 'em alone takes all one's time, and you want to sack the laborer. But I tell you straight, I'm not going to do a man's work! I'll go and lie on the top of the oven same as you, and let everything go to pot! You may do what you like.

PETER (*to* AKOULÍNA). Go and see about the feeding, will you? it's time.

AKOULÍNA. The feeding? All right.

(*Puts on a coat and takes a rope.*)

ANÍSYA. I'm not going to work for you. You go and work yourself. I've had enough of it, so there!

PETER. That'll do. What are you raving about? Like a sheep with the staggers!

ANÍSYA. You're a crazy cur, you are! One gets neither work nor pleasure from you. Eating your fill, that's all you do, you palsied cur, you!

PETER (*spits and puts on coat*). Faugh! The Lord have mercy! I'd better go myself and see what's up. (*Exit.*)

ANÍSYA (*after him*). Scurvy long-nosed devil!

AKOULÍNA. What are you swearing at dad for?

ANÍSYA. Hold your noise, you idiot!

AKOULÍNA (*going to the door*). I know why you're swearing at him. You're an idiot yourself, you bitch. I'm not afraid of you.

ANÍSYA. What do you mean? (*Jumps up and looks round for something to hit her with.*) Mind, or I'll give you one with the poker.

AKOULÍNA (*opening the door*). Bitch! devil! that's what you are. Devil! bitch! bitch! devil! (*Runs off.*)

ANÍSYA (*ponders*). "Come and dance at my wedding!" What new plan is this? Marry? Mind, Nikíta, if that's your intention, I'll go and... No, I can't live without him. I won't let him go.

NIKÍTA (*enters, looks round, and, seeing* ANÍSYA *alone, approaches quickly. In a low tone*). Here's a go; I'm in a regular fix! That governor of mine wants to take me away, — tells me I'm to come home. Says quite straight I'm to marry and live at home.

ANÍSYA. Well, go and marry! What's that to me?

NIKÍTA. Is that it? Why, here am I reckoning how best to consider matters, and just hear her! She tells me to go and marry. Why's that? (*Winking.*) Has she forgotten?

ANÍSYA. Yes, go and marry! What do I care?

NIKÍTA. What are you spitting for? Just see, she won't even let
me stroke her... What's the matter?

ANÍSYA. This! That you want to play me false... If you do —
why, I don't want you either. So now you know!

NIKÍTA. That'll do, Anísya. Do you think I'll forget you? Never
while I live! I'll not play you false, that's flat. I've been
thinking that supposing they do go and make me marry, I'd
still come back to you. If only he don't make me live at home.

ANÍSYA. Much need I'll have of you, once you're married.

NIKÍTA. There's a go now. How is it possible to go against one's
father's will?

ANÍSYA. Yes, I daresay, shove it all on your father. You know
it's your own doing. You've long been plotting with that slut
of yours, Marína. It's she has put you up to it. She didn't
come here for nothing t'other day.

NIKÍTA. Marína? What's she to me? Much I care about her!...
Plenty of them buzzing around.

ANÍSYA. Then what has made your father come here? It's you
have told him to. You've gone and deceived me.   (Cries.)

NIKÍTA. Anísya, do you believe in a God or not? I never so
much as dreamt of it. I know nothing at all about it. I
never even dreamt of it — that's flat. My old dad has got it
all out of his own pate.

ANÍSYA. If you don't wish it yourself who can force you? He
can't drive you like an ass.

NIKÍTA. Well, I reckon it's not possible to go against one's parent.
But it's not by my wish.

ANÍSYA. Don't you budge, that's all about it!

NIKÍTA. There was a fellow wouldn't budge, and the village elder
gave him such a hiding.... That's what it might come to!
I've no great wish for that sort of thing. They say it touches
one up....

ANÍSYA. Shut up with your nonsense. Nikíta, listen to me: if
you marry that Marína I don't know what I won't do to myself.
... I shall lay hands on myself! I have sinned, I have gone
against the law, but I can't go back now. If you go away
I'll...

NIKÍTA. Why should I go? Had I wanted to go — I should

have gone long ago. There was Iván Semyónitch t'other day — offered me a place as his coachman.... Only fancy what a life that would have been! But I did not go. Because, I reckon, I am good enough for any one. Now if you did not love me it would be a different matter.

ANÍSYA. Yes, and that's what you should remember. My old man will die one of these fine days, I'm thinking; then we could cover our sin, make it all right and lawful, and then you'll be master here.

NIKÍTA. Where's the good of making plans? What do I care? I work as hard as if I were doing it for myself. My master loves me, and his missus loves me. And if the wenches run after me, it's not my fault, that's flat.

ANÍSYA. And you'll love me?

NIKÍTA (embracing her). There, as you have ever been in my heart...

MATRYÓNA (enters and crosses herself a long time before the icón. NIKÍTA and ANÍSYA step apart). What I saw I didn't perceive, what I heard, I didn't hearken to. Playing with the lass, eh? Well — even a calf will play. Why shouldn't one have some fun when one's young? But your master is out in the yard a-calling you, sonny.

NIKÍTA. I only came to get the axe.

MATRYÓNA. I know, sonny, I know; them sort of axes are mostly to be found where the women are.

NIKÍTA (stooping to pick up axe). I say, mother, is it true you want me to marry? As I reckon, that's quite unnecessary. Besides, I've got no wish that way.

MATRYÓNA. Eh, honey! why should you marry? Go on as you are. It's all the old man. You'd better go, sonny; we can talk these matters over without you.

NIKÍTA. It's a queer go! One moment I'm to be married, the next, not. I can't make head or tail of it. (Exit.)

ANÍSYA. What's it all about, then? Do you really wish him to get married?

MATRYÓNA. Eh, why should he marry, my jewel? It's all nonsense, all my old man's drivel. "Marry, marry." But he's reckoning without his host. You know the saying, "From oats and hay, why should horses stray?" When you've enough

to spare, why look elsewhere? And so in this case. (*Winks*.)
Don't I see which way the wind blows?

ANÍSYA. Where's the good of my pretending to you, Mother
Matryóna? You know all about it. I have sinned. I love
your son.

MATRYÓNA. Dear me, here's news! D'you think Mother Matryóna
didn't know? Eh, lassie — Mother Matryóna's been ground,
and ground again, ground fine! This much I can tell you,
my jewel: Mother Matryóna can see through a brick wall
three feet thick. I know it all, my jewel! I know what young
wives need sleeping draughts for, so I've brought some along.

(*Unties a knot in her handkerchief and brings out paper-packets.*)
As much as is wanted, I see, and what's not wanted I neither
see nor perceive! There! Mother Matryóna has also been
young. I had to know a thing or two to live with my old fool.
I know seventy-and-seven dodges. But I see your old man's
quite seedy, quite seedy! How's one to live with such as
him? Why, if you pricked him with a hayfork it wouldn't
fetch blood. See if you don't bury him before the spring.
Then you'll need some one in the house. Well, what's wrong
with my son? He'll do as well as another. Then where's
the advantage of my taking him away from a good place?
Am I my child's enemy?

ANÍSYA. Oh, if only he does not go away!

MATRYÓNA. He won't go away, birdie. It's all nonsense. You
know my old man. His wits are always wool-gathering; yet
sometimes he takes a thing into his pate, and it's as if it were
wedged in, you can't knock it out with a hammer.

ANÍSYA. And what started this business?

MATRYÓNA. Well, you see, my jewel, you yourself know what a
fellow with women the lad is — and he's handsome too, though
I say it as shouldn't. Well, you know, he was living at the
railway, and they had an orphan wench there to cook for them.
Well, that same wench took to running after him.

ANÍSYA. Marína?

MATRYÓNA. Yes, the plague seize her! Whether anything happened or not, anyhow something got to my old man's ears.
Maybe he heard from the neighbors, maybe she's been and
blabbed...

ANÍSYA. Well, she is a bold hussy!

MATRYÓNA. So my old man — the old blockhead — off he goes: "Marry, marry," he says, "he must marry her and cover the sin," he says. "We must take the lad home," he says, "and he shall marry," he says. Well, I did my best to make him change his mind, but, dear me, no. So, all right, thinks I — I'll try another dodge. One always has to entice them fools in this way, just pretend to be of their mind, and when it comes to the point one goes and turns it all one's own way. You know, a woman has time to think seventy-and-seven thoughts while falling off the oven, so how's such as he to see through it? "Well, yes," says I, "it would be a good job — only we must consider well beforehand. Why not go and see our son, and talk it over with Peter Ignátitch and hear what he has to say?" So here we are.

ANÍSYA. Oh dear, oh dear, how will it all end? Supposing his father just orders him to marry her?

MATRYÓNA. Orders, indeed! Chuck his orders to the dogs! Don't you worry; that affair will never come off. I'll go to your old man myself, and sift and strain this matter clear — there will be none of it left. I have come here only for the look of the thing. A very likely thing! Here's my son living in happiness and expecting happiness, and I'll go and match him with a slut! No fear, I'm not a fool!

ANÍSYA. And she — this Marína — came dangling after him here! Mother, would you believe, when they said he was going to marry, it was as if a knife had gone right through my heart. I thought he cared for her.

MATRYÓNA. Oh, my jewel! Why, you don't think him such a fool, that he should go and care for a homeless baggage like that? Nikíta is a sensible fellow, you see. He knows whom to love. So don't you go and fret, my jewel. We'll not take him away, and we won't marry him. No, we'll let him stay on, if you'll only oblige us with a little money.

ANÍSYA. All I know is, that I could not live if Nikíta went away.

MATRYÓNA. Naturally, when one's young it's no easy matter! You, a wench in full bloom, to be living with the dregs of a man like that husband of yours.

ANÍSYA. Mother Matryóna, would you believe it? I'm that
sick of him, that sick of this long-nosed cur of mine, I can
hardly bear to look at him.

MATRYÓNA. Yes, I see, it's one of them cases. Just look here.
(*Looks round and whispers.*) I've been to see that old man, you
know he's given me simples of two kinds. This, you see, is a
sleeping draught. "Just give him one of these powders," he
says, "and he'll sleep so sound you might jump on him!"
And this here, "This is that kind of simple," he says, "that
if you give one some of it to drink it has no smell whatever, but
its strength is very great. There are seven doses here, a pinch
at a time. Give him seven pinches," he says, "and she won't
have far to look for freedom," he says.

ANÍSYA. O-o-oh! What's that?

MATRYÓNA. "No sign whatever,' he says. He's taken a rouble
for it. "Can't sell it for less," he says. Because it's no easy
matter to get 'em, you know. I paid him, dearie, out of my
own money. If she takes them, thinks I, it's all right; if she
don't, I can let old Michael's daughter have them.

ANÍSYA. O-o-oh! But mayn't some evil come of them? I'm
frightened!

MATRYÓNA. What evil, my jewel? If your old man was hale and
hearty, 'twould be a different matter, but he's neither alive nor
dead as it is. He's not for this world. Such things often
happen.

ANÍSYA. O-o-oh, my poor head! I'm afeared, Mother Matryóna,
lest some evil come of them. No. That won't do.

MATRYÓNA. Just as you like. I might even return them to him.

ANÍSYA. And are they to be used in the same way as the others?
Mixed in water?

MATRYÓNA. Better in tea, he says. "You can't notice anything,"
he says, "no smell nor nothing." He's a cute old fellow, too.

ANÍSYA (*taking the powder*). O-oh, my poor head! Could I have
ever thought of such a thing if my life were not a very hell?

MATRYÓNA. You'll not forget that rouble? I promised to take
it to the old man. He's had some trouble, too.

ANÍSYA. Of course?   (*Goes to her box and hides the powders.*)

MATRYÓNA. And now, my jewel, keep it as close as you can, so that no one should find it out. Heaven defend that it should happen, but *if* anyone notices it, tell 'em it's for the black-beetles. (*Takes the rouble.*) It's also used for beetles. (*Stops short.*)

(*Enter* AKÍM, *who crosses himself in front of the icón, and then* PETER, *who sits down.*)

PETER. Well, then, how's it to be, Daddy Akím?

AKÍM. As it's best, Peter Ignátitch, as it's best... I mean — as it's best. 'Cos why? I'm afeared of what d'you call 'ems, some tomfoolery, you know. I'd like to, what d'you call it... to start, you know, start the lad honest, I mean. But supposing you'd rather, what d'you call it, we might, I mean, what's name? As it's best...

PETER. All right. All right. Sit down and let's talk it over. (AKÍM *sits down.*) Well, then, what's it all about? You want him to marry?

MATRYÓNA. As to marrying, he might bide a while, Peter Ignátitch. You know our poverty, Peter Ignátitch. What's he to marry on? We've hardly enough to eat ourselves. How can he marry then?...

PETER. You must consider what will be best.

MATRYÓNA. Where's the hurry for him to get married? Marriage is not that sort of thing, it's not like ripe raspberries that drop off if not picked in time.

PETER. If he were to get married, 'twould be a good thing in a way.

AKÍM. We'd like to... what d'you call it? 'Cos why, you see. I've what d'you call it... a job. I mean, I've found a paying job in town, you know.

MATRYÓNA. And a fine job too — cleaning out cesspools. The other day when he came home, I could do nothing but spew and spew. Faugh!

AKÍM. It's true, at first it does seem what d'you call it... knocks one clean over, you know — the smell, I mean. But one gets used to it, and then it's nothing, no worse than malt grain, and then it's, what d'you call it,... pays, pays, I mean. And as to the smell being, what d'you call it, it's not for the likes of us to complain. And one changes one's clothes. So we'd

like to take what's his name... Nikíta, I mean, home. Let
him manage things at home while I, what d'you call it — earn
something in town.

PETER. You want to keep your son at home? Yes, that would
be well: but how about the money he has had in advance?

AKÍM. That's it, that's it! It's just as you say, Ignátitch, it's
just what d'you call it. 'Cos why? If you go into service,
it's as good as if you had sold yourself, they say. That will
be all right. I mean he may stay and serve his time, only he
must, what d'you call it, get married. I mean — so: you let
him off for a little while, that he may, what d'you call it?

PETER. Yes, we could manage that.

MATRYÓNA. Ah, but it's not yet settled between ourselves, Peter
Ignátitch. I'll speak to you as I would before God, and you
may judge between my old man and me. He goes on harping
on that marriage. But just ask — who it is he wants him to
marry. If it were a girl of the right sort now —— I am not
my child's enemy, but the wench is not honest.

AKÍM. No, that's wrong! Wrong, I say. 'Cos why? She, that
same girl — it's my son as has offended, offended the girl
I mean.

PETER. How offended?

AKÍM. That's how. She's what d'you call it, with him, with my
son, Nikíta. With Nikíta, what d'you call it, I mean.

MATRYÓNA. You wait a bit, my tongue runs smoother — let me
tell it. You know, this lad of ours lived at the railway before he came to you. There was a girl there as kept dangling
after him. A girl of no account, you know; her name's Marína.
She used to cook for the men. So now this same girl accuses
our son, Nikíta, that he, so to say, deceived her.

PETER. Well, there's nothing good in that.

MATRYÓNA. But she's no honest girl herself; she runs after the
fellows like a common slut.

AKÍM. There you are again, old woman, and it's not at all what
d'you call it, it's all not what d'you call it, I mean...

MATRYÓNA. There now, that's all the sense one gets from my old
owl — "what d'you call it, what d'you call it," and he doesn't
know himself what he means. Peter Ignátitch, don't listen

to me, but go yourself and ask anyone you like about the girl, everybody will say the same. She's just a homeless good-for-nothing.

PETER. You know, Daddy Akím, if that's how things are, there's no reason for him to marry her. A daughter-in-law's not like a shoe, you can't kick her off.

AKÍM (*excitedly*). It's false, old woman, it's what d'you call it, false; I mean, about the girl; false! 'Cos why? The lass is a good lass, a very good lass, you know. I'm sorry, sorry for the lassie, I mean.

MATRYÓNA. It's an old saying: "For the wide world old Miriam grieves, and at home without bread her children she leaves." He's sorry for the girl, but not sorry for his own son! Sling her round your neck and carry her about with you! That's enough of such empty cackle!

AKÍM. No, it's not empty.

MATRYÓNA. There, don't interrupt, let me have my say.

AKÍM (*interrupts*). No, not empty! I mean, you twist things your own way, about the lass or about yourself. Twist them, I mean, to make it better for yourself; but God, what d'you call it, turns them His way. That's how it is.

MATRYÓNA. Eh! One only wears out one's tongue with you.

AKÍM. The lass is hard-working and spruce, and keeps everything round herself... what d'you call it. And in our poverty, you know, it's a pair of hands, I mean; and the wedding needn't cost much. But the chief thing's the offence, the offence to the lass, and she's a what d'you call it, an orphan, you know; that's what she is, and there's the offence.

MATRYÓNA. Eh! they'll all tell you a tale of that sort...

ANÍSYA. Daddy Akím, you'd better listen to us women; we can tell you a thing or two.

AKÍM. And God, how about God? Isn't she a human being, the lass? A what d'you call it — also a human being I mean, before God. And how do you look at it?

MATRYÓNA. Eh!... started off again?...

PETER. Wait a bit, Daddy Akím. One can't believe all these girls say, either. The lad's alive, and not far away; send for him, and find out straight from him if it's true. He won't

wish to lose his soul.   Go and call the fellow (ANÍSYA *rises*),
and tell him his father wants him.   (*Exit* ANÍSYA.)

MATRYÓNA.   That's right, dear friend; you've cleared the way
clean, as with water.   Yes, let the lad speak for himself.   Nowadays, you know, they'll not let you force a son to marry;
one must first of all ask the lad.   He'll never consent to marry
her and disgrace himself, not for all the world.   To my thinking, it's best he should go on living with you and serving you
as his master.   And we need not take him home for the summer
either; we can hire a help.   If you would only give us ten
roubles now, we'll let him stay on.

PETER.   All in good time.   First let us settle one thing before we
start another.

AKÍM.   You see, Peter Ignátitch, I speak.   'Cos why? you know
how it happens.   We try to fix things up as seems best for ourselves, you know; and as to God, we what d'you call it, we
forget Him.   We think it's best so, turn it our own way, and
lo! we've got into a fix, you know.   We think it will be best,
I mean; and lo! it turns out much worse — without God,
I mean.

PETER.   Of course one must not forget God.

AKÍM.   It turns out worse!   But when it's the right way — God's
way — it what d'you call it, it gives one joy; seems pleasant,
I mean.   So I reckon, you see, get him, the lad, I mean, get
him to marry her, to keep him from sin, I mean, and let him
what d'you call it at home, as it's lawful, I mean, while I go
and get the job in town.   The work is of the right sort — it's
payin', I mean.   And in God's sight it's what d'you call it —
it's best, I mean.   Ain't she an orphan?   Here, for example,
a year ago some fellows went and took timber from the steward
— thought they'd do the steward, you know.   Yes, they did
the steward, but they couldn't what d'you call it — do God,
I mean.   Well, and so...

(*Enter* NIKÍTA *and* NAN.)

NIKÍTA.   You called me?

(*Sits down and takes out his tobacco-pouch.*)

PETER (*in a low, reproachful voice*).   What are you thinking about —

have you no manners?   Your father is going to speak to you, and you sit down and fool about with tobacco.   Come, get up!

(NIKÍTA *rises, leans carelessly with his elbow on the table, and smiles.*)

AKÍM. It seems there's a complaint, you know, about you, Nikíta — a complaint, I mean, a complaint.

NIKÍTA. Who's been complaining?

AKÍM. Complaining?   It's a maid, an orphan maid, complaining, I mean.   It's her, you know — a complaint against you, from Marína, I mean.

NIKÍTA (*laughs*). Well, that's a good one.   What's the complaint? And who's told you — she herself?

AKÍM. It's I am asking you, and you must now, what d'you call it, give me an answer.   Have you got mixed up with the lass, I mean — mixed up, you know?

NIKÍTA. I don't know what you mean.   What's up?

AKÍM. Foolin', I mean, what d'you call it? foolin'.   Have you been foolin' with her, I mean?

NIKÍTA. Never mind what's been!   Of course one does have some fun with a cook now and then to while away the time. One plays the concertina and gets her to dance.   What of that?

PETER. Don't shuffle, Nikíta, but answer your father straight out.

AKÍM (*solemnly*). You can hide it from men but not from God, Nikíta.   You, what d'you call it — think, I mean, and don't tell lies.   She's an orphan; so, you see, anyone is free to insult her.   An orphan, you see.   So you should say what's rightest.

NIKÍTA. But what if I have nothing to say?   I have told you everything — because there isn't anything to tell, that's flat! (*Getting excited.*)   She can go and say anything about me, same as if she was speaking of one as is dead.   Why don't she say anything about Fédka Mikíshin?   Besides, how's this, that one mayn't even have a bit of fun nowadays?   And as for her, well, she's free to say anything she likes.

AKÍM. Ah, Nikíta, mind!   A lie will out.   Did anything happen?

NIKÍTA (*aside*). How he sticks to it; it's too bad.   (*To* AKÍM.) I tell you, I know nothing more.   There's been nothing be- tween us.   (*Angrily.*)   By God! and may I never leave this spot (*crosses himself*) if I know anything about it.   (*Silence.*

Then still more excitedly.) Why! have you been thinking of getting me to marry her? What do you mean by it? — it's a confounded shame. Besides, nowadays you've got no such rights as to force a fellow to marry. That's plain enough. Besides, haven't I sworn I know nothing about it?

MATRYÓNA (*to her husband*). There now, that's just like your silly pate to believe all they tell you. He's gone and put the lad to shame all for nothing. The best thing is to let him live as he is living, with his master. His master will help us in our present need, and give us ten roubles, and when the time comes...

PETER. Well, Daddy Akím, how's it to be?

AKÍM (*looks at his son, clicking his tongue disapprovingly*). Mind, Nikíta, the tears of one that's been wronged never, what d'you call it — never fall beside the mark but always on, what's name — the head of the man as did the wrong. So mind, don't what d'you call it.

NIKÍTA (*sits down*). What's there to mind? mind yourself.

NAN (*aside*). I must run and tell mother. (*Exit.*)

MATRYÓNA (*to* PETER). That's always the way with this old mumbler of mine, Peter Ignátitch. Once he's got anything wedged in his pate there's no knocking it out. We've gone and troubled you all for nothing. The lad can go on living as he has been. Keep him; he's your servant.

PETER. Well, Daddy Akím, what do you say?

AKÍM. Why, the lad's his own master, if only he what d'you call it.... I only wish that, what d'you call it, I mean.

MATRYÓNA. You don't know yourself what you're jawing about. The lad himself has no wish to leave. Besides, what do we want with him at home? We can manage without him.

PETER. Only one thing, Daddy Akím — if you are thinking of taking him back in summer, I don't want him here for the winter. If he is to stay at all, it must be for the whole year.

MATRYÓNA. And it's for a year he'll bind himself. If we want help when the press of work comes, we can hire help, and the lad shall remain with you. Only give us ten roubles now....

PETER. Well then, is it to be for another year?

AKÍM (*sighing*). Yes, it seems, it what d'you call it... if it's so, I mean, it seems that it must be what d'you call it.

MATRYÓNA. For a year, counting from St. Dimítry's day. We know you'll pay him fair wages. But give us ten roubles now. Help us out of our difficulties. (*Gets up and bows to* PETER.)

(*Enter* NAN *and* ANÍSYA. *The latter sits down at one side.*)

PETER. Well, if that's settled we might step across to the inn and have a drink. Come, Daddy Akím, what do you say to a glass of vódka?

AKÍM. No, I never drink that sort of thing.

PETER. Well, you'll have some tea?

AKÍM. Ah, tea! yes, I do sin that way. Yes, tea's the thing.

PETER. And the women will also have some tea. Come. And you, Nikíta, go and drive the sheep in and clear away the straw.

NIKÍTA. All right. (*Exeunt all but* NIKÍTA. NIKÍTA *lights a cigarette. It grows darker.*) Just see how they bother one. Want a fellow to tell 'em how he larks about with the wenches! It would take long to tell 'em all those stories — "Marry her," he says. Marry them all! One would have a good lot of wives! And what need have I to marry? Am as good as married now! There's many a chap as envies me. Yet how strange it felt when I crossed myself before the icón. It was just as if someone shoved me. The whole web fell to pieces at once. They say it's frightening to swear what's not true. That's all humbug. It's all talk, that is. It's simple enough.

AKOULÍNA (*enters with a rope, which she puts down. She takes off her outdoor things and goes into closet*). You might at least have got a light.

NIKÍTA. What, to look at you? I can see you well enough without.

AKOULÍNA. Oh, bother you!

(NAN *enters and whispers to* NIKÍTA.)

NAN. Nikíta, there's a person wants you. There is!

NIKÍTA. What person?

NAN. Marína from the railway; she's out there, round the corner.

NIKÍTA. Nonsense!

NAN. Blest if she isn't!

NIKÍTA. What does she want?

NAN. She wants you to come out. She says, "I only want to say a word to Nikíta." I began asking, but she won't tell, but only says, "Is it true he's leaving you?" And I say, "No, only his father wanted to take him away and get him to marry, but he won't, and is going to stay with us another year." And she says, "For goodness' sake send him out to me. I must see him," she says, "I must say a word to him somehow." She's been waiting a long time. Why don't you go?

NIKÍTA. Bother her! What should I go for?

NAN. She says, "If he don't come, I'll go into the hut to him." Blest if she didn't say she'd come in!

NIKÍTA. Not likely. She'll wait a bit and then go away.

NAN. "Or is it," she says, "that they want him to marry Akoulína?"

(Re-enter AKOULÍNA, passing near NIKÍTA to take her distaff.)

AKOULÍNA. Marry whom to Akoulína?

NAN. Why, Nikíta.

AKOULÍNA. A likely thing! Who says it?

NIKÍTA *(looks at her and laughs)*. It seems people do say it. Would you marry me, Akoulína?

AKOULÍNA. Who, you? Perhaps I might have afore, but won't now.

NIKÍTA. And why not now?

AKOULÍNA. 'Cos you wouldn't love me.

NIKÍTA. Why not?

AKOULÍNA. 'Cos you'd be forbidden to.   *(Laughs.)*

NIKÍTA. Who'd forbid it?

AKOULÍNA. Who? My step-mother. She does nothing but grumble, and is always staring at you.

NIKÍTA *(laughing)*. Just hear her! Ain't she cute?

AKOULÍNA. Who? Me? What's there to be cute about? Am I blind? She's been rowing and rowing at dad all day. The fat-muzzled witch!   *(Goes into closet.)*

NAN *(looking out of window)*. Look, Nikíta, she's coming! I'm blest if she isn't! I'll go away.   *(Exit.)*

MARÍNA *(enters)*. What are you doing with me?

NIKÍTA. Doing? I'm not doing anything.

MARÍNA. You mean to desert me.

NIKÍTA (*gets up angrily*). What does this look like, your coming here?

MARÍNA. Oh, Nikíta!

NIKÍTA. Well, you are strange! What have you come for?

MARÍNA. Nikíta!

NIKÍTA. That's my name. What do you want with Nikíta? Well, what next? Go away, I tell you!

MARÍNA. I see, you do want to throw me over.

NIKÍTA. Well, and what's there to remember? You yourself don't know. When you stood out there round the corner and sent Nan for me, and I didn't come, wasn't it plain enough that you're not wanted? It seems pretty simple. So there — go!

MARÍNA. Not wanted! So now I'm not wanted! I believed you when you said you would love me. And now that you've ruined me, I'm not wanted.

NIKÍTA. Where's the good of talking? This is quite improper. You've been telling tales to father. Now, do go away, will you?

MARÍNA. You know yourself I never loved anyone but you. Whether you married me or not, I'd not have been angry. I've done you no wrong, then why have you left off caring for me? Why?

NIKÍTA. Where's the use of baying at the moon? You go away. Goodness me! what a duffer!

MARÍNA. It's not that you deceived me when you promised to marry me that hurts, but that you've left off loving. No, it's not that you've stopped loving me either, but that you've changed me for another, that's what hurts. I know who it is!

NIKÍTA (*comes up to her viciously*). Eh! what's the good of talking to the likes of you, that won't listen to reason? Be off, or you'll drive me to do something you'll be sorry for.

MARÍNA. What, will you strike me, then? Well then, strike me! What are you turning away for? Ah, Nikíta!

NIKÍTA. Supposing someone came in. Of course, it's quite improper. And what's the good of talking?

MARÍNA. So this is the end of it! What has been has flown. You want me to forget it? Well, then, Nikíta, listen. I kept my maiden honor as the apple of my eye. You have ruined me for nothing, you have deceived me. You have no pity on a fatherless and motherless girl! (*Weeping.*) You have deserted, you have killed me, but I bear you no malice. God forgive you! If you find a better one you'll forget me, if a worse one you'll remember me. Yes, you will remember, Nikíta! Good-bye, then, if it is to be. Oh, how I loved you! Good-bye for the last time.

(*Takes his head in her hands and tries to kiss him.*)

NIKÍTA (*tossing his head back*). I'm not going to talk with the likes of you. If you won't go away I will, and you may stay here by yourself.

MARÍNA (*screams*). You are a brute. (*In the doorway.*) God will give you no joy. (*Exit, crying.*)

AKOULÍNA (*comes out of closet*). You're a dog, Nikíta!

NIKÍTA. What's up?

AKOULÍNA. What a cry she gave! (*Cries.*)

NIKÍTA. What's up with you?

AKOULÍNA. What's up? You've hurt her so. That's the way you'll hurt me also. You're a dog. (*Exit into closet.*)

(*Silence.*)

NIKÍTA. Here's a fine muddle. I'm as sweet as honey on the lasses, but when a fellow's sinned with 'em it's a bad look-out!

CURTAIN

ACT II

The scene represents the village street. To the left the outside of PETER's *hut, built of logs, with a porch in the middle; to the right of the hut the gates and a corner of the yard buildings.* ANÍSYA *is beating hemp in the street near the corner of the yard. Six months have elapsed since the First Act.*

ANÍSYA (*stops and listens*). Mumbling something again. He's probably got off the stove.

(AKOULÍNA *enters, carrying two pails on a yoke.*)

ANÍSYA. He's calling. You go and see what he wants, kicking up such a row.

AKOULÍNA. Why don't you go?

ANÍSYA. Go, I tell you! (*Exit* AKOULÍNA *into hut.*) He's bothering me to death. Won't let out where the money is, and that's all about it. He was out in the passage the other day. He must have been hiding it there. Now, I don't know myself where it is. Thank goodness he's afraid of parting with it, so that at least it will stay in the house. If only I could manage to find it. He hadn't it on him yesterday. Now I don't know where it can be. He has quite worn the life out of me.

(*Enter* AKOULÍNA, *tying her kerchief over her head.*)

ANÍSYA. Where are you off to?

AKOULÍNA. Where? Why, he's told me to go for Aunt Martha. "Fetch my sister," he says. "I am going to die," he says. "I have a word to say to her."

ANÍSYA (*aside*). Asking for his sister? Oh, my poor head! Sure he wants to give it her. What shall I do? Oh! (*To* AKOULÍNA.) Don't go! Where are you off to?

AKOULÍNA. To call Aunt.

ANÍSYA. Don't go I tell you, I'll go myself. You go and take the clothes to the river to rinse. Else you'll not have finished by the evening.

AKOULÍNA. But he told me to go.

ANÍSYA. You go and do as you're bid. I tell you I'll fetch Martha myself. Take the shirts off the fence.

AKOULÍNA. The shirts? But maybe you'll not go. He's given the order.

ANÍSYA. Didn't I say I'd go? Where's Nan?

AKOULÍNA. Nan? Minding the calves.

ANÍSYA. Send her here. I dare say they'll not run away.

(AKOULÍNA *collects the clothes, and exit.*)

ANÍSYA. If one doesn't go he'll scold. If one goes he'll give the money to his sister. All my trouble will be wasted. I don't myself know what I'm to do. My poor head's splitting.

(*Continues to work.*)

(*Enter* MATRYÓNA, *with a stick and a bundle, in outdoor clothes.*)

MATRYÓNA. May the Lord help you, honey.

ANÍSYA (*looks round, stops working, and claps her hands with joy*). Well, I never expected this! Mother Matryóna, God has sent the right guest at the right time.

MATRYÓNA. Well, how are things?

ANÍSYA. Ah, I'm driven well-nigh crazy. It's awful!

MATRYÓNA. Well, still alive, I hear?

ANÍSYA. Oh, don't talk about it. He doesn't live and doesn't die!

MATRYÓNA. But the money — has he given it to anybody?

ANÍSYA. He's just sending for his sister Martha — probably about the money.

MATRYÓNA. Well, naturally! But hasn't he given it to anyone else?

ANÍSYA. To no one. I watch like a hawk.

MATRYÓNA. And where is it?

ANÍSYA. He doesn't let out. And I can't find out in any way. He hides it now here, now there, and I can't do anything because of Akoulína. Idiot though she is, she keeps watch, and is always about. Oh my poor head! I'm bothered to death.

MATRYÓNA. Oh, my jewel, if he gives the money to anyone but you, you'll never cease regretting it as long as you live! They'll turn you out of house and home without anything. You've been worriting, and worriting all your life with one you don't love, and will have to go a-begging when you are a widow.

ANÍSYA. No need to tell me, mother. My heart's that weary, and I don't know what to do. No one to get a bit of advice from. I told Nikíta, but he's frightened of the job. The only thing he did was to tell me yesterday it was hidden under the floor.

MATRYÓNA. Well, and did you look there?

ANÍSYA. I couldn't. The old man himself was in the room. I notice that sometimes he carries it about on him, and sometimes he hides it.

MATRYÓNA. But you, my lass, must remember that if once he gives you the slip there's no getting it right again! (*Whispering.*) Well, and did you give him the strong tea?

ANÍSYA. Oh! oh!... (*About to answer, but sees neighbor and stops.*)
     (*The neighbor (a woman) passes the hut, and listens to a call from within.*)

NEIGHBOR (*to* ANÍSYA). I say, Anísya! Oh, Anísya! There's your old man calling, I think.

ANÍSYA. That's the way he always coughs — just as if he were screaming. He's getting very bad.

NEIGHBOR (*approaches* MATRYÓNA). How do you do, granny? Have you come far?

MATRYÓNA. Straight from home, dear. Come to see my son. Brought him some shirts — can't help thinking of these things, you see, when it's one's own child.

NEIGHBOR. Yes, that's always so. (*To* ANÍSYA.) And I was thinking of beginning to bleach the linen, but it is a bit early, no one has begun yet.

ANÍSYA. Where's the hurry?

MATRYÓNA. Well, and has he had communion?

ANÍSYA. Oh, dear, yes, the priest was here yesterday.

NEIGHBOR. I had a look at him yesterday. Dearie me! one wonders his body and soul keep together. And, O Lord, the other day he seemed just at his last gasp, so that they laid him under the holy icóns.[1] They started lamenting and got ready to lay him out.

ANÍSYA. He came to, and creeps about again.

MATRYÓNA. Well, and is he to have extreme unction?

ANÍSYA. The neighbors advise it. If he lives till tomorrow we'll send for the priest.

NEIGHBOR. Oh, Anísya dear, I should think your heart must be heavy. As the saying goes, "Not he is sick that's ill in bed, but he that sits and waits in dread."

ANÍSYA. Yes, if it were only over one way or other!

NEIGHBOR. Yes, that's true, dying for a year, it's no joke. You're bound hand and foot like that.

MATRYÓNA. Ah, but a widow's lot is also bitter. It's all right as long as one's young, but who'll care for you when you're old? Oh yes, old age is not pleasure. Just look at me. I've not walked very far, and yet am so footsore I don't know how to stand. Where's my son?

ANÍSYA. Ploughing. But you come in and we'll get the samovár ready; the tea'll set you up again.

---

[1] It was customary to place a dying person under the icón. One or more icóns hung in the hut of each Orthodox peasant.

MATRYÓNA (*sitting down*). Yes, it's true, I'm quite done up, my dears. As to extreme unction, that's absolutely necessary. Besides, they say it's good for the soul.

ANÍSYA. Yes, we'll send tomorrow.

MATRYÓNA. Yes, you had better. And we've had a wedding down in our parts.

NEIGHBOR. What, in spring? [1]

MATRYÓNA. Ah, now if it were a poor man, then, as the saying is, it's always unseasonable for a poor man to marry. But it's Simon Matvéyitch, he's married that Marína.

ANÍSYA. What luck for her!

NEIGHBOR. He's a widower. I suppose there are children?

MATRYÓNA. Four of 'em. What decent girl would have him! Well, so he's taken her, and she's glad. You see, the vessel was not sound, so the wine trickled out.

NEIGHBOR. Oh, my! And what do people say to it? And he, a rich peasant!

MATRYÓNA. They are living well enough so far.

NEIGHBOR. Yes, it's true enough. Who wants to marry where there are children? There now, there's our Michael. He's such a fellow, dear me...

PEASANT'S VOICE. Hullo, Mávra. Where the devil are you? Go and drive the cow in. (*Exit* NEIGHBOR.)

MATRYÓNA (*while the* NEIGHBOR *is within hearing speaks in her ordinary voice*). Yes, lass, thank goodness, she's married. At any rate my old fool won't go bothering about Nikíta. Now (*suddenly changing her tone*), she's gone! (*Whispers.*) I say, did you give him the tea?

ANÍSYA. Don't speak about it. He'd better die of himself. It's no use — he doesn't die, and I have only taken a sin on my soul. O-oh, my head, my head! Oh, why did you give me those powders?

MATRYÓNA. What of the powders? The sleeping powders, lass — why not give them? No evil can come of them.

ANÍSYA. I am not talking of the sleeping ones, but the others, the white ones.

---

[1] Peasant weddings were usually in autumn. They were forbidden in Lent, and soon after Easter the peasants become too busy to marry till harvest is over.

MATRYÓNA. Well, honey, those powders are medicinal.

ANÍSYA (*sighs*). I know, yet it's frightening. Though he's worried me to death.

MATRYÓNA. Well, and did you use many?

ANÍSYA. I gave two doses.

MATRYÓNA. Was anything noticeable?

ANÍSYA. I had a taste of the tea myself — just a little bitter. And he drank them with the tea and says, "Even tea disgusts me," and I say, "Everything tastes bitter when one's sick." But I felt that scared, mother.

MATRYÓNA. Don't go thinking about it. The more one thinks the worse it is.

ANÍSYA. I wish you'd never given them to me and led me into sin. When I think of it something seems to tear my heart. Oh, dear, why did you give them to me?

MATRYÓNA. What do you mean, honey? Lord help you! Why are you turning it on to me? Mind, lass, don't go twisting matters from the sick on to the healthy. If anything were to happen, I stand aside! I know nothing! I'm aware of nothing! I'll kiss the cross on it; I never gave you any kind of powders, never saw any, never heard of any, and never knew there were such powders. You think about yourself, lass. Why, we were talking about you the other day. "Poor thing, what torture she endures. The step-daughter an idiot; the old man rotten, sucking her life-blood. What wouldn't one be ready to do in such a case!"

ANÍSYA. I'm not going to deny it. A life such as mine could make one do worse than that. It could make you hang yourself or throttle him. Is this a life?

MATRYÓNA. That's just it. There's no time to stand gaping; the money must be found one way or other, and then he must have his tea.

ANÍSYA. O-oh, my head, my head! I can't think what to do. I am so frightened; he'd better die of himself. I don't want to have it on my soul.

MATRYÓNA (*viciously*). And why doesn't he show the money? Does he mean to take it along with him? Is no one to have it? Is that right? God forbid such a sum should be lost all for nothing. Isn't that a sin? What's he doing? Is he worth considering?

ANÍSYA. I don't know anything. He's worried me to death.

MATRYÓNA. What is it you don't know? The business is clear. If you make a slip now, you'll repent it all your life. He'll give the money to his sister and you'll be left without.

ANÍSYA. O-oh dear! Yes, and he did send for her — I must go.

MATRYÓNA. You wait a bit and light the samovár first. We'll give him some tea and search him together — we'll find it, no fear.

ANÍSYA. Oh dear, oh dear; supposing something were to happen.

MATRYÓNA. What now? What's the good of waiting? Do you want the money to slip from your hand when it's just in sight? You go and do as I say.

ANÍSYA. Well, I'll go and light the samovár.

MATRYÓNA. Go, honey, do the business so as not to regret it afterwards. That's right!

(ANÍSYA *turns to go.* MATRYÓNA *calls her back.*)

MATRYÓNA. Just a word. Don't tell Nikíta about the business. He's silly. God forbid he should find out about the powders. The Lord only knows what he would do. He's so tender-hearted. D'you know, he usen't to be able to kill a chicken. Don't tell him. 'Twould be a fine go, he wouldn't understand things. (*Stops horror-struck as* PETER *appears in the doorway.*)

PETER (*holding on to the wall, creeps out into the porch and calls with a faint voice*). How's it one can't make you hear? Oh, oh, Anísya! Who's there? (*Drops on the bench.*)

ANÍSYA (*steps from behind the corner*). Why have you come out? You should have stayed where you were lying.

PETER. Has the girl gone for Martha? It's very hard.... Oh, if only death would come quicker!

ANÍSYA. She had no time. I sent her to the river. Wait a bit, I'll go myself when I'm ready.

PETER. Send Nan. Where's she? Oh, I'm that bad! Oh, death's at hand!

ANÍSYA. I've sent for her already.

PETER. Oh, dear! Then where is she?

ANÍSYA. Where's she got to, the plague seize her!

PETER. Oh, dear! I can't bear it. All my inside's on fire. It's as if a gimlet were boring me. Why have you left me as if I were a dog?... no one to give me a drink.... Oh... send Nan to me.

ANÍSYA. Here she is. Nan, go to father.

(NAN *runs in.* ANÍSYA *goes behind the corner of the house.*)

PETER. Go you. Oh... to Aunt Martha, tell her father wants her; say she's to come, I want her.

NAN. All right.

PETER. Wait a bit. Tell her she's to come quick. Tell her I'm dying. O-oh!

NAN. I'll just get my shawl and be off. (*Runs off.*)

MATRYÓNA (*winking*). Now, then, mind and look sharp, lass. Go into the hut, hunt about everywhere, like a dog that's hunting for fleas: look under everything, and I'll search him.

ANÍSYA (*to* MATRYÓNA). I feel a bit bolder, somehow, now you're here. (*Goes up to porch.* *To* PETER.) Hadn't I better light the samovár? Here's Mother Matryóna come to see her son; you'll have a cup of tea with her?

PETER. Well, then, light it.

(ANÍSYA *goes into the house.* MATRYÓNA *comes up to the porch.*)

PETER. How do you do?

MATRYÓNA (*bowing*). How d'you do, my benefactor; how d'you do, my precious... still ill, I see. And my old man, he's that sorry! "Go," says he, "see how he's getting on." He sends his respects to you. (*Bows again.*)

PETER. I'm dying.

MATRYÓNA. Ah, yes, Peter Ignátitch, now I look at you I see, as the saying has it, "Sickness lives where men live." You've shrivelled, shrivelled, all to nothing, poor dear, now I come to look at you. Seems illness does not add to good looks.

PETER. My last hour has come.

MATRYÓNA. Oh well, Peter Ignátitch, it's God's will you know, you've had communion, and you'll have unction, God willing. Your missus is a wise woman, the Lord be thanked; she'll give you a good burial, and have prayers said for your soul, all most respectable! And my son, he'll look after things meanwhile.

PETER. There'll be no one to manage things! She's not steady.
Has her head full of folly — why, I know all about it, I know.
And my girl is silly and young. I've got the homestead together, and there's no one to attend to things. One can't
help feeling it.   (*Whimpers.*)

MATRYÓNA. Why, if it's money, or something, you can leave orders.

PETER (*to* ANÍSYA *inside the house*). Has Nan gone?

MATRYÓNA (*aside*). There now, he's remembered!

ANÍSYA (*from inside*). She went then and there. Come inside,
won't you? I'll help you in.

PETER. Let me sit here a bit for the last time. The air's so stuffy
inside. Oh, how bad I feel! Oh, my heart's burning....
Oh, if death would only come!

MATRYÓNA. If God don't take a soul, the soul can't go out. Death
and life are in God's will, Peter Ignátitch. You can't be
sure of death either. Maybe you'll recover yet. There
was a man in our village just like that, at the very point of
death....

PETER. No, I feel I shall die today, I feel it.
                              (*Leans back and shuts his eyes.*)

ANÍSYA (*enters*). Well, now, are you coming in or not? You do
keep one waiting. Peter! eh, Peter!

MATRYÓNA (*steps aside and beckons to* ANÍSYA *with her finger*). Well?

ANÍSYA (*comes down the porch steps*). Not there.

MATRYÓNA. But have you searched everywhere? Under the
floor?

ANÍSYA. No, it's not there either. In the shed perhaps; he was
rummaging there yesterday.

MATRYÓNA. Go, search, search for all you're worth. Go all
over everywhere, as if you licked with your tongue! But
I see he'll die this very day, his nails are turning blue and his
face looks earthy. Is the samovár ready?

ANÍSYA. Just on the boil.

NIKÍTA (*comes from the other side, if possible on horseback, up to the
gate, and does not see* PETER. *To* MATRYÓNA). How d'you do,
mother, is all well at home?

MATRYÓNA. The Lord be thanked, we're all alive and have a
crust to bite.

NIKÍTA. Well, and how's master?

MATRYÓNA. Hush, there he sits. *(Points to porch.)*

NIKÍTA. Well, let him sit. What's it to me?

PETER *(opens his eyes)*. Nikíta, I say, Nikíta, come here!

(NIKÍTA *approaches.* ANÍSYA *and* MATRYÓNA *whisper together.*)

PETER. Why have you come back so early?

NIKÍTA. I've finished ploughing.

PETER. Have you done the strip beyond the bridge?

NIKÍTA. It's too far to go there.

PETER. Too far? From here it's still farther. You'll have to go on purpose now. You might have made one job of it.

(ANÍSYA, *without showing herself, stands and listens.*)

MATRYÓNA *(approaches)*. Oh, sonny, why don't you take more pains for your master? Your master is ill and depends on you; you should serve him as you would your own father, straining every muscle just as I always tell you to.

PETER. Well, then — o-oh!... Get out the seed potatoes, and the women will go and sort them.

ANÍSYA *(aside)*. No fear, I'm not going. He's again sending everyone away; he must have the money on him now, and wants to hide it somewhere.

PETER. Else... o-oh! when the time comes for planting, they'll all be rotten. Oh, I can't stand it! *(Rises.)*

MATRYÓNA *(runs up into the porch and holds* PETER *up)*. Shall I help you into the hut?

PETER. Help me in. *(Stops.)* Nikíta!

NIKÍTA *(angrily)*. What now?

PETER. I shan't see you again... I'll die today.... Forgive me,[1] for Christ's sake, forgive me if I have ever sinned against you.... If I have sinned in word or deed.... There's been all sorts of things. Forgive me!

NIKÍTA. What's there to forgive? I'm a sinner myself.

MATRYÓNA. Ah, sonny, have some feeling.

PETER. Forgive me, for Christ's sake. *(Weeps.)*

NIKÍTA *(snivels)*. God will forgive you, Daddy Peter. I have

---

[1] A formal request for forgiveness was customary among Russians, but was often no mere formality. Nikíta's first reply is evasive; his second reply, "God will forgive you," is the correct one sanctioned by custom.

no cause to complain of you. You've never done me any wrong. You forgive me; maybe I've sinned worse against you. (*Weeps.*)

(PETER *goes in whimpering,* MATRYÓNA *supporting him.*)

ANÍSYA. Oh, my poor head! It's not without some reason he's hit on that. (*Approaches* NIKÍTA.) Why did you say the money was under the floor? It's not there.

NIKÍTA (*does not answer, but cries*). I have never had anything bad from him, nothing but good, and what have I gone and done!

ANÍSYA. Enough now! Where's the money?

NIKÍTA (*angrily*). How should I know? Go and look for it yourself!

ANÍSYA. What's made you so tender?

NIKÍTA. I am sorry for him — that sorry. How he cried! Oh, dear!

ANÍSYA. Look at him — seized with pity! He has found someone to pity too! He's been treating you like a dog, and even just now was giving orders to have you turned out of the house. You'd better show me some pity!

NIKÍTA. What are you to be pitied for?

ANÍSYA. If he dies, and the money's been hidden away...

NIKÍTA. No fear, he'll not hide it...

ANÍSYA. Oh, Nikíta darling! he's sent for his sister, and wants to give it to her. It will be a bad lookout for us. How are we going to live, if he gives her the money? They'll turn me out of the house! You try and manage somehow! You said he went to the shed last night.

NIKÍTA. I saw him coming from there, but where he's shoved it to, who can tell?

ANÍSYA. Oh, my poor head! I'll go and have a look there.

(NIKÍTA *steps aside.*)

MATRYÓNA (*comes out of the hut and down the steps of the porch to* ANÍSYA *and* NIKÍTA). Don't go anywhere. He's got the money on him. I felt it on a string round his neck.

ANÍSYA. Oh my head, my head!

MATRYÓNA. If you don't keep wide awake now, then you may whistle for it. If his sister comes — then good-bye to it!

ANÍSYA. That's true. She'll come and he'll give it her. What's to be done? Oh, my poor head!

MATRYÓNA. What is to be done? Why, look here: the samovár is boiling, go and make the tea and pour him out a cup, and then (*whispers*) put in all that's left in the paper. When he's drunk the cup, then just take it. He'll not tell, no fear.

ANÍSYA. Oh! I'm afeared!

MATRYÓNA. Don't be talking now, but look alive, and I'll keep his sister off if need be. Mind, don't make a blunder! Get hold of the money and bring it here, and Nikíta will hide it.

ANÍSYA. Oh my head, my head! I don't know how I'm going to...

MATRYÓNA. Don't talk about it I tell you, do as I bid you. Nikíta!

NIKÍTA. What is it?

MATRYÓNA. You stay here — sit down — in case something is wanted.

NIKÍTA (*waves his hand*). Oh, these women, what won't they be up to? Muddle one up completely. Bother them! I'll really go and fetch out the potatoes.

MATRYÓNA (*catches him by the arm*). Stay here, I tell you.

(NAN *enters.*)

ANÍSYA. Well?

NAN. She was down in her daughter's vegetable plot — she's coming.

ANÍSYA. Coming! What shall we do?

MATRYÓNA. There's plenty of time if you do as I tell you.

ANÍSYA. I don't know what to do; I know nothing, my brain's all in a whirl. Nan! Go, daughter, and see to the calves, they'll have run away, I'm afraid.... Oh dear, I haven't the courage.

MATRYÓNA. Go on! I should think the samovár's boiling over.

ANÍSYA. Oh my head, my poor head! (*Exit.*)

MATRYÓNA (*approaches* NIKÍTA). Now then, sonny. (*Sits down beside him.*) Your affairs must also be thought about, and not left anyhow.

NIKÍTA. What affairs?

MATRYÓNA. Why, this affair — how you're to live your life.

NIKÍTA. How to live my life? Others live, and I shall live!

MATRYÓNA. The old man will probably die today.

NIKÍTA. Well, if he dies, God give him rest! What's that to me?

MATRYÓNA (*keeps looking towards the porch while she speaks*). Eh, sonny! Those that are alive have to think about living. One needs plenty of sense in these matters, honey. What do you think? I've tramped all over the place after your affairs, I've got quite footsore bothering about matters. And you must not forget me when the time comes.

NIKÍTA. And what's it you've been bothering about?

MATRYÓNA. About your affairs, about your future. If you don't take trouble in good time you'll get nothing. You know Iván Moséitch? Well, I've been to him too. I went there the other day. I had something else to settle, you know. Well, so I sat and chatted awhile and then came to the point. "Tell me, Iván Moséitch," says I, "how's one to manage an affair of this kind? Supposing," says I, "a peasant as is a widower married a second wife, and supposing all the children he has is a daughter by the first wife, and a daughter by the second. Then," says I, "when that peasant dies, could an outsider get hold of the homestead by marrying the widow? Could he," says I, "give both the daughters in marriage and remain master of the house himself?" "Yes, he could," says he, "but," says he, "it would mean a deal of trouble; still the thing could be managed by means of money, but if there's no money it's no good trying."

NIKÍTA (*laughs*). That goes without saying, only fork out the money. Who does not want money?

MATRYÓNA. Well then, honey, so I spoke out plainly about the affair. And he says, "First and foremost, your son will have to get himself on the register of that village — that will cost something. The elders will have to be treated. And they, you see, they'll sign. Everything," says he, "must be done sensibly." Look (*unwraps her kerchief and takes out a paper*), he's written out this paper; just read it, you're a scholar, you know.   (NIKÍTA *reads*.)

NIKÍTA. This paper's only a decision for the elders to sign. There's no great wisdom needed for that.

MATRYÓNA. But you just hear what Iván Moséitch bids us do. "Above all," he says, "mind and don't let the money slip away, dame. If she don't get hold of the money," he says, "they'll not let her do it. Money's the great thing!" So look out, sonny, things are coming to a head.

NIKÍTA. What's that to me? The money's hers — so let her look out.

MATRYÓNA. Ah, sonny, how you look at it! How can a woman manage such affairs? Even if she does get the money, is she capable of arranging it all? One knows what a woman is! You're a man anyhow. You can hide it, and all that. You see, you've after all got more sense, in case of anything happening.

NIKÍTA. Oh, your woman's notions are all so inexpedient!

MATRYÓNA. Why inexpedient? You just collar the money, and the woman's in your hands. And then should she ever turn snappish you'd be able to tighten the reins!

NIKÍTA. Bother you all — I'm going.

ANÍSYA (*quite pale, runs out of the hut and round the corner to* MATRYÓNA). So it was, it was on him! Here it is!

(*Shows that she has something under her apron.*)

MATRYÓNA. Give it to Nikíta; he'll hide it. Nikíta, take it and hide it somewhere.

NIKÍTA. All right, give here!

ANÍSYA. O-oh, my poor head! No, I'd better do it myself.

(*Goes toward the gate.*)

MATRYÓNA (*seizing her by the arm*). Where are you going to? You'll be missed. There's the sister coming; give it him; he knows what to do. Eh, you blockhead!

ANÍSYA (*stops irresolutely*). Oh, my head, my head!

NIKÍTA. Well, give it here. I'll shove it away somewhere.

ANÍSYA. Where will you shove it to?

NIKÍTA (*laughing*). Why, are you afraid?

(*Enter* AKOULÍNA, *carrying clothes from the wash.*)

ANÍSYA. O-oh, my poor head! (*Gives the money.*) Mind, Nikíta.

NIKÍTA. What are you afraid of? I'll hide it so that I'll not be able to find it myself. (*Exit.*)

ANÍSYA (*stands in terror*). Oh dear, and supposing he...

MATRYÓNA. Well, is he dead?

ANÍSYA. Yes, he seems dead. He did not move when I took it.

MATRYÓNA. Go in, there's Akoulína.

ANÍSYA. Well there, I've done the sin and he has the money....

MATRYÓNA. Have done and go in! There's Martha coming!

ANÍSYA. There now, I've trusted him. What's going to happen now? (*Exit.*)

MARTHA (*enters from one side*, AKOULÍNA *enters from the other. To* AKOULÍNA). I should have come before, but I was at my daughter's. Well, how's the old man? Is he dying?

AKOULÍNA (*puts down the clothes*). Don't know; I've been to the river.

MARTHA (*pointing to* MATRYÓNA). Who's that?

MATRYÓNA. I'm from Zoúevo. I'm Nikíta's mother from Zoúevo, my dearie. Good afternoon to you. He's withering, withering away, poor dear — your brother, I mean. He came out himself. "Send for my sister," he said, "because," said he... Dear me, why, I do believe he's dead!

ANÍSYA (*runs out screaming. Clings to a post, and begins wailing*).[1] Oh, oh, ah! who-o-o-o-m have you left me to, why-y-y have you dese-e-e-e-rted me — a miserable widow... to live my life alone... Why have you closed your bright eyes...

(*Enter* NEIGHBOR. MATRYÓNA *and* NEIGHBOR *catch hold of* ANÍSYA *under the arms to support her*. AKOULÍNA *and* MARTHA *go into the hut. A crowd assembles.*)

A VOICE IN THE CROWD. Send for the old women to lay out the body.

MATRYÓNA (*rolls up her sleeves*). Is there any water in the copper? But I daresay the samovár is still hot. I'll also go and help a bit.

CURTAIN

---

[1] Loud public wailing of this kind is customary, and considered indispensable, among the peasants.

ACT III

The same hut.   Winter.   Nine months have passed since Act II.
ANÍSYA, *plainly dressed, sits before a loom weaving.* NAN *is on the oven.*

MÍTRITCH (*an old laborer, enters and slowly takes off his outdoor things*).
   Oh Lord, have mercy!   Well, hasn't the master come home yet?

ANÍSYA.   What?

MÍTRITCH.   Nikíta isn't back from town, is he?

ANÍSYA.   No.

MÍTRITCH.   Must have been on the spree.   Oh Lord!

ANÍSYA.   Have you finished in the stackyard?

MÍTRITCH.   What d'you think?   Got it all as it should be, and
   covered everything with straw!   I don't like doing things by
   halves!   Oh Lord! holy Nicholas!   (*Picks at the corns on his
   hands.*)   But it's time he was back.

ANÍSYA.   What need has he to hurry?   He's got money.   Merry-
   making with that girl, I daresay....

MÍTRITCH.   Why shouldn't one make merry if one has the money?
   And why did Akoulína go to town?

ANÍSYA.   You'd better ask her.   How do I know what the devil
   took her there!

MÍTRITCH.   What! to town?   There's all sorts of things to be got
   in town if one's got the means.   Oh Lord!

NAN.   Mother, I heard myself.   "I'll get you a little shawl," he
   says, blest if he didn't; "you shall choose it yourself," he says.
   And she got herself up so fine; she put on her velveteen coat
   and the French shawl.

ANÍSYA.   Really, a girl's modesty reaches only to the door.   Step
   over the threshold and it's forgotten.   She is a shameless
   creature.

MÍTRITCH.   Oh my!   What's the use of being ashamed?   While
   there's plenty of money make merry.   Oh Lord!   It is too soon
   to have supper, eh?   (ANÍSYA *does not answer.*)   I'll go and get
   warm meanwhile.   (*Climbs on the stove.*)   Oh Lord!   Blessed
   Virgin Mother!   Holy Nicholas!

NEIGHBOR (*enters*).   Seems your goodman's not back yet?

ANÍSYA.   No.

NEIGHBOR. It's time he was. Hasn't he perhaps stopped at our inn? My sister, Thekla, says there's heaps of sledges standing there as have come from the town.

ANÍSYA. Nan! Nan, I say!

NAN. Yes?

ANÍSYA. You run to the inn and see! Mayhap, being drunk, he's gone there.

NAN (*jumps down from the oven and dresses*). All right.

NEIGHBOR. And he's taken Akoulína with him?

ANÍSYA. Else he'd not have had any need of going. It's because of her he's unearthed all the business there. "Must go to the bank," he says; "it's time to receive the payments," he says. But it's all her fooling.

NEIGHBOR (*shakes her head*). It's a bad look-out. (*Silence.*)

NAN (*at the door*). And if he's there, what am I to say?

ANÍSYA. You only see if he's there.

NAN. All right. I'll be back in a winking. (*Long silence.*)

MÍTRITCH (*roars*). Oh Lord! merciful Nicholas!

NEIGHBOR (*starting*). Oh, how he scared me! Who is it?

ANÍSYA. Why, Mítritch, our laborer.

NEIGHBOR. Oh dear, oh dear, what a fright he did give me! I had quite forgotten. But tell me, dear, I've heard someone's been wooing Akoulína?

ANÍSYA (*gets up from the loom and sits down by the table*). There was someone from Dédlovo; but it seems the affair's got wind there too. They made a start, and then stopped; so the thing fell through. Of course, who'd care to?

NEIGHBOR. And the Lizounófs from Zoúevo?

ANÍSYA. They made some steps too, but it didn't come off either. They won't even see us.

NEIGHBOR. Yet it's time she was married.

ANÍSYA. Time and more than time! Ah, my dear, I'm that impatient to get her out of the house; but the matter does not come off. He does not wish it, nor she either. He's not yet had enough of his beauty, you see.

NEIGHBOR. Eh, eh, eh, what doings! Only think of it. Why, he's her step-father!

ANÍSYA. Ah, friend, they've taken me in completely. They've

done me so fine it's beyond saying. I, fool that I was, noticed nothing, suspected nothing, and so I married him. I guessed nothing, but they already understood one another.

NEIGHBOR. Oh dear, what goings on!

ANÍSYA. So it went on from bad to worse, and I see they begin hiding from me. Ah, friend, I was that sick — that sick of my life! It's not as if I didn't love him.

NEIGHBOR. That goes without saying.

ANÍSYA. Ah, how hard it is to bear such treatment from him! Oh, how it hurts!

NEIGHBOR. Yes, and I've heard say he's becoming too free with his fists?

ANÍSYA. And that too! There was a time when he was gentle when he'd had a drop. He used to hit out before, but of me he was always fond! But now when he's in temper he goes for me and is ready to trample me under his feet. The other day he got both my hands entangled in my hair so that I could hardly get away. And the girl's worse than a serpent; it's a wonder the earth bears such furies.

NEIGHBOR. Ah, ah, my dear, now I look at you, you are a sufferer! To suffer like that is no joke. To have given shelter to a beggar, and he to lead you such a dance! Why don't you pull in the reins?

ANÍSYA. Ah, but, my dear, if it weren't for my heart! Him as is gone was stern enough, still I could twist him about any way I liked; but with this one I can do nothing. As soon as I see him all my anger goes. I haven't a grain of courage before him; I go about like a drowned hen.

NEIGHBOR. Ah, neighbor, you must be under a spell. I've heard that Matryóna goes in for that sort of thing. It must be her.

ANÍSYA. Yes, dear; I think so myself sometimes. Gracious me, how hurt I feel at times! I'd like to tear him to pieces. But when I set eyes on him, my heart won't go against him.

NEIGHBOR. It's plain you're bewitched. It don't take long to blight a body. There now, when I look at you, what you have dwindled to!

ANÍSYA. Growing a regular spindle-shanks. And just look at that fool Akoulína. Wasn't the girl a regular untidy slattern, and just look at her now! Where has it all come from? Yes, he has fitted her out. She's grown so smart, so puffed up, just like a bubble that's ready to burst. And, though she's a fool, she's got it into her head. "I'm the mistress," she says; "the house is mine; it's me father wanted him to marry." And she's that vicious! Lord help us, when she gets into a rage she's ready to tear the thatch off the house.

NEIGHBOR. Oh dear, what a life yours is, now I come to look at you. And yet there's people envying you: "They're rich," they say; but it seems that gold don't keep tears from falling.

ANÍSYA. Much reason for envy indeed! And the riches, too, will soon be made ducks and drakes of. Dear me, how he squanders money!

NEIGHBOR. But how's it, dear, you've been so simple to give up the money? It's yours.

ANÍSYA. Ah, if you knew all! The thing is that I've made one little mistake.

NEIGHBOR. Well, if I were you, I'd go straight and have the law of him. The money's yours; how dare he squander it? There's no such rights.

ANÍSYA. They don't pay heed to that nowadays.

NEIGHBOR. Ah, my dear, now I come to look at you, you've got that weak.

ANÍSYA. Yes, quite weak, dear, quite weak. He's got me into a regular fix. I don't myself know anything. Oh, my poor head!

NEIGHBOR (listening). There's someone coming, I think.

(The door opens and AKÍM enters.)

AKÍM (crosses himself, knocks the snow off his feet, and takes off his coat). Peace be to this house! How do you do? Are you well, daughter?

ANÍSYA. How d'you do, father? Do you come straight from home?

AKÍM. I've been a-thinking I'll go and see what's name, go to see my son, I mean — my son. I didn't start early — had my dinner, I mean; I went, and it's so what d'you call it — so snowy, hard walking, and so there I'm what d'you call it — late, I mean. And my son — is he at home? At home? My son, I mean.

ANÍSYA. No; he's gone to the town.

AKÍM (*sits down on a bench*). I've some business with him, d'you see, some business, I mean. I told him t'other day, told him I was in need — told him, I mean, that our horse was done for, our horse, you see. So we must what d'ye call it, get a horse, I mean, some kind of a horse, I mean. So there, I've come, you see.

ANÍSYA. Nikíta told me. When he comes back you'll have a talk. (*Goes to the oven.*) Have some supper now, and he'll soon come. Mítritch, eh, Mítritch, come have your supper.

MÍTRITCH. Oh Lord! merciful Nicholas!

ANÍSYA. Come to supper.

NEIGHBOR. I shall go now. Good-night. (*Exit.*)

MÍTRITCH (*gets down from the oven*). I never noticed how I fell asleep. Oh, Lord! gracious Nicholas! How d'you do, Daddy Akím?

AKÍM. Ah, Mítritch! What are you, what d'ye call it, I mean?...

MÍTRITCH. Why, I'm working for your son, Nikíta.

AKÍM. Dear me! What d'ye call... working for my son, I mean. Dear me!

MÍTRITCH. I was living with a tradesman in town, but drank all I had there. Now I've come back to the village. I've no home, so I've gone into service. (*Gapes.*) Oh Lord!

AKÍM. But how's that, what d'you call it, or what's name, Nikíta, what does he do? Has he some business, I mean besides, that he should hire a laborer, a laborer, I mean, hire a laborer?

ANÍSYA. What business should he have? He used to manage, but now he's other things on his mind, so he's hired a laborer.

MÍTRITCH. Why shouldn't he, seeing he has money?

AKÍM. Now that's what d'you call it, that's wrong, I mean, quite wrong, I mean. That's spoiling oneself.

ANÍSYA. Oh, he has got spoilt, that spoilt, it's just awful.

AKÍM. There now, what d'you call it, one thinks how to make things better, and it gets worse I mean. Riches spoil a man, spoil, I mean.

MÍTRITCH. Fatness makes even a dog go mad; how's one not to get spoilt by fat living? Myself now; how I went on with fat living. I drank for three weeks without being sober. I drank

my last breeches. When I had nothing left, I gave it up. Now
I've determined not to. Bother it!

AKÍM. And where's what d'you call, your old woman?

MÍTRITCH. My old woman has found her right place, old fellow.
She's hanging about the gin-shops in town. She's a swell too;
one eye knocked out, and the other black, and her muzzle
twisted to one side. And she's never sober; drat her!

AKÍM. Oh, oh, oh, how's that?

MÍTRITCH. And where's a soldier's wife to go? She has found
her right place.   (Silence.)

AKÍM (to ANÍSYA). And Nikíta — has he what d'you call it, taken
anything up to town? I mean, anything to sell?

ANÍSYA (laying the table and serving up). No, he's taken nothing.
He's gone to get money from the bank.

AKÍM (sitting down to supper). Why? D'you wish to put it to another
use, the money I mean?

ANÍSYA. No, we don't touch it. Only some twenty or thirty
roubles as have come due; they must be taken.

AKÍM. Must be taken. Why take it, the money I mean? You'll
take some today I mean, and some tomorrow; and so you'll
what d'you call it, take it all, I mean.

ANÍSYA. We get this besides. The money is all safe.

AKÍM. All safe? How's that, safe? You take it, and it what
d'you call it, it's all safe. How's that? You put a heap of
meal into a bin, or a barn, I mean, and go on taking meal,
will it remain there, what d'you call it, all safe, I mean? That's,
what d'you call it, it's cheating. You'd better find out, or else
they'll cheat you. Safe indeed! I mean you what d'ye call...
you take it and it remains all safe there?

ANÍSYA. I know nothing about it. Iván Moséitch advised us at
the time. "Put the money in the bank," he said, "the money
will be safe, and you'll get interest," he said.

MÍTRITCH (having finished his supper). That's so. I've lived with a
tradesman. They all do like that. Put the money in the
bank, then lie down on the oven and it will keep coming in.

AKÍM. That's queer talk. How's that — what d'ye call, coming
in, how's that coming in, and they, who do they get it from I
mean, the money I mean?

ANÍSYA. They take the money out of the bank.

MÍTRITCH. Get along! 'Tain't a thing a woman can understand! You look here, I'll make it all clear to you. Mind and remember. You see, suppose you've got some money, and I, for instance, have spring coming on, my land's idle, I've got no seeds, or I have to pay taxes. So, you see, I go to you. "Akím," I say, "give us a ten-rouble note, and when I've harvested in autumn I'll return it, and till two acres for you besides, for having obliged me!" And you, seeing I've something to fall back on — a horse say, or a cow — you say, "No, give two or three roubles for the obligation," and there's an end of it. I'm stuck in the mud, and can't do without. So I say, "All right!" and take a tenner. In the autumn, when I've made my turnover, I bring it back, and you squeeze the extra three roubles out of me.

AKÍM. Yes, but that's what peasants do when they what d'ye call it, when they forget God. It's not honest, I mean, it's no good, I mean.

MÍTRITCH. You wait. You'll see it comes just to the same thing. Now don't forget how you've skinned me. And Anísya, say, has got some money lying idle. She does not know what to do with it, besides, she's a woman, and does not know how to use it. She comes to you. "Couldn't you make some profit with my money too?" she says. "Why not?" say you, and you wait. Before the summer I come again and say, "Give me another tenner, and I'll be obliged." Then you find out if my hide isn't all gone, and if I can be skinned again you give me Anísya's money. But supposing I'm clean shorn — have nothing to eat — then you see I can't be fleeced any more, and you say, "Go your way, friend," and you look out for another, and lend him your own and Anísya's money and skin him. That's what the bank is. So it goes round and round. It's a cute thing, old fellow!

AKÍM (excitedly). Gracious me, whatever is that like? It's what d'ye call it, it's filthy! The peasants — what d'ye call it, the peasants do so I mean, and know it's, what d'ye call it, a sin! It's what d'you call, not right, not right, I mean. It's filthy! How can people as have learnt... what d'ye call it...

(Akím takes off his leg-bands and bast-shoes. Anísya washes up.)

MÍTRITCH. That, old fellow, is just what they're fond of! **And** remember, them that are stupid, or the women folk, as can't put their money into use themselves, they take it to the bank, and they there, deuce take 'em, clutch hold of it, and with this money they fleece the people. It's a cute thing!

AKÍM (*sighing*). Oh dear, I see, what d'ye call it, without money it's bad, and with money it's worse! How's that? God told us to work, but you, what d'you call… I mean you put money into the bank and go to sleep, and the money will what d'ye call it, will feed you while you sleep. It's filthy, that's what I call it; it's not right.

MÍTRITCH. Not right? Eh, old fellow, who cares about that nowadays? And how clean they pluck you, too! That's the fact of the matter.

AKÍM (*sighs*). Ah, yes, seems the time's what d'ye call it, the time's growing ripe. There, I've had a look at the closets in town. What they've come to! It's all polished and polished I mean, it's fine, it's what d'ye call it, it's like inside an inn. And what's it all for? What's the good of it? Oh, they've forgotten God. Forgotten, I mean. We've forgotten, forgotten God, God, I mean! Thank you, my dear, I've had enough. I'm quite satisfied.

(*Rises.* MÍTRITCH *climbs on to the oven.*)

ANÍSYA (*eats, and collects the dishes*). If his father would only take him to task! But I'm ashamed to tell him.

AKÍM. What d'you say?

ANÍSYA. Oh! it's nothing.

(*Enter* NAN.)

AKÍM. Here's a good girl, always busy! You're cold, I should think?

NAN. Yes, I am, terribly. How d'you do, grandfather?

ANÍSYA. Well? Is he there?

NAN. No. But Andriyán is there. He's been to town, and he says he saw them at an inn in town. He says Dad's as drunk as drunk can be!

ANÍSYA. Do you want anything to eat? Here you are.

NAN (*goes to the oven*). Well, it *is* cold. My hands are quite numb.

(AKÍM *takes off his leg-bands and bast-shoes.* ANÍSYA *washes up.*)

ANÍSYA. Father!

AKÍM. Well, what is it?

ANÍSYA. And is Marína living well?

AKÍM. Yes, she's living all right. The little woman is what d'ye call it, clever and steady; she's living, and what d'ye call it, doing her best. She's all right; the little woman's of the right sort I mean; painstaking and what d'ye call it, submissive; the little woman's all right I mean, all right, you know.

ANÍSYA. And is there no talk in your village that a relative of Marína's husband thinks of marrying our Akoulína? Have you heard nothing of it?

AKÍM. Ah; that's Mirónof. Yes, the women did chatter something. But I didn't pay heed, you know. It don't interest me I mean, I don't know anything. Yes, the old women did say something, but I've a bad memory, bad memory, I mean. But the Mirónofs are what d'ye call it, they're all right, I mean they're all right.

ANÍSYA. I'm that impatient to get her settled.

AKÍM. And why?

NAN (listens). They've come!

ANÍSYA. Well, don't you go bothering them.

(Goes on washing the spoons without turning her head.)

NIKÍTA (enters). Anísya! Wife! who has come?

(ANÍSYA looks up and turns away in silence.)

NIKÍTA (severely). Who has come? Have you forgotten?

ANÍSYA. Now don't humbug. Come in!

NIKÍTA (still more severely). Who's come?

ANÍSYA (goes up and takes him by the arm). Well, then, husband has come. Now then, come in!

NIKÍTA (holds back). Ah, that's it! Husband! And what's husband called? Speak properly.

ANÍSYA. Oh bother you! Nikíta!

NIKÍTA. Where have you learnt manners? The full name.

ANÍSYA. Nikíta Akímitch! Now then!

NIKÍTA (still in the doorway). Ah, that's it! But now — the surname?

ANÍSYA (laughs and pulls him by the arm). Tchilíkin. Dear me, what airs!

NIKÍTA. Ah, that's it. (*Holds on to the door-post.*) No, now say with which foot Tchilíkin steps into this house!

ANÍSYA. That's enough! You're letting the cold in!

NIKÍTA. Say with which foot he steps? You've got to say it — that's flat.

ANÍSYA (*aside*). He'll go on worrying. (*To* NIKÍTA.) Well then, with the left. Come in!

NIKÍTA. Ah, that's it.

ANÍSYA. You look who's in the hut!

NIKÍTA. Ah, my parent! Well, what of that? I'm not ashamed of my parent. I can pay my respects to my parent. How d'you do, father? (*Bows and puts out his hand.*) My respects to you.

AKÍM (*does not answer*). Drink, I mean drink, what it does! It's filthy!

NIKÍTA. Drink, what's that? I've been drinking? I'm to blame, that's flat! I've had a glass with a friend, drank his health.

ANÍSYA. Go and lie down, I say.

NIKÍTA. Wife, say where am I standing?

ANÍSYA. Now then, it's all right, lie down!

NIKÍTA. No, I'll first drink a samovár with my parent. Go and light the samovár. Akoulína, I say, come here!

(*Enter* AKOULÍNA, *smartly dressed and carrying their purchases.*)

AKOULÍNA. Why have you thrown everything about? Where's the yarn?

NIKÍTA. The yarn? The yarn's there. Hullo, Mítritch, where are you? Asleep? Asleep? Go and put the horse up.

AKÍM (*not seeing* AKOULÍNA *but looking at his son*). Dear me, what is he doing? The old man's what d'ye call it, quite done up, I mean — been thrashing — and look at him, what d'ye call it, putting on airs! Put up the horse! Faugh, what filth!

MÍTRITCH (*climbs down from the oven, and puts on felt boots*). Oh, merciful Lord! Is the horse in the yard? Done it to death, I dare say. Just see how he's been swilling, the deuce take him. Up to his very throat. Oh Lord, Holy Nicholas!

(*Puts on sheepskin and exit.*)

NIKÍTA (*sits down*). You must forgive me, father. It's true I've had a drop; well, what of that? Even a hen will drink. Ain't it true? So you must forgive me. Never mind Mítritch, he doesn't mind, he'll put it up.

ANÍSYA. Shall I really light the samovár?

NIKÍTA. Light it! My parent has come. I wish to talk to him, and shall drink tea with him. (*To* AKOULÍNA.) Have you brought all the parcels?

AKOULÍNA. The parcels? I've brought mine, the rest's in the sledge. Hi, take this, this isn't mine!

(*Throws a parcel on the table and puts the others into her box. NAN watches her while she puts them away. AKÍM does not look at his son, but puts his leg-bands and bast-shoes on the oven.*)

ANÍSYA (*going out with the samovár*). Her box is full as it is, and still he's bought more!

NIKÍTA (*pretending to be sober*). You must not be cross with me, father. You think I'm drunk? I am all there, that's flat! As they say, "Drink, but keep your wits about you." I can talk with you at once, father. I can attend to any business. You told me about the money; your horse is worn-out — I remember! That can all be managed. That's all in our hands. If it was an enormous sum that's wanted, then we might wait; but as it is I can do everything. That's the case.

AKÍM (*goes on fidgeting with the leg-bands*). Eh, lad, "It's ill sledging when the thaw has set in."

NIKÍTA. What do you mean by that? "And it's ill talking with one who is drunk?" But don't you worry, let's have some tea. And I can do anything; that's flat! I can put everything to rights.

AKÍM (*shakes his head*). Eh, eh, eh!

NIKÍTA. The money, here it is. (*Puts his hand in his pocket, pulls out pocket-book, handles the notes in it and takes out a ten-rouble note.*) Take this to get a horse; I can't forget my parent. I shan't forsake him, that's flat. Because he's my parent! Here you are, take it! Really now, I don't grudge it. (*Comes up and pushes the note towards* AKÍM, *who won't take it.* NIKÍTA *catches hold of his father's hand.*) Take it, I tell you. I don't grudge it.

AKÍM. I can't what d'you call it, I mean, can't take it! And

can't what d'ye call it, talk to you, because you're not yourself,
I mean.

NIKÍTA. I'll not let you go! Take it!

(*Puts the money into* AKÍM's *hand.*)

ANÍSYA (*enters, and stops*). You'd better take it, he'll give you
no peace!

AKÍM (*takes it, and shakes his head*). Oh! that liquor. Not like a
man, I mean!

NIKÍTA. That's better! If you repay it you'll repay it, if not
I'll make no bother. That's what I am. (*Sees* AKOULÍNA.)
Akoulína, show your presents.

AKOULÍNA. What?

NIKÍTA. Show your presents.

AKOULÍNA. The presents, what's the use of showing 'em? I've
put 'em away.

NIKÍTA. Get them, I tell you. Nan will like to see 'em. Undo
the shawl. Give it here.

AKÍM. Oh, oh! It's sickening! (*Climbs on the oven.*)

AKOULÍNA (*gets out the parcels and puts them on the table*). Well,
there you are — what's the good of looking at 'em?

NAN. Oh, how lovely! It's as good as Stepanída's.

AKOULÍNA. Stepanída's? What's Stepanída's compared to this?
(*Brightening up and undoing the parcels.*) Just look here — see
the quality! It's a French one.

NAN. The print *is* fine. Mary has a dress like it, only lighter on
a blue ground. This *is* pretty.

NIKÍTA. Ah, that's it!

(ANÍSYA *passes angrily into the closet, returns with a tablecloth
and the chimney of the samovár, and goes up to the table.*)

ANÍSYA. Drat you, littering the table!

NIKÍTA. You look here!

ANÍSYA. What am I to look at? Have I never seen anything?
Put it away! (*Sweeps the shawl onto the floor with her arm.*)

AKOULÍNA. What are you pitching things down for? You pitch
your own things about! (*Picks up the shawl.*)

NIKÍTA. Anísya! Look here!

ANÍSYA. Why am I to look?

NIKÍTA. You think I have forgotten you? Look here! (*Shows her a parcel and sits down on it.*) It's a present for you. Only you must earn it! Wife, where am I sitting?

ANÍSYA. Enough of your humbug. I'm not afraid of you. Whose money are you spreeing on and buying your fat wench presents with? Mine!

AKOULÍNA. Yours indeed? No fear! You wished to steal it, but it did not come off! Get out of the way!

(*Pushes her while trying to pass.*)

ANÍSYA. What are you shoving for? I'll teach you to shove!

AKOULÍNA. Shove me? You try! (*Presses against* ANÍSYA.)

NIKÍTA. Now then, now then, you women. Have done now!

(*Steps between them.*)

AKOULÍNA. Comes shoving herself in! You ought to keep quiet and remember your doings! You think no one knows!

ANÍSYA. Knows what? Out with it, out with it! What do they know?

AKOULÍNA. I know something about you!

ANÍSYA. You're a slut who goes with another's husband!

AKOULÍNA. And you did yours to death!

ANÍSYA (*throwing herself on* AKOULÍNA). You're raving!

NIKÍTA (*holding her back*). Anísya, you seem to have forgotten!

ANÍSYA. Want to frighten me! I'm not afraid of you!

NIKÍTA (*turns* ANÍSYA *round and pushes her out*). Be off!

ANÍSYA. Where am I to go? I'll not go out of my own house!

NIKÍTA. Be off, I tell you, and don't dare to come in here!

ANÍSYA. I won't go! (NIKÍTA *pushes her*, ANÍSYA *cries and screams and clings to the door.*) What! am I to be turned out of my own house by the scruff of the neck? What are you doing, you scoundrel? Do you think there's no law for you? You wait a bit!

NIKÍTA. Now then!

ANÍSYA. I'll go to the Elder! To the policeman!

NIKÍTA. Off, I tell you! (*Pushes her out.*)

ANÍSYA (*behind the door*). I'll hang myself!

NIKÍTA. No fear!

NAN. Oh, oh, oh! Mother, dear, darling! (*Cries.*)

NIKÍTA. Me frightened of her! A likely thing! What are you crying for? She'll come back, no fear. Go and see to the samovár. (*Exit* NAN.)

AKOULÍNA (*collects and folds her presents*). The mean wretch, how she's messed it up. But wait a bit, I'll cut up her jacket for her! Sure I will!

NIKÍTA. I've turned her out; what more do you want?

AKOULÍNA. She's dirtied my new shawl. If that bitch hadn't gone away, I'd have torn her eyes out!

NIKÍTA. That's enough. Why should you be angry? Now if I loved her...

AKOULÍNA. Loved her? She's worth loving, with her fat mug! If you'd have given her up, then nothing would have happened. You should have sent her to the devil. And the house was mine all the same, and the money was mine! Says she is the mistress, but what sort of mistress is she to her husband? She's a murderess, that's what she is! She'll serve you the same way!

NIKÍTA. Oh dear, how's one to stop a woman's jaw? You don't yourself know what you're jabbering about!

AKOULÍNA. Yes, I do. I'll not live with her! I'll turn her out of the house! She can't live here with me. The mistress indeed! She's not the mistress — that jailbird!

NIKÍTA. That's enough! What have you to do with her? Don't mind her. You look at me! I am the master! I do as I like. I've ceased to love her, and now I love you. I love who I like! The power is mine, she's under me. That's where I keep her. (*Points to his feet.*) A pity we've no concertina. (*Sings.*)

> "We have loaves on the stoves,
> We have porridge on the shelf.
> So we'll live and be gay,
> Making merry every day,
> And when death comes,
> Then we'll die!
> We have loaves on the stoves,
> We have porridge on the shelf..."

(*Enter* MÍTRITCH. *He takes off his outdoor things and climbs on the oven.*)

MÍTRITCH. Seems the women have been fighting again! Tearing each other's hair. Oh Lord, gracious Nicholas!

AKÍM (*sitting on the edge of the oven, takes his leg-bands and shoes and begins putting them on*). Get in, get into the corner.

MÍTRITCH. Seems they can't settle matters between them. Oh Lord!

NIKÍTA. Get out the liquor, we'll have some with our tea.

NAN (*to* AKOULÍNA). Sister, the samovár is just boiling over.

NIKÍTA. And where's your mother?

NAN. She's standing and crying out there in the passage.

NIKÍTA. Oh, that's it! Call her, and tell her to bring the samovár. And you, Akoulína, get the tea things.

AKOULÍNA. The tea things? All right. (*Brings the things.*)

NIKÍTA (*unpacks spirits, rusks, and salt herrings*). That's for myself. This is yarn for the wife. The paraffin is out there in the passage, and here's the money. Wait a bit (*takes a counting-frame*); I'll add it up. (*Adds.*) Wheat-flour, 80 kopéykas, oil… Father, 10 roubles…. Father, come let's have some tea!

(*Silence.* AKÍM *sits on the oven and winds the bands round his legs. Enter* ANÍSYA *with samovár.*)

ANÍSYA. Where shall I put it?

NIKÍTA. Here on the table. Well! have you been to the Elder? Ah, that's it! Have your say and then eat your words. Now then, that's enough. Don't be cross; sit down and drink this. (*Fills a wine-glass for her.*) And here's your present.

(*Gives her the parcel he had been sitting on.* ANÍSYA *takes it silently and shakes her head.*)

AKÍM (*gets down and puts on his sheepskin, then comes up to the table and puts down the money*). Here, take your money back! Put it away.

NIKÍTA (*does not see the money*). Why have you put on your things?

AKÍM. I'm going, going, I mean; forgive me, for the Lord's sake. (*Takes up his cap and belt.*)

NIKÍTA. My gracious! Where are you going to at this time of night?

AKÍM. I can't, I mean what d'ye call 'em, in your house, what d'ye call 'em, can't stay I mean, stay, can't stay, forgive me.

NIKÍTA. But are you going without having any tea?

AKÍM (*fastens his belt*). Going because, I mean, it's not right in your house, I mean, what d'you call it, not right, Nikíta, in the house, what d'ye call it, not right! I mean, you are living a bad life, Nikíta, bad — I'll go.

NIKÍTA. Eh, now! Have done talking! Sit down and drink your tea!

ANÍSYA. Why, father, you'll shame us before the neighbors.. What has offended you?

AKÍM. Nothing what d'ye call it, nothing has offended me, nothing at all! I mean only, I see, what d'you call it, I mean, I see my son, to ruin, I mean, to ruin, I mean my son's on the road to ruin, I mean.

NIKÍTA. What ruin? Just prove it!

AKÍM. Ruin, ruin; you're in the midst of it! What did I tell you that time?

NIKÍTA. You said all sorts of things!

AKÍM. I told you, what d'ye call it, I told you about the orphan lass. That you had wronged an orphan — Marína, I mean, wronged her!

NIKÍTA. Eh! he's at it again. Let bygones be bygones... All that's past!

AKÍM (excited). Past! No, lad, it's not past. Sin, I mean, fastens onto sin — drags sin after it, and you've stuck fast, Nikíta, fast in sin! Stuck fast in sin! I see you're fast in sin. Stuck fast, sunk in sin, I mean!

NIKÍTA. Sit down and drink your tea, and have done with it!

AKÍM. I can't, I mean can't what d'ye call it, can't drink tea. Because of your filth, I mean; I feel what d'ye call it, I feel sick, very sick! I can't what d'ye call it, I can't drink tea with you.

NIKÍTA. Eh! There he goes rambling! Come to the table.

AKÍM. You're in your riches same as in a net — you're in a net, I mean. Ah, Nikíta, it's the soul that God needs!

NIKÍTA. Now really, what right have you to reprove me in my own house? Why do you keep on at me? Am I a child that you can pull by the hair? Nowadays those things have been dropped!

AKÍM. That's true. I have heard that nowadays, what d'ye call it, that nowadays children pull their fathers' beards, I mean! But that's ruin, that's ruin, I mean!

NIKÍTA (*angrily*). We are living without help from you, and it's you who came to us with your wants!

AKÍM. The money? There's your money! I'll go begging, begging I mean, before I'll take it, I mean.

NIKÍTA. That's enough! Why be angry and upset the whole company! (*Holds him by the arm.*)

AKÍM (*shrieks*). Let go! I'll not stay. I'd rather sleep under some fence than in the midst of your filth! Faugh! God forgive me! (*Exit.*)

NIKÍTA. Here's a go!

AKÍM (*reopens the door*). Come to your senses, Nikíta! It's the soul that God wants! (*Exit.*)

AKOULÍNA (*takes cups*). Well, shall I pour out the tea?
(*Takes a cup. All are silent.*)

MÍTRITCH (*roars*). Oh Lord be merciful to me a sinner! (*All start.*)

NIKÍTA (*lies down on the bench*). Oh, it's dull, it's dull! (*To Akoulína.*) Where's the concertina?

AKOULÍNA. The concertina? He's bethought himself of it. Why, you took it to be mended. I've poured out your tea. Drink it!

NIKÍTA. I don't want it! Put out the light... Oh, how dull I feel, how dull! (*Sobs.*)

CURTAIN

ACT IV

Autumn. Evening. The moon is shining. The stage represents the interior of courtyard. The scenery at the back shows, in the middle, the back porch of the hut. To the right the winter half of the hut and the gate; to the left the summer half and the cellar. To the right of the stage is a shed. The sound of tipsy voices and shouts are heard from the hut.[1] SECOND NEIGHBOR WOMAN comes out of the hut and beckons to FIRST NEIGHBOR WOMAN.

SECOND NEIGHBOR. How's it Akoulína has not shown herself?

FIRST NEIGHBOR. Why hasn't she shown herself? She'd have

[1] Where not otherwise mentioned in the stage directions, it is always the winter half of the hut that is referred to as "the hut." The summer half is not heated, and not used in winter under ordinary circumstances.

been glad to; but she's too ill, you know. The suitor's relatives
have come, and want to see the girl; and she, my dear, she's
lying in the cold hut and can't come out, poor thing!

SECOND NEIGHBOR. But how's that?

FIRST NEIGHBOR. They say she's been bewitched by an evil eye!
She's got pains in the stomach!

SECOND NEIGHBOR. You don't say so?

FIRST NEIGHBOR. What else could it be? (*Whispers.*)

SECOND NEIGHBOR. Dear me! There's a go! But his relatives
will surely find it out?

FIRST NEIGHBOR. They find it out! They're all drunk! Besides,
they are chiefly after her dowry. Just think what they give
with the girl! Two furs, my dear, six dresses, a French shawl,
and I don't know how many pieces of linen, and money as
well — two hundred roubles, it's said!

SECOND NEIGHBOR. That's all very well, but even money can't
give much pleasure in the face of such a disgrace.

FIRST NEIGHBOR. Hush!... There's his father, I think.

(*They cease talking and go into the hut.*)

(*The* SUITOR'S FATHER *comes out of the hut hiccoughing.*)

THE FATHER. Oh, I'm all in a sweat. It's awfully hot! Will just
cool myself a bit. (*Stands puffing.*) The Lord only knows
what — something is not right. I can't feel happy. — Well, it's
the old woman's affair.

(*Enter* MATRYÓNA *from hut.*)

MATRYÓNA. And I was just thinking, where's the father? Where's
the father? And here you are, dear friend.... Well, dear
friend, the Lord be thanked! Everything is as honorable as
can be! When one's arranging a match one should not boast.
And I have never learnt to boast. But as you've come about
the right business, so with the Lord's help, you'll be grateful
to me all your life! She's a wonderful girl! There's no other
like her in all the district!

THE FATHER. That's true enough, but how about the money?

MATRYÓNA. Don't you trouble about the money! All she had
from her father goes with her. And it's more than one gets
easily, as things are nowadays. Three times fifty roubles!

THE FATHER. We don't complain, but it's for our own child. Naturally we want to get the best we can.

MATRYÓNA. I'll tell you straight, friend: if it hadn't been for me, you'd never have found anything like her! They've had an offer from the Karmílins, but I stood out against it. And as for the money, I'll tell you truly: when her father, God be merciful to his soul, was dying, he gave orders that the widow should take Nikíta into the homestead — of course I know all about it from my son — and the money was to go to Akoulína. Why, another one might have thought of his own interests, but Nikíta gives everything clean! It's no trifle. Fancy what a sum it is!

THE FATHER. People are saying that more money was left her? The lad's sharp too!

MATRYÓNA. Oh, dear soul alive! A slice in another's hand always looks big; all she had will be handed over. I tell you, throw doubts to the wind and make all sure! What a girl she is! as fresh as a daisy!

THE FATHER. That's so. But my old woman and I were only wondering about the girl; why has she not come out? We've been thinking, suppose she's sickly?

MATRYÓNA. Ah, ah.... Who? She? Sickly? Why, there's none to compare with her in the district. The girl's as sound as a bell; you can't pinch her. But you saw her the other day! And as for work, she's wonderful! She's a bit deaf, that's true, but there are spots on the sun, you know. And her not coming out, you see, it's from an evil eye! A spell's been cast on her! And I know the bitch who's done the business! They know of the betrothal and they bewitched her. But I know a counter-spell. The girl will get up tomorrow. Don't you worry about the girl!

THE FATHER. Well, of course, the thing's settled.

MATRYÓNA. Yes, of course! Don't you turn back. And don't forget me, I've had a lot of trouble. Don't forget...

(*A woman's voice from the hut.*)

VOICE. If we are to go, let's go. Come along, Iván!

THE FATHER. I'm coming.

(*Exeunt. Guests crowd together in the passage and prepare to go away.*)

NAN (*runs out of the hut and calls to* ANÍSYA). Mother!

ANÍSYA (*from inside*). What d'you want?

NAN. Mother, come here, or they'll hear.

(ANÍSYA *enters and they go together to the shed.*)

ANÍSYA. Well? What is it? Where's Akoulína?

NAN. She's gone into the barn. It's awful what she's doing there! I'm blest! "I can't bear it," she says. "I'll scream," she says, "I'll scream out loud." Blest if she didn't.

ANÍSYA. She'll have to wait. We'll see our visitors off first.

NAN. Oh, mother! She's so bad! And she's angry too. "What's the good of their drinking my health?" she says. "I shan't marry," she says. "I shall die," she says. Mother, supposing she does die! It's awful. I'm so frightened!

ANÍSYA. No fear, she'll not die. But don't you go near her. Come along. (*Exit* ANÍSYA *and* NAN.)

MÍTRITCH (*comes in at the gate and begins collecting the scattered hay*). Oh, Lord! Merciful Nicholas! What a lot of liquor they've been and swilled, and the smell they've made! It smells even out here! But no, I don't want any, drat it! See how they've scattered the hay about. They don't eat it, but only trample it under foot. A truss gone before you know it. Oh, that smell, it seems to be just under my nose! Drat it! (*Yawns.*) It's time to go to sleep! But I don't care to go into the hut. It seems to float just round my nose! It has a strong scent, the damned stuff! (*The guests are heard driving off.*) They're off at last. Oh Lord! Merciful Nicholas! There they go, binding themselves and gulling one another. And it's all gammon!

(*Enter* NIKÍTA.)

NIKÍTA. Mítritch, you get off to sleep and I'll put this straight.

MÍTRITCH. All right, you throw it to the sheep. Well, have you seen 'em all off?

NIKÍTA. Yes, they're off! But things are not right! I don't know what to do!

MÍTRITCH. It's a fine mess. But there's the Foundlings' [1] for

---

[1] The Foundlings' Hospital in Moscow, where 80 to 90 per cent of the children were said to die.

that sort of thing. Whoever likes may drop one there; they'll take 'em all. Give 'em as many as you like, they ask no questions, and even pay — if the mother goes in as a wet-nurse. It's easy enough nowadays.

NIKÍTA. But mind, Mítritch, don't go blabbing.

MÍTRITCH. It's no concern of mine. Cover the tracks as you think best. Dear me, how you smell of liquor. I'll go in. Oh, Lord! *(Exit, yawning.)*

(NIKÍTA is long silent. Sits down on a sledge.)

NIKÍTA. Here's a go!

(Enter ANÍSYA.)

ANÍSYA. Where are you?

NIKÍTA. Here.

ANÍSYA. What are you doing there? There's no time to be lost! We must take it out directly!

NIKÍTA. What are we to do?

ANÍSYA. I'll tell you what you are to do. And you'll have to do it!

NIKÍTA. You'd better take it to the Foundlings' — if anything.

ANÍSYA. Then you'd better take it there yourself if you like! You've a hankering for smut, but you're weak when it comes to settling up, I see!

NIKÍTA. What's to be done?

ANÍSYA. Go down into the cellar, I tell you, and dig a hole!

NIKÍTA. Couldn't you manage, somehow, some other way?

ANÍSYA *(imitating him)*. "Some other way?" Seems we can't "some other way!" You should have thought about it a year ago. Do what you're told to!

NIKÍTA. Oh, dear, what a go!

(Enter NAN.)

NAN. Mother! Grandmother's calling! I think sister's got a baby! I'm blest if it didn't scream!

ANÍSYA. What are you babbling about? Plague take you! It's kittens whining there. Go into the hut and sleep, or I'll give it you!

NAN. Mammy dear, truly, I swear...

ANÍSYA *(raising her arm as if to strike)*. I'll give it you! You be off and don't let me catch sight of you! (NAN *runs into hut.* *To* NIKÍTA.) Do as you're told, or else mind! (*Exit.*)

NIKÍTA (*alone.* *After a long silence*). Here's a go! Oh, these women! What a fix! Says you should have thought of it a year ago. When's one to think beforehand? When's one to think? Why, last year this Anísya dangled after me. What was I to do? Am I a monk? The master died; and I covered my sin as was proper, so I was not to blame there. Aren't there lots of such cases? And then those powders. Did I put her up to that? Why, had I known what the bitch was up to, I'd have killed her! I'm sure I should have killed her! She's made me her partner in these horrors — that jade! And she became loathsome to me from that day! She became loathsome, loathsome to me as soon as mother told me about it. I can't bear the sight of her! Well, then, how could I live with her? And then it begun.... That wench began hanging round. Well, what was I to do! If I had not done it, someone else would. And this is what comes of it! Still I'm not to blame in this either. Oh, what a go! (*Sits thinking.*) They are bold, these women! What a plan to think of! But I won't have a hand in it!

(*Enter* MATRYÓNA *with a lantern and spade, panting.*)

MATRYÓNA. Why are you sitting there like a hen on a perch? What did your wife tell you to do? You just get things ready!

NIKÍTA. What do you mean to do?

MATRYÓNA. We know what to do. You do your share!

NIKÍTA. You'll be getting me into a mess!

MATRYÓNA. What? You're not thinking of backing out, are you? Now it's come to this, and you back out!

NIKÍTA. Think what a thing it would be! It's a living soul.

MATRYÓNA. A living soul indeed! Why, it's more dead than alive. And what's one to do with it? Go and take it to the Foundlings' — it will die just the same, and the rumor will get about, and people will talk, and the girl be left on our hands.

NIKÍTA. And supposing it's found out?

MATRYÓNA. Not manage to do it in one's own house? We'll manage it so that no one will have an inkling. Only do as

I tell you. We women can't do it without a man. There, take the spade, and get it done there — I'll hold the light.

NIKÍTA. What am I to get done?

MATRYÓNA (*in a low voice*). Dig a hole; then we'll bring it out and get it out of the way in a trice! There, she's calling again. Now then, get in, and I'll go.

NIKÍTA. Is it dead then?

MATRYÓNA. Of course it is. Only you must be quick, or else people will notice! They'll see or they'll hear! The rascals must needs know everything. And the policeman went by this evening. Well then, you see (*gives him the spade*), you get down into the cellar and dig a hole right in the corner; the earth is soft there, and you'll smooth it over. Mother earth will not blab to anyone; she'll keep it close. Go then; go, dear.

NIKÍTA. You'll get me into a mess, bother you! I'll go away! You do it alone as best you can!

ANÍSYA (*through the doorway*). Well? Has he dug it?

MATRYÓNA. Why have you come away? What have you done with it?

ANÍSYA. I've covered it with rags. No one can hear it. Well, has he dug it?

MATRYÓNA. He doesn't want to!

ANÍSYA (*springs out enraged*). Doesn't want to! How will he like feeding vermin in prison! I'll go straight away and tell everything to the police! It's all the same if one must perish. I'll go straight and tell!

NIKÍTA (*taken aback*). What will you tell?

ANÍSYA. What? Everything! Who took the money? You! (NIKÍTA *is silent.*) And who gave the poison? I did! But you knew! You knew! You knew! We were in agreement!

MATRYÓNA. That's enough now. Nikíta dear, why are you obstinate? What's to be done now? One must take some trouble. Go, honey.

ANÍSYA. See the fine gentleman! He doesn't like it! You've put upon me long enough! You've trampled me under foot! Now it's my turn! Go, I tell you, or else I'll do what I said.... There, take the spade; there, now go!

NIKÍTA. Drat you! Can't you leave a fellow alone! (*Takes the spade, but shrinks.*) If I don't choose to, I'll not go!

ANÍSYA. Not go? (*Begins to shout.*) Neighbors! Heh! heh!

MATRYÓNA (*closes her mouth*). What are you about? You're mad! He'll go.... Go, sonny, go, my own.

ANÍSYA. I'll cry murder!

NIKÍTA. Now stop! Oh, what people! You'd better be quick.... As well be hung for a sheep as a lamb! (*Goes towards the cellar.*)

MATRYÓNA. Yes, that's just it, honey. If you know how to amuse yourself, you must know how to hide the consequences.

ANÍSYA (*still excited*). He's trampled on me... he and his slut! But it's enough! I'm not going to be the only one! Let him also be a murderer! Then he'll know how it feels!

MATRYÓNA. There, there! How she flares up! Don't you be cross, lass, but do things quietly little by little, as it's best. You go to the girl, and he'll do the work.

(*Follows* NIKÍTA *to the cellar with the lantern. He descends into the cellar.*)

ANÍSYA. And I'll make him strangle his dirty brat! (*Still excited.*) I've worried myself to death all alone, with Peter's bones weighing on my mind! Let him feel it too! I'll not spare myself; I've said I'll not spare myself!

NIKÍTA (*from the cellar*). Show a light!

MATRYÓNA (*holds up the lantern to him. To* ANÍSYA). And I'll go and bring it.

ANÍSYA. You stay with him, or he'll go away, the wretch. And I'll go and bring it.

MATRYÓNA. Mind, don't forget to baptize it, or I will if you like. Have you a cross?

ANÍSYA. I'll find one. I know how to do it. (*Exit.*)

See at end of Act, Variation, which may be used instead of the following.

MATRYÓNA. How the woman bristled up! But one must allow she's been put upon. Well, but with the Lord's help, when we've covered this business, there'll be an end of it. We'll shove the girl off without any trouble. My son will live in comfort. The house, thank God, is as full as an egg. They'll not forget me either. Where would they have been without Matryóna? They'd not have known how to contrive things. (*Peering into the cellar.*) Is it ready, sonny?

NIKÍTA (*puts out his head*). What are you about there? Bring it quick! What are you dawdling for? If it is to be done, let it be done.

MATRYÓNA (*goes towards door of the hut and meets ANÍSYA. ANÍSYA comes out with a baby wrapped in rags*). Well, have you baptized it?

ANÍSYA. Why, of course. It was all I could do to take it away — she wouldn't give it up! (*Comes forward and hands it to NIKÍTA.*)

NIKÍTA (*does not take it*). You bring it yourself!

ANÍSYA. Take it, I tell you! (*Throws the baby to him.*)

NIKÍTA (*catches it*). It's alive! Gracious me, it's moving! It's alive! What am I to...

ANÍSYA (*snatches the baby from him and throws it into the cellar*). Be quick and smother it, and then it won't be alive! (*Pushes NIKÍTA down.*) It's your doing, and you must finish it.

MATRYÓNA (*sits on the doorstep of the hut*). He's tender-hearted. It's hard on him, poor dear. Well, what of that? Isn't it also his sin? (*ANÍSYA stands by the cellar.*)

MATRYÓNA (*sits looking at her and discourses*). Oh, oh, oh! How frightened he was: well, but what of that? If it *is* hard, it's the only thing to be done. Where was one to put it? And just think, how often it happens that people pray to God to have children! But no, God gives them none; or they are all still-born. Look at our priest's wife now.... And here, where it's not wanted, here it lives. (*Looks towards the cellar.*) I suppose he's finished. (*To ANÍSYA.*) Well?

ANÍSYA (*looking into the cellar*). He's put a board on it and is sitting on it. It must be finished!

MATRYÓNA. Oh, oh! One would be glad not to sin, but what's one to do?

(*Re-enter NIKÍTA from cellar, trembling all over.*)

NIKÍTA. It's still alive! I can't! It's alive!

ANÍSYA. If it's alive, where are you off to? (*Tries to stop him.*)

NIKÍTA (*rushes at her*). Go away! I'll kill you! (*Catches hold of her arms; she escapes, he runs after her with the spade.* MATRYÓNA *runs towards him and stops him.   ANÍSYA runs into the porch.   MATRY-ÓNA tries to wrench the spade from him.   To his mother.)* I'll kill you!   I'll kill you!   Go away!   (MATRYÓNA *runs to* ANÍSYA *in the porch.   NIKÍTA stops.)*   I'll kill you!   I'll kill you all!!

MATRYÓNA. That's because he's so frightened!   Never mind, it will pass!

NIKÍTA. What have they made me do?   What have they made me do?   How it whimpered.... How it crunched under me!   What have they done with me?... And it's really alive, still alive!   (*Listens in silence.*)   It's whimpering... There, it's whimpering.   (*Runs to the cellar.*)

MATRYÓNA (*to* ANÍSYA). He's going; it seems he means to bury it.   Nikíta, you'd better take the lantern!

NIKÍTA (*does not heed her, but listens by the cellar door*). I can hear nothing!   I suppose it was fancy!   (*Moves away, then stops.*)   How the little bones crunched under me.   Krr...kr... What have they made me do?   (*Listens again.*)   Again whimpering!   It's really whimpering!   What can it be?   Mother!   Mother, I say!   (*Goes up to her.*)

MATRYÓNA. What is it, sonny?

NIKÍTA. Mother, my own mother, I can't do any more!   Can't do any more!   My own mother, have some pity on me!

MATRYÓNA. Oh dear, how frightened you are, my darling!   Come, come, drink a drop to give you courage!

NIKÍTA. Mother, mother!   It seems my time has come!   What have you done with me?   How the little bones crunched, and how it whimpered!   My own mother!   What have you done with me?   (*Steps aside and sits down on the sledge.*)

MATRYÓNA. Come, my own, have a drink!   It certainly does seem uncanny at night-time.   But wait a bit.   When the day breaks, you know, and one day and another passes, you'll forget even to think of it.   Wait a bit; when the girl's married we'll even forget to think of it.   But you go and have a drink; have a drink!   I'll go and put things straight in the cellar myself.

NIKÍTA (*rouses himself*). Is there any drink left?   Perhaps I can drink it off!   (*Exit.*)

(ANÍSYA, *who has stood all the time by the door, silently makes way for him.*)

MATRYÓNA. Go, go, honey, and I'll set to work! I'll go down
myself and dig! Where has he thrown the spade to? (*Finds
the spade, and goes down into the cellar.*) Anísya, come here!
Hold the light, will you?

ANÍSYA. And what of him?

MATRYÓNA. He's so frightened! You've been too hard with
him. Leave him alone, he'll come to his senses. God help
him! I'll set to work myself. Put the lantern down here.
I can see. (MATRYÓNA *disappears into the cellar.*)

ANÍSYA (*looking towards the door by which* NIKÍTA *entered the hut*).
Well, have you had enough spree? You've been puffing
yourself up, but now you'll know how it feels! You'll lose some
of your bluster!

NIKÍTA (*rushes out of the hut towards the cellar*). Mother! Mother,
I say!

MATRYÓNA (*puts out her head*). What is it, sonny?

NIKÍTA (*listening*). Don't bury it, it's alive! Don't you hear?
Alive! There — it's whimpering! There... quite plain!

MATRYÓNA. How can it whimper? Why, you've flattened it
into a pancake! The whole head is smashed to bits!

NIKÍTA. What is it then? (*Stops his ears.*) It's still whimpering!
I am lost! Lost! What have they done with me?... Where
shall I go? (*Sits down on the step.*)

CURTAIN

VARIATION

*Instead of the end of Act IV (from the words, "*ANÍSYA. I'll find one.
I know how to do it. [Exit]*") the following variation may be read,
and is the one usually acted.*

SCENE II — *The interior of the hut as in Act I.*

NAN *lies on the bench, and is covered with a coat.* MÍTRITCH *is sitting
on the oven smoking.*

MÍTRITCH. Dear me! How they've made the place smell! Drat
'em! They've been spilling the fine stuff. Even tobacco don't
get rid of the smell! It keeps tickling one's nose so. Oh
Lord! But it's bedtime, I guess.

(*Approaches the lamp to put it out.*)

NAN (*jumps up, and remains sitting up*). Daddy dear,[1] don't put it out!

MÍTRITCH. Not put it out? Why?

NAN. Didn't you hear them making a row in the yard? (*Listens.*) D'you hear, there in the barn again now?

MÍTRITCH. What's that to you? I guess no one's asked you to mind! Lie down and sleep! And I'll turn down the light. (*Turns down lamp.*)

NAN. Daddy darling! Don't put it right out; leave a little bit if only as big as a mouse's eye, else it's so frightening!

MÍTRITCH (*laughs*). All right, all right. (*Sits down by her.*) What's there to be afraid of?

NAN. How can one help being frightened, daddy! Sister did go on so! She was beating her head against the box! (*Whispers.*) You know, I know... a little baby is going to be born.... It's already born, I think....

MÍTRITCH. Eh, what a little busybody it is! May the frogs kick her! Must needs know everything. Lie down and sleep! (NAN *lies down.*) That's right! (*Tucks her up.*) That's right! There now, if you know too much you'll grow old too soon.

NAN. And you are going to lie on the oven?

MÍTRITCH. Well, of course! What a little silly you are, now I come to look at you! Must needs know everything. (*Tucks her up again, then stands up to go.*) There now, lie still and sleep! (*Goes up to the oven.*)

NAN. It gave just one cry, and now there's nothing to be heard.

MÍTRITCH. Oh Lord! Gracious Nicholas! What is it you can't hear?

NAN. The baby.

MÍTRITCH. There is none, that's why you can't hear it.

NAN. But I heard it! Blest if I didn't hear it! Such a thin voice!

MÍTRITCH. Heard indeed! Much you heard! Well, if you know — why then it was just such a little girl as you that the bogey popped into his bag and made off with.

NAN. What bogey?

MÍTRITCH. Why, just his very self! (*Climbs up onto the oven.*) The oven is beautifully warm tonight. Quite a treat! Oh Lord! Gracious Nicholas!

NAN. Daddy! are you going to sleep?

---

[1] Nan calls Mítritch "daddy" merely as a term of endearment.

MÍTRITCH. What else? Do you think I'm going to sing songs? *(Silence.)*

NAN. Daddy! Daddy, I say! They are digging! they're digging — don't you hear? Blest if they're not, they're digging!

MÍTRITCH. What are you dreaming about? Digging! Digging in the night! Who's digging? The cow's rubbing herself, that's all. Digging indeed! Go to sleep I tell you, else I'll just put out the light!

NAN. Daddy darling, don't put it out! I won't... truly, truly, I won't. It's so frightful!

MÍTRITCH. Frightful? Don't be afraid and then it won't be frightful. Look at her, she's afraid, and then says it's frightful. How can it help being frightful if you are afraid? Eh, what a stupid little girl! *(Silence. The cricket chirps.)*

NAN *(whispers)*. Daddy! I say, daddy! Are you asleep?

MÍTRITCH. Now then, what d'you want?

NAN. What's the bogey like?

MÍTRITCH. Why, like this! When he finds such a one as you, who won't sleep, he comes with a sack and pops the girl into it, then in he gets himself, head and all, lifts her dress, and gives her a fine whipping!

NAN. What with?

MÍTRITCH. He takes a birch-broom with him.

NAN. But he can't see there — inside the sack!

MÍTRITCH. He'll see, no fear!

NAN. But I'll bite him.

MÍTRITCH. No, friend, him you can't bite!

NAN. Daddy, there's someone coming! Who is it? Oh gracious goodness! Who can it be?

MÍTRITCH. Well, if someone's coming, let them come! What's the matter with you? I suppose it's your mother!

(Enter ANÍSYA.*)*

ANÍSYA *(*NAN *pretends to be asleep)*. Mítritch!

MÍTRITCH. What?

ANÍSYA. What's the lamp burning for? We are going to sleep in the summer-hut.

MÍTRITCH. Why, you see I've only just got straight. I'll put the light out all right.

ANÍSYA (*rummages in her box and grumbles*). When a thing's wanted one never can find it!

MÍTRITCH. Why, what is it you are looking for?

ANÍSYA. I'm looking for a cross. Suppose it were to die unbaptized! It would be a sin, you know!

MÍTRITCH. Of course it would! Everything in due order.... Have you found it?

ANÍSYA. Yes, I've found it. (*Exit.*)

MÍTRITCH. That's right, else I'd have lent her mine. Oh Lord!

NAN (*jumps up trembling*). Oh, oh, daddy! Don't go to sleep; for goodness' sake, don't! It's so frightful!

MÍTRITCH. What's frightful?

NAN. It will die — the little baby will! At Aunt Irene's the old woman also baptized the baby, and it died!

MÍTRITCH. If it dies, they'll bury it!

NAN. But maybe it wouldn't have died, only old Granny Matryóna's there! Didn't I hear what granny was saying? I heard her! Blest if I didn't!

MÍTRITCH. What did you hear? Go to sleep, I tell you. Cover yourself up, head and all, and let's have an end of it!

NAN. If it lived, I'd nurse it!

MÍTRITCH (*roars*). Oh Lord!

NAN. Where will they put it?

MÍTRITCH. In the right place! It's no business of yours! Go to sleep I tell you, else mother will come; she'll give it you!

(*Silence.*)

NAN. Daddy! Eh, daddy! That girl, you know, you were telling about — they didn't kill her?

MÍTRITCH. That girl? Oh yes. That girl turned out all right!

NAN. How was it? You were saying you found her?

MÍTRITCH. Well, we just found her!

NAN. But where did you find her? Do tell!

MÍTRITCH. Why, in their own house; that's where! We came to a village, the soldiers began hunting about in the house, when suddenly there's that same little girl lying on the floor, flat on her stomach. We were going to give her a knock on the head, but all at once I felt that sorry, that I took her up in my arms; but no, she wouldn't let me! Made herself so heavy, quite a hundredweight, and caught hold where she could with her hands, so that one couldn't get them off! Well, so I began stroking her head. It was so bristly — just like a hedgehog! So I stroked and stroked, and she quieted down at last. I soaked a bit of rusk and gave it her. She understood that, and began nibbling. What were we to do with her? We took her; took her, and began feeding and feeding her, and she got so used to us that we took her with us on the march, and so she went about with us. Ah, she was a fine girl!

NAN. Yes, and not baptized?

MÍTRITCH. Who can tell! They used to say, not altogether. 'Cos why, those people weren't our own.

NAN. Germans?

MÍTRITCH. What an idea! Germans! Not Germans, but Asiatics. They are just the same as Jews, but still not Jews. Polish, yet Asiatics. Curls... or, Curdlys is their name.... I've forgotten what it is![1] We called the girl Sáshka. She was a fine girl, Sáshka was! There now, I've forgotten everything I used to know! But that girl — the deuce take her — seems to be before my eyes now! Out of all my time of service, I remember how they flogged me, and I remember that girl. That's all I remember! She'd hang round one's neck, and one 'ud carry her so. That was a girl — if you wanted a better you'd not find one! We gave her away afterwards. The captain's wife took her to bring up as her daughter. So — she was all right! How sorry the soldiers were to let her go!

NAN. There now, daddy, and I remember when father was dying — you were not living with us then. Well, he called Nikíta and says, "Forgive me, Nikíta!" he says, and begins to cry. (Sighs.) That also felt very sad!

MÍTRITCH. Yes; there now, so it is...

NAN. Daddy! Daddy, I say! There they are again, making a noise in the cellar! Oh gracious heavens! Oh dear! Oh dear! Oh, daddy! They'll do something to it! They'll make away with it, and it's so little! Oh, oh! (Covers up her head and cries.)

MÍTRITCH (listening). Really they're up to some villainy, blow them to shivers! Oh, these women are vile creatures! One

[1] Probably Kurds.

can't say much for men either; but women!…. They are like wild beasts, and stick at nothing!

NAN (*rising*). Daddy; I say, daddy!

MÍTRITCH. Well, what now?

NAN. The other day a traveller stayed the night; he said that when an infant died its soul goes up straight to heaven. Is that true?

MÍTRITCH. Who can tell? I suppose so. Well?

NAN. Oh, it would be best if I died too. (*Whimpers.*)

MÍTRITCH. Then you'd be off the list!

NAN. Up to ten one's an infant, and maybe one's soul would go to God. Else one's sure to go to the bad!

MÍTRITCH. And how to the bad? How should the likes of you not go to the bad? Who teaches you? What do you see? What do you hear? Only vileness! I, though I've not been taught much, still know a thing or two. I'm not quite like a peasant woman. A peasant woman, what is she? Just mud! There are many millions of the likes of you in Russia, and all as blind as moles — knowing nothing! All sorts of spells: how to stop the cattle-plague with a plough, and how to cure children by putting them under the perches in the hen-house! That's what they know!

NAN. Yes, mother also did that!

MÍTRITCH. Yes — there it is — just so! So many millions of girls and women, and all like beasts in a forest! As she grows up, so she dies! Never sees anything; never hears anything. A peasant — he may learn something at the pub, or maybe in prison, or in the army — as I did. But a woman? Let alone about God, she doesn't even know rightly what Friday it is! Friday! Friday! But ask her what's Friday? She don't know! They're like blind puppies, creeping about and poking their noses into the dung-heap…. All they know are their silly songs. Ho, ho, ho, ho! But what they mean by ho-ho, they don't know themselves!

NAN. But I, daddy, I do know half the Lord's Prayer!

MÍTRITCH. A lot you know! But what can one expect of you? Who teaches you? Only a tipsy peasant — with the strap perhaps! That's all the teaching you get! I don't know who'll have to answer for you. For a recruit, the drill-sergeant or the corporal has to answer; but for the likes of you there's no one responsible! Just as the cattle that have no herdsman are the most mischievous, so with you women — you are the stupidest class! The most foolish class is yours!

NAN. Then what's one to do?

MÍTRITCH. That's what one has to do.... You just cover up your head and sleep! Oh Lord! (*Silence. The cricket chirps.*)

NAN (*jumps up*). Daddy! Someone's screaming awfully! Blest if someone isn't screaming! Daddy darling, it's coming here!

MÍTRITCH. Cover up your head, I tell you!

(*Enter* NIKÍTA, *followed by* MATRYÓNA.)

NIKÍTA. What have they done with me? What have they done with me?

MATRYÓNA. Have a drop, honey; have a drop of drink! What's the matter? (*Fetches the spirits and sets the bottle before him.*)

NIKÍTA. Give it here! Perhaps the drink will help me!

MATRYÓNA. Mind! They're not asleep! Here you are, have a drop!

NIKÍTA. What does it all mean? Why did you plan it? You might have taken it somewhere!

MATRYÓNA (*whispers*). Sit still a bit and drink a little more, or have a smoke. It will ease your thoughts!

NIKÍTA. My own mother! My turn seems to have come! How it began to whimper, and how the little bones crunched... krr... I'm not a man now!

MATRYÓNA. Eh, now, what's the use of talking so silly! Of course it does seem fearsome at night, but wait till the daylight comes, and a day or two passes, and you'll forget to think of it! (*Goes up to* NIKÍTA *and puts her hand on his shoulder.*)

NIKÍTA. Go away from me! What have you done with me?

MATRYÓNA. Come, come, sonny! Now, really, what's the matter with you? (*Takes his hand.*)

NIKÍTA. Go away from me! I'll kill you! It's all one to me now! I'll kill you!

MATRYÓNA. Oh, oh, how frightened he's got! You should go and have a sleep now!

NIKÍTA. I have nowhere to go; I'm lost!

MATRYÓNA (*shaking her head*). Oh, oh, I'd better go and tidy things up. He'll sit and rest a bit, and it will pass!   (*Exit.*)

(NIKÍTA *sits with his face in his hands.* MÍTRITCH *and* NAN *seem stunned.*)

NIKÍTA. It's whining! It's whining! It is really — there, there, quite plain! She'll bury it, really she will!   (*Runs to the door.*) Mother, don't bury it, it's alive....

(*Enter* MATRYÓNA.)

MATRYÓNA (*whispers*). Now then, what is it? Heaven help you! Why won't you get to rest? How can it be alive? All its bones are crushed!

NIKÍTA. Give me more drink.   (*Drinks.*)

MATRYÓNA. Now go, sonny. You'll fall asleep now all right.

NIKÍTA (*stands listening*). Still alive... there... it's whining! Don't you hear?... There!

MATRYÓNA (*whispers*). No! I tell you!

NIKÍTA. Mother! My own mother! I've ruined my life! What have you done with me? Where am I to go?

(*Runs out of the hut;* MATRYÓNA *follows him.*)

NAN. Daddy dear, darling, they've smothered it!

MÍTRITCH (*angrily*). Go to sleep, I tell you! Oh dear, may the frogs kick you! I'll give it to you with the broom! Go to sleep, I tell you!

NAN. Daddy, my treasure! Something is catching hold of my shoulders, something is catching hold with its paws! Daddy dear... really, really... I must go! Daddy, darling! let me get up on the oven with you! Let me, for Heaven's sake! Catching hold... catching hold! Oh!   (*Runs to the stove.*)

MÍTRITCH. See how they've frightened the girl.... What vile creatures they are! May the frogs kick them! Well then, climb up.

NAN (*climbs on oven*). But don't you go away!

MÍTRITCH. Where should I go? Climb up, climb up! Oh Lord! Gracious Nicholas! Holy Mother!... How they have frightened the girl. (*Covers her up.*) There's a little fool — really a little fool! How they've frightened her; really, they are vile creatures! The deuce take 'em!

CURTAIN

ACT V

SCENE I

In front of scene a stack-stand, to the left a thrashing ground, to the right a barn. The barn doors are open. Straw is strewn about in the doorway. The hut with yard and out-buildings is seen in the background, whence proceeds sounds of singing and of a tambourine. Two GIRLS *are walking past the barn towards the hut.*

FIRST GIRL. There, you see we've managed to pass without so much as getting our boots dirty! But to come by the street is terribly muddy! (*Stop and wipe their boots on the straw.* FIRST GIRL *looks at the straw and sees something.*) What's that?

SECOND GIRL (*looks where the straw lies and sees someone*). It's Mítritch, their laborer. Just look how drunk he is!

FIRST GIRL. Why, I thought he didn't drink.

SECOND GIRL. It seems he didn't, until it was going around.

FIRST GIRL. Just see! He must have come to fetch some straw. Look! he's got a rope in his hand, and he's fallen asleep.

SECOND GIRL (*listening*). They're still singing the praises.[1] So I s'pose the bride and bridegroom have not yet been blessed! They say Akoulína didn't even lament![2]

FIRST GIRL. Mammie says she is marrying against her will. Her stepfather threatened her, or else she'd not have done it for the world! Why, you know what they've been saying about her?

MARÍNA (*catching up the* GIRLS). How d'you do, lassies?

GIRLS. How d'you do?

MARÍNA. Going to the wedding, my dears?

FIRST GIRL. It's nearly over! We've come just to have a look.

MARÍNA. Would you call my old man for me? Simon, from Zoúevo; but surely you know him?

FIRST GIRL. To be sure we do; he's a relative of the bridegroom's, I think?

MARÍNA. Of course; he's my old man's nephew, the bridegroom is.

---

[1] This refers to the songs customary at the wedding of Russian peasants, praising the bride and bridegroom.

[2] It is etiquette for a bride to bewail the approaching loss of her maidenhood.

SECOND GIRL. Why don't you go yourself? Fancy not going to a wedding!

MARÍNA. I have no mind for it, and no time either. It's time for us to be going home. We didn't mean to come to the wedding. We were taking oats to town. We only stopped to feed the horse, and they made my old man go in.

FIRST GIRL. Where did you put up then? At Fyódoritch's?

MARÍNA. Yes. Well then, I'll stay here and you go and call him, my dear — my old man. Call him, my pet, and say "Your missis, Marína, says you must go now!" His mates are harnessing.

FIRST GIRL. Well, all right — if you won't go in yourself.

(*The* GIRLS *go away towards the house along a footpath. Sounds of songs and tambourine.*)

MARÍNA (*alone, stands thinking*). I might go in, but I don't like to, because I have not met him since that day he threw me over. It's more than a year now. But I'd have liked to have a peep and see how he lives with his Anísya. People say they don't get on. She's a coarse woman, and with a character of her own. I should think he's remembered me more than once. He's been caught by the idea of a comfortable life and has changed me for it. But, God help him, I don't cherish ill-will! Then it hurt! Oh dear, it was pain! But now it's worn away and been forgotten. But I'd like to have seen him. (*Looks towards hut and sees* NIKÍTA.) Look there! Why, he is coming here! Have the girls told him? How's it he has left his guests? I'll go away! (NIKÍTA *approaches, hanging his head down, swinging his arms, and muttering.*) And how sullen he looks.

NIKÍTA (*sees and recognizes* MARÍNA). Marína, dearest friend, little Marina, what do you want?

MARÍNA. I have come for my old man.

NIKÍTA. Why didn't you come to the wedding? You might have had a look round, and a laugh at my expense!

MARÍNA. What have I to laugh at? I've come for my husband.

NIKÍTA. Ah, Marína dear! (*Tries to embrace her.*)

MARÍNA (*steps angrily aside*). You'd better drop that sort of thing, Nikíta! What has been is past! I've come for my husband. Is he in your house?

NIKÍTA. So I must not remember the past? You won't let me?

MARÍNA. It's no use recalling the past! What used to be is over now!

NIKÍTA. And can never come back, you mean?

MARÍNA. And will never come back! But why have you gone away? You, the master — and to go away from the feast!

NIKÍTA (sits down on the straw). Why have I gone away? Eh, if you knew, if you had any idea... I'm dull, Marína, so dull that I wish my eyes would not see! I rose from the table and left them, to get away from the people. If I could only avoid seeing anyone!

MARÍNA (coming nearer to him). How's that?

NIKÍTA. This is how it is: when I eat, it's there! When I drink, it's there! When I sleep, it's there! I'm so sick of it — so sick! But it's chiefly because I'm all alone that I'm so sick, Marína. I have no one to share my trouble.

MARÍNA. You can't live your life without trouble, Nikíta. However, I've wept over mine and wept it away.

NIKÍTA. The former, the old trouble! Ah, dear friend, you've wept yours away, and I've got mine up to there!

(Puts his hand to his throat.)

MARÍNA. But why?

NIKÍTA. Why, I'm sick of my whole life! I am sick of myself! Ah, Marína, why did you not know how to keep me? You've ruined me, and yourself too! Is this life?

MARÍNA (stands by the barn crying, but restrains herself). I do not complain of my life, Nikíta! God grant everyone a life like mine. I do not complain. I confessed to my old man at the time, and he forgave me. And he does not reproach me. I'm not discontented with my life. The old man is quiet, and is fond of me, and I keep his children clothed and washed! He is really kind to me. Why should I complain? It seems God willed it so. And what's the matter with your life? You are rich...

NIKÍTA. My life!... It's only that I don't wish to disturb the wedding feast, or I'd take this rope here (takes hold of the rope on the straw) and throw it across that rafter there. Then I'd make a noose and stretch it out, and I'd climb on to that rafter and jump down with my head in the noose! That's what my life is!

MARÍNA. That's enough! Lord help you!

NIKÍTA. You think I'm joking? You think I'm drunk? I'm not drunk! Today even drink takes no hold on me! I'm devoured by misery! Misery is eating me up completely, so that I care for nothing! Oh little Marína, it's only with you I ever lived! Do you remember how we used to while away the nights together at the railway?

MARÍNA. Don't you rub the sores, Nikíta! I'm bound legally now, and you too. My sin has been forgiven, don't disturb...

NIKÍTA. What shall I do with my heart? Where am I to turn to?

MARÍNA. What's there to be done? You've got a wife. Don't go looking at others, but keep to your own! You loved Anísya, then go on loving her!

NIKÍTA. Oh, that Anísya, she's gall and wormwood to me, but she's round my feet like rank weeds!

MARÍNA. Whatever she is, still she's your wife.... But what's the use of talking; you'd better go to your visitors, and send my husband to me.

NIKÍTA. Oh dear, if you knew the whole business... but there's no good talking!

(Enter MARÍNA's *husband, red and tipsy, and* NAN.)

MARÍNA'S HUSBAND. Marína! Missis! My old woman! are you here?

NIKÍTA. There's your husband calling you. Go!

MARÍNA. And you?

NIKÍTA. I? I'll lie down here for a bit! *(Lies down on the straw.)*

HUSBAND. Where is she then?

NAN. There she is, near the barn.

HUSBAND. What are you standing there for? Come to the feast! The hosts want you to come and do them honor! The wedding party is just going to start, and then we can go too.

MARÍNA *(going towards her husband)*. I didn't want to go in.

HUSBAND. Come on, I tell you! You'll drink a glass to our nephew Peter's health, the rascal! Else the hosts might take offense! There's plenty of time for our business.

*(*MARÍNA's *husband puts his arm around her, and goes reeling out with her.)*

NIKÍTA (*rises and sits down on the straw*). Ah, now that I've seen her, life seems more sickening than ever! It was only with her that I ever really lived! I've ruined my life for nothing! I've done for myself! (*Lies down.*) Where can I go? If mother earth would but open and swallow me!

NAN (*sees* NIKÍTA, *and runs towards him*). Daddy, I say, daddy! They're looking for you! Her godfather and all of them have already blessed her. Truly they have, they're getting cross!

NIKÍTA (*aside*). Where can I go to?

NAN. What? What are you saying?

NIKÍTA. I'm not saying anything! Don't bother!

NAN. Daddy! Come, I say! (NIKÍTA *is silent*, NAN *pulls him by the hand*.) Dad, go and bless them! My word, they're angry, they're grumbling!

NIKÍTA (*drags away his hand*). Leave me alone!

NAN. Now then!

NIKÍTA (*threatens her with the rope*). Go, I say! I'll give it you!

NAN. Then I'll send mother! (*Runs away.*)

NIKÍTA (*rises*). How can I go? How can I take the holy icón in my hands? How am I to look her in the face! (*Lies down again.*) Oh, if there were a hole in the ground, I'd jump in! No one should see me, and I should see no one! (*Rises again.*) No, I shan't go.... May they all go to the devil, I shan't go! (*Takes the rope and makes a noose, and tries it on his neck.*) That's the way!

(*Enter* MATRYÓNA. NIKÍTA *sees his mother, takes the rope off his neck, and again lies down in the straw.*)

MATRYÓNA (*comes in hurriedly*). Nikíta! Nikíta, I say! He don't even answer! Nikíta, what's the matter? Have you had a drop too much? Come, Nikíta dear; come, honey! The people are tired of waiting.

NIKÍTA. Oh dear, what have you done with me? I'm a lost man!

MATRYÓNA. But what is the matter then? Come, my own; come give them your blessing, as is proper and honorable, and then it'll all be over! Why, the people are waiting!

NIKÍTA. How can I give blessings?

MATRYÓNA. Why, in the usual way! Don't you know?

NIKÍTA. I know, I know! But who is it I am to bless? What have I done to her?

MATRYÓNA. What have you done? Eh, now he's going to remember it! Why, who knows anything about it? Not a soul! And the girl is going of her own accord.

NIKÍTA. Yes, but how?

MATRYÓNA. Because she's afraid, of course. But still she's going. Besides, what's to be done now? She should have thought sooner! Now she can't refuse. And his kinsfolks can't take offense either. They saw the girl twice, and get money with her too! It's all safe and sound!

NIKÍTA. Yes, but what's in the cellar?

MATRYÓNA (laughs). In the cellar? Why, cabbages, mushrooms, potatoes, I suppose! Why remember the past?

NIKÍTA. I'd be only too glad to forget it; but I can't! When I let my mind go, it's just as if I heard…. Oh, what have you done with me?

MATRYÓNA. Now, what are you humbugging for?

NIKÍTA (turns face downward). Mother! Don't torment me! I've got it up to there! (Puts his hand to his throat.)

MATRYÓNA. Still it has to be done! As it is, people are talking. "The master's gone away and won't come; he can't make up his mind to give his blessing." They'll be putting two and two together. As soon as they see you're frightened they'll begin guessing. "The thief none suspect who walks bold and erect!" But you'll be getting out of the frying-pan into the fire! Above all, lad, don't show it; don't lose courage, else they'll find out all the more!

NIKÍTA. Oh dear! You have snared me into a trap!

MATRYÓNA. That'll do, I tell you; come along! Come in and give your blessing, as is right and honorable; — and there's an end of the matter!

NIKÍTA (lies face down). I can't!

MATRYÓNA (aside). What has come over him? He seemed all right, and suddenly this comes over him! It seems he's bewitched! Get up, Nikíta! See! There's Anísya coming; she's left her guests!

(ANÍSYA *enters, dressed up, red and tipsy.*)

ANÍSYA. Oh, how nice it is, mother! So nice, so respectable! And how the people are pleased.... But where is he?

MATRYÓNA. Here, honey, he's here; he's laid down on the straw and there he lies! He won't come!

NIKÍTA (*looking at his wife*). Just see, she's tipsy too! When I look at her my heart seems to turn! How can one live with her? (*Turns on his face.*) I'll kill her some day! It'll be worse then!

ANÍSYA. Only look, how he's got all among the straw! Is it the drink? (*Laughs.*) I'd not mind lying down there with you, but I've no time! Come, I'll lead you! It is so nice in the house! It's a treat to look on! A concertina! And the women singing so well! All tipsy! Everything so respectable, so nice!

NIKÍTA. What's nice?

ANÍSYA. The wedding — such a jolly wedding! They all say it's quite an uncommon fine wedding. All so respectable, so nice! Come along! We'll go together! I have had a drop, but I can give you a hand yet! (*Takes his hand.*)

NIKÍTA (*pulls it back with disgust*). Go alone! I'll come!

ANÍSYA. What are you humbugging for? We've got rid of all the bother, we've got rid of her as came between us; now we have nothing to do but to live and be merry! And all so respectable, and quite legal! I'm so pleased! I have no words for it! It's just as if I were going to marry you over again! And oh, the people, they *are* pleased! They're all thanking us! And the guests are all of the best: Ivan Moséitch is there, and the Police Officer; they've also been singing songs of praise!

NIKÍTA. Then you should have stayed with them! What have you come for?

ANÍSYA. True enough, I must go back! Else what does it look like! The hosts both go and leave the visitors! And the guests are all of the best!

NIKÍTA (*gets up and brushes the straw off himself*). Go, and I'll come at once!

MATRYÓNA. Just see! He listens to the young bird, but wouldn't listen to the old one! He would not hear me, but he follows his wife at once! (MATRYÓNA *and* ANÍSYA *turn to go.*) Well, are you coming?

NIKÍTA. I'll come directly! You go and I'll follow! I'll come and give my blessing! (*The women stop.*) Go on! I'll follow! Now then, go! (*Exit women. Sits down and takes his boots off.*) Yes, I'm going! A likely thing! No, you'd better look at the rafter for me! I'll fix the noose and jump with it from the rafter, then you can look for me! And the rope is here just handy. (*Ponders.*) I'd have got over it, over any sorrow — I'd have got over that. But this now — here it is, deep in my heart, and I can't get over it! (*Looks towards the yard.*) Surely she's not coming back? (*Imitates* ANÍSYA.) "So nice, so nice. I'd lie down here with you." Oh, the baggage! Well, then, here I am! Come and cuddle when they've taken me down from the rafter! There's only one way!

(*Takes the rope and pulls it.*)

(MÍTRITCH, *who is tipsy, sits up and won't let go of the rope.*)

MÍTRITCH. Shan't give it up! Shan't give it to no one! I'll bring it myself! I said I'd bring the straw — and so I will! Nikíta, is that you? (*Laughs.*) Oh, the devil! Have you come to get the straw?

NIKÍTA. Give me the rope!

MÍTRITCH. No, you wait a bit! The peasants sent me! I'll bring it... (*Rises to his feet and begins getting the straw together, but reels for a time, then falls.*) It has beaten me. It's stronger...

NIKÍTA. Give me the rope!

MÍTRITCH. Didn't I say I won't! Oh, Nikíta, you're as stupid as a hog! (*Laughs.*) I love you, but you're a fool! You see that I'm drunk... devil take you! You think I need you?... You just look at me; I'm a Non... fool, can't say it — Non-commissioned officer of Her Majesty's very First Regiment of Grenadier Guards! I've served Tsar and country, loyal and true! But who am I? You think I'm a warrior? No, I'm not a warrior; I'm the very least of men, a poor lost orphan! I swore not to drink, and now I had a smoke, and... Well then, do you think I'm afraid of you? No fear; I'm afraid of no man! I've taken to drink, and I'll drink! Now I'll go it for a fortnight; I'll go it hard! I'll drink my last shirt; I'll drink my cap; I'll pawn my passport; and I'm afraid of no one! They flogged me in the army to stop me drinking! They switched and switched! "Well," they say, "will you leave off?" "No," says I! Why should I be afraid of them? Here I am! Such as I am, God made me! I swore off drinking, and didn't drink. Now I've took to drink, and I'll drink! And I fear no man! 'Cos I don't lie; but just as... Why should one mind them — such muck as they are! "Here you are," I say; that's me. A priest told me, the devil's the biggest bragger! "As soon," says he, "as you begin to brag, you get frightened; and as soon as you fear men, then the hoofed one just collars you and pushes you where he likes!" But as I don't fear men, I'm easy! I can spit in the devil's beard, and at the sow his mother! He can't do me no harm! There, put that in your pipe!

NIKÍTA (*crossing himself*). True enough! What was I about?

(*Throws down the rope.*)

MÍTRITCH. What?

NIKÍTA (*rises*). You tell me not to fear men?

MÍTRITCH. Why fear such muck as they are? You look at 'em in the bath-house! All made of one paste! One has a bigger belly, another a smaller; that's all the difference there is! Fancy being afraid of 'em! Deuce take 'em!

MATRYÓNA (*from the yard*). Well, are you coming?

NIKÍTA. Ah! Better so! I'm coming! (*Goes toward yard.*)

SCENE II

Interior of hut, full of people, some sitting round tables and others standing. In the front corner AKOULÍNA *and the* BRIDEGROOM. *On one of the tables an Icón and a loaf of rye bread. Among the visitors are* MARÍNA, *her husband, and a* POLICE OFFICER, *also a* HIRED DRIVER, *the* MATCHMAKER, *and the* BEST MAN. *The women are singing.* ANÍSYA *carries round the drink. The singing stops.*

THE DRIVER. If we are to go, let's go! The church ain't so near.

THE BEST MAN. All right; you wait a bit till the stepfather has given his blessing. But where is he?

ANÍSYA. He is coming — coming at once, dear friends! Have another glass, all of you; don't refuse!

THE MATCHMAKER. Why is he so long? We've been waiting such a time!

ANÍSYA. He's coming; coming directly, coming in no time!

He'll be here before one could plait a girl's hair who's had her hair cropped! Drink, friends! (*Offers the drink.*) Coming at once! Sing again, my pets, meanwhile!

THE DRIVER. They've sung all their songs, waiting here!

(*The women sing. NIKÍTA and AKÍM enter during the singing.*)

NIKÍTA (*holds his father's arm and pushes him in before him*). Go, father; I can't do without you!

AKÍM. I don't like — I mean what d'ye call it...

NIKÍTA (*to the women*). Enough! Be quiet! (*Looks round the hut.*) Marína, are you there?

THE MATCHMAKER. Go, take the icón, and give them your blessing!

NIKÍTA. Wait a while! (*Looks round.*) Akoulína, are you there?

MATCHMAKER. What are you calling everybody for? Where should she be? How queer he seems!

ANÍSYA. Gracious goodness! Why, he's barefoot!

NIKÍTA. Father, you are here! Look at me! Christian Commune, you are all here, and I am here! I am...

(*Falls on his knees.*)

ANÍSYA. Nikíta, darling, what's the matter with you? Oh, my head, my head!

MATCHMAKER. Here's a go!

MATRYÓNA. I did say he was taking too much of that French wine! Come to your senses; what are you about?

(*They try to lift him; he takes no heed of them, but looks in front of him.*)

NIKÍTA. Christian Commune! I have sinned, and I wish to confess!

MATRYÓNA (*shakes him by the shoulder*). Are you mad? Dear friends, he's gone crazy! He must be taken away!

NIKÍTA (*shakes her off*). Leave me alone! And you, father, hear me! And first, Marína, look here! (*Bows to the ground to her and rises.*) I have sinned towards you! I promised to marry you, I tempted you, and forsook you! Forgive me, in Christ's name! (*Again bows to the ground before her.*)

ANÍSYA. And what are you drivelling about? It's not becoming! No one wants to know! Get up! It's like your impudence!

MATRYÓNA. Oh, oh, he's bewitched! And how ever did it happen? It's a spell! Get up! what nonsense are you jabbering?

(*Pulls him.*)

NIKÍTA (*shakes his head*). Don't touch me! Forgive me my sin towards you, Marína! Forgive me, for Christ's sake!

(MARÍNA *covers her face with her hands in silence*.)

ANÍSYA. Get up, I tell you! Don't be so impudent! What are you thinking about — to recall it? Enough humbug! It's shameful! Oh my poor head! He's quite crazy!

NIKÍTA (*pushes his wife away and turns to* AKOULÍNA). Akoulína, now I'll speak to you! Listen, Christian Commune! I'm a fiend, Akoulína! I have sinned against you! Your father died no natural death! He was poisoned!

ANÍSYA (*screams*). Oh my head! What's he about?

MATRYÓNA. The man's beside himself! Lead him away!

(*The folk come up and try to seize him*.)

AKÍM (*motions them back with his arms*). Wait! You lads, what d'ye call it, wait, I mean!

NIKÍTA. Akoulína, I poisoned him! Forgive me, in Christ's name!

AKOULÍNA (*jumps up*). He's telling lies! I know who did it!

MATCHMAKER. What are you about? You sit still!

AKÍM. Oh Lord, what sins, what sins!

POLICE OFFICER. Seize him, and send for the Elder! We must draw up an indictment and have witnesses to it! Get up and come here!

AKÍM (*to* POLICE OFFICER). Now you — with the bright buttons — I mean, you wait! Let him, what d'ye call it, speak out, I mean!

POLICE OFFICER. Mind, old man, and don't interfere! I have to draw up an indictment!

AKÍM. Eh, what a fellow you are; wait, I say! Don't talk, I mean about, what d'ye call it, 'ditements. Here God's work is being done.... A man is confessing, I mean! And you, what d'ye call it... 'ditements!

POLICE OFFICER. The Elder!

AKÍM. Let God's work be done, I mean, and then you, I mean, you, do your business!

NIKÍTA. And, Akoulína, my sin is great towards you; I seduced you; forgive me in Christ's name! (*Bows to the ground before her*.)

AKOULÍNA (*leaves the table*). Let me go! I shan't be married! He told me to, but I shan't now!

POLICE OFFICER. Repeat what you have said.

NIKÍTA. Wait, sir, let me finish!

AKÍM (*with rapture*). Speak, my son! Tell everything — you'll feel better! Confess to God, don't fear men! God — God! It is He!

NIKÍTA. I poisoned the father, dog that I am, and I ruined the daughter! She was in my power, and I ruined her, and her baby!

AKOULÍNA. True, that's true!

NIKÍTA. I smothered the baby in the cellar with a board! I sat on it and smothered it — and its bones crunched! (*Weeps.*) And I buried it! I did it, all alone!

AKOULÍNA. He raves! I told him to!

NIKÍTA. Don't shield me! I fear no one now! Forgive me, Christian Commune! (*Bows to the ground.*)

(*Silence.*)

POLICE OFFICER. Bind him! The marriage is evidently off!

(*Men come up with their belts.*)

NIKÍTA. Wait, there's plenty of time! (*Bows to the ground before his father.*) Father, dear father, forgive me too — fiend that I am! You told me from the first, when I took to bad ways, you said then, "If a claw is caught, the bird is lost!" I would not listen to your words, dog that I was, and it has turned out as you said! Forgive me, for Christ's sake!

AKÍM (*rapturously*). God will forgive you, my own son! (*Embraces him.*) You have had no mercy on yourself; He will show mercy on you! God — God! It is He!

(*Enter* ELDER.)

ELDER. There are witnesses enough here.

POLICE OFFICER. We will have the examination at once.

(NIKÍTA *is bound.*)

AKOULÍNA (*goes and stands by his side*). I shall tell the truth! Ask me!

NIKÍTA (*bound*). No need to ask! I did it all myself. The design was mine, and the deed was mine. Take me where you like. I will say no more!

CURTAIN

PELLÉAS AND MÉLISANDE

By MAURICE MAETERLINCK

Translated by RICHARD HOVEY

On its first publication this play was dedicated as follows:

TO

OCTAVE MIRBEAU

IN WITNESS OF DEEP FRIENDSHIP
ADMIRATION AND GRATITUDE

M. M.

MAURICE MAETERLINCK

MAURICE MAETERLINCK was born at Ghent, Belgium, August 27, 1862, of a Flemish line extending back many centuries. As a youth in school he showed ability in Latin translation, and studied for the law. Visiting Paris in 1886 he came under the influence of Villiers de l'Isle Adam and the symbolists. His first story was entitled "The Massacre of the Innocents," and was published in *The Pleiade*. Of "La Princesse Maleine," brought out in 1889 by *La jeune Belgique*, Octave Mirbeau wrote: "I do not know M. Maurice Maeterlinck.... I know only that he has created a masterpiece." And he compared Maeterlinck with Shakespeare, by whom, and by the later Elizabethan dramatists, he has been much influenced. Returning to Flanders after his years in Paris, Maeterlinck established himself in the country, where, keeping bees and growing flowers, he developed a sensitive intimacy with the secrets of nature. His plays have been translated into English by Richard Hovey, Bernard Miall, Charlotte Porter, Alfred Sutro, William Archer and Alexander Teixeira de Mattos.

Maeterlinck's work as a playwright falls into two clearly marked stages. In the first period he is the proponent of the static school of dramatic writing. Though Maeterlinck's theories during his first period have been clouded with a great deal of mystical expression, his service for the art of the theater has been neither vague nor mystical. He was in fact the first playwright to compose plays for production under the new theories of stage art, many of which he anticipated. In particular he anticipated Gordon Craig in raising the question of the place of the actor in the production. By his new conceptions of setting, and by eliminating the factor of will from drama, he prepared the way for the generation of stage designers. This was his most important period during which he influenced such diverse geniuses as D'Annunzio, Strindberg, Andreyev, and Claudel. During his second period, Maeterlinck repudiated much for which he had stood in his more significant work. He now writes, "Do what one will, discover what marvels one may, the sovereign law of the stage, its essential demand, will always be action." (*The Double Garden*.)

MAURICE MAETERLINCK

Maurice Maeterlinck was born at Ghent, Belgium,

PELLÉAS AND MÉLISANDE

THE form of drama represented by this play diverges from both
naturalism and romanticism. It is evident at first view that the
author seeks neither to give a photographic expression to external
phenomena, nor to adorn a fable by phrasing it in beautiful
literary language. In fact, the play constrains both the factors
of action and of speech. So static is the treatment, so colorless
and anemic is the speech, that whatever ends the play may serve
must be sought elsewhere than in the usual interests of playwriting.
When we seek to find what those ends are, we reach two answers.
There is little doubt that *Pelléas and Mélisande* is in form a libretto
for a new kind of stage production, which includes not music alone,
but new theories of setting, of tempo, of action, and of the function
of the actor. Like many of Maeterlinck's early plays, it is a play
for puppets. In production it was most successful when completed by Debussy's music. Though the play should be considered
as primarily a technical achievement of first importance and very
great influence in the history of the theater, its spiritual and philo-
sophical values should not be ignored. So considered *Pelléas and
Mélisande* belongs to the class of symbolism. Symbolism in drama
is essentially a modern form which borrows from the religious
drama of the late Middle Ages the quality of implying more
than it says. It is a commonplace to trace Maeterlinck's early
plays to the influence of the Symbolist Movement in France.
This movement has not elsewhere found a foothold in the French
Theater, and it is to be questioned whether the source of Maeterlinck's early genius does not derive rather from the German
romanticism of Tieck, Novalis, and Hoffmann than from the
decadent poets of the French Symbolist School. *Pelléas and
Mélisande* was published in 1892, and produced May 16, 1893, at
Paris. With incidental music by Claude Debussy, it was produced at the Opéra Comique, Paris, April 30, 1902. When it was
presented in Germany in 1898, Max Reinhardt played the part of
the King. In 1903, Reinhardt produced the play as one of the
first offerings of the Neues Theater.

PERSONS

ARKËL, *King of Allemonde*
GENEVIÈVE, *mother of Pelléas and Golaud*
PELLÉAS }
GOLAUD } *grandsons of Arkël*
MÉLISANDE, *wife of Golaud*
YNIOLD, *son of Golaud (by a former marriage)*
A PHYSICIAN
THE PORTER
            Servants, Beggars, etc.

ACT I

SCENE I — *The gate of the castle.*

MAIDSERVANTS (*within*). Open the gate! Open the gate!

PORTER (*within*). Who is there? Why do you come and wake me up? Go out by the little gates; there are enough of them!...

A MAIDSERVANT (*within*). We have come to wash the threshold, the gate, and the steps; open, then! open!

ANOTHER MAIDSERVANT (*within*). There are going to be great happenings!

THIRD MAIDSERVANT (*within*). There are going to be great fêtes! Open quickly!

THE MAIDSERVANTS. Open! open!

PORTER. Wait! wait! I do not know whether I shall be able to open it;... it is never opened.... Wait till it is light....

FIRST MAIDSERVANT. It is light enough without; I see the sunlight through the chinks....

PORTER. Here are the great keys.... Oh! oh! how the bolts and the locks grate!... Help me! help me!...

MAIDSERVANTS. We are pulling; we are pulling....

SECOND MAIDSERVANT. It will not open....

FIRST MAIDSERVANT. Ah! ah! It is opening! it is opening slowly!

PORTER. How it shrieks! how it shrieks! It will wake up everybody....

SECOND MAIDSERVANT (*appearing on the threshold*). Oh, how light it is already out-of-doors!

FIRST MAIDSERVANT. The sun is rising on the sea!

PORTER. It is open.... It is wide open!

(*All the maidservants appear on the threshold and pass over it.*)

FIRST MAIDSERVANT. I am going to wash the sill first....

SECOND MAIDSERVANT. We shall never be able to clean all this.

OTHER MAIDSERVANTS. Fetch the water! fetch the water!

PORTER. Yes, yes; pour on water; pour on water; pour on all the water of the Flood! You will never come to the end of it....

Scene II — *A forest.* Mélisande *discovered at the brink of a spring.*
(*Enter* Golaud.)

golaud. I shall never be able to get out of this forest again. —
God knows where that beast has led me. And yet I thought
I had wounded him to death; and here are traces of blood.
But now I have lost sight of him; I believe I am lost myself —
my dogs can no longer find me — I shall retrace my steps....
I hear weeping... Oh! oh! what is there yonder by the water's
edge?... A little girl weeping by the water's edge? (*He coughs.*)
She does not hear me. I cannot see her face. (*He approaches
and touches* Mélisande *on the shoulder.*) Why weepest thou?
(Mélisande *trembles, starts up, and would flee.*) Do not be afraid.
You have nothing to fear. Why are you weeping here all
alone?

mélisande. Do not touch me! do not touch me!

golaud. Do not be afraid.... I will not do you any... Oh, you
are beautiful!

mélisande. Do not touch me! do not touch me! or I throw myself
in the water!...

golaud. I will not touch you.... See, I will stay here, against the
tree. Do not be afraid. Has any one hurt you?

mélisande. Oh! yes! yes! yes!...   (*She sobs profoundly.*)

golaud. Who has hurt you?

mélisande. Every one! every one!

golaud. What hurt have they done you?

mélisande. I will not tell! I cannot tell!...

golaud. Come; do not weep so. Whence come you?

mélisande. I have fled!... fled... fled....

golaud. Yes; but whence have you fled?

mélisande. I am lost!... lost!... Oh! oh! lost here.... I am not of
this place.... I was not born there....

golaud. Whence are you? Where were you born?

mélisande. Oh! oh! far away from here!... far away... far
away....

golaud. What is it shining so at the bottom of the water?

mélisande. Where? — Ah! it is the crown he gave me. It fell
as I was weeping....

GOLAUD. A crown? — Who was it gave you a crown? — I will try to get it....

MÉLISANDE. No, no; I will have no more of it! I will have no more of it!... I had rather die... die at once....

GOLAUD. I could easily pull it out. The water is not very deep.

MÉLISANDE. I will have no more of it! If you take it out, I throw myself in its place!...

GOLAUD. No, no; I will leave it there. It could be reached without difficulty, nevertheless. It seems very beautiful. — Is it long since you fled?

MÉLISANDE. Yes, yes!... Who are you?

GOLAUD. I am Prince Golaud — grandson of Arkël, the old King of Allemonde.

MÉLISANDE. Oh, you have gray hairs already....

GOLAUD. Yes; some, here, by the temples...

MÉLISANDE. And in your beard, too.... Why do you look at me so?

GOLAUD. I am looking at your eyes. — Do you never shut your eyes?

MÉLISANDE. Oh, yes; I shut them at night....

GOLAUD. Why do you look so astonished?

MÉLISANDE. You are a giant.

GOLAUD. I am a man like the rest....

MÉLISANDE. Why have you come here?

GOLAUD. I do not know, myself. I was hunting in the forest. I was chasing a wild boar. I mistook the road. — You look very young. How old are you?

MÉLISANDE. I am beginning to be cold.

GOLAUD. Will you come with me!

MÉLISANDE. No, no; I will stay here.

GOLAUD. You cannot stay here all alone. You cannot stay here all night long.... What is your name?

MÉLISANDE. Mélisande.

GOLAUD. You cannot stay here, Mélisande. Come with me....

MÉLISANDE. I will stay here....

GOLAUD. You will be afraid, all alone. We do not know what there may be here... all night long... all alone... it is impossible. Mélisande, come, give me your hand....

MÉLISANDE. Oh, do not touch me!...

GOLAUD. Do not scream.... I will not touch you again. But come
  with me. The night will be very dark and very cold. Come
  with me....

MÉLISANDE. Where are you going?...

GOLAUD. I do not know.... I am lost too....   (*Exeunt.*)

SCENE III — *A hall in the castle.*   ARKËL *and* GENEVIÈVE *discovered.*

GENEVIÈVE. Here is what he writes to his brother Pelléas: "I found
  her all in tears one evening, beside a spring in the forest where
  I had lost myself. I do not know her age, nor who she is, nor
  whence she comes, and I dare not question her, for she must
  have had a sore fright; and when you ask her what has happened
  to her, she falls at once a-weeping like a child, and sobs so heavily
  you are afraid. Just as I found her by the springs, a crown of
  gold had slipped from her hair and fallen to the bottom of the
  water. She was clad, besides, like a princess, though her garments had been torn by the briers. It is now six months since
  I married her and I know no more about it than on the day of
  our meeting. Meanwhile, dear Pelléas, thou whom I love
  more than a brother, although we were not born of the same
  father; meanwhile make ready for my return.... I know my
  mother will willingly forgive me. But I am afraid of the King,
  our venerable grandsire, I am afraid of Arkël, in spite of all his
  kindness, for I have undone by this strange marriage all his
  plans of state, and I fear the beauty of Mélisande will not excuse
  my folly to eyes so wise as his. If he consents nevertheless to
  receive her as he would receive his own daughter, the third
  night following this letter, light a lamp at the top of the tower
  that overlooks the sea. I shall perceive it from the bridge of our
  ship; otherwise I shall go far away again and come back no
  more...." What say you of it?

ARKËL. Nothing. He has done what he probably must have done.
  I am very old, and nevertheless I have not yet seen clearly for
  one moment into myself; how would you that I judge what
  others have done? I am not far from the tomb and do not
  succeed in judging myself.... One always mistakes when one
  does not close his eyes. That may seem strange to us; but
  that is all. He is past the age to marry and he weds, like a child,

a little girl he finds by a spring.... That may seem strange to us, because we never see but the reverse of destinies... the reverse even of our own.... He has always followed my counsels hitherto; I had thought to make him happy in sending him to ask the hand of Princess Ursula.... He could not remain alone; since the death of his wife he has been sad to be alone; and that marriage would have put an end to long wars and old hatreds.... He would not have it so. Let it be as he would have it; I have never put myself athwart a destiny; and he knows better than I his future. There happen perhaps no useless events....

GENEVIÈVE. He has always been so prudent, so grave and so firm. ... If it were Pelléas, I should understand.... But he... at his age.... Who is it he is going to introduce here? — An unknown found along the roads.... Since his wife's death, he has no longer lived for aught but his son, the little Yniold, and if he were about to marry again, it was because you had wished it.... And now... a little girl in the forest.... He has forgotten everything.... — What shall we do?...

(*Enter* PELLÉAS.)

ARKËL. Who is coming in there?

GENEVIÈVE. It is Pelléas. He has been weeping.

ARKËL. Is it thou, Pelléas? — Come a little nearer, that I may see thee in the light....

PELLÉAS. Grandfather, I received another letter at the same time as my brother's; a letter from my friend Marcellus.... He is about to die and calls for me. He would see me before dying....

ARKËL. Thou wouldst leave before thy brother's return? — Perhaps thy friend is less ill than he thinks....

PELLÉAS. His letter is so sad you can see death between the lines.... He says he knows the very day when death must come.... He tells me I can arrive before it if I will, but that there is no more time to lose. The journey is very long, and if I await Golaud's return, it will be perhaps too late....

ARKËL. Thou must wait a little while, nevertheless.... We do not know what this return has in store for us. And, besides, is not thy father here, above us, more sick perhaps than thy friend.... Couldst thou choose between the father and the friend?...

(*Exit.*)

GENEVIÈVE. Have a care to keep the lamp lit from this evening, Pelléas.... *(Exeunt severally.)*

SCENE IV — *Before the castle.*

(Enter GENEVIÈVE *and* MÉLISANDE.*)*

MÉLISANDE. It is gloomy in the gardens. And what forests, what forests all about the palaces....

GENEVIÈVE. Yes; that astonished me too when I came hither; it astonishes everybody. There are places where you never see the sun. But one gets used to it so quickly.... It is long ago, it is long ago.... It is nearly forty years that I have lived here.... Look toward the other side, you will have the light of the sea....

MÉLISANDE. I hear a noise below us....

GENEVIÈVE. Yes; it is some one coming up toward us.... Ah! it is Pelléas.... He seems still tired from having waited so long for you....

MÉLISANDE. He has not seen us.

GENEVIÈVE. I think he has seen us but does not know what he should do.... Pelléas, Pelléas, is it thou?...

(Enter PELLÉAS.*)*

PELLÈAS. Yes!... I was coming toward the sea....

GENEVIÈVE. So were we; we were seeking the light. It is a little lighter here than elsewhere; and yet the sea is gloomy.

PELLÉAS. We shall have a storm tonight. There has been one every night for some time, and yet it is so calm now.... One might embark unwittingly and come back no more.

MÉLISANDE. Something is leaving the port....

PELLÉAS. It must be a big ship.... The lights are very high, we shall see it in a moment, when it enters the band of light....

GENEVIÈVE. I do not know whether we shall be able to see it... there is still a fog on the sea....

PELLÉAS. The fog seems to be rising slowly....

MÉLISANDE. Yes; I see a little light down there, which I had not seen....

PELLÉAS. It is a lighthouse; there are others we cannot see yet.

MÉLISANDE. The ship is in the light.... It is already very far away....

PELLÉAS. It is a foreign ship. It looks larger than ours....

MÉLISANDE. It is the ship that brought me here!...

PELLÉAS. It flies away under full sail....

MÉLISANDE. It is the ship that brought me here. It has great sails.... I recognized it by its sails.

PELLÉAS. There will be a rough sea tonight.

MÉLISANDE. Why does it go away tonight?... You can hardly see it any longer.... Perhaps it will be wrecked....

PELLÉAS. The night falls very quickly....   (*A silence.*)

GENEVIÈVE. No one speaks any more?... You have nothing more to say to each other?... It is time to go in. Pelléas, show Mélisande the way. I must go see little Yniold a moment.

                                                              (*Exit.*)

PELLÉAS. Nothing can be seen any longer on the sea....

MÉLISANDE. I see more lights.

PELLÉAS. It is the other lighthouses.... Do you hear the sea?... It is the wind rising.... Let us go down this way. Will you give me your hand?

MÉLISANDE. See, see, my hands are full....

PELLÉAS. I will hold you by the arm, the road is steep and it is very gloomy there.... I am going away perhaps tomorrow....

MÉLISANDE. Oh!... why do you go away?   (*Exeunt.*)

ACT II

SCENE I — *A fountain in the park.*

(*Enter* PELLÉAS *and* MÉLISANDE.)

PELLÉAS. You do not know where I have brought you? — I often come to sit here, toward noon, when it is too hot in the gardens. It is stifling today, even in the shade of the trees.

MÉLISANDE. Oh, how clear the water is!...

PELLÉAS. It is as cool as winter. It is an old abandoned spring. It seems to have been a miraculous spring — it opened the eyes of the blind — they still call it "Blind Man's Spring."

MÉLISANDE. It no longer opens the eyes of the blind?

PELLÉAS. Since the King has been nearly blind himself, no one comes any more....

MÉLISANDE. How alone one is here!... There is no sound.

PELLÉAS. There is always a wonderful silence here.... One could hear the water sleep.... Will you sit down on the edge of the marble basin? There is one linden where the sun never comes....

MÉLISANDE. I am going to lie down on the marble. — I should like to see the bottom of the water....

PELLÉAS. No one has ever seen it. It is as deep, perhaps, as the sea. It is not known whence it comes. Perhaps it comes from the bottom of the earth....

MÉLISANDE. If there were anything shining at the bottom, perhaps one could see it....

PELLÉAS. Do not lean over so....

MÉLISANDE. I would like to touch the water....

PELLÉAS. Have a care of slipping.... I will hold your hand....

MÉLISANDE. No, no, I would plunge both hands in it.... You would say my hands were sick today....

PELLÉAS. Oh! oh! take care! take care! Mélisande!... Mélisande! ... Oh! your hair!...

MÉLISANDE (*starting upright*). I cannot... I cannot reach it....

PELLÉAS. Your hair dipped in the water....

MÉLISANDE. Yes, it is longer than my arms.... It is longer than I....
(*A silence.*)

PELLÉAS. It was at the brink of a spring, too, that he found you?

MÉLISANDE. Yes....

PELLÉAS. What did he say to you?

MÉLISANDE. Nothing; — I no longer remember....

PELLÉAS. Was he quite near you?

MÉLISANDE. Yes; he would have kissed me.

PELLÉAS. And you would not?

MÉLISANDE. No.

PELLÉAS. Why would you not?

MÉLISANDE. Oh! oh! I saw something pass at the bottom of the water....

PELLÉAS. Take care! take care! — You will fall! What are you playing with?

MÉLISANDE. With the ring he gave me.

PELLÉAS. Take care; you will lose it....

MÉLISANDE. No, no; I am sure of my hands....

PELLÉAS. Do not play so, over so deep a water....

MÉLISANDE. My hands do not tremble.

PELLÉAS. How it shines in the sunlight! Do not throw it so high in the air....

MÉLISANDE. Oh!...

PELLÉAS. It has fallen?

MÉLISANDE. It has fallen into the water!

PELLÉAS. Where is it? where is it?...

MÉLISANDE. I do not see it sink!...

PELLÉAS. I think I see it shine....

MÉLISANDE. My ring?

PELLÉAS. Yes, yes; down yonder.....

MÉLISANDE. Oh! oh! It is so far away from us!... no, no, that is not it... that is not it... It is lost... lost.... There is nothing any more but a great circle on the water.... What shall we do? What shall we do now?...

PELLÉAS. You need not be so troubled for a ring. It is nothing. ... We shall find it again, perhaps. Or else we shall find another....

MÉLISANDE. No, no; we shall never find it again; we shall never find any others either.... And yet I thought I had it in my hands.... I had already shut my hands, and it is fallen in spite of all.... I threw it too high, toward the sun....

PELLÉAS. Come, come, we will come back another day;... come, it is time. They will come to meet us. It was striking noon at the moment the ring fell.

MÉLISANDE. What shall we say to Golaud if he asks where it is?

PELLÉAS. The truth, the truth, the truth.... *(Exeunt.)*

SCENE II — *An apartment in the castle.* GOLAUD *discovered, stretched upon his bed;* MÉLISANDE, *by his bedside.*

GOLAUD. Ah! ha! all goes well; it will amount to nothing. But I cannot understand how it came to pass. I was hunting quietly in the forest. All at once my horse ran away, without cause. Did he see anything unusual?... I had just heard the twelve strokes of noon. At the twelfth stroke he suddenly took fright and ran like a blind madman against a tree. I heard no more. I do not yet know what happened. I fell, and he must have fallen on me. I thought I had the whole forest on my breast; I thought my heart was crushed. But my heart is sound. It is nothing, apparently....

MÉLISANDE. Would you like a little water?

GOLAUD. Thanks, thanks; I am not thirsty.

MÉLISANDE. Would you like another pillow?... There is a little spot of blood on this.

GOLAUD. No, no; it is not worth while. I bled at the mouth just now. I shall bleed again, perhaps....

MÉLISANDE. Are you quite sure?... You are not suffering too much?

GOLAUD. No, no; I have seen a good many more like this. I was made of iron and blood.... These are not the little bones of a child; do not alarm yourself....

MÉLISANDE. Close your eyes and try to sleep. I shall stay here all night....

GOLAUD. No, no; I do not wish you to tire yourself so. I do not need anything; I shall sleep like a child.... What is the matter, Mélisande? Why do you weep all at once?...

MÉLISANDE (bursting into tears). I am... I am ill too....

GOLAUD. Thou art ill?... What ails thee, then; what ails thee, Mélisande?...

MÉLISANDE. I do not know.... I am ill here.... I had rather tell you today; my lord, my lord, I am not happy here....

GOLAUD. Why, what has happened, Mélisande? What is it?... And I suspecting nothing.... What has happened?... Someone has done thee harm?... Someone has given thee offense?

MÉLISANDE. No, no; no one has done me the least harm.... It is not that.... It is not that.... But I can live here no longer. I do not know why.... I would go away, go away!... I shall die if I am left here....

GOLAUD. But something has happened? You must be hiding something from me?... Tell me the whole truth, Mélisande.... Is it the King?... Is it my mother?... Is it Pelléas?...

MÉLISANDE. No, no; it is not Pelléas. It is not anybody.... You could not understand me....

GOLAUD. Why should I not understand?... If you tell me nothing, what will you have me do?... Tell me everything and I shall understand everything.

MÉLISANDE. I do not know myself what it is.... I do not know just what it is.... If I could tell you, I would tell you.... It is something stronger than I....

GOLAUD. Come; be reasonable, Mélisande. — What would you have me do? — You are no longer a child. — Is it I whom you would leave?

MÉLISANDE. Oh! no, no; it is not that.... I would go away with you.... It is here that I can live no longer.... I feel that I shall not live a long while....

GOLAUD. But there must be a reason, nevertheless. You will be thought mad. It will be thought child's dreams. — Come, is it Pelléas, perhaps? — I think he does not often speak to you.

MÉLISANDE. Yes, yes; he speaks to me sometimes. I think he does not like me; I have seen it in his eyes.... But he speaks to me when he meets me....

GOLAUD. You must not take it ill of him. He has always been so. He is a little strange. And just now he is sad; he thinks of his friend Marcellus, who is at the point of death, and whom he cannot go to see.... He will change, he will change, you will see; he is young....

MÉLISANDE. But it is not that... it is not that....

GOLAUD. What is it, then? — Can you not get used to the life one leads here? Is it too gloomy here? — It is true the castle is very old and very somber.... It is very cold, and very deep. And all those who dwell in it, are already old. And the country may seem gloomy too, with all its forests, all its old forests without light. But that may all be enlivened if we will. And then, joy, joy, one does not have it every day; we must take things as they come. But tell me something; no matter what; I will do everything you could wish....

MÉLISANDE. Yes, yes; it is true.... You never see the sky here. I saw it for the first time this morning....

GOLAUD. It is that, then, that makes you weep, my poor Mélisande? — It is only that, then? — You weep, not to see the sky? — Come, come, you are no longer at the age when one may weep for such things.... And then, is not the summer yonder? You will see the sky every day. — And then, next year.... Come, give me your hand; give me both your little hands. (*He takes her hands.*) Oh! oh! these little hands that I could crush like flowers.... — Hold! where is the ring I gave you?

MÉLISANDE. The ring?

GOLAUD. Yes; our wedding-ring, where is it?

MÉLISANDE. I think... I think it has fallen....

GOLAUD. Fallen? — Where has it fallen? — You have not lost it?

MÉLISANDE. No, no; it fell... it must have fallen... but I know where it is....

GOLAUD. Where is it?

MÉLISANDE. You know... you know well... the grotto by the sea-shore?...

GOLAUD. Yes.

MÉLISANDE. Well then, it is there.... It must be it is there.... Yes, yes; I remember.... I went there this morning to pick up shells for little Yniold.... There were some very fine ones.... It slipped from my finger... then the sea came in; and I had to go out before I had found it.

GOLAUD. Are you sure it is there?

MÉLISANDE. Yes, yes; quite sure.... I felt it slip... then, all at once, the noise of the waves....

GOLAUD. You must go look for it at once.

MÉLISANDE. I must go look for it at once?

GOLAUD. Yes.

MÉLISANDE. Now? — at once? — in the dark?

GOLAUD. Now, at once, in the dark. You must go look for it at once. I had rather have lost all I have than have lost that ring. You do not know what it is. You do not know whence it came. The sea will be very high tonight. The sea will come to take it before you.... Make haste. You must go look for it at once....

MÉLISANDE. I dare not.... I dare not go alone....

GOLAUD. Go, go with no matter whom. But you must go at once, do you understand? — Make haste; ask Pelléas to go with you.

MÉLISANDE. Pelléas? — With Pelléas? — But Pelléas would not....

GOLAUD. Pelléas will do all you ask of him. I know Pelléas better than you do. Go, go; hurry! I shall not sleep until I have the ring.

MÉLISANDE. Oh! oh! I am not happy!... I am not happy!...

(*Exit, weeping.*)

SCENE III — *Before a grotto.*

(*Enter* PELLÉAS *and* MÉLISANDE.)

PELLÉAS (*speaking with great agitation*). Yes; it is here; we are there. It is so dark you cannot tell the entrance of the grotto from the rest of the night.... There are no stars on this side. Let us wait till the moon has torn through that great cloud; it will light up the whole grotto, and then we can enter without danger. There are dangerous places, and the path is very narrow between two lakes whose bottom has not yet been found. I did not think to bring a torch or a lantern, but I think the light of the sky will be enough for us. — You have never gone into this grotto?

MÉLISANDE. No....

PELLÉAS. Let us go in; let us go in.... You must be able to describe the place where you lost the ring, if he questions you.... It is very big and very beautiful. There are stalactites that look like plants and men. It is full of blue darks. It has not been explored to the end. There are great treasures hidden there, it seems. You will see the remains of ancient shipwrecks there. But you must not go far in it without a guide. There have been some who never have come back. I myself dare not go forward too far. We will stop the moment we no longer see the light of the sea or the sky. When you strike a little light there, you would say the vault was covered with stars like the sky. It is bits of crystal or salt, they say, that shine so in the rock. — Look, look, I think the sky is going to clear.... Give me your hand; do not tremble, do not tremble so. There is no danger; we will stop the moment we no longer see the light of the sea.... Is it the noise of the grotto that frightens you? It is the noise of night or the noise of silence.... Do you hear the sea behind us? — It does not seem happy tonight.... Ah! look, the light!...

(*The moon lights up abundantly the entrance and part of the darkness of the grotto; and at a certain depth are seen three old beggars with white hair, seated side by side, leaning upon each other and asleep against a boulder.*)

MÉLISANDE. Ah!

PELLÉAS. What is it?

MÉLISANDE. There are... there are....

(*She points out the three beggars.*)

PELLÉAS. Yes, yes; I have seen them too....

MÉLISANDE. Let us go!... Let us go!...

PELLÉAS. Yes... it is three old poor men fallen asleep.... There is a famine in the country.... Why have they come to sleep here?...

MÉLISANDE. Let us go!... Come, come.... Let us go!...

PELLÉAS. Take care; do not speak so loud.... Let us not wake them.... They are still sleeping heavily.... Come.

MÉLISANDE. Leave me, leave me; I prefer to walk alone....

PELLÉAS. We will come back another day....   (*Exeunt.*)

SCENE IV — *An apartment in the castle.* ARKËL *and* PELLÉAS *discovered.*

ARKËL. You see that everything retains you here just now and forbids you this useless journey. We have concealed your father's condition from you until now; but it is perhaps hopeless; and that alone should suffice to stop you on the threshold. But there are so many other reasons.... And it is not in the day when our enemies awake, and when the people are dying of hunger and murmur about us, that you have the right to desert us. And why this journey? Marcellus is dead; and life has graver duties than the visit to a tomb. You are weary, you say, of your inactive life; but activity and duty are not found on the highways. They must be waited for upon the threshold, and let in as they go by; and they go by every day. You have never seen them? I hardly see them any more myself; but I will teach you to see them, and I will point them out to you the day when you would make them a sign. Nevertheless, listen to me; if you believe it is from the depths of your life this journey is exacted, I do not forbid your undertaking it, for you must know better than I the events you must offer to your being or your fate. I shall ask you only to wait until we know what must take place ere long....

PELLÉAS. How long must I wait?

ARKËL. A few weeks; perhaps a few days....

PELLÉAS. I will wait....

ACT III

SCENE I — *An apartment in the castle*. PELLÉAS *and* MÉLISANDE *discovered*. MÉLISANDE *plies her distaff at the back of the room*.

PELLÉAS. Yniold does not come back; where has he gone?

MÉLISANDE. He had heard something in the corridor; he has gone to see what it is.

PELLÉAS. Mélisande...

MÉLISANDE. What is it?

PELLÉAS. ... Can you see still to work there?...

MÉLISANDE. I work as well in the dark....

PELLÉAS. I think everybody is already asleep in the castle. Golaud does not come back from the chase. It is late, nevertheless.... He no longer suffers from his fall?...

MÉLISANDE. He said he no longer suffered from it.

PELLÉAS. He must be more prudent; his body is no longer as supple as at twenty years.... I see the stars through the window and the light of the moon on the trees. It is late; he will not come back now. (*Knocking at the door*.) Who is there?... Come in!...

(*Little* YNIOLD *opens the door and enters the room*.)

It was you knocking so?... That is not the way to knock at doors. It is as if a misfortune had arrived; look, you have frightened little mother.

YNIOLD. I only knocked a tiny little bit.

PELLÉAS. It is late; little father will not come back tonight; it is time for you to go to bed.

YNIOLD. I shall not go to bed before you do.

PELLÉAS. What?... What is that you are saying?

YNIOLD. I say... not before you... not before you...

(*Bursts into sobs and takes refuge by* MÉLISANDE.)

MÉLISANDE. What is it, Yniold?... What is it? why do you weep all at once?

YNIOLD (*sobbing*). Because... oh! oh! because...

MÉLISANDE. Because what?... Because what?... Tell me..

YNIOLD. Little mother... little mother... you are going away....

MÉLISANDE. But what has taken hold of you, Yniold?... I have never dreamed of going away....

YNIOLD. Yes, you have; yes, you have; little father has gone away. ... Little father does not come back, and you are going to go away too.... I have seen it... I have seen it....

MÉLISANDE. But there has never been any idea of that, Yniold.... Why, what makes you think that I would go away?...

YNIOLD. I have seen it... I have seen it.... You have said things to uncle that I could not hear...

PELLÉAS. He is sleepy.... He has been dreaming.... Come here, Yniold; asleep already?... Come and look out at the window; the swans are fighting with the dogs....

YNIOLD (*at the window*). Oh! oh! they are chasing the dogs!... They are chasing them!... Oh! oh! the water!... the wings!... the wings!... they are afraid....

PELLÉAS (*coming back by* MÉLISANDE). He is sleepy; he is struggling against sleep; his eyes were closing....

MÉLISANDE (*singing softly as she spins*).

　　　　　Saint Daniel and Saint Michaël....
　　　　　Saint Michaël and Saint Raphaël....

YNIOLD (*at the window*). Oh! oh! little mother!...

MÉLISANDE (*rising abruptly*). What is it, Yniold?... What is it?...

YNIOLD. I saw something at the window!

　　　　　(PELLÉAS *and* MÉLISANDE *run to the window*.)

PELLÉAS. What is there at the window?... What have you seen?...

YNIOLD. Oh! oh! I saw something!...

PELLÉAS. But there is nothing. I see nothing....

MÉLISANDE. Nor I....

PELLÉAS. Where did you see something? Which way?...

YNIOLD. Down there, down there!... It is no longer there....

PELLÉAS. He does not know what he is saying. He must have seen the light of the moon on the forest. There are often strange reflections... or else something must have passed on the highway... or in his sleep. For see, see, I believe he is quite asleep....

YNIOLD (*at the window*). Little father is there! little father is there!

PELLÉAS (*going to the window*). He is right; Golaud is coming into the courtyard.

YNIOLD. Little father!... little father!... I am going to meet him!...

(*Exit, running. — A silence.*)

PELLÉAS. They are coming up the stair.

(*Enter* GOLAUD *and little* YNIOLD *with a lamp.*)

GOLAUD. You are still waiting in the dark?

YNIOLD. I have brought a light, little mother, a big light!...
(*He lifts the lamp and looks at* MÉLISANDE.) You have been
weeping, little mother?... You have been weeping?... (*He lifts
the lamp toward* PELLÉAS *and looks in turn at him.*) You too, you
too, you have been weeping?... Little father, look, little father;
they have both been weeping....

GOLAUD. Do not hold the light under their eyes so....

SCENE II — *One of the towers of the castle.   A watchman's round passes
under a window in the tower.*

MÉLISANDE (*at the window, combing her unbound hair*).

My long locks fall foaming
    To the threshold of the tower —
My locks await your coming
    All along the tower,
    And all the long, long hour,
    And all the long, long hour.

Saint Daniel and Saint Michaël,
Saint Michaël and Saint Raphaël.

I was born on a Sunday,
    A Sunday at high noon....

(*Enter* PELLÉAS *by the watchman's round.*)

PELLÉAS. Holà! Holà! ho!...

MÉLISANDE. Who is there?

PELLÉAS. I, I, and I!... What art thou doing there at the window,
singing like a bird that is not native here?

MÉLISANDE. I am doing my hair for the night....

PELLÉAS. Is it that I see upon the wall?... I thought you had some
light....

MÉLISANDE. I have opened the window; it is too hot in the tower.... It is beautiful tonight....

PELLÉAS. There are innumerable stars; I have never seen so many as tonight;... but the moon is still upon the sea.... Do not stay in the shadow, Mélisande; lean forward a little till I see your unbound hair....

MÉLISANDE. I am frightful so....   (*She leans out at the window.*)

PELLÉAS. Oh! oh! Mélisande!... oh, thou art beautiful!... thou art beautiful so!... Lean out! lean out!... Let me come nearer thee...

MÉLISANDE. I cannot come nearer thee.... I am leaning out as far as I can....

PELLÉAS. I cannot come up higher;... give me at least thy hand tonight... before I go away.... I leave tomorrow....

MÉLISANDE. No, no, no!...

PELLÉAS. Yes, yes, yes; I leave, I shall leave tomorrow.... Give me thy hand, thy hand, thy little hand upon my lips....

MÉLISANDE. I give thee not my hand if thou wilt leave....

PELLÉAS. Give, give, give!...

MÉLISANDE. Thou wilt not leave?

PELLÉAS. I will wait; I will wait....

MÉLISANDE. I see a rose in the shadows....

PELLÉAS. Where?... I see only the boughs of the willow hanging over the wall....

MÉLISANDE. Farther down, farther down, in the garden; farther down, in the somber green....

PELLÉAS. It is not a rose.... I will go see by and by, but give me thy hand first; first thy hand....

MÉLISANDE. There, there;... I cannot lean out farther....

PELLÉAS. I cannot reach thy hand with my lips....

MÉLISANDE. I cannot lean out farther.... I am on the point of falling.... — Oh! oh! my hair is falling down the tower!

(*Her tresses fall suddenly over her head, as she is leaning out so, and stream over* PELLÉAS.)

PELLÉAS. Oh! oh! what is it?... Thy hair, thy hair is falling down to me!... All thy locks, Mélisande, all thy locks have fallen down the tower!... I hold them in my hands; I hold them in my mouth.... I hold them in my arms; I put them about my neck. ... I will not open my hands again tonight....

MÉLISANDE. Let me go! let me go!... Thou wilt make me fall!...

PELLÉAS. No, no, no;... I have never seen such hair as thine, Mélisande!... See, see, see; it comes from so high and yet it floods me to the heart!... And yet it floods me to the knees!... And it is sweet, sweet as if it fell from heaven!... I see the sky no longer through thy locks. Thou seest, thou seest?... I can no longer hold them with both hands; there are some on the boughs of the willow.... They are alive like birds in my hands,... and they love me, they love me more than thou!...

MÉLISANDE. Let me go; let me go!... Someone might come....

PELLÉAS. No, no, no; I shall not set thee free tonight.... Thou art my prisoner tonight; all night, all night!...

MÉLISANDE. Pelléas! Pelléas!...

PELLÉAS. I tie them, I tie them to the willow boughs.... Thou shalt not go away now;... thou shalt not go away now.... Look, look, I am kissing thy hair.... I suffer no more in the midst of thy hair.... Hearest thou my kisses along thy hair?... They mount along thy hair.... Each hair must bring thee some.... Thou seest, thou seest, I can open my hands.... My hands are free, and thou canst not leave me now....

MÉLISANDE. Oh! oh! thou hurtest me.... (*Doves come out of the tower and fly about them in the night.*) — What is that, Pelléas? — What is it flying about me?

PELLÉAS. It is the doves coming out of the tower.... I have frightened them; they are flying away....

MÉLISANDE. It is my doves, Pelléas. — Let us go away, let me go; they will not come back again....

PELLÉAS. Why will they not come back again?

MÉLISANDE. They will be lost in the dark.... Let me go; let me lift my head.... I hear a noise of footsteps.... Let me go! — It is Golaud!... I believe it is Golaud!... He has heard us....

PELLÉAS. Wait! Wait!... Thy hair is about the boughs.... It is caught there in the darkness.... Wait, wait!.... It is dark....

(*Enter* GOLAUD, *by the watchman's round.*)

GOLAUD. What do you here?

PELLÉAS. What do I here?... I...

GOLAUD. You are children.... Mélisande, do not lean out so at

the window; you will fall.... Do you not know it is late? It is
nearly midnight. — Do not play so in the darkness. — You are
children... (*Laughing nervously.*) What children!... What children!... (*Exit, with* PELLÉAS.)

SCENE III — *The vaults of the castle.*

(*Enter* GOLAUD *and* PELLÉAS.)

GOLAUD. Take care; this way, this way. — You have never
penetrated into these vaults?

PELLÉAS. Yes; once, of old; but it was long ago....

GOLAUD. They are prodigious great; it is a succession of enormous
crypts that end, God knows where. The whole castle is builded
on these crypts. Do you smell the deathly odor that reigns here?
— That is what I wished to show you. In my opinion, it comes
from the little underground lake I am going to have you see.
Take care; walk before me, in the light of my lantern. I will
warn you when we are there. (*They continue to walk in silence.*)
Hey! hey! Pelléas! stop! stop! (*He seizes him by the arm.*) For
God's sake!... Do you not see? — One step more, and you had
been in the gulf!....

PELLÉAS. But I did not see it!... The lantern no longer lighted me....

GOLAUD. I made a misstep... but if I had not held you by the
arm... Well, this is the stagnant water that I spoke of to you....
Do you perceive the smell of death that rises? — Let us go to the
end of this overhanging rock, and do you lean over a little.
It will strike you in the face.

PELLÉAS. I smell it already;... you would say a smell of the tomb.

GOLAUD. Farther, farther.... It is this that on certain days has poisoned the castle. The King will not believe it comes from here.
— The crypt should be walled up in which this standing water
is found. It is time, besides, to examine these vaults a little.
Have you noticed those lizards on the walls and pillars of the
vaults? — There is a labor hidden here you would not suspect;
and the whole castle will be swallowed up one of these nights,
if it is not looked out for. But what will you have? Nobody
likes to come down this far.... There are strange lizards in many
of the walls.... Oh! here... do you perceive the smell of death
that rises?

PELLÉAS. Yes; there is a smell of death rising about us....

GOLAUD. Lean over; have no fear.... I will hold you... give me... no, no, not your hand... it might slip... your arm, your arm!... Do you see the gulf? (*Moved.*) — Pelléas? Pelléas?...

PELLÉAS. Yes; I think I see the bottom of the gulf.... Is it the light that trembles so?... You...

(He straightens up, turns, and looks at GOLAUD.*)*

GOLAUD (*with a trembling voice*). Yes; it is the lantern.... See, I shook it to lighten the walls....

PELLÉAS. I stifle here;... let us go out....

GOLAUD. Yes; let us go out.... *(Exeunt in silence.)*

SCENE IV — *A terrace at the exit of the vaults.*

(Enter GOLAUD *and* PELLÉAS.*)*

PELLÉAS. Ah! I breathe at last!... I thought, one moment, I was going to be ill in those enormous crypts; I was on the point of falling.... There is a damp air there, heavy as a laden dew, and darkness thick as a poisoned paste.... And now, all the air of all the sea!... There is a fresh wind, see; fresh as a leaf that has just opened, over the little green waves.... Hold! the flowers have just been watered at the foot of the terrace, and the smell of the verdure and the wet roses comes up to us.... It must be nearly noon; they are already in the shadow of the tower.... It is noon; I hear the bells ringing, and the children are going down to the beach to bathe.... I did not know that we had stayed so long in the caverns....

GOLAUD. We went down toward eleven o'clock....

PELLÉAS. Earlier; it must have been earlier; I heard it strike half past ten.

GOLAUD. Half past ten or a quarter to eleven....

PELLÉAS. They have opened all the windows of the castle. It will be unusually hot this afternoon.... Look, there is mother with Mélisande at a window of the tower....

GOLAUD. Yes; they have taken refuge on the shady side. — Speaking of Mélisande, I heard what passed and what was said last night. I am quite aware all that is but child's play; but it need not be repeated. Mélisande is very young and very impressionable; and she must be treated the more circumspectly that she is perhaps with child at this moment.... She is very delicate, hardly woman; and the least emotion might bring on a mishap. It is not the first time I have noticed there might be something between you.... You are older than she; it will suffice to have told you.... Avoid her as much as possible; without affectation, moreover; without affectation.... — What is it I see yonder on the highway toward the forest?...

PELLÉAS. Some herds they are leading to the city....

GOLAUD. They cry like lost children; you would say they smelt the butcher already. — It will be time for dinner. — What a fine day! What a capital day for the harvest!... (*Exeunt.*)

SCENE V — *Before the castle.*

(*Enter* GOLAUD *and little* YNIOLD.)

GOLAUD. Come, we are going to sit down here, Yniold; sit on my knee; we shall see from here what passes in the forest. I do not see you any more at all now. You abandon me too; you are always at little mother's.... Why, we are sitting just under little mother's windows. — Perhaps she is saying her evening prayer at this moment.... But tell me, Yniold, she is often with your Uncle Pelléas, isn't she?

YNIOLD. Yes, yes; always, little father; when you are not there, little father....

GOLAUD. Ah! — Look; someone is going by with a lantern in the garden. — But I have been told they did not like each other.... It seems they often quarrel;... no? Is it true?

YNIOLD. Yes, yes; it is true.

GOLAUD. Yes? — Ah! ah! — But what do they quarrel about?

YNIOLD. About the door.

GOLAUD. What? — about the door? — What are you talking about? — No, come, explain yourself; why do they quarrel about the door?

YNIOLD. Because it won't stay open.

GOLAUD. Who wants it to stay open? — Come, why do they quarrel?

YNIOLD. I don't know, little father; about the light.

GOLAUD. I am not talking to you about the light; we will talk of that by and by. I am talking to you about the door. Answer what I ask you; you must learn to talk; it is time.... Do not put your hand in your mouth so;.... come....

YNIOLD. Little father! little father!... I won't do it any more....
(He cries.)

GOLAUD. Come; what are you crying for now? What has happened?

YNIOLD. Oh! oh! little father, you hurt me....

GOLAUD. I hurt you? — Where did I hurt you? I did not mean to....

YNIOLD. Here, here; on my little arm....

GOLAUD. I did not mean to; come, don't cry any more, and I will give you something tomorrow.

YNIOLD. What, little father?

GOLAUD. A quiver and some arrows; but tell me what you know about the door.

YNIOLD. Big arrows?

GOLAUD. Yes, yes; very big arrows. — But why don't they want the door to be open? — Come, answer me sometime! — No, no; do not open your mouth to cry. I am not angry. We are going to have a quiet talk, like Pelléas and little mother when they are together. What do they talk about when they are together?

YNIOLD. Pelléas and little mother?

GOLAUD. Yes; what do they talk about?

YNIOLD. About me; always about me.

GOLAUD. And what do they say about you?

YNIOLD. They say I am going to be very big.

GOLAUD. Oh, plague of my life!... I am here like a blind man searching for his treasure at the bottom of the ocean!... I am here like a new-born child lost in the forest, and you... Come, come, Yniold, I was wandering; we are going to talk seriously. Do Pelléas and little mother never speak of me when I am not there?...

YNIOLD. Yes, yes, little father; they are always speaking of you.

GOLAUD. Ah!... And what do they say of me?

YNIOLD. They say I shall grow as big as you are.

GOLAUD. You are always by them?

YNIOLD. Yes, yes, always, always, little father.

GOLAUD. They never tell you to go play somewhere else?

YNIOLD. No, little father; they are afraid when I am not there.

GOLAUD. They are afraid?.... What makes you think they are afraid?

YNIOLD. Little mother always says, "Don't go away; don't go away!"... They are unhappy, but they laugh....

GOLAUD. But that does not prove they are afraid.

YNIOLD. Yes, yes, little father; she is afraid....

GOLAUD. Why do you say she is afraid?

YNIOLD. They always weep in the dark.

GOLAUD. Ah! ah!...

YNIOLD. That makes one weep too.

GOLAUD. Yes, yes!...

YNIOLD. She is pale, little father.

GOLAUD. Ah! ah!... patience, my God, patience!...

YNIOLD. What, little father?

GOLAUD. Nothing, nothing, my child. — I saw a wolf go by in the forest. — Then they get on well together? — I am glad to learn they are on good terms. — They kiss each other sometimes? — No?...

YNIOLD. Kiss each other, little father? — No, no — ah! yes, little father, yes, yes; once... once when it rained....

GOLAUD. They kissed? — But how, how did they kiss?

YNIOLD. So, little father, so!... (*He gives him a kiss on the mouth, laughing.*) Ah! ah! your beard, little father!... It pricks! it pricks! it pricks! It is getting all gray, little father, and your hair, too; all gray, all gray, all gray.... (*The window under which they are sitting is lighted up at this moment, and the lights falls upon them.*) Ah! ah! little mother has lit her lamp. It is light, little father; it is light....

GOLAUD. Yes; it is beginning to be light....

YNIOLD. Let us go there, too, little father; let us go there, too....

GOLAUD. Where do you want to go?

YNIOLD. Where it is light, little father.

GOLAUD. No, no, my child; let us stay in the dark a little longer....
One cannot tell, one cannot tell yet.... Do you see those poor people down there trying to kindle a little fire in the forest? —

It has rained. And over there, do you see the old gardener trying to lift that tree the wind has blown down across the road? — He cannot; the tree is too big; the tree is too heavy, and it will lie where it fell. All that cannot be helped.... I think Pelléas is mad....

YNIOLD. No, little father, he is not mad; he is very good.

GOLAUD. Do you want to see little mother?

YNIOLD. Yes, yes; I want to see her!

GOLAUD. Don't make any noise; I am going to hoist you up to the window. It is too high for me, for all I am so big.... (*He lifts the child.*) Do not make the least noise; little mother would be terribly afraid.... Do you see her? — Is she in the room?

YNIOLD. Yes.... Oh, how light it is!

GOLAUD. She is alone?

YNIOLD. Yes;... no, no; Uncle Pelléas is there, too.

GOLAUD. He — ...!

YNIOLD. Ah! ah! little father! you have hurt me!...

GOLAUD. It is nothing; be still; I will not do it any more; look, look, Yniold!... I stumbled; speak lower. What are they doing? —

YNIOLD. They are not doing anything, little father; they are waiting for something.

GOLAUD. Are they near each other?

YNIOLD. No, little father.

GOLAUD. And... and the bed? Are they near the bed?

YNIOLD. The bed, little father? — I can't see the bed.

GOLAUD. Lower, lower; they will hear you. Are they speaking?

YNIOLD. No, little father; they do not speak.

GOLAUD. But what are they doing? — They must be doing something....

YNIOLD. They are looking at the light.

GOLAUD. Both?

YNIOLD. Yes, little father.

GOLAUD. They do not say anything?

YNIOLD. No, little father; they do not close their eyes.

GOLAUD. They do not come near each other?

YNIOLD. No, little father; they do not stir.

GOLAUD. They are sitting down?

YNIOLD. No, little father; they are standing upright against the wall.

GOLAUD. They make no gestures? — They do not look at each other? — They make no signs?...

YNIOLD. No, little father. — Oh! oh! little father; they never close their eyes.... I am terribly afraid....

GOLAUD. Be still. They do not stir yet?

YNIOLD. No, little father. — I am afraid, little father; let me come down!...

GOLAUD. Why, what are you afraid of? — Look! look!...

YNIOLD. I dare not look any more, little father!... Let me come down!...

GOLAUD. Look! look!...

YNIOLD. Oh! oh! I am going to cry, little father! — Let me come down! let me come down!...

GOLAUD. Come; we will go see what has happened. (*Exeunt.*)

ACT IV

SCENE I — *A corridor in the castle.*
(*Enter* PELLÉAS *and* MÉLISANDE, *meeting.*)

PELLÉAS. Where goest thou? I must speak to thee tonight. Shall I see thee?

MÉLISANDE. Yes.

PELLÉAS. I have just left my father's room. He is getting better. The physician has told us he is saved.... And yet this morning I had a presentiment this day would end ill. I have had a rumor of misfortune in my ears for some time.... Then, all at once there was a great change; today it is no longer anything but a question of time. All the windows in his room have been thrown open. He speaks; he seems happy. He does not speak yet like an ordinary man, but already his ideas no longer all come from the other world.... He recognized me. He took my hand and said with that strange air he has had since he fell sick: "Is it thou, Pelléas? Why, why, I had not noticed it before, but thou hast the grave and friendly look of those who will not live long.... You must travel; you must travel...." It is strange;

I shall obey him.... My mother listened to him and wept for joy. — Hast thou not been aware of it? — The whole house seems already to revive, you hear breathing, you hear speaking, you hear walking.... Listen; I hear some one speaking behind that door. Quick, quick! answer quickly! where shall I see thee?

MÉLISANDE. Where wouldst thou?

PELLÉAS. In the park; near "Blind Man's Spring." — Wilt thou? — Wilt thou come?

MÉLISANDE. Yes.

PELLÉAS. It will be the last night; — I am going to travel, as my father said. Thou wilt not see me more....

MÉLISANDE. Do not say that, Pelléas.... I shall see thee always; I shall look upon thee always....

PELLÉAS. Thou wilt look in vain.... I shall be so far away thou couldst no longer see me.... I shall try to go very far away.... I am full of joy, and you would say I had all the weight of heaven and earth on my body today....

MÉLISANDE. What has happened, Pelléas? — I no longer understand what you say....

PELLÉAS. Go, go; let us separate. I hear someone speaking behind that door.... It is the strangers who came to the castle this morning.... They are going out.... Let us go; it is the strangers....   (*Exeunt severally.*)

SCENE II — *An apartment in the castle.* ARKËL *and* MÉLISANDE
discovered.

ARKËL. Now that Pelléas's father is saved, and sickness, the old handmaid of Death, has left the castle, a little joy and a little sunlight will at last come into the house again.... It was time! — For, since thy coming, we have only lived here whispering about a closed room.... And truly I have pitied thee, Mélisande.... Thou camest here all joyous, like a child seeking a gala-day, and at the moment thou enteredst in the vestibule I saw thy face change, and probably thy soul, as the face changes in spite of us when we enter at noon into a grotto too gloomy and too cold.... And since — since, on account of all that, I have often no longer understood thee.... I observed thee, thou wert there, listless, perhaps, but with the strange, astray look of one awaiting

ever a great trouble, in the sunlight, in a beautiful garden....
I cannot explain.... But I was sad to see thee so; for thou art
too young and too beautiful to live already day and night under
the breath of death.... But now all that will change. At my
age — and there, perhaps, is the surest fruit of my life — at my
age I have gained I know not what faith in the fidelity of events,
and I have always seen that every young and beautiful being
creates about itself young, beautiful, and happy events....
And it is thou who wilt now open the door for the new era I have
glimpses of.... Come here; why dost thou stay there without
answering and without lifting thine eyes? — I have kissed thee
but once only hitherto — the day of thy coming; and yet old
men need sometimes to touch with their lips a woman's forehead
or a child's cheek, to believe still in the freshness of life and avert
awhile the menaces.... Art thou afraid of my old lips? How
I have pitied thee these months!...

MÉLISANDE. Grandfather, I have not been unhappy....

ARKËL. Perhaps you were of those who are unhappy without
knowing it,... and they are the most unhappy.... Let me look
at thee, so, quite near, a moment:... we have such need of
beauty beside Death....

(Enter GOLAUD.*)*

GOLAUD. Pelléas leaves tonight.

ARKËL. Thou hast blood on thy forehead. — What hast thou done?

GOLAUD. Nothing, nothing.... I have passed through a hedge of
thorns.

MÉLISANDE. Bend down your head a little, my lord.... I will wipe
your forehead....

GOLAUD *(repulsing her).* I will not that you touch me, do you understand? Go, go! — I am not speaking to you. — Where is my
sword? — I come to seek my sword....

MÉLISANDE. Here; on the praying-stool.

GOLAUD. Bring it. *(To* ARKËL.*)* They have just found another
peasant dead of hunger, along by the sea. You would say they
all meant to die under our eyes. *(To* MÉLISANDE.*)* Well, my
sword? — Why do you tremble so? — I am not going to kill
you. I would simply examine the blade. I do not employ the

sword for these uses. Why do you examine me like a beggar? —
I do not come to ask alms of you. You hope to see something
in my eyes without my seeing anything in yours? — Do you
think I may know something? (*To* ARKËL.) — Do you see
those great eyes? — It is as if they were proud of their richness....

ARKËL. I see there only a great innocence....

GOLAUD. A great innocence!... They are greater than innocence.
... They are purer than the eyes of a lamb.... They would give
God lessons in innocence! A great innocence! Listen: I am
so near them I feel the freshness of their lashes when they wink;
and yet I am less far away from the great secrets of the other
world than from the smallest secret of those eyes!... A great
innocence!... More than innocence! You would say the angels
of heaven celebrated there an eternal baptism!... I know those
eyes! I have seen them at their work! Close them! close them!
or I shall close them for a long while!... Do not put your right
hand to your throat so; I am saying a very simple thing.... I
have no under-thought.... If I had an under-thought, why
should I not say it? Ah! ah! — Do not attempt to flee! — Here!
— Give me that hand! — Ah! your hands are too hot.... Go
away! Your flesh disgusts me!... Here! — There is no more
question of fleeing now! (*He seizes her by the hair.*) You shall
follow me on your knees! — On your knees! — On your knees
before me! — Ah! ah! your long hair serves some purpose at
last!... Right,... left! — Left,... right! — Absalom! Absalom.
— Forward! back! To the ground! to the ground!... You
see, you see; I laugh already like an old man....

ARKËL (*running up*). Golaud!...

GOLAUD (*affecting a sudden calm*). You will do as you may please,
look you. — I attach no importance to that. — I am too old;
and, besides, I am not a spy. I shall await chance; and then...
Oh! then!... simply because it is the custom; simply because
it is the custom.... (*Exit.*)

ARKËL. What ails him? — He is drunk?

MÉLISANDE (*in tears*). No, no; he does not love me any more....
I am not happy!... I am not happy!...

ARKËL. If I were God, I would have pity on men's hearts....

SCENE III — *A terrace of the castle. Little* YNIOLD *discovered, trying to lift a boulder.*

YNIOLD. Oh, this stone is heavy!... It is heavier than I am.... It is heavier than everybody.... It is heavier than everything that ever happened.... I can see my golden ball between the rock and this naughty stone, and I cannot reach it.... My little arm is not long enough,... and this stone won't be lifted.... I can't lift it,... and nobody could lift it.... It is heavier than the whole house;... you would think it had roots in the earth.... (*The bleatings of a flock heard far away.*) — Oh! oh! I hear the sheep crying.... (*He goes to look, at the edge of the terrace.*) Why! there is no more sun.... They are coming... the little sheep... they are coming.... There is a lot of them!... There is a lot of them! ... They are afraid of the dark.... They crowd together! They crowd together!... They can hardly walk any more.... They are crying! They are crying! And they go quick!... They go quick!... They are already at the great crossroads. Ah! ah! They don't know where they ought to go any more.... They don't cry any more.... They wait.... Some of them want to go to the right.... They all want to go to the right.... They cannot!... The shepherd is throwing earth at them.... Ah! ah! They are going to pass by here.... They obey! They obey! They are going to pass under the terrace.... They are going to pass under the rocks. I am going to see them near by.... Oh! oh! what a lot of them!... What a lot of them! The whole road is full of them!... They all keep still now.... Shepherd! shepherd! why don't they speak any more?

THE SHEPHERD (*who is out of sight*). Because it is no longer the road to the stable...

YNIOLD. Where are they going? — Shepherd! shepherd! — Where are they going? — He doesn't hear me any more. They are too far away already.... They go quick.... They are not making a noise any more.... It is no longer the road to the stable.... Where are they going to sleep tonight? — Oh! oh! — It is too dark.... I am going to tell something to somebody.... (*Exit.*)

SCENE IV — *A fountain in the park.*

(*Enter* PELLÉAS.)

PELLÉAS. It is the last evening... the last evening. It must all end. I have played like a child about a thing I did not guess.... I have played a-dream about the snares of fate.... Who has awakened me all at once? I shall flee, crying out for joy and woe like a blind man fleeing from his burning house.... I am going to tell her I shall flee.... My father is out of danger; and I have no more reason to lie to myself.... It is late; she does not come.... I should do better to go away without seeing her again. ... I must look well at her this time.... There are some things that I no longer recall.... It seems at times as if I had not seen her for a hundred years.... And I have not yet looked upon her look.... There remains nought to me if I go away thus. And all those memories... it is as if I were to take away a little water in a muslin bag.... I must see her one last time, to the bottom of her heart.... I must tell her all that I have never told her.

(*Enter* MÉLISANDE.)

MÉLISANDE. Pelléas!

PELLÉAS. Mélisande! — Is it thou, Mélisande?

MÉLISANDE. Yes.

PELLÉAS. Come hither; do not stay at the edge of the moonlight. — Come hither. We have so many things to tell each other.... Come hither in the shadow of the linden.

MÉLISANDE. Let me stay in the light....

PELLÉAS. We might be seen from the windows of the tower. Come hither; here, we have nothing to fear. — Take care; we might be seen...

MÉLISANDE. I wish to be seen....

PELLÉAS. Why, what doth ail thee? — Thou wert able to come out without being seen?

MÉLISANDE. Yes; your brother slept....

PELLÉAS. It is late. — In an hour they will close the gates. We must be careful. Why art thou come so late?

MÉLISANDE. Your brother had a bad dream. And then my gown

was caught on the nails of the gate. See, it is torn. I lost all this time, and ran....

PELLÉAS. My poor Mélisande!... I should almost be afraid to touch thee.... Thou art still out of breath, like a hunted bird.... It is for me, for me, thou doest all that?... I hear thy heart beat as if it were mine.... Come hither... nearer, nearer me....

MÉLISANDE. Why do you laugh?

PELLÉAS. I do not laugh; — or else I laugh for joy, unwittingly.... It were a weeping matter, rather....

MÉLISANDE. We have come here before.... I recollect....

PELLÉAS. Yes... yes... Long months ago. — I knew not then.... Knowest thou why I asked thee to come here tonight?

MÉLISANDE. No.

PELLÉAS. It is perhaps the last time I shall see thee.... I must go away forever....

MÉLISANDE. Why sayest thou always thou wilt go away?...

PELLÉAS. I must tell thee what thou knowest already? — Thou knowest not what I am going to tell thee?

MÉLISANDE. Why, no; why, no; I know nothing —...

PELLÉAS. Thou knowest not why I must go afar.... Thou knowest not it is because... (*He kisses her abruptly.*) I love thee....

MÉLISANDE (*in a low voice*). I love thee, too....

PELLÉAS. Oh! oh! What saidst thou, Mélisande?... I hardly heard it!... Thou sayest that in a voice coming from the end of the world!... I hardly heard thee.... Thou lovest me? — Thou lovest me, too?... Since when lovest thou me?...

MÉLISANDE. Since always.... Since I saw thee....

PELLÉAS. Oh, how thou sayest that!... Thy voice seems to have blown across the sea in spring!... I have never heard it until now;... one would say it had rained on my heart!... Thou sayest that so frankly!... Like an angel questioned!... I cannot believe it, Mélisande!... Why shouldst thou love me? — Nay, why dost thou love me? — Is what thou sayest true? — Thou dost not mock me? — Thou dost not lie a little, to make me smile?...

MÉLISANDE. No; I never lie; I lie but to thy brother....

PELLÉAS. Oh, how thou sayest that!... Thy voice! thy voice!... It is cooler and more frank than the water is!... It is like pure water on my lips!... It is like pure water on my hands.... Give me, give me thy hands!... Oh, how small thy hands are!... I did not know thou wert so beautiful!... I have never seen anything so beautiful before thee.... I was full of unrest; I sought throughout the country.... And I found not beauty.... And now I have found thee!... I have found thee!... I do not think there could be on the earth a fairer woman!... Where art thou? — I no longer hear thee breathe....

MÉLISANDE. Because I look on thee....

PELLÉAS. Why dost thou look so gravely on me? — We are already in the shadow. — It is too dark under this tree. — Come into the light. We cannot see how happy we are. Come, come; so little time remains to us....

MÉLISANDE. No, no; let us stay here.... I am nearer thee in the dark....

PELLÉAS. Where are thine eyes? — Thou art not going to fly me? — Thou dost not think of me just now.

MÉLISANDE. Oh, yes; oh, yes; I only think of thee....

PELLÉAS. Thou wert looking elsewhere....

MÉLISANDE. I saw thee elsewhere....

PELLÉAS. Thy soul is far away.... What ails thee, then? — Meseems thou art not happy....

MÉLISANDE. Yes, yes; I am happy, but I am sad....

PELLÉAS. One is sad often when one loves....

MÉLISANDE. I weep always when I think of thee....

PELLÉAS. I, too.... I, too, Mélisande.... I am quite near thee; I weep for joy and yet... (*He kisses her again.*) — Thou art strange when I kiss thee so.... Thou art so beautiful that one would think thou wert about to die....

MÉLISANDE. Thou, too....

PELLÉAS. There, there.... We do not what we will.... I did not love thee the first time I saw thee....

MÉLISANDE. Nor I... nor I.... I was afraid....

PELLÉAS. I could not admit thine eyes.... I would have gone away at once... and then....

MÉLISANDE. And I — I would not have come.... I do not yet know why — I was afraid to come....

PELLÉAS. There are so many things one never knows. We are

ever waiting; and then.... What is that noise? — They are closing the gates!...

MÉLISANDE. Yes, they have closed the gates....

PELLÉAS. We cannot go back now? — Hearest thou the bolts? — Listen! listen!... The great chains!... The great chains!... It is too late; it is too late!...

MÉLISANDE. All the better! all the better! all the better!...

PELLÉAS. Thou — ...? Behold, behold!... It is no longer we who will it so!... All's lost, all's saved! All is saved tonight! — Come, come.... My heart beats like a madman — up to my very throat.... (*They embrace.*) Listen! Listen! My heart is almost strangling me.... Come! come!... Ah, how beautiful it is in the shadows!...

MÉLISANDE. There is someone behind us!

PELLÉAS. I see no one....

MÉLISANDE. I heard a noise....

PELLÉAS. I hear only thy heart in the dark....

MÉLISANDE. I heard the crackling of dead leaves....

PELLÉAS. Because the wind is silent all at once.... It fell as we were kissing....

MÉLISANDE. How long our shadows are tonight!...

PELLÉAS. They embrace to the very end of the garden. Oh, how they kiss far away from us!... Look! look!...

MÉLISANDE (*in a stifled voice*). A-a-h! — He is behind a tree!

PELLÉAS. Who?

MÉLISANDE. Golaud!

PELLÉAS. Golaud! — Where? — I see nothing....

MÉLISANDE. There... at the end of our shadows....

PELLÉAS. Yes, yes; I saw him.... Let us not turn abruptly....

MÉLISANDE. He has his sword....

PELLÉAS. I have not mine....

MÉLISANDE. He saw us kiss....

PELLÉAS. He does not know we have seen him.... Do not stir; do not turn your head.... He would rush headlong on us.... He will remain there while he thinks we do not know. He watches us.... He is still motionless.... Go, go at once this way.... I will wait for him.... I will stop him....

MÉLISANDE. No, no, no!...

PELLÉAS. Go! Go! He has seen all!... He will kill us!...

MÉLISANDE. All the better! all the better! all the better!...

PELLÉAS. He comes! He comes!... Thy mouth!... Thy mouth!...

MÉLISANDE. Yes!... yes! yes!...   (*They kiss desperately.*)

PELLÉAS. Oh! oh! All the stars are falling!...

MÉLISANDE. Upon me, too! upon me, too!

PELLÉAS. Again! Again!... Give! Give!

MÉLISANDE. All! all! all!...

(GOLAUD *rushes upon them, sword in hand, and strikes* PELLÉAS, *who falls at the brink of the fountain.* MÉLISANDE *flees terrified.*)

MÉLISANDE (*fleeing*). Oh! Oh! I have no courage!... I have no courage!...   (GOLAUD *pursues her through the wood in silence.*)

ACT V

SCENE I — *A lower hall in the castle. The women servants discovered, gathered together, while without children are playing before one of the ventilators of the hall.*

AN OLD SERVANT. You will see, you will see, my daughters; it will be tonight. — Someone will come to tell us by and by....

ANOTHER SERVANT. They will not come to tell us.... They don't know what they are doing any longer....

THIRD SERVANT. Let us wait here....

FOURTH SERVANT. We shall know well enough when we must go up....

FIFTH SERVANT. When the time is come, we shall go up of ourselves....

SIXTH SERVANT. There is no longer a sound heard in the house....

SEVENTH SERVANT. We ought to make the children keep still, who are playing before the ventilator.

EIGHTH SERVANT. They will be still of themselves by and by.

NINTH SERVANT. The time has not yet come....

(*Enter an old Servant.*)

THE OLD SERVANT. No one can go in the room any longer. I have listened more than an hour.... You could hear the flies walk on the doors.... I heard nothing....

FIRST SERVANT. Has she been left alone in the room?

THE OLD SERVANT. No, no; I think the room is full of people.

FIRST SERVANT. They will come, they will come, by and by....

THE OLD SERVANT. Lord! Lord! It is not happiness that has come into the house.... One may not speak, but if I could say what I know....

SECOND SERVANT. It was you who found them before the gate?

THE OLD SERVANT. Why, yes! why, yes! It was I who found them. The porter says it was he who saw them first; but it was I who waked them. He was sleeping on his face and would not get up. — And now he comes saying, "It was I who saw them first." Is that just? — See, I burned myself lighting a lamp to go down cellar. Now what was I going to do down cellar? — I can't remember any more what I was going to do down cellar. — At any rate, I got up very early; it was not yet very light; I said to myself, I will go across the courtyard, and then I will open the gate. Good; I go down the stairs on tiptoe, and I open the gate as if it were an ordinary gate.... My God! My God! What do I see? Divine a little what I see!...

FIRST SERVANT. They were before the gate?

THE OLD SERVANT. They were both stretched out before the gate!... Exactly like poor folk that are too hungry.... They were huddled together like little children who are afraid.... The little princess was nearly dead, and the great Golaud had still his sword in his side.... There was blood on the sill....

SECOND SERVANT. We ought to make the children keep still.... They are screaming with all their might before the ventilator....

THIRD SERVANT. You can't hear yourself speak....

FOURTH SERVANT. There is nothing to be done: I have tried already; they won't keep still....

FIRST SERVANT. It seems he is nearly cured?

THE OLD SERVANT. Who?

FIRST SERVANT. The great Golaud.

THIRD SERVANT. Yes, yes; they have taken him to his wife's room. I met them just now, in the corridor. They were holding him up as if he were drunk. He cannot yet walk alone.

THE OLD SERVANT. He could not kill himself; he is too big. But she is hardly wounded, and it is she who is going to die.... Can you understand that?

FIRST SERVANT. You have seen the wound?

THE OLD SERVANT. As I see you, my daughter.— I saw everything, you understand…. I saw it before all the others…. A tiny little wound under her little left breast — a little wound that wouldn't kill a pigeon. Is it natural?

FIRST SERVANT. Yes, yes; there is something underneath….

SECOND SERVANT. Yes; but she was delivered of her babe three days ago….

THE OLD SERVANT. Exactly!… She was delivered on her death-bed; is that a little sign? — And what a child! Have you seen it? — A wee little girl a beggar would not bring into the world. … A little wax figure that came much too soon;… a little wax figure that must live in lambs' wool…. Yes, yes; it is not happiness that has come into the house….

FIRST SERVANT. Yes, yes; it is the hand of God that has been stirring….

SECOND SERVANT. Yes, yes; all that did not happen without reason….

THIRD SERVANT. It is as good Lord Pelléas… where is he? — No one knows….

THE OLD SERVANT. Yes, yes; everybody knows…. But nobody dare speak of it…. One does not speak of this;… one does not speak of that;… one speaks no more of anything;… one no longer speaks truth…. But *I* know he was found at the bottom of Blind Man's Spring;… but no one, no one could see him…. Well, well, we shall only know all that at the last day….

FIRST SERVANT. I dare not sleep here any longer….

THE OLD SERVANT. Yes, yes; once ill-fortune is in the house, one keeps silence in vain….

THIRD SERVANT. Yes; it finds you all the same….

THE OLD SERVANT. Yes, yes; but we do not go where we would….

FOURTH SERVANT. Yes, yes; we do not do what we would….

FIRST SERVANT. They are afraid of us now….

SECOND SERVANT. They all keep silence….

THIRD SERVANT. They cast down their eyes in the corridors.

FOURTH SERVANT. They do not speak any more except in a low voice.

FIFTH SERVANT. You would think they had all done it together.

SIXTH SERVANT. One doesn't know what they have done....

SEVENTH SERVANT. What is to be done when the masters are afraid?... (*A silence.*)

FIRST SERVANT. I no longer hear the children screaming.

SECOND SERVANT. They are sitting down before the ventilator.

THIRD SERVANT. They are huddled against each other.

THE OLD SERVANT. I no longer hear anything in the house....

FIRST SERVANT. You no longer even hear the children breathe....

THE OLD SERVANT. Come, come; it is time to go up....

(*Exeunt, in silence.*)

SCENE II — *An apartment in the castle.* ARKËL, GOLAUD, *and the* PHYSICIAN *discovered in one corner of the room.* MÉLISANDE *is stretched upon her bed.*

THE PHYSICIAN. It cannot be of that little wound she is dying; a bird would not have died of it.... It is not you, then, who have killed her, good my lord; do not be so disconsolate.... She could not have lived.... She was born without reason... to die; and she dies without reason.... And then, it is not sure we shall not save her....

ARKËL. No, no; it seems to me we keep too silent, in spite of ourselves, in her room.... It is not a good sign.... Look how she sleeps... slowly, slowly;... it is as if her soul was cold forever....

GOLAUD. I have killed her without cause! I have killed her without cause!... Is it not enough to make the stones weep?... They had kissed like little children.... They had simply kissed.... They were brother and sister.... And I, and I at once!... I did it in spite of myself, look you.... I did it in spite of myself....

THE PHYSICIAN. Stop; I think she is waking....

MÉLISANDE. Open the window;... open the window....

ARKËL. Shall I open this one, Mélisande?

MÉLISANDE. No, no; the great window... the great window.... It is to see...

ARKËL. Is not the sea air too cold tonight?

THE PHYSICIAN. Do it; do it....

MÉLISANDE. Thanks.... Is it sunset?

ARKËL. Yes; it is sunset on the sea; it is late. — How are you, Mélisande?

MÉLISANDE. Well, well. — Why do you ask that? I have never been better. — And yet it seems to me I know something....

ARKËL. What sayest thou? — I do not understand thee....

MÉLISANDE. Neither do I understand all I say, you see.... I do not know what I am saying.... I do not know what I know.... I no longer say what I would....

ARKËL. Why, yes! why, yes!... I am quite happy to hear thee speak so; thou hast raved a little these last days, and one no longer understood thee.... But now all that is far away....

MÉLISANDE. I do not know.... — Are you all alone in the room, grandfather?

ARKËL. No; there is the physician, besides, who cured thee....

MÉLISANDE. Ah!...

ARKËL. And then there is still someone else....

MÉLISANDE. Who is it?

ARKËL. It is... thou must not be frightened.... He does not wish thee the least harm, be sure.... If thou'rt afraid, he will go away.... He is very unhappy....

MÉLISANDE. Who is it?

ARKËL. It is thy... thy husband.... It is Golaud....

MÉLISANDE. Golaud is here? Why does he not come by me?

GOLAUD (*dragging himself toward the bed*). Mélisande... Mélisande....

MÉLISANDE. Is it you, Golaud? I should hardly recognize you any more.... It is the evening sunlight in my eyes.... Why look you on the walls? You have grown thin and old.... Is it a long while since we saw each other?

GOLAUD. (*To* ARKËL *and the* PHYSICIAN.) Will you withdraw a moment, if you please, if you please?... I will leave the door wide open.... One moment only.... I would say something to her; else I could not die.... Will you? — Go clear to the end of the corridor; you can come back at once, at once.... Do not refuse me this.... I am a wretch.... (*Exit* ARKËL *and the* PHYSICIAN.) — Mélisande, hast thou pity on me, as I have pity on thee?... Mélisande?... Dost thou forgive me, Mélisande?...

MÉLISANDE. Yes, yes, I do forgive thee.... What must I forgive?...

GOLAUD. I have wrought thee so much ill, Mélisande....
I cannot tell thee the ill I have wrought thee.... But I see it,
I see it so clearly today... since the first day.... And all I did
not know till now leaps in my eyes tonight.... And it is all my
fault, all that has happened, all that will happen.... If I could
tell it, thou wouldst see as I do!... I see all! I see all!... But
I loved thee so!... I loved thee so!... But now there is someone
dying.... It is I who am dying.... And I would know... I would
ask thee.... Thou'lt bear me no ill-will... I would.... The
truth must be told to a dying man.... He must know the truth,
or else he could not sleep.... Swearest thou to tell me the truth?

MÉLISANDE. Yes.

GOLAUD. Didst thou love Pelléas?

MÉLISANDE. Why, yes; I loved him. — Where is he?

GOLAUD. Thou dost not understand me? — Thou wilt not understand me? — It seems to me... it seems to me... Well, then,
here: I ask thee if thou lovedst him with a forbidden love?...
Wert thou... were you guilty? Say, say, yes, yes, yes!...

MÉLISANDE. No, no; we were not guilty. — Why do you ask that?

GOLAUD. Mélisande!... tell me the truth, for the love of God!

MÉLISANDE. Why have I not told the truth?

GOLAUD. Do not lie so any more, at the moment of death!

MÉLISANDE. Who is dying? — Is it I?

GOLAUD. Thou, thou! And I, I too, after thee!... And we must
have the truth.... We must have the truth at last, dost thou
understand?... Tell me all! Tell me all! I forgive thee all!...

MÉLISANDE. Why am I going to die? — I did not know it....

GOLAUD. Thou knowest it now!... It is time! It is time!...
Quick! quick!... The truth! the truth!...

MÉLISANDE. The truth... the truth...

GOLAUD. Where art thou? — Mélisande! — Where art thou? —
It is not natural! Mélisande! Where art thou! — Where
goest thou? (*Perceiving* ARKËL *and the* PHYSICIAN *at the door of
the room.*) — Yes, yes; you may come in.... I know nothing; it is
useless.... It is too late; she is already too far away from us....
I shall never know!... I shall die here like a blind man!...

ARKËL. What have you done? You will kill her....

GOLAUD. I have already killed her....

ARKËL. Mélisande....

MÉLISANDE. Is it you, grandfather?

ARKËL. Yes, my daughter.... What would you have me do?

MÉLISANDE. Is it true that the winter is beginning?...

ARKËL. Why dost thou ask?

MÉLISANDE. Because it is cold, and there are no more leaves....

ARKËL. Thou art cold? — Wilt thou have the windows closed?

MÉLISANDE. No, no,... not till the sun be at the bottom of the sea.
— It sinks slowly; then it is the winter beginning?

ARKËL. Yes. — Thou dost not like the winter?

MÉLISANDE. Oh! no. I am afraid of the cold. — I am so afraid of
the great cold....

ARKËL. Dost thou feel better?

MÉLISANDE. Yes, yes; I have no longer all those qualms....

ARKËL. Wouldst thou see thy child?

MÉLISANDE. What child?

ARKËL. Thy child. — Thou art a mother.... Thou hast brought
a little daughter into the world....

MÉLISANDE. Where is she?

ARKËL. Here....

MÉLISANDE. It is strange. I cannot lift my arms to take her....

ARKËL. Because you are still very weak.... I will hold her myself;
look....

MÉLISANDE. She does not laugh.... She is little.... She is going to
weep too.... I pity her....

(*The room has been invaded, little by little, by the women servants
of the castle, who range themselves in silence along the walls
and wait.*)

GOLAUD (*rising abruptly*). What is the matter? — What are all these
women coming here for?

THE PHYSICIAN. It is the servants....

ARKËL. Who was it called them?

THE PHYSICIAN. It was not I....

GOLAUD. Why do you come here? — No one has asked for you....
What come you here to do? — But what is it, then? — Answer
me!...

(*The servants make no answer.*)

ARKËL. Do not speak too loud.... She is going to sleep; she has
closed her eyes....

GOLAUD. It is not...?

THE PHYSICIAN. No, no; see, she breathes....

ARKËL. Her eyes are full of tears. — It is her soul weeping now....
Why does she stretch her arms out so? — What would she?

THE PHYSICIAN. It is toward the child, without doubt.... It is the
struggle of motherhood against...

GOLAUD. At this moment? — At this moment? — You must say.
Say! Say!...

THE PHYSICIAN. Perhaps.

GOLAUD. At once?... Oh! oh! I must tell her.... — Mélisande!
... Mélisande!... Leave me alone! leave me alone with her!...

ARKËL. No, no; do not come near.... Trouble her not.... Speak
no more to her.... You know not what the soul is....

GOLAUD. It is not my fault!... It is not my fault!

ARKËL. Hush!... Hush!... We must speak softly now. — She
must not be disturbed.... The human soul is very silent....
The human soul likes to depart alone.... It suffers so timorously.
... But the sadness, Golaud... the sadness of all we see!...
Oh! oh! oh!...

> (*At this moment, all the servants fall suddenly on their knees at the
> back of the chamber.*)

ARKËL (*turning*). What is the matter!

THE PHYSICIAN (*approaching the bed and feeling the body*). They are
right.... (*A long silence.*)

ARKËL. I saw nothing. — Are you sure?

THE PHYSICIAN. Yes, yes.

ARKËL. I heard nothing.... So quick, so quick!... All at once!...
She goes without a word....

GOLAUD (*sobbing*). Oh! oh! oh!

ARKËL. Do not stay here, Golaud.... She must have silence now....
Come, come.... It is terrible, but it is not your fault.... 'Twas
a little being, so quiet, so fearful, and so silent.... 'Twas a poor
little mysterious being, like everybody.... She lies there as if
she were the big sister of her child.... Come, come.... My God!
My God!... I shall never understand it at all.... Let us not stay
here. — Come; the child must not stay here in this room....
She must live now in her place.... It is the poor little one's
turn.... (*They go out in silence.*)

THE WEAVERS

A DRAMA OF THE FORTIES

By GERHART HAUPTMANN

Translated from the German by MARY MORISON

I DEDICATE THIS DRAMA

TO MY FATHER

ROBERT HAUPTMANN

You, dear Father, know what feelings lead me to dedicate this work to you, and I am not called upon to analyse them here. Your stories of my grandfather, who in his young days sat at the loom, a poor weaver like those here depicted, contained the germ of my drama. Whether it possesses the vigor of life or is rotten at the core, it is the best, "so poor a man as Hamlet is" can offer.

Yours,

GERHART.

GERHART HAUPTMANN

THE early career of Hauptmann is identified with the development of naturalism in the German theater and the establishment of the Freie Bühne. But even while he was supplying naturalism with some of its incentives and its lasting monuments, Hauptmann was no wholeheartedly a naturalist. He was rather an exceedingly impressionable and flexible poetic genius who in his career as a dramatist turned his hand with almost equal skill to naturalism, fantasy, bourgeois drama, and historical drama. Hauptmann's grandfather had begun life as a weaver; his father was an innkeeper of some culture. Gerhart went in 1874 from Obersalzbrunn in Silesia, where he had been born in 1862, to Realschule at Breslau. In his youthful efforts he was encouraged by his brother Carl, who himself became a poet and dramatist. In 1880 he went to the Royal College of Art at Breslau, and in 1882 was, with his brother, a student at Jena. The young man wavered between sculpture and poetry. On a trip to the Mediterranean he was inspired to write his first published poem, "Promethidenlos," published in 1885. This Byronesque effort was later withdrawn by the author. With his marriage at twenty-two he turned to the theater, took lessons in the art of acting, and saturated himself with the influence of Ibsen, Zola, and Tolstoy. His first attempt in playwriting was a tragedy *Germanen und Römer*, long lost, and rediscovered by the author in 1927. The second was *Das Erbe des Tiberius*, offered to the theaters at Berlin and Oldenburg in 1884 and not accepted. This is now lost. His first naturalistic work was a narrative, *Barnwärter Theil*, published in 1888. Other fiction written by Hauptmann was *Der Apostel*, 1899; *Der Narr in Christo, Emanuel Quint*, 1910; and *Phantom*, 1923.

THE WEAVERS

THE naturalistic movement in the German theater is partly a social and partly a literary movement. It grew out of the unexampled social ferment of the latter years of the nineteenth century within Germany as this was played upon in the world of art by the influence from abroad of the work of Tolstoy, Zola, and Ibsen. Notable in the movement in Germany was the establishment of the magazine *Gesellschaft*, edited by Michael Conrad, and the organization of the revolutionary art society, *Durch*, 1886, of which the moving spirits were Michael Conrad, the Hart brothers, and Arno Holz. One of the notable results of the naturalistic movement was the establishment of the Freie Bühne in 1889 by Paul Schlenther and Otto Brahm. To these agencies we owe the fostering of the early genius of Hauptmann.

We are now far enough away from the movement of naturalism to see that many of its imperatives and sacred doctrines which it was treason to question in the nineties have lost something in authority. For one thing many men, among these Hauptmann himself, who early pledged themselves to naturalism as a social and art evangel, rather speedily forgot their vows. For another thing it soon became apparent that naturalism itself was an ideal that was practically impossible of achievement. Though influenced by Zola and Tolstoy and following them faithfully in his first two plays, *Before Sunrise* and *The Coming of Peace*, the sensitive spirit of the young playwright, in which there was much of the feeling for form, revolted against the excesses of this one-sided naturalism. Without discarding sympathy for the unfortunate and oppressed, he determined to write a play in which observation should operate freely over all fields of the action, and a wise pity should be general and not particular. The result was *Die Waber*, one of the best examples of pure naturalism, unburdened with special pleading, produced by the modern theater.

As first published in 1892, the play was written in complete Silesian dialect. Before it came to the stage this local color had been made more mild. Under the title *Die Weber*, the play was accepted for production by L'Arronge in the Deutsches Theater. The resulting outcry was so great that the Kaiser gave up his loge at the theater and the play was forbidden by the censor. Thereupon it was presented by the Freie Bühne, in 1893, the last of the author's first four plays to be presented by this private theater. In 1894 it was produced by Antoine in Paris, the first German play to be presented in Paris after the war of 1870. The first production in America was at the Irving Place Theater, New York, in 1905. The play was long in the repertory of Max Reinhardt's Grosses Schauspielhaus in Berlin.

"Naturalism is not so much a strict recipe as a collection of desiderata which one meets in the theater and novel of the period: taste for the minute event, for detail in description; in the worship of verity, an absolute freedom in the painting of the humble and the debased, and a preference for these things, a depiction of environment with an especial leaning to the life of the people; the use of a language approaching spoken discourse, with interruptions, faults, with the flat vocabulary of the vulgar, sometimes slangy and dialectical. In general a drab and often sad atonality. Naturalism applies scientific — not artistic — principles to letters and the theater."

RENE LAURET, *Le Theatre Allemand d'Aujourdhui.*

COMPLETE LIST OF CHARACTERS

DREISSIGER, *fustian manufacturer*

MRS. DREISSIGER

PFEIFER, *manager*

NEUMANN, *cashier*

AN APPRENTICE } *in* DREISSIGER'S *employment*

JOHN, *coachman*

A MAID

WEINHOLD, *tutor to* DREISSIGER'S *sons*

PASTOR KITTELHAUS

MRS. KITTELHAUS

HEIDE, *Police Superintendent*

KUTSCHE, *policeman*

WELZEL, *publican*

MRS. WELZEL

ANNA WELZEL

WIEGAND, *joiner*

A COMMERCIAL TRAVELER

A PEASANT

A FORESTER

SCHMIDT, *surgeon*

HORNIG, *rag dealer*

WITTIG, *smith*

WEAVERS

BECKER

MORITZ JAEGER

OLD BAUMERT

MOTHER BAUMERT

BERTHA } BAUMERT
EMMA

FRITZ, EMMA'S *son* (*four years old*)

AUGUST BAUMERT

OLD ANSORGE

MRS. HEINRICH

OLD HILSE
MOTHER HILSE
GOTTLIEB HILSE
LUISE, GOTTLIEB'S *wife*
MIELCHEN, *their daughter* (*six years old*)
REIMANN, *weaver*
HEIBER, *weaver*
A WEAVER'S WIFE

A number of weavers, young and old, of both sexes.

The action passes in the Forties, at Kaschbach, Peterswaldau and Langen-bielau, in the Eulengebirge.

THE FIRST ACT

A large whitewashed room on the ground floor of DREISSIGER'S *house at Peterswaldau, where the weavers deliver their finished webs and the fustian is stored. To the left are uncurtained windows, in the back wall there is a glass door, and to the right another glass door, through which weavers, male and female, and children, are passing in and out. All three walls are lined with shelves for the storing of the fustian. Against the right wall stands a long bench, on which a number of weavers have already spread out their cloth. In the order of arrival each presents his piece to be examined by* PFEIFER, DREISSIGER'S *manager, who stands, with compass and magnifying-glass, behind a large table, on which the web to be inspected is laid. When* PFEIFER *has satisfied himself, the weaver lays the fustian on the scale, and an office apprentice tests its weight. The same boy stores the accepted pieces on the shelves.* PFEIFER *calls out the payment due in each case to* NEUMANN, *the cashier, who is seated at a small table.*

It is a sultry day toward the end of May. The clock is on the stroke of twelve. Most of the waiting work-people have the air of standing before the bar of justice, in torturing expectation of a decision that means life or death to them. They are marked, too, by the anxious timidity character- istic of the receiver of charity, who has suffered many humiliations, and, conscious that he is barely tolerated, has acquired the habit of self-efface- ment. Add to this an expression on every face that tells of constant, fruit- less brooding. There is a general resemblance among the men. They have something about them of the dwarf, something of the schoolmaster. The majority are flat-breasted, short-winded, sallow, and poor looking — creatures of the loom, their knees bent with much sitting. At a first glance the women show fewer typical traits. They look over-driven, worried, reckless, whereas the men still make some show of a pitiful self-respect; and their clothes are ragged, while the men's are patched and mended. Some of the young girls are not without a certain charm, consisting in a wax-like pallor, a slender figure, and large, projecting, melancholy eyes.

NEUMANN (*counting out money*). Comes to one and sevenpence halfpenny.

WEAVER'S WIFE (*about thirty, emaciated, takes up the money with trembling fingers*). Thank you, sir.

NEUMANN (*seeing that she does not move on*). Well, something wrong this time, too?

WEAVER'S WIFE (*agitated, imploringly*). Do you think I might have a few pence in advance, sir? I need it that bad.

NEUMANN. And I need a few pounds. If it was only a question of needing it — ! (*Already occupied in counting out another weaver's money, shortly.*) It's Mr. Dreissiger who settles about pay in advance.

WEAVER'S WIFE. Couldn't I speak to Mr. Dreissiger himself, then, sir?

PFEIFER (*now manager, formerly weaver. The type is unmistakable, only he is well fed, well dressed, clean-shaven; also takes snuff copiously. He calls out roughly.*) Mr. Dreissiger would have enough to do if he had to attend to every trifle himself. That's what we are here for. (*He measures, and then examines through the magnifying-glass.*) Mercy on us! what a draught! (*Puts a thick muffler round his neck.*) Shut the door, whoever comes in.

APPRENTICE (*loudly to* PFEIFER). You might as well talk to stocks and stones.

PFEIFER. That's done! — Weigh! (*The weaver places his web on the scales.*) If you only understood your business a little better! Full of lumps again.... I hardly need to look at the cloth to see them. Call yourself a weaver, and "draw as long a bow" as you've done there!

(BECKER *has entered. A young, exceptionally powerfully-built weaver; offhand, almost bold in manner.* PFEIFER, NEUMANN, *and the* APPRENTICE *exchange looks of mutual understanding as he comes in.*)

BECKER. Devil take it! This is a sweating job, and no mistake.

FIRST WEAVER (*in a low voice*). This blazing heat means rain.

(OLD BAUMERT *forces his way in at the glass door on the right, through which the crowd of weavers can be seen, standing shoulder to shoulder, waiting their turn. The old man stumbles forward and lays his bundle on the bench, beside* BECKER'S. *He sits down by it, and wipes the sweat from his face.*)

OLD BAUMERT. A man has a right to a rest after that.

BECKER. Rest's better than money.

OLD BAUMERT. Yes, but we *needs* the money, too. Good-mornin' to you, Becker!

BECKER. Morning, Father Baumert! Goodness knows how long we'll have to stand here again.

FIRST WEAVER. And what does that matter? What's to hinder a weaver waitin' for an hour, or for a day if need be? What else is he there for?

PFEIFER. Silence there! We can't hear our own voices.

BECKER (*in a low voice*). This is one of his bad days.

PFEIFER (*to the weaver standing before him*). How often have I told you that you must bring cleaner cloth? What sort of mess is this? Knots, and straw, and all kinds of dirt.

REIMANN. It's for want of a new picker, sir.

APPRENTICE (*has weighed the piece*). Short weight, too.

PFEIFER. I never saw such weavers. I hate to give out the yarn to them. It was another story in my day! I'd have caught it finely from my master for work like that. The business was carried on in different style then. A man had to know his trade — that's the last thing that's thought of nowadays. Reimann, one shilling.

REIMANN. But there's always a pound allowed for waste.

PFEIFER. I've no time. Next man! — What have you to show?

HEIBER (*lays his web on the table. While* PFEIFER *is examining it, he goes close up to him; eagerly in a low tone*). Beg pardon, Mr. Pfeifer, but I wanted to ask you, sir, if you would perhaps be so very kind as do me the favor an' not take my advance money off this week's pay.

PFEIFER (*measuring and examining the texture; jeeringly*). Well! What next, I wonder? This looks very much as if half the weft had stuck to the bobbins again.

HEIBER (*continues*). I'll be sure to make it all right next week, sir. But this last week I've had to put in two days' work on the estate. And my missus is ill in bed....

PFEIFER (*giving the web to be weighed*). Another piece of real slop-work. (*Already examining a new web.*) What a selvage! Here it's broad, there it's narrow; here it's drawn in by the wefts goodness knows how tight, and there it's torn out again by the temples. And hardly seventy threads weft to the inch.

What's come of the rest? Do you call this honest work? I never saw anything like it.

(HEIBER, *repressing tears, stands humiliated and helpless*.)

BECKER (*in a low voice to* BAUMERT). To please that brute you would have to pay for extra yarn out of your own pocket.

(*The* WEAVER'S WIFE, *who has remained standing near the cashier's table, from time to time looking round appealingly, takes courage and once more comes forward*.)

WEAVER'S WIFE (*to cashier imploringly*). I don't know what's to come of me, sir, if you won't give me a little advance this time — O Lord, O Lord!

PFEIFER (*calls across*). It's no good whining, or dragging the Lord's name into the matter. You're not so anxious about Him at other times. You look after your husband and see that he's not to be found so often lounging in the public house. We can give no pay in advance. We have to account for every penny. It's not our money. People that are industrious, and understand their work, and do it in the fear of God, never need their pay in advance. So now you know.

NEUMANN. If a Bielau weaver got four times as much pay, he would squander it four times over and be in debt into the bargain.

WEAVER'S WIFE (*in a loud voice, as if appealing to the general sense of justice*). No one can't call me idle, but I'm not fit now for what I once was. I've twice had a miscarriage. And as to John, he's but a poor creature. He's been to the shepherd at Zerlau, but he couldn't do him no good, and... you can't do more than you've strength for.... We works as hard as ever we can. This many a week I've been at it till far on into the night. An' we'll keep our heads above water right enough if I can just get a bit of strength into me. But you must have pity on us, Mr. Pfeifer, sir. (*Eagerly, coaxingly*.) You'll please be so very kind as to let me have a few pence on the next job, sir?

PFEIFER (*paying no attention*). Fiedler, one and twopence.

WEAVER'S WIFE. Only a few pence, to buy bread with. We can't get no more credit. We've a lot of little ones.

NEUMANN (*half aside to the* APPRENTICE, *in a serio-comic tone*). "Every year brings a child to the linen-weaver's wife, heigh-ho, heigh-ho, heigh."

APPRENTICE (*takes up the rhyme, half singing*). "And the little brat it's blind the first weeks of its life, heigh-ho, heigh-ho, heigh."

REIMANN (*not touching the money which the cashier has counted out to him*). We've always got one and fourpence for the web.

PFEIFER (*calls across*). If our terms don't suit you, Reimann, you have only to say so. There's no scarcity of weavers — especially of your sort. For full weight we give full pay.

REIMANN. How anything can be wrong with the weight is past...

PFEIFER. You bring a piece of fustian with no faults in it, and there will be no fault in the pay.

REIMANN. It's not possible that there's too many knots in this web.

PFEIFER (*examining*). If you want to live well, then be sure you weave well.

HEIBER (*has remained standing near* PFEIFER, *so as to seize on any favorable opportunity. He laughs at* PFEIFER's *little witticism, then steps forward and again addresses him*). I wanted to ask you, sir, if you would perhaps have the great kindness not to take my advance of sixpence off today's pay? My missus has been bedridden since February. She can't do a hand's turn for me, and I've to pay a bobbin girl. And so...

PFEIFER (*takes a pinch of snuff*). Heiber, do you think I have no one to attend to but you? The others must have their turn.

REIMANN. As the warp was given me I took it home and fastened it to the beam. I can't bring back better yarn than I get.

PFEIFER. If you are not satisfied, you need come for no more. There are plenty ready to tramp the soles off their shoes to get it.

NEUMANN (*to* REIMANN). Do you not want your money?

REIMANN. I can't bring myself to take such pay.

NEUMANN (*paying no further attention to* REIMANN). Heiber, one shilling. Deduct sixpence for pay in advance. Leave sixpence.

HEIBER (*goes up to the table, looks at the money, stands shaking his head as if unable to believe his eyes, then slowly takes it up*). Well, I never! — (*Sighing.*) Oh, dear, oh, dear!

OLD BAUMERT (*looking into* HEIBER's *face*). Yes, Franz, that's so! There's matter enough for sighing.

HEIBER (*speaking with difficulty*). I've a girl lying sick at home, too, an' she needs a bottle of medicine.

OLD BAUMERT. What's wrong with her?

HEIBER. Well, you see, she's always been a sickly bit of a thing. I don't know.... I needn't mind tellin' you — she brought her trouble with her. It's in her blood, and it breaks out here, there, and everywhere.

OLD BAUMERT. It's always the way. Let folks be poor, and one trouble comes to them on the top of another. There's no help for it and there's no end to it.

HEIBER. What are you carryin' in that cloth, Father Baumert?

OLD BAUMERT. We haven't so much as a bite in the house, and so I've had the little dog killed. There's not much on him, for the poor beast was half starved. A nice little dog he was! I couldn't kill him myself. I hadn't the heart to do it.

PFEIFER (has inspected BECKER's web — calls). Becker, one and threepence.

BECKER. That's what you might give to a beggar: it's not pay.

PFEIFER. Everyone who has been attended to must clear out. We haven't room to turn round in.

BECKER (to those standing near, without lowering his voice). It's a beggarly pittance, nothing else. A man works his treadle from early morning till late at night, an' when he has bent over his loom for days an' days, tired to death every evening, sick with the dust and the heat, he finds he's made a beggarly one and threepence!

PFEIFER. No impudence allowed here.

BECKER. If you think I'll hold my tongue for your telling, you're much mistaken.

PFEIFER (exclaims). We'll see about that! (Rushes to the glass door and calls into the office.) Mr. Dreissiger, Mr. Dreissiger, will you be good enough to come here?

(Enter DREISSIGER. About forty, full-bodied, asthmatic. Looks severe.)

DREISSIGER. What is it, Pfeifer?

PFEIFER (spitefully). Becker says he won't be told to hold his tongue.

DREISSIGER (draws himself up, throws back his head, stares at BECKER; his nostrils tremble). Oh, indeed! — Becker. (To PFEIFER.) Is he the man?... (The clerks nod.)

BECKER (insolently). Yes, Mr. Dreissiger, yes! (Pointing to himself.)

This is the man. (*Pointing to* DREISSIGER.) And that's a man, too!

DREISSIGER (*angrily*). Fellow, how dare you?

PFEIFER. He's too well off. He'll go dancing on the ice once too often, though.

BECKER (*recklessly*). You shut up, you Jack-in-the-box. Your mother must have gone dancing once too often with Satan to have got such a devil for a son.

DREISSIGER (*now in a violent passion, roars*). Hold your tongue this moment, sir, or... (*He trembles and takes a few steps forward.*)

BECKER (*holding his ground steadily*). I'm not deaf. My hearing's quite good yet.

DREISSIGER (*controls himself, asks in an apparently cool business tone*). Was this fellow not one of the pack...?

PFEIFER. He's a Bielau weaver. When there's any mischief going, they are sure to be in it.

DREISSIGER (*trembling*). Well, I give you all warning: if the same thing happens again as last night — a troop of half-drunken cubs marching past my windows singing that low song...

BECKER. Is it "Bloody Justice" you mean?

DREISSIGER. You know well enough what I mean. I tell you that if I hear it again I'll get hold of one of you, and — mind, I'm not joking — before the justice he shall go. And if I can find out who it was that made up that vile doggerel...

BECKER. It's a beautiful song, that's what it is!

DREISSIGER. Another word and I send for the police on the spot, without more ado. I'll make short work with you young fellows. I've got the better of very different men before now.

BECKER. I believe you there. A real thoroughbred manufacturer will get the better of two or three hundred weavers in the time it takes you to turn round — swallow them up, and not leave as much as a bone. He's got four stomachs like a cow, and teeth like a wolf. That's nothing to him at all!

DREISSIGER (*to his clerks*). That man gets no more work from us.

BECKER. It's all the same to me whether I starve at my loom or by the roadside.

DREISSIGER. Out you go, then, this moment!...

BECKER (*determinedly*). Not without my pay.

DREISSIGER. How much is owing to the fellow, Neumann?

NEUMANN. One and threepence.

DREISSIGER (*takes the money hurriedly out of the cashier's hand, and flings it on the table, so that some of the coins roll off onto the floor*). There you are, then; and now, out of my sight with you!

BECKER. Not without my pay.

DREISSIGER. Do you not see it lying there? If you don't take it and go... It's exactly twelve now... The dyers are coming out for their dinner...

BECKER. I get my pay into my hand — here.

(*Points with the fingers of his right hand at the palm of his left.*)

DREISSIGER (*to the* APPRENTICE). Pick up the money, Tilgner.

(*The* APPRENTICE *lifts the money and puts it into* BECKER'S *hand.*)

BECKER. Everything in proper order.

(*Deliberately takes an old purse out of his pocket and puts the money into it.*)

DREISSIGER (*as* BECKER *still does not move away*). Well? Do you want me to come and help you?

(*Signs of agitation are observable among the crowd of weavers. A long, loud sigh is heard, and then a fall. General interest is at once diverted to this new event.*)

DREISSIGER. What's the matter there?

CHORUS OF WEAVERS AND WOMEN. "Someone's fainted." — "It's a little sickly boy."— "Is it a fit, or what?"

DREISSIGER. What do you say? Fainted?   (*He goes nearer.*)

OLD WEAVER. There he lies, anyway.

(*They make room. A boy of about eight is seen lying on the floor as if dead.*)

DREISSIGER. Does anyone know the boy?

OLD WEAVER. He's not from our village.

OLD BAUMERT. He's like one of Weaver Heinrich's boys. (*Looks at him more closely.*) Yes, that's Heinrich's little Philip.

DREISSIGER. Where do they live?

OLD BAUMERT. Up near us in Kaschbach, sir. He goes round playin' music in the evenings, and all day he's at the loom. They've nine children an' a tenth a-coming.

CHORUS OF WEAVERS AND WOMEN. "They're terrible put to it."—

"The rain comes through their roof."— "The woman hasn't two shirts among the nine."

OLD BAUMERT (*taking the boy by the arm*). Now then, lad, what's wrong with you? Wake up, lad.

DREISSIGER. Some of you help me, and we'll get him up. It's disgraceful to send a sickly child this distance. Bring some water, Pfeifer.

WOMAN (*helping to lift the boy*). Surely you're not going to die, lad!

DREISSIGER. Brandy, Pfeifer, brandy will be better.

BECKER (*forgotten by all, has stood looking on. With his hand on the door-latch, he now calls loudly and tauntingly*). Give him something to eat, an' he'll soon be all right. (*Goes out.*)

DREISSIGER. That fellow will come to a bad end. — Take him under the arm, Neumann. Easy now, easy; we'll get him into my room. What?

NEUMANN. He said something, Mr. Dreissiger. His lips are moving.

DREISSIGER. What — what is it, boy?

BOY (*whispers*). I'm h—hungry.

WOMAN. I think he says...

DREISSIGER. We'll find out. Don't stop. Let us get him into my room. He can lie on the sofa there. We'll hear what the doctor says.

(DREISSIGER, NEUMANN, *and the woman lead the boy into the office. The weavers begin to behave like school-children when their master has left the classroom. They stretch themselves, whisper, move from one foot to the other, and in the course of a few moments are conversing loudly.*)

OLD BAUMERT. I believe as how Becker was right.

CHORUS OF WEAVERS AND WOMEN. "He did say something like that."— "It's nothing new here to fall down from hunger."— "God knows what's to come of them in winter if this cutting down of wages goes on."— "An' this winter the potatoes aren't no good at all."— "Things'll get worse and worse till we're all done for together."

OLD BAUMERT. The best thing a man could do would be to put a rope round his neck and hang hisself on his own loom, like Weaver Nentwich. (*To another old weaver.*) Here, take a pinch. I was at Neurode yesterday. My brother-in-law, he works in the snuff factory there, and he give me a grain or two. Have you anything good in your handkercher?

OLD WEAVER. Only a little pearl barley. I was coming along behind Ulbrich the miller's cart, and there was a slit in one of the sacks. I can tell you we'll be glad of it.

OLD BAUMERT. There's twenty-two mills in Peterswaldau, but of all they grind, there's never nothing comes our way.

OLD WEAVER. We must keep up heart. There's always something comes to help us on again.

HEIBER. Yes, when we're hungry, we can pray to all the saints to help us, and if that don't fill our bellies we can put a pebble in our mouths and suck it. Eh, Baumert?

(Re-enter DREISSIGER, PFEIFER, AND NEUMANN.)

DREISSIGER. It was nothing serious. The boy is all right again. *(Walks about excitedly, panting.)* But all the same it's a disgrace. The child's so weak that a puff of wind would blow him over. How people, how any parents can be so thoughtless is what passes my comprehension. Loading him with two heavy pieces of fustian to carry good six miles! No one would believe it that hadn't seen it. It simply means that I shall have to make a rule that no goods brought by children will be taken over. *(He walks up and down silently for a few moments.)* I sincerely trust such a thing will not occur again.— Who gets all the blame for it? Why, of course the manufacturer. It's entirely our fault. If some poor little fellow sticks in the snow in winter and goes to sleep, a special correspondent arrives posthaste, and in two days we have a blood-curdling story served up in all the papers. Is any blame laid on the father, the parents, that send such a child?— Not a bit of it. How should they be to blame? It's all the manufacturer's fault — he's made the scapegoat. They flatter the weaver, and give the manufacturer nothing but abuse — he's a cruel man, with a heart like a stone, a wicked fellow, at whose calves every cur of a journalist may take a bite. He lives on the fat of the land, and pays the poor weavers starvation wages. In the flow of his eloquence the writer forgets to mention that such a man has his cares too and his sleepless nights; that he runs risks of which the workman never dreams; that he is often driven distracted by all the calculations he has to make, and all the different things he has to take into account; that he has to struggle for his very life against competition; and that no day passes without some annoyance or some loss. And think of the manufacturer's responsibilities, think of the numbers that depend on him, that look to him for their daily bread. No, No! none of you need wish yourselves in my shoes — you would soon have enough of it. (*After a moment's reflection.*) You all saw how that fellow, that scoundrel Becker, behaved. Now he'll go and spread about all sorts of tales of my hardheartedness, of how my weavers are turned off for a mere trifle, without a moment's notice. Is that true? Am I so very unmerciful?

CHORUS OF VOICES. No, sir.

DREISSIGER. It doesn't seem to me that I am. And yet these ne'er-do-wells come round singing low songs about us manufacturers — prating about hunger, with enough in their pockets to pay for quarts of bad brandy. If they would like to know what want is, let them go and ask the linen-weavers: they can tell something about it. But you here, you fustian-weavers, have every reason to thank God that things are no worse than they are. And I put it to all the old, industrious weavers present: Is a good workman able to gain a living in my employment, or is he not?

MANY VOICES. Yes, sir; he is, sir.

DREISSIGER. There now! You see! Of course such a fellow as that Becker can't. I advise you to keep these young lads in check. If there's much more of this sort of thing, I'll shut up shop — give up the business altogether, and then you can shift for yourselves, get work where you like — perhaps Mr. Becker will provide it.

FIRST WEAVER'S WIFE (*has come close to* DREISSIGER, *obsequiously removes a little dust from his coat*). You've been an' rubbed ag'in' something, sir.

DREISSIGER. Business is as bad as it can be just now, you know that yourselves. Instead of making money, I am losing it every day. If, in spite of this, I take care that my weavers are kept in work, I look for some little gratitude from them. I have thousands of pieces of cloth in stock, and don't know if I'll ever be able to sell them. Well, now, I've heard how many weavers hereabouts are out of work, and — I'll leave Pfeifer to give the particulars — but this much I'll tell you, just to show you my good will.... I can't deal out charity all round; I'm not rich enough for that; but I can give the people who are out of work the chance of earning at any rate a little. It's a great business risk I run by doing it, but that's my affair. I say to myself: Better that a man should work for a bite of bread than that he should starve altogether. Am I not right?

CHORUS OF VOICES. Yes, yes, sir.

DREISSIGER. And therefore I am ready to give employment to two hundred more weavers. Pfeifer will tell you on what conditions. *(He turns to go.)*

FIRST WEAVER'S WIFE *(comes between him and the door, speaks hurriedly, eagerly, imploringly)*. Oh, if you please, sir, will you let me ask you if you'll be so good... I've been twice laid up for...

DREISSIGER *(hastily)*. Speak to Pfeifer, good woman. I'm too late as it is. *(Passes on, leaving her standing.)*

REIMANN *(stops him again. In an injured, complaining tone)*. I have a complaint to make, if you please, sir. Mr. Feifer refuses to... I've always got one and twopence for a web...

DREISSIGER *(interrupts him)*. Mr. Pfeifer's my manager. There he is. Apply to him.

HEIBER *(detaining DREISSIGER; hurriedly and confusedly)*. O sir, I wanted to ask if you would p'r'aps, if I might p'r'aps... if Mr. Feifer might... might...

DREISSIGER. What is it you want?

HEIBER. That advance pay I had last time, sir; I thought p'r'aps you would kindly....

DREISSIGER. I have no idea what you are talking about.

HEIBER. I'm awful hard up, sir, because...

DREISSIGER. These are things Pfeifer must look into — I really have not the time. Arrange the matter with Pfeifer.

(He escapes into the office. The supplicants look helplessly at one another, sigh, and take their places again among the others.)

PFEIFER (*resuming his task of inspection*). Well, Annie, let us see what yours is like.

OLD BAUMERT. How much are we to get for the web, then, Mr. Pfeifer?

HEIBER. One shilling a web.

OLD BAUMERT. Has it come to that!

(*Excited whispering and murmuring among the weavers.*)

THE SECOND ACT

A small room in the house of WILHELM ANSORGE, *weaver and house-owner in the village of Kaschbach, in the Eulengebirge.*

In this room, which does not measure six feet from the dilapidated wooden floor to the smoke-blackened rafters, sit four people. Two young girls, EMMA *and* BERTHA BAUMERT, *are working at their looms;* MOTHER BAUMERT, *a decrepit old woman, sits on a stool beside the bed, with a winding-wheel in front of her; her idiot son* AUGUST *sits on a footstool, also winding. He is twenty, has a small body and head, and long, spider-like legs and arms.*

Faint, rosy evening light makes its way through two small windows in the right wall, which have their broken panes pasted over with paper or stuffed with straw. It lights up the flaxen hair of the girls, which falls loose on their slender white necks and thin bare shoulders, and their coarse chemises. These, with a short petticoat of the roughest linen, form their whole attire. The warm glow falls on the old woman's face, neck, and breast — a face worn away to a skeleton, with shriveled skin and sunken eyes, red and watery with smoke, dust, and working by lamplight; a long goître neck, wrinkled and sinewy; a hollow breast covered with faded, ragged shawls.

Part of the right wall is also lighted up, with stove, stove-bench, bed-stead, and one or two gaudily colored sacred prints. On the stove rail rags are hanging to dry, and behind the stove is a collection of worthless lumber. On the bench stand some old pots and cooking-utensils, and potato-parings are laid out on it, on paper, to dry. Hanks of yarn and reels hang from the rafters; baskets of bobbins stand beside the looms. In the back wall there is a low door without fastening. Beside it a bundle of willow wands is set up against the wall, and beyond them lie some damaged quarter-bushel baskets.

The room is full of sound — the rhythmic thud of the looms, shaking floor and walls, the click and rattle of the shuttles passing back and forward, and the steady whirr of the winding-wheels, like the hum of gigantic bees.

MOTHER BAUMERT (*in a querulous, feeble voice, as the girls stop weaving and bend over their webs*). Got to make knots again already, have you?

EMMA (*the elder of the two girls, about twenty-two, tying a broken thread*). It's the plaguyest web, this!

BERTHA (*fifteen*). Yes, it's real bad yarn they've given us this time.

EMMA. What can have happened to father? He's been away since nine.

MOTHER BAUMERT. You may well ask. Where in the wide world can he be?

BERTHA. Don't you worry yourself, mother.

MOTHER BAUMERT. I can't help it, Bertha lass.

(EMMA *begins to weave again.*)

BERTHA. Stop a minute, Emma!

EMMA. What is it!

BERTHA. I thought I heard someone.

EMMA. It'll be Ansorge coming home.

(*Enter* FRITZ, *a little, barefooted, ragged boy of four.*)

FRITZ (*whimpering*). I'm hungry, mother.

EMMA. Wait, Fritzel, wait a bit! Gran'father will be here very soon, an' he's bringin' bread along with him, an' coffee, too.

FRITZ. But I'm awful hungry, mother.

EMMA. Be a good boy now, Fritz. Listen to what I'm tellin' you. He'll be here this minute. He's bringin' nice bread an' nice corn-coffee; an' when we stop working mother'll take the tater peelin's and carry them to the farmer, and the farmer'll give her a drop o' good skim milk for her little boy.

FRITZ. Where's grandfather gone?

EMMA. To the manufacturer, Fritz, with a web.

FRITZ. To the manufacturer?

EMMA. Yes, yes, Fritz; down to Dreissiger's at Peterswaldau.]

FRITZ. Is it there he gets the bread?

EMMA. Yes; Dreissiger gives him money, and then he buys the bread.

FRITZ. Does he give him a heap of money?

EMMA (*impatiently*). Oh, stop that chatter, boy.

> (*She and* BERTHA *go on weaving for a time, and then both stop again.*)

BERTHA. August, go and ask Ansorge if he'll give us a light.

> (AUGUST *goes out accompanied by* FRITZ.)

MOTHER BAUMERT (*overcome by her childish apprehension, whimpers*). Emma! Bertha! where can father be?

BERTHA. He'll have looked in to see Hauffen.

MOTHER BAUMERT (*crying*). What if he's sittin' drinkin' in the public house?

EMMA. Don't cry, mother! You know well enough father's not the man to do that.

MOTHER BAUMERT (*half distracted by a multitude of gloomy forebodings*). What... what... what's to become of us if he doesn't come home? — if he drinks the money, and brings us nothin' at all? There's not so much as a handful of salt in the house — not a bite o' bread, nor a bit o' wood for the fire.

BERTHA. Wait a bit, mother! It's moonlight just now. We'll take August with us and go into the wood and get some sticks.

MOTHER BAUMERT. Yes, an' be caught by the forester.

(ANSORGE, *an old weaver of gigantic stature, who has to bend down to get into the room, puts his head and shoulders in at the door. Long, unkempt hair and beard.*)

ANSORGE. What's wanted?

BERTHA. Light, if you please.

ANSORGE (*in a muffled voice, as if speaking in a sick-room*). There's good daylight yet.

MOTHER BAUMERT. Are we to sit in the dark next?

ANSORGE. I've to do the same myself. (*Goes out.*)

BERTHA. It's easy to see that he's a miser.

EMMA. Well, there's nothin' for it but to sit an' wait his pleasure.

(*Enter* MRS. HEINRICH, *a woman of thirty, enceinte; an expression of torturing anxiety and apprehension on her worn face.*)

MRS. HEINRICH. Good-evenin' t' you all.

MOTHER BAUMERT. Well, Jenny, and what's your news?

MRS. HEINRICH (*who limps*). I've got a piece o' glass into my foot.

BERTHA. Come an' sit down, then, an' I'll see if I can get it out.

(MRS. HEINRICH *seats herself.* BERTHA *kneels down in front of her, and examines her foot.*)

MOTHER BAUMERT. How are you all at home, Jenny?

MRS. HEINRICH (*breaks out despairingly*). Things is in a terrible way with us!

(*She struggles in vain against a rush of tears; then weeps silently.*)

MOTHER BAUMERT. The best thing as could happen to the likes of us, Jenny, would be if God had pity on us an' took us away out o' this weary world.

MRS. HEINRICH (*no longer able to control herself, screams, still crying*). My children's starvin'. (*Sobs and moans.*) I'm at my wits' ends. Let me work till I fall down — I'm more dead than alive — it's all no use. Am I able to fill nine hungry mouths? We got a bit o' bread last night, but it wasn't enough even for the two smallest ones. Who was I to give it to, eh? They all cried: Me, me, mother! give it to me!... An' if it's like this while I'm still on my feet, what'll it be when I've to take to bed? Our few taters was washed away. We haven't a thing to put in our mouths.

BERTHA (*has removed the bit of glass and washed the wound*). We'll put a rag round it. Emma, see if you can find one.

MOTHER BAUMERT. We're no better off than you, Jenny.

MRS. HEINRICH. You have your girls, anyway. You've a husband as can work. Mine was taken with one of his fits last week again — so bad that I didn't know what to do with him, and was half out o' my mind with fright. And when he's had a turn like that, he can't stir out of bed under a week.

MOTHER BAUMERT. Mine's no better. His breathin' 's bad now as well as his back. An' there's not a farthin' nor a farthin's worth in the house. If he don't bring a few pence with him today, I don't know what we're to do.

EMMA. It's the truth she's tellin' you, Jenny. We had to let father take the little dog with him today, to have him killed, that we might get a bite into our stomachs again!

MRS. HEINRICH. Have you not got as much as a handful of flour to spare?

MOTHER BAUMERT. And that we have not, Jenny. There's not as much as a grain of salt in the house.

MRS. HEINRICH. Oh, whatever am I to do? (*Rises; stands still, brooding.*) I don't know what'll be the end of this! It's more nor I can bear. (*Screams in rage and despair.*) I would be contented if it was nothin' but pigs' food! — But I can't go home again empty-handed — that I can't. God forgive me, I see no other way out of it. (*She limps quickly out.*)

MOTHER BAUMERT (*calls after her in a warning voice*). Jenny, Jenny! don't you be doin' anything foolish, now!

BERTHA. She'll do herself no harm, mother. You needn't be afraid.

EMMA. That's the way she always goes on.

(*Seats herself at the loom and weaves for a few seconds.*)

(AUGUST *enters, carrying a tallow candle, and lighting his father,* OLD BAUMERT, *who follows close behind him, staggering under a heavy bundle of yarn.*)

MOTHER BAUMERT. Oh, father, where have you been all this long time? Where have you been?

OLD BAUMERT. Come now, mother, don't fall on a man like that. Give me time to get my breath first. An' look who I've brought with me.

(MORITZ JAEGER *comes stooping in at the low door. Reserve soldier, newly discharged. Middle height, rosy-cheeked, military carriage. His cap on the side of his head, hussar fashion, whole clothes and shoes, a clean shirt without collar. Draws himself up and salutes.*)

JAEGER (*in a hearty voice*). Good-evening, Auntie Baumert!

MOTHER BAUMERT. Well, well, now! And to think you've got back! An' you've not forgotten us? Take a chair, then, lad.

EMMA (*wiping a wooden chair with her apron, and pushing it toward* MORITZ). An' so you've come to see what poor folks are like again, Moritz?

JAEGER. I say, Emma, is it true that you've got a boy nearly old enough to be a soldier? Where did you get hold of him, eh?

(BERTHA, *having taken the small supply of provisions which her father has brought, puts meat into a saucepan, and shoves it into the oven, while* AUGUST *lights the fire.*)

BERTHA. You knew Weaver Finger, didn't you?

MOTHER BAUMERT. We had him here in the house with us. He was ready enough to marry her; but he was too far gone in consumption; he was as good as a dead man. It didn't happen for want of warning from me. But do you think she would listen? Not she. Now he's dead an' forgotten long ago, an' she's left with the boy to provide for as best she can. But now tell us how you've been gettin' on, Moritz.

OLD BAUMERT. You've only to look at him, mother, to know that. He's had luck. It'll be about as much as he can do to speak to the likes of us. He's got clothes like a prince, an' a silver watch, an' thirty shillings in his pocket into the bargain.

JAEGER (stretching himself consequentially, a knowing smile on his face). I can't complain. I didn't get on at all badly in the regiment.

OLD BAUMERT. He was the major's own servant. Just listen to him — he speaks like a gentleman.

JAEGER. I've got so accustomed to it that I can't help it.

MOTHER BAUMERT. Well, now, to think that such a good-for-nothing as you were should have come to be a rich man. For there wasn't nothing to be made of you. You would never sit still to wind more than a hank of yarn at a time, that you wouldn't. Off you went to your tom-tit boxes an' your robin redbreast snares — they was all you cared about. Is it not the truth I'm telling?

JAEGER. Yes, yes, auntie, it's true enough. It wasn't only redbreasts. I went after swallows, too.

EMMA. Though we were always tellin' you that swallows were poison.

JAEGER. What did I care? — But how have you all been getting on, Auntie Baumert?

MOTHER BAUMERT. Oh, badly, lad, badly these last four years. I've had the rheumatics — just look at them hands. And it's more than likely as I've had a stroke o' some kind, too, I'm that helpless. I can hardly move a limb, an' nobody knows the pains I suffers.

OLD BAUMERT. She's in a bad way, she is. She'll not hold out long.

BERTHA. We've to dress her in the mornin' an' undress her at night, an' to feed her like a baby.

MOTHER BAUMERT (*speaking in a complaining, tearful voice*). Not a thing can I do for myself. It's far worse than bein' ill. For it's not only a burden to myself I am, but to everyone else. Often and often do I pray to God to take me. For oh! mine's a weary life. I don't know... p'r'aps they think... but I'm one that's been a hard worker all my days. An' I've always been able to do my turn too; but now, all at once (*she vainly attempts to rise*), I can't do nothing.—I've a good husband an' good children, but to have to sit here and see them... ! Look at the girls! There's hardly any blood left in them — faces the color of a sheet. But on they must work at these weary looms whether they earn enough to keep theirselves or not. What sort o' life is it they lead? Their feet never off the treadle from year's end to year's end. An' with it all they can't scrape together as much as 'll buy them clothes that they can let theirselves be seen in; never a step can they go to church, to hear a word of comfort. They're liker scarecrows than young girls of fifteen and twenty.

BERTHA (*at the stove*). It's beginnin' to smoke again!

OLD BAUMERT. There now; look at that smoke. And we can't do nothin' for it. The whole stove's goin' to pieces. We must let it fall, and swallow the soot. We're coughin' already, one worse than the other. We may cough till we choke, or till we cough our lungs up — nobody cares.

JAEGER. But this here is Ansorge's business; he must see to the stove.

BERTHA. He'll see us out of the house first; he has plenty against us without that.

MOTHER BAUMERT. We've only been in his way this long time past.

OLD BAUMERT. One word of complaint an' out we go. He's had no rent from us this last half-year.

MOTHER BAUMERT. A well-off man like him needn't be so hard.

OLD BAUMERT. He's no better off than we are, mother. He's hard put to it, too, for all he holds his tongue about it.

MOTHER BAUMERT. He's got his house.

OLD BAUMERT. What are you talkin' about, mother? Not one stone in the wall is the man's own.

JAEGER (*has seated himself, and taken a short pipe with gay tassels out of one coat pocket, and a quart bottle of brandy out of another*). Things can't go on like this. I'm dumbfoundered when I see the life the people live here. The very dogs in the towns live better.

OLD BAUMERT (*eagerly*). That's what I say! Eh? eh? You know it, too! But if you say that here, they'll tell you that it's only bad times.

(*Enter* ANSORGE, *an earthenware pan with soup in one hand, in the other a half-finished quarter-bushel basket.*)

ANSORGE. Glad to see you again, Moritz!

JAEGER. Thank you, Father Ansorge — same to you!

ANSORGE (*shoving his pan into the oven*). Why, lad, you look like a duke!

OLD BAUMERT. Show him your watch, Moritz! An' he's got a new suit of clothes besides them he's on, an' thirty shillings in his purse.

ANSORGE (*shaking his head*). Is that so? Well, well!

EMMA (*puts the potato-parings into a bag*). I must be off; I'll maybe get a drop o' skim milk for these.   (*Goes out.*)

JAEGER (*the others hanging on his words*). You know how you all used to be down on me. It was always: Wait, Moritz, till your soldiering time comes — you'll catch it then. But you see how well I've got on. At the end of the first half-year I had got my good conduct stripes. You've got to be willing — that's where the secret lies. I brushed the sergeant's boots; I groomed his horse; I fetched his beer. I was as sharp as a needle. Always ready, accoutrements clean and shining — first at stables, first at rollcall, first in the saddle. And when the bugle sounded to the assault — why, then, blood and thunder, and ride to the devil with you!! I was as keen as a pointer. Says I to myself: There's no help for it now, my boy, it's got to be done; and I set my mind to it and did it. Till at last the major said before the whole squadron: There's a hussar now that shows you what a hussar should be!
                                   (*Silence. He lights his pipe.*)

ANSORGE (*shaking his head*). Well, well, well! You had luck with you, Moritz.

      (*Sits down on the floor, with his willow twigs beside him, and continues mending the basket, which he holds between his legs.*)

OLD BAUMERT. Let's hope you've brought some of it to us.— Are we to have a drop to drink your health in?

JAEGER. Of course you are, Father Baumert. And when this bottle's done, we'll send for more. (*He flings a coin on the table.*)

ANSORGE (*open-mouthed with amazement*). Oh, my! Oh, my! What goings on to be sure! Roast meat frizzlin' in the oven! A bottle o' brandy on the table! (*He drinks out of the bottle.*) Here's to you, Moritz! — Well, well, well!

(*The bottle circulates freely after this.*)

OLD BAUMERT. If we could anyway have a bit o' meat on Sundays and holidays, instead of never seein' the sight of it from year's end to year's end! Now we'll have to wait till another poor little dog finds its way into the house like this one did four weeks gone by — an' that's not likely to happen soon again.

ANSORGE. Have you killed the little dog?

OLD BAUMERT. We had to do that or starve.

ANSORGE. Well, well!

MOTHER BAUMERT. A nice, kind little beast he was, too!

JAEGER. Are you as keen as ever on roast dog hereabouts?

OLD BAUMERT. My word, if we could only get enough of it!

MOTHER BAUMERT. A nice little bit o' meat like that does you a lot o' good.

OLD BAUMERT. Have you lost the taste for it, Moritz? Stay with us a bit, and it'll soon come back to you.

ANSORGE (*sniffing*). Yes, yes! That will be a tasty bite — what a good smell it has!

OLD BAUMERT (*sniffing*). Splendid!

ANSORGE. Come, then, Moritz, tell us your opinion, you that's been out and seen the world. Are things at all like improving for us weavers, eh?

JAEGER. They would need to.

ANSORGE. We're in an awful state here. It's not livin' an' it's not dyin'. A man fights to the bitter end, but he's bound to be beat at last — to be left without a roof over his head, you may say without ground under his feet. As long as he can work at the loom he can earn some sort o' poor, miserable livin'. But it's many a day since I've been able to get that sort o' job. Now I tries to put a bite into my mouth with this here basket-

makin'. I sits at it late into the night, and by the time I tumbles
into bed I've earned three-halfpence. I put it to you if a
man can live on that, when everything's so dear? Nine shillin'
goes in one lump for house tax, three shillin' for land tax, nine
shillin' for mortgage interest — that makes one pound one.
I may reckon my year's earnin' at just double that money,
and that leaves me twenty-one shillin' for a whole year's food,
an' fire, an' clothes, an' shoes; and I've got to keep up some
sort of a place to live in. Is it any wonder if I'm behindhand
with my interest payments?

OLD BAUMERT. Someone would need to go to Berlin an' tell the
King how hard put to it we are.

JAEGER. Little good that would do, Father Baumert. There's
been plenty written about it in the newspapers. But the rich
people, they can turn and twist things round... as cunning
as the devil himself.

OLD BAUMERT (*shaking his head*). To think they've no more sense
than that in Berlin!

ANSORGE. And is it really true, Moritz? Is there no law to
help us? If a man hasn't been able to scrape together enough
to pay his mortgage interest, though he's worked the very
skin off his hands, must his house be taken from him? The
peasant that's lent the money on it, he wants his rights —
what else can you look for from him? But what's to be the
end of it all, I don't know. — If I'm put out o' the house...
(*In a voice choked by tears.*) I was born here, and here my father
sat at his loom for more than forty year. Many was the time
he said to mother: Mother, when I'm gone, the house'll still
be here. I've worked hard for it. Every nail means a night's
weaving, every plank a year's dry bread. A man would think
that...

JAEGER. They're quite fit to take the last bite out of your mouth —
that's what they are.

ANSORGE. Well, well, well! I would rather be carried out than
have to walk out now in my old days. Who minds dyin'?
My father, he was glad to die. At the very end he got frightened,
but I crept into bed beside him, an' he quieted down again.
I was a lad of thirteen then. I was tired and fell asleep beside

him — I knew no better — and when I woke he was quite cold.

MOTHER BAUMERT (*after a pause*). Give Ansorge his soup out o' the oven, Bertha.

BERTHA. Here, Father Ansorge, it'll do you good.

ANSORGE (*eating and shedding tears*). Well, well, well!

(OLD BAUMERT *has begun to eat the meat out of the saucepan.*)

MOTHER BAUMERT. Father, father, can't you have patience an' let Bertha serve it up properly?

OLD BAUMERT (*chewing*). It's two years now since I took the sacrament. I went straight after that an' sold my Sunday coat, an' we bought a good bit o' pork, an' since then never a mouthful of meat has passed my lips till tonight.

JAEGER. How should *we* need meat? The manufacturers eat it for us. It's the fat of the land *they* live on. Whoever doesn't believe that has only to go down to Bielau and Peterswaldau. He'll see fine things there — palace upon palace, with towers and iron railings and plate-glass windows. Who do they all belong to? Why, of course, the manufacturers! No signs of bad times there! Baked and boiled and fried — horses and carriages and governesses — they've money to pay for all that and goodness knows how much more. They're swelled out to bursting with pride and good living.

ANSORGE. Things was different in my young days. Then the manufacturers let the weaver have his share. Now they keep everything to theirselves. An' would you like to know what's at the bottom of it all? It's that the fine folks nowadays believes neither in God nor devil. What do they care about commandments or punishments? And so they steal our last scrap o' bread, an' leave us no chance of earnin' the barest living. For it's their fault. If our manufacturers was good men, there would be no bad times for us.

JAEGER. Listen, then, and I'll read you something that will please you. (*He takes one or two loose papers from his pocket.*) I say, August, run and fetch another quart from the public-house. Eh, boy, do you laugh all day long?

MOTHER BAUMERT. No one knows why, but our August's always happy — grins an' laughs, come what may. Off with you, then, quick! (*Exit* AUGUST *with the empty brandy bottle.*) You've got something good now, eh, father?

OLD BAUMERT (*still chewing; spirits rising from the effect of food and drink*). Moritz, you're the very man we want. You can read an' write. You understand the weavin' trade, and you've a heart to feel for the poor weavers' sufferin's. You should stand up for us here.

JAEGER. I'd do that quick enough! There's nothing I'd like better than to give the manufacturers round here a bit of a fright — dogs that they are! I'm an easy-going fellow, but let me once get worked up into a real rage, and I'll take Dreissiger in the one hand and Dittrich in the other, and knock their heads together till the sparks fly out of their eyes.— If we could only arrange all to join together, we'd soon give the manufacturers a proper lesson... without help from King or Government... all we'd have to do would be to say, We want this and that, and we don't want the other thing. There would be a change of days then. As soon as they see that there's some pluck in us, they'll cave in. I know the rascals; they're a pack of cowardly hounds.

MOTHER BAUMERT. There's some truth in what you say. I'm not an ill-natured woman. I've always been the one to say as how there must be rich folks as well as poor. But when things come to such a pass as this...

JAEGER. The devil may take them all, for what I care. It would be no more than they deserve.

(OLD BAUMERT *has quietly gone out.*)

BERTHA. Where's father?

MOTHER BAUMERT. I don't know where he can have gone.

BERTHA. Do you think he's not been able to stomach the meat, with not gettin' none for so long?

MOTHER BAUMERT (*in distress, crying*). There, now, there! He's not even able to keep it down when he's got it. Up it comes again, the only bite o' good food as he's tasted this many a day.

(*Re-enter* OLD BAUMERT, *crying with rage.*)

OLD BAUMERT. It's no good! I'm too far gone! Now that I've at last got hold of somethin' with a taste in it, my stomach won't keep it. (*He sits down on the bench by the stove crying.*)

JAEGER (*with a sudden violent ebullition of rage*). And yet there are people not far from here, justices they call themselves too, over-fed brutes, that have nothing to do all the year round but invent new ways of wasting their time. And these people say that the weavers would be quite well off if only they weren't so lazy.

ANSORGE. The men as say that are no men at all, they're monsters.

JAEGER. Never mind, Father Ansorge; we're making the place hot for 'em. Becker and I have been and given Dreissiger a piece of our mind, and before we came away we sang him "Bloody Justice."

ANSORGE. Good Lord! Is that the song?

JAEGER. Yes; I have it here.

ANSORGE. They call it Dreissiger's song, don't they?

JAEGER. I'll read it to you.

MOTHER BAUMERT. Who wrote it?

JAEGER. That's what nobody knows. Now listen.

(*He reads, hesitatingly like a schoolboy, with incorrect accentuation, but unmistakably strong feeling. Despair, suffering, rage, hatred, thirst for revenge, all find utterance.*)

> The justice to us weavers dealt
> Is bloody, cruel, and hateful;
> Our life's one torture, long drawn out:
> For Lynch law we'd be grateful.
>
> Stretched on the rack day after day,
> Hearts sick and bodies aching,
> Our heavy sighs their witness bear
> To spirits slowly breaking.

(*The words of the song make a strong impression on* OLD BAUMERT. *Deeply agitated, he struggles against the temptation to interrupt* JAEGER. *At last he can keep quiet no longer.*)

OLD BAUMERT (*to his wife, half laughing, half crying, stammering*). Stretched on the rack day after day. Whoever wrote that, mother, wrote the truth. You can bear witness... eh, how does it go? "Our heavy sighs their witness bear"... what's the rest?

JAEGER. "To spirits slowly breaking."

OLD BAUMERT. You know the way we sigh, mother, day and night, sleepin' and wakin'.

(ANSORGE *has stopped working, and cowers on the floor, strongly agitated.* MOTHER BAUMERT *and* BERTHA *wipe their eyes frequently during the course of the reading.*)

JAEGER (*continues to read*).

> The Dreissigers true hangmen are,
> Servants no whit behind them;
> Masters and men with one accord
> Set on the poor to grind them.
>
> You villains all, you brood of hell...

OLD BAUMERT (*trembling with rage, stamping on the floor*). Yes, brood of hell!!!

JAEGER (*reads*).

> You fiends in fashion human,
> A curse will fall on all like you,
> Who prey on man and woman.

ANSORGE. Yes, yes, a curse upon them!

OLD BAUMERT (*clenching his fist threateningly*). You prey on man and woman.

JAEGER (*reads*).

> Our life's one torture, long drawn out;
> For Lynch law we'd be grateful.

(*struck out*)

> The suppliant knows he asks in vain,
> Vain every word that's spoken.
> "If not content, then go and starve —
> Our rules cannot be broken."

OLD BAUMERT. What is it? "The suppliant knows he asks in vain"? Every word of it's true... every word... as true as the Bible. He knows he asks in vain.

ANSORGE. Yes, yes! It's all no good.

JAEGER (*reads*).

> Then think of all our woe and want,
> O ye who hear this ditty!
> Our struggle vain for daily bread
> Hard hearts would move to pity.

But pity's what *you've* never known —
You'd take both skin and clothing,
You cannibals, whose cruel deeds
Fill all good men with loathing.

OLD BAUMERT (*jumps up, beside himself with excitement*). Both skin and clothing. It's true, it's all true! Here I stand, Robert Baumert, master-weaver of Kaschbach. Who can bring up anything against me? I've been an honest, hard-working man all my life long, an' look at me now! What have I to show for it? Look at me! See what they've made of me! Stretched on the rack day after day. (*He holds out his arms.*) Feel that! Skin and bone! "You villains all, you brood of hell!!"

(*He sinks down on a chair, weeping with rage and despair.*)

ANSORGE (*flings his basket from him into a corner, rises, his whole body trembling with rage, gasps*). And the time's come now for a change, I say. We'll stand it no longer! We'll stand it no longer! Come what may!

THE THIRD ACT

The common room of the principal public-house in Peterswaldau. A large room with a raftered roof supported by a central wooden pillar, round which a table runs. In the back wall, a little to the right of the pillar, is the entrance door, through the opening of which the spacious lobby or outer room is seen, with barrels and brewing utensils. To the right of this door, in the corner, is the bar — a high wooden counter with receptacles for beer-mugs, glasses, etc.; a cupboard with rows of brandy and liqueur bottles on the wall behind, and between counter and cupboard a narrow space for the barkeeper. In front of the bar stands a table with a gay-colored cover, a pretty lamp hanging above it, and several cane chairs placed around it. Not far off, in the right wall, is a door with the inscription: Bar Parlor. Nearer the front on the same side an old eight-day clock stands ticking. At the back, to the left of the entrance door, is a table with bottles and glasses, and beyond this, in the corner, is the great stove. In the left wall there are three small windows. Below them runs a long bench; and in front of each stands a large oblong wooden table, with the end towards the wall. There are benches with backs along the sides of these tables, and at the end of each facing the window stands a wooden chair. The walls are washed blue and decorated with advertisements, colored prints and oleographs, among the latter a portrait of Frederick William III.

WELZEL, *the publican, a good-natured giant, upwards of fifty, stands behind the counter, letting beer run from a barrel into a glass.*

MRS. WELZEL *is ironing by the stove. She is a handsome, tidily dressed woman in her thirty-fifth year.*

ANNA WELZEL, *a good-looking girl of seventeen, with a quantity of beautiful, fair, reddish hair, sits, nicely dressed, with her embroidery, at the table with the colored cover. She looks up from her work for a moment and listens, as the sound of a funeral hymn sung by school-children is heard in the distance.*

WIEGAND, *the joiner, in his working clothes, is sitting at the same table, with a glass of Bavarian beer before him. His face shows that he understands what the world requires of a man if he is to attain his ends — namely, craftiness, sharpness, and relentless determination.*

A COMMERCIAL TRAVELER *is seated at the pillar-table, vigorously masticating a beefsteak. He is of middle height, stout and thriving-looking, inclined to jocosity, lively, and impudent. He is dressed in the fashion of the day, and his portmanteau, pattern-case, umbrella, overcoat, and traveling-rug lie on chairs beside him.*

WELZEL (*carrying a glass of beer to the* TRAVELER, *but addressing* WIEGAND). The devil's loose in Peterswaldau today.

WIEGAND (*in a sharp, shrill voice*). That's because it's delivery day at Dreissiger's.

MRS. WELZEL. But they don't generally make such an awful row.

WIEGAND. It's maybe because of the two hundred new weavers that he's going to take on.

MRS. WELZEL (*at her ironing*). Yes, yes, that'll be it. If he wants two hundred, six hundred's sure to have come. There's no lack of *them*.

WIEGAND. You may well say that. There's no fear of their dying out, let them be ever so badly off. They bring more children into the world than we know what to do with. (*The strains of the funeral hymn are suddenly heard more distinctly.*) There's a funeral today, too. Weaver Nentwich is dead, as no doubt you know.

WELZEL. He's been long enough about it. He's been goin' about like a livin' ghost this many a long day.

WIEGAND. You never saw such a little coffin, Welzel; it was the tiniest, miserablest little thing I ever glued together. And what a corpse! It didn't weigh ninety pounds.

TRAVELER (*his mouth full*). What I don't understand's this.... Take up whatever paper you like and you'll find the most heartrending accounts of the destitution among the weavers. You get the impression that three quarters of the people in this neighborhood are starving. Then you come and see a funeral like what's going on just now. I met it as I came into the village. Brass band, schoolmaster, schoolchildren, pastor, and such a procession behind them that you would think it was the Emperor of China that was getting buried. If the people have money to spend on this sort of thing, well... ! (*He takes a drink of beer; puts down the glass; suddenly and jocosely.*) What do you say to it, Miss? Don't you agree with me?

(ANNA *gives an embarrassed laugh, and goes on working busily.*)

TRAVELER. Now, I'll take a bet that these are slippers for papa.

WELZEL. You're wrong, then; I wouldn't put such things on my feet.

TRAVELER. You don't say so! Now, I would give half of what I'm worth if these slippers were for me.

MRS. WELZEL. Oh, you don't know nothing about such things.

WIEGAND (*has coughed once or twice, moved his chair, and prepared himself to speak*). You were saying, sir, that you wondered to see such a funeral as this. I tell you, and Mrs. Welzel here will bear me out, that it's quite a small funeral.

TRAVELER. But, my good man... what a monstrous lot of money it must cost! Where does that all come from?

WIEGAND. If you'll excuse me for saying so, sir, there's a deal of foolishness among the poorer working-people hereabouts. They have a kind of inordinate idea, if I may say so, of the respect an' duty an' honor they're bound to show to such as are taken from their midst. And when it comes to be a case of parents, then there's no bounds whatever to their superstitiousness. The children and the nearest family scrapes together every farthing they can call their own, an' what's still wanting, that they borrow from some rich man. They run themselves into debt over head and ears; they're owing money to the pastor, to the sexton, and to all concerned. Then there's the victuals an' the drink, an' such like. No, sir, I'm far from speaking against dutifulness to parents; but it's too much when it goes the length of the mourners having to bear the weight of it for the rest of their lives.

TRAVELER. But surely the pastor might reason them out of such foolishness.

WIEGAND. Begging your pardon, sir, but I must mention that every little place hereabouts has its church an' its respected pastor to support. These honorable gentlemen has their advantages from big funerals. The larger the attendance is, the larger the offertory is bound to be. Whoever knows the circumstances connected with the working classes here, sir, will assure you that the pastors are strong against quiet funerals.

(*Enter* HORNIG, *the rag-dealer, a little bandy-legged old man, with a strap round his chest.*)

HORNIG. Good-mornin', ladies and gentlemen! A glass of schnapps, if you please, Mr. Welzel. Has the young mistress anything for me today? I've got beautiful ribbons in my cart, Miss Anna, an' tapes, an' garters, an' the very best of pins an' hairpins an' hooks an' eyes. An' all in exchange for a few rags. (*He changes his voice.*) An' out of them rags fine white paper's to be made, for your sweetheart to write you a letter on.

ANNA. Thank you, but I've nothing to do with sweethearts.

MRS. WELZEL (*putting a bolt into her iron*). No, she's not that kind. She'll not hear of marrying.

TRAVELER (*jumps up, affecting delighted surprise, goes forward to* ANNA's *table, and holds out his hand to her across it*). That's right, miss. You and I think alike in this matter. Give me your hand on it. We'll both remain single.

ANNA (*blushing scarlet, gives him her hand*). But you are married already!

TRAVELER. Not a bit of it. I only pretend to be. You think so because I wear a ring. I only have it on my finger to protect my charms against shameless attacks. I'm not afraid of you, though. (*He puts the ring into his pocket.*) But tell me, truly, miss, are you quite determined never, never, never, to marry?

ANNA (*shakes her head*). Oh, get along with you!

MRS. WELZEL. You may trust her to remain single unless something very extra good turns up.

TRAVELER. And why should it not? I know of a rich Silesian proprietor who married his mother's lady's maid. And there's Dreissiger, the rich manufacturer, his wife is an innkeeper's daughter too, and not half so pretty as you, miss, though she rides in her carriage now, with servants in livery. And why not? (*He marches about, stretching himself, and stamping his feet.*) Let me have a cup of coffee, please.

(*Enter* ANSORGE *and* OLD BAUMERT, *each with a bundle. They seat themselves meekly and silently beside* HORNIG, *at the front table to the left.*)

WELZEL. How are you, Father Ansorge? Glad to see you once again.

HORNIG. Yes, it's not often as you crawl down from that smoky old nest.

ANSORGE (*visibly embarrassed, mumbles*). I've been fetchin' myself a web again.

BAUMERT. He's goin' to work at a shilling the web.

ANSORGE. I wouldn't have done it, but there's no more to be made now by basket-weavin'.

WIEGAND. It's always better than nothing. He does it only to give you employment. I know Dreissiger very well. When I was up there taking out his double windows last week we were talking about it, him and me. It's out of pity that he does it.

ANSORGE. Well, well, well! That may be so.

WELZEL (*setting a glass of schnapps on the table before each of the weavers*). Here you are, then. I say, Ansorge, how long is it since you had a shave? The gentleman over there would like to know.

TRAVELER (*calls across*). Now, Mr. Welzel, you know I didn't say that. I was only struck by the venerable appearance of the master-weaver. It isn't often one sees such a gigantic figure.

ANSORGE (*scratching his head, embarrassed*). Well, well!

TRAVELER. Such specimens of primitive strength are rare nowadays.   We're all rubbed smooth by civilization... but I can still take pleasure in nature untampered with.... These bushy eyebrows!   That tangled length of beard!

HORNIG.   Let me tell you, sir, that these people haven't the money to pay a barber, and as to a razor for themselves, that's altogether beyond them.   What grows, grows.   They haven't nothing to throw away on their outsides.

TRAVELER.   My good friend, you surely don't imagine that I would...   (*Aside to* WELZEL.)   Do you think I might offer the hairy one a glass of beer?

WELZEL.   No, no; you mustn't do that.   He wouldn't take it. He's got some queer ideas in that head of his.

TRAVELER.   All right, then, I won't.   With your permission, miss. (*He seats himself at* ANNA's *table.*)   I declare, miss, that I've not been able to take my eyes off your hair since I came in — such glossy softness, such a splendid quantity!   (*Ecstatically kisses his fingertips.*)   And what a color!... like ripe wheat.   Come to Berlin with that hair and you'll create no end of a sensation. On my honor, with hair like that you may go to Court.... (*Leans back, looking at it.*)   Glorious, simply glorious!

WIEGAND.   They've given her a name because of it.

TRAVELER.   And what may that be?

HORNIG.   The chestnut filly, isn't it?

WELZEL.   Come, now, we've had enough o' this.   I'm not goin' to have the girl's head turned altogether.   She's had a-plenty of silly notions put into it already.   She'll hear of nothing under a count today, and tomorrow it'll be a prince.

MRS. WELZEL.   You let her alone, father.   There's no harm in wantin' to rise in the world.   It's as well that people don't all think as you do, or nobody would get on at all.   If Dreissiger's grandfather had been of your way of thinkin', they would be poor weavers still.   And now they're rollin' in wealth.   An' look at old Tromtra.   He was nothing but a weaver, too, and now he owns twelve estates, an' he's been made a nobleman into the bargain.

WIEGAND.   Yes, Welzel, you must look at the thing fairly.   Your wife's in the right this time.   I can answer for that.   I'd never be where I am, with seven workmen under me, if I had thought like you.

HORNIG. Yes, you understand the way to get on; that your worst enemy must allow. Before the weaver has taken to bed, you're gettin' his coffin ready.

WIEGAND. A man must attend to his business if he's to make anything of it.

HORNIG. No fear of you for that. You know before the doctor when death's on the way to knock at a weaver's door.

WIEGAND (*attempting to laugh, suddenly furious*). And you know better than the police where the thieves are among the weavers, that keep back two or three bobbins full every week. It's rags you ask for, but you don't say No, if there's a little yarn among them.

HORNIG. An' your corn grows in the churchyard. The more that are bedded on the sawdust, the better for you. When you see the rows of little children's graves, you pats yourself on the belly, and says you: This has been a good year; the little brats have fallen like cockchafers off the trees. I can allow myself a quart extra in the week again.

WIEGAND. And supposing this is all true, it still doesn't make me a receiver of stolen goods.

HORNIG. No; perhaps the worst you do is to send in an account twice to the rich fustian manufacturers, or to help yourself to a plank or two at Dreissiger's when there's building goin' on and the moon happens not to be shinin'.

WIEGAND (*turning his back*). Talk to anyone you like, but not to me. (*Then suddenly.*) Hornig the liar!

HORNIG. Wiegand the coffin-jobber!

WIEGAND (*to the rest of the company*). He knows charms for bewitching cattle.

HORNIG. If you don't look out, I'll try one of 'em on you.

(WIEGAND *turns pale.*)

MRS. WELZEL (*had gone out; now returns with the* TRAVELER'S *coffee; in the act of putting it on the table*). Perhaps you would rather have it in the parlor, sir?

TRAVELER. Most certainly not! (*With a languishing look at* ANNA.) I could sit here till I die.

(*Enter a* YOUNG FORESTER *and a* PEASANT, *the latter carrying a whip. They wish the others "Good-Morning," and remain standing at the counter.*)

PEASANT. Two brandies, if you please.

WELZEL. Good-morning to you, gentlemen.

(*He pours out their beverage; the two touch glasses, take a mouthful, and then set the glasses down on the counter.*)

TRAVELER (*to* FORESTER). Come far this morning, sir?

FORESTER. From Steinseiffersdorf — that's a good step.

(*Two old* WEAVERS *enter, and seat themselves beside* ANSORGE, BAUMERT, *and* HORNIG.)

TRAVELER. Excuse me asking, but are you in Count Hochheim's service?

FORESTER. No. I'm in Count Keil's.

TRAVELER. Yes, yes, of course — that was what I meant. One gets confused here among all the counts and barons and other gentlemen. It would take a giant's memory to remember them all. Why do you carry an axe, if I may ask?

FORESTER. I've just taken this one from a man who was stealing wood.

OLD BAUMERT. Yes, their lordships are mighty strict with us about a few sticks for the fire.

TRAVELER. You must allow that if everyone were to help himself to what he wanted...

OLD BAUMERT. By your leave, sir, but there's a difference made here as elsewhere between the big an' the little thieves. There's some here as deals in stolen wood wholesale, and grows rich on it. But if a poor weaver...

FIRST OLD WEAVER (*interrupts* BAUMERT). We're forbid to take a single branch; but their lordships, they take the very skin off of us — we've assurance money to pay, an' spinning-money, an' charges in kind — we must go here an' go there, an' do so an' so much field work, all willy-nilly.

ANSORGE. That's just how it is — what the manufacturer leaves us, their lordships takes from us.

SECOND OLD WEAVER (*has taken a seat at the next table*). I've said it to his lordship himself. By your leave, my lord, says I, it's not possible for me to work on the estate so many days this year. For why — my own bit of ground, my lord, it's been next to carried away by the rains. I've to work both night and day if I'm to live at all. For oh, what a flood that was!... There I stood an' wrung my hands, an' watched the good soil come pourin' down the hill, into the very house! And all that dear, fine seed!... I could do nothing but roar an' cry until I couldn't see out o' my eyes for a week. And then I had to start an' wheel eighty heavy barrow-loads of earth up that hill, till my back was all but broken.

PEASANT (*roughly*). You weavers here make such an awful outcry. As if we hadn't all to put up with what Heaven sends us. An' if you *are* badly off just now, whose fault is it but your own? What did you do when trade was good? Drank an' squandered all you made. If you had saved a bit then, you'd have it to fall back on now when times is bad, and not need to be goin' stealin' yarn and wood.

FIRST YOUNG WEAVER (*standing with several comrades in the lobby or outer room, calls in at the door*). What's a peasant but a peasant, though he lies in bed till nine?

FIRST OLD WEAVER. The peasant an' the count, it's the same story with 'em both. Says the peasant when a weaver wants a house: I'll give you a little bit of a hole to live in, an' you'll pay me so much rent in money, an' the rest of it you'll make up by helpin' me to get in my hay an' my corn — an' if that doesn't please you, why, then you may go elsewhere. He tries another, and the second he says the same as the first.

BAUMERT (*angrily*). The weaver's like a bone that every dog takes a gnaw at.

PEASANT (*furious*). You starving curs, you're no good for anything. Can you yoke a plough? Can you draw a straight furrow or throw a bundle of sheaves onto a cart? You're fit for nothing but to idle about an' go after the women. A pack of scoundrelly ne'er-do-wells!

(*He has paid and now goes out. The* FORESTER *follows, laughing.* WELZEL, *the joiner, and* MRS. WELZEL *laugh aloud; the* TRAVELER *laughs to himself. Then there is a moment's silence.*)

HORNIG. A peasant like that's as stupid as his own ox. As if I didn't know all about the distress in the villages round here. Sad sights I've seen! Four and five lyin' naked on one sack of straw.

TRAVELER (*in a mildly remonstrative tone*). Allow me to remark, my good man, that there's a great difference of opinion as to the amount of distress here in the Eulengebirge. If you can read...

HORNIG. I can read straight off, as well as you. An' I know what I've seen with my own eyes. It would be queer if a man that's traveled the country with a pack on his back these forty years an' more didn't know something about it. There was Fullern, now. You saw the children scraping about among the dung-heaps with the peasants' geese. The people up there died naked, on the bare stone floors. In their sore need they ate the stinking weavers' glue. Hunger carried them off by the hundred.

TRAVELER. You must be aware, since you are able to read, that strict investigation has been made by the Government, and that...

HORNIG. Yes, yes, we all know what that means. They send a gentleman that knows all about it already better nor if he had seen it, an' he goes about a bit in the village, at the lower end, where the best houses are. He doesn't want to dirty his shining boots. Thinks he to himself: All the rest'll be the same as this. An' so he steps into his carriage, an' drives away home again, an' then writes to Berlin that there's no distress in the place at all. If he had but taken the trouble to go higher up into a village like that, to where the stream comes in, or across the stream onto the narrow side — or, better still, if he'd gone up to the little out-o'-the-way hovels on the hill above, some of 'em that black an' tumble-down as it would be the waste of a good match to set fire to 'em — it's another kind of report he'd have sent to Berlin. They should have come to me, these government gentlemen that wouldn't believe there was no distress here. I would have shown them something. I'd have opened their eyes for 'em in some of these starvation holes.

(*The strains of the Weavers' Song are heard, sung outside.*)

WELZEL. There they are, roaring at that devil's song again.

WIEGAND. They're turning the whole place upside down.

MRS. WELZEL. You'd think there was something in the air.

(JAEGER *and* BECKER *arm in arm, at the head of a troop of young weavers, march noisily through the outer room and enter the bar.*)

JAEGER. Halt! To your places!

(*The new arrivals sit down at the various tables, and begin to talk to other weavers already seated there.*)

HORNIG (*calls out to* BECKER). What's up now, Becker, that you've got together a crowd like this?

BECKER (*significantly*). Who knows but something may be going to happen? Eh, Moritz?

HORNIG. Come, come, lads. Don't you be a-gettin' of yourselves into mischief.

BECKER. Blood's flowed already. Would you like to see it?

(*He pulls up his sleeve and shows bleeding tattoo-marks on the upper part of his arm. Many of the other young weavers do the same.*)

BECKER. We've been at Father Schmidt's gettin' ourselves vaccinated.

HORNIG. Now the thing's explained. Little wonder there's such an uproar in the place, with a band of young rapscallions like you paradin' round.

JAEGER (*consequentially, in a loud voice*). You may bring two quarts at once, Welzel! I pay. Perhaps you think I haven't got the needful. You're wrong, then. If we wanted we could sit an' drink your best brandy an' swill coffee till tomorrow morning with any bagman in the land.

(*Laughter among the young weavers.*)

TRAVELER (*affecting comic surprise*). Is the young gentleman kind enough to take notice of me?

(*Host, hostess, and their daughter,* WIEGAND, *and the* TRAVELER *all laugh.*)

JAEGER. If the cap fits wear it.

TRAVELER. Your affairs seem to be in a thriving condition, young man, if I may be allowed to say so.

JAEGER. I can't complain. I'm a traveler in made-up goods.

I go shares with the manufacturers. The nearer starvation the weaver is, the better I fare. His want butters my bread.

BECKER. Well done, Moritz! You gave it to him that time. Here's to you!

(WELZEL *has brought the corn-brandy. On his way back to the counter he stops, turns round slowly, and stands, an embodiment of phlegmatic strength, facing the weavers.*)

WELZEL (*calmly but emphatically*). You let the gentleman alone. He's done you no harm.

YOUNG WEAVERS. And we're doing him no harm.

(MRS. WELZEL *has exchanged a few words with the* TRAVELER. *She takes the cup with the remains of his coffee and carries it into the parlor. The* TRAVELER *follows her amidst the laughter of the weavers.*)

YOUNG WEAVERS (*singing*).

"The Dreissigers the hangmen are,
Servants no whit behind them."

WELZEL. Hush-sh! Sing that song anywhere else you like, but not in my house.

FIRST OLD WEAVER. He's quite right. Stop that singin', lads.

BECKER (*roars*). But we must march past Dreissiger's, boys, and let them hear it once more.

WIEGAND. You'd better take care — you may march once too often.

(*Laughter and cries of Ho, ho!*)

(WITTIG *has entered; a gray-haired old smith bareheaded, with leather apron and wooden shoes, sooty from the smithy. He is standing at the counter waiting for his schnapps.*)

YOUNG WEAVER. Wittig, Wittig!

WITTIG. Here he is. What do you want with him?

YOUNG WEAVERS. "It's Wittig!" — "Wittig, Wittig!" — "Come here, Wittig."— "Sit beside us, Wittig."

WITTIG. Do you think I would sit beside a set of rascals like you?

JAEGER. Come and take a glass with us.

WITTIG. Keep your brandy to yourselves. I pay for my own drink. (*Takes his glass and sits down beside* BAUMERT *and* ANSORGE. *Clapping the latter on the stomach.*) What's the weavers' food so nice? Sauerkraut and roasted lice!

OLD BAUMERT (*excitedly*). But what would you say now if they'd made up their minds as how they would put up with it no longer.

WITTIG (*with pretended astonishment, staring open-mouthed at the old weaver*). Heinerle! you don't mean to tell me that that's you? (*Laughs immoderately.*) O Lord, O Lord! I could laugh myself to death. Old Baumert risin' in rebellion! We'll have the tailors at it next, and then there'll be a rebellion among the baa-lambs, and the rats and the mice. Damn it all, but we'll see some sport. (*He nearly splits with laughter.*)

OLD BAUMERT. You needn't go on like that, Wittig. I'm the same man I've always been. I still say 'twould be better if things could be put right peaceably.

WITTIG. Peaceably! How could it be done peaceably? Did they do it peaceably in France? Did Robespeer tickle the rich men's palms? No! It was: Away with them, every one! To the gilyoteen with them! Allongs onfong! You've got your work before you. The geese'll not fly ready roasted into your mouths.

OLD BAUMERT. If I could make even half a livin' ——

FIRST OLD WEAVER. The water's up to our chins now, Wittig.

SECOND OLD WEAVER. We're afraid to go home. It's all the same whether we works or whether we lies abed; it's starvation both ways.

FIRST OLD WEAVER. A man's like to go mad at home.

OLD ANSORGE. It's that length with me now that I don't care how things go.

OLD WEAVERS (*with increasing excitement*). "We've no peace anywhere."— "We've no spirit left to work."— "Up with us in Steenkunzendorf you can see a weaver sittin' by the stream washin' hisself the whole day long, naked as God made him. It's driven him clean out of his mind."

THIRD OLD WEAVER (*moved by the spirit, stands up and begins to "speak with tongues," stretching out his hand threateningly*). Judgment is at hand! Have no dealings with the rich and the great! Judgment is at hand! The Lord God of Sabaoth...

(*Some of the weavers laugh. He is pulled down onto his seat.*)

WELZEL. That's a chap that can't stand a single glass — he gets wild at once.

THIRD OLD WEAVER (*jumps up again*). But they — they believe not in God, not in hell, not in heaven. They mock at religion...

FIRST OLD WEAVER. Come, come now, that's enough!

BECKER. You let him do his little bit o' preaching. There's many a one would be the better for taking it to heart.

VOICES (*in excited confusion*). "Let him alone!" — "Let him speak!"

THIRD OLD WEAVER (*raising his voice*). But hell is opened, saith the Lord; its jaws are gaping wide, to swallow up all those that oppress the afflicted and pervert judgment in the cause of the poor. (*Wild excitement.*)

THIRD OLD WEAVER (*suddenly declaiming schoolboy fashion*).

> When one has thought upon it well,
> It's still more difficult to tell
> Why they the linen-weaver's work despise.

BECKER. But we're fustian-weavers, man. (*Laughter.*)

HORNIG. The linen-weavers is ever so much worse off than you. They're wandering about among the hills like ghosts. You people here have still got the pluck left in you to kick up a row.

WITTIG. Do you suppose the worst's over here? It won't be long till the manufacturers drain away that little bit of strength they still have left in their bodies.

BECKER. You know what he said: It will come to the weavers working for a bite of bread. (*Uproar.*)

SEVERAL OLD AND YOUNG WEAVERS. Who said that?

BECKER. Dreissiger said it.

A YOUNG WEAVER. The damned rascal should be hung up by the heels.

JAEGER. Look here, Wittig. You've always jawed such a lot about the French Revolution, and a good deal too about your own doings. A time may be coming, and that before long, when everyone will have a chance to show whether he's a braggart or a true man.

WITTIG (*flaring up angrily*). Say another word if you dare! Have you heard the whistle of bullets? Have you done outpost duty in an enemy's country?

JAEGER. You needn't get angry about it. We're comrades. I meant no harm.

WITTIG. None of your comradeship for me, you impudent young fool.

(Enter KUTSCHE, *the policeman.)*

SEVERAL VOICES. Hush — sh! Police!

(This calling goes on for some time, till at last there is complete silence, amidst which KUTSCHE *takes his place at the central pillar-table.)*

KUTSCHE. A small brandy, please. *(Again complete silence.)*

WITTIG. I suppose you've come to see if we're all behaving ourselves, Kutsche?

KUTSCHE *(paying no attention to* WITTIG*)*. Good-morning, Mr. Wiegand.

WIEGAND *(still in the corner in front of the counter)*. Good-morning t'you, sir.

KUTSCHE. How's trade?

WIEGAND. Thank you, much as usual.

BECKER. The chief constable's sent him to see if we're spoiling our stomach on these big wages we're getting. *(Laughter.)*

JAEGER. I say, Welzel, you will tell him how we've been feasting on roast pork an' sauce an' dumplings and sauerkraut, and now we're sitting at our champagne wine. *(Laughter.)*

WELZEL. The world's upside down with them today.

KUTSCHE. An' even if you had the champagne wine and the roast meat, you wouldn't be satisfied. I've to get on without champagne wine as well as you.

BECKER *(referring to* KUTSCHE's *nose)*. He waters his beet-root with brandy and gin. An' it thrives upon it, too. *(Laughter.)*

WITTIG. A p'liceman like that has a hard life. Now it's a starving beggar boy he has to lock up, then it's a pretty weaver girl he has to lead astray; then he has to get roarin' drunk an' beat his wife till she goes screamin' to the neighbors for help; and there's the ridin' about on horseback and the lyin' in bed till nine — nay, faith, but it's no easy job!

KUTSCHE. Jaw away; you'll jaw a rope round your neck in time. It's long been known what sort of a fellow you are. The magistrates know all about that dangerous tongue of yours. I know who'll drink wife and child into the poorhouse an' himself into jail before long, who it is that'll go on agitatin' and agitatin' till he brings down judgment on himself and all concerned.

WITTIG (*laughs bitterly*). It's true enough — no one knows what'll
be the end of it. You may be right yet. (*Bursts out in fury.*)
But if it does come to that, I know who I've got to thank for it,
who it is that's blabbed to the manufacturers an' all the gentlemen round, an' blackened my character to that extent that
they never give me a hand's turn of work to do — an' set the
peasants an' the millers against me, so that I'm often a whole
week without a horse to shoe or a wheel to put a tire on.   I
know who's done it.   I once pulled the damned brute off his
horse, because he was givin' a little stupid boy the most awful
flogging for stealin' a few unripe pears.   But I tell you this,
Kutsche, and you know me — if you get me put into prison,
you may make your own will.   If I hear as much as a whisper
of it, I'll take the first thing as comes handy, whether it's a
horseshoe or a hammer, a wheel-spoke or a pail; I'll get hold
of you if I've to drag you out of bed from beside your wife, and
I'll beat in your brains, as sure as my name's Wittig.

        (*He has jumped up and is going to rush at* KUTSCHE.)

OLD AND YOUNG WEAVERS (*holding him back*). Wittig, Wittig! Don't
lose your head!

KUTSCHE (*has risen involuntarily, his face pale. He backs toward the
door while speaking. The nearer the door the higher his courage rises.
He speaks the last words on the threshold, and then instantly disappears*).
What are you goin' on at me about?   I didn't meddle with you.
I came to say something to the weavers.   My business is with
them an' not with you, and I've done nothing to you.   But
I've this to say to you weavers: The Superintendent of Police
herewith forbids the singing of that song — Dreissiger's song,
or whatever it is you call it.   And if the yelling of it on the
streets isn't stopped at once, he'll provide you with plenty of
time and leisure for going on with it in jail.   You may
sing there, on bread and water, to your hearts' content.

        (*Goes out.*)

WITTIG (*roars after him*). He's no right to forbid it — not if we were
to roar till the windows shook an' they could hear us at Reichenbach — not if we sang till the manufacturers' houses tumbled
about their ears an' all the Superintendents' helmets danced
on the top of their heads.   It's nobody's business but our own.

(BECKER *has in the meantime got up, made a signal for singing, and now leads off, the others joining in.*)

> The justice to us weavers dealt
>   Is bloody, cruel, and hateful;
> Our life's one torture, long drawn out;
>   For Lynch law we'd be grateful.

(WELZEL *attempts to quiet them but they pay no attention to him.* WIEGAND *puts his hands to his ears and rushes off. During the singing of the next verse the weavers rise and form into procession behind* BECKER *and* WITTIG, *who have given pantomimic signs for a general break-up.*)

> Stretched on the rack, day after day,
>   Hearts sick and bodies aching,
> Our heavy sighs their witness bear
>   To spirit slowly breaking.

(*Most of the weavers sing the following verse out on the street, only a few young fellows, who are paying, being still in the bar. At the conclusion of the verse no one is left in the room except* WELZEL *and his wife and daughter,* HORNIG, *and* OLD BAUMERT.)

> You villains all, you brood of hell,
>   You fiends in fashion human,
> A curse will fall on all like you
>   Who prey on man and woman.

WELZEL (*phlegmatically collecting the glasses*). Their backs are up today, and no mistake.

HORNIG (*to* OLD BAUMERT, *who is preparing to go*). What in the name of Heaven are they up to, Baumert?

BAUMERT. They're goin' to Dreissiger's to make him add something onto the pay.

WELZEL. And are you joining in these foolish ongoings?

OLD BAUMERT. I've no choice, Welzel. The young men may an' the old men must. (*Goes out rather shamefacedly.*)

HORNIG. It'll not surprise me if this ends badly.

WELZEL. To think that even old fellows like him are goin' right off their heads!

HORNIG. We all set our hearts on something!

THE FOURTH ACT

Peterswaldau.   Private room of DREISSIGER, *the fustian manufacturer — luxuriously furnished in the chilly taste of the first half of this century. Ceiling, doors, and stove are white, and the wall paper, with its small, straight-lined floral pattern, is dull and cold in tone.   The furniture is mahogany, richly-carved, and upholstered in red.   On the right, between two windows with crimson damask curtains, stands the writing-table, a high bureau with falling flap.   Directly opposite to this is the sofa, with the strong-box beside it; in front of the sofa a table, with chairs and easy-chairs arranged about it.   Against the back wall is a gun-cupboard.   All three walls are decorated with bad pictures in gilt frames.   Above the sofa is a mirror with a heavily gilt rococo frame.   On the left an ordinary door leads into the hall.   An open folding-door at the back shows the drawing-room, over-furnished in the same style of comfortless splendor.   Two ladies,* MRS. DREISSIGER *and* MRS. KITTELHAUS, *the Pastor's wife, are seen in the drawing-room, looking at pictures.* PASTOR KITTELHAUS *is there too, engaged in conversation with* WEINHOLD, *the tutor, a theological graduate.*

KITTELHAUS (*a kindly little elderly man, enters the front room, smoking and talking to the tutor, who is also smoking; he looks round and shakes his head in surprise at finding the room empty*).   You are young, Mr. Weinhold, which explains everything.   At your age we old fellows held — well, I won't say the same opinions — but certainly opinions of the same tendency.   And there's something fine about youth — youth with its grand ideals.   But unfortunately, Mr. Weinhold, they don't last; they are as fleeting as April sunshine.   Wait till you are my age.   When a man has said his say from the pulpit for thirty years — fifty-two times every year, not including saints' days — he has inevitably calmed down.   Think of me, Mr. Weinhold, when you come to that length.

WEINHOLD (*nineteen, pale, thin, tall, with lanky fair hair; restless and nervous in his movements*).   With all due respect, Mr. Kittelhaus — I can't think — people have such different natures.

KITTELHAUS.   My dear Mr. Weinhold, however restless-minded and unsettled a man may be — (*in a tone of reproof*) — and you are a case in point — however violently and wantonly he may attack the existing order of things, he calms down in the end. I grant you, certainly, that among our professional brethren individuals are to be found, who, at a fairly advanced age, still play youthful pranks. One preaches against the drink evil and founds temperance societies, another publishes appeals which undoubtedly read most effectively. But what good do they do? The distress among the weavers, where it does exist, is in no way lessened — but the peace of society is undermined. No, no; one feels inclined in such cases to say: Cobbler, stick to your last; don't take to caring for the belly, you who have the care of souls. Preach the pure Word of God, and leave all else to Him who provides shelter and food for the birds, and clothes the lilies of the field. But I should like to know where our good host, Mr. Dreissiger, has suddenly disappeared to.

(Mrs. Dreissiger, *followed by* Mrs. Kittelhaus, *now comes forward. She is a pretty woman of thirty, of a healthy, florid type. A certain discordance is noticeable between her deportment and way of expressing herself and her rich, elegant toilette.*)

mrs. dreissiger. That's what I want to know, too, Mr. Kittelhaus. But it's what William always does. No sooner does a thing come into his head than off he goes and leaves me in the lurch. I've said enough about it, but it does no good.

kittelhaus. It's always the way with business men, my dear Mrs. Dreissiger.

weinhold. I'm almost certain that something has happened downstairs.

(Dreissiger *enters, hot and excited.*)

dreissiger. Well, Rosa, is coffee served?

mrs. dreissiger (*sulkily*). Fancy your needing to run away again!

dreissiger (*carelessly*). Ah! these are things you don't understand.

kittelhaus. Excuse me — has anything happened to annoy you, Mr. Dreissiger?

dreissiger. Never a day passes without that, my dear sir. I am accustomed to it. What about that coffee, Rosa?

(Mrs. Dreissiger *goes ill-humoredly and gives one or two violent tugs at the broad embroidered bellpull.*)

DREISSIGER. I wish you had been downstairs just now, Mr. Weinhold. You'd have gained a little experience. Besides... But now let us have our game of whist.

KITTELHAUS. By all means, sir. Shake off the dust and burden of the day, Mr. Dreissiger; forget it in our company.

DREISSIGER (*has gone to the window, pushed aside a curtain, and is looking out*). Vile rabble!! Come here, Rosa! (*She goes to the window.*) Look... that tall red-haired fellow there!...

KITTELHAUS. That's the man they call Red Becker.

DREISSIGER. Is he the man that insulted you the day before yesterday? You remember what you told me — when John was helping you into the carriage?

MRS. DREISSIGER (*pouting, carelessly*). I'm sure I don't know.

DREISSIGER. Come now, what's the use of being cross? I must know. If he's the man, I mean to have him arrested. (*The strains of the Weavers' Song are heard.*) Listen to that! Just listen!

KITTELHAUS (*highly incensed*). Is there to be no end to this nuisance? I must acknowledge now that it is time for the police to interfere. Permit me. (*He goes forward to the window.*) See, see, Mr. Weinhold! These are not only young people. There are numbers of steady-going old weavers among them, men whom I have known for years and looked upon as most deserving and God-fearing. There they are, taking part in this intolerable uproar, trampling God's law under foot. Do you mean to tell me that you still defend these people?

WEINHOLD. Certainly not, Mr. Kittelhaus. That is, sir... *cum grano salis*. For after all, they are hungry and they are ignorant. They are giving expression to their dissatisfaction in the only way they understand. I don't expect that such people...

MRS. KITTELHAUS (*short, thin, faded, more like an old maid than a married woman*). Mr. Weinhold, Mr. Weinhold, how can you?

DREISSIGER. Mr. Weinhold, I am sorry to be obliged to... I didn't bring you into my house to give me lectures on philanthropy, and I must request that you will confine yourself to the education of my boys, and leave my other affairs entirely to me — entirely! Do you understand?

WEINHOLD (*stands for a moment rigid and deathly pale, then bows, with a strained smile. In a low voice*). Certainly, of course I understand. I have seen this coming. It is my wish too.

(*Goes out.*)

DREISSIGER (*rudely*). As soon as possible then, please. We require the room.

MRS. DREISSIGER. William, William!

DREISSIGER. Have you lost your senses, Rosa, that you're taking the part of a man who defends a low, blackguardly libel like that song?

MRS. DREISSIGER. But, William, he didn't defend it.

DREISSIGER. Mr. Kittelhaus, did he defend it or did he not?

KITTELHAUS. His youth must be his excuse, Mr. Dreissiger.

MRS. KITTELHAUS. I can't understand it. The young man comes of such a good, respectable family. His father held a public appointment for forty years, without a breath on his reputation. His mother was overjoyed at his getting this good situation here. And now... he himself shows so little appreciation of it.

PFEIFER (*suddenly opens the door leading from the hall and shouts in*). Mr. Dreissiger, Mr. Dreissiger! they've got him! Will you come, please? They've caught one of them.

DREISSIGER (*hastily*). Has someone gone for the police?

PFEIFER. The Superintendent's on his way upstairs.

DREISSIGER (*at the door*). Glad to see you, sir. We want you here.

(KITTELHAUS *makes signs to the ladies that it will be better for them to retire. He, his wife, and* MRS. DREISSIGER *disappear into the drawing-room.*)

DREISSIGER (*exasperated, to the* POLICE SUPERINTENDENT, *who has now entered*). I have at last had one of the ringleaders seized by my dyers. I could stand it no longer — their insolence was beyond all bounds — quite unbearable. I have visitors in my house, and these blackguards dare to... They insult my wife whenever she shows herself; my boys' lives are not safe. My visitors run the risk of being jostled and cuffed. Is it possible that in a well-ordered community incessant public insult offered to unoffending people like myself and my family should pass unpunished? If so... then... then I must confess that I have other ideas of law and order.

SUPERINTENDENT (*a man of fifty, middle height, corpulent, full-blooded. He wears cavalry uniform with a long sword and spurs*). No, no, Mr. Dreissiger... certainly not! I am entirely at your disposal. Make your mind easy on the subject. Dispose of me as you will. What you have done is quite right. I am delighted that you have had one of the ringleaders arrested. I am very glad indeed that a settling day has come. There are a few disturbers of the peace here whom I have long had my eye on.

DREISSIGER. Yes, one or two raw lads, lazy vagabonds, that shirk every kind of work, and lead a life of low dissipation, hanging about the public-houses until they've sent their last halfpenny down their throats. But I'm determined to put a stop to the trade of these professional blackguards once and for all. It's in the public interest to do so, not only my private interest.

SUPERINTENDENT. Of course it is! Most undoubtedly, Mr. Dreissiger! No one can possibly blame you. And everything that lies in my power...

DREISSIGER. The cat-o'-nine tails is what should be taken to the beggarly pack.

SUPERINTENDENT. You're right, quite right. We must make an example.

(KUTSCHE, *the policeman, enters and salutes. The door is open, and the sound of heavy steps stumbling up the stair is heard.*)

KUTSCHE. I have to inform you, sir, that we have arrested a man.

DREISSIGER (*to* SUPERINTENDENT). Do you wish to see the fellow?

SUPERINTENDENT. Certainly, most certainly. We must begin by having a look at him at close quarters. Oblige me, Mr. Dreissiger, by not speaking to him at present. I'll see to it that you get complete satisfaction, or my name's not Heide.

DREISSIGER. That's not enough for me, though. He goes before the magistrates. My mind's made up.

(JAEGER *is led in by five dyers, who have come straight from their work — faces, hands, and clothes stained with dye. The prisoner, his cap set jauntily on the side of his head, presents an appearance of impudent gayety; he is excited by the brandy he has just drunk.*)

JAEGER. Hounds that you are! — Call yourselves workingmen! —

Pretend to be comrades! Before I would do such a thing as lay my hands on a mate, I'd see my hand rot off my arm!

(*At a sign from the* SUPERINTENDENT, KUTSCHE *orders the dyers to let go their victim.* JAEGER *straightens himself up, quite free and easy. Both doors are guarded.*)

SUPERINTENDENT (*shouts to* JAEGER). Off with your cap, sir. (JAEGER *takes it off, but very slowly, still with an impudent grin on his face.*) What's your name!

JAEGER. What's yours? I'm not your swineherd.

(*Great excitement is produced among the audience by this reply.*)

DREISSIGER. This is too much of a good thing.

SUPERINTENDENT (*changes color, is on the point of breaking out furiously, but controls his rage*). We'll see about this afterwards.— Once more, what's your name? (*Receiving no answer, furiously.*) If you don't answer at once, fellow, I'll have you flogged on the spot.

JAEGER (*perfectly cheerful, not showing by so much as the twitch of an eyelid that he has heard the* SUPERINTENDENT'S *angry words, calls over the heads of those around him to a pretty servant girl, who has brought in the coffee and is standing open-mouthed with astonishment at the unexpected sight*). Hullo, Emmy, do you belong to this company now? The sooner you find your way out of it, then, the better. A wind may begin to blow here, an' blow everything away overnight.

(*The girl stares at* JAEGER, *and as soon as she comprehends that it is to her he is speaking, blushes with shame, covers her eyes with her hands, and rushes out, leaving the coffee things in confusion on the table. Renewed excitement among those present.*)

SUPERINTENDENT (*half beside himself, to* DREISSIGER). Never in all my long service... such a case of shameless effrontery...

(JAEGER *spits on the floor.*)

DREISSIGER. I'll thank you to remember that this is not a stable.

SUPERINTENDENT. My patience is at an end now. For the last time: What's your name?

(KITTELHAUS, *who has been peering out at the partly opened drawing-room door, listening to what has been going on, can no longer refrain from coming forward to interfere. He is trembling with excitement.*)

KITTELHAUS. His name is Jaeger, sir. Moritz... is it not? Moritz Jaeger. (*To* JAEGER.) And, Jaeger, you know me.

JAEGER (*seriously*). You are Pastor Kittelhaus.

KITTELHAUS. Yes, I am your pastor, Jaeger! It was I who received you, a babe in swaddling clothes, into the Church of Christ. From my hands you took for the first time the body of the Lord. Do you remember that, and how I toiled and strove to bring God's Word home to your heart? Is this your gratitude?

JAEGER (*like a scolded schoolboy, in a surly voice*). I paid my half-crown like the rest.

KITTELHAUS. Money, money... Do you imagine that the miserable little bit of money... Such utter nonsense! I'd much rather you kept your money. Be a good man, be a Christian! Think of what you promised. Keep God's law. Money, money!...

JAEGER. I'm a Quaker now, sir. I don't believe in anything.

KITTELHAUS. Quaker! What are you talking about? Try to behave yourself, and don't use words you don't understand. Quaker, indeed! They are good Christian people, and not heathens like you.

SUPERINTENDENT. Mr. Kittelhaus, I must ask you... (*He comes between the Pastor and* JAEGER.) Kutsche! tie his hands!

(*Wild yelling outside:* "*Jaeger, Jaeger! come out!*")

DREISSIGER (*like the others, slightly startled, goes instinctively to the window*). What's the meaning of this next?

SUPERINTENDENT. Oh, I understand well enough. It means that they want to have the blackguard out among them again. But we're not going to oblige them. Kutsche, you have your orders. He goes to the lock-up.

KUTSCHE (*with the rope in his hand, hesitating*). By your leave, sir, but it'll not be an easy job. There's a confounded big crowd out there — a pack of raging devils. They've got Becker with them, and the smith...

KITTELHAUS. Allow me one more word! — So as not to rouse still worse feeling, would it not be better if we tried to arrange things peaceably? Perhaps Jaeger will give his word to go with us quietly, or...

SUPERINTENDENT. Quite impossible! Think of my responsibility.

I couldn't allow such a thing. Come, Kutsche! lose no more time.

JAEGER (*putting his hands together, and holding them out*). Tight, tight, as tight as ever you can! It's not for long.

(KUTSCHE, *assisted by the workmen, ties his hands*.)

SUPERINTENDENT. Now, off with you, march! (*To* DREISSIGER.) If you feel anxious, let six of the weavers go with them. They can walk on each side of him, I'll ride in front, and Kutsche will bring up the rear. Whoever blocks the way will be cut down.

(*Cries from below:* "Cock-a-doodle-doo-oo-oo! Bow, wow, wow!")

SUPERINTENDENT (*with a threatening gesture in the direction of the window*). You rascals, I'll cock-a-doodle-doo and bow-wow you! Forward! March!

(*He marches out first, with drawn sword; the others, with* JAEGER, *follow*.)

JAEGER (*shouts as he goes*). An' Mrs. Dreissiger there may play the lady as proud as she likes, but for all that she's no better than us. Many a hundred times she's served my father with a half penny-worth of schnapps. Left wheel — march!

(*Exit laughing*.)

DREISSIGER (*after a pause, with apparent calmness*). Well, Mr. Kittelhaus, shall we have our game now? I think there will be no further interruption. (*He lights a cigar, giving short laughs as he does so; when it is lighted, bursts into a regular fit of laughing.*) I'm beginning now to think the whole thing very funny. That fellow! (*Still laughing nervously.*) It really is too comical: first came the dispute at dinner with Weinhold — five minutes after that he takes leave — off to the other end of the world; then this affair crops up — and now we'll proceed with our whist.

KITTELHAUS. Yes, but... (*Roaring is heard outside.*) Yes, but... that's a terrible uproar they're making outside.

DREISSIGER. All we have to do is to go into the other room; it won't disturb us in the least there.

KITTELHAUS (*shaking his head*). I wish I knew what has come over these people. In so far I must agree with Mr. Weinhold, or at least till quite lately I was of his opinion, that the weavers were a patient, humble, easily-led class. Was it not your idea of them, too, Mr. Dreissiger?

DREISSIGER. Most certainly that is what they used to be — patient, easily managed, peaceable people. They were that as long as these so-called humanitarians let them alone. But for ever so long now they've had the awful misery of their condition held up to them. Think of all the societies and associations for the alleviation of the distress among the weavers. At last the weaver believes in it himself, and his head's turned. Some of them had better come and turn it back again, for now he's fairly set a-going there's no end to his complaining. This doesn't please him, and that doesn't please him. He must have everything of the best.

(A loud roar of "Hurrah!" is heard from the crowd.)

KITTELHAUS. So that with all their humanitarianism they have only succeeded in almost literally turning lambs into wolves.

DREISSIGER. I won't say that, sir. When you take time to think of the matter coolly, it's possible that some good may come of it yet. Such occurrences as this will not pass unnoticed by those in authority, and may lead them to see that things can't be allowed to go on as they are doing — that means must be taken to prevent the utter ruin of our home industries.

KITTELHAUS. Possibly. But what is the cause, then, of this terrible falling off of trade?

DREISSIGER. Our best markets have been closed to us by the heavy import duties foreign countries have laid on our goods. At home the competition is terrible, for we have no protection, none whatever.

PFEIFER *(staggers in, pale and breathless)*. Mr. Dreissiger, Mr. Dreissiger!

DREISSIGER *(in the act of walking into the drawing-room, turns round, annoyed)*. Well, Pfeifer, what now?

PFEIFER. Oh, sir! Oh, sir!... It's worse than ever!

DREISSIGER. What are they up to next?

KITTELHAUS. You're really alarming us — what is it?

PFEIFER *(still confused)*. I never saw the like. Good Lord! — The Superintendent himself... they'll catch it for this yet.

DREISSIGER. What's the matter with you, in the devil's name? Is anyone's neck broken?

PFEIFER (*almost crying with fear, screams*). They've set Moritz Jaeger free — they've thrashed the Superintendent and driven him away — they've thrashed the policeman and sent him off to — without his helmet... his sword broken... Oh dear, oh dear!

DREISSIGER. I think you've gone crazy, Pfeifer.

KITTELHAUS. This is actual riot.

PFEIFER (*sitting on a chair, his whole body trembling*). It's turning serious, Mr. Dreissiger! Mr. Dreissiger, it's serious now!

DREISSIGER. Well, if that's all the police...

PFEIFER. Mr. Dreissiger, it's serious now!

DREISSIGER. Damn it all, Pfeifer, will you hold your tongue?

MRS. DREISSIGER (*coming out of the drawing-room with* MRS. KITTELHAUS). This is really too bad, William. Our whole evening's being spoiled. Here's Mrs. Kittelhaus saying that she'd better go home.

KITTELHAUS. You mustn't take it amiss, dear Mrs. Dreissiger, but perhaps, under the circumstances, it *would* be better...

MRS. DREISSIGER. But, William, why in the world don't you go out and put a stop to it?

DREISSIGER. Go you and try if you can do it. Try! Go and speak to them! (*Standing helplessly in front of the pastor.*) Am I such a tyrant? Am I a cruel master?

(*Enter* JOHN *the coachman.*)

JOHN. If you please, m'm, I've put to the horses. Mr. Weinhold's put Georgie and Charlie into the carriage. If it comes to the worst, we're ready to be off.

MRS. DREISSIGER. If what comes to the worst?

JOHN. I'm sure I don't know, m'm. But the crowd's gettin' bigger and bigger, an' they've sent the Superintendent an' the p'liceman to the right-about.

PFEIFER. It's serious now, Mr. Dreissiger! It's serious!

MRS. DREISSIGER (*with increasing alarm*). What's going to happen? — What do the people want? — They're never going to attack us, John?

JOHN. There's some rascally hounds among 'em, ma'am.

PFEIFER. It's serious now! serious!

DREISSIGER. Hold your tongue, fool! — Are the doors barred?

KITTELHAUS. I ask you as a favor, Mr. Dreissiger... as a favor...
I am determined to... I ask you as a favor... (*To* JOHN.) What
demands are the people making?

JOHN (*awkwardly*). It's higher wages they're after, the blackguards.

KITTELHAUS. Good, good! — I shall go out and do my duty.
I shall speak seriously to these people.

JOHN. Oh, sir, please, sir, don't do any such thing. Words is
quite useless.

KITTELHAUS. One little favor, Mr. Dreissiger. May I ask you to
post men behind the door, and to have it closed at once after
me?

MRS. KITTELHAUS. O Joseph, Joseph! you're not really going out?

KITTELHAUS. I am. Indeed I am. I know what I'm doing.
Don't be afraid. God will protect me.

> (MRS. KITTELHAUS *presses his hand, draws back, and wipes
> tears from her eyes.*)

KITTELHAUS (*while the murmur of a great, excited crowd is heard un-
interruptedly outside*). I'll go... I'll go out as if I were simply
on my way home. I shall see if my sacred office... if the
people have not sufficient respect for me left to... I shall try...
(*He takes his hat and stick.*) Forward, then, in God's name!

> (*Goes out accompanied by* DREISSIGER, PFEIFER, *and* JOHN.)

MRS. KITTELHAUS. Oh, dear Mrs. Dreissiger! (*She bursts into tears
and embraces her.*) I do trust nothing will happen to him.

MRS. DREISSIGER (*absently*). I don't know how it is, Mrs. Kittelhaus,
but I... I can't tell you how I feel. I didn't think such a
thing was possible. It's... it's as if it was a sin to be rich.
If I had been told about all this beforehand, Mrs. Kittelhaus,
I don't know but what I would rather have been left in my
own humble position.

MRS. KITTELHAUS. There are troubles and disappointments in
every condition of life, Mrs. Dreissiger.

MRS. DREISSIGER. True, true, I can well believe that. And suppose we have more than other people... goodness me! we
didn't steal it. It's been honestly got, every penny of it. It's
not possible that the people can be going to attack us! If
trade's bad, that's not William's fault, is it?

> (*Loud, confused yelling is heard outside. While the two women*

stand gazing at each other, pale and startled, DREISSIGER *rushes in.)*

DREISSIGER. Quick, Rosa — put on something, and get into the carriage. I'll be after you this moment.

(*He rushes to the strong-box, and takes out papers and various articles of value.*)

(*Enter* JOHN.)

JOHN. We're ready to start. But come quickly, before they get round to the back door.

MRS. DREISSIGER (*in a transport of fear, throwing her arms around* JOHN's *neck*). John, John, dear, good John! Save us, John. Save my boys! Oh, what is to become of us?

DREISSIGER. Rosa, try to keep your head. Let John go.

JOHN. Yes, yes, ma'am! Don't you be frightened. Our good horses'll soon leave them all behind; an' whoever doesn't get out of the way'll be driven over.

MRS. KITTELHAUS (*in helpless anxiety*). But my husband... my husband? But, Mr. Dreissiger, my husband?

DREISSIGER. He's in safety now, Mrs. Kittelhaus. Don't alarm yourself; he's all right.

MRS. KITTELHAUS. Something dreadful has happened to him. I know it. You needn't try to keep it from me.

DREISSIGER. You mustn't take it to heart — they'll be sorry for it yet. I know exactly whose fault it was. Such a detestable, shameful outrage will not go unpunished. A community laying hands on its own pastor and maltreating him — abominable! Mad dogs they are — raging brutes — and they'll be treated as such. (*To his wife who still stands petrified.*) Go, for my sake, Rosa, go quickly! (*The clatter of window panes being smashed on the ground floor is heard.*) They've gone quite mad. There's nothing for it but to get away as fast as we can.

(*Cries of* "Feifer, come out!" — "We want Feifer!" — "Feifer, come out!" *are heard.*)

MRS. DREISSIGER. Feifer, Feifer, they want Feifer!

PFEIFER (*dashes in*). Mr. Dreissiger, there are people at the back gate already, and the house door won't hold much longer. The smith's battering it in with a stable pail.

(*The cry sounds louder and clearer: "Feifer! Feifer! Feifer! come out!"* MRS. DREISSIGER *rushes off as if pursued.* MRS. KITTELHAUS *follows.* PFEIFER *listens, and changes color as he hears what the cry is. A perfect panic of fear seizes him; he weeps, entreats, whimpers, writhes, all at the same moment. He overwhelms* DREISSIGER *with childish caresses, strokes his cheeks and arms, kisses his hands, and at last, like a drowning man, throws his arms round him and prevents him moving.*)

PFEIFER. Dear, good, kind Mr. Dreissiger, don't leave me behind. I've always served you faithfully. I've always treated the people well. I couldn't give them more wages than the fixed rate. Don't leave me here — they'll do for me! If they find me, they'll kill me. O God! O God! My wife, my children!

DREISSIGER (*making his way out, vainly endeavoring to free himself from* PFEIFER'S *clutch*). Can't you let me go, fellow? It'll be all right; it'll be all right.

(*For a few seconds the room is empty. Windows are broken in the drawing-room. A loud crash resounds through the house, followed by shouts of "Hurrah!" For an instant there is silence. Then gentle, cautious steps are heard on the stair, then timid, hushed ejaculations: "To the left!" — "Up with you!" — "Hush!" — "Slow, slow!" — "Don't shove like that!" — "It's a wedding we're goin' to!" — "Stop that crowding!" — "You go first!" — "No, you go!"*)

(*Young weavers and weaver girls appear at the door leading from the hall, not daring to enter, but each trying to shove the other in. In the course of a few moments their timidity is overcome, and the poor, thin, ragged or patched figures, many of them sickly-looking, disperse themselves through* DREISSIGER'S *room and the drawing-room, first gazing timidly and curiously at everything, then beginning to touch things. Girls sit down on the sofas, whole groups admire themselves in the mirrors, men stand up on chairs, examine the pictures and take them down. There is a steady influx of miserable-looking creatures from the hall.*)

FIRST OLD WEAVER (*entering*). No, no, this is carryin' it too far. They've started smashing things downstairs. There's no sense nor reason in that. There'll be a bad end to it. No man in his wits would do that. I'll keep clear of such ongoings.

(JAEGER, BECKER, WITTIG *carrying a wooden pail,* BAUMERT, *and a number of other old and young weavers, rush in as if in pursuit of something, shouting hoarsely.*)

JAEGER. Where has he gone?

BECKER. Where's the cruel brute?

BAUMERT. If we can eat grass, he may eat sawdust.

WITTIG. We'll hang him whenever we catch him.

FIRST YOUNG WEAVER. We'll take him by the legs and fling him out at the window, onto the stones. He'll never get up again.

SECOND YOUNG WEAVER (*enters*). He's off!

ALL. Who?

SECOND YOUNG WEAVER. Dreissiger.

BECKER. Feifer too?

VOICES. Let's get hold of Feifer. Look for Feifer!

BAUMERT. Yes, yes! Feifer! Tell him there's a weaver here for him to starve. (*Laughter.*)

JAEGER. If we can't lay hands on that brute Dreissiger himself... we'll at any rate make a poor man of him.

BAUMERT. As poor as a church mouse... we'll see to that!

(*All, bent on the work of destruction, rush towards the drawing-room door.*)

BECKER (*who is leading, turns round and stops the others*). Halt! Listen to me! This is nothing but a beginning. When we're done here, we'll go straight to Bielau, to Dittrich's, where the steam power-looms are. The whole mischief's done by these factories.

OLD ANSORGE (*enters from hall. Takes a few steps, then stops and looks round, bewildered; shakes his head, taps his forehead*). Who am I? Weaver Anton Ansorge. Has he gone mad, Old Ansorge? My head's goin' round like a humming-top, sure enough. What's he doing here? He'll do whatever he's a mind to. Where is Ansorge? (*He taps his forehead repeatedly.*) Something's wrong! I'm not answerable! I'm off my head! Off with you, off with you, rioters that you are! Heads off, legs off, hands off! If you take my house, I take your house. Forward, forward!

(*Goes yelling into the drawing-room, followed by a yelling, laughing mob.*)

THE FIFTH ACT

Langen-Bielau. OLD WEAVER HILSE'S *workroom. On the left a small window, in front of which stands the loom. On the right a bed, with a table pushed close to it. Stove, with stove-bench, in the right-hand corner. Family worship is going on.* HILSE, *his old, blind, and almost deaf wife, his son* GOTTLIEB, *and* LUISE, GOTTLIEB'S *wife, are sitting at the table, on the bed and wooden stools. A winding-wheel and bobbins on the floor between table and loom. Old spinning, weaving, and winding implements are disposed of on the smoky rafters; hanks of yarn are hanging down. There is much useless lumber in the low narrow room. The door, which is in the back wall, and leads into the big outer passage, or entry-room of the house, stands open. Through another open door on the opposite side of the passage, a second, in most respects similar weaver's room is seen. The large passage, or entry-room of the house, is paved with stone, has damaged plaster, and a tumble-down wooden staircase leading to the attics; a washing-tub on a stool is partly visible; dirty linen of the most miserable description and poor household utensils lie about untidily. The light falls from the left into all three apartments.*

OLD HILSE *is a bearded man of strong build, but bent and wasted with age, toil, sickness, and hardship. He is an old soldier, and has lost an arm. His nose is sharp, his complexion ashen-gray, and he shakes; he is nothing but skin and bone, and has the deep-set, sore weaver's eyes.*

OLD HILSE (*stands up, as do his son and daughter-in-law; prays*). O Lord, we know not how to be thankful enough to Thee, for that Thou hast spared us this night again in thy goodness... an' hast had pity on us... an' hast suffered us to take no harm. Thou art the All-Merciful, an' we are poor, sinful children of men — that bad that we are not worthy to be trampled under thy feet. Yet Thou art our loving Father, an' Thou will look upon us an' accept us for the sake of thy dear Son, our Lord and Saviour Jesus Christ. "Jesus' blood and righteousness, Our covering is and glorious dress." An' if we're sometimes too sore cast down under thy chastening — when the fire of thy purification burns too raging hot — oh, lay it not to our charge; forgive us our sin. Give us patience, heavenly Father, that after all these sufferin's we may be made partakers of thy eternal blessedness. Amen.

MOTHER HILSE (*who has been bending forward, trying hard to hear*). What a beautiful prayer you do say, father!

 (LUISE *goes off to the wash-tub,* GOTTLIEB *to the room on the other side of the passage.*)

OLD HILSE. Where's the little lass?

LUISE. She's gone to Peterswaldau, to Dreissiger's. She finished all she had to wind last night.

OLD HILSE (*speaking very loud*). You'd like the wheel now, mother, eh?

MOTHER HILSE. Yes, father, I'm quite ready.

OLD HILSE (*setting it down before her*). I wish I could do the work for you.

MOTHER HILSE. An' what would be the good of that, father? There would I be, sittin' not knowin' what to do.

OLD HILSE. I'll give your fingers a wipe, then, so that they'll not grease the yarn. (*He wipes her hands with a rag.*)

LUISE (*at her tub*). If there's grease on her hands, it's not from what she's eaten.

OLD HILSE. If we've no butter, we can eat dry bread — when we've no bread, we can eat potatoes — when there's no potatoes left, we can eat bran.

LUISE (*saucily*). An' when that's all eaten, we'll do as the Wenglers did — we'll find out where the skinner's buried some stinking old horse, an' we'll dig it up an' live for a week or two on rotten carrion — how nice that'll be!

GOTTLIEB (*from the other room*). There you are, letting that tongue of yours run away with you again.

OLD HILSE. You should think twice, lass, before you talk that god-less way. (*He goes to his loom, calls.*) Can you give me a hand, Gottlieb? — there's a few threads to pull through.

LUISE (*from her tub*). Gottlieb, you're wanted to help father.

(GOTTLIEB *comes in, and he and his father set themselves to the trouble-some task of "drawing and slaying," that is, pulling the strands of the warp through the "heddles" and "reed" of the loom. They have hardly begun to do this when* HORNIG *appears in the outer room.*)

HORNIG (*at the door*). Good luck to your work!

HILSE AND HIS SON. Thank you, Hornig.

GOTTLIEB. I say, Hornig, when do you take your sleep? You're on your rounds all day, and on watch all night.

HORNIG. Sleep's gone from me nowadays.

LUISE. Glad to see you, Hornig!

OLD HILSE. And what's the news?

HORNIG. It's queer news this mornin'. The weavers at Peterswaldau have taken the law into their own hands, an' chased Dreissiger an' his whole family out of the place.

LUISE (*perceptibly agitated*). Hornig's at his lies again.

HORNIG. No, missus, not this time, not today.— I've some beautiful pinafores in my cart.— No, it's God's truth I'm telling you. They've sent him to the rightabout. He came down to Reichenbach last night, but, Lord love you! they daren't take him in there, for fear of the weavers — off he had to go again, all the way to Schweinitz.

OLD HILSE (*has been carefully lifting threads of the web and approaching them to the holes, through which, from the other side,* GOTTLIEB *pushes a wire hook, with which he catches them and draws them through*). It's about time you were stopping now, Hornig!

HORNIG. It's as sure as I'm a livin' man. Every child in the place'll soon tell you the same story.

OLD HILSE. Either your wits are a-wool-gatherin' or mine are.

HORNIG. Not mine. What I'm telling you's as true as the Bible. I wouldn't believe it myself if I hadn't stood there an' seen it with my own eyes — as I see you now, Gottlieb. They've wrecked his house from the cellar to the roof. The good china came flyin' out at the garret windows, rattlin' down the roof. God only knows how many pieces of fustian are lying soakin' in the river! The water can't get away for them — it's running over the banks, the color of washin'-blue with all the indigo they've poured out at the windows — it was flyin' like clouds of sky-blue dust. Oh, it's a terrible destruction they've worked! And it's not only the house — it's the dye-works, too — an' the stores! They've broken the stair rails, they've torn up the fine flooring — smashed the lookin'-glasses — cut an' hacked an' torn an' smashed the sofas an' the chairs. — It's awful — it's worse than war.

OLD HILSE. An' you would have me believe that my fellow weavers did all that?

> (*He shakes his head incredulously. Other tenants of the house have collected at the door and are listening eagerly.*)

HORNIG. Who else, I'd like to know? I could put names to every one of 'em. It was me took the sheriff through the house, an' I spoke to a whole lot of 'em, an' they answered me back quite friendly like. They did their business with little noise, but my word! they did it well. The sheriff spoke to them, and they answered him mannerly, as they always do. But there wasn't no stoppin' of them. They hacked on at the beautiful furniture as if they were workin' for wages.

OLD HILSE. *You* took the sheriff through the house?

HORNIG. An' what would I be frightened of? Everyone knows me. I'm always turning up, like a bad penny. But no one has anything agin' me. They're all glad to see me. Yes, I went the rounds with him, as sure as my name's Hornig. An' you may believe me or not as you like, but my heart's sore yet from the sight — an' I could see by the sheriff's face that he felt queer enough, too. Not a living word did we hear — they were doin' their work and holdin' their tongues. It was a solemn an' a woeful sight to see the poor starving creatures for once in a way takin' their revenge.

LUISE (*with irrepressible excitement, trembling, wiping her eyes with her apron*). An' right they are! It's only what should be!

VOICES AMONG THE CROWD AT THE DOOR. "There's some of the same sort here." — "There's one no farther away than across the river." — "He's got four horses in his stable an' six carriages, an' he starves his weavers to keep them."

OLD HILSE (*still incredulous*). What was it set them off?

HORNIG. Who knows? Who knows? One says this, another says that.

OLD HILSE. What do they say?

HORNIG. The story as most of them tells is that it began with Dreissiger sayin' that if the weavers were hungry they might eat grass.

> (*Excitement at the door, as one person repeats this to the other, with signs of indignation.*)

OLD HILSE. Well, now, Hornig — if you was to say to me: Father Hilse, says you, you'll die tomorrow, I would answer back: That may be — an' why not? You might even go to the length of saying: You'll have a visit tomorrow from the King of Prussia. But to tell me that weavers, men like me an' my son, have done such things as that — never! I'll never in this world believe it.

MIELCHEN (*a pretty girl of seven, with long, loose flaxen hair, carrying a basket on her arm, comes running in, holding out a silver spoon to her mother*). Mammy, mammy! look what I've got! An' you're to buy me a new frock with it.

LUISE. What d' you come tearing in like that for, girl? (*With increased excitement and curiosity.*) An' what's that you've got hold of now? You've been runnin' yourself out o' breath, an' there — if the bobbins aren't in her basket yet? What's all this about?

OLD HILSE. Mielchen, where did that spoon come from?

LUISE. She found it, maybe.

HORNIG. It's worth its seven or eight shillin's at least.

OLD HILSE (*in distressed excitement*). Off with you, lass — out of the house this moment — unless you want a lickin'! Take that spoon back where you got it from. Out you go! Do you want to make thieves of us all, eh? I'll soon drive that out of you.

(*He looks round for something to beat her with.*)

MIELCHEN (*clinging to her mother's skirts, crying*). No, grandfather, no! don't lick me! We — we did find them. All the other bob — bobbin... girls has... has them too.

LUISE (*half frightened, half excited*). I was right, you see. She found it. Where did you find it, Mielchen?

MIELCHEN (*sobbing*). At — at Peterswal — dau. We — we found them in front of — in front of Drei — Dreissiger's house.

OLD HILSE. This is worse an' worse! Get off with you this moment, unless you would like me to help you.

MOTHER HILSE. What's all the to-do about?

HORNIG. I'll tell you what, Father Hilse. The best way'll be for Gottlieb to put on his coat an' take the spoon to the police office.

OLD HILSE. Gottlieb, put on your coat.

GOTTLIEB (*pulling it on, eagerly*). Yes, an' I'll go right in to the office an' say they're not to blame us for it, for what can a child like that understand about it? an' I brought the spoon back at once. Stop your crying now, Mielchen!

(*The crying child is taken into the opposite room by her mother, who shuts her in and comes back.*)

HORNIG. I believe it's worth as much as nine shillin's.

GOTTLIEB. Give us a cloth to wrap it in, Luise, so that it'll take no harm. To think of the thing bein' worth all that money!

(*Tears come into his eyes while he is wrapping up the spoon.*)

LUISE. If it was only ours, we could live on it for many a day.

OLD HILSE. Hurry up, now! Look sharp! As quick as ever you can. A fine state o' matters, this! Get that devil's spoon out o' the house. (GOTTLIEB *goes off with the spoon.*)

HORNIG. I must be off now, too.

(*He goes, is seen talking to the people in the entry-room before he leaves the house.*)

SURGEON SCHMIDT. (*A jerky little ball of a man, with a red, knowing face, comes into the entry-room.*) Good-morning, all! These are fine goings on! Take care! Take care! (*Threatening with his finger.*) You're a sly lot — that's what you are. (*At* HILSE's *door without coming in.*) Morning, Father Hilse. (*To a woman in the outer room.*) And how are the pains, mother? Better, eh? Well, well. And how's all with you, Father Hilse? (*Enters.*) Why the deuce! what's the matter with mother?

LUISE. It's the eye veins, sir — they've dried up, so as she can't see at all now.

SURGEON SCHMIDT. That's from the dust and weaving by candle-light. Will you tell me what it means that all Peterswaldau's on the way here? I set off on my rounds this morning as usual, thinking no harm; but it wasn't long till I had my eyes opened. Strange doings these! What in the devil's name has taken possession of them, Hilse? They're like a pack of raging wolves. Riot — why, it's revolution! they're plundering and laying waste right and left... Mielchen! where's Mielchen? (MIEL-CHEN, *her face red with crying, is pushed in by her mother.*) Here, Mielchen, put your hand into my coat pocket. (MIELCHEN *does so.*) The ginger-bread nuts are for you. Not all at once, though, you baggage! And a song first! The fox jumped up on a... come, now... The fox jumped up... on a moonlight...

Mind, I've heard what you did. You called the sparrows on the churchyard hedge a nasty name, and they're gone and told the pastor. Did anyone ever hear the like? Fifteen hundred of them agog — men, women, and children. (*Distant bells are heard.*) That's at Reichenbach — alarm-bells! Fifteen hundred people! Uncomfortably like the world coming to an end!

OLD HILSE. An' is it true that they're on their way to Bielau?

SURGEON SCHMIDT. That's just what I'm telling you. I've driven through the middle of the whole crowd. What I'd have liked to do would have been to get down and give each of them a pill there and then. They were following on each other's heels like grim death, and their singing was more than enough to turn a man's stomach. I was nearly sick, and Frederick was shaking on the box like an old woman. We had to take a stiff glass at the first opportunity. I wouldn't be a manufacturer, not though I could drive my carriage and pair. (*Distant singing.*) Listen to that! It's for all the world as if they were beating at some broken old boiler. We'll have them here in five minutes, friends. Good-bye! Don't you be foolish. The troops will be upon them in no time. Keep your wits about you. The Peterswaldau people have lost theirs. (*Bells ring close at hand.*) Good gracious! There are our bells ringing too! Everyone's going mad.

(*He goes upstairs.*)

GOTTLIEB. (*Comes back. In the entry-room, out of breath.*) I've seen them, I've seen them! (*To a woman.*) They're here, auntie, they're here! (*At the door.*) They're here, father, they're here! They've got bean-poles, an' ox-goads, an' axes. They're standin' outside the upper Dittrich's kickin' up an awful row. I think he's payin' them money. O Lord! whatever's goin' to happen? What a crowd! Oh, you never saw such a crowd! Dash it all — if once they make a rush, our manufacturers'll be hard put to it.

OLD HILSE. What have you been runnin' like that for? You'll go racin' till you bring on your old trouble, and then we'll have you on your back again, strugglin' for breath.

GOTTLIEB (*almost joyously excited*). I had to run, or they would have caught me an' kept me. They were all roarin' to me to join them. Father Baumert was there too, and says he to me: You come an' get your sixpence with the rest — you're a poor starving weaver too. An' I was to tell you, father, from him, that you were to come an' help to pay out the manufacturers for their grindin' of us down. Other times is coming, he says. There's going to be a change of days for us weavers. An' we're all to come an' help to bring it about. We're to have our half-pound of meat on Sundays, and now and again on a holiday sausage with our cabbage. Yes, things is to be quite different, by what he tells me.

OLD HILSE (*with repressed indignation*). An' that man calls himself your godfather! and he bids you take part in such works of wickedness? Have nothing to do with them, Gottlieb. They've let themselves be tempted by Satan, an' it's his works they're doin'.

LUISE (*no longer able to restrain her passionate excitement, vehemently*). Yes, Gottlieb, get into the chimney corner, an' take a spoon in your hand, an' a dish of skim milk on your knee, an' put on a petticoat an' say your prayers, an' then father'll be pleased with you. And *he* sets up to be a man!

(*Laughter from the people in the entry-room.*)

OLD HILSE (*quivering with suppressed rage*). An' you set up to be a good wife, eh? You call yourself a mother, an' let your evil tongue run away with you like that? You think yourself fit to teach your girl, you that would egg on your husband to crime an' wickedness?

LUISE (*has lost all control of herself*). You an' your piety an' religion — did they serve to keep the life in my poor children? In rags an' dirt they lay, all the four — it didn't as much as keep them dry. Yes! I set up to be a mother, that's what I do — an' if you'd like to know it, that's why I would send all the manufacturers to hell — because I'm a mother! — Not one of the four could I keep in life! It was cryin' more than breathin' with me from the time each poor little thing came into the world till death took pity on it. The devil a bit you cared! You sat there prayin' and singin', and let me run about till my feet bled, tryin' to get one little drop o' skim milk. How many hundred nights have I lain an' racked my head to think what I could do to cheat the churchyard of my little one? What harm has a baby

like that done that it must come to such a miserable end — eh?
An' over there at Dittrich's they're bathed in wine an' washed
in milk. No! you may talk as you like, but if they begin here,
ten horses won't hold me back. An' what's more — if there's
a rush on Dittrich's, you'll see me in the forefront of it — an'
pity the man as tries to prevent me — I've stood it long enough,
so now you know it.

OLD HILSE. You're a lost soul — there's no help for you.

LUISE (*frenzied*). It's you there's no help for! Tatter-breeched
scarecrows — that's what you are — an' not men at all. Whey-
faced gutter-scrapers that take to your heels at the sound of
a child's rattle. Fellows that say "thank you" to the man as
gives you a hidin'. They've not left that much blood in you as
that you can turn red in the face. You should have the whip
taken to you, an' a little pluck flogged into your rotten bones.

(She goes out quickly.)

(Embarrassed pause.)

MOTHER HILSE. What's the matter with Liesl, father?

OLD HILSE. Nothin', mother! What should be the matter with
her?

MOTHER HILSE. Father, is it only me that's thinkin' it, or are the
bells ringin'?

OLD HILSE. It'll be a funeral, mother.

MOTHER HILSE. An' I've got to sit waitin' here yet. Why must
I be so long a-dyin', father?   (*Pause.*)

OLD HILSE (*leaves his work, holds himself up straight; solemnly*). Gottlieb! — you heard all your wife said to us. Look here, Gottlieb!
(*He bares his breast.*) Here they cut out a bullet as big as a
thimble. The King knows where I lost my arm. It wasn't the
mice as ate it. (*He walks up and down.*) Before that wife of yours
was ever thought of, I had spilled my blood by the quart fo'
King an' country. So let her call what names she likes — an'
welcome! It does me no harm. — Frightened? Me frightened?
What would I be frightened of, will you tell me that? Of the
few soldiers, maybe, that'll be comin' after the rioters? Good
gracious me! That would be a lot to be frightened at! No, no,
lad; I may be a bit stiff in the back, but there's some strength
left in the old bones; I've got the stuff in me yet to make a stand

against a few rubbishin' bay'nets. — An' if it came to the worst! Willin', willin' would I be to say good-bye to this weary world. Death would be welcome — welcomer to me today than tomorrow. For what is it we leave behind? That old bundle of aches an' pains we call our body, the care an' the oppression we call by the name of life. We may be glad to get away from it. — But there's something to come after, Gottlieb! — an' if we've done ourselves out of that too — why, then it's all over with us!

GOTTLIEB. Who knows what's to come after? Nobody's seen it.

OLD HILSE. Gottlieb! don't you be throwin' doubts on the one comfort us poor people have. Why have I sat here an' worked my treadle like a slave this forty year an' more? — sat still an' looked on at him over yonder livin' in pride an' wastefulness — why? Because I have a better hope, something as supports me in all my troubles. (Points out at the window.) You have your good things in this world — I'll have mine in the next. That's been my thought. An' I'm that certain of it — I'd let myself be torn in pieces. Have we not His promise? There's a Day of Judgment coming; but it's not us as are the judges — no: vengeance is mine, saith the Lord.

(A cry of "Weavers, come out!" is heard outside the window.)

OLD HILSE. Do what you will for me. (He seats himself at his loom.) I stay here.

GOTTLIEB (after a short struggle). I'm going to work, too — come what may. (Goes out.)

(The Weavers' Song is heard, sung by hundreds of voices quite close at hand; it sounds like a dull monotonous wail.)

INMATES OF THE HOUSE (in the entry-room). "Oh, mercy on us! there they come swarmin' like ants!" — "Where can all these weavers be from?" — "Don't shove like that, I want to see too." — "Look at that great maypole of a woman leadin' on in front!" — "Gracious! they're comin' thicker an' thicker."

HORNIG (comes into the entry-room from outside). There's a theayter play for you now! That's what you don't see every day. But you should go up to the other Dittrich's an' look what they've done there. It's been no half work. He's got no house now, nor no factory, nor no wine-cellar, nor nothing. They're drinkin' out of the bottles — not so much as takin' the time to get out the corks. One, two, three, an' off with the neck, an' no matter whether they cut their mouths or not. There's some of them runnin' about bleedin' like stuck pigs. — Now they're goin' to do for this Dittrich. *(The singing has stopped.)*

INMATES OF THE HOUSE. There's nothin' so very wicked-like about them.

HORNIG. You wait a bit! you'll soon see! All they're doin' just now is makin' up their minds where they'll begin. Look, they're inspectin' the palace from every side. Do you see that little stout man there, him with the stable pail? That's the smith from Peterswaldau — an' a dangerous little chap he is. He batters in the thickest doors as if they were made o' pie-crust. If a manufacturer was to fall into his hands it would be all over with him!

INMATES OF THE HOUSE. "That was a crack!"—"There went a stone through the window!" — "There's old Dittrich, shakin' with fright." — "He's hangin' out a board." — "Hangin' out a board?" — "What's written on it?" — "Can you not read?" — "It would be a bad job for me if I couldn't read!" — "Well, read it, then!" — "'You — shall have — full — satisfaction! You — shall have full satisfaction.'"

HORNIG. He might ha' spared himself the trouble — *that* won't help him. It's something else they've set their minds on here. It's the factories. They're goin' to smash up the power-looms. For it's them that are ruinin' the hand-loom weaver. Even a blind man might see that. No! the good folks know what they're after, an' no sheriff an' no p'lice superintendent'll bring them to reason — much less a bit of a board. Him as has seen them at work already knows what's comin'.

INMATES OF THE HOUSE. "Did anyone ever see such a crowd?" — "What can these ones be wantin'?" — *(Hastily.)* "They're crossin' the bridge!" — *(Anxiously.)* "They're never comin' over on this side, are they?" — *(In excitement and terror.)* "It's to us they're comin'!" — "They're comin' to us!" — "They're comin' to fetch the weavers out of their houses!"

(General flight. The entry-room is empty. A crowd of dirty, dusty rioters rush in, their faces scarlet with brandy and excitement; tattered, untidy-looking, as if they had been up all night. With

the shout: "Weavers, come out!" they disperse themselves through the house. BECKER and several other young weavers, armed with cudgels and poles, come into OLD HILSE's room. When they see the old man at his loom they start, and cool down a little.)

BECKER. Come, Father Hilse, stop that. Leave your work to them as wants to work. There's no need now for you to be doin' yourself harm. You'll be well taken care of.

FIRST YOUNG WEAVER. You'll never need to go hungry to bed again.

SECOND YOUNG WEAVER. The weaver's goin' to have a roof over his head and a shirt on his back once more.

OLD HILSE. An' what's the devil sendin' you to do now, with your poles an' axes?

BECKER. These are what we're goin' to break on Dittrich's back.

SECOND YOUNG WEAVER. We'll heat them red hot an' stick them down the manufacturers' throats, so as they'll feel for once what burnin' hunger tastes like.

THIRD YOUNG WEAVER. Come along, Father Hilse! We'll give no quarter.

SECOND YOUNG WEAVER. No one had mercy on us — neither God nor man. Now we're standin' up for our rights ourselves.

(OLD BAUMERT enters, somewhat shaky on the legs, a newly killed cock under his arm.)

OLD BAUMERT *(stretching out his arms)*. My brothers — we're all brothers! Come to my arms, brothers! *(Laughter.)*

OLD HILSE. And that's the state you're in, Willem?

OLD BAUMERT. Gustav, is it you? My poor starvin' friend! Come to my arms, Gustav!

OLD HILSE *(mutters)*. Let me alone.

OLD BAUMERT. I'll tell you what, Gustav. It's nothin' but luck that's wanted. You look at me. What do I look like? Luck's what's wanted. Do I not look like a lord? *(Pats his stomach.)* Guess what's in there! There's food fit for a prince in that belly. When luck's with him a man gets roast hare to eat an' champagne wine to drink. — I'll tell you all something: We've made a big mistake — we must help ourselves.

ALL (*speaking at once*). We must help ourselves, hurrah!

OLD BAUMERT. As soon as we get the first good bite inside us we're different men. Damn it all! but you feel the power comin' into you till you're like an ox, an' that wild with strength that you hit out right an' left without as much as takin' time to look. Dash it, but it's grand!

JAEGER (*at the door, armed with an old cavalry sword*). We've made one or two first-rate attacks.

BECKER. We know how to set about it now. One, two, three, an' we're inside the house. Then, at it like lightning — bang, crack, shiver! till the sparks are flyin' as if it was a smithy.

FIRST YOUNG WEAVER. It wouldn't be half bad to light a bit o' fire.

SECOND YOUNG WEAVER. Let's march to Reichenbach and burn the rich folks' houses over their heads!

JAEGER. That would be nothing but butterin' their bread. Think of all the insurance money they'd get. (*Laughter.*)

BECKER. No, from here we'll go to Freiburg, to Tromtra's.

JAEGER. What would you say to givin' all them as holds Government appointments a lesson? I've read somewhere as how all our troubles come from them birocrats, as they call them.

SECOND YOUNG WEAVER. Before long we'll go to Breslau, for more an' more'll be joining us.

OLD BAUMERT (*to* HILSE). Won't you take a drop, Gustav?

OLD HILSE. I never touches it.

OLD BAUMERT. That was in the old world; we're in a new world today, Gustav.

FIRST YOUNG WEAVER. Christmas comes but once a year.

(*Laughter.*)

OLD HILSE (*impatiently*). What is it you want in my house, you limbs of Satan?

OLD BAUMERT (*a little intimidated, coaxingly*). I was bringin' you a chicken, Gustav. I thought it would make a drop o' soup for mother.

OLD HILSE (*embarrassed, almost friendly*). Well, you can tell mother yourself.

MOTHER HILSE (*who has been making efforts to hear, her hand at her ear, motions them off*). Let me alone. I don't want no chicken soup.

OLD HILSE. That's right, mother. An' I want none, an' least of all that sort. An' let me say this much to you, Baumert: The devil stands on his head for joy when he hears the old ones jabberin' and talkin' as if they was infants. An' to you all I say — to every one of you: Me and you, we've got nothing to do with each other. It's not with my will that you're here. In law an' justice you've no right to be in my house.

A VOICE. Him that's not with us is against us.

JAEGER (roughly and threateningly). You're a cross-grained old chap, and I'd have you remember that we're not thieves.

A VOICE. We're hungry men, that's all.

FIRST YOUNG WEAVER. We want to *live* — that's all. An' so we've cut the rope we were hung up with.

JAEGER. And we were in our right! (Holding his fist in front of the old man's face.) Say another word, and I'll give you one between the eyes.

BECKER. Come now, Jaeger, be quiet. Let the old man alone. — What we say to ourselves, Father Hilse, is this: Better dead than begin the old life again.

OLD HILSE. Have I not lived that life for sixty years an' more?

BECKER. That doesn't help us — there's got to be a change.

OLD HILSE. On the Judgment Day.

BECKER. What they'll not give us willingly we're going to take by force.

OLD HILSE. By force. (Laughs.) You may as well go an' dig your graves at once. They'll not be long showin' you where the force lies. Wait a bit, lad!

JAEGER. Is it the soldiers you're meaning? We've been soldiers, too. We'll soon do for a company or two of them.

OLD HILSE. With your tongues, maybe. But supposin' you did — for two that you'd beat off, ten'll come back.

VOICES (call through the window). The soldiers are comin'! Look out!

(General, sudden silence. For a moment a faint sound of fifes and drums is heard; in the ensuing silence a short, involuntary exclamation, "The devil! I'm off!" followed by general laughter.)

BECKER. Who was that? Who speaks of running away?

JAEGER. Which of you is it that's afraid of a few paltry helmets? You have me to command you, and I've been in the trade. I know their tricks.

OLD HILSE. An' what are you goin' to shoot with? Your sticks, eh?

FIRST YOUNG WEAVER. Never mind that old chap; he's wrong in the upper story.

SECOND YOUNG WEAVER. Yes, he's a bit off his head.

GOTTLIEB (*has made his way unnoticed among the rioters; catches hold of the speaker*). Would you give your impudence to an old man like him?

SECOND YOUNG WEAVER. Let me alone. 'Twasn't anything bad I said.

OLD HILSE (*interfering*). Let him jaw, Gottlieb. What would you be meddlin' with him for? He'll soon see who it is that's been off his head today, him or me.

BECKER. Are you comin', Gottlieb?

OLD HILSE. No, he's goin' to do no such thing.

LUISE (*comes into the entry-room, calls*). What are you puttin' off your time with prayin' hypocrites like them for? Come quick to where you're wanted! Quick! Father Baumert, run all you can! The Major's speakin' to the crowd from horseback. They're to go home. If you don't hurry up, it'll be all over.

JAEGER (*as he goes out*). That's a brave husband of yours.

LUISE. Where is he? I've got no husband!

(*Some of the people in the entry-room sing.*)

> Once on a time a man so small,
>   Heigh-ho, heigh!
> Set his heart on a wife so tall,
>   Heigh diddle-di-dum-di!

WITTIG, THE SMITH (*comes downstairs, still carrying the stable pail; stops on his way through the entry-room*). Come on! all of you that are not cowardly scoundrels! — hurrah!

(*He dashes out, followed by* LUISE, JAEGER, *and others, all shouting "Hurrah!"*)

BECKER. Good-bye, then, Father Hilse; we'll see each other again.
                                                              (*Is going.*)

OLD HILSE. I doubt that. I've not five years to live, and that'll be the soonest you'll get out.

BECKER (*stops, not understanding*). Out o' what, Father Hilse?

OLD HILSE. Out of prison — where else?

BECKER (*laughs wildly*). Do you think I would mind that? There's bread to be had there anyhow!   (*Goes out.*)

OLD BAUMERT (*has been cowering on a low stool, painfully beating his brains; he now gets up*). It's true, Gustav, as I've had a drop too much. But for all that I know what I'm about. You think one way in this here matter; I think another. I say Becker's right: even if it ends in chains an' ropes — we'll be better off in prison than at home. You're cared for there, an' you don't need to starve. I wouldn't have joined them, Gustav, if I could have let it be; but once in a lifetime a man's got to show what he feels. (*Goes slowly toward the door.*) Good-bye, Gustav. If anything happens, mind you put in a word for me in your prayers.

(*Goes out.*)

(*The rioters are now all gone. The entry-room gradually fills again with curious onlookers from the different rooms of the house. OLD HILSE knots at his web. GOTTLIEB has taken an axe from behind the stove and is unconsciously feeling its edge. He and the old man are silently agitated. The hum and roar of a great crowd penetrate into the room.*)

MOTHER HILSE. The very boards is shakin', father — what's goin' on? What's goin' to happen to us? (*Pause.*)

OLD HILSE. Gottlieb!

GOTTLIEB. What is it?

OLD HILSE. Let that axe alone.

GOTTLIEB. Who's to split the wood, then?

(*He leans the axe against the stove. Pause.*)

MOTHER HILSE. Gottlieb, you listen to what father says to you.

(*Someone sings outside the window.*)

Our little man does all that he can,
   Heigh-ho, heigh!
At home he cleans the pots an' the pan,
   Heigh-diddle-di-dum-di! (*Passes on.*)

GOTTLIEB (*jumps up, shakes his clenched fist at the window*). Brute that you are, would you drive me crazy?

(*A volley of musketry is heard.*)

MOTHER HILSE (*starts and trembles*). Good Lord! is that thunder again?

OLD HILSE (*instinctively folding his hands*). Oh, our Father in heaven! defend the poor weavers, protect my poor brothers!

(*A short pause ensues.*)

OLD HILSE (*to himself, painfully agitated*). There's blood flowing now.

GOTTLIEB (*had started up and grasped the axe when the shooting was heard; deathly pale, almost beside himself with excitement*). And am I to lie to heel like a dog still?

A GIRL (*calls from the entry-room*). Father Hilse, Father Hilse! get away from the window. A bullet's just flown in at ours upstairs.
(*Disappears.*)

MIELCHEN (*puts her head in at the window, laughing*). Gran'father, gran'father, they've shot with their guns. Two or three's been knocked down, an' one of them's turnin' round and round like a top, an' one's twistin' himself like a sparrow when its head's bein' pulled off. An' oh, if you saw all the blood that came pourin' —! (*Disappears.*)

A WEAVER'S WIFE. Yes, there's two or three'll never get up again.

AN OLD WEAVER (*in the entry-room*). Look out! They're goin' to make a rush on the soldiers.

A SECOND WEAVER (*wildly*). Look, look, look at the women! — skirts up, an' spittin' in the soldiers' faces already!

A WEAVER'S WIFE (*calls in*). Gottlieb, look at your wife. She's more pluck in her than you. She's jumpin' about in front o' the bay'nets as if she was dancin' to music.

(*Four men carry a wounded rioter through the entry-room. Silence, which is broken by someone saying in a distinct voice, "It's Weaver Ulbrich." Once more silence for a few seconds, when the same voice is heard again: "It's all over with him; he's got a bullet in his ear." The men are heard climbing the wooden stair. Sudden shouting outside: "Hurrah, hurrah!"*)

VOICES IN THE ENTRY-ROOM. "Where did they get the stones from?" — "Yes, it's time you were off!" — "From the new road." — "Ta-ta, soldiers!" — "It's raining paving-stones."

(*Shrieks of terror and loud roaring outside, taken up by those in the entry-room. There is a cry of fear, and the house door is shut with a bang.*)

VOICES IN THE ENTRY-ROOM. "They're loading again." — "They'll fire another volley this minute." — "Father Hilse, get away from that window."

GOTTLIEB (*clutches the axe*). What! are we mad dogs? Are we to eat powder an' shot now instead of bread? (*Hesitating an instant: to the old man.*) Would you have me sit here an' see my wife shot? Never! (*As he rushes out.*) Look out! I'm coming!

OLD HILSE. Gottlieb, Gottlieb!

MOTHER HILSE. Where's Gottlieb gone?

OLD HILSE. He's gone to the devil.

VOICES FROM THE ENTRY-ROOM. Go away from the window, Father Hilse.

OLD HILSE. Not I! Not if you all go crazy together! (*To* MOTHER HILSE, *with rapt excitement.*) My heavenly Father has placed me here. Isn't that so, mother? Here we'll sit, an' do our bounden duty — ay, though the snow was to go on fire.

(*He begins to weave.*)

(*Rattle of another volley.* OLD HILSE, *mortally wounded, starts to his feet and then falls forward over the loom. At the same moment loud shouting of "Hurrah!" is heard. The people who till now have been standing in the entry-room dash out, joining in the cry. The old woman repeatedly asks: "Father, father, what's wrong with you?" The continued shouting dies away gradually in the distance.* MIELCHEN *comes rushing in.*)

MIELCHEN. Gran'father, gran'father, they're drivin' the soldiers out of the village; they've got into Dittrich's house, an' they're doin' what they did at Dreissiger's. Gran'father!

(*The child grows frightened, notices that something has happened, puts her finger in her mouth, and goes up cautiously to the dead man.*)

Gran'father!

MOTHER HILSE. Come now, father, can't you say something? You're frightenin' me.

LIGHT–O'–LOVE

(LIEBELEI)

By ARTHUR SCHNITZLER

Translated from the German by BAYARD QUINCY MORGAN

ARTHUR SCHNITZLER

Born in Vienna in 1862 Arthur Schnitzler was the son of a physician. He studied medicine and received his degree in 1885, thereafter serving until 1888 in a hospital. He published a medical work on laryngology in 1895. Before this he had begun to write plays of airy grace and haunting sentiment. The most characteristic and popular of his works were those which were written early. These include the Anatol sequence (1893) of gay and tender Viennese sketches gracefully adapted by Granville-Barker, and *Liebelei*, translated as *Light-o'-Love*. Schnitzler received the Grillparzer Prize in 1908. As Schnitzler grew older his work became heavier. *Reigen*, made up of dialogues written in 1900, was not performed until 1920. Among novels and romances are *Frau Berta Garlan*, 1901; *Der Weg ins Frei*, 1908; *Casanova's Heimfahrt*. Schnitzler died in 1931.

LIGHT–O'–LOVE

THERE is nothing naturalistic in this play. Schnitzler does not pretend to solve problems; nor does he seek to present with verisimilitude the external features of social life. Between the structure of the play and the substance of life itself there is a veil of haunting sentiment. And in the legend he seeks not so much to present an action that is typical of life as an action that has been heightened and intensified by all the graces of the playwright. This play then is one form of that most popular and manifold of all theatrical forms, the play of artifice. It should be stipulated at once that when one speaks of artifice on the stage one does not imply untruth. One implies rather a particular kind of truth, the truth of the theater. Many of the greatest playwrights have been dramatists of artifice, and nothing else. When the playwright adds to his artifice, to his dramatic craftsmanship, a real knowledge of men and women, sympathy for their weaknesses and sorrows, and a delicate gift alike of insight and of suggestion, his craftsmanship and artifice reach the standards of high art. It may be said of Schnitzler that he does this. As a craftsman he derives from Scribe, but he is a deeper man and a more subtle artist than the typical exponent of the "well-made play." Like many Austrians he reflects a French influence. Alfred Kerr said of him that he writes "Comedy with a hint of profundity, not completely profound and not entirely comedy." Perhaps one of the signs of artifice in him is the fact that he never precisely discovered his bent. There was something of Musset in him and that was very fine. There was something of Donnay in him and that was impressive and not so fine. He did not seek to see life objectively, but through a medium of careless grace. His chief mood was one of contemplation, disillusion, nostalgia. He likes to deal with the lives of young women who "love in the city and marry in the suburbs." *Light-o'-Love* was one of the earliest and most successful of his plays. It was produced at the Vienna Burg Theater in October, 1895. In February, 1905, it was produced as *The Flirtation* by the Progressive Stage Society of New York. As *The Reckoning* it was produced in 1907; and as *Playing with Love* in 1929. It was played in German in New York in 1896 and again in 1912.

CHARACTERS

HANS VYRING, *violinist at the city theater*
CHRISTINE, *his daughter*
TONI SCHLAGER, *milliner*
CATHERINE BINDER, *wife of a stocking-maker*
LENA, *her nine-year-old daughter*
FRITZ LOHEIMER, } *young men*
THEODORE KAISER, }
A GENTLEMAN

The action takes place in Vienna at the present day

ACT ONE

FRITZ's *room. Cozy but elegantly furnished.*

THEODORE. (*Enters in advance. He carries a stick, has an overcoat flung over his arm; takes off his hat upon entering.*)

FRITZ (*outside*). So nobody has been here?

VOICE. No, sir.

FRITZ (*entering*). I suppose we might let the carriage go?

THEODORE. Of course. I thought you had.

FRITZ (*goes to the door*). Send the carriage away. And... you can go, too. I don't need you any more. (*Returning.*) Why don't you lay down your things?

THEODORE (*at the desk*). Here are a couple of letters.

(*Throws coat and hat on a chair, keeps his stick.*)

FRITZ (*hastens to the desk*). Oh!...

THEODORE. Now, now!... I believe you're frightened!

FRITZ. From dad.... (*Opens a second letter.*) From Lensky.

THEODORE. Don't let me disturb you.

FRITZ. (*Skims the letters.*)

THEODORE. What does your father say?

FRITZ. Nothing special.... He wants me to spend a week on the estate at Whitsuntide.

THEODORE. Excellent plan. I'd like to send you there for six months.

FRITZ. (*Turns to face him.*)

THEODORE. I certainly would! — riding, driving, fresh air, dairy-maids ——

FRITZ. Idiot, there aren't any dairy-farms out there.

THEODORE. Well, you know what I mean, don't you?

FRITZ. Will you come along?

THEODORE. You know I can't.

FRITZ. Why not?

THEODORE. My dear fellow, I have my doctor's exam. coming! If I went along, it would be only for the sake of keeping you there.

FRITZ. Oh, come, you needn't worry about me.

THEODORE. You see, all you need is fresh air; I'm convinced of that — I saw that today. Out yonder in the open where we found the genuine green springtime, you were a very pleasant fellow again.

FRITZ. Thanks.

THEODORE. And now — now of course you are collapsing. We're too close to the dangerous atmospheric zone again.

FRITZ. (*Makes a gesture of irritation.*)

THEODORE. Why, you've no idea how jolly you were out there. You were actually reasonable for once; it was like the good old days. And then a couple of days ago, when we were out with those two jolly little girls, you were very nice; but now — that's all over again, and you find it absolutely necessary to think — (*With ironical pathos.*) — of that woman.

FRITZ. (*Rises, vexed.*)

THEODORE. You don't know me, my dear fellow. I don't intend to stand that any longer.

FRITZ. My goodness, but you're ambitious!

THEODORE. Oh, I don't demand of you that you forget — (*as before*) — that woman.... I only hope — (*warmly*) — my dear Fritz, that this miserable affair, that keeps me trembling for you all the time, means no more to you than any trivial love affair.... Look here, Fritz, some day, when you stop worshiping "that woman," you'll be surprised how congenial she is to you. Then you'll find out that there's nothing demoniac in her at all, but that she is a very sweet little woman — one that you can have plenty of fun with, just as you can with all women that are young and pretty, and that have a little temperament.

FRITZ. Why do you say "tremble for me"?

THEODORE. You know why.... I must confess that I am in constant terror that you will run off with her some fine day.

FRITZ. That was what you meant?

THEODORE (*after a short pause*). That isn't the only danger.

FRITZ. Right you are, Theodore — there are others, too.

THEODORE. But then we never do anything silly.

FRITZ (*to himself*). There are others, too....

THEODORE. What's the matter?... You're thinking of something in particular.

FRITZ. Oh, no, I'm not... (*Glances at the window.*) She was deceived once before.

THEODORE. What?... What's that?... I don't understand you.

FRITZ. Oh, nothing.

THEODORE. What? Do talk sense.

FRITZ. She's been afraid lately... at times.

THEODORE. Why? — There must be a reason for it.

FRITZ. Not at all. Nervousness — (*ironically*) — an uneasy conscience, if you will.

THEODORE. You say she was deceived once ——

FRITZ. Well, yes — and again today, I suppose.

THEODORE. Today — well, what does all this mean?

FRITZ (*after a slight pause*). She thinks... we are watched.

THEODORE. What?

FRITZ. She sees apparitions; really, she has actual hallucinations. (*At the window.*) She sees some person standing on the street corner,... through the crack in the curtain, and thinks —— (*Breaks off.*) Is it possible, anyway, to recognize a face at this distance?

THEODORE. Scarcely.

FRITZ. Why, that's what I say. But then that's terrible. She's afraid to go out; she has all sorts of queer feelings; she gets hysterical; she wants to die with me ——

THEODORE. Of course.

FRITZ (*short pause*). Today I had to go down and take a look. Went down as cheerfully as if I were leaving the house alone; of course there wasn't a familiar face to be seen anywhere....

THEODORE. (*Is silent.*)

FRITZ. Well, that ought to set fears at rest, oughtn't it? A man can't suddenly be swallowed up by the earth, hey?... Answer, can't you?

THEODORE. What sort of an answer do you want? Of course a man can't be swallowed up. But a man can hide inside the gates.

FRITZ. I looked behind them all.

THEODORE. You must have looked very innocent at that.

FRITZ. There was nobody there. I tell you it's hallucinations.

THEODORE. Certainly. But it ought to teach you to be more careful.

FRITZ. And I couldn't have helped knowing it, if he suspected it. Why, I ate supper with them yesterday after the play — with him and her — and it was so pleasant!... ridiculous, I tell you!

THEODORE. I beg of you Fritz, be sensible; do me that favor. Give up this whole cursed affair, for my sake, if nothing else. I have nerves, too... I know you're not the kind of man who can escape from such an affair unaided, and so I made it so easy for you — gave you a chance to save yourself by starting another...

FRITZ. You did?

THEODORE. Well, didn't I take you along with me when I had an appointment with little Miss Toni a while back? And didn't I ask her to bring along her prettiest friend? And can you deny that you like her?

FRITZ. Certainly, she is sweet!... So sweet! And you have no idea how I longed for such an affection as that, so sweet and quiet, that would hover about me and soothe me, and help me to recover from these everlasting irritations and torments.

THEODORE. That's exactly it. Recover! That's the deeper purpose of it. They help us to recover. That's why I'm against these so-called interesting women. It's not the business of women to be interesting, but to be agreeable. You must seek happiness where I have sought and found it — where there are no grand scenes, no dangers, no tragic entanglements — where the beginning has no special difficulties, and the ending no torments — where you take your first kiss with a smile, and part with very gentle emotion.

FRITZ. Yes, that's it.

THEODORE. Those women are so happy in their healthy every-day womanhood — what compels us to make demons or angels out of them at all cost?

FRITZ. She is really a treasure. So affectionate, so dear. Often it seems to me she is too dear for me.

THEODORE. You're incorrigible, apparently. If you intend to take that affair seriously again....

FRITZ. No, no, not a thought of it. We are agreed, I need to recover.

THEODORE. If you did, I'd give you up for good. I've had enough of your love-tragedies. You bore me with them. And if you feel like coming at me with your famous "conscience," I'll give you my simple rule for treating such cases: Better it were I than someone else. For that "someone else" is as sure as fate itself.

(*There is a ring.*)

FRITZ. What's that now?...

THEODORE. Go and see. There you are, all pale again! Set your fears at rest. It's the two sweet little girls.

FRITZ (*agreeably surprised*). What?

THEODORE. I took the liberty of inviting them here today.

FRITZ (*going out*). Oh, you — why didn't you tell me? Now I've sent away my man.

THEODORE. So much the cozier.

FRITZ (*outside*). Greetings, Toni.

TONI. (*Enters, carrying a package.*)

FRITZ (*re-enters behind her*). And where's Christine?

TONI. She'll be here soon. Greetings, Dore.

THEODORE. (*Kisses her hand.*)

TONI. You'll have to excuse us, Mr. Fritz; but Theodore invited us....

FRITZ. Why, it was a splendid idea. Only he forgot something, Theodore did.

THEODORE. Theodore forgot nothing! (*Takes the package from* TONI.) Did you bring everything I wrote down for you?

TONI. Of course. (*To* FRITZ.) Where can I put it?

FRITZ. Just give it to me, Toni; we'll put it on the sideboard for the present.

TONI. I bought something else, Dore, besides what you told me.

FRITZ. Give me your hat, Toni, that's right. (*Lays it on the piano, also her boa.*)

THEODORE (*dubiously*). What?

TONI. A coffee cream-cake.

THEODORE. Oh, what a sweet tooth!

FRITZ. Well, but tell me, why didn't Christine come with you?

TONI. She's going to take her father to the theater first. Then she'll come along on the street car.

THEODORE. What an affectionate daughter!...

TONI. I should say so, and especially since he went into mourning.

THEODORE. Why, who died there, anyway?

TONI. The old gentleman's sister.

THEODORE. Ah, a widow?

TONI. No, it was an old maiden lady, who has lived with them always. Well, and so he feels so lonesome, somehow.

THEODORE. He's a little man with short gray hair — her father — isn't he?

TONI (*shakes her head*). No, he has long hair.

FRITZ. How do you come to know him?

THEODORE. Recently I was in the theater with Lensky, and I took a look at the men playing the bass-viols.

TONI. Why, he doesn't play the bass-viol — he plays the violin.

THEODORE. Oh, is that so? I thought he played the bass-viol. (TONI *laughs*.) Nothing funny about that; how should I know, child?

TONI. What a beautiful place you have, Mr. Fritz — just wonderful! What view is that?

FRITZ. This window opens on Straw Lane, and in the next room ——

THEODORE (*quickly*). Do tell me, why are you so formal, you two?

TONI. At supper we'll get better acquainted.

THEODORE. A lady of principle, I see. Well, that's some comfort, just the same. How's your mother, anyhow?

TONI (*turns to him, her face suddenly showing concern*). Only think, she's got ——

THEODORE. Toothache, I know, I know. Your mother always has the toothache. She ought to go to a dentist one of these times.

TONI. But the doctor says it's only rheumatic pains.

THEODORE (*laughing*). Well, if it's rheumatic...

TONI (*an album in her hand*). Nothing but pretty things. (*Turning the pages.*) Who is that?... Why, that's you, Mr. Fritz,... in uniform? You're in the army?

FRITZ. Yes.

TONI. Dragoon! — Are you in the yellows or the blacks?

FRITZ (*smiling*). In the yellows.

TONI (*as in a reverie*). The yellows.

THEODORE. There she goes a-dreaming. Wake up, Toni!

TONI. But now you're lieutenant in the reserves?

FRITZ. Surely.

TONI. You must look very nice in the fur cap.

THEODORE. How much she knows about it! — Look here, Toni, I'm in the army, too.

TONI. Are you in the dragoons, too?

THEODORE. Yes.

TONI. Well, why can't you tell a body that?

THEODORE. I want to be loved for myself.

TONI. Come, Dore, you must put on your uniform some time when we're going out together.

THEODORE. In August there will be maneuvers, anyway.

TONI. Heavens! by August ——

THEODORE. Yes, that's so — eternal love doesn't last that long.

TONI. Who thinks about August in May? Isn't that so, Mr. Fritz? — Say, Mr. Fritz, why did you run away from us yesterday?

FRITZ. What do you mean?

TONI. Why — after the play.

FRITZ. Didn't Theodore make my excuses to you?

THEODORE. To be sure, I excused you.

TONI. What good do your excuses do me, or rather Christine? When a man makes a promise, he ought to keep it.

FRITZ. I really would rather have gone with you.

TONI. Really?

FRITZ. But I couldn't. You saw yourselves I was in a box with friends, and afterward I couldn't get away from them.

TONI. Yes, you couldn't get away from the pretty ladies. Do you think we didn't see you from the gallery?

FRITZ. Well, I saw you, too.

TONI. You were sitting backwards in the box.

FRITZ. Not all the time.

TONI. But most of it. Behind a lady with a black velvet dress you sat and kept — (*imitating*) — looking forward like this.

FRITZ. You must have watched me closely.

TONI. Why, it's nothing to me. But if I were Christine... Why did Theodore have time after the play? Why doesn't he have to take supper with friends?

THEODORE (*proudly*). Why don't I have to take supper with friends? (*There is a ring.* FRITZ *hastens out.*)

THEODORE. Toni, you can do me a favor.

TONI. (*Assumes questioning expression.*)

THEODORE. Forget your military recollections — at least, for a time.

TONI. Why, I haven't any.

THEODORE. Come, now, you didn't learn all that just by accident, that's plain enough.

CHRISTINE (*enters with flowers in her hand.* FRITZ *behind her. With a trace of embarrassment*). Good-evening. (*General salutation. To* FRITZ.) Are you glad we came — You're not angry?

FRITZ. But — my dear child! Sometimes, you know Theodore is cleverer than I am.

THEODORE. Well, is your father fiddling by now?

CHRISTINE. Surely; I took him to the theater.

FRITZ. Toni told us.

CHRISTINE (*to* TONI). And Catherine stopped me, too.

TONI. Oh, pshaw! the false cat!

CHRISTINE. Oh, no, she isn't false at all; she is very good to me.

TONI. You trust everyone, anyway.

CHRISTINE. Why should she be false to me?

FRITZ. Who is Catherine?

TONI. The wife of a stocking-maker; and she's always vexed because some girls are younger than she is.

CHRISTINE. Why, she's quite young herself.

FRITZ. Bother Catherine! — What have you got there?

CHRISTINE. I brought along a few flowers for you.

FRITZ (*takes them from her and kisses her hand*). You're a little angel. Here, we'll put them in the vase.

THEODORE. No, no! You've no talent as decorator. The flowers will be scattered at random on the table.... That is, later on, when the table is set. We really ought to fix it so that they would fall from the ceiling. But that can't be done.

FRITZ (*laughing*). Scarcely.

THEODORE. Meanwhile we'll put them in here, after all (*puts them into the vase*).

TONI. Children, it's getting dark!

FRITZ (*helps* CHRISTINE *to take off her coat, and she takes off her hat. He puts hat and coat on a chair in the background*). We'll light the lamp right away.

THEODORE. Lamp! I should say not! Candles we must have. Their light is so much prettier. Come, Toni, you can help me. (*He and* TONI *light the candles, in the branched candelabra before the pierglass, one on the desk, two candles on the sideboard. Meanwhile* FRITZ *and* CHRISTINE *converse.*)

FRITZ. How are you, sweetheart?

CHRISTINE. I'm all right now.

FRITZ. Well, but not at other times?

CHRISTINE. I have longed so for you.

FRITZ. Why, we saw each other only yesterday.

CHRISTINE. Saw each other... from away off.... (*Shyly.*) Fritz, it wasn't very nice of you to...

FRITZ. Yes, I know; Toni told me. But you're always a child. I couldn't get away. You've got to understand such things.

CHRISTINE. Yes.... Fritz,... who were the people in the box?

FRITZ. Friends of mine — it doesn't matter what their names are.

CHRISTINE. Well, who was the lady in the black velvet dress?

FRITZ. Child, I have no memory for dresses.

CHRISTINE (*coaxingly*). Come, come!

FRITZ. That is to say,... I do have a sort of a memory for them — in certain cases. For example, I remember very well that dark-blue waist you had on the first time we saw each other. And the black and white one you wore to the theater yesterday.

CHRISTINE. Why, I'm wearing it today!

FRITZ. Sure enough;... from the distance, you know, it looks different — I mean it! Oh, and that medallion — I know that, too.

CHRISTINE (*smiling*). When did I wear that?

FRITZ. Oh — that time we went walking in the public gardens, where all the children were playing — isn't that right?

CHRISTINE. Yes... So you do think of me sometimes?

FRITZ. Rather frequently, my child.

CHRISTINE. Not so often as I think of you. I am always thinking of you... all day long;... and I can only be happy when I see you.

FRITZ. Then don't we see each other often enough?

CHRISTINE. Often...

FRITZ. Certainly. In the summer we shan't see each other so much. Just think! Suppose, for example, I went away for a couple of weeks — what would you say?

CHRISTINE (*anxiously*). What? You are going away?

FRITZ. No.... And still it might be possible that I would like the notion of being all alone for a week.

CHRISTINE. Oh, why?

FRITZ. I'm simply talking about possibilities. I know myself, I get such notions. And you, too, might some time take the whim of not wanting to see me for a few days.... I'll always understand that.

CHRISTINE. No, I'll never have that whim, Fritz.

FRITZ. You can't tell about that.

CHRISTINE. But I can.... I love you.

FRITZ. I love you, too, very much.

CHRISTINE. But you are everything to me, Fritz; for you I could —— (*Breaks off.*) No, I can't imagine an hour ever coming when I wouldn't want to see you. As long as I live, Fritz ——

FRITZ (*interrupts*). Child, I beseech you,... don't say anything like that.... I don't like big words. We won't talk about eternity.

CHRISTINE (*smiling sadly*). Have no fear, Fritz..... I know this can't be for always.

FRITZ. You misunderstand me, child. Of course it's possible — (*laughing*) — that we simply won't be able to live without each other, but we can't tell for sure, can we? We're only human.

THEODORE (*pointing to the lighted candles*). Kindly turn your eyes upon that.... Isn't that different from a stupid lamp?

FRITZ. You're really a born decorator.

THEODORE. Children, what do you say — shall we think about eating?

TONI. Yes!... Come, Christine.

FRITZ. Wait; I'll show you where to find everything.

TONI. First of all, we need a table-cloth.

THEODORE (*with German accent, as on the vaudeville stage*). "A table-clot'?"

FRITZ. What?

THEODORE. Don't you remember that fellow in the Orpheum? "Dot is a table-clot'." "Dot is a shtool." "Dot is a liddle piannino."

TONI. Say, Dore, when are you going to the Orpheum with me? You promised me a little while ago. Then Christine will come along, and Mr. Fritz, too. (*She is just taking from* FRITZ *the table-cloth which he has taken out of the sideboard.*) Then we'll be your friends in the box.

FRITZ. Yes, yes.

TONI. Then the lady with the black velvet dress can go home alone.

FRITZ. Why do you keep thinking about that lady in black? It's too stupid.

TONI. Oh, we don't think about her.... There.... And the silver? (FRITZ *shows her the things in the open sideboard.*) Yes.... And the plates?... Yes, thanks.... There, now we can do it alone all right. Go, go away now, you're only getting in our way.

THEODORE (*has meanwhile stretched out on the couch;* FRITZ *advances toward him*). You'll excuse me.

TONI. Did you see the picture of Fritz in his uniform?

CHRISTINE. No.

TONI. You must have a look at it. Swell! (*They talk on.*)

THEODORE. Such evenings are my delight, Fritz.

FRITZ. Well, they are nice.

THEODORE. Then I feel so cozy.... Don't you?

FRITZ. Oh, I wish I could always feel so contented.

TONI. Tell me, Mr. Fritz, is there coffee in the machine?

FRITZ. Yes. You can start the lamp under it right away — it takes a good hour on that machine, before the coffee is done.

THEODORE. I'd give a dozen demoniac women for a sweet girl like that.

FRITZ. There's no comparison.

THEODORE. You see, we hate the women that we love — and only love the women that are indifferent to us.

FRITZ. (*Laughs.*)

TONI. What's the joke? We'd like to hear it, too.

THEODORE. Nothing for you, children. We're philosophizing. — If this were to be our last meeting with these girls, we'd be just as jolly, wouldn't we?

FRITZ. The last time?... Well, there's certainly something melancholy about that. Parting always gives pain, even if you've been looking forward to it eagerly for a long time.

CHRISTINE. Say, Fritz, where's the small silver?

FRITZ (*goes rear to the sideboard*). Here it is, sweetheart.

TONI. (*Comes forward, runs her hand through* THEODORE's *hair; he still reclining on the couch.*)

THEODORE. You pussy-cat!

FRITZ (*opens the package* TONI *brought*). Grand!

CHRISTINE (*to* FRITZ). You have everything in such good order.

FRITZ. Yes. (*Arranges the things* TONI *brought — sardines, cold meat, butter, cheese.*)

CHRISTINE. Fritz... won't you tell me?

FRITZ. Tell you what?

CHRISTINE (*very timidly*). Who the lady was.

FRITZ. No; don't make me cross. (*More gently.*) You see, that's one thing we agreed upon expressly: No questions asked. That's the nice thing about it. When I am with you the world disappears, like that —— (*Snaps his fingers.*) I don't ask you any questions, either.

CHRISTINE. You can ask me anything you like.

FRITZ. But I don't. I don't want to know anything.

TONI (*returns to table*). Goodness, what a mess you're making! (*Takes the edibles, puts them on the plates.*) There....

THEODORE. Say, Fritz, have you anything to drink here?

FRITZ. Oh, yes, I think I can find something. (*Exit into front room.*)

THEODORE (*raises himself and inspects the table*). Good.

TONI. There, I think we've got everything now.

FRITZ (*returns with some bottles*). Here's something to drink, too.

THEODORE. Where are the roses that fall from the ceiling?

TONI. That's right, we forgot the roses. (*She takes the roses out of the vase, climbs on a chair, and lets the roses fall on the table.*) There!

CHRISTINE. My, what a wild girl you are tonight!

THEODORE. Here, not on the plates.

FRITZ. Where do you want to sit, Christine?

THEODORE. Where is the cork-screw?

FRITZ (*gets one from the sideboard*). Here is one.

TONI. (*Tries to open a bottle.*)

FRITZ. No, let me do that.

THEODORE. No, let me do it.... (*Takes bottle and cork-screw from him.*) Meanwhile you might —— (*Moves his fingers as at the piano.*)

TONI. Yes, yes, that's grand!... (*She runs to the piano, takes the things off it, and opens it.*)

FRITZ (*to* CHRISTINE). Shall I?

CHRISTINE. Oh, please do, I've wanted that for so long.

FRITZ (*at the piano*). You can play a little too?

CHRISTINE (*with a gesture*). Oh goodness.

TONI. She plays fine, Christine does... she can sing too.

FRITZ. Really? You never told me that.

CHRISTINE. Did you ever ask me?

FRITZ. Where did you learn to sing?

CHRISTINE. I really never learned. Father taught me a little — but I haven't got much voice. And you know, since auntie died, the one that always lived with us, it's even quieter at home than it was before.

FRITZ. What do you do, anyway, all day long?

CHRISTINE. Oh, I have plenty to do!

FRITZ. Around the house, I suppose?

CHRISTINE. Yes. And then I copy notes quite a lot.

THEODORE. Music notes?

CHRISTINE. Surely.

THEODORE. They must pay you tremendously for that. (*The others laugh.*) Well, I'd pay tremendously for it. Music copying must be a terrible task, I think.

TONI. There's no sense in her working so hard, either. If I had as much voice as you have, I'd have been in the theater long ago.

THEODORE. You wouldn't even need a voice.... Of course you do nothing all day, hey?

TONI. Well, I like that! I have two little brothers that are going to school. I have to dress them in the morning. And then I help them with their lessons ——

THEODORE. That's a lie, every word of it.

TONI. Well, if you won't believe me. — And until last autumn I was in a store from eight in the morning till eight at night.

THEODORE (*mockingly*). Where was that?

TONI. In a millinery store. Mother wants me to go back there.

THEODORE (*as above*). Why did you leave it?

FRITZ (*to* CHRISTINE). Then you must sing something for us.

THEODORE. Come on, children, let's eat first, and then you'll play, won't you?

FRITZ (*rising, to* CHRISTINE). Come, sweetheart. (*Leads her to the table.*)

TONI. The coffee! There's the coffee boiling over, and we haven't begun to eat.

THEODORE. Nothing matters now.

TONI. But it's boiling over! (*Blows out the flame.*)

(*All sit down at the table.*)

THEODORE. What will you have, Toni? But let me tell you this: the cake comes last!... First you've got to eat nothing but sour things.

FRITZ. (*Pours out the wine.*)

THEODORE. Not that way: we do it differently now. Don't you know the latest fashion? (*Stands up, affects magniloquence; to* CHRISTINE, *bottle in hand.*) Special quality, genuine Johannisberger, eighteen hundred —— (*Mumbles the last figures. Fills glass, then goes to* TONI, *to* FRITZ, *repeating the same ceremony and words; finally stands at his own place, and repeats as before. Seats himself.*)

TONI (*laughing*). He's always doing something silly.

THEODORE (*raises his glass; all clink*). Prosit.

TONI. Your health, Theodore.

THEODORE (*rising*). Ladies and Gentlemen...

FRITZ. Oh, not yet!

THEODORE (*sits again*). Well, I can wait.

TONI. Oh, that's what I like — after-dinner speeches. I have a cousin that always makes his speeches in rhymes.

THEODORE. What regiment is he in?

TONI. Come, stop that... He talks it off by heart and in rhyme, and it's just splendid, Christine. And he's an elderly gentleman now, too.

THEODORE. Oh, it sometimes happens that elderly gentlemen can still talk in rhyme.

FRITZ. But you're not drinking at all, Christine! (*Clinks with her.*)

THEODORE (*clinks with* TONI). To the old gentleman who talks in rhymes.

TONI (*merrily*). To the young gentlemen, even if they don't talk at all... for example, to Mr. Fritz.... Say, Mr. Fritz, now we'll drink to our better acquaintance, if you wish — and Christine must do the same with Theodore.

THEODORE. But not with this wine, that's not the right kind for it. (*Rises, takes another bottle, same ceremony as before.*) Xeres de la Frontera mille huit cent cinquante ——

TONI (*sips*). Ah ——

THEODORE. Can't you wait till we all drink together? Now then, children... Before we solemnly drink to our better acquaintance, let us drink to the happy chance that, that... and so forth...

TONI. Yes, that's enough. (*They drink,* FRITZ *taking* TONI'S *arm,* THEODORE CHRISTINE'S.)

FRITZ. (*Kisses* TONI.)

THEODORE. (*Starts to kiss* CHRISTINE.)

CHRISTINE. Is that necessary?

THEODORE. Absolutely, else the whole ceremony is null.... (*Kisses her.*) There, and now to your seats!...

TONI. But it's getting terribly hot in the room.

FRITZ. That's because of all the candles Theodore lit.

TONI. And the wine, too. (*She leans back in her chair.*)

THEODORE. Come here, the best of all is coming now. (*He cuts off a slice of the cake and puts it in her mouth.*) There, sweet tooth — that good?

TONI. Awfully!... (*He gives her another.*)

THEODORE. Come, Fritz, now's the time. Now you might play something.

FRITZ. Do you want me to, Christine?

CHRISTINE. Please do!

TONI. Play something swell.

THEODORE. (*Fills the glasses.*)

TONI. No more. (*Drinks.*)

CHRISTINE (*sipping*). The wine is so heavy.

THEODORE (*pointing to the glass*). Fritz.

FRITZ. (*Empties the glass, goes to piano.*)

CHRISTINE. (*Goes and sits by him.*)

TONI. Mr. Fritz, play the "Double Eagle."

FRITZ. The "Double Eagle" — how does it go?

TONI. Dore, can't you play it?

THEODORE. I can't play at all.

FRITZ. I know the thing; but I can't think of it.

TONI. I'll sing for you.... La... la... lalalala....

FRITZ. Aha, now I know. (*Does not play quite correctly.*)

TONI (*goes to the piano*). No, this way. (*Plays the melody with one finger.*)

FRITZ. Yes, yes.... (*He plays,* TONI *sings.*)

THEODORE. Recollections again, hey?

FRITZ (*plays wrong again and stops*). Can't do it. I've got no ear.

(*He starts to improvise.*)

TONI (*after the first measure*). That's no good.

FRITZ (*laughs*). Don't say that, I made it up.

TONI. But it's no good for dancing.

FRITZ. Just try it once....

THEODORE (*to* TONI). Come, let's try. (*They dance.*)

CHRISTINE. (*Sits by the piano and looks at the keys.*)

(*There is a ring.*)

FRITZ. (*Suddenly stops playing;* THEODORE *and* TONI *dance on.*)

THEODORE AND TONI (*together*). What's all this? Come!

FRITZ. The bell just rang.... (*To* THEODORE.) Did you invite anybody else?

THEODORE. I should say not — you don't need to answer the bell.

CHRISTINE (*to* FRITZ). What's the matter with you?

FRITZ. Nothing.... (*There is another ring.*)

FRITZ. (*Stands up, rooted to the spot.*)

THEODORE. You are simply not at home.

FRITZ. You can hear the piano out in the corridor.... And you can see from the street that the room is lit.

THEODORE. What folly is this? You're simply not at home.

FRITZ. But it makes me nervous.

THEODORE. Well, what do you suppose it's going to be? A letter

— or a telegram —— You're not going to have a visitor at (*looks at his watch*) nine o'clock. (*There is another ring.*)

FRITZ. Rubbish, I must go and see —— (*Exit.*)

TONI. But you're not a bit swell ——

(*Strikes a few keys on the piano.*)

THEODORE. Here, stop that now! — (*To* CHRISTINE.) What ails you? Does the bell make you nervous too?

FRITZ. (*Returns, in forced calm.*)

THEODORE AND CHRISTINE (*together*). Well, who was it? — Who was it?

FRITZ (*with a forced smile*). You must be good enough to excuse me for a moment. Go in there meanwhile.

THEODORE. What is it?

CHRISTINE. Who is it?

FRITZ. Nothing, child, I simply have to say a few words to a gentleman....

(FRITZ *has opened the door of the adjoining room, conducts the girls into it.* THEODORE, *going in last, looks questioningly at* FRITZ.)

FRITZ (*in a low voice, with an expression of horror*). He!

THEODORE. Ah!

FRITZ. In with you!

THEODORE. I beg of you, don't do anything stupid, it may be a trap....

FRITZ. Go... go.... (THEODORE *exit.* FRITZ *goes rapidly through the room to the corridor, so that the stage is empty for a few seconds. Then he enters again, allowing an elegantly dressed gentleman of about thirty-five years to precede him.* THE GENTLEMAN *wears a yellow mantle, holds his hat in his gloved hand. While entering.*) Pardon me for making you wait.... I beg you....

THE GENTLEMAN (*in a very easy tone*). Oh, that is nothing. I regret extremely to have disturbed you.

FRITZ. By no means. Will you not.... (*Indicates a chair.*)

THE GENTLEMAN. Why, I see that I have disturbed you? A little entertainment, I presume?

FRITZ. A few friends.

THE GENTLEMAN (*seating himself, amicable*). A masquerade, no doubt?

FRITZ (*embarrassed*). Why do you say that?

THE GENTLEMAN. Well, your friends have ladies' hats and cloaks.

FRITZ. Well yes.... (*Smiling.*) There may be lady friends among them.... (*Silence.*)

THE GENTLEMAN. Life is at times very merry... yes...

(*Looks rigidly at* FRITZ.)

FRITZ (*endures the glance a while, then looks away*). I presume I may permit myself to inquire what gives me the pleasure of your visit?

THE GENTLEMAN. Certainly.... (*Calmly.*) You see, my wife forgot to take her veil away from here.

FRITZ. Your wife... here? Her... (*Smiling.*) The jest is a trifle strange....

THE GENTLEMAN (*suddenly rising, very loudly, almost wildly, supporting himself by resting one hand on the chair arm*). She did forget it.

FRITZ. (*Rises also, and the two men stand facing each other.*)

THE GENTLEMAN (*raises his clenched fist, as if to launch it at* FRITZ; *in fury and loathing*). Oh!...

FRITZ. (*Makes a parrying motion, takes a short step backward.*)

THE GENTLEMAN (*after a long pause*). Here are your letters. (*He throws on the desk a packet of letters which he has taken from his overcoat pocket.*) I wish those which you have received.

FRITZ. (*Parrying motion.*)

THE GENTLEMAN (*vehemently, significantly*). I do not wish to have them found — later — in your rooms.

FRITZ (*very loudly*). They will not be found.

THE GENTLEMAN. (*Looks at him. Pause.*)

FRITZ. What else do you wish of me?

THE GENTLEMAN (*scornfully*). What else?

FRITZ. I am at your disposal....

THE GENTLEMAN (*bows coolly*). Very well.

(*He casts a glance around the room; as he again sees the table and the girls' hats, a sudden flash crosses his face, as if he would burst into a new fit of rage.*)

FRITZ (*notices this*). I am wholly at your disposal. — I shall be at home tomorrow till noon.

THE GENTLEMAN. (*Bows and turns to go.*)

FRITZ (*accompanies him to the door,* THE GENTLEMAN *motioning him away. When he is gone,* FRITZ *goes to the desk and stands there a moment. Then he hastens to the window, looks through a crack in the blind, and can be seen to follow the motions of the gentleman passing along the street. Leaving the window he looks down for a moment; then goes to the door of the adjoining room, opens it halfway, and calls).* Theodore, one moment.

(The following scene very rapid.)

THEODORE *(excited)*. Well?...

FRITZ. He knows.

THEODORE. He knows nothing. You simply fell into his trap. I'll wager you even confessed. You're a fool, I tell you.... You...

FRITZ *(pointing to the letters)*. He brought me back my letters.

THEODORE *(startled)*. Oh!... *(After a pause.)* I always say, a man ought not to write letters.

FRITZ. It was he, this noon, down below.

THEODORE. Well, what happened? — Tell me about it.

FRITZ. You must do me a great service now, Theodore.

THEODORE. I'll fix up the whole business for you.

FRITZ. That is out of the question now.

THEODORE. Then...

FRITZ. In any case it will be well.... *(Breaks off.)* — But we can't let the poor girls wait so long.

THEODORE. Let them wait. What were you going to say?

FRITZ. It will be well if you go to Lensky today.

THEODORE. At once, if you wish.

FRITZ. You won't find him now... but between eleven and twelve he will surely come into the coffee-house... perhaps the two of you will then come here....

THEODORE. Come, don't make up such a face... ninety-nine times out of a hundred it turns out all right....

FRITZ. He will see to it that this one doesn't turn out all right.

THEODORE. But I beg you, remember that affair of last year, between Doctor Billinger and Herz — that was exactly the same.

FRITZ. None of that! You know yourself he ought to have shot me down right here in the room — it would have come to the same thing.

THEODORE *(acting)*. Well, that is fine, I must say. That's a grand idea.... And so Lensky and I count for nothing? You think we'll agree that...

FRITZ. I beg of you, no more of that!... You simply accept what is proposed.

THEODORE. Ah ——

FRITZ. What's the sense of all this, Theodore? As if you didn't know.

THEODORE. Nonsense. And anyway, it's all a matter of luck.... You have just as much chance of...

FRITZ (*without listening to him*). She foreboded it. We both foreboded it. We knew it....

THEODORE. Come, Fritz....

FRITZ (*goes to the desk, locks up the letters*). Oh, what is she doing this minute? Did he... Theodore, you must find out tomorrow what happened over there.

THEODORE. I will try.

FRITZ. And see to it that no useless delay...

THEODORE. It can scarcely be before day after tomorrow in the morning.

FRITZ (*almost horrified*). Theodore!

THEODORE. And so... head up. — You believe a little in inward conviction, don't you — and I have a firm conviction that everything will turn out all right. (*With forced merriment.*) I don't know why myself, but I have the conviction, anyway!

FRITZ (*smiling*). What a good fellow you are. But what shall we say to the girls?

THEODORE. That doesn't matter. Let's simply send them away.

FRITZ. No, no. Let's be as merry as we can. Christine must not suspect anything. I'll sit down at the piano again; and you call them in. (THEODORE *turns to do this, with discontented face.*) And what shall you say to them?

THEODORE. That it's none of their business.

FRITZ (*who has sat down at the piano, turning toward him*). No, no ——

THEODORE. That it's about a friend — I'll invent something.

FRITZ. (*Plays a few notes.*)

THEODORE. Ladies, I beg you to enter. (*Has opened the door.*)

TONI. Well, at last! Has he gone?

CHRISTINE (*hastening to* FRITZ). Who was here, Fritz?

FRITZ (*at the piano, playing*). Curious again.

CHRISTINE. I beg you, Fritz, tell me.

FRITZ. Sweetheart, I can't tell you; it really concerns people that you don't know at all.

CHRISTINE (*coaxingly*). Come, Fritz, tell me the truth.

THEODORE. Of course she won't leave you in peace.... But mind you tell her nothing! You promised him.

TONI. Come, don't be so tiresome, Christine, let them have their fun. They're simply putting on airs.

THEODORE. I must finish that waltz with Miss Toni. (*German accent.*) Bleaze, Mister Music-maker — a liddle museek.

FRITZ. (*Plays.*)   (THEODORE and TONI *dance a few measures.*)

TONI (*after a few moments*). I can't.   (*She falls back into a chair.*)

THEODORE. (*Kisses her, seats himself beside her on the chair-arm.*)

FRITZ. (*Stays at the piano, takes both* CHRISTINE's *hands, looks at her.*)

CHRISTINE (*as if awakening*). Why don't you play on?

FRITZ (*smiling*). Enough for today....

CHRISTINE. That's the way I'd like to be able to play.

FRITZ. Do you play much?

CHRISTINE. I don't get much chance; there's always something in the house that needs to be done. And then you know we have such a poor piano.

FRITZ. I'd like to try it once. I'd like to see your room once, anyway.

CHRISTINE (*smiling*). It isn't as pretty as here.

FRITZ. And something else I'd like: to have you tell me about yourself... a whole lot... I really know so little about you.

CHRISTINE. There isn't much to tell. — And I haven't any secrets either... like some others.

FRITZ. You never loved any man before?

CHRISTINE. (*Merely looks at him.*)

FRITZ. (*Kisses her hands.*)

CHRISTINE. And never shall love any other.

FRITZ (*with an almost pained expression*). Don't say that... don't... What do you know about it?... Does your father love you very much, Christine?

CHRISTINE. Oh, how much!... And there was a time when I used to tell him everything.

FRITZ. Well, child, don't reproach yourself. People have to have secrets once in a while — that's the way of the world.

CHRISTINE. If I only knew that you loved me — it would all be right.

FRITZ. Then don't you know?

CHRISTINE. If you would always talk to me like that then....

FRITZ. Christine! You haven't a very comfortable seat, though.

CHRISTINE. Let me be — this is all right.

(She lays her head against the piano.)

FRITZ. *(Stands up and strokes her hair.)*

CHRISTINE. Oh, that feels good. *(The room is quiet.)*

THEODORE. Where are the cigars, Fritz?

FRITZ. *(Advances to him as he stands by the sideboard looking.)*

TONI. *(Has fallen asleep.)*

FRITZ *(hands him a small box of cigars)*. And black coffee.

(He pours two cups.)

THEODORE. Children, don't you want some coffee, too?

FRITZ. Toni, shall I pour a cup?...

THEODORE. Let them sleep. — You ought not to drink coffee today. You ought to go to bed as soon as possible and try to sleep well.

FRITZ. *(Looks at him and laughs bitterly.)*

THEODORE. Well, things are as they are... and now it's not a question of being magnificent or deep, but of being as sensible as you can... that's the point... in such cases.

FRITZ. You'll bring Lensky to me tonight, will you?

THEODORE. That's nonsense. Tomorrow is time enough.

FRITZ. I beg you, bring him.

THEODORE. All right, then.

FRITZ. Will you take the girls home?

THEODORE. Yes, and right away, too. — Toni!... Get up!

TONI. Oh, you're drinking black coffee. Give me some, too.

THEODORE. Here you are, child.

FRITZ *(to CHRISTINE, going to her)*. Tired, my sweetheart?

CHRISTINE. How sweet, when you talk that way.

FRITZ. Very tired?

CHRISTINE *(smiling)*. It's the wine. — And I have a little headache, too.

FRITZ. Well, that will pass off in the open air.

CHRISTINE. Are we going now? Will you go with us?

FRITZ. No, child. I'm going to stay right here. I have some things to do.

CHRISTINE (*recollecting*). Now... What have you got to do now?

FRITZ (*almost sternly*). Christine, that's something you must stop. — (*Gently.*) You see, I'm all used up... we walked around in the country for two hours today, Theodore and I.

THEODORE. Oh, that was delightful. One of these days we'll all drive out into the country together.

TONI. Yes, that will be swell. And you'll put on your uniform.

THEODORE. There's feeling for nature!

CHRISTINE. When shall I see you again?

FRITZ (*somewhat nervously*). I'll write you.

CHRISTINE (*sadly*). Good-bye.   (*Turns to go.*)

FRITZ (*notices her sadness*). Tomorrow, Christine.

CHRISTINE (*happily*). Truly?

FRITZ. In the public gardens out there — at — say at six o'clock.... Will that suit you?

CHRISTINE. (*Nods.*)

TONI (*to* FRITZ). Are you going with us, Fritz?

FRITZ. No, I shall stay here.

TONI. He has an easy time of it. Think of the long journey home we have.

FRITZ. But Toni, you have left almost the whole of that cake. Wait, I'll wrap it up for you, shall I?

TONI (*to* THEODORE). Is that proper?

FRITZ. (*Wraps up the cake.*)

CHRISTINE. She's like a little child.

TONI (*to* FRITZ). Wait, I'll help you put out the candles. (*Puts out one after another. The candle on the desk is left burning.*)

CHRISTINE. Shan't I open the window for you? The air is so heavy.   (*She opens the window, looks at the house opposite.*)

FRITZ. There, children. Now I'll light you down the stairs.

TONI. Are the lights out on the stairs?

THEODORE. Why, of course.

CHRISTINE. Oh, the air is nice, coming in here.

TONI. May breezes.... (*At the door to* FRITZ, *who holds the candlestick.*) Well, we thank you for a warm welcome.

THEODORE (*urging her forward*). Come, come, come, come....

FRITZ. (*Goes out with them. The door stays open. The voices are heard outside. The outer door is heard to open.*)

TONI. Bah!

THEODORE. Look out for the steps there.

TONI. Thanks for the cake.

THEODORE. Shh, you'll wake people up.

CHRISTINE. Good night.

THEODORE. Good night.

      (FRITZ *can be heard to close and bolt the outer door. As he enters and puts the light on the desk, the street-door is heard to open and close.*)

FRITZ. (*Goes to the window and bows, looking down.*)

CHRISTINE. Good night.

TONI (*in high spirits*). Good night, my darling child.

THEODORE (*reprovingly*). Toni! (*One can hear his words, her laughter; the steps die away.* THEODORE *whistles the melody of the "Double Eagle," which is the last thing heard.* FRITZ *looks out a few moments longer, then sinks down on the chair nearest the window.*)

ACT TWO

CHRISTINE'S *room. Modest and neat.*

CHRISTINE. (*Is dressing to go out.*)

CATHERINE (*enters after knocking*). Good evening, Miss Christine.

CHRISTINE (*standing before the mirror, turns around*). Good evening.

CATHERINE. You're just going out?

CHRISTINE. I'm not in such a great hurry.

CATHERINE. My husband sent me to ask if you wouldn't go and take supper with us in the Zoological Garden; there's a band there tonight.

CHRISTINE. Thank you very much, Mrs. Binder. I can't tonight. Another time, perhaps? — But you're not angry?

CATHERINE. Not a bit, why should I be? You'll probably have a better time than with us.

CHRISTINE. (*Looks at her.*)

CATHERINE. Has your father gone to the theater?

CHRISTINE. Oh, no; he comes home first. It doesn't begin till half past seven now.

CATHERINE. That's so, I keep forgetting. I'll just wait for him. I've wanted for a long time to ask him about free tickets to the new piece. I suppose they can be had now?

CHRISTINE. Surely, nobody goes there any more now, when the evenings are so lovely.

CATHERINE. People like us never get a chance to go, unless we happen to know somebody in a theater. — But don't let me keep you, Miss Christine, if you have to go. To be sure, my husband will be very sorry... and somebody else too.

CHRISTINE. Who?

CATHERINE. Binder's cousin goes with us, of course. Do you know, Miss Christine, that he has a steady job now?

CHRISTINE (*indifferently*). Oh.

CATHERINE. And a very nice salary. And such a fine young fellow. And he has such respect for you ——

CHRISTINE. Well — good-bye, Mrs. Binder.

CATHERINE. A body could tell him anything about you — he wouldn't believe a word of it....

CHRISTINE. (*Looks at her.*)

CATHERINE. There are such men.

CHRISTINE. Good-bye, Mrs. Binder.

CATHERINE. Good-bye.... (*Not too maliciously.*) See that you aren't late to your appointment, Miss Christine.

CHRISTINE. What do you want of me, anyway?

CATHERINE. Why, nothing; you're quite right. You can't be young but once.

CHRISTINE. Good-bye.

CATHERINE. But I'd like to give you one piece of advice, just the same, Miss Christine: you ought to be a little more careful.

CHRISTINE. Why, what do you mean?

CATHERINE. Look — Vienna is such a big city.... Do you have to have your meetings a hundred paces from your house?

CHRISTINE. I suppose that's nobody's business.

CATHERINE. I didn't want to believe it, when Binder told me. He saw you, you know.... Come, I said to him, you were mistaken, you saw somebody else. Miss Christine is not the girl to go walking with elegant young gentlemen in the evening, and if she did, she would be wise enough not to go walking through these streets. Well, says he, you can ask her yourself. And, says he, it's no wonder, either — she doesn't come to see us any more at all. Instead of that she's going around all the time with Toni Schlager, and what sort of company is that for a decent young girl? — see, men are so low-minded, Miss Christine. — And of course he had to go and tell everything to Franz right away too; but he got fine and angry, he did, and for Miss Christine he'd burn his hand off, and anybody that said anything about her would have to deal with him. And you're so domestic and were always so sweet with your old auntie — God grant her eternal rest — and you live so modestly and so retiringly and all that.... (*Pause.*) Perhaps you'll come to hear the music, after all?

CHRISTINE. No....

VYRING (*enters, a laurel branch in his hand*). Good evening. — Ah, Mrs. Binder. How are you?

CATHERINE. Thank you, well.

VYRING. And little Lena? And your husband?

CATHERINE. All well, God be praised.

VYRING. Well, that's fine. (*To* CHRISTINE.) You're still at home in all this fine weather?

CHRISTINE. I was just going out.

VYRING. That's right. The air outside — it's something wonderful, eh, Mrs. Binder? I just came through the public gardens; the lilacs are in bloom, simply gorgeous. I broke the law a little, too.   (*Gives the branch to* CHRISTINE.)

CHRISTINE. Thank you, father.

CATHERINE. Thank your lucky stars that the guard didn't catch you.

VYRING. Just go out there once, Mrs. Binder. It smells just as good as if I hadn't plucked the little twig.

CATHERINE. But if everybody thought the same —

VYRING. Well, that would be a mistake, to be sure.

CHRISTINE. Good-bye, father.

VYRING. If you could wait a few minutes, you might go to the theater with me.

CHRISTINE. I... I promised Toni that I would go for her....

VYRING. Oh, yes. Well, that's wiser, too. Youth belongs with youth. Good-bye, Christine.

CHRISTINE (*kisses him*). Good-bye, Mrs. Binder.

(*Exit.* VYRING's *eyes follow her tenderly.*)

CATHERINE. That's a very close friendship with her and Miss Toni.

VYRING. Yes — I'm really glad that she has such company and doesn't have to sit at home all the time. What sort of a life does that girl have, anyway?

CATHERINE. Yes, to be sure.

VYRING. I can't tell you, Mrs. Binder, how it hurts me sometimes when I come home from rehearsal and find her sitting there and sewing; and then we've scarcely got up from the table at noon when she sits down again and goes to copying notes.

CATHERINE. Yes, yes, the millionaires have an easier time of it, to be sure, than we do. But how about her singing?

VYRING. It's not much. Her voice is big enough for a room, and her singing is good enough for her father — but you can't live on that.

CATHERINE. That's too bad.

VYRING. I am glad she sees it herself. She at least will be spared from disappointments. Of course I could get her into the chorus in our theater.

CATHERINE. Of course, with such a figure!

VYRING. But there's no future there.

CATHERINE. A girl brings really a good many cares. When I think that in five or six years my little Lena will be a grown girl too ——

VYRING. But why don't you sit down, Mrs. Binder?

CATHERINE. Oh, thanks; my husband is coming for me right away — I only came to invite Christine.

VYRING. Invite?...

CATHERINE. Yes, to hear the band in the Zoological Gardens. I thought that might cheer her up a bit. She really needs it.

VYRING. Couldn't do her a bit of harm, especially after this sad winter. Why doesn't she go with you?

CATHERINE. I don't know.... Perhaps because Binder's cousin is with us.

VYRING. Ah, that's possible. You know she can't stand him. She told me that herself.

CATHERINE. Well, why not? Franz is a very decent fellow — and now he's even got a steady job, and that's a piece of good fortune nowadays for a...

VYRING. For a... poor girl ——

CATHERINE. For any girl.

VYRING. Now, tell me, Mrs. Binder, is a blooming young creature like that really made for nothing but for some such decent fellow who happens to have a steady job?

CATHERINE. Why, that's the best thing, after all. You can't wait for a count, and when one happens to come along, he usually takes his leave before he's married you. (VYRING *is at the window. Pause.*) Well, and that's why I always say you can't be careful enough of a young girl, especially of the company she keeps ——

VYRING. Well, I wonder if it's worth while to throw away all your young years like that. — And what good does all her goodness do a poor creature like that, even if, after years of waiting, the stocking-maker actually comes?

CATHERINE. Mr. Vyring, if my husband is a stocking-maker, he is an honest and good man, that I've never had to complain of....

VYRING (*soothingly*). Why, Mrs. Binder, do you think I'm aiming at you?... You didn't fling your youth out of the window, either.

CATHERINE. I have forgotten all about that.

VYRING. Don't say that. — You can say what you like, memories are, after all, the best thing in your life.

CATHERINE. I haven't any memories.

VYRING. Now, now....

CATHERINE. And if a body does have such memories as you mean, what remains behind?... Regret.

VYRING. Well, and what remains behind — if she — doesn't even have anything to remember? If her whole life simply goes by (*Simply and without emotion*), day after day, without happiness or love — I suppose you think that's better?

CATHERINE. But, Mr. Vyring, just think of the old lady, of your sister.... But it still pains you to have her spoken of, Mr. Vyring.

VYRING. It still pains me, yes.

CATHERINE. Of course... when two people have clung to each other so warmly.... I always said that brothers like you aren't found every day.

VYRING. (*Makes a gesture of deprecation.*)

CATHERINE. Well, it's true. You had to be both father and mother to her, and such a young man.

VYRING. Yes, yes ——

CATHERINE. And that must be a kind of consolation, too. Then you know that you have been the benefactor and the protector of a poor girl like that ——

VYRING. Yes, I imagined that, too — when she was still a pretty young girl — and God knows how clever and noble I thought myself. But then, later on, when the gray hairs came and the wrinkles, and one day passed like all the others — and her whole youth — and the girl gradually (you scarcely notice such things) turned into the old maid — then for the first time I began to see what I had done.

CATHERINE. But Mr. Vyring ——

VYRING. I still see her before me, as she often used to sit opposite me in the evening, sitting by the lamp here in the room, and used to look at me with her quiet smile, with a certain resigned expression — as if she wanted to thank me for something; — and I — I could have gladly gone down on my knees to her, and begged her forgiveness that I had guarded her so well against all dangers — and all happiness! (*Pause.*)

CATHERINE. And many a girl would be happy just the same, if she always had such a brother by her side... and nothing to regret....

TONI (*enters*). Good evening.... Why, it's all dark here, you can scarcely see a thing. — Ah, Mrs. Binder. Your husband is downstairs waiting for you, Mrs. Binder.... Isn't Christine at home?

VYRING. She went out a quarter of an hour ago.

CATHERINE. Didn't you meet her? She was going to meet you.

TONI. No... we evidently missed each other. — You're going to hear the band tonight, your husband says.

CATHERINE. Yes, he is so fond of it. What a charming little hat you have on, Miss Toni. Isn't it a new one?

TONI. I should say not. — Don't you know this style any more? Last spring's style, only freshly trimmed.

CATHERINE. Did you trim it yourself?

TONI. Well, of course.

VYRING. So clever!

CATHERINE. Oh, yes — I keep forgetting that you worked for a year in a milliner shop.

TONI. I shall probably go back again. Mother wants me to, and that settles it.

CATHERINE. How is your mother?

TONI. Well enough — she has a little toothache — but the doctor says it's rheumatic pains.

VYRING. Well, it's time for me....

CATHERINE. I'll go right down with you, Mr. Vyring.

TONI. I'll go, too. But take your overcoat, Mr. Vyring; it's going to be quite cool later on.

VYRING. You think so?

CATHERINE. Yes, indeed.— How can you be so foolish?

CHRISTINE. (Enters.)

TONI. Why, there she is.

CATHERINE. Back from your walk already?

CHRISTINE. Yes. Hello, Toni — I have a headache. (Seats herself.)

VYRING. Headache?

CATHERINE. That's from the air.

VYRING. Come, what's the matter, Christine? — Please, Miss Toni, will you light the lamp?

TONI. (Sets about it.)

CHRISTINE. But I can do that myself.

VYRING. Let me see your face, Christine.

CHRISTINE. But, father, it is nothing; it's just the air outside.

CATHERINE. Lots of people can't stand the spring air.

VYRING. Miss Toni, you'll stay with Christine, won't you?

TONI. Of course I will.

CHRISTINE. But it isn't anything, father.

TONI. My mother doesn't make such a fuss over me, when I have a headache.

VYRING (to CHRISTINE, still sitting). Are you so tired?

CHRISTINE (standing up). I'll get right up again. (Smiling.)

VYRING. There — now you look quite different again. (To CATHERINE.) She looks quite different when she smiles, don't you think? Well, good-bye Christine. (*Kisses her.*) And see to it that your little head isn't aching when I come home.

(*He is at the door.*)

CATHERINE (*softly to* CHRISTINE). Have you quarreled?

CHRISTINE. (*Makes an angry gesture.*)

VYRING (*at the door*). Mrs. Binder!

TONI. Good-bye. (*Exeunt* VYRING AND CATHERINE.)

TONI. Do you know what your headache comes from? From the sweet wine yesterday. I'm surprised that I don't feel the effects of it. But it was jolly, wasn't it?

CHRISTINE. (*Nods.*)

TONI. They're swell people, aren't they? — both of them, you can't say anything different, can you? — And such nice rooms as Fritz has, really splendid. At Dore's place… (*Interrupts herself.*) Oh, well. — Say, have you still got such a headache? Why don't you talk?… What's the matter with you?

CHRISTINE. Only think — he didn't come.

TONI. Left you in the lurch, did he? Serves you right.

CHRISTINE. Why, what do you mean? What have I done?

TONI. You spoil him, that's all; you're too nice to him. A man just can't help getting tyrannical.

CHRISTINE. You don't know what you're talking about.

TONI. I do know quite well. — I've been angry with you this long time. He comes late to his appointments; he doesn't take you home; he goes into a theater-box with strangers; he leaves you in the lurch — and you take it all calmly and make sheep's eyes (*imitating*) at him into the bargain.

CHRISTINE. Oh, don't talk so, don't make yourself out worse than you are. You love Theodore too.

TONI. Love him — of course I love him. But he won't find me grieving about him, and no man will, not any more. There isn't one of these men that is worth it.

CHRISTINE. I never heard you talk so, never!

TONI. No. Tina — we never talked like this before. I never dared, you see. You don't know how afraid of you I was!… But I always thought this: when you once get it, you'll get it bad. And the first time it certainly does give you a shaking up. — But you can be thankful that you've got such a good friend to help you through your first love affair.

CHRISTINE. Toni!

TONI. Don't you believe me when I say I'm a good friend to you? If I wasn't here to tell you that he's just a man like the rest, and that the whole manpack isn't worth a single bad hour, God knows what thoughts might come into your head. But I always will say, you never can believe a word men say.

CHRISTINE. What do you mean by saying men, men — what do I care about men! — I'm not asking about the others.— As long as I live I shall never think about another man.

TONI. Well, what are you thinking of?.... has he?... Of course — such things have happened; but then you ought to have gone at the affair differently.

CHRISTINE. Do keep still!

TONI. Well, what do you want? I can't help it if it's so.— You have to think about a thing like that. You simply have to wait till somebody comes that you can see is in earnest from his face....

CHRISTINE. Toni, I can't stand such words today; they hurt me.

TONI (*good-humoredly*). Oh, now, come ——

CHRISTINE. Leave me alone... don't be angry... leave me alone!

TONI. Why should I be angry? I'll go. I didn't want to hurt you, Christine, truly not. (*Turns to go.*) Ah, Mr. Fritz.

FRITZ (*has entered*). Good evening.

CHRISTINE (*with a joyous cry*). Fritz! Fritz! (*Rushes into his arms.*)

TONI. (*Steals out, her face saying: I'm not needed here.*)

FRITZ (*freeing himself*). But ——

CHRISTINE. They all say you will forsake me! But you won't, will you — not yet — not just yet?

FRITZ. Who says it? What ails you? (*Patting her.*) But, sweetheart,... I really thought you would be startled when I suddenly came walking in here.

CHRISTINE. Oh — so long as I have you!

FRITZ. Come, calm yourself — did you wait long for me?

CHRISTINE. Why didn't you come?

FRITZ. I was detained and that made me late. Just now I was in the gardens and didn't find you — and was going home again. Suddenly I had such a longing, such a longing for your dear little face...

CHRISTINE (*happily*). Oh, truly?

FRITZ. And then, too, I had such an indescribable desire to see where you live — yes, really — I just had to see it once. And so I couldn't stand it and came up here... and so you really don't mind?

CHRISTINE. Oh, the idea!

FRITZ. Nobody saw me; and I knew your father was in the theater.

CHRISTINE. What do I care about people!

FRITZ. So this is — (*Looks around the room.*) — this is your room? Very pretty.

CHRISTINE. You can't see anything.

(*Is about to take the shade off the lamp.*)

FRITZ. No, don't do that, the light blinds me, it's better this way. So that's the window you've told me about, where you always sit and work, eh? — And the pretty view! (*Smiling.*) But just look at all the roofs you see.— And over there — what's that black thing I see over yonder?

CHRISTINE. That's Bald Mountain.

FRITZ. Sure enough. You really have a better view than I.

CHRISTINE. Oh!

FRITZ. I'd like to live up so high, and be able to overlook all the roofs; I think that is very nice. And I suppose the alley is quiet?

CHRISTINE. Oh, in the daytime there's noise enough.

FRITZ. Do any teams go past?

CHRISTINE. Not often, but there's a locksmith in the house opposite.

FRITZ. Oh, that's very unpleasant. (*He has sat down.*)

CHRISTINE. You get used to it; you don't hear it any more.

FRITZ (*rises again hastily*). Is this really my first visit? Everything seems so familiar to me.... I have imagined everything just this way. (*He starts to look around the room.*)

CHRISTINE. No, you mustn't look at anything.

FRITZ. What are those pictures?

CHRISTINE. Oh, stop!

FRITZ. Ah, I want to look at them.

(*He takes the lamp and lights the pictures.*)

CHRISTINE. "Parting and Return."

FRITZ. Sure enough — "Parting and Return."

CHRISTINE. I know well enough that the pictures aren't pretty.—
There is a much better one in father's room.

FRITZ. What picture is it?

CHRISTINE. It is a girl looking out of the window, and outside it's
winter, you know — and it's name is "Forsaken."

FRITZ. Oh.— (*Puts down the lamp.*) Ah, and that's your library.
(*Sits down beside the little book-rack.*)

CHRISTINE. You'd better not look at them.

FRITZ. Why not? Ah! Schiller... Hauff... Pocket Encyclopedia
... Goodness gracious!

CHRISTINE. It only goes to G.

FRITZ (*smiling*). Oh.... A book for old and young.... You look at
the pictures in it, I suppose?

CHRISTINE. Of course I've looked at the pictures.

FRITZ (*still seated*). Who is the gentleman there on the stove?

CHRISTINE. Why, don't you know? That's Schubert.

FRITZ (*rising*). Sure enough.

CHRISTINE. Because father likes him so much. Father used to
compose songs himself, very beautiful ones.

FRITZ. And now he doesn't?

CHRISTINE. Not any more. (*Pause.*)

FRITZ (*sits down*). How cosy it is here.

CHRISTINE. Do you really like it?

FRITZ. Very much.... What is that?
(*Takes up a vase of artificial flowers standing on the table.*)

CHRISTINE. He's found something else!

FRITZ. No, child, that doesn't belong in here.... It looks so dusty.

CHRISTINE. But they certainly aren't dusty.

FRITZ. Artificial flowers always look dusty.... Real flowers ought
to be in your room, flowers that are fresh and sweet-smelling.
From now I shall... (*Breaks off, turns to conceal his emotion.*)

CHRISTINE. What? What were you going to say?

FRITZ. Nothing, nothing.

CHRISTINE (*rises. Tenderly*). What was it?

FRITZ. I was going to say that I would send you fresh flowers
tomorrow.

CHRISTINE. Well, and did you want to take it back so soon? —
Of course! Tomorrow you won't be thinking of me any more.

FRITZ. (*Deprecatory gesture.*)

CHRISTINE. Certainly, it's out of sight, out of mind, with you.

FRITZ. What are you saying?

CHRISTINE. Oh, yes, I know. I can tell.

FRITZ. How can you imagine such a thing?

CHRISTINE. You are to blame yourself. Because you're always keeping secrets from me.... Because you never tell me about yourself.— What do you do all day?

FRITZ. Why, sweetheart, that's very simple. I go to lectures — sometimes — then I go into the coffeehouse... then I read... or sometimes I play the piano — then I chat with somebody — then I go calling... but all that is of no account. It's tiresome to talk about it.— But now I must go, child.

CHRISTINE. So soon ——

FRITZ. Your father will soon be here.

CHRISTINE. Not for a long time yet, Fritz.— Stay awhile — just a minute — stay awhile.

FRITZ. And then I have... Theodore is expecting me.... I have something to talk over with him.

CHRISTINE. Today?

FRITZ. Surely today.

CHRISTINE. You can see him tomorrow, too.

FRITZ. Perhaps I shan't be in Vienna tomorrow.

CHRISTINE. Not in Vienna?

FRITZ (*noticing her alarm, calmly, cheerfully*). Well, that wouldn't be anything wonderful, would it? I'm going away for a day — or perhaps for two, you child, you.

CHRISTINE. Where to?

FRITZ. Where?... Oh, anywhere.— Good heavens, don't make up such a face.... I'm going out to my father's estate.... Well, is that so terrible to you?

CHRISTINE. And you never tell me about him, either.

FRITZ. No; what a child you are.... You don't understand how nice it is to be all alone together. Tell me, don't you feel that?

CHRISTINE. No, it isn't nice at all that you never tell me anything about yourself.... You see, I'm interested in everything that touches you... yes, everything.— I'd like to have more of you than just the one hour in the evening that we can spend together sometimes. Then you are gone again, and I don't know anything.... Then the whole night goes and a whole day, with so many hours in it — and still I don't know anything. And that often makes me so sad.

FRITZ. Why does that make you sad?

CHRISTINE. Why, because I have such a longing for you as if you weren't in the same city at all, as if you were somewhere else. You simply disappear, as far as I am concerned, so far away....

FRITZ (*somewhat impatient*). But ——

CHRISTINE. Well, it's true!

FRITZ. Come here to me. (*She does so.*) After all, the only thing you know is that I — that you love me at this moment.... (*She wishes to speak.*) Don't talk about eternity. (*More to himself.*) Perhaps there are moments that scatter around them the aroma of eternity.— That is the only one that we can understand, the only one that belongs to us. (*He kisses her. Pause. He rises. With a sudden outburst.*) Oh, how beautiful it is here, how beautiful! (*He stands at the window.*) So far from the world you are in here, among all the many houses.... I seem to be so alone here, just with you.... (*Softly.*) So sheltered.

CHRISTINE. If you always talked like that... I could almost believe...

FRITZ. Believe what, child?

CHRISTINE. That you loved me as I dreamed it — the day you kissed me the first time,... do you remember?

FRITZ (*passionately*). I do love you! — (*He embraces her; tears himself from her.*) But now let me go.

CHRISTINE. Are you sorry you said it, so soon again? You are free, you know you are free — you can go and leave me whenever you like... you haven't promised me anything — and I haven't demanded anything of you.... It doesn't matter what becomes of me, then: I've been happy for once, and that's all I ask of life. I only want you to know that and to believe that I never — loved any man before you, and that I never shall love any man — when you get tired of me ——

FRITZ (*more to himself*). Don't say it, don't say it — it sounds — so sweet.   (*There is a knock.*)

FRITZ (*starts*). That's probably Theodore.

CHRISTINE (*startled*). He knows that you are here?

THEODORE (*enters*). Good evening.— Impudent of me, eh?

CHRISTINE. Do you have such important matters to discuss with him?

THEODORE. I certainly have; and have been looking everywhere for him.

FRITZ (*in a low voice*). Why didn't you wait below?

CHRISTINE. What are you whispering to him?

THEODORE (*wishing her to hear*). Why I didn't wait below.... Well, if I had absolutely known that you were here.... But I couldn't risk walking up and down outside for two hours.

FRITZ (*pointedly*). Then... you will go with me tomorrow?

THEODORE (*comprehending*). Surely.

FRITZ. That's right.

THEODORE. But I've been hurrying so that I must beg permission to sit down for a few seconds.

CHRISTINE. Please do.   (*Busies herself at the window.*)

FRITZ (*softly*). Anything new? — Did you find out about her?

THEODORE. No. I merely came to get you because you are so incautious. What's the use of these unnecessary excitements? You ought to try to sleep.... It's rest you need....

(CHRISTINE *is near them again.*)

FRITZ. Tell me, isn't this a dear little room?

THEODORE. Yes, it is very nice. (*To* CHRISTINE.) Do you stay here at home all day long? — Really, it is very homelike here. A little high up for my taste.

FRITZ. That's just what I like about it.

THEODORE. But now I'm going to take Fritz away from you; we've got to get up early in the morning.

CHRISTINE. Then you are really going away?

THEODORE. He will come again, Miss Christine.

CHRISTINE. Will you write to me?

THEODORE. But if he comes back tomorrow ——

CHRISTINE. Oh, I know he's going to stay longer than that.

FRITZ. (*Starts.*)

THEODORE (*notices it*). Well, does he have to write immediately? I wouldn't have thought you so sentimental.... Well,... kiss each other good-bye, since it'll be so long.... (*Breaks off.*) I'm simply not here. (FRITZ *and* CHRISTINE *kiss.*)

THEODORE (*takes out a cigarette-case and puts a cigarette in his mouth; seeks vainly for a match*). Tell me, dear Christine, haven't you a match?

CHRISTINE. Oh, yes, there are some.

(*Points to a holder on the chest of drawers.*)

THEODORE. It's empty.

CHRISTINE. I'll get you one. (*Hurries into adjoining room.*)

FRITZ (*looking after her*). Oh, God, how such hours lie to us!

THEODORE. Why, what hours?

FRITZ. I'm almost ready to believe that my happiness is here, that this sweet girl — (*breaks off*) — but this hour is a tremendous liar....

THEODORE. Absurd talk.... How you will laugh at it.

FRITZ. I don't think I shall have any time for that.

CHRISTINE (*returns*). Here you are.

THEODORE. Thanks very much.... Good-bye, then.— (*To* FRITZ.) Well, what do you want now?

FRITZ (*looks back and forth around the room, as if to deepen the impression in his mind*). It's hard to leave it.

CHRISTINE. Oh, make fun of it if you like.

THEODORE (*firmly*). Come.— Good-bye, Christine.

FRITZ. Farewell.

CHRISTINE. Till we meet again. (THEODORE *and* FRITZ *exeunt. She stands a moment, anxious, then goes to the open door, softly.*) Fritz!

FRITZ (*comes back again and presses her to his heart*). Farewell.

ACT THREE

The same scene as the second act. It is noon.

CHRISTINE. (*Alone, sitting sewing by the window; lays down her work.*)

LENA (*enters*). Good day, Miss Christine.

CHRISTINE (*very absent-mindedly*). Good day, child; what is it?

LENA. Mother sent me to see if I could get the theater tickets.

CHRISTINE. Father hasn't got home yet, child; will you wait?

LENA. No, Miss Christine; then I'll come after lunch again.

CHRISTINE. Very well.

LENA (*going, turns back*). And mother said to ask Miss Christine if her headache was gone yet.

CHRISTINE. Yes, child.

LENA. Good-bye, Miss Christine.

CHRISTINE. Good-bye.

TONI. (*Enters just as* LENA *is going out.*)

LENA. Good day, Miss Toni.

TONI. Hello, little monkey!

LENA. (*Exit.*)

CHRISTINE (*rises to meet* TONI). Then they are back?

TONI. How should I know?

CHRISTINE. And you haven't any letter, nothing?

TONI. No.

CHRISTINE. You have no letter, either?

TONI. What should we write to each other?

CHRISTINE. They've been gone since day before yesterday.

TONI. Yes, yes, that's not such a long time. You needn't make such a fuss on that account. I don't understand you... and how you look — your face is all tear-stained. Your father will surely notice it when he comes home.

CHRISTINE (*simply*). My father knows everything.

TONI (*almost frightened*). What?

CHRISTINE. I told him.

TONI. That's another of your bright ideas. But of course your face shows everything. And does he know who it is?

CHRISTINE. Yes.

TONI. And did he scold?

CHRISTINE. (*Shakes her head.*)

TONI. What did he say, then?

CHRISTINE. Nothing.... He went away very quietly, as usual.

TONI. And still it was stupid of you to tell. You'll see.... Do you know why your father said nothing? Because he thinks Fritz will marry you.

CHRISTINE. Why do you speak of that?

TONI. Do you know what I think?

CHRISTINE. Well, what?

TONI. That this whole story of a journey is a lie.

CHRISTINE. What?

TONI. Perhaps they haven't gone away at all.

CHRISTINE. They have gone — I know they have. Yesterday evening I went past his house; the blinds were down; he isn't there.

TONI. Oh, I believe that. They're away all right. But they won't come back — at least not to us.

CHRISTINE (*anxiously*). Oh ——

TONI. Well, it's possible.

CHRISTINE. You say that so calmly.

TONI. Why yes — whether it happens today or tomorrow — or in six months — it comes to the same thing.

CHRISTINE. Oh, you don't know what you are saying.... You don't know Fritz.... He isn't like what you think. I found that out when he was here in my room the other day. Often he only pretends to be indifferent — but he does love me.... (*As if she divined* TONI'S *reply.*) Yes, yes, not forever, I know that... but it can't stop all at once!

TONI. Well, I don't know Fritz so well.

CHRISTINE. He will come back, and Theodore will come back too; I am sure of it.

TONI. (*Makes a gesture indicating indifference.*)

CHRISTINE. Toni... do me a favor.

TONI. Don't be so excited — what is it you want?

CHRISTINE. Go to Theodore's, it's right near here.... Ask in the house whether he's got back yet, and if he isn't back, perhaps they'll know when he's coming.

TONI. I'm not going to run after a man.

CHRISTINE. He doesn't need to find it out. Perhaps you'll happen to meet him. It's almost one o'clock now — he'll be just going to lunch.

TONI. Why don't you go and ask at Fritz's house?

CHRISTINE. I'm afraid to — he doesn't like that.... And he is certainly not back yet. But perhaps Theodore is back by now and knows when Fritz is coming. Oh, please Toni!

TONI. You're so childish sometimes.

CHRISTINE. Do it for me! Go and ask! It won't do any harm.

TONI. Well, if it means so much to you I'll go. But it won't do much good. I'm sure they aren't back yet.

CHRISTINE. And you'll come right back, won't you?

TONI. Yes, yes; mother can wait lunch a little.

CHRISTINE. I thank you, Toni, you're so good.

TONI. Of course I'm good — but now you be sensible, won't you?... Well, so long.

CHRISTINE. Oh, thank you!

TONI. (*Exit.*)

CHRISTINE. (*Arranges the room, folds up her sewing, etc. Then she goes to window and looks out. After a moment* VYRING *enters without her seeing him at first. He is in great excitement, looks anxiously at his daughter.*)

VYRING. She knows nothing yet, nothing.

(*He remains standing in the doorway and does not venture to take a step into the room.*)

CHRISTINE. (*Turns, sees him, starts.*)

VYRING (*tries to smile. He steps in*). Well, Christine.... (*As if calling her to him.*)

CHRISTINE. (*Goes to him, as if to fall before him.*)...

VYRING (*prevents her*). Well... what are you thinking of, Christine? We... (*With a new resolve.*) We'll just forget it, shall we?

CHRISTINE. (*Raises her head.*)

VYRING. Why yes... I — and you!

CHRISTINE. Father, didn't you understand me this morning?

VYRING. Well, what would you have, Christine?... I surely must tell you what I think about it, don't you think so? Well, then...

CHRISTINE. Father, what does this mean?

VYRING. Come here, my child.... Listen to me quietly. You know I listened quietly to you, when you told me. We must ——

CHRISTINE. Oh, I beg you, don't speak to me so, father. If you have thought it over, and find that you can't forgive me, then drive me away — but don't speak that way.

VYRING. Just listen quietly to me, Christine. You can still do whatever you will.... See, Christine, you are so young. Haven't you ever thought... (*with great hesitation*) that the whole thing might be a mistake?

CHRISTINE. Why do you say that to me, father? I know so well what I have done — and I don't ask anything — not from you

and not from anybody in the world, if it has been a mistake....
I just told you, drive me away, but...

VYRING (*interrupting*). How can you talk so.... Even if it was a
mistake, is that any reason for getting desperate right away,
such a young creature as you are? Just think how beautiful,
how wonderful life is. Just think how many things there are
to give you joy, how much youth and how much happiness
still lies before you.... See, I don't have much of the world
any more, and even for me life is still beautiful — and I can
still look forward to so many things. How we shall be together — how we shall plan our life, you and I — how you will
begin to sing again, now that the beautiful days are here —
and how we'll take a whole day off, when summer comes, and
go out into the green country — Oh, there are so many lovely
things... so many. It is silly to give up everything, because one
must give up his first happiness, or anything that he thought
was that.

CHRISTINE. Why... (*anxiously*) then must I give it up?

VYRING. Well, was it happiness? Do you really think, Christine,
that you had to tell your father today? I have known it for a
long time — and I knew too that you would tell me. No, it
never was happiness for you.... Don't I know those eyes?
There wouldn't have been tears in them so often, and those
cheeks wouldn't have been pale so much, if you had loved a
man who was worthy of it.

CHRISTINE. Why, how can you... what do you know... what
have you heard?

VYRING. Nothing, nothing at all.... But you yourself told me
what he is.... A young fellow like that — what does he know?
Has he the faintest idea of what falls into his hands — does he
know the difference between the true and the false — and
all your mad love — did he ever understand that?

CHRISTINE (*more and more alarmed*). You and he.... Were you at
his house?

VYRING. Why, what are you thinking of! He went away, didn't
he? But Christine, I still have a head on my shoulders, and my
eyes in my head. Come, child, forget about it, do! Your
future lies in an altogether different place. You can, you

will still be as happy as you deserve. You will find a man sometime who will know what a treasure he has in you.

CHRISTINE. (*Has hurried to the chest of drawers to get her hat.*)

VYRING. What are you doing?

CHRISTINE. I'm going out.

VYRING. Where to?

CHRISTINE. To him... to him.

VYRING. What are you thinking of?

CHRISTINE. You're keeping something from me — let me go.

VYRING (*holding her firmly*). Come to your senses, child. He isn't there at all. Perhaps he's gone away for a very long time.... Stay here; what do you want there?... Tomorrow or this evening I'll go there with you. You can't go out on the street like that... do you know how you look?

CHRISTINE. You will go with me?

VYRING. I promise you I will. Only stay here now; sit down and come to your senses again. It's enough to make a man laugh, almost, to look at you... and all for nothing. Can't you stand it here with your father at all any more?

CHRISTINE. What is it you know?

VYRING (*more and more helpless*). What should I know?... I know that I love you, that you are my only child, that you must stay with me all the time ——

CHRISTINE. Enough — let me go.

(*She wrests herself from him and opens the door;* TONI *appears in it.*)

TONI (*utters a little cry, as* CHRISTINE *rushes toward her*). Why do you frighten me so?

CHRISTINE. (*Steps back, seeing* THEODORE *behind* TONI.)

THEODORE. (*Remains in the doorway; he is dressed in black.*)

CHRISTINE. What... what is... (*No answer. She looks* THEODORE *in the face; he cannot meet her eyes.*) Where is he, where is he?... (*In the greatest terror. No answer; all faces are embarrassed and sad.*) Where is he? (*To* THEODORE.) Speak, can't you?

THEODORE. (*Tries to speak.*)

CHRISTINE (*looks at him wide-eyed, looks around her, comprehends the look on their faces, her face shows the dawn of this understanding, she utters a terrible cry*). Theodore... he is...

THEODORE. (*Nods.*)

CHRISTINE (*seizes her forehead, cannot understand it; she goes to* THEODORE, *takes him by the arm, as if demented*). He is... dead? (*As if asking herself.*)

VYRING. My child ——

CHRISTINE (*thrusting him away*). Speak, Theodore, speak!

THEODORE. You know all.

CHRISTINE. I know nothing.... I don't know what has happened ... do you think... I can't hear everything now?... how did it happen... Father... Theodore... (*To* TONI.) You know it too.

THEODORE. An unfortunate accident.

CHRISTINE. What, what?

THEODORE. He fell.

CHRISTINE. What does that mean: he...

THEODORE. He fell in a duel.

CHRISTINE (*shrieks. She is about to fall,* VYRING *sustains her, motions to* THEODORE *to go. She notes it and seizes him*). Stay here.... I must know all. Do you think you can keep anything from me now?

THEODORE. What else do you want to know?

CHRISTINE. Why — why did he fight a duel?

THEODORE. I don't know the reason.

CHRISTINE. With whom, with whom?... You surely know who killed him?... Well, well, who...

THEODORE. Nobody you know.

CHRISTINE. Who, who?

TONI. Christine!

CHRISTINE Who? You tell me! (*To* TONI.)... Father, you tell me... (*No answer. She starts to go out.* VYRING *holds her back.*) Can't I know who killed him, and for what cause?

THEODORE. It was... a trivial cause...

CHRISTINE. You're not telling the truth... why, why...

THEODORE. Dear Christine....

CHRISTINE (*as if about to interrupt, goes up to him; looks at him in silence, then suddenly shrieks*). On account of a woman?

THEODORE. No ——

CHRISTINE. Yes — for a woman... (*turning to* TONI) for that woman — for that woman that he loved. And her husband — yes,

yes, her husband killed him... And I... what am I? What was I to him?... Theodore... haven't you anything for me at all... didn't he write down anything?... Didn't he tell you anything for me? Didn't you find anything... a letter... a note...

THEODORE. (*Shakes his head.*)

CHRISTINE. And that evening... when he was here, when you came to get him... he knew it, he knew then that he perhaps would never... And he went away from here to be killed for another woman. No, no, it is not possible... didn't he know what he was to me... didn't...

THEODORE. He did know. On the last morning, when we drove out together... he spoke of you too.

CHRISTINE. He spoke of me too! Of me too! And of what else? Of how many other people, of how many other things, that meant just as much to him as I did? Of me too! Oh, God!... And of his father and his mother and his room and of the spring-time and of the city and of everything, everything that belonged to his life and that he had to give up just as much as he gave up me — of everything he talked to you... and of me too...

THEODORE (*moved*). He surely loved you.

CHRISTINE. Love? He? I was nothing to him but a pastime — and he died for another woman! And I — I worshiped him! Didn't he know that?... That I gave him everything I could give, that I would have died for him — that he was my God and my bliss of Heaven — didn't he see that at all? He could go away from me with a smile, out of my room, and be shot down for another woman.... Father, father, can you understand that?

VYRING (*goes to her*). Christine!

THEODORE (*to* TONI). Child, you might have spared me this.

TONI. (*Looks at him venomously.*)

THEODORE. I have had enough distress... these last days...

CHRISTINE (*with sudden resolve*). Theodore, take me to him — I want to see him — once more I want to see him — his face — Theodore, take me to him.

THEODORE (*with a gesture, hesitatingly*). No.....

CHRISTINE. Why "no"? You can't refuse me that! Surely I can see him once more?

THEODORE. It is too late.

CHRISTINE. Too late? To see his corpse... is it too late? Yes... yes... (*She does not understand.*)

THEODORE. He was buried this morning.

CHRISTINE (*with the greatest horror*). Buried... And I didn't know about it? They shot him... and put him in his coffin and carried him out and buried him down in the earth — and I couldn't even see him once more? He's been dead two days — and you didn't come and tell me?

THEODORE (*much moved*). In these two days I have... You cannot dream all that I... Consider that it was my duty to notify his parents — I had to think of many things — and then my own state of mind.

CHRISTINE. Your...

THEODORE. And then the... it was done very quietly.... Only the closest relatives and friends...

CHRISTINE. The closest ——? And I ——?... What am I?

TONI. They would have asked that.

CHRISTINE. What am I? Less than all the rest ——? Less than his relatives, less than — you?

VYRING. My child, my child. Come to me, to me... (*He embraces her. To* THEODORE.) Go... leave me alone with her.

THEODORE. I am very... (*With tears in his voice.*) I never suspected...

CHRISTINE. Never suspected what? That I loved him? (VYRING *draws her to him;* THEODORE *looks down;* TONI *stands near* CHRISTINE. *Freeing herself.*) Take me to his grave!

VYRING. No, no ——

TONI. Don't go, Christine.

THEODORE. Christine... later... tomorrow... when you are calmer ——

CHRISTINE. Tomorrow? When I shall be calmer? And in a month completely consoled, eh? And in six months I can laugh again, can I? (*Laughing shrilly.*) And then when will the next lover come?

VYRING. Christine...

CHRISTINE. Stay here, then... I can find the way alone...

VYRING AND TONI (*together*). Don't go.

CHRISTINE. It's even better... if I... let me go, let go.

VYRING. Christine, stay here.

TONI. Don't go! Perhaps you'll find the other one there — praying.

CHRISTINE (*to herself, her eyes fixed*). I won't pray there... no...
(*She rushes out; the others speechless for the moment.*)

VYRING. Hurry after her.   (THEODORE *and* TONI *exeunt.*)

VYRING. I can't, I can't... (*He goes painfully from the door to the window.*)   What does she want... what does she want...
(*He looks through the window.*)   She won't come back — she won't
come back!   (*He sinks to the floor, sobbing loudly.*)

THE END

FRANCESCA DA RIMINI

By GABRIELE D'ANNUNZIO

GABRIELE D'ANNUNZIO

GABRIELE D'ANNUNZIO, whose real name is said to be Rapagnetta, was born on board the yacht *Irene* on the Adriatic in 1863. His childhood was spent in Abruzzi; in 1878 he was at school in Tuscany. By 1890 he was writing verse for the ultra-modern *Cronica Bizantina*, had joined a fashionable and fast society, and was writing voluptuous autobiographical fiction. As a poet he was influenced by Carducci; his first volume of verse was *Primo Vere*. His first dramatic works were published in *La Nuova Antologia* in 1897 and in *Mattino di Napoli* in 1898. These are three parables in verse, not for production, based on the parables of the Foolish and Wise Virgins, the Rich Man and Poor Lazarus, and the Prodigal Son. With his two *Dreams of the Seasons* his active career as a dramatist begins. During his most important period as a dramatist he was under the influence of the great Eleanora Duse, for whom his best plays were written, and who gave them in production the stamp of her incomparable genius. D'Annunzio's chief plays are *The Dead City*, *Gioconda*, *Francesca da Rimini*, and *The Daughter of Jorio*. A poet of a wide but perhaps shallow erudition, especially in out-of-the-way places, in the occult and in the bizarre, there is a note of eccentricity in D'Annunzio's work. But this does not reduce the sheer dramatic sweep of his drama or the beauty of his verse. During and after the World War his genius turned away from the romance of the imagination to an equally imaginative intrusion into political and nationalistic affairs.

FRANCESCA DA RIMINI

It is interesting to compare Maeterlinck's *Pelléas and Mélisande* and D'Annunzio's *Francesca da Rimini*. The legends upon which they are based are similar if not derived from the same source. But while Maeterlinck's play is written for a new theater, employing standards of production which had not yet been worked out, were indeed as yet hardly guessed by the playwright himself, D'Annunzio's play is clearly composed as a vehicle for the romantic orders of production. While Maeterlinck's method impedes expression and breaks it into fragments, D'Annunzio's method magnifies expression and pours it forth through tirades of eloquence. While D'Annunzio glorifies the actor, Maeterlinck reduces the actor to a puppet. While D'Annunzio's play is a tragedy of contending wills, Maeterlinck's play is a tragedy of fate without will. This is to say that *Francesca da Rimini* is an almost perfect example of the modern romantic play. Needless to say it does not follow directly in the path of nineteenth-century dramatic romance. There is much more of Alfred de Vigny in it than of Victor Hugo. Probably the most impressionable of modern playwrights, D'Annunzio is not a man of the theater first and foremost. His plays have been written under a multitude of influences, from Greek tragedy down, and all have been written at white heat. Perhaps that is the reason why, when the flame died down, he could write no more plays. But the plays written at the top of his genius are the best examples of free romantic imagination at work in the theater of our time. *Francesca da Rimini* is written in blank verse, of a flexible order approaching *vers libre*. In style it is influenced by Leopardi. Symons says that the play is more than a tragedy of two lovers. It is a study of an age of blood, the thirteenth century in Italy. At the first presentation of the play by the company of Eleanora Duse at the Teatro Costanzi in Rome, December 9, 1901, the production took five hours. Its reception was tumultuous. Translated by Arthur Symons, it was published in English in 1902. It was translated into French in the *Revue de Paris*, 1910–11, by Georges Hérelle, who also translated *The Daughter of Jorio*. A musical version was made by Riccardo Zandonai. The play was presented at the Playhouse, Cleveland, in 1924.

CHARACTERS

OSTASIO
BANNINO
FRANCESCA
SAMARITANA } *Sons and Daughters of* GUIDO MINORE DA POLENTA

BIANCOFIORE
ALDA
GARSENDA
ALTICHIARA
ADONELLA
The Slave } *Francesca's Women*

SER TOLDO BERARDENGO
ASPINELLO ARSENDI
VIVIANO DE' VIVII
BERTRANDO LURO
An Archer } *Partisans of* GUIDO

GIOVANNI, "The Lame,"
known as GIANCIOTTO
PAOLO "The Beautiful"
MALATESTINO "The
One-eyed" } *Sons of* MALATESTA DA VERRUCCHIO

ODDO DALLE CAMINATE
FOSCOLO D'OLNANO
Archers
Men-at-Arms } *Partisans of* MALATESTA

The Merchant.   The Merchant's Boy.   The Doctor.
The Jester.   The Astrologer.   The Musicians.
The Torchbearers.

The action takes place in Ravenna and Rimini, in the thirteenth century.

ACT ONE

A Court in the House of the Polentani, adjacent to a garden that shines brightly through a marble screen, pierced in the form of a transept. A loggia runs round it above, leading on the right to the women's apartments, and in front, supported on small pillars, affords a double view. On the left is a flight of steps leading down to the threshold of the enclosed garden. At the back is a large door, and a low, barred window, through which can be seen a range of arches surrounding another larger court. Near the steps is a Byzantine sarcophagus, without a lid, filled with earth, like a flower pot, in which grows a crimson rosebush.

The WOMEN *are seen, leaning over the loggia, and coming down the stairs, gazing curiously at the* JESTER, *who carries his viol hanging by his side, and in his hand an old jerkin.*

ALDA. Jester, hey, Jester!

GARSENDA. Adonella, Adonella, here is the Jester
  In the court! O Biancofiore,
  The Jester! he has come!

ADONELLA. Are the gates open yet?

BIANCOFIORE. Let's make the Jester sing.

ALDA. Hey, tell me, are you that Gianni...

JESTER. Sweet ladies...

ALDA. That Gianni who was coming from Bologna?
  Gian Figo?

GARSENDA. Are you Gordello who is coming from Ferrara?

JESTER. Dear ladies...

ADONELLA. What are you seeking there?

JESTER. The trail of the scent.

BIANCOFIORE. We brew in limbecs oils of lavender,
  And oils of spikenard.

JESTER. I am no apothecary's pedlar, I.

ALTICHIARA. You shall have a bunch though, my good nightingale,
  If you will sing.

GARSENDA. Look at him, how he droops!

JESTER. Fair ladies, have you...

BIANCOFIORE. Yes,

Heaps upon heaps.

ADONELLA. Bags full

And coffers full of it. Madonna Francesca

Can dip her beauty, if she has a mind to,

In oil of lavender.

JESTER. I thought rather to find the smell of blood

In the house of Guido.

ALDA. Blood of the Traversari: in the streets,

In the streets you will find it.

ALL. Polenta! Polenta! Down with the Traversari!

JESTER. Heigho! Catch who catch can, go free who may!

The sparrows are becoming sparrow-hawks.

(*Shouts of laughter ring down the staircase, between the twi-
horned head-dresses.*)

ALL. Grapple with the Ghibelline!

JESTER. Be quiet now, don't let the archer hear you,

Or he will fetch me suddenly such a bolt

As will lay me out my length for all my life.

ALDA. You swear you are a Guelph?

JESTER. By San Mercuriale of Forlì

(That sets the belfry crumbling on the pate

Of the Feltran people) I tell you I am Guelph,

As Guelph as Malatesta da Verrucchio.

GARSENDA. Good then, you are safe; only be circumspect:

You have leave to smell.

JESTER. To smell? And not to eat?

I am a dog, then?

How many bitches are there in the place?

Let's see.

(*He goes down on hands and feet like a dog, and makes for the
women.*)

GARSENDA. Ah, nasty dog!

ALDA. Filthy dog!

ALTICHIARA. Wicked dog!

Take that!

JESTER. Ahi, ahi, you have smashed my viol,

You have broken my bow.

ADONELLA. Take that!

GARSENDA. And that!

BIANCOFIORE. And that!

JESTER. They are all in heat!

I would I knew which one of you the most!

> (*They all strike him on the back with their fists, laughing. And as the* JESTER *jumps about amongst them like a dog, they begin to dance round him, shaking out their perfumed skirts.*)

BIANCOFIORE. Take hands, and dance a round!

ADONELLA. Do you smell the spice,
Lavender and spikenard?

ALTICHIARA. I am flame and ice,
I am flame and ice!

BIANCOFIORE. Fresh in cool linen is sweet lavender!

ALDA. Come in, bright eyes, into my garden fair!

ALTICHIARA. An odour comes, no garden can I find.

ADONELLA. How comes this lovely odour on the wind?

ALL. Smell! Smell!

GARSENDA. Sweet shift that long in lavender has lain;
Sweetheart, the time of May has come again.

ALL. Smell! Smell!

ADONELLA. I would I had my sweetheart near my side,
And nearer than my shift is near to me.
Dear love is dear to me!
Dear love is dear to me!

ALL. Smell! smell! smell!

JESTER (*standing up and trying to catch one of them*). Catch who catch can!

If I catch one of you...

> (*With cries of laughter, they run up the stairs, then stand panting with merriment.*)

ALDA (*with a contemptuous gesture*). You are no sheep dog, you!

GARSENDA. You are a pantry dog.
Poor Jester! have you not
More stomach now for food than bantering?

JESTER (*scratching his throat*). Maybe I have. I dined some while ago.
Fine scents fill no lean paunches.

GARSENDA. Well then, well,

Go rather to the Archbishop Bonifazio,
He is the biggest glutton
That eats in the world: the Genoese. This house
Is Guido da Polenta's.

JESTER. Yellow with flower of the black hellebore
Because there is no juniper in the world,
May all be salt to me,
Ravenna women have it... in the round,
Salt be to me!

GARSENDA. Round-pated you yourself!
You thought to get the better of us, eh?
We have got the better of you.

BIANCOFIORE. Sing, Jester!

ALDA. Dance, Jester!

JESTER (*picking up his rag*). You have pulled me all to pieces,
Mischief o' me! Have you, by chance, a little...

GARSENDA. A little bacon?

JESTER. Have you a little scarlet?

ADONELLA. Are you for jesting with us? We are ready.

BIANCOFIORE. But who are you? that Gianni...

ALTICHIARA. O, Biancofiore, look what clothes he has!
The doublet is at loggerheads with the hose.

GARSENDA. He is Gian Figo, who was coming from Bologna.

BIANCOFIORE. Come from Bologna without a bolognino.

ALDA. I am sure he is of the Lambertazza party.

GARSENDA. An evil race!

ALDA. He has been put to shame
By the Geremei.

ALTICHIARA. Have you not lost a princedom, noble sir?

GARSENDA. O, Adonella, look at him: he has fled
In nothing but his trousers.

JESTER. And you will have them off me.

ADONELLA. What a poor thing! Look at yourself in the glass,
As crooked as a cross-bow on its stock.

BIANCOFIORE. Now you will sing the spoiling of Bologna,
And how King Enzo was made prisoner.

GARSENDA. Have I not told you he is from Ferrara?

JESTER (*impatiently*). I am from Ferrara and I am from Bologna.

GARSENDA. Was it then you
  Who escorted from Bologna to Ferrara
  Ghisolabella de' Caccianimici
  To the good Marchese Opizzo?
JESTER. Just so, just so, 'twas I, just as you say.
GARSENDA. It was you too who made
  The match between the sister of the Marquese
  And that old and rich judge, him of Gallura,
  A shrivelled, wizened thing
  That had the help of his big man-servant?
JESTER. Just so, 'twas I, just as you say; and I had
  In thanks for it...
ALDA. A bone?
ADONELLA. Two chestnuts?
BIANCOFIORE. Three
  Walnuts and a hazel-nut?
ALTICHIARA. A stump of pimpernel?
GARSENDA. A pair of snails
  And an acorn?
JESTER. This mantle that you see, of Irish frieze?
  No; or of purple Tyrian samite? no;
  But all of velvet crimson-coloured, lined
  With skins of miniver.
GARSENDA. Look, look, Altichiara,
  The thing he is holding!
ALTICHIARA. A little threadbare cloak.
GARSENDA. No, no, it is a Romagna jerkin.
ALDA. Then
  You are Gordello, you are not Gian Figo.
ADONELLA. But no, he is a Jew.
BIANCOFIORE. He is the huckster Lotto
  Of Porto Sisi.
ALTICHIARA. Sells fripperies and songs.
ADONELLA. What have you with you?
  Have you rags or ballads?
JESTER. Fool that I am, I thought to find myself
  In the palace of the nobles of Polenta,
  And here I am in a chirping nest of swallows.

GARSENDA. Comfort yourself, I am satisfied by now
    That I have taught you, Master Merrymaker,
    Ravenna women are not easily beaten
    At the game of banter.
JESTER. And of the pole, too.
GARSENDA. You chuckle over it?
ADONELLA. Will you whet your whistle?
BIANCOFIORE. No, Alda: come now, make him sing to us.
GARSENDA. Do you not see the sorry sort of viol
    He trails here, Adonella?
    It seems to me a sort of pumpkin cowled,
    With its big belly and its monstrous neck.
    The rose is meanly cut,
    Here's a peg missing, here
    The bass and tierce are gone.
    Well, if he barks, his viol gapes in answer.
    Go, scrawl arpeggios
    Upon a rebeck, let the bow alone.
BIANCOFIORE. You let the joke alone, then, Mona Berta.
    Let us see now if he knows how to sing.
    Come on then, Jester,
    And sing us, if you can, a pretty song.
    Do you know any of that Troubadour
    Who calls himself the Notary of Lentino?
    Madonna Francesca knows a lovely one
    Beginning this way: "Very mightily
    Love holds me captive." Do you know the song?
JESTER. Yes, I will say it now,
    If you have a little scarlet.
ALTICHIARA. But what is it you want then, with your scarlet?
ADONELLA. We are waiting, we are waiting!
JESTER. I want you, if you will,
    To put a patch for me
    Upon this jerkin.
ALTICHIARA. What a mad idea,
    To patch Romagna woollen, and with scarlet!
JESTER. I pray you, if you have it, do for me
    This service. There is one tear here, in front,

Another on the elbow; here it is.
Have you two scraps?

ALTICHIARA. I will put it right for you
If you will sing to us.
But I assure you, 'tis a novelty
To set the two together.

JESTER. I go about in search of novelties,
As novel as myself:
That's just the reason.
But not long since I found a novelty,
As I was on my way:
I met with one,
Not two miles out of here,
That had his head of iron,
His legs of wood, and talked with both his shoulders.

BIANCOFIORE. This is a novelty in very deed,
But tell us how.

ADONELLA. We are waiting! we are waiting!

JESTER. Listen, and I will tell you. I met with one
That wore an iron headpiece on his head
And went to gather fir-cones in the wood
Here at Ravenna, and he went on crutches,
And when I asked him had he seen about
A little friend of mine, he shrugged his shoulders,
Saying by this means
He had not seen him.

BIANCOFIORE (contemptuously). But this is a true thing.

JESTER. Am I not novel,
That tell true things for fables? Catch who catch can!
So, you will do then what I asked of you?
And after you have done it,
You shall wait no great while before you learn,
The occasion offering, that Gian Figo...

GARSENDA. Ah!
You have let it out at last.

ALL. He is Gian Figo!

JESTER. Before you learn Gian Figo is as wise
As Dinadan the King of Orbeland's son,
That found his wisdom by forgetting love.

ALTICHIARA. But now enough of this: time for a song!

BIANCOFIORE. "There comes a time to rise..."

    Do you not know the song King Enzo made,
    The King that lost his kingdom in a battle
    Against Bologna, and was put in prison
    In a big iron cage, and ended his life there,
    Singing his sorrows?
    Seven years ago in March: I can remember,
    "There comes a time to rise, a time to fall,
    A time for speaking and for keeping silence."

ADONELLA. No, no, Gian Figo,

    Tell us instead the song
    Made by King John, John of Jerusalem,
    "For the flower of all the lands."

GARSENDA. No, tell us that of good King Frederick,

    "A song of pure delight"
    (Madonna Francesca, the flower of all Ravenna
    Knows it) made for the flower
    Of Soria when the sire of Suabia
    Loved a most worthy maiden
    His wife had brought with her from over sea,
    And brought to honour; and this wife of the King
    Of Suabia was no other than the daughter
    Of John, King of Jerusalem, and her name
    Was Isabella, and she died, and then
    King Frederick took for his wife the sister
    Of the simple Henry of England; and he loved her
    Exceedingly, because, like our Madonna
    Francesca, she was skilled
    In music, and all ways of lovely speech;
    And this was the third wedding; and she, then,
    That sang and played all day and all night long,
    Had...   (BIANCOFIORE *covers her mouth with her hand.*)

JESTER. What a bibble babble! O poor King Enzo,

    There never is a time here to be silent.
    What's to be done with all your merchandise,
    Gian Figo, chitter, chatter, chattering,
    Here are four voices, and more like a thousand!

ALTICHIARA. Listen to me now, Jester. Let the King
Alone. He is dead and buried. Say instead
"O mother mine,
Give me a husband." "Tell me why, my child."
"That he may give me happy..."

ALDA. That is old:
Listen to me, Jester.

ALTICHIARA. Then, "Monna Lapa,
She spun and span..."

ALDA. No!

ALTICHIARA. Then: "O garden-close,
I enter and nobody knows."

ALDA. Hush!

ALTICHIARA. Then: "Let's all
Have seven lovers,
That's one for every day of the week."

ALDA. Hush!

ALTICHIARA. Then:
"Monna Aldruda, don't be a prude, a
Piece of good news..."

ALDA. O hush! Biancofiore,
Do shut her mouth. Jester, listen to me:
These are old songs...

ADONELLA. There's a new troubadour
Known at Bologna: surely you have heard him?
He's the new fashion;
They call him Messer Guido... Messer Guido
Di...di...

JESTER. Di Guinizello.
He was one that went out with the Lambertazzi,
Took refuge at Verona, and there died.

ALDA. Good, let him die: he's for the Emperor.
May he go now and make his rhymes in hell!
Listen to me, Jester; tell us a story
Of knights.

BIANCOFIORE. Yes, yes, the knights of the Round Table!
Do you know their stories?
The love of Iseult of the golden hair?

JESTER. I know the histories of all the knights
And all the knightly deeds of chivalry
Done in King Arthur's time,
And specially I know of Messer Tristan
And Messer Lancelot of the Lake, and Messer
Percival of the Grail, that took the blood
Of our Lord Jesus Christ, and of Galahad,
And of Gawain, and the rest. I know them all.

ALDA. Of Guenevere?

ADONELLA. Good luck, Jester, good luck!
We will tell Madonna Francesca what you know,
Will we not, Alda?
She takes delight in them;
Jester, she will reward you bountifully.

JESTER. She will give me the remainder...

ADONELLA. What remainder?

JESTER. Why, the two scraps of scarlet.

ADONELLA. She will give you
Quite other gifts, the bountifullest gifts.
Rejoice that she is marrying;
Messer Guido marries her to a Malatesta;
The wedding day is close at hand.

BIANCOFIORE. Meanwhile
Tell us a story: we are all ears. "There is time
To listen," said the prisoner.

(*They group themselves about the* JESTER, *leaning towards him:
he begins.*)

JESTER. How the fay Morgana sent to Arthur's Court
The shield foretelling the great love to be
Between good Tristan and the flower-like Iseult;
And this shall be between the loveliest lady
And the most knightly knight in all the world.
And how Iseult and Tristan drank together
The draught of love that Iseult's mother, Lotta,
Had destined for her daughter and King Mark.
And how the draught of love, being perfect, brought
Both these two lovers to one single death.

(*The* WOMEN *stand listening, the* JESTER *preludes on the viol and
sings.*)

Now, when the dawn of day was nigh at hand,
King Mark of Cornwall and good Tristan rose...

THE VOICE OF OSTASIO (*behind the scenes*). Tell him, the Puglian thief,
Tell him, I say, that I will wash my hands
And feet in his heart's blood!

ALDA. Messer Ostasio!

GARSENDA. Come away, come, come!

    (*They scatter, and rush up the stairs, with laughter and cries
    and along the loggia.*)

JESTER. My jerkin, my good jerkin! I commend you,
My jerkin, and the scarlet!

ALTICHIARA (*leaning over the loggia*). Come back at noon:
It shall be ready.

(OSTASIO DA POLENTA *enters by the great door at the back, accompanied
by* SER TOLDO BERARDENGO.)

OSTASIO (*seizing the terrified* JESTER). What are you doing here, rascal?
Who were you talking with, the women? How
Did you come here? Answer me, I say. Are you
From Messer Paola Malatesta? Now,
Answer!

JESTER. O sir, you are holding me too hard.
Ahi!

OSTASIO. Did you come here with Messer Paolo?

JESTER. No, sir.

OSTASIO. You lie!

JESTER. Yes, sir.

OSTASIO. You were talking with
The women; what did you say? something, no doubt,
Concerning Messer Paolo. What was it?

JESTER. No, sir, no, sir, only of Messer Tristan.

OSTASIO. Take care — you do not trifle with me twice,
Or you shall keep this tryst of yours with Tristan
Longer than you intend, unseemly fool.

JESTER. Ahi, ahi! what have I done to vex you, sir?
I was only singing something.
I was only singing a song of the Round Table.
The ladies asked me for a history

Of knights... I am a Jester and I sing
From hunger, and my hunger
Hoped better things than beating in the house
Of the most noble Messer Guido. I,
That keep no hack, have footed
From the Castle of Calbeli
All the way here: I left
Messer Rinieri fortifying his keep
With some seven hundred strong
Of infantry.

OSTASIO. You come from Calbeli?

JESTER. Yes, sir.

OSTASIO. Were you ever with the Malatesti
    At Rimino?

JESTER. No, sir; never, sir.

OSTASIO. Then
You do not know Messer Paolo, the Beautiful,
That dotes on jesters, and would have them sing
And play at all times in his company?

JESTER. Unluckily I do not know him, sir,
But I would gladly know him. And if I find him,
I pray to be found always at his side.
Long life to Messer Paolo Malatesta!

(He is about to retire hastily. OSTASIO *catches hold of him again
    and calls the* ARCHER *who is on guard in the other Court.)*

OSTASIO. Jacomello!

JESTER. What have I done, and why
Do you do me violence?

OSTASIO. Too much talk.

JESTER. I am mute.
It is hunger barking in me. Keep me prisoner
In the kitchen, and I will be as still as oil.

OSTASIO. Will you be silent, rascal? Jacomello!
I give this prattle-seller to your charge,
See that you bit and bib him.

JESTER. A spice cake,
Give me a spice cake.

OSTASIO. Give him a box on the ears.

JESTER (*as the* ARCHER *thrusts him out*). When Madonna Francesca
    knows how you have used me...
    I am to sing at her wedding.
    Long life to Messer Paolo Malatesta!
        (*Raging, and full of suspicion,* OSTASIO *draws the* NOTARY *to-
        wards the sarcophagus.*)

OSTASIO. These jesters and the like men of the Court
    Here in Romagna are a very plague,
    Worse than the Emperor's rabble. They are tongues
    Of women; they know everything, say everything;
    They go about the world
    Spreading abroad their news and novelties;
    Their ears are at the keyholes of us all.
    Who wants to know how the good Papal Rector
    Lay with the wife of Lizio da Valbona?
    Who wants to know
    How much Rinieri da Calbeli has taken
    Out of the purses of the Geremei?
    As for this rascal
    That gossiped with the women of Francesca,
    If he had been a jester
    Of the Malatesti
    By now the women had heard all the news
    There is to tell of Paolo,
    And all the cunning plan had been vain,
    Ser Toldo, that you counselled
    Out of your manifold wisdom.

SER TOLDO. As for him,
    He was so poor and threadbare,
    How could I take him for a follower
    Of such a lordly knight as Paolo,
    He being so bountiful
    With gentry such as these?
    But you are well-advised in bitting him.
    These creatures of the Court
    May be by way of being soothsayers,
    And often steal the trade
    Of the astrologers.

OSTASIO. True. And this slave
    Of Cyprus, that my sister loves so dearly,
    I have my doubts of her; she too, I think,
    Is something of a soothsayer; I know
    That she interprets dreams. The other day
    I saw my sister full of heavy thoughts,
    And almost sorrowful,
    As if some evil dream had come to her;
    And only yesterday
    I heard her heave such a long, heavy sigh
    As if she had a trouble in her heart,
    And I heard Samaritana
    Say to her: "What is it, sister? Why do you weep?"
SER TOLDO. Messer Ostasio, it is the month of May.
OSTASIO. In truth there is no peace for us until
    This marriage is well over. And I fear,
    Ser Toldo, lest some scandal come of it.
SER TOLDO. Yet you know well, what sort
    Of woman is your sister, and how high
    Of heart and mind. If she see this Gianciotto,
    So lamed and bent, and with those eyes of his,
    As of an angry devil,
    Before the marriage-contract
    Be signed and sealed, why, neither will your father
    Nor you, nor any, of a certainty
    Bring her to take
    The man for husband, not although you set
    Your dagger at her throat, or haled her through
    Ravenna by the hair.
OSTASIO. I know it well, Ser Toldo, for my father
    Gave her for foster-mother
    A sword of his of a miraculous edge,
    That he had tempered in Cesena blood
    When he was Podestà.
SER TOLDO. Well then, I say,
    If this be so, and you desire the match,
    There is no other way to compass it.
    And seeing that Paolo Malatesta comes

As procurator of Gianciotto here,
And with full powers
For the betrothal of Madonna Francesca,
I say you should proceed
Instantly to the marriage,
If you would sleep in peace, Messer Ostasio.
Paolo is a fair and pleasant youth,
And makes a brave decoy,
Undoubtedly; yet it is far too easy
To learn that he is married to Orabile.
And you, did you not beat this jester but
For fear of idle talk?

OSTASIO. Yes, you are right,
Ser Toldo; we must put an end to this.
My father is returning from Valdoppio
This very night; we will have all prepared
And ready for tomorrow.

SER TOLDO. Very good,
Messer Ostasio.

OSTASIO. Yet... What will come of it?

SER TOLDO. If you do all, as all this should be done,
With secrecy and prudence, Madonna Francesca
Will find out nothing till at Rimino,
She wakes, the morning after
Her wedding day, and sees
Beside her...

OSTASIO. Ah, it is like some vile revenge!

SER TOLDO. And sees beside her rise
Gianciotto.

OSTASIO. O, she is so beautiful!
And we avenge ourselves upon her beauty,
Almost as if she wronged our house and us
In coming to be born
Here like a flower in the midst of so much iron.
We are giving her to the lame Malatesta
For the sake of that poor hundred infantry!
But is she not herself
Worth more than all the lordship of Romagna?

False notary, how did you poison first
My father's mind? All this
Is your base bargaining. I will not have it.
Do you understand?

SER TOLDO. Why, what tarantula bites you,
Messer Ostasio?
Surely you will not find
A better match to make in all Romagna?

OSTASIO. The Malatesti? Who then after all
Are these Verrucchio folk? By this alliance
Shall we have got Cesena,
Cervia, Faenza, Forlì, Civitella,
Half of Romagna?
A hundred infantry!
To hunt the Traversara region, O
The mighty succour!
And Dovadella, and Zello, and Montaguto
Already in our power perhaps. Gianciotto!
But who is he, Gianciotto? When I think
How that Traversarian widow,
That ancient scabby bitch, has mated with
(After the nephew of the Pope) the son
Of Andrea, the King of Hungary....

SER TOLDO. What is the King of Hungary to you?

OSTASIO. But here are we, with this
Puglian clodhopper,
This Guglielmetto that now vaunts himself
As the legitimate heir
Of Paolo Traversari,
And harries us; and we shall never break him
With this mere hundred infantry, and he
Will surely come again with help from Foglia.
What shall we hope for then
From Malatesta?

SER TOLDO. Malatesta is the chief of all the Guelphs
Now in Romagna, and the chief defender
Of the Church, and he has the favour of the Pope,
And he was made the governor of Florence

Under King Charles, and whosoever seeks
A captain......

OSTASIO. Notary!
Guido di Montefeltro shattered him,
Once, at the bridge of San Procolo. Notary,
Guglielmino de' Pazzi drove him back
At Reversano, and has made him since
Give up the fortress of Cesena.

SER TOLDO. Ay,
But the victory at Colle di Valdelsa
Against the Sienese,
The time he slaughtered Provenzan Salvani?
But when he made Count Guido prisoner
On the borders of Ancona, and brought him back,
Him and his men, to Rimino? But when
He intercepted
The famous secret letters
From the Emperor Baldwin to King Manfred? Come,
In truth it seems to me,
Messer Ostasio,
Your memory is then no longer Guelph.

OSTASIO. If the Devil comes to me and lends me a hand
That I may root and ruin the evil race
Of the slave Pasquetta and the Puglian hag,
I am for the Devil, notary.

SER TOLDO. Ah, ah! I guessed the truth:
It is the tarantula of Puglia bites you.

OSTASIO. The Emperor Frederick (God, for this thing
Grant him a cup of water down in hell!)
Had utterly destroyed the seed of them,
When he hurled Aica Traversari headlong
Into the fiery furnace.
And lo, one day there comes into Ravenna
A certain slave, Pasquetta, with her sweetheart,
And tells you: "I am Aica,"
And comes on one Filippo, an Archbishop,
And he affirms her the legitimate heir,
And with the taking over of the Dukedom

Makes her the lady mistress! And from that
The filthy vagabond of a husband holds
The headship of the very Ghibelline party
Against the house of Polenta! O Ser Toldo,
Now we are doing deeds of chivalry
Against Guglielmo Francisio, bastard
Of shepherd-folk. Do you understand?

SER TOLDO.   But you,
Have you not driven him out of Ravenna?

OSTASIO.   With the infantry of Gianciotto Malatesta?

SER TOLDO.   You are ungrateful, Messer Ostasio.
Gianciotto Malatesta in two days
Broke all the bars and gratings in the streets;
Between Sant' Agata and Porta San Mamante,
He massacred the gang
Of the Anastagi;
Between San Simone and Porta San Vittore
His heavy cross-bolts cleared
The whole pack in a breath.
Nor is he ever one to spare himself,
But proved his courage,
There, with a buckler braced about his arm,
A rapier in his hand;
And always in the crush
Set on his priceless horse,
A raging beast that gave his enemies
What travail more he could, so that he had
Always some dozen more or less of men
Under his horse's hoof; and Stefano
Sibaldo, that stood by,
Swears, when the Lamester does
A feat of arms, it is beautiful to see him;
He is a master in the art of war!

OSTASIO.   O Ser Toldo, you had certainly your share
Of the booty! You will take away their skill
From those who sang the song of the twelve barons
Of Charlemagne,
Lord of the flowing beard. How much, I pray,
Came to your share?

SER TOLDO. The tarantula of Puglia
    Is a certain sort of spider,
    That brings all kinds of luck to those he bites.
    I am not now, alas,
    All that I have been once!
    But the Malatesti always have been ill
    Bearers of shame, and now Gianciotto knows
    The way by which one gets inside the walls
    Here at Ravenna.... But you might give your sister,
    No doubt, to the Prince Royal of Salerno,
    Or to the Doge of Venice.

OSTASIO (absorbed). Ah! is she
    Not worth a kingdom? How beautiful she is!
    There never was a sword that went so straight
    As her eyes go, if they but look at you.
    Yesterday she was saying: "Who is it
    You give me to?" When she walks, and her hair
    Falls all about her to her waist, and down
    To her strong knees (she is strong, though very pale)
    And her head sways a little, she gives forth joy
    Like flags that wave in the wind
    When one sets forth against a mighty city
    In polished armour. Then
    She seems as if she held
    The eagle of Polenta
    Fast in her fist, like a trained hawk, to fling him
    Forth to the prey. Yesterday she was saying:
    "Who is it you give me to?"
    Why should I see her die?

SER TOLDO. Now you might give your sister
    To the King of Hungary
    Or better, to the Paleologue.

OSTASIO. Be silent,
    Ser Toldo, for today
    I am not patient.

THE VOICE OF BANNINO. Ostasio! Ostasio!

OSTASIO. By God! here is Bannino, here is the bastard
    That pants and lolls his tongue.
    I knew it.

(BANNINO *appears at the door at the back of the stage, panting
    and dishevelled, like a fugitive, with* ASPINELLO ARSENDI,
    VIVIANO DE' VIVII, *and* BERTRANDO LURO, *who are bleeding
    and covered with dust.*)

BANNINO. Ostasio!

The men of Forlì have attacked the waggons
Of salt, by Cervia;
They have put to flight the convoy and overturned
The waggons....

OSTASIO (*shouting*). Ah, I knew it!
But they have not cut your throat?

ASPINELLO. The Ghibellines that were exiled from Bologna,
With those too of Faenza and Forlì
Gather in companies over all the land
And are laying all things waste with fire and sword.

OSTASIO. Jesu our Lord, good tidings for your Vicar!

VIVIANO. And they have burned Monte Vecchio, Valcapra,
Pianetto. They have laid waste Strabatanza and Biserno
For Lizio da Valbona,
They have laid waste, for the Count
Ugo da Cerfugnano,
The country of Rontana and of Quarmento.

OSTASIO. God of mercy, still good tidings,
Good things to thy servants, and good tidings!

BERTRANDO. Guido di Montefeltro
Takes horse to Calbeli
With engines, and balistas;
And he will have the castle.

OSTASIO. More! More!
Christ Jesus, to thy praise always!

VIVIANO. There was Scarpetta
Of the Ordelaffi with the Forlì folk.

BANNINO. They have put to flight the convoy and overturned
The waggons and taken cattle
And horses, and have killed
Malvincino da Lozza
And many soldiers, and made prisoner
Pagano Coffa; and the others in disorder
Have fled in search of safety towards the sea.

OSTASIO. And you, you towards the land,
  As fast as horse could carry you. I knew it,
  I knew it well.
  Where did you leave your sword?
  And you have thrown away your helmet too.
  Save himself he who can! That is your cry.

BANNINO. My sword? I broke my sword
  In the very rage of striking blows with it.
  There were three hundred, maybe four, against us.
  Aspinello, Bertrando,
  Say, both of you, and you
  Viviano, say if I did well or no.
  I had against me more than twenty men
  That would have taken me; and I carved my life
  With my own hand out of their flesh and bone.
  Say, all of you!

OSTASIO. You see
  They cannot answer for you; they are tasked
  To stanch the flowing of their blood, and wipe
  The dust away that clings about their faces.
  But you are clean, you; cuirass, sleeves, all clean,
  Spotless. Your enemies
  Had got no veins then in their bodies? You
  Have not a scratch upon your whited face,
  O mighty man of valour in your words!

    (*The* THREE SOLDIERS, *taking their harness off their backs,
    and wiping it, move away.*)

BANNINO. Ostasio! Ostasio! Enough!

OSTASIO. I knew it well,
  I had but laughter when
  My father picked you out
  To lead the waggon safely in. I said:
  "May the good Bishop of Cervia
  Preserve him with his crozier! In Ravenna
  'Tis very certain we shall have no salt."
  Did I say wrong? Go, go, Bannino, go
  And mince the lungs of hares into a dish
  For sparrow-hawks.

BANNINO. You should be silent. You,
    While I was in the fray,
    Stayed safe at home, plotting with notaries.

OSTASIO. O lord and leader of harlots, you shall know
    That if the men of Forlì did not catch you,
    Because you were too nimble,
    'Tis I will catch you.

BANNINO. What? with treachery,
    After your fashion?

OSTASIO. I will do it so that you,
    This time at least, do not go whimpering home
    To tell my father.

SER TOLDO. Peace! Peace!

BANNINO. I will tell him
    Something I know, this time.

OSTASIO. What do you know?

BANNINO. You know the thing I mean.

SER TOLDO. Peace, peace, O peace!
    Be brothers!

OSTASIO. He is from another nest.

SER TOLDO. Messer Ostasio, he is but a boy.

OSTASIO. Speak then, if you know how to wound a man
    At any rate with your tongue.

BANNINO. You know the thing
    I mean. I keep my counsel.

OSTASIO. No, pour out
    Your gall, that is now painted in your face,
    Or I will wring you up as if I wrung
    A wet rag out.

BANNINO. Ostasio,
    I am not so skilled in pouring out my gall
    As you your wine
    With an unshaken hand.

OSTASIO. What wine?

BANNINO. Your wine, pure wine, pure wine, I mean.

OSTASIO. Listen to me, bastard!

BANNINO. Our good old father
    Fell sick one day. With what a tenderness

You watched about him, O you best of sons!
Do you know now? do you know? I know a thing
That you too know.
God dry your right hand up!

OSTASIO. Ah, what a woman's lie is that! O bastard,
Your day has come at last;
No use in flying from the enemy!

> (*He draws his sword and rushes upon* BANNINO, *who leaps aside and avoids the blow. He is about to follow him, when* SER TOLDO *tries to draw him back.*)

SER TOLDO. Messer Ostasio, what is it you would do?
Let him alone! Let him alone! He is
Your brother. What would you do to him?

> (*The* SLAVE *comes out on the loggia and watches.*)

BANNINO (*terrified*). O father,
O father, help! Francesca, O sister, help!
No! you will kill me. Wretch! Wretch! No, no, pardon,
Ostasio! No, I will not tell...

> (*Seeing the point at his throat, he kneels down.*)

The poison
Was not yours.

> (*The* THREE SOLDIERS, *unarmed, have come back.*)

No, I will not tell! O pardon!

> (OSTASIO *wounds him in the cheek. He swoons.*)

OSTASIO. Nothing, nothing, it is nothing.

> (*He leans over and looks at him.*)

It is nothing;
He has fainted; I have only pricked the skin;
Not in a bad place, no; and not in anger.
I pricked him just a little
That he might learn not to fear naked steel,
That he might bear him better in the fray
And not lose sword and helmet
When he turns tail next on the Ghibelline.

> (*The* THREE SOLDIERS *lift* BANNINO.)

Take him away to Maestro Gabbadeo,
And let his wounds be staunched
With salt out of the Cervia salt-mines.

*(He watches the wounded man as he is borne away, then closes the
    great door with a clang. The* SLAVE *silently retires from the
    loggia.)*

Come,

Ser Toldo, let us go.

SER TOLDO. What will your father

Say when he comes?

OSTASIO. My father

Is much too kind to this young bastardling.

(He looks gloomily on the ground.)

He is from another nest, and he was hatched

Not by the eagle, no, but by a jay.

Did you not hear what he was stuttering?

About a wine, a wine...   *(He pauses grimly.)*

It was a stock

Suborned by someone of the Anastagi.

Christ guard my father and my house from traitors!

SER TOLDO. And Madonna Francesca, then?

OSTASIO. Yes, we will give her

To the Malatesta.

SER TOLDO. May God prosper it!

OSTASIO. The vengeances that wait for us are great

And many, and some tears shall flow in the world,

Please God, more bitter than the salt in all

The salt-mines of this Cervia. Come with me,

Ser Toldo, Paolo Malatesta waits.   *(They go out.)*

(The SLAVE *reappears, carrying a bucket and a sponge. She
    comes down the stairs in silence, barefooted. She looks at the
    bloodstains on the pavement and goes down on her knees to wash
    them up. From the rooms above is heard the song of the*
    WOMEN.)

CHORUS OF WOMEN. Ah me, the sorrow of heart

In the heart that loves too well. Ah me!

Ah me, if the heart could tell

How love in the heart is a flame. Ah me!

*(*FRANCESCA *and* SAMARITANA *are seen coming out on the loggia
    side by side, with their arms about each other. The chorus of*
    WOMEN *follows them, carrying distaffs of different colours;*

but pauses on the lighted loggia, standing as in a singing gallery, while the two sisters go down the stairs to the level of the garden. The SLAVE, *having washed out the stains, hurriedly pours the bloodstained water in her bucket into the sarcophagus among the flowers.*)

FRANCESCA (*pausing on the stairs*). It is love makes them sing!

> (*She throws back her head a little, as if abandoning herself to the breath of the melody, light and palpitating.*)

WOMEN. Ah me, the sorrow and shame,

In the sad heart on the morrow. Ah me!

FRANCESCA. They are intoxicated with these odours.

Do you not hear them? With a sighing fall

Sadly they sing

The things of perfect joy.

> (*She withdraws her arm from her sister's waist, and moves a little away, pausing while the other takes another step downward.*)

WOMEN. Ah me, the bitter sorrow.

All life long. Ah me!

FRANCESCA. Like running water

That goes and goes, and the eye sees it not,

So is my soul.

SAMARITANA (*with a sudden alarm, clinging closer to her sister*).

Francesca,

Where are you going, who is taking you?

FRANCESCA. Ah, you awaken me.

> (*The song pauses. The* WOMEN *turn their backs, looking down into the other court. They seem to be on the watch. The twi-horned headdresses and the tall distaffs shine in the sun, and now and then there is a whispering and rustling of lips and garments in the clear sunlight.*)

SAMARITANA. O, sister, sister,

Listen to me: stay with me still! O stay

With me! we were born here,

Do not forsake me, do not go away,

Let me still keep my bed

Beside your bed, and let me still at night

Feel you beside me.

FRANCESCA. He has come.

SAMARITANA. Who? Who has come
     To take you from me?
FRANCESCA. Sister, he has come.
SAMARITANA. He has no name, he has no countenance,
     And we have never seen him.
FRANCESCA. It may be
     That I have seen him.
SAMARITANA. I have never been apart
     From you, and from your breath;
     My life has never seen but with your eyes;
     O, where can you have seen him, and not I
     Seen him as well?
FRANCESCA. Where you
     Can never come, sweetheart, in a far place
     And in a lonely place
     Where a great flame of fire
     Burns, and none feed that flame.
SAMARITANA. You speak to me in riddles,
     And there is like a veil over your face.
     Ah, and it seems as if you had gone away,
     And from far off
     Turned and looked back; and your voice sounds to me
     As out of a great wind.
FRANCESCA. Peace, peace, dear soul,
     My little dove. Why are you troubled? Peace;
     You also, and ere long,
     Shall see your day of days,
     And leave our nest as I have left it; then
     Your little bed shall stand
     Empty beside my bed; and I no more
     Shall hear through dreams at dawn
     Your little naked feet run to the window,
     And no more see you, white and barefooted,
     Run to the window, O my little dove,
     And no more hear you say to me: "Francesca,
     Francesca, now the morning-star is born,
     And it has chased away the Pleiades."
SAMARITANA. So we will live, ah me,

So we will live forever;
And time shall flee away,
Flee away always!

FRANCESCA. And you will no more say to me at morn:
"What was it in your bed that made it creak
Like reeds in the wind?" Nor shall I answer you:
"I turned about to sleep,
To sleep and dream, and saw,
As I was sleeping, in the dream I dreamed..."
Ah I shall no more tell you what is seen
In dreams. And we will die,
So we will die forever;
And time shall flee away,
Flee away always!

SAMARITANA. O Francesca, O Francesca, you hurt my heart,
And see, Francesca,
You make me tremble all over.

FRANCESCA. Little one, peace,
Peace, be at rest.

SAMARITANA. You told me of the dream
You dreamed last night, and while
You spoke I seemed to hear
A sound of voices calling out in anger,
And then a cry, and then
The sound of a door shutting; and then silence.
You did not finish telling me your dream,
For then
The women began singing, and you stopped;
And you have left my heart in pain for you.
Whom is it that our father gives you to?

FRANCESCA. Sister, do you remember how one day
In August we were on the tower together?
We saw great clouds rise up out of the sea,
Great clouds heavy with storm,
And there was a hot wind that gave one thirst;
And all the weight of the great heavy sky
Weighed over on our heads; and we saw all
The forest round about, down to the shore

Of Chiassi, turn to blackness, like the sea;
And we saw birds flying in companies
Before the murmurs growing on the wind.
Do you remember? We were on the tower;
And then, all of a sudden, there was dead
Silence. The wind was silent, and I heard
Only the beating of your little heart;
And then a hammer beat,
As by the roadside some flushed plunderer,
Hot for more plunder, bent
Shoeing his horse in haste.
The forest was as silent as the shadow
Over the tombs;
Ravenna, dusk and hollow as a city
Sacked by the enemy, at nightfall. We,
We two, under that cloud
(Do you remember?) felt as if death came
Nearer, yet moved no eyelid, but stood there,
Waiting the thunder.

    (*She turns to the* SLAVE, *who stands motionless beside*
      the sarcophagus.)

O Smaragdi, who,
Who was it, in the song among your people,
That stood, shoeing his horse under the moon,
And when his mother spoke to him, and said:
"My son, I pray you take not in your course
The sister when you take the brother, nor
Lovers that love each other, with true love,"
Answered her sourly back:
"If three I find, three I take; if I find
Two, I take one; and if I find but one,
I take the one I find"?
What was the name they gave him in your land?
SLAVE. An evil name
It is not good for any man to name.
FRANCESCA. Tell me, what will you do without me here,
Smaragdi? What is there that I can leave you
When I go hence?

SLAVE. Three cups of bitterness
    Leave me:
    The first that I may drink at early morning;
    The second, on the stroke
    Of mid-day; and the third,
    Soon after vespers.

FRANCESCA. No, I will not leave
    Three cups of bitterness, but you shall come
    With me, Smaragdi, to the city of Rimino,
    And you shall be with me, and we will have
    A window opening upon the sea,
    And I will tell you over all my dreams,
    Because you see unveiled
    The face of sorrow and the face of joy;
    And I will speak to you of that most sweet
    Sister, my little dove;
    And you will stand, and, looking through the window,
    See all the skiffs and galleys on the sea,
    And you will sing: "My galley of Barbary,
    What is the port you make for, and the shore
    Where you would anchor? Cyprus I would make for,
    And at Limisso anchor,
    And land my sailors for a kiss, my captain,
    For love!" Come now, must I not take you with me
    To Rimino, Smaragdi?

SLAVE. To go with you
    It were a happiness to tread on thorns,
    And to pass through the flames
    To be with you.
    You are the heaven with stars,
    The sea with waves.

FRANCESCA. The sea with waves!
    But tell me, what are you doing with the bucket,
    Smaragdi?

SLAVE. I have watered
    The roses.

FRANCESCA. Why then have you watered them
    Out of their season? Why? Samaritana

Will be angry with you.　She
Gives water to the roses
As soon as the bell sounds for vespers.　Come,
What do you say, Samaritana?
SAMARITANA.　I would let them die, because,
Francesca, you are going away from us.
FRANCESCA.　O beautiful, and perchance
A holy thing, being born in this most ancient
Sarcophagus that was the sepulchre
Perchance of some great martyr or of some
Glorious virgin!

> (*She walks round the sarcophagus, touching with her fingers the
> carvings on the four sides.*)

The Redeemer treads
Under his feet the lion and the snake;
Mary saluted by Elizabeth;
Our Lady, and the angel bids "All hail!"
The stags are drinking at the running brook.

> (*She stretches out her arms towards the rose-tree.*)

And now the blood of martyrdom reflowers
In purple and in fire.　Behold, behold,
Sister, the ardent flame,
Behold the roses that are full of fire!
Here did our own hands plant them, on a day,
It was October, on a day of battle
That crimsoned the red eagle of Polenta.
Do you remember?　How the trumpets sounded
From Porta Gaza to the Torre Zancana,
As the new flag unfurled,
The flag our father
Had bid us make for him with forty yards
Of crimson cloth: it was a mighty flag-pole.
Do you remember?
And we had broidered round about the hem
A border fringe of gold.
It conquered!　And from then
We held these roses
To be a blessed thing, we held them spotless

And undefiled as a white virginal robe;
And there was never plucked
One of these roses, and three springtides through
They blossomed into flower and fell to dust
In the sarcophagus.
But never have they flowered until this May,
Such floods, such floods of them.
There are a hundred.   Look!
They burn me if I touch them.
The virgins vowed to Saint Apollinaris
Burn not with such an ardour in their heaven
Of gold.   Samaritana,
Samaritana, which of them say you
Found here a sepulchre
After her glorious martyrdom?   O, which
Of these was sepulchred
Here, tell me, here, after her martyrdom?
Look, look: it is the miracle of the blood!

SAMARITANA (*frightened, drawing her towards herself*).   Sister, what is
    it, sister?
You speak as if you raved.
What is it?   Speak!

BIANCOFIORE (*from the loggia*).   Madonna Francesca!

ADONELLA.   Madonna
    Francesca!

FRANCESCA.   Who calls for me?

ADONELLA.   Come up here!   O come quick!

ALDA.   Here, here, Madonna Francesca, come up here
And see!

ADONELLA.   Come quickly.   It is your betrothed
Who is passing.

BIANCOFIORE.   He is passing through the court,
He is with your brother, Messer Ostasio;
And here too is Ser Toldo Berardengo,
The notary, he is with them.

ALDA.   Here, here!   Madonna Francesca, come up quickly.
He is there, he is there!

        (FRANCESCA *goes hastily up the stairs*.   SAMARITANA *is about to
        follow her, but stops, overcome*.)

ADONELLA (*pointing him out to* FRANCESCA, *who leans over to look*).
　　See, there is he who comes
　　To be your husband.
GARSENDA. O most happy lady,
　　Most happy lady,
　　He is the fairest knight in all the world,
　　In very truth. See now
　　How his hair falls, and waves about his shoulders
　　In the new way, the Angevin way!
ALDA. And how
　　Well made he is, a proper man, well girded
　　About the surcoat with the hanging sleeves
　　That almost touch the ground.
ALDA. And what a splendid clasp and what an aglet!
BIANCOFIORE. And tall! And slender! And a royal carriage!
ADONELLA. And how his teeth are white!
　　He smiled a little, and I saw them glitter.
　　Did you not see, did you
　　Not see?
GARSENDA. O, happy, happy shall she be
　　That kisses him on the mouth!
FRANCESCA. Be silent.
ALDA. He has gone. He is passing now
　　Under the portico.
　　　　(*The* SLAVE *opens the grating, closes it furtively behind her, and
　　　　disappears into the garden.*)
FRANCESCA. Be silent, be silent!
　　　　(*She turns, covering her face with both her hands; when she with-
　　　　draws them, her face appears transfigured. She goes down the
　　　　first stairs slowly, then with a sudden rapidity throws herself
　　　　into the arms of her sister, who awaits her at the foot of the
　　　　staircase.*)
ALTICHIARA. Messer Ostasio is coming back alone.
BIANCOFIORE. The slave, where is she going? She is running
　　Down through the garden.
GARSENDA. Smaragdi runs and runs
　　Like a hound unleashed. Where is she going?
ADONELLA. Sing

Together, sing the song of the fair Isotta:
"O date, O leafy date!..."

> (*The* WOMEN *form into a circle on the* loggia.)

CHORUS OF WOMEN. O date, O leafy date.

O love, O lovely love,

What wilt thou do to me?

> (FRANCESCA, *held close in her sister's arms, suddenly begins to*
> *weep. The chorus breaks off. The* WOMEN *speak together*
> *in low voices.*)

BIANCOFIORE. Madonna weeps.

ADONELLA. She weeps!

ALDA. Why does she weep?

ALTICHIARA. She weeps because her heart is sick with joy.

GARSENDA. Straight to the heart

He wounded her. If she is beautiful,

He is beautiful, the Malatesta!

ADONELLA. Born

One for the other

Under one star.

GARSENDA. O happy he and she!

ALDA. Long may he live who crowns

Their heads with garlands!

BIANCOFIORE. First rain of the season

To the corn brings increase;

And the first tears of love

To the lover bring peace.

ADONELLA. She smiles, she smiles

Now.

BIANCOFIORE. And her tears

Laugh like the hoar-frost.

GARSENDA. Go, warm the bath,

Get the combs ready.

> (*The* WOMEN *scatter over the* loggia, *with their garments fluttering,*
> *nimble as birds on the bough, while the tall staves of their distaffs*
> *pass and repass, shaken like torches against the blue strip of*
> *the sky. Some go into the rooms and come out again. Others*
> *stand as if watching. And they talk in subdued voices and*
> *they move without sound of footsteps.*)

BIANCOFIORE. These smelling-bottles
　　Of bright new silver
　　We have to fill
　　With water of orange flower and water of roses.
ALDA. We have to fill
　　Four mighty coffers
　　With sheets of linen fringed with silken lace.
ALTICHIARA. And stores of pillows
　　We have wrought for a marvel.
　　We have wrought so many
　　That never in dreams the people of Rimino
　　Have seen such store!
ADONELLA. Ah, we have much to be doing!
GARSENDA. And we must fold the quilts
　　Of cloth of linen
　　And all the embroidered coverlets of gold.
BIANCOFIORE. And count the nets and ribbons for the hair
　　And all the girdles and the belts of gold.
ADONELLA. We have much to be doing!
GARSENDA. I take my oath
　　A better dowry brings to Malatesta
　　The daughter of Messer Guido than the daughter
　　Of Boemondo, King of Servia,
　　To the Doge of Venice.
ADONELLA. And if she go by sea we have store enough
　　Of oil and lavender
　　To perfume all the sea.
ALDA. And we will teach the women
　　Of Rimino, that are a little raw,
　　The art of odours.
BIANCOFIORE. And the art of playing
　　And of singing and of dancing.
ALTICHIARA. O, I forgot
　　That I have yet to put a patch of scarlet
　　On the jerkin of Gian Figo.
　　He comes again at noonday.
BIANCOFIORE. He will do well to finish
　　The story of Morgana and the shield,
　　And of the magic potion.

ALDA. Hey, hey, the wedding in May!
  The table must be laid for thirty dishes
  And for a hundred trenchers.
BIANCOFIORE. We must bring word
  To Mazarello
  To have the music ready.
ADONELLA. Ah, we have much to be doing!
GARSENDA. Hey, hey, to work, to work!
ADONELLA. Come, lay our distaffs down
  And take our garlands up.

     (*They go into the room with a murmur, like a swarm of bees into
     the hive.* FRANCESCA *has raised her head, and her tears are
     suddenly lit up by a smile. While the* WOMEN *on the loggia
     were chattering in a low voice among themselves, she wiped the
     tears from her face and the face of her sister with her fingers.
     Now she speaks, and her first words are heard through the last
     words of the* WOMEN.)

FRANCESCA. O sister, sister,
  Weep no more. Now I weep no more. See now,
  I am smiling. Tears and smiles
  Are not enough now. Close
  And narrow is the heart to hold this power,
  And weeping is a virtue all outspent,
  And laughter is a little idle play;
  And all my life seems now,
  With all the veins of it,
  And all the days of it,
  And all old things in it, far away things,
  From long ago in the old time, the blind
  And silent time, when I
  Was but an infant on my mother's breast,
  And you were not,
  Seems all to tremble
  In one long shuddering
  Over the earth;
  And now through all the streams
  That laugh and weep in the places
  That I have never known,

The forces of my being are cast abroad;
And I hear the air cry with a terrible cry,
And I hear the light
Sound like a trumpet-peal,
And the shouting that I hear
And the tumult cry out louder than the sound
In days of vengeance, sister, when the blood
Colours the portals of our father's house.

SAMARITANA. O Francesca, my Francesca, O dear soul,
What have you seen?   What is it you have seen?

FRANCESCA. No, do not be afraid!
What is it your eyes speak?
What sickness am I stricken with, and what,
What have I seen?
It is life runs away,
Runs away like a river,
Ravening, and yet cannot find its sea;
And the roar is in my ears.
But you, but you,
Take me, dear sister, take me with you now,
And let me be with you!
Carry me to my room,
And shut the shutters fast.
And give me a little shade,
And give me a draught of water,
And lay me down upon your little bed,
And with a covering cover me and make
A silence of the shouting, make a silence
Of the shouting and the tumult
I hear within my soul!
Bring stillness back to me,
That I may hear again
The bees of May
Beat on the window, and the cry of the swallows,
And some of your soft words,
Your words of yesterday,
Your words of long ago
And long ago,

Out of an hour that comes to me again
Like an enchantment.
And hold me close, dear sister,
And hold me close to you!
And we will wait for night,
Night with its prayer and sleep,
Sister; and for the morning we will wait
That brings that morning-star.

GARSENDA (*rushing in upon the loggia*). He is coming, he is coming!
O Madonna
Francesca! see he is coming by the way
Of the garden. I have seen him from the room
Of the coffers, I have seen him
Under the cypresses. Smaragdi shows him
The way.

(*The* WOMEN *join her, curious and mirthful; and they have
garlands on their heads for joy: and they have with them three
GIRLS, lute-players and viol-players and flute-players.*)

FRANCESCA (*white with fear, and beside herself*). No, no, no! Run,
Run, women, run!
Let him not come! Run, run!
Women, go out to meet him,
Let him not come! Shut to
The gates, and bar the way, and say to him
Merely that I salute him! and you, you,
Samaritana, help me,
Because I cannot fly; but my knees fail
And my sight fails me.
But you, my women, run,
Run now, and meet him,
And bid him turn again! Go out to meet him,
And say that I salute him!

THE WOMEN. He is here!
He is here, he is here at hand!

(*Aided by her sister,* FRANCESCA *is about to go up the stairs;
but suddenly she sees* PAOLO MALATESTA, *close to her, on the
other side of the marble screen. She stands motionless, and he
stops, in the midst of the arbutuses; and they stand facing one*

*another, separated by the railing, looking at one another, without
word or movement.   The* SLAVE *is hidden behind the leaves.
The* WOMEN *on the loggia form, in a circle, and the* PLAYERS
sound their instruments.)

CHORUS OF WOMEN.   Over the land of May.

  The archer with his band

  Goes out to seek his prey.

  At a feast of fears,

  In a far-off land,

  A heart sighs with tears.

     (FRANCESCA *leaves her sister and goes slowly towards the sar-
cophagus.   She picks a large red rose, and offers it to* PAOLO
MALATESTA *across the bars.* SAMARITANA *with bowed
head goes up the stairs weeping.   The women take up the song.
At the barred window, at the back,* BANNINO *appears, with
his face bandaged; then drawing back, he beats at the door closed
by* OSTASIO.   FRANCESCA *trembles.)*

THE VOICE OF BANNINO.   Francesca, open, Francesca!

ACT TWO

*A cross-shaped room, in the house of the Malatesti, with projecting
side beams and strong pillars, two of which, at the back, support an arch
which leads through a narrow closed entrance between two walls pierced
by loopholes, to the platform of a round tower.   Two side staircases of
twelve steps run from the entrance to the leads of the tower; a third staircase, between the two, runs from the leads to the floor underneath, passing
through a trap-door.   Through the archway are seen the square battlements of the Guelfs, provided with block-houses and openings for pouring
down molten lead.   A huge catapult lifts its head out of its supports
and stretches out its framework of twisted ropes.   Heavy crossbows, with
large-headed, short, and square bolts, balistas, arcobalistas, and other rope-
artillery, are placed around, with their cranks, pulleys, wheels, wires, and
levers.   The summit of the tower, crowned with engines and arms that
stand out in the murky air, overlooks the city of Rimino, where can be
dimly seen the wing-shaped battlements of the highest Ghibelline tower.*

On the right of the room is a door; on the left, a narrow fortified window looking out on the Adriatic.

In the closed entrance is seen a MAN-AT-ARMS *stirring the fire under a smoking cauldron. He has piled against the wall the tubes, syphons and boles of the fiery staves and darts, and heaped about them all sorts of prepared fires. On the tower, beside the catapult, a young* ARCHER *stands on guard.*

MAN-AT-ARMS. The meadow of the Commune is still empty?

ARCHER. As clean and polished as my buckler.

MAN-AT-ARMS. Still not a soul stirring!

ARCHER. Not the shadow even
Of a Gambancerro or of an Omodeo.

MAN-AT-ARMS. They seem then to be dead already, those
That have to die.

ARCHER. Quite otherwise than dead!
If all we did not buckle breastplates well,
And if the gates were not cross-bolted fast,
You would soon hear a hammering of hearts
In the regions about Rimino.... Ah, there goes
A donkey.

MAN-AT-ARMS. It is Messer Montagna, eh?
Of the Parcitadi, or Messer Ugolino
Cignatta.

ARCHER. Both of them, by Berlingerio,
Stand with the right foot ready
In the stirrup of the crossbow, for the sign
To come out and to face the bolts and bars.

MAN-AT-ARMS. What sign? The Parcitade
Lacks his astrologer. He waits and hopes
For succour from Urbino.
But long before Count Guido comes to us,
By the body of San Giulian the martyr,
We shall have burnt the city to the ground.
We have enough to do with burning down
Half of Romagna. 'Tis warm work this time,
I warrant you! The Lamester
Wanted to singe his horse's mane with one

Of these fire-bearers:
Sure sign we are in salamander weather.
ARCHER. He loves the stench of singeing, it would seem,
More than the civet of his wedded wife,
That woman of Ravenna! another thing
Than firebrands or this sulphur and bitumen!
A smile of hers would set the city alight
And all the country and the territory.
MAN-AT-ARMS. She smiles but little. She is always overcast
With thinking, and with anger. She is restless.
I see her almost every day come up
Upon this tower. She scarcely speaks. She watches
The sea, and if she sees
Some galley or some frigate on the sea,
She follows it with her eyes
(Blacker than pitch, her eyes!)
Until it fades away,
As if she waited for a message or
Longed to set sail. She goes
From tower to tower,
From the Mastra to the Rubbia,
And from the Gemmana to the Tanaglia,
Like a lost swallow. And sometimes I fear,
When she is on the platform,
That she will take a flying leap and fall.
Misericordia!
ARCHER. The Lamester is well made
To ride astride upon the Omodeo,
To batter strongholds, and to ford the streams,
And to force palisades,
To plunder and to pillage all the earth,
But not to labour in the lovely vineyard
That God has given him.
MAN-AT-ARMS. Hush! You must not speak
So loud; we should not hear him if he came.
He goes about more softly than a panther,
You cannot hear him when he comes. He makes
A goodly pair with Messer Malatestino,

That comes upon you always suddenly
Without your knowing how or whence he came,
And gives you the same start,
Always, as if you had come upon a ghost.

ARCHER. This is the day we are to lay about us.
The women will be all shut up.

MAN-AT-ARMS. This one
Is not a lady to be frightened. Look,
See what is stirring.

ARCHER (*returning to his post*). I see the friars,
The hermits of Sant' Agostino, pass
To the exorcising. I can smell the stench
Of singeing in the cool air.

MAN-AT-ARMS. And the gate
Of the Gattalo is closed still?

ARCHER. Ay, closed still.
Our men, that had to come Verrucchio way,
Will be by now with trumpets and flags flying
At the bridge of the Maone. Messer Paolo
Came with the infantry by the postern gate
Of the sea.

MAN-AT-ARMS. The mixture now
Is ready brewed. Since midday I have stirred
The ladle, mixed and moulded it together.
We are to sling barrels and casks of it
Upon the excommunicated houses.
But what is it we wait for? The conjunction
Of Mars with Venus? This astrologer,
Come from Baldach, does not quite seem to me
A modern Balaam. God be on our side!
Look if you see him now
Upon the belfry of Santa Colomba.
He is to ring the bell three times, to say
The fates are in our favour.

ARCHER. I can see
A great long beard.

MAN-AT-ARMS. May he be tarred all over with his tow,
And brayed in a mortar! I suspect him.

He was with Ezelino at Padua,
And other of hell's own Ghibellines. I know not
Why Messer Malatesta
Keeps in his company.

ARCHER. Guido Bonatto, of Forlì, I know
To be a true astrologer of battles.
I saw him on the great day of Valbona,
And his prognostic never faulted.

MAN-AT-ARMS. Now
The cursed Feltran has him. Thunder strike
His eyesight and his astrolabe!

> (FRANCESCA *enters by the door on the right, and advances as far
> as the pillar that supports the arch. She wears about her face a
> dark band that passes under her chin and joins a kind of skull-cap
> that covers her hair, leaving visible the tresses knotted on her neck.*)

ARCHER. The dust
Begins to rise over toward Aguzano.

MAN-AT-ARMS. Are they Count Guido's horsemen
That ought to come from Petramala?

ARCHER. No.
May God cast down their eyes
Out of their visors into the dust!

MAN-AT-ARMS. But who,
Who are they?

FRANCESCA. Berlingerio!

MAN-AT-ARMS (*starting*). O, Madonna Francesca!

> (THE ARCHER *remains silent and stares at her blankly, leaning
> on the catapult.*)

FRANCESCA. Messer Giovanni
Is at the Mastra yet?

MAN-AT-ARMS. Not yet, Madonna. We expect him now.

FRANCESCA. And no one else?

MAN-AT-ARMS. Yes, Messer Malatesta,
The old man.   He himself it was who made
The mixing in the cauldron; and I am here
Since midday with this ladle, stirring it.

FRANCESCA (*going nearer*). And no one else?

MAN-AT-ARMS. And no one else, Madonna.

FRANCESCA. What are you doing here?

MAN-AT-ARMS. Making Greek fire,
Distaffs and staves and spouts and lines and pots
And fiery darts, and much
Other caresses for the Parcitadi,
Because we trust to come to blows today
And give them from this quarter what shall prove
A good part-payment of their coming hell.

FRANCESCA (*looking wonderingly at the boiling mass in the cauldron*).
Greek fire! Who can escape it? I have never
Seen it before. Tell me, is it not true
That there is nothing known so terrible
In battles for a torture?

MAN-AT-ARMS. This is indeed most terrible; 'tis a secret
That Messer Malatesta
Had from an aged man of Pisa, who
Was with the Christians at the famous taking
Of Damiata.

FRANCESCA. Tell me, is it true
That it flames in the sea,
Flames in the stream,
Burns up the ships,
Burns down the towers,
Stifles and sickens,
Drains a man's blood in his veins,
Straightway, and makes
Of his flesh and his bones
A little black ashes,
Draws from the anguish
Of man the wild cry of the beast,
That it maddens the horse,
Turns the valiant to stone?
Is it true that it shatters
The rock, and consumes
Iron, and bites
Hard to the heart
Of a breastplate of diamond?

MAN-AT-ARMS. It bites and eats

All kinds of things that are, living and dead;
Sand only chokes it out,
But also vinegar
Slacks it.

FRANCESCA. But how do you
Dare, then, to handle it?

MAN-AT-ARMS. We have the license
Of Beelzebub, that is the prince of devils,
And comes to take the part
Of the Malatesti.

FRANCESCA. How do you scatter it?

MAN-AT-ARMS. With tubes and syphons
Of a long range; or at the point of pikes
With distaffs full of flax
We shoot it by the help of our balistas.
See here, Madonna, these are very good
Distaffs; they are
The distaffs of the Guelfs
That without spindle weave the death of men.

(He takes up a staff prepared for the fire and shows it to FRANCESCA,
who takes it by the handle and shakes it vehemently.)

FRANCESCA. Light one for me.

MAN-AT-ARMS. The signal is not yet
Given.

FRANCESCA. I would have you light this one for me.

MAN-AT-ARMS. Who is to put it out?

FRANCESCA. O, I must see
The flame that I have never seen as yet.
Light it! Is it not true that when you light it
It darts marvellous colours, like no other
Creature of flight,
Colours of such a mingling that the eye
Cannot endure them,
Of an unspeakable
Variety, innumerable
In fervour and in splendour, that alone
Live in the wandering planets and within
The vials of alchemists,

And in volcanoes full of many metals,
And in the dreams of blind men? Is it true?
MAN-AT-ARMS. In very deed, Madonna,
It is a beautiful and pleasant thing
To see at night these lighted distaffs fly
And light upon a camp
Of the imperial ragamuffianry;
And that knows well Messer Giovanni, your
Good husband, who takes pleasure to behold it.
FRANCESCA. Light it, then, Man-At-Arms! for I must see it.
MAN-AT-ARMS. 'Tis not yet night, nor is the signal given.
FRANCESCA. Light it! I bid you.
And I will hide myself here in the dark
To see it, by the stairway leading down,
Where it is darker.
MAN-AT-ARMS. Do you want to burn
The tower with all the archers,
And please the Parcitade folk?

    (FRANCESCA *dips the fiery staff into the cauldron, then rapidly*
    lights it with a firebrand.)

FRANCESCA. And I
Light it!

    (*The violent and many-coloured flame crackles at the point of the*
    pike that she holds in her hand like a torch, fearlessly.)

O, fair flame, conqueror of day!
Ah, how it lives, how it lives vibrating,
The whole staff vibrates with it, and my hand
And my arm vibrate with it, and my heart.
I feel it nearer me
Than if I held it in my palm. Wouldst thou
Devour me, fair flame, wouldst thou make me thine?
I feel that I am maddening for thee.

    (*Her voice rises like a song. The* MAN-AT-ARMS *and the* ARCHER
    gaze in astonishment at the flame and the woman, as at some
    work of sorcery.)

And how it roars!
It roars to seek its prey.
It roars and longs for flight;

And I would fling it up into the clouds.
Come, charge the arbalest.
The sun is dead, and this,
This is the daughter that he had of death.
O, I would fling it up into the clouds.
Why do you linger? No, I am not mad,
No, no, poor Man-At-Arms, who look at me
In wonderment.   (*She laughs.*)
No, but this flame is so
Beautiful, I am drunk with it. I feel
As I were in the flame and it in me.
You, you, do you not see how beautiful,
How beautiful it is? The bitter smoke
Has spoilt your eyes for seeing. If it shines
So gloriously by day, how will it shine
By night?

> (*She approaches the trap-door through which the stairs go down into the tower, and lowers the burning staff into the darkness.*)

A miracle! A miracle!

MAN-AT-ARMS. Madonna, God preserve us, you will burn
The whole tower down.
Madonna, I pray you!

> (*He hastily draws back out of the way of sparks the staves prepared for fire which are lying about.*)

FRANCESCA (*intent on the light*). It is a miracle!
It is the joy of the eyes, and the desire
Of splendour and destruction. In the heart
Of silence of this high and lonely mount
Shall I spread forth these gems of frozen fire,
That all the terror of the flame unloose
And bring to birth new ardours in the soul?
Tremendous life of swiftness, mortal beauty!
Swift through the night, swift through the starless night,
Fall in the camp, and seize the armèd man,
Enswathe his sounding armour, glide between
Strong scale and scale, hunt down
The life of veins, and break
The bones asunder, suck the marrow out,

Stifle him, rend him, blind him, but before
The final darkness falls upon his eyes,
Let all the soul within him without hope
Shriek in the splendour that is slaying him.

(She listens in the direction of the trap-door.)

Someone is coming up the stairs here. Who
Is coming?

MAN-AT-ARMS. On each floor
We have a hundred men,
Archers and those that work the manganels,
Hidden, and bidden not to move or breathe,
Crammed in together like a sheaf of arrows
Inside a quiver. Perhaps
They saw the flame.

FRANCESCA. It is one man alone.
His armour clanks upon him.
Who is it coming?

MAN-AT-ARMS. Lift up the staff, turn it away, Madonna
Francesca, it is surely not an enemy.
Or you are like to burn him in the face.
Perhaps it is Messer Giovanni.

FRANCESCA *(bending over the opening)*. Who are you?
Who are you?

THE VOICE OF PAOLO. Paolo!

(FRANCESCA *is silent; she draws back the fiery staff, and the
flame, heightened by the sudden movement, lights up the helmet
and gorgerin of* PAOLO MALATESTA. PAOLO *appears, up
to the waist, in the opening of the stairs, and turns to* FRANCESCA,
*who has moved back against the wall, still holding in her hand
the iron handle of the staff, which she has lowered to the ground,
so that the fire burns perilously near her feet. The* ARCHER
has returned to his post.)

MAN-AT-ARMS. You have come just in time, Messer Paolo, just
In time, for all we here
Were like to have been roasted living, we
And all the towers along with us. You see:
Madonna plays
With the Greek fire

As if she held
A lap-dog in a leash.

> (FRANCESCA, *pale and leaning against the wall, laughs with a
> troubled laugh, letting the staff fall from her hand.*)

It is a miracle
That we are not all here in open hell.
You see!

> (*He pours sand on the flame in order to extinguish it.* PAOLO
> *runs up the remaining steps; as he sets foot on the platform of
> the tower, the* ARCHER *points towards the city, to show where
> the battle is beginning.*)

ARCHER. There is tumult in the San Cataldo quarter.
It is breaking out at the Membruto bridge
Over the Patara trench.
And they are fighting at the fullers' mill
Under the gun tower, there, by the Masdogna.

> (FRANCESCA *moves away, stepping uncertainly among the arrows
> and engines heaped around, and goes towards the door by which
> she had come; she pauses by the pillar that hides her from the
> eyes of* PAOLO.)

MAN-AT-ARMS. We are still waiting
For the signal, Messer Paolo.
It is almost vespers. What are we to do?

> (PAOLO *does not seem to hear, possessed by a single thought, a
> single anguish. Seeing* FRANCESCA *has gone, he leaves the
> tower, and goes down one of the little side staircases to rejoin her.*)

PAOLO. Francesca!
FRANCESCA. Give the signal. Paolo, give
The signal! Do not fear
For me, Paolo. Let me stay here and hear
The twanging of the bows.
I cannot breathe
When I am shut into my room, among
My trembling women, and I know there is fighting
Out in the city. I would have you give me,
My lord and kinsman, a fair helmet.
PAOLO. I
Will give you one.

FRANCESCA. Have you come from Cesena?

PAOLO. I came today.

FRANCESCA. You stayed
A long while there.

PAOLO. It took us forty days
With Guido di Monforte in the field
To take Cesena and the castle.

FRANCESCA. Ah!
You have toiled, I think, too much.
You are a little thinner and a little
Paler, it seems to me.

PAOLO. There is an Autumn fever
Among the thickets on the Savio.

FRANCESCA. No,
But you are sick? You tremble. And Orabile,
Has she no medicine for you?

PAOLO. This fever
Feeds on itself; I ask no medicine,
I seek no herb to heal my sickness, sister.

FRANCESCA. I had a healing herb
When I was in my father's house, the house
Of my good father, God protect him, God
Protect him! I had a herb, a healing herb,
There in the garden where you came one day
Clothed in a garment that is called, I think,
Fraud, in the gentle world;
But you set foot on it, and saw it not,
And it has never come up any more,
However light your foot may be, my lord
And kinsman. It was dead.

PAOLO. I saw it not,
I knew not where I was,
Nor who had led my feet into that way,
I did not speak, I did not hear a word,
I had no bounds to cross,
No barriers to break down,
I only saw a rose
That offered itself up to me more living

Than the lips of a fresh wound, and a young song
I heard in the air, and I heard angry blows
Beaten upon a loud and terrible door,
And I heard an angry voice that cried your name
In anger. Only that, nothing but that.
Nor from that way did I come back by will
Of coming back;
Because the ways of death
Are not so secret as that other way,
O sister, if God wills.

FRANCESCA.   I also saw
With my own eyes the dawn,
The dawn that brings with it the morning star,
The nurse of the young heavens,
That had but newly waked to give its milk
When the last dream of sleep
Came to my pillow; and I also saw,
With my own eyes I saw,
With horror and with shame,
About me as it were an impure stream
Of water flung suddenly outraging
A palpitating face
Lifted to drink the light.
This did I see with my own eyes; and this
I shall see always till the night has fallen,
The night that has no dawn,
Brother.

PAOLO.   The shame and horror be on me!
The light that came again
Found me awake.
Peace had forever fled
Out of the soul of Paolo Malatesta;
It has not come again, it will not come
Ever again;
Peace and the soul of Paolo Malatesta
Are enemies from now in life or death.
And all things were as enemies to me
From the hour that you set foot

Upon the threshold, and without escape,
And I turned back and followed with the guide.
Violent deeds
Were the one medicine for my disease,
That night: violent deeds.
And then I killed Tindaro Omodei
And burned his roofs about him.
I gave to the harsh guide another prey.

FRANCESCA. God shall forgive you this,
God shall forgive you all the blood you shed,
And all the rest,
But not the tears I did not weep, but not
The eyes that were still dry when the dawn came.
I cannot weep now, brother! Another draught
You gave me at the ford
Of the beautiful river, do you remember it?
With your false heart,
Filled full with madness and with treachery,
That was the last, that was the last that quenched
My thirst; and now no water
Can quench my thirst, not any more, my lord.
And then we saw the walls of Rimino,
And then we saw the Galeana gate,
And the sun was going down upon the hills,
And all the horses neighed against the walls,
And then I saw your face,
Silent, between the spears
Of the horsemen.   And a wicked thing it was
That you did not let me drift upon the stream,
That would have taken me and laid me down
Softly upon the seashore of Ravenna,
And someone would have found me, and brought me back
To my good father, to my most kind father
That without thought of wrong had given me
To whom he would, yes, without thought of wrong;
God have him in his keeping, give him always
More and more lordship!

PAOLO. Your rebuke, Francesca,

Is cruel over-much, sweet over-much,
And my heart melts within me, and my sad soul
Is shed before the strangeness of your voice.
My soul is shed before you,
All that is in me have I cast away,
And I will no more stoop to pick it up.
How would you have me die?

FRANCESCA. Like to the galley-slave
Rowing in the galley that is called Despair,
So would I have you die; and there and then
The memory of that draught
You gave me at the ford
Of the beautiful river,
Before we had come to the water of treachery
And to the walls of fraud, should burn in you
And should consume you. My brother in God,
In the Most High God,
And in Saint John, better it were for you
That you should lose your life than stain your soul.

> (*The bells of Santa Colomba are heard. Both shiver as if re-
> turning to consciousness.*)

Ah! where are we?   Who is it calling us?

PAOLO. What hour is that?
What are you doing?

> (*The* MAN-AT-ARMS *and the* ARCHER, *busy loading the balistas
> and cocking the fiery staves, start at the sound.*)

MAN-AT-ARMS. The signal!   It is the signal!
It is the bells of Santa Colomba!

ARCHER. Fire!
Fire! Long live Malatesta!

> (*A troop of* ARCHERS *hurry shouting up through the trap-door,
> and through the platform of the tower, and seize weapons and
> engines.*)

ARCHERS. Long live Messer Malatesta and the Guelfs!
Down with Messer Parcitade and the Ghibellines!

> (*On the battlements is a great sheaf of fiery staves, which glows
> in the dusky air. PAOLO MALATESTA takes his helmet from
> his head and gives it to* FRANCESCA.)

PAOLO. Here is the helmet that I have to give you.

FRANCESCA. Paolo!

> (PAOLO *rushes upon the tower. His bare head overtops the* MEN-AT-ARMS *as they work.* FRANCESCA, *throwing down the helmet, follows, calling to him through the noise and clamour.*)

PAOLO. Give me a crossbow!

FRANCESCA. Paolo! Paolo!

PAOLO. A bow! A crossbow!

FRANCESCA. Paolo! Paolo!

> (*An* ARCHER *is knocked over by a bolt which takes him in the throat.*)

MAN-AT-ARMS. Madonna, get you gone, for God's sake; now
They are beginning here to bite the leads.

> (*Some* ARCHERS *raise their large painted shields in the way of* FRANCESCA *as she tries to follow* PAOLO.)

ARCHERS. The Galeana Tower is answering!
Cignatta's men are coming
By the Masdogna!
Long live Messer Malatesta and the Guelfs!
Verrucchio! Verrucchio!

> (FRANCESCA *tries to get past the* ARCHERS, *who stop her way.*)

MAN-AT-ARMS. Madonna,
By any God you worship! Messer Paolo,
Pay a little heed here! Here is Madonna Francesca
Out in the open. It is death here.

> (PAOLO, *snatching a crossbow, stands on the rampart, firing furiously, in full view of the enemy, like a madman.*)

FRANCESCA. Paolo!

> (PAOLO *turns at the cry, and sees the woman in the glare of the fires. He snatches a shield from one of the* ARCHERS *and covers her.*)

PAOLO. Ah, Francesca, go, go! What is this madness?

> (*He pushes her toward shelter, holding the shield over her; she gazes at his angry and beautiful face from under the shield.*)

FRANCESCA. You
Are the madman! You are the madman!

PAOLO. And was I not to die?

> (*He leads her back to shelter and throws down the shield, still holding the crossbow.*)

FRANCESCA. Not now, not now,
  It is not yet the hour.

ARCHERS. — Malatesta! Malatesta!
  — Cignatta's men are there, under the Rubbia!
  — This side, this side!

> (*They come down by the stairs on the left and set the crossbows to
> the arrow-slits in the walls. The bells ring in all directions.
> A distant sound of trumpets is heard.*)

  — Verrucchio! Down with the Parcitade! Death
To the Ghibelline!
  — Long live Messer Malatesta!
Long live the Guelfs!

PAOLO. This is the hour, if you will see me die,
  If you will lift my head out of the dust
  With your two hands. What other could I have?
  I will not die the death of the galley-slave.

FRANCESCA. Paolo, steel your heart against your fate,
  Be silent as that day
  Under the heavy guidance, as that day
  Among the spears of the spearmen. And let me not
  Stain my own soul for your sake!

PAOLO. Ay, to play
  With fate is what I will,
  Is what my false heart wills,
  Filled full of madness and of treachery.

> (*With an impetuous gesture he draws her towards the fortified
> window, and puts into her hand the cord that hangs from the
> portcullis.*)

Throw the portcullis open!
A child's hand opens it,
The mere touch of an innocent hand.

> (*He gathers a bundle of arrows and throws them at the feet of*
> FRANCESCA. *Then he loads the crossbow.*)

FRANCESCA. Ah, madman!
  Madman! And do you think
  My hand will tremble? Do you think to tempt
  My soul after this fashion? I am ready
  For any mortal game men play with fate,

Knowing I shall not lose,
Seeing that all is lost.
But you now stand
Upon tremendous limits, where God help you!
I open for you. See!
Look straight before you,
And take the sign, if you would not have me laugh.

(*She pulls the portcullis open with the cord, and through the opening is seen the open sea, shining under the last rays of light.*)

The sea! The sea! (PAOLO *aims the crossbow and fires.*)

PAOLO. A good stroke! It is gone
Through neck and neckpiece.
That's my good forerunner
In the land of darkness!

(FRANCESCA *lowers the portcullis, and the return arrow is heard
against it.* PAOLO *reloads the crossbow.*)

ARCHER (*on the tower*).— Victory!
Victory! Death, death to the Parcitadi!
Long live Messer Malatesta and the Guelfs!
— Victory! Victory! the Ghibelline is broken
At the Patara bridge.
— The fullers' mill is empty!
— Messer Giovanni galloping with the spears
At the Gattolo gate! Cignatta scampering!
— Be careful not to wound
Our own folk in the fray!
— Victory to Malatesta!

FRANCESCA (*in great emotion*). I have seen the sea,
The eternal sea,
The witness of the Lord,
And on the sea a sail
That the Lord set to be a sign of saving.
Paolo, brother of God,
I make a vow
If the Lord of mercy
Have you in keeping!

PAOLO. Raise the portcullis up!

FRANCESCA. I will not let it down again. This hazard

Shall be God's judgment, this judgment of the arrow.
Man is deceit, but God is very truth.
Brother in God, the stain of fraud you have
Upon your soul,
Let it be pardoned to you with all love,
And let the judgment of God
Make proof of you
Now by the arrow
That it touch you not;
Or it were better
That you give your life,
And I with you.

> (*Holding the tightened cord in her hand she kneels and prays, with her wide-open eyes fixed on* PAOLO's *unarmed head. Through the raised portcullis can be seen the shining sea.* PAOLO *loads and fires the crossbow without a pause. From time to time* GHIBELLINE *missiles enter by the window and strike on the opposite wall or fall on the pavement without wounding him. The cruel suspense convulses the face of the woman in prayer. The syllables hardly form themselves on her parted lips.*)

Our Father which art in heaven,
Hallowed be thy name,
Thy Kingdom come,
Thy will be done in earth
As it is in heaven.
Father, give us this day
Our daily bread.

> (PAOLO, *having failed in several shots, takes aim more carefully, as if for a master-stroke. He fires; a clamour is heard among the enemy.*)

PAOLO (*with fierce delight*). Ah, Ugolino, I have found you out!

FRANCESCA. And forgive us our debts, as we
Forgive our debtors.
And lead us not
Into temptation,
But deliver us from evil.
So be it, Amen.

> (*Meanwhile there is great rejoicing among the* ARCHERS *on the*

tower. *Some carry the killed and wounded down through the trap-door.*)

ARCHERS.— Victory to Malatesta!

— Death to the Parcitadi and the Ghibellines!
Montagna's men are flying
By the San Cataldo gate.— See, see, the fire
Is spreading. There's a powder-barrel burst
Over the house of Accarisio. See,
The fire is spreading! — Victory! Malatesta!
— Ah, Messer Ugolino
Cignatta has fallen from his horse. He is dead!
— A bolt from a crossbow took him in the mouth.
Who was it killed him? Was it Bartolo
Gambitta?
— Who, who killed him? One of ours?
A splendid stroke!
— Deserves a hundred lire,
A thousand golden crowns! — Victory! Victory!

(*A shaft grazes the head of* PAOLO MALATESTA, *passing through his hair.* FRANCESCA *utters a cry, letting go the cord; starting to her feet, she takes his head in her hands, feeling for the wound. A mortal pallor overspreads his face at the touch. The crossbow falls at his feet.*)

FRANCESCA. Paolo! Paolo!

(*She looks at her hands to see if they are stained with blood. They are white. She again searches anxiously.*)

O, what is this? Oh, God!
Paolo! Paolo! You are not bleeding, and you have
No single drop of blood upon your head,
Yet you look deathly. Paolo!

PAOLO (*in a choking voice*). I am not dying,
Francesca. Iron has not touched me.

FRANCESCA. Saved!

O saved and pure! Cleansed utterly of fraud!
Give thanks to God! Kneel, brother!

PAOLO. But your hands
Have touched me, and the soul
Has fainted in my heart, and icy cold

Takes hold on all my veins, and no more strength
Is in me now to live;
But of this other life
That comes to meet me —

FRANCESCA. Kneel, kneel, on your life!

PAOLO. Ah! an unspeakable fear takes hold on me,
And a scorn deeper even than the fear ——

FRANCESCA. Kneel! Kneel!

PAOLO. Since I have lived
With such an infinite force,
Fighting apart, yet ever on the lonely
Height of your prayer,
And in the fiery solitude of your eyes ——

FRANCESCA. Kneel! Kneel! Give thanks to God!
I will not lose you now over again!

PAOLO. Fighting apart, and slaying
Men ——

FRANCESCA. You are pardoned now,
And you are cleansed, and yet you will be lost!

PAOLO. And all my courage drawn
Vehemently about my angry heart,
And all within me now
The power of my most evil love sealed up.

FRANCESCA. Lost! Lost! Say you are mad,
Say, on your life, that you are mad, and say
That your most wretched soul
Has heard no word of all your mouth has said!
By the arrow that passed by
And struck you not,
By the death that touched you with its finger-tip
And took you not,
Say that your life shall never, never speak
Those words again!

ARCHERS. Long live Messer Giovanni Malatesta!

> (GIOVANNI MALATESTA *comes up by the stairs of the Mastra*
> *Tower, armed from head to foot, and holding a Sardinian rod*
> *in his hand. He limps up the stairs, and, when he has reached*
> *the top, raises his terrible spear, while his harsh voice cuts through*
> *the clamour.*)

GIANCIOTTO. By God, you craven creatures,
You cut-throat spawn,
I am well minded
To pitch you all headlong into the Ausa,
Like carrion that you are.

FRANCESCA. Your brother!   (PAOLO *picks up the crossbow.*)

GIANCIOTTO. You are more ready
To cry rejoicings
Than to belabour this tough Ghibelline hide.
How should you work your crossbows without sinews?
Had I not come to aid you with my horse,
Cignatta would have battered down your gates;
God break the arms of all of you for cowards!

ARCHERS.— We had used almost all our stock of arrows.
  — The Astrologer was late in signalling.
  — We have silenced them on the Galassa tower.
  — We have piled up a heap on the Masdogna.

GIANCIOTTO. Poor fire, by God! There are not many houses
To be seen burning. Badly thrown, your fire.

ARCHERS.— The house of Accarisio is still burning.
  — And the good Cignatta, who unhorsed him then?
  —It was one of us that slit his windpipe for him?

GIANCIOTTO. Which one of you was standing at the window?

ARCHERS.— Was not this one here something of the cut?
A thousand golden crowns to the company!

GIANCIOTTO. Who was it at the window?

ARCHERS.— We have been slaving on an empty stomach.
  — We are dead with hunger and with thirst.
  — Long live
Messer Gianciotto the never-satisfied!

    (PAOLO *picks up his helmet, puts it on and goes towards the
    tower.* FRANCESCA *goes towards the door by which she had
    entered, opens it and calls.*)

FRANCESCA. O Smaragdi! Smaragdi!

GIANCIOTTO (*to the* ARCHERS). Be silent there. Your tongues
dry up in you!
No talking while you work: I like you silent.
But come now, there is a great cask to hurl;

I will teach you the right way of it; and I will send it
To the old Parcitade for leave-taking
In my good father's name.   Here, Berlingerio,
Where is my brother Paolo?
Did he not come up here?

> (*The* SLAVE *appears at the door; then, after an order from her
> mistress, disappears.*   FRANCESCA *remains standing on the
> threshold.*)

PAOLO.   Here.   I am here, Gianciotto.   It was I
Who shot out of the window.   The dumb thing
Struck through the throat of one whose mouth was open
To jest at you.   (*There is a murmur among the* ARCHERS.)

GIANCIOTTO.   Brother, much thanks for this.

> (*He turns to the* MEN-AT-ARMS.)

So sure a shot must needs
Come from a Malatesta,
My braggart bowmen.

> (*The* SLAVE *reappears with a jar and a cup.*   FRANCESCA *comes
> forward.*   GIANCIOTTO *comes down towards his brother.*)

Paolo, I bring you news,
Good news.   (*He sees his wife.*   *His voice changes to a gentler tone.*)
Francesca!

FRANCESCA.   All hail, my lord; you bring the victory.

> (*He goes up to her and embraces her.*)

GIANCIOTTO.   Dear lady, why are you in such a place?

> (*She draws back from the embrace.*)

FRANCESCA.   You have blood upon your armour.

GIANCIOTTO.   Have I painted you?

FRANCESCA.   You are all over dust.

GIANCIOTTO.   Lady, the dust
Is bread to me.

FRANCESCA.   You are not wounded?

GIANCIOTTO.   Wounds?
  I feel none.

FRANCESCA.   But you must be thirsty.

GIANCIOTTO.   Yes,
  I am very thirsty.

FRANCESCA.   Smaragdi, bring the wine.

> (*The* SLAVE *comes forward with the jar and the cup.*)

GIANCIOTTO (*with delighted surprise*). What, my dear lady, you have
    taken thought
  I might be thirsty? Why, you must have set
  Your slave to watch for me, that you should know
  My coming to the minute.

> (FRANCESCA *pours out the wine and hands the cup to her husband.*
> PAOLO *stands aside in silence, watching the men who are*
> *preparing the fiery cask.*)

FRANCESCA. Drink, it is wine of Scios.

GIANCIOTTO. Drink first, I pray you.
  A draught.

FRANCESCA. I have not poisoned it, my lord.

GIANCIOTTO. You laugh at me. Not for suspicion's sake,
  But for the favour, for the favour of it,
  Francesca, my true wife.
  I have no fear of treachery from you.
  My horse has not yet stumbled under me.
  Drink, lady.   (FRANCESCA *touches the cup with her lips.*)
  It is sweet,
  After the fight, to see your face again,
  To take a strong wine from your hands, and drink it
  Down at a draught.   (*He empties the cup.*)
  So. Why this warms my heart.
  And Paolo? Where is Paolo?
  Why has he not a word for you? He comes
  Back from Cesena, and not
  A word of welcome has my kinsman from you.
  Paolo, come here. Are you not thirsty? Leave
  Greek fire for Greek wine. Then
  We will burn up the Parcitadi living!
  Lady, pour out for him a cup brimful
  And drink with him a draught, to do him honour;
  And welcome him, welcome the perfect archer.

FRANCESCA. I have already greeted him.

GIANCIOTTO. But when?

FRANCESCA. When he was shooting.

PAOLO. Do you know, Gianciotto,
  I came up on the tower

And found her in the act of making trial
With Berlingerio of a fiery dart?

GIANCIOTTO. Is that the truth?

PAOLO. She played
With lighted fire, and the poor man-at-arms
Was crying out for fear the tower should burn,
And she the while was laughing. I heard her laugh,
While the fire lay as gentle at her feet
As a greyhound in leash.

GIANCIOTTO. Is that the truth,
Francesca?

FRANCESCA. I was weary of my rooms
And of my whimpering women. And of a truth
I had rather look, my lord, on open war
Than feed fear closeted.

GIANCIOTTO. Daughter of Guido,
Your father's seal is on you. May God make you
Fruitful to me, that you may give me many
And many a lion's cub!   (FRANCESCA *knits her brow*.)
Paolo, you have not drunk!
Drink, you are pale. Pour out a cup for him,
My woman warrior, full, and drink a draught.
He shot a splendid bolt.

PAOLO. Do you know, Gianciotto,
Who lifted up the window while I shot?
She! In her hand she held the little cord
That lifts it, like the children of our soldiers;
And steady was her hand and firm her eye.

GIANCIOTTO. Why, come then, come, my lady, and make war
Among the castles! I will make for you
A breastplate of fine gold, and you shall go
Riding with sword and spear,
Like the brave Countess Aldruda di Bertinoro,
When she went out to fight with Marchesella
Against the Councillor of Magonza. Ah!
You have been apart from me too long, dear lady.
Now with that dark band underneath your chin
And round your neck, you seem to wear a gorget:

It gives you a wild sort of grace. True, eh,
Paozzo? But you have not yet drunk! Drink, now.
Drink, you are pale. You have worked well. This night
We shall not sleep, two in our beds. So, lady,
Pour out the wine.

FRANCESCA. See, I am pouring it.

GIANCIOTTO. It is almost dark here; one can hardly see;
    You might have spilt it.

FRANCESCA. Drink, my lord and kinsman,
    Out of the cup in which your brother drank.
    God give you both good fortune,
    Each as the other, and alike to me!

            (PAOLO *drinks, looking straight into* FRANCESCA'S *eyes.*)

GIANCIOTTO. Good fortune, Paolo.
    I had begun to tell you, and I stopped;
    I have happy tidings for you. In the hour
    Of victory there came to our good father
    Envoys from Florence, saying you are elected
    The Captain of the People and the Commune
    Of Florence.

PAOLO. Envoys came!

GIANCIOTTO. Why, yes. You are sorry?

PAOLO. No, I will go.

        (FRANCESCA *turns her face to the shadow and moves a few steps
        nearer the tower. The* SLAVE *retires to one side and stands
        motionless.*)

GIANCIOTTO. You must go within three days.
    You will have time to go to Ghiaggiolo
    To your Orabile, who is used by now
    To being a widow. And from there you will go
    To the city of gay living that has thriven
    Under the guidance of the joyous friars,
    Full of fat merchants, and of merrymakers,
    And gentry of the Court, and there the tables
    Are spread both night and morning, and they dance there
    And sing there, and you can sport to heart's content.

            (*His face clouds over and he becomes bitter again.*)
    We will stay here and set the trap for wolves

And slit the throats of lambkins. Iron shall knock
On iron for the pleasure of our ears,
Sardinian rod and hatchet of Orezzo
On bolt with rounded edge, morning and night
And night and morning. Here then we will wait
Till in some escalade another stone
Fracture another knee. And then, why, then,
Giovanni, the old Lamester, Gianni Ciotto,
Shall have himself tied tightly on the back
Of a stallion with the staggers, and so slung
Neck and crop ravaging down the ways of hell.

    (FRANCESCA *moves restlessly to and fro in the shadow. Through
    the archway is seen the evening sky reddened by the flames.*)

PAOLO. Giovanni, are you angry with me?
GIANCIOTTO. No,
    Did you not split the tongue of him who cried
    His jests against me? "At him! At him! Ha!
    The Lamester with the lovely wife!" cried out
    Ugolino as he rode. His voice was loud:
    Did it reach you at the window? I was there,
    Eye upon eye, and stirrup against stirrup,
    When your good shaft went straight
    Into his snarling mouth,
    And through, and out the back way of the head.
    And yet you might have missed.
    I felt the feathers of the arrow-shaft
    Whistle against my face. You might have missed.
PAOLO. But since I did not miss, why think of it?
GIANCIOTTO. It is your way to run these sorts of risks.
    At Florence be more cautious. You are going
    To a hard post. Have sharp and rapid sight
    But also prudent hand.
PAOLO. Since you advise me,
    Does it not seem to you, brother, as if
    'Twere wiser let it go? We shall have need
    Of all our forces here. The year is turning
    Not over fortunately for the Guelfs,
    Since the defeat of that Giovanni d'Appia

And the rebellion since in Sicily.
In favour of the Angevins.

GIANCIOTTO. We must needs
Accept, and that without delay. You now
Shall be the keeper of the peace where once
Our mighty father was the Governor
Under King Charles, in the one great Guelf city
That prospers still. And so beyond the bounds
Of our Romagna shall the name of us
Sound high and spread abroad; and each of us
Shall follow where his rising star leads on.
I go my way, my sword has eyes for me;
My horse has not yet stumbled under me.

(*While he speaks,* MALATESTINO *is brought, wounded, down
the stairs of the tower, between lighted torches, like a corpse.
The shadow grows darker.*)

FRANCESCA (*from the back*). O, what is this? Horror! Do you
not see

Malatestino, there, Malatestino,
The soldiers carrying him in their arms
Between the torches? They have killed his father!

(*She runs towards the* MEN, *who are coming down the side stairs,
and passing through the midst of the* ARCHERS, *who leave off
their work and make way in silence.* GIANCIOTTO *and* PAOLO
run forward. ODDO DALLE CAMINATE *and* FOSCOLO
D'OLNANG *are carrying the bleeding* YOUTH. *Four* ARCHERS
with long quivers accompany them with torches.)

FRANCESCA (*bending over the* YOUTH). Malatestino! O God,
His eye is black with blood,
His eye is cut and torn. How have they killed him?
O, has his father seen it? Does he know?

(GIANCIOTTO *feels over his body and listens to his heart.*)

GIANCIOTTO. Francesca, no, he is not dead! He breathes,
His heart is beating still. Do you not see?
He is coming to. The blow has struck him senseless;
But he is coming to.
The life is sound in him; he has good teeth
To keep it back from going. Courage, now!

Set him down gently here, here on this heap
Of ropes.

> (*As the* BEARERS *are setting him down, the* YOUTH *begins to
> revive.*)

Oddo, how was it?

ODDO. From a stone
While they were scaling the Galassa tower.

FOSCOLO. All by himself he had made prisoner
Montagna Parcitade,
And bound him with his sword-belt, and led him back
To Messer Malatesta; and returned
To take the Tower.

ODDO. Just as he was, without
A visor to his helmet, heedlessly:
You know how hot he is!

FOSCOLO. And he was angry
Because his father would not suffer him
To cut the prisoner's throat.

> (FRANCESCA *pours a few drops of wine between the lips of the*
> YOUTH.   PAOLO *follows every movement greedily with his eyes.*)

GIANCIOTTO (*looking at the wound*). A stone out of the hand; not
from a sling.
Come, it is nothing.
Lean as he is, he needs
Crow-bar and catapult to put him under.
This is a heart of metal, a tough liver.
He bears the sign of God now, as I do,
In warfare. He shall be
Named, from henceforth, as I am, by his scar.

> (*He kisses him on the forehead.*)

Malatestino!

> (*The* YOUTH *shakes himself and recovers consciousness.*)

Drink, Malatestino!

> (*He drinks some of the wine, which* FRANCESCA *puts to his lips.
> Then he shakes his head, and is about to raise to his wounded left
> eye the hand still wearing its gauntlet.* FRANCESCA *prevents him.*)

MALATESTINO (*as if suddenly awaking, with violence*). He will escape,
I say. He is not safe

In prison. I tell you he will find a way
To escape presently. Father, give me leave
To cut his throat! I took him for you! Father,
Dear Father, let me kill him. I am sure
He will find a way to escape presently.
He is an evil one. Well, you then, give him
One hammer-stroke upon the head; one blow,
And he will turn upon himself three times.

FRANCESCA. Malatestino, what do you see? You are raving,
What do you see, Malatestino?

ODDO. Still
He is raging at Montagna.

GIANCIOTTO. Malatestino, do you not know me? See,
You are on the Mastra Tower.
Montagna is in good clutches. Be assured
He will not run away from you.

MALATESTINO. Giovanni,
Where am I? O Francesca, and you too?

(He again raises his hand to his eyes.)

What is the matter with my eye?

GIANCIOTTO. A stone
That caught you in it.

FRANCESCA. Are you suffering much?

(The YOUTH rises to his feet and shakes his head.)

MALATESTINO. The stone-throw of a Ghibelline camp-follower
To make me suffer?
Come, come, there's no use now,
No time to weave new linen with old thread.
Put on a bandage, quick,
Give me to drink, and then
To horse, to horse!

(FRANCESCA takes off the band that surrounds her chin and throat.)

GIANCIOTTO. Can you see?

MALATESTINO. One's enough for me.

GIANCIOTTO. Try now
If the left one is lost. *(He takes a torch from one of the* ARCHERS.)*
Close your right eye. Francesca,
Put your hand over it. He has his gauntlet.

(She closes his eyelid with her fingers. GIANCIOTTO *puts the torch before his face.)*

Look! Do you see this torch?

MALATESTINO. No.

GIANCIOTTO. Not a glimmer?

MALATESTINO. No, no!

(He takes FRANCESCA'S *wrist and pushes it away.)*

But I can see with one.

ARCHER *(excited by the* YOUTH'S *courage)*. Long live
Messer Malatestino! Malatesta!

MALATESTINO. To horse, to horse!
Giovanni, though the day is won, yet, yet,
Is not old Parcitade living still,
And waiting reinforcements? We must not
Be blinded. Oddo, Foscolo, the best
Is still to have.

GIANCIOTTO *(turning to the* ARCHERS*)*. The cask! is the cask ready?

(He goes towards the tower, to direct the operations of the catapult.)

ODDO. You will fall half-way there.

FRANCESCA. Stay, Malatestino,
Do not go back into the fight! Stay here,
And I will bathe and heal you. Run, Smaragdi,
Prepare the water and the linen; send
For Maestro Almodoro.

MALATESTINO. No, kinswoman,
Put on a bandage, quick,
And let me go. I will come back again
To find the doctor: bid the doctor wait.
I feel no pain at all.
But bandage me, I beg of you, kinswoman,
With the band that you have taken off your face.

FRANCESCA. I will do the best I can for you, God knows,
But it will not be well done.

(She binds up his eye. He observes PAOLO, *who has not taken his eyes off* FRANCESCA.*)*

MALATESTINO. O, Paozzo,
What are you doing there? dreaming?

FRANCESCA. 'Twill not
Be well done.

MALATESTINO. You have been elected Captain
Of the People at Florence. When I haled Montagna
Up to our father, bound, I saw the envoys,
The Guelfs of the Red Lily,
Who were with him then.

    (*A guttural cry is heard as the* MEN *raise the cask upon the cata-
pult. Above the battlements the glow of the fire spreads over
the sky. The bells ring in all directions. Trumpets are heard.*)

They have shut up Montagna
In the sea prison. He will get away.
I begged my father, I begged him, on my knees,
To let me finish.
The envoys smiled. My father would not let me,
Because of them, I know,
To seem magnanimous. Another night
Montagna must not spend here. Will you help me?
Come to the prison! Have you done, kinswoman?
But do not tremble.

FRANCESCA (*tying the knot*). Yes, yes, but it is not well done. Your
    forehead
Is burning. You are feverish. Do not go,
Malatestino. Listen to me. Stay,
For God's sake!

GIANCIOTTO (*on the tower*). Heave it! Let it go!

    (*The noise of the catapult is heard as it discharges the cask with its
lighted fuses.*)

ARCHER. Long life
To Malatesta! Long life to the Guelfs!
Death to the Ghibellines and Parcitade!

MALATESTINO (*turning and running forward*). To horse! to horse!
    to horse!

    (ODDO, FOSCOLO, *and the* ARCHERS *with their torches follow him.*)
    (*The stage darkens. The reflection of the fire reddens the shadow
in which* PAOLO *and* FRANCESCA *remain alone.*)

PAOLO. Farewell, Francesca.

    (*As he approaches her, she draws back with terror.*)

GIANCIOTTO (*from the tower*). Paolo! Paolo!

FRANCESCA. Brother, farewell! Brother!

(PAOLO *goes towards the Tower, from which the fiery staves are again being thrown.* FRANCESCA, *left alone in the shadow, makes the sign of the cross and falls on her knees, bowing herself to the ground. At the back a still brighter illumination lights up the sky.*)

ARCHER. Fire! fire! Death to the Ghibellines! Fire! Death
To Parcitade and the Ghibellines!
Long live the Guelfs and long live Malatesta!

(*The fiery shafts are let fly through the battlements. The bells ring in all directions. The trumpets sound in the confusion of cries rising from the streets of the burning and blood-stained city.*)

ACT THREE

A room painted in fresco, elegantly divided into panels, portraying stories out of the romance of Tristan, between birds, beasts, flowers, and fruits. Under the moulding, around the walls, runs a frieze in the form of festoons, on which are written some words from a love-song:

"*Meglio m'è dormire gaudendo*
C'avere penzieri veghiando."

On the right is a beautiful alcove hidden by rich curtains; on the left a doorway covered by a heavy hanging; at the back a long window with many panes, divided by little columns, looking out on the Adriatic; a pot of basil is on the window-sill. Near the door, raised two feet above the floor, is a musicians' gallery, with compartments decorated with open carvings. Near the window is a reading desk, on which is open "The History of Launcelot of the Lake," composed of large illuminated pages, firmly bound together by thin boards covered in crimson velvet. Beside it is a couch, a sort of long chair without back or arms, with many cushions of samite, almost on the level of the window-sill, on which anyone leaning back can see over the whole seashore of Rimini. A chamber organ of small size, with chest, pipes, keys, bellows, and registers finely worked, stands in the corner, a lute and a viol beside it. On a small table is a silver mirror, amongst scent-bottles, glasses, purses, girdles, and other trinkets. Large iron candlesticks stand beside the alcove and the musicians' gallery. Footstools are scattered about, and in the midst of the floor is seen the bolt of a trap-door, through which a passage leads to the lower rooms.

(FRANCESCA *is reading in the book. The* WOMEN, *seated on the footstools in a circle, embroidering the border of a coverlet, listen to the story; each of them has a little phial of seed pearls and gold threads hanging from her girdle. The March sunlight beats on the crimson taffeta, and sheds a diffused light on the faces bent over the needlework. The* SLAVE *is near the windowsill, gazing into the sky.*)

FRANCESCA (*reading*). "Thereat Galeotto comes to her and says:
'Lady, have pity on him, for God's sake,
And do for me as I would do for you,
If you should ask it of me.' 'What is this
That I should pity?' 'Lady, you well know
How much he loves you, and has done for you,
More than knight ever did for any lady.'
'In truth he has done more for me than I
Can ever do for him again, and he
Could ask of me nothing I would not do;
But he asks nothing of me, and he has
So deep a sadness, that I marvel at it.'
And Galeotto says: 'Lady, have pity.'
'That will I have,' says she, 'and even such
As you would have me; but he asks of me
Nothing…' "

    (*The* WOMEN *laugh.* FRANCESCA *throws herself back on the cushions, troubled and enervated.*)

GARSENDA. Madonna,
How ever could a knight, and Launcelot,
Have been so shamefaced?

ALDA. All the while the queen,
The poor queen, only longing she might give
Her lover what he would not ask of her!

BIANCOFIORE. She should have said to him: "Most worthy knight,
Your sadness will avail you not a mite."

ALTICHIARA. Guenevere did but jest with him, and chose
To wait her time; but nothing in the world
Was in her mind more than a speedy bed.

ADONELLA. And Galeotto, though indeed he was
A noble prince, knew well enough the art
That is called —

FRANCESCA. Adonella, hush! I tire
Of listening to your chattering so long.
Smaragdi, tell me, is the falcon back?

SLAVE. No, lady; he has lost his way.

FRANCESCA. Do you hear
His little golden bell?

SLAVE. I cannot hear it.
My eyes are good, and yet I cannot see him.
He has flown too high.

(FRANCESCA *turns to the window and gazes out.*)

ALDA. He will be lost, Madonna.
It was not well to let him out of leash.
He was a little haughty.

GARSENDA. He was one
They call the Ventimillia breed, brave birds;
This one had thirteen feathers in his tail.

ALTICHIARA. Their home is on an island;
He will have flown back to his island home.

BIANCOFIORE. He followed cranes, was good at catching them;
And Simonetto begs of you, Madonna,
That he may have a crane, to make two fifes
Of the two leg-bones, and he says they sound
Sweetly as might be.

GARSENDA. No,
He is not coming back; he was too proud;
Ah, like the one who gave him to you, Messer
Malatestino, I would say: may he
Not hear me! If you had but rubbed his beak,
At dead of night,
With horse's belly-grease,
He would have come to love you so, Madonna,
He never would have flown out of your hand.

(*The* WOMEN *burst out laughing.*)

ADONELLA. Now listen to the learned doctoress!

ALTICHIARA. At dead of night with horse's belly-grease!

GARSENDA. Why, yes, I have read the book that Danchi wrote,
The first and best master of falconry;
It gives you all the rules.

FRANCESCA. Go, Adonella,
  Run to the falconer, tell him what has happened,
  And bid him go with his decoy, and call
  And search all over. He has flown, perhaps,
  Up to some tower, and perched there. Bid him go
  And search all over. (ADONELLA *drops her needle and hurries out.*)

ALTICHIARA. He has fled away,
  Madonna after the first swallows.

ALDA. See,
  The blood of all the swallows
  Is raining on the sea.

BIANCOFIORE (*singing*). "Fresh in the Calends of March,
  O swallows, coming home,
  Fresh from the quiet lands beyond the sea."

FRANCESCA. O, yes, yes, Biancofiore!
  Some music, give me music!
  Sing over a low song
  In the minor key!
  Leave off your sewing, go
  And bring me music.
  Look   (*The* WOMEN *rise quickly and fold up the taffeta.*)
  For Simonetto, Biancofiore.

BIANCOFIORE. Yes, Madonna.

FRANCESCA. And you, Alda, look for Bordo
  And Signorello and Rosso,
  And bid them come and bring the instruments
  And bring the tablature
  For making music in the room here.

ALDA. Yes, Madonna.

FRANCESCA. Altichiara, if you see
  The doctor, send him to me.

ALTICHIARA. Yes, Madonna.

FRANCESCA. And you, Garsenda, if you come across
  The merchant who is here from Florence bid him
  Come hither.

GARSENDA. Yes, Madonna, I will seek him.

FRANCESCA. Bring me a garland of March violets.
  Today 'tis the March calends.

BIANCOFIORE. Madonna, you shall have one, and a fair one.

(*All go out.*)

(FRANCESCA *turns to the* SLAVE, *who is still gazing into the sky.*)

FRANCESCA. O Smaragdi, he is not coming back?

SLAVE. He is not coming back.
 The falconer will bring him back again.
 Do not be troubled.

FRANCESCA. But I am troubled, yes; Malatestino
 Will be enraged with me, because I have kept
 His gifts so ill. He tells me that he gave me
 The king of falcons. I have lost it.

SLAVE. Wild
 And thankless and unkind, if so it flies
 From the face of man. (FRANCESCA *is silent for a few instants.*)

FRANCESCA. I am afraid of him.

SLAVE. Afraid of whom, lady?

FRANCESCA. I am afraid
 Of Malatestino.

SLAVE. Is it his blind eye
 That frightens you?

FRANCESCA. No, no, the other one,
 The one he sees with: it is terrible.

SLAVE. Let him not see you, lady.

FRANCESCA. Ah, Smaragdi, what was the wine you brought
 That night, upon the Mastra tower, when all
 The city was in arms? Was it bewitched?

SLAVE. Lady, what are you saying?

FRANCESCA. It is as if you brought me a drugged wine;
 The poison is taking hold
 Upon the veins of her that drank of it,
 And all my fate grows cruel to me again.

SLAVE. What is this sadness, lady?
 Although the falcon has not yet come back,
 He has come back to you,
 Lady, who is the sun that your soul loves.

FRANCESCA (*turning pale, and speaking with repressed anger*).
 Unhappy woman!
 How do you dare to speak it? Treachery

Even in you? Accursed be the hour
In which you brought him to me, and his fraud
With him! Was it not you
Who made the way that leads me to my death?
Three cups of bitterness I do not leave you;
It is you that set them down before me, you
That brim them up each day, without a tear.

(The SLAVE *flings herself on the ground.)*

SLAVE. Tread on me, tread on me! Between two stones
Crush in my head!

FRANCESCA *(more calmly)*. Rise up,
It is no fault of yours, my poor Smaragdi,
It is no fault of yours.
Suddenly like a spirit of my heart
You ran to meet my joy! On your eyes too
There was a veil; and veiled by the same fate
Was the iniquity of my father. We,
All of us, were made powerless and unpitying,
Wretched and ignorant,
Upon the bank of a river,
Unblamable all of us,
Upon the bank of a loud rushing river.
I crossed it, I alone,
I had no thought of you;
I found myself upon the other side.
And we are thrust apart,
Ah me, and never to be one again.
And I now say to you:
I cannot. And you say:
Cross and come back.
And I: I do not know.

*(She gives to the last words almost the cadence of a melody; then
she laughs a dry and bitter laugh, which seems as if torn out
of her. But the sound of her own laughter frightens her. The*
SLAVE *stands trembling.)*

O my poor reason, rule
Still, do not turn away!
What is this demon that has hold on me?

The enemy was laughing in my heart:
Did you not hear him?
I cannot pray now, I can pray no longer.

SLAVE (*in a low voice*). Shall I not call him?

FRANCESCA (*starting*). Who?

> (*She looks about her anxiously: her eye turns to the motionless
> curtain over the door. Her craving overcomes her, her voice
> sounds hoarse.*)

Smaragdi, did you see Messer Giovanni
Take horse?

SLAVE. Yes, lady, with the old man too,
With Messer Malatesta, the old man.
They are going surely to an act of peace
With the Lord Bishop. They are riding now
By Sant' Arcangelo.

FRANCESCA (*darkly*). You watch, Smaragdi; you see all, hear all,
Know all; well, be so always.

SLAVE. Doubt me not,
Lady. Sleep safe and sound. Could I but give you
Joy, as the stone whose name I bear could give you!

FRANCESCA. And do you know where Malatestino is?

SLAVE. At Roncofreddo, sent there by his father
With thirty horse.

FRANCESCA. I am afraid of him.
Keep him away from me.

SLAVE. But why so, lady?
When he was sick, did you not care for him,
Day and night, like a sister?

FRANCESCA. O, that name
Is like a poison here. Samaritana,
Where are you? and the stream of your young freshness,
Where does it run, that now can never slake
My thirst when I am nigh to perishing?
I see about me, in the shadow about me,
Eyes, savage eyes, that spy on me, the eyes
Of wild beasts only waiting to take hold
And fight over their prey;
And they are all veined with the selfsame blood,

They are all brothers;
One mother gave them birth. Ah me! what sad
Sorcery have I suffered? Who has set
Thus, thus, upon the threshold of my life
This mortal sin? You, creature of the earth,
Who dig about the roots of poisonous flowers,
Say, where was this unnatural evil born?
It is from you I know
The old hard song:
"If three I find, three I take!" Now the demon
Has taken them all together, three has taken,
And me with them.

SLAVE. Call not upon the enemy!
Be it forgiven to you, body and soul!
You are deceived in this.
The shadow is a glass to you, and therein
You see your own eyes burn.
Call not upon your head
Some evil fortune! May the Lord God watch
Over you as your slave will surely watch!

FRANCESCA. There is no escape, Smaragdi. You have said it:
The shadow is a glass to me; and God
Lets me be lost. What days
And nights I spent alone by the bedside
Of the sick man, that I might purge myself
Of evil thoughts that faded, faded out.
I touched the horrible wound,
Praying; I washed away
That evil foulness with my prayers. And then
My soul, amid that horror, seemed to see
Grace and salvation; then it was I found
The beast desire that wakened in the veins
Of that too violent life. Do you understand?
The gaping wound under the forehead closed
And another opened, far more horrible,
Within the breast. And thoughts
That had faded out, my old despairing thoughts,
Seemed to infect me with a blacker venom,

More cruelly; and my flesh
Upon my sorrow like a covering
Intolerable;
And exiled from the world
All the sweet things of springtide and of sleep;
And the very face of love
Turned into stone, and turned
To a terror; only hatred and desire,
Bewildered in the darkness of the world,
And reeling blindly in their work of death,
Like drunken slaughterers,
That, full of wine
And fury, slay each other witlessly.

SLAVE (*in a low voice*). Do not despair!   Listen, listen!   I know
A spell to cast on him who makes you fear;
I know a drink that drives these thoughts away
And cures remembrance.   You must give it him
With the left hand
When he dismounts wearied and hungering.
I will teach you how to say the spell.

FRANCESCA. Smaragdi,
If it avails at all, give it to me,
And let me drink it, and be free again.
But there is no escape.   Will you interpret
The dream I always dream,
Night after night?

SLAVE. Lady, tell me the dream;
I will interpret it.

FRANCESCA. Night after night I see the savage hunt
Nastagio degli Onesti saw one day
In the pine-wood of Ravenna, as I heard
Bannino tell the story when we went
Down to the shore at Chiassi.   In my dream
I see it as it was in very truth.
A naked woman, through the depth of the wood,
Dishevelled, torn by branches and by thorns,
Weeping and crying for mercy,
Runs, followed by two mastiffs at her heels

That bite her cruelly when they overtake her;
See, and behind her through the depth of the wood,
Mounted on a black charger,
A dark knight, strong and angry in the face,
Sword in hand, threatening her
With a swift death in terrifying words.
Then the dogs, taking hold
Of the woman's naked side,
Stop her; and the fierce knight, coming abreast,
Dismounts from off his horse,
And with his sword in hand
Runs at the woman so,
And she, upon her knees, pinned to the earth
By the two mastiffs, cries to him for mercy;
And he thereat drives at her with full strength,
Pierces her in the breast
So that the sword goes through her; and she falls
Forward, upon her face,
Still always weeping; and the knight draws forth
A dagger, and opens her
By the hip-bone, and draws
Her heart out, and the rest,
And throws it to the dogs that hungrily
Devour it of a sudden.   But she has lain
Not long before, as if she were not dead,
She rises up and she begins again
Her lamentable running toward the sea;
And the two dogs after her, tearing her,
Always, and always after her the knight,
Upon his horse again,
And with his sword in hand,
Always threatening her.
Tell me, can you interpret me my dream,
Smaragdi?   (*The* SLAVE, *as she listens, seems stricken with terror.*)
Are you frightened?

(GARSENDA *enters followed by the* MERCHANT *and his* BOY *carrying a pack.*)

GARSENDA (*gaily*). Madonna, here is the merchant with his goods.
May he come in? He is the Florentine,
Who came to Rimino yesterday with the escort
Of Messer Paolo.

> (FRANCESCA, *her face suddenly flushing, shakes off her gloomy thoughts, and seems eager to seek forgetfulness of her mortal anguish; but a kind of painful tension accompanies her volubility.*)

FRANCESCA. Come in, come in, we are minded to renew
Our robes with the new season.
Come in, come in. I would have something made
Of sarcenet woven of many coloured threads,
Of many colours, of a hundred colours,
So that at each turn and return of light
And of sight the aspect changes; O Smaragdi,
A raiment of pure joy! (*The* MERCHANT *inclines humbly.*)
Good merchant, what have you to offer me?

MERCHANT. Noble Madonna, everything that suits
With your nobility; light taffetas,
Highly embroidered, circlet upon circlet,
Sarcenet, samite, and damask,
Grogram and bombasin,
Camlet, barracan, fustian,
Serge, Neapolitan doublets,
Sicilian tunics,
Watered silk, high or low, watered with gold
And silver thread, and waved;
Linen of Lucca, Osta, Dondiscarte,
Of Bruges, of Tournai, and of Terremonde,
And of Mostavolieri in Normandy,
Fine serge from Como, changeable taffeta,
Cloth of silk worked in trees and squares and eyelets
And patterns toothed and fish-boned,
Velvets of every sort
And every make,

Velvets one piled, and two piled, and three piled.

(GARSENDA *bursts out laughing.*)

FRANCESCA. Enough! enough! And have you found a warehouse
In Rimino for so many goods?

MERCHANT. I am
Giotto di Bernarduccio Boninsegni,
The agent of the Company of Piero
Di Niccolaio degli Oricellari,
That has its thousand samples in the warehouses
Of Calimala and of Calimaruzza,
And sends its agents over all the west,
As far as Ireland, and, in the Levant,
As far as the Cattaio, noble Madonna.

(GARSENDA *laughs. The* MERCHANT *turns and looks at her.*)

GARSENDA. A florin or two, eh?
You lent to Prester John,
(Poor wretch!) or to the Khan of Babylon.

(*The* MERCHANT *opens the pack before* FRANCESCA, *who stands
at the reading desk, and exhibits his goods.*)

MERCHANT. We go to Armalecco, to buy vair,
Sable and ermine,
And marten-skins, and lynx, and other skins;
And to buy woollen too,
To the monasteries of England, and to China,
To Bilignass, Croccostrande, and Isticchi,
To Diolacresca, Giúttebi, and Bufeltro,
In Cornwall. (GARSENDA *laughs.*)

GARSENDA. Then you saw
King Mark in Cornwall, then
The fair-haired Iseult bought brocades from you
Sky-coloured, of a surety? Or you carried
Her Tristan, hidden in your pack of goods,
Into her chamber.

MERCHANT. They say that in Romagna
All fowling, nay, all gulling, is permitted;
But the blackbird has already crossed the stream
And his mate has crossed the Po already.

GARSENDA. Shafts
Of Florence make and Lombard: bastard shafts.

They neither shine nor sting,
Because I do not know them.

        (FRANCESCA *seems intent on turning over the stuffs.*)

FRANCESCA. This is good,
    Brocade with golden pomegranates. And how,
    Giotto, did you come here to Rimino?

MERCHANT. Noble Madonna, full of perils is
    The life of merchants. Needs must be we take
    Every occasion that is offered us.
    I, by good fortune, chanced to come upon
    The escort of the noble Messer Paolo,
    And had good leave to follow it in safety.
    So swift a journey may I ever make
    Again; with Messer Paolo you ride
    The whole day long, and never sleep at all.

        (FRANCESCA *feels over the stuffs, outwardly calm, but an uncon-*
        querable smile burns in her eyes. GARSENDA *has gone down*
        on her knees to see the stuffs.)

FRANCESCA. You rode so swiftly?

MERCHANT. Without rest or stay,
    With tightened bridles, if I might so put it;
    And every stream they forded, could not wait
    Until the flood had ebbed. And Messer Paolo
    Laboured his horse with spur in such a haste
    That there was always between him and us,
    A mile or so of distance. I should say
    He has some urgent business here. He asked
    The Commune leave of absence
    After two months, or little more, that he
    Had entered into office; truth it is
    That the whole city sorrows at it, never
    A more accustomed and more civil knight
    Was Captain of the People there in Florence.

FRANCESCA. I will take this brocade.

MERCHANT. Good, very good,
    Madonna. And Bernardino della Porta
    Of Parma, they have chosen
    To take his place, is worth,

Why not so much as one hair of the head
Of Messer Paolo.

FRANCESCA. And this samite too.

MERCHANT. Madonna, this with patterns all of gold...

FRANCESCA. Yes, I like this one too. It seems to me
You Florentines keep feast on feast, and make
The year a holiday, and care for nothing
Except for games and sports and banquetings
And dances.

MERCHANT. Yes, Madonna, 'tis a sweet
And blessed land, our Florence: 'tis the flower
Of the others, Fiorenza!

FRANCESCA. I will take this silk too with the silver lines.
And the Captain of the People,
Was he well liked by all the companies
Of knights and ladies?

MERCHANT. Each rivalled with each
Of all the companies
To have his presence, as the most well-spoken
And gallant man he indeed is; but he,
By what I know, would hold himself apart,
A trifle haughtily, and rare it was
To see him at their suppers. And in time
Of Carnival, in Santa Felicita
Beyond the Arno, I know by Messer Betto
De' Rossi that they made a company,
A thousand men or more, all dressed in white,
And Messer Paolo by this company
Was chosen Lord of Love,
But he would not consent...

FRANCESCA. Here, this shot sarcenet
And this buff-coloured cotton. You were saying,
Giotto...

> (GARSENDA *takes the stuffs selected, and puts them aside, first*
> *holding them up to the light.*)

MERCHANT. I have seen him sometimes go about
With Guido of the Messers Cavalcante
Dei Cavalcanti; he that is, they say,

One of the best logicians in the world,
And a most manifest
Natural philosopher,
And, as they say, he seeks,
Among the tombs, to find
There never was a God.

FRANCESCA. Garsenda, you may have this violet samite.

GARSENDA. O Madonna, much thanks!

MERCHANT. 'Tis a fine violet,
One of the finest colours of the dye.

FRANCESCA. And for you, Smaragdi? You were saying, Giotto...

MERCHANT. Often he had with him
Good singers and good players, specially
Casella da Pistoia the musician,
A master in the art of singing songs
Of love...

FRANCESCA. For you, Smaragdi, you shall have
This green-brown serge. And Altichiara too
And Biancofiore, each of you must have
A new dress.

MERCHANT. This, Madonna, is a colour
Of the newest fashion, it is called the seamew,
A very marvel, with its golden bunches;
Mona Giuglia degli Adimari, the other week,
Bought from me full ten yards of it. And this
With the goose pattern. Capon's foot, bear's ear,
Young pigeon, angel's wing,
Iris, corn-flower, new colours...

(FRANCESCA *rises impetuously, as if breaking some constraint.*)

FRANCESCA. Merchant, leave it,
And I will choose at leisure.

(*She turns towards the window and looks out on the shining sea,
shading her eyes with her hand.*)

How the sun
Is strong, this March, and fierce!
There goes a little ship with a red sail!
Here are the swallows coming back in flocks!

GARSENDA (*to the* MERCHANT). How long shall you be staying in
Rimino?

MERCHANT. Three days. And then I have to make my way
  To Barletta and from Barletta I take ship
  For Cyprus.

> (*The* SLAVE *lights up, hearing the name of her country.*)

GARSENDA. Listen, listen,
  Smaragdi!

SLAVE (*anxiously*). Do you go to Cyprus, merchant?

MERCHANT. I go there yearly. We have warehouses
  At Famagosta, and there yearly sell
  Thousands and thousands besants' worth of goods.
  Are you from Cyprus?

SLAVE. Salute for me the Mount Chionodes,
  His head in snow and olives at his feet;
  And drink for me at the spring of Chitria
  A draught for my heart's sake.

FRANCESCA (*turning*). "And Cyprus I would make for,
  And at Limisso anchor,
  And land my sailors for a kiss, my captains
  For love!"

> (*Instruments and merry voices are heard preluding while she goes
>   towards the bed, droopingly, as if to lie down on it.*)

SLAVE. And who is king there? Sire Ughetto?

MERCHANT. Ughetto died young. Ugo di Lusignano,
  His cousin, is king now. And there have been
  Most evil deeds,
  And poisonings of women,
  And treachery of barons and the plague,
  Locusts and earthquakes,
  And Venus, queen of devils, has appeared.

> (*The sounds of music and voices and laughter come nearer.* FRAN-
>   CESCA *lies back on the bed between the half-closed cur-
>   tains.*)

> (*The* WOMEN, *with the exception of* ADONELLA, *enter, followed by
>   the* DOCTOR, *the* ASTROLOGER, *the* JESTER *and the* MUSICIANS,
>   *who tune their instruments and prelude on them. The* DOCTOR *wears
>   a dressing-gown, down to the heels, of a dark tan-colour; the* ASTROL-
>   OGER *a green-brown robe and a black turban striped with yellow;*

the JESTER *a scarlet jerkin.* *The* MUSICIANS *go up on their gallery, and range themselves in order.)*

ALTICHIARA. Madonna, here is Maestro Almodoro.

ALDA. And we have found the astrologer, Madonna.

BIANCOFIORE. And the Jester too, Gian Figo, that procures
Recipes against melancholy with songs
And stories and the dust of No-Man's Land.

ALDA. And the voices and the players
On bagpipe, flute and lute,
Rebec and monochord.

(Standing upright between the curtains, FRANCESCA *looks before her as if bewildered, neither smiling nor speaking.)*

BIANCOFIORE *(coming forward).* Here is the garland
Of violets. May it chase your melancholy!

(She offers it to her gracefully. FRANCESCA *takes it, while* ALTICHIARA *takes the mirror from the table and holds it up before her face as she puts on the garland. The* SLAVE *slowly goes out.)*

GARSENDA. O Maestro Almodoro,
Galen, Hippocrates, and Avicenna
Returned to earth inside one doctor's gown,
Can you tell us what is melancholy?

(The DOCTOR *places himself in their midst, and assumes a solemn air.)*

DOCTOR. Melancholy
Is a dark humour many call black bile,
And it is cold and dry,
And has its situation in the spine;
Its nature is of the earth
And of the autumn. Nec dubium est quidem
Melancholicus morbus
Ab impostore Diabolo...

(The JESTER *puts himself in front of him, covering him. The* WOMEN *and the* MUSICIANS *laugh and whisper.)*

JESTER. When
Your devil was born, my devil had found his legs.
Melancholy is to drink as the Germans do,
Madonna; to backbite as the Greeks do,

To sing as the French do,
To dance as the Moors do,
To sleep as the English do,
And to stand steady like
Messer Ferragunze the Cordelier.
Madonna, I have had from you those two
Pieces of scarlet in advance: but see,
The jerkin that was new has become old.
Have you two other pieces, may it please you,
Of velvet?

> (*The* WOMEN *laugh. He eyes the* MERCHANT'S *wares, scattered over the couch.*)

GARSENDA. The Astrologer! Speak now,
Astrologer of Syria who sees all things!

> (*The bearded* ASTROLOGER *puts on a gloomy look and speaks with a voice that seems to come from a deep cave.*)

ASTROLOGER. All darts he sees not, who sees every dart;
But he who blindly aims against the heart
Takes aim from thence, whence doth all life depart.
JESTER. And I believe not in your art.

> (FRANCESCA *looks sharply at the* SARACEN *as if fearing something.*)

FRANCESCA. What do you mean by this dark riddle? Speak,
Maestro Isacco, explain.
ASTROLOGER. Lady, who inward looks,
Looks not, but he who wills that which he looks.
JESTER. And yet the man of Friuli has said:
He who wants woman wants a lord and master,
And he who wants a lord and master wants —
Catch who catch can! And then
In the book of Madam Mogias of Egypt,
That is called the Book of Piercing to the Heart,
It is declared that woman's enemies
Are seventeen —

> (ADONELLA *enters, carrying five garlands of white narcissi, hanging from a gold wire that binds them together.*)

ADONELLA. Madonna, the falconer
Has called the falcon back. Some of his feathers

Are bent or broken a little; but warm water
And a soft bandage will soon set them right.

ASTROLOGER. The falcon's beak thou shalt not shear or break,
But scanty clippings take;
For these, well mixed with wool, long talons make.

FRANCESCA. You speak in riddles, then,
Today, Maestro Isacco?

ASTROLOGER. Not everyone who speaketh speaks, but he
Who sleeps must silent be;
Evils in life and truth in prophecy.

JESTER. So may it be, amen! Bring in the bier.
O Saracen Isacco,
You are a very great astronomer;
You prophesy, besides;
But you must make a little matter plain.
Tell me, which is the easier to know,
The things that are now past,
Or else the things that are to come?

ASTROLOGER. O fool,
Who does not know the things that he has seen,
The things that are behind?

JESTER. Good, very good; we'll see how well you know them.
Now tell me this,
What were you doing on the last March calends,
A year ago! (*The* ASTROLOGER *thinks.*)
Well, then, six months ago?

(*The* ASTROLOGER *thinks. The* WOMEN *laugh. The* JESTER
speaks rapidly.)

I will ask you, then, one last time: can you tell me
What weather it was three months ago?

(*The* ASTROLOGER *thinks and stares before him. The* JESTER
plucks him by the robe.)

Isacco,
Don't cast nativities, you need not gape,
Stand steady. Now, what ship
Came here, a month ago? What ship set sail?
What do you gape at? Did you eat indoors
Or out of doors a fortnight since?

ASTROLOGER. Wait, wait
  A little.
JESTER. Wait! What? But I will not wait.
  Come now, what were you doing,
  A week ago today?
ASTROLOGER. Give me a little respite.
JESTER. Why, what respite
  Should such as I give such as you who know
  The things that are to come? What did you eat
  Four days ago?
ASTROLOGER. Ah, I will tell you that.
JESTER. What did you say?
ASTROLOGER. You are in such haste.
JESTER. What haste? Well, tell me now, what did you eat
  Yesterday morning? Tell me!

  (*The* ASTROLOGER, *annoyed, turns his back upon him. He
    plucks him by the sleeve.*)

  Stop! Look at me a moment!
  I lay you ten to one you do not know
  If you are wide awake or if you dream.
ASTROLOGER. I know I do not sleep, and that you are
  The greatest fool now living in the world!
JESTER. But I assure you that you do not know.
  Come here. Don't go like that against the wind
  Of Mongibello. Tell me, have you not
  Hundreds of times gone up and down the stairs
  Of the belfry-tower of Santa Colomba? Well,
  How many stairs are there? Come here, I say!
  Don't run away from me. Have you ever eaten
  Medlars? How many pips are in a medlar?

  (*The infuriated* ASTROLOGER *frees himself from the grip of the
    JESTER, amidst much laughter.*)

  Then if you don't know that,
  How can you know things that are in the sky,
  And in the hearts of women, and in hair?
  Find a cordwainer, bid him make a rope
  Out of your beard, and hang you to a star.
BIANCOFIORE. Madonna has smiled!

Gian Figo has made even Madonna smile!
Go, go, dear doctor, to your house again,
And take your medicine and your Latin with you,
Today is the March calends! Song means dance
Today, and dance means song.
Play, Simonetto, play!

> (*The* MUSICIANS *begin a prelude. Those standing near go to
> the back, so as to leave room for the dance.* ADONELLA *un-
> looses the gold wire, and distributes the garlands of narcissi
> to her companions, who put them on; and retains for herself the
> one that bears two swallows' wings.* ALDA *takes out of a
> little bag four painted wooden swallows that have a kind of
> small handle under the breast, and gives one to each of her
> companions; who, standing ready for the dance, hold them each
> raised in the left hand.* ADONELLA *whistles, in imitation of
> the chirruping of swallows, and, while the other four dance
> and sing, she utters at intervals, according to the rhythm, the
> loud chirping that heralds the spring.*)

ALDA. Fresh, fresh, in the calends of March,
　　O swallows, coming home
　　Fresh from the quiet lands beyond the sea;
　　First to bring back the great good messages
　　Of joy, and first to taste the good wild scent.
　　O creature of pure joy,
　　Come in your garments white and black, fly hither,
　　And bring your springtide gladness to our dance!

ALTICHIARA. March comes, and February
　　Goes with the wind today;
　　Bring out your taffety
　　And put the vair away.
　　And come with me, I pray,
　　Across the streams in flood,
　　Under the branching wood that leans along,
　　With dancing and with song in company
　　With fleet-foot lovers, or upon the lea
　　Gather the violets,
　　Where the grass smells more sweet because her feet,
　　Have passed that way, the naked feet of Spring!

GARSENDA. Today the earth appears
  New-wedded like a girl;
  The face that the sea wears
  Today is like a pearl.
  Hark, hark, is that the merle
  Deep in the thicket? Hark,
  How swift upsoars the lark into the sky!
  The cruel wind goes by, and in his mouth
  Bears ravished nests! O swallow of the south,
  Thy tail's an arrow feather,
  And like the twanging of a bow thy cry
  Whereby the spring will strike, the hands of Spring!

BIANCOFIORE. O creature of delight,
  Lead thou the dancing feet,
  In robe of black and white,
  As is thy usage sweet.
  Make here thy stay, O fleet
  Swallow, here in this room
  Wherein is seen, in gloom or light of day,
  The tale of Iseult, the fair flower of Ireland,
  As here thou seest, and this shall be thy garland,
  Thy nest, no prison-mesh,
  Seeing that the fresh fair lady seated here
  Is not Francesca, but is very —

> (*The* DANCERS *return rapidly, towards* FRANCESCA *and form in a line, stretching out towards her the hand that holds the swallow, and the other; and they all sing with* BIANCOFIORE, *without interval, the last word of the stanza.*)

ALL. Spring!

(*At the beginning of the last movement the* SLAVE *appears on the threshold. As the* MUSICIANS *play the last notes, she goes up to* FRANCESCA *hurriedly and whispers to her something that suddenly disturbs her.*)

FRANCESCA (*impetuously*). Biancofiore, Altichiara, Alda, Adonella,
  Garsenda, for the new
  Delight of this new dance,
  I must give you something new:
  These dresses, take them, each!
> (*She picks up some of the scattered goods and gives them.*)

Here's for you, and for you!

> (*The* JESTER *comes forward in a sidelong way.*)

And for you too,
Gian Figo, but no jesting.   (*The* JESTER *takes it and decamps.*)
Garsenda, take this too for the Musicians,
They can make jackets of it,
With stripes of red and yellow. And see, too, Merchant,
You set aside two lengths of some good serge
For Maestro Almodoro, and Maestro Isacco.
Now go, I have given you something, all of you,
For the March calends' sake. Go now, and, going,
Sing in the court the song of the March swallows.
You must come back again, Merchant; Garsenda
Will bring you word. You may leave your wares here now.
Go, and be merry, until vesper-time;
Adonella, lead the way into the court.
A happy spring to you!

> (*The* MUSICIANS *come down from their gallery, playing, and go
> out. The* JESTER *skips after them. All the others bow before*
> FRANCESCA *and take the gifts they have received, following the*
> MUSICIANS *with whispering and laughter. The* SLAVE
> *remains, busy wrapping up the wares in bundles.* FRANCESCA
> *abandons herself to her anxiety. She takes several steps, blindly;*
> *with a sudden movement, she draws the curtains of the alcove,*
> *which are half open, showing the bed. Then she sits down before*
> *the reading-desk, and glances at the open book, but, in turning,*
> *the train of her dress catches in the lute, which falls, and lies*
> *on the ground. She trembles.*)

No, no, Smaragdi! Run, and tell him not
To come!

> (*The sounds die away in the distance. The* SLAVE, *having*
> *finished, goes towards the door.* FRANCESCA *takes a step*
> *towards her as if to call her back.*)

Smaragdi!   (*The* SLAVE *goes out.*)

> (*After a few moments, a hand raises the curtain, and* PAOLO MALATESTA
> *appears. The door closes behind him. As* PAOLO *and* FRANCESCA
> *gaze at one another, for a moment, without finding words, both*

change colour. The sound of MUSIC *dies away through the palace.*
The room is gilded by the rays of the setting sun, which shine through
the long window.)

FRANCESCA. Welcome, my lord and kinsman.

PAOLO. I have come,
Hearing a sound of music, to bring greetings,
My greetings of return.

FRANCESCA. You have come back
Speedily, sir; indeed with the first swallow.
My women even now
Were singing a new song that they have made
To welcome March. And there was also here
The merchant out of Florence, who had come
Among your following. Of him I had
Tidings of you.

PAOLO. But I, of you, no tidings,
None, I heard nothing there,
Nothing of you at all,
From that day onward, when, one perilous night
You put a cup of wine into my hands,
And said to me, "farewell!"
And said to me, "God-speed!"

FRANCESCA. I have no memory,
My lord, concerning this. I have prayed much.

PAOLO. You have forgotten, then?

FRANCESCA. I have prayed much.

PAOLO. And I have suffered much.
If it be true that he who suffers conquers,
I think I must needs conquer....

FRANCESCA. What?

PAOLO. My fate,
Francesca.

FRANCESCA. And yet you have come back?

PAOLO. I have come back
To live.

FRANCESCA. Not to die now?

PAOLO. Ah, you remember
The death I was to die,

And you that would not!   So much, at the least,
You have remembered.

> (*She draws back towards the window, as if withdrawing herself from his scarcely repressed violence.*)

FRANCESCA.   Paolo, give me peace!
It is so sweet a thing to live forgetting,
But one hour only, and be no more tossed,
Out of the tempest.
Do not call back, I pray,
The shadow of that time in this fresh light
That slakes my thirst at last
Like that long draught
That at the ford I drank,
Out of the living water.
And now, I desire now
To think my soul has left
That shore to come into this sheltering shore,
Where music and where hope are sisters; so
To forget all the sorrow that has been
Yesterday, and shall be
Tomorrow, and so let
All of my life, and all the veins of it,
And all the days of it,
And all old things in it, far-away things,
But for one hour, one hour,
Slip away quietly, a quiet tide,
Unto that sea,
Even these eyes might behold smilingly,
Were it not hidden by the tears that tremble
And do not fall.   O peace, peace in that sea
That was so wild with waves
Yesterday, and today is like a pearl.
Give me peace!

PAOLO.   It is the voice of spring
I hear, and from your lips the music runs
Over the world, that I have seemed to hear,
Riding against the wind,
Sing in the voice of the wind,

At every turn of the way,
At every glade and high
On the hill-tops, and on the edges of the woods,
And under them the streams,
When my desire bent back,
Burning with breath, the mane of my wild horse,
Over the saddle-bow, and the soul lived,
In the swiftness of that flight,
On swiftness,
Like a torch carried in the wind, and all
The thoughts of all my soul, save one, save one,
Were all blown backward, spent
Like sparks behind me.

FRANCESCA. Ah, Paolo, like sparks
All your words are, and still they take no rest,
And all your soul lives still
In the strong wind and swiftness of your coming,
And drags me with it, and I am full of fear.
I pray you, I pray you now,
That you will give me peace
For this hour only,
My fair friend, my sweet friend,
That I may quiet and put to sleep in me
The old sick pain, and forget all the rest;
Only bring back into my eyes the first
Look that took hold on me out of your face,
Unknown to me; for these dry eyelids have
No need of any healing but that dew,
Only to bring back and to have in them
Again the miracle of that first look;
And they will feel that grace has come to them,
As they felt once, out of the heart of a dream,
The coming near of the dawn;
And feel that they are to be comforted,
Perhaps in the shade
Of the new garland.

PAOLO. And so garlanded
With violets I saw you yesterday

In a meadow, as I stayed,
Pausing in journeying,
And being alone, and having far outstripped
My escort. I could hear
Only the champing bit
Of my horse pasturing, and see from there
The towers of Meldola in a wood. And all
Palpitated with you
In the high morning. And you came to me
With violets, and returning to your lips
I heard again a word that you had spoken,
Saying: I pardon you, and with much love!
FRANCESCA. That word was spoken
And perfect joy awaits upon the word.

(PAOLO'S *eyes wander over the room.*)

Ah, do not look around
Upon these things,
Silent, as if with joy,
And only full of sorrow and of shame.
No autumn withered them,
They shall not be awakened with the spring.
Look on the sea, the sea
That has borne witness for us once with God
To certain words once spoken, vast and calm
And shining where the battle came between,
And silent where the rage of clamour came
Between, and one sail passed upon the sea,
Going alone upon its way, like this,
See, yonder? And our souls
Were tried, as if with fire.
But now sit here, upon the window-seat,
And not with weapons now for killing men,
But without cruelty. See, Paolo,
With this mere sprig of basil.

(*She takes a cluster from her head, and offers it to him; as he steps
     nearer, his foot strikes against the catch of the trap-door, and he
     stops.*)

You have struck your foot

Against the ring of the trap-door. It leads
From here into another room beneath.

(PAOLO *stoops to look at it.*)

PAOLO. Ah, you can go from here into a room
Beneath.

FRANCESCA (*giving him the sprig of basil*). Come, take it, smell it;
    it is good.
Smaragdi planted it in memory
Of Cyprus, in this vase;
And when she waters it,
She sings: "Under your feet
I spread sweet basil,
I bid you sleep there,
I bid you pluck it,
I bid you smell it,
And remember the giver!"
At Florence all the women
Have their sweet basil on the window-sill.
Do you not know? But come,
Will you not tell me something of your life?
Sit here, and tell me something of yourself,
How you have lived.

PAOLO. Why do you ask of me
To live the misery of my life twice over?
All that was joy to others was to me
Sorrow and heaviness. One only thing,
Music, could ever give me pleasant hours.
I went sometimes to a great singer's house,
He was by name Casella,
And there were met many of gentle birth,
Among them Guido Cavalcanti, and these
Were wont to make rhymes in the vulgar tongue;
And there was Ser Brunetto,
Returned from Paris, wise
With rhetoric of the schools,
Also a youth
Of the Alighieri, Dante was his name,
And I much loved this youth, he was so full

Of thoughts of love and sorrow,
So burning and so loverlike for song.
And something like a healing influence passed
Out of his heart to mine,
That seemed shut up in me; for the exceeding
And too much sweetness hid
Sometimes within the song moved him to weep.
Silently, silent tears,
And seeing his weeping, I too wept with him.

> (*Her eyes fill with tears and her voice trembles.*)

FRANCESCA. You wept?

PAOLO. Francesca!

FRANCESCA. Wept? Ah, Paolo mine.
Blessed be he that taught your heart such tears,
Such tears! I will pray always for his peace.
For now I see you, now I see you again
As you were then, sweet friend.
The grace has come with healing to my eyes.

> (*She appears as if transfigured with perfect joy. With a slow
> movement she takes the garland from her head and lays it on the
> open book beside her.*)

PAOLO. Why do you take the garland from your head?

FRANCESCA. Because it was not you who gave it me.
I gave you once a rose
From that sarcophagus.
But now, poor flowers, I feel
Your freshness is all spent!

> (PAOLO *rises, and goes up to the reading-desk and touches the
> violets.*)

PAOLO. 'Tis true! Do you remember? on that night
Of fire and blood, you asked of me the gift
Of a fair helmet; and I gave it you:
'Twas finely tempered.
The steel and gold of it have never known
What rust is, soiling. And you let it fall.
Do you remember?
I picked it up, and I have held it dear
As a king's crown.

Since then, when I have set it on my head,
I feel twice bold, and there is not a thought
Within my heart that is not as a flame. (*He bends over the book.*)
Ah, listen, the first words that meet my eye!
"Made richer by that gift than had you given him
The gift of all the world."
What book is this?

FRANCESCA. The famous history
Of Launcelot of the Lake.

(*She rises and goes over to the reading-desk.*)

PAOLO. And have you read
The book all through?

FRANCESCA. I have but....
Come in my reading to this point.

PAOLO. To where?
Here, where the mark is? (*He reads.*)
"... but you ask of me
Nothing...." Will you go on?

FRANCESCA. Look how the sea is growing white with light!

PAOLO. Will you not read the page with me, Francesca?

FRANCESCA. Look yonder, how a flight
Of swallows comes, and coming sets a shadow
On the white sea!

PAOLO. Will you not read, Francesca?

FRANCESCA. And there is one sail, and so red it seems
Like fire.

PAOLO (*reading*). " 'Assuredly, my lady' says
Thereat Galeotto, 'he is not so hot,
He does not ask you any single thing
For love of you, because he fears, but I
Make suit to you for him; and know that I
Had never asked it of you, but that you
Were better off for it, seeing it is
The richest treasure you shall ever compass.'
Whereas says she...."

(PAOLO *draws* FRANCESCA *gently by the hand.*)

But now, will you not read
What she says? Will you not be Guenevere?

See now how sweet they are,
Your violets
That you have cast away! Come, read a little.

            (Their heads lean together over the book.)

FRANCESCA (*reading*). "Whereat says she: 'This know I well, and I
    Will do whatever thing you ask of me.'
    And Galeotto answers her: 'Much thanks,
    Lady! I ask you that you give to him
    Your love....' "   *(She stops.)*

PAOLO. But read on.

FRANCESCA. No, I cannot see
    The words.

PAOLO. Read on. It says: "Assuredly...."

FRANCESCA. " 'Assuredly,' says she, 'I promise it,
    But let him be mine own and I all his,
    And let there be set straight all crooked things
    And evil....' " Enough, Paolo.

PAOLO (*reading: hoarsely and tremulously*). " 'Lady!' says he, 'much
    thanks, but kiss him then,
    Now, and before my face, for a beginning
    Of a true love....' " You, you! what does she say?
    Now, what does she say? Here.

        *(Their white faces lean over the book, until their cheeks almost
           touch.)*

FRANCESCA (*reading*). "Says she: 'For what
    Shall I be then entreated. But I will it
    More than he wills it...' "

PAOLO (*following brokenly*). "And they draw apart
    And the queen looks on him and sees that he
    Cannot take heart on him to do aught more.
    Thereat she takes him by the chin, and slowly
    Kisses him on the mouth...."

        (He makes the same movement towards FRANCESCA, *and kisses
          her. As their mouths separate,* FRANCESCA *staggers and
          falls back on the cushions.)*

FRANCESCA (*faintly*). No, Paolo!

ACT FOUR

An octagonal hall, of gray stone, with five of its sides in perspective. High up, on the bare stone, is a frieze of unicorns on a gold background. On the wall at the back is a large window with glass panes, looking out on the mountain, furnished with benches in the recess. On the wall at right angles to it, on the right, is a grated door leading to the subterranean prison. Against the opposite wall, to the left, is a long wooden seat with a high back, in front of which is a long narrow table laid with fruit and wine. In each of the other two sides facing, is a door; the left, near the table, leads to the room of FRANCESCA, *the right to the corridor and stairs. All round are placed torchbearers of iron; on brackets are hung shoulder-belts, waist-belts, quivers, and different portions of armour; pikes, lances, halberds, spears, axes, balistas lean against them.*

(FRANCESCA *is seated at the window, and* MALATESTINO *stands at her feet.*)

FRANCESCA. You would be justicer, Malatestino!
    Your cradle, of a surety, was hewn out
    From some old tree-trunk by a savage axe
    That had cut many heads off before then.

MALATESTINO (*laughs convulsively*). Kinswoman, do I fright you?
    And should I please you better
    If I had had my cradle in the rose
    Of a calm lute?

FRANCESCA. You are a cruel boy to take revenge
    Upon a falcon!
    Why did you kill him, if you held him dear?

MALATESTINO. Merely for justice' sake.
    See, I had let him loose upon a crane,
    The crane went up, the falcon followed him
    And went up far above him, and under him
    Saw a young eagle flying, and he took him
    And struck him to the ground, and held him so
    Till he had killed him.
    I ran to take him, thinking him the crane,
    But found it was an eagle.

Then I was angry, and struck off the head
Of the fair falcon who had killed his lord.

FRANCESCA. It was a foolish deed.

MALATESTINO. But he had killed
His lord. I did but justice.

FRANCESCA. It was a wicked folly, Malatestino.

MALATESTINO. The fool shall pass, and with the fool his folly,
And the time passes, but not every time.

FRANCESCA. Why do you speak so strangely?
You are athirst for blood
Always, always at watch,
The enemy of all things. In all your words
There is a secret menace;
Like a wild beast you bite
And tear and claw whatever comes your way.
Where were you born? Your mother gave you milk
As to another? And you are so young!
The down is scarcely shadowed on your cheek.

MALATESTINO (*with sudden violence*). You are a goad to me,
The thought of you is like a goad to me,
Always. You are my wrath.

> (FRANCESCA *rises and moves away from the window, as if to
> escape from a snare. She stands near the wall against which
> arms are heaped up.*)

FRANCESCA. Malatestino, enough! Have you no shame?
Your brother will be here.

MALATESTINO (*following her*). You strain me like a bow,
That vibrates in an hour
A thousand times, and pierces at a venture.
Your hand is terrible,
That holds my force in it,
And casts it out to wound where it has flown.
I fly you, and you follow.
You are with me suddenly,
Like a sharp storm of rain,
In the fields and on the ways,
When I go out
Against the enemy.

I breathe you when I breathe the dust of battles.
The cloud that rises from the trampled earth
Takes on your very form,
And you live and breathe and you dissolve again
Under the pawing of the panting horses
In the tracks that redden and fill up with blood.
I will clasp you, I will clasp you now at last!

(FRANCESCA *retreats along the wall until she comes to the grated door.*)

FRANCESCA. You do not touch me, madman, or I call
Your brother! Get you gone. I pity you.
You are a boy. If you would not be whipped,
Get you gone. You are a boy,
A wicked boy.

MALATESTINO. Whom would you call?

FRANCESCA. Your brother.

MALATESTINO. Which?

(FRANCESCA *starts, hearing a cry rise up from below, through the door against which she is standing.*)

FRANCESCA. Who cried there? Did you not hear it?

MALATESTINO. One
Who has to die.

FRANCESCA. Montagna
Dei Parcitadi? (*Another cry comes from the prison.*)

MALATESTINO. I too will say: Enough!
Enough, Francesca, today you seal your fate.

FRANCESCA. Ah, now I cannot hear him; but at night
He howls, howls like a wolf;
His crying rises to me in my room.
What have you done to him?
Have you put him to the torture?

MALATESTINO. Listen to me. Giovanni
Sets out at Vespers for the Podesteria
Of Pesaro. You have prepared for him
Food for the journey. (*He points to the table.*)
Listen. I can give him
Food for another journey.

FRANCESCA. What do you mean?

MALATESTINO. Look well at me. I can still see with one.

FRANCESCA. What do you mean? You threaten me? You net
  Some treachery against your brother.

MALATESTINO. Treachery?

I would have thought, kinswoman, that such a word
Had burnt your tongue; I see
Your lips are scathless, though
A little paler. I but spoke at random.
My judgment was at fault. Only I say
This one time more....

  (*The crying of the* PRISONER *is again heard.*)

FRANCESCA (*trembling with horror*). How he cries! How he cries!
  Who tortures him, or what new agony
  Have you found out for him?
  Have you walled him up alive? Will he cry so
  All his life long? Go, put an end to it,
  And take him from his torture.
  I will not hear his crying any more.

MALATESTINO. Well, I will go. I will see that you shall have
  A quiet night and an untroubled sleep,
  Because tomorrow you must sleep alone,
  While my good brother rides to Pesaro.

  (*He goes up to the wall and chooses an axe from among the weapons
    piled up against it.*)

FRANCESCA. What are you doing?

MALATESTINO. I?

I would be justicer,
And by your wish and will,
Kinswoman.

  (*He examines the blade of the weapon; then unbolts the barred
    door, which opens upon black darkness.*)

FRANCESCA. You are going to kill him? Ah,
  Wild beast, but you have lived too long, I think,
  Since I bound up your wound for you, and you
  Raved at your father. Still I hear you. Then
  You bit the hand that gave you medicine,
  Cared for you in your sickness, soothed your pain.
  Accursed be the hour in which I bent
  Over your pillow to give ease to you!

MALATESTINO. Francesca, listen, Francesca: even so sure
  As death is in the point of this good weapon
  I hold here in my hand, so sure is life
  In that one word
  You still may say to me,
  Full-blooded life, do you not understand?
  And full of winds, and full of conquering days.

  (FRANCESCA *replies slowly, in an equable voice, as in a momen-
      tary respite from horror and anxiety.*)

FRANCESCA. What is the word?   Who is there that could say it?
  You live in a loud noise,
  But where I live is silence.   The prisoner
  Is not so far and lonely
  As you are far and lonely, O poor blind
  Slaughterman, drunk with shoutings, and with blows!
  But fate is very silent.

MALATESTINO. Ah, if you could but see the countenance
  Of the overhanging fate!
  There is a wretched knot within my head,
  A knot of thoughts like pent-up lightnings: soon
  They will break out.   But listen,
  Listen!   If your hand will but touch my hand,
  If your hair will lean over me again,
  Over my fever, and...

                     (*A more prolonged cry is heard from below.*)

FRANCESCA. O horror!   horror!
        (*She moves back to the embrasure of the window, sits down, and
          puts her elbows on her knees, and her head between her hands.*)

MALATESTINO (*looking aside at her*). This shall be from you.
        (*He takes down a torch, puts the axe on the ground, takes the
          steel, strikes it, and lights the torch, while he speaks.*)

  I go.   You will not hear him any more.
  I will see that you shall have
  A quiet night and an untroubled sleep,
  And I will give my father quiet too;
  He fears his flight.   And I would have Giovanni
  In passing by Gradara, give him this
  Most certain token.

O kinswoman, good vespers!

(FRANCESCA *remains motionless as if hearing nothing. He picks up the weapon and goes into the darkness with his silent cat-like step, holding the lighted torch in his left hand. The little door remains open.* FRANCESCA *rises and watches the light fade away in the opening; suddenly she runs to the door, and stops, shuddering. The barred door grates in the silence. She turns, and moves away with slow steps, her head bent, as if under a heavy weight.*)

FRANCESCA (*in a low voice, to herself*). And an untroubled sleep!

(*Through the great door on the right is heard the harsh voice of* GIANCIOTTO. FRANCESCA *stops suddenly.*)

GIOVANNI. Look you for Messer Paolo my brother,
And tell him I set out for Pesaro
In an hour's time from now,
And that I wait him.

          (*He enters fully armed. Seeing his wife, he goes up to her.*)
Ah, my dear lady, you are waiting me!
Why do you tremble, why are you so pale? (*He takes her hand.*)
And you are cold too, cold as if with fear.
But why?

FRANCESCA. Malatestino
Had scarcely entered when I heard again
The crying of the prisoner,
Who cries these many days so horribly
Out of the earth; and, seeing me distraught,
Flamed into anger and went suddenly
Down to the prison by the door there, armed
With a great axe, saying that he would kill him,
Against the express commandments of his father
That fretted him too much.
Cruel he is, your brother, my good lord,
And does not love me.

GIANCIOTTO. Do not tremble, lady.
Where has your valiance gone? But now you were
Fearless among the fighters,
And saw men fall with arrows in their throats,
And flung about the Greek fire in your hands.

Why does the life, then, of an enemy
So greatly trouble you? and a cry affright you,
Or an axe brandished?

FRANCESCA. To fight in battle is a lovely thing,
But secret slaying in the dark I hate.

GIANCIOTTO. Malatestino tired of keeping watch
So long, and so long waiting for the ransom
That the old Parcitade would not pay,
The old foul miser that in taking flight
Took with him certain rights and privileges
Of the Commune at Rimino... But why
Do you say he does not love you?

FRANCESCA. I do not know. It seems so.

GIANCIOTTO. Is he unkind with you?

FRANCESCA. He is a boy, and like
Young mastiffs, he must bite. But come, my lord,
Take food and drink
Before you go your journey.

GIANCIOTTO. But perhaps
Malatestino...

FRANCESCA. Come, why do you think
Of what I said but lightly? "Heart of metal,
Tough liver": I remember your own word,
And when you said it. He will love his horse
Until the horse falls sick;
His armour, till the steel begins to wear.
I have no mind to trouble you with him,
My lord. 'Tis almost vespers.
Come, here is food and drink. Do you mean to go
The way of the seashore?

> (GIANCIOTTO *is moody, while he follows* FRANCESCA *toward the spread table. He takes off his basnet, unclasps his gorget, and gives them to his wife, who sets them down on a seat, with sudden graceful movements, talking rapidly.*)

You will have all the freshness of the night.
It is September, and the nights are soft;
Just before midnight the moon rises. When
Do you reach Pesaro,
Messere il Podestà?

GIANCIOTTO. Tomorrow at the third hour,
  For I must stay a little with my father
  In passing through Gradara.

        (He unbuckles his sword-belt and gives it to his wife.)
FRANCESCA. Is it for long that you must stay at Pesaro,
  Before you come again?

      (The terrible cry of MONTAGNA *is heard from below.* FRANCESCA
      shudders, and lets fall the sword, which slips from its scabbard.)
GIANCIOTTO. It is done now.
  Do not be frightened, lady. There will be
  Nothing but silence now. May God so take
  The heads of all our enemies! From this forth
  There shall no wind root into Rimino
  This evil seed between the stones of it.
  And may God scatter it out of all Romagna
  In this most bloody year, if it so be
  He wills to have his holy Easter held
  By the Guelfs of Calboli with the Ghibelline blood
  Of Aldobrandin degli Argogliosi!

              (He stoops and picks up the bare blade.)
             Pope
Martino is dead and good King Carlo went
Before him into paradise. That's ill!
As for this Pietro di Stefano that Onorio
Sends us for governor,
  I doubt him, he's no friend,
He's not a Polentani, not your father's,
Francesca. We shall still have need to keep
Our swords unsheathed, and eyes in all our swords.

    (He puts himself on guard, then looks along the blade from the hilt.)
  This is inflexible!   *(He puts it back in its scabbard.)*
FRANCESCA. Give it to me, my lord,
  I will not let it fall
  Twice over. And sit down, take food and drink.

    (He gives her the sword and sits down on the bench before the table.)
GIANCIOTTO. Good so, my own dear lady.
  I talk of war to you, now I think
  That I have never given you a flower.

Ah, we are hard. I give you arms in heaps
To hold in those white hands,
Malatestino gave to you at least
A falcon. Paolo gives you
Flowers perhaps. The Captain of the People
Learnt all the courteous virtues in his Florence,
But left his force upon the banks of Arno
And now is more in love with idleness
Than any labour. He is always with
His music-makers.

> (*He breaks the bread and pours out the wine, while* FRANCESCA
> *sits beside him, at the table, with her hands on the hilt of the*
> *sword.*)

But you,
Francesca, love your chamber-music, too.
Are not your women ever tired of singing?
Their voices must have covered
The cries of Parcitade,
Surely? You turn the tower
Of the Malatesti
Into a singing wood of nightingales. (*He eats and drinks.*)
FRANCESCA. I and Samaritana,
My sister, at Ravenna, in our home,
Lived always, always in the midst of singing.
Our mother had indeed a throat of gold.
From our first infancy
Music flowed over us and bent our souls
As the water bends the grass upon the bank.
And our mother said to me:
Sweet singing can put out all harmful things.
GIANCIOTTO. My mother said to us:
Do you know what woman is a proper woman?
She that in spinning thinks upon the spindle,
She that in spinning spins without a knot,
She that in spinning lets not fall the spindle,
She that winds thread in order about thread,
She that knows when the spindle is full or halfway.
FRANCESCA. Then why did you not seek for such a woman,
My lord, through all the country?

(*A knocking is heard at the little barred door.* FRANCESCA *rises to her feet, drops the sword on the table and turns to go out.*)

Malatestino back!

I will not wait to see him.

THE VOICE OF MALATESTINO. Who has shut it?

Kinswoman, are you there? Have you shut me in?

(*He kicks at the door.*)

GIANCIOTTO. Wait, wait, and I will open!

THE VOICE OF MALATESTINO. Ah, Giovanni!

Open, and I will bring you

A good ripe heavy fruit,

Food for your journey:

A ripe September fig.

And how it weighs!

(GIANCIOTTO *goes to the door to open it.* FRANCESCA *follows his limping steps for some instants with her eyes, then moves towards the door that leads to her rooms, and goes out.*)

Be quick!

GIANCIOTTO. Why, here I am.

(*He opens the door, and* MALATESTINO *appears in the narrow door-way holding in his left hand the lighted torch, in his right, by a knotted cord, the head of* MONTAGNA *wrapped in a cloth.*)

MALATESTINO (*handing the torch to his brother*). Here, brother, put it out. (GIOVANNI *stamps out the flame under his foot.*)

Was not your wife

With you?

GIANCIOTTO (*roughly*). She was with me.

What do you want of her?

MALATESTINO. Ah, then you know

What fruit it is I am bringing to your table?

GIANCIOTTO. Did you not fear to disobey our father?

MALATESTINO. Feel how it weighs! now feel!

(*He hands the bundle to* GIOVANNI, *who weighs it in his hand, and lets it fall on the pavement with a dull thud.*)

It is yours; it is the head

Of Montagna dei Parcitade; take it.

It is for your saddle bow,

For you to carry with you to Gradara
And leave it with our father, and say to him:
"Malatestino sends you
This token, lest you doubt his guardianship,
And pledges you his word
He will not let the prisoner escape;
And asks you in return
The three foot black white-spotted horse you said
That you would give him
With saddle set with gold."
How hot it is!

(*He wipes the sweat from his forehead.* GIANCIOTTO *has
seated himself again at the table.*)

I tell you,
When the light struck upon his eyes, he snorted,
As a horse does when it shies. Give me to drink.

(*He drains a cup that stands full.* GIANCIOTTO *seems gloomy,
and chews in silence, without swallowing, like an ox ruminating.
The slayer of* MONTAGNA *sits where* FRANCESCA *had been
sitting. The blood-stained bundle lies on the pavement; through
the window can be seen the sun as it sets behind the Apennines,
crimsoning the peaks and the clouds.*)

You are not wroth with me?
You did not want to have us wait a year
In hopes of ransom from the Perdecittade?
I tell you we should not have had the ransom,
Sure as a florin's yellow.
From this day backwards
The Malatesti never have given quarter,
Since they first cut their teeth.
It is not two months now, at Cesena, our father
Just saved his skin by a mere miracle
From the clutches of Corrado Montefeltvo.
And the bastard Filipuccio is still living!
Heaven bless and save
Frate Alberigo,
Who knows full well the way to spare at once
Both trunk and branches!

It is time now for every Ghibelline
To come to his desert,
As the gay Knight would have us.

> (*He takes the sword lying across the table, and strikes the scabbard with his hand.*)

And here is the dessert for every feast
Of peace and amity.
Do not be wroth with me,
Giovanni, I am yours.
Are you not called the Lamester
And am I not the One-eyed?...

> (*He is silent an instant, deceitfully.*)

But Paolo is the Beautiful!

> (GIANCIOTTO *lifts his head and gazes fixedly at* MALATESTINO. *In the silence is heard the jingling of his spurs as he moves his foot restlessly on the floor.*)

GIANCIOTTO. You are a babbler too?

> (MALATESTINO *is about to pour out more wine. His brother arrests his hand.*)

No, do not drink,
But answer me. What is it you have done
To vex Francesca?
What have you done to her?
MALATESTINO. I! What is it she says?
GIANCIOTTO. You have changed colour.
MALATESTINO. What is it she says?
GIANCIOTTO. Answer me now!
MALATESTINO (*pretending to be confused*). I cannot answer you.
GIANCIOTTO. What do you harbour against her in your mind?
MALATESTINO (*with a gleam in his eye*). She told you this? And did
she not change colour
While she was saying it?
GIANCIOTTO. Enough, Malatestino!
Look at me in the eyes.
I limp in going, but I go straight before me.
You go a crooked way, and you smooth out
The sound your feet have made. Only, take heed
I do not set my mind upon you. There

You would writhe your best in vain.
So now I say to you:
Woe to you if you touch my lady! You,
You should know, having seen me at the work,
That a less time it is
Between the touch of the spur and the first leap
Of the Barbary horse
Than between my saying and doing. Think of it.

MALATESTINO (*in a low voice, with downcast eye*). And if the brother
    sees that there is one
That touches of a truth his brother's wife,
And is incensed at it, and stirs himself
To wipe the shame out, does he therefore sin?
And if, for this, he is accused to have
Harboured ill thought against the woman, say:
Is the accusation just?

    (GIANCIOTTO *springs up and raises his fists as if to crush the
    youth. But he restrains himself, his arms fall.*)

GIANCIOTTO. Malatestino, scourge of hell, if you
Would have me not put out
The other eye by which your blinking soul
Offends the world, speak now,
And tell me what it is that you have seen.

    (MALATESTINO *rises and goes with his silent, cat-like steps to the
    door near the table. He listens for some instants; then opens
    the door suddenly with a swift movement, and looks. He sees
    no one. He goes back to his brother's side.*)

Speak.

MALATESTINO. Not for threats. You frighten me, I say.
Because I wore no visor, I was made
Blind of one eye; but you must wear indoors
Visor and headpiece, chin-piece, eye-piece, all
Of tempered steel, without a flaw in it!
You will see nothing, nothing can come through
The iron-barred approaches to your brain.

GIANCIOTTO. Come, come, the thing! None of your talk! The
    thing!
Tell me what you have seen! Tell me the man!

MALATESTINO. Were you nowise surprised
 When someone who had gone away from here
 No later than December, suddenly
 Gave up his post at Florence
 And was already back by February?

  (*One of the silver cups is heard to crack, as it is crushed in* GIAN-
  CIOTTO'*s hand.*)

GIANCIOTTO. Paolo? No, no. It is not.

  (*He rises, leaves the table, and walks to and fro in the room,
  grimly, with overclouded eyes. He stumbles against the blood-
  stained bundle. He goes towards the window, whose panes
  glitter in the light of the setting sun. He sits down on the
  window-seat, and takes his head between his hands, as if to
  collect his thoughts.* MALATESTINO *plays with the sword,
  drawing it half in and half out of the scabbard.*)

 Malatestino, here!

  (*The youth comes across to him swiftly, almost without sound,
  as if his feet were shod with felt.* GIANCIOTTO *enfolds him
  in his arms, and holds him tightly between his armoured knees,
  and speaks to him breath to breath.*)

 Are you sure? Have you seen this?

MALATESTINO. Yes.

GIANCIOTTO. How and when?

MALATESTINO. I have seen him often enter...

GIANCIOTTO. Enter where?

MALATESTINO. Enter the room.

GIANCIOTTO. Well? That is not enough.
 He is a kinsman. They might talk together.
 There are the women..... You have seen him go
 With the musicians, it may be....

MALATESTINO. At night.
 For God's sake, do not hurt me! Not so hard!
 You have your iron gauntlets. Let me go.

        (*He writhes in his grasp.*)

GIANCIOTTO. Have I heard right? You said...
 Say it again.

MALATESTINO. At night,
 At night, I say, I have seen him.

GIANCIOTTO. If you should lie, I will break
    Your body in two.

MALATESTINO. At night,
    I have seen him enter, and go out at dawn.
    You were in arms against the Urbinati.

GIANCIOTTO. I will break you, if you lie.

MALATESTINO. Would you like to see and feel?

GIANCIOTTO. I must do so.
    If you have any will to go alive
    Out of these mortal pincers.

MALATESTINO. Then, tonight?

GIANCIOTTO. Tonight, then.

MALATESTINO. But can you find out the way
    To cheat, to smile? Ah, no, you cannot smile.

GIANCIOTTO. Let my revenge teach me the way to smile,
    If my delight could never.

MALATESTINO. Can you kiss
    Both, one after the other, and not bite
    Instead?

GIANCIOTTO. Yes, I will kiss them, thinking them
    Already dead.

MALATESTINO. You must put both your arms
    About them, you must talk to them, and not
    Tremble.

GIANCIOTTO. Ah, you are playing with my sorrow!
    Beware! it has two edges.

MALATESTINO. Do not hurt me,
    For God's sake!

GIANCIOTTO. Good; but tell me how you think:
    The way, and speedily.

MALATESTINO. You must take your leave,
    And go from here, take horse, and by the gate
    Of San Genesio with all your escort
    Set out for Pesaro. I will come with you.
    You will say you are wroth with me
    For the Parcitade's head's sake, and desire
    To take me to our father at Gradara,
    That he may punish me or pardon me.

So they will think
That they are left alone. Do you understand?
Then, half-way through the night,
We will leave the escort, and come back again,
And enter by the gate of the Gattolo
Before the moon is up. We will give the signal
To Rizio. But let me dispose of that.
Saddle your swiftest horse, and take with you
A little linen
To bind about his hoofs, in case of need,
Because at night the stones
Upon the noisy way
May well be traitors, brother.

GIANCIOTTO. Then shall I see?
You are sure? Then I shall take them in the act....

MALATESTINO. Not so hard! Now I think,
There is the slave, there is the Cyprian slave....
She is their go-between.
Sly is she, works with charms....
I have seen her as she goes
Snuffing the wind.... I must find a way to lead her
Into a snare, and blindfold her. But this,
Leave this to me: you need not think of anything
Till you are at the door.

GIANCIOTTO. On your life now, shall I take them in the act?

MALATESTINO. Enough of this, by God!
Let me go, now, let me go! I am not
Your prey. (*Through the door is heard the voice of* PAOLO.)

PAOLO (*outside*). Where is Giovanni?

(GIANCIOTTO *lets* MALATESTINO *go, and rises with a white face.*)

MALATESTINO. Look to it now,
Look to it; no suspicion!

(*As* PAOLO *opens the door and enters,* MALATESTINO *pretends
to be angry with* GIANCIOTTO.)

Ah, at last
You have let me go! (*He pretends to suffer in his wrists.*)
By God, it is well for you

You were born my elder brother, otherwise....
Ah, Paolo, well met!

> (PAOLO *wears a long rich surtout falling below his knees
> nearly to the ankle, girt at the waist by a jewelled belt through
> which is thrust a beautiful damascened dagger. His curled
> hair, not parted, but waving in a mass, surrounds his face
> like a cloud.*)

PAOLO. What is the matter?

MALATESTINO. See,
Giovanni is enraged
Because I have lost all patience at the last
And have struck dumb Montagna, being weary
Of listening to his cries (Francesca too
Could get no sleep) and weary too of hearing
My father say twice over,
By word of mouth and message:
"Will you keep watch on him?
Are you sure you can keep watch?
I know he will escape;
I know that you will let him go, and then,
When he has gone, you will not bring him back!"
By God, I was tired of it. There is his head.

PAOLO. You cut it off yourself?

MALATESTINO. Yes, I myself,
And neatly.

> (PAOLO *looks at the bundle, but draws back so as not to stain
> himself with the dripping blood.*)

Ah, you draw back, it seems
You fear to stain your garments?
I did not know I had
Two sisters, both so dainty!

GIANCIOTTO. Enough of jesting! Paolo,
I have to take him with me to Gradara,
To our father; he must plead
His cause himself,
For disobeying. What do you say to it?

PAOLO. I say that it is well for him to go, Giovanni.

MALATESTINO. I am content.

But I must bear the token;
I will hang it to my saddle: that is staunch.

(*He takes up the bundle by the cord.*)

I have no fear our father will be angry.
He will be filled with joy,
I tell you, when the knots are all untied.
And he will give me the black horse for war,
And maybe the grey jennet for the chase.

GIANCIOTTO. Get ready, then, and without lingering,
    It is already evening.

(MALATESTINO *takes up the bundle to carry it away.*)

PAOLO (*to* GIOVANNI). I see your men are armed at front and back,
    And wait the clarion.

    (*The two brothers go towards the window lit up by the sunset,
    and sit down.*)

MALATESTINO (*going*). Ah, but how heavy! and without a helmet!
    The Parcitadi always were gross oxen,
    Fatted for slaughtering, great horned heads.
    Ah, Paozzo, where you go
    You leave behind a scent of orange-water.
    Take care, a drop may drip upon your clothes.   (*He goes out.*)

PAOLO. He is all teeth and claws, ready for biting.
    Our men at arms used once
    To say he always slept with one eye closed
    And one eye open, even in his sleep.
    Now I believe he never sleeps at all,
    Nor slacks the sinews of his cruelty.
    He was made to conquer lands, and die some day
    Of extreme cold, God keep him, our good brother!
    So you are Podestà of Pesaro!
    Our father from Gradara scans the hill
    Of Pesaro as if he watched his prey.
    You, with your strength and wisdom,
    Should give it to him soon,
    Giovanni.

GIANCIOTTO. It is not a year yet since
    You went to Florence, Captain of the People,
    And now I go as Podestà.   Not long

You stayed at Florence. I shall stay there long,
Because it is not well for me to yield
The office to another. Yet to leave
Francesca for so long,
Goes to my heart a little.

PAOLO. You can come back again from time to time,
Pesaro is not far.

GIANCIOTTO. The Podestà is not allowed to leave
His post, so long as lasts
His office, as you know, nor bring with him
His wife. But I will leave her in your care,
Brother, my most dear wife; you will be here.

PAOLO. I have held her always
As a dear sister might be held.

GIANCIOTTO. I know,
Paolo.

PAOLO. Be very sure
That I will guard her for you well.

GIANCIOTTO. I know,
Paolo. You from Ravenna
Brought her a virgin to your brother's bed
And you will keep her for me from all harm.

PAOLO. I will tell Orabile
To leave Ghaggiolo and come
To Rimino to keep her company.

GIANCIOTTO. See that they love each other, Paolo,
For they are kinswomen.

PAOLO. Francesca often
Sends gifts to her.

GIANCIOTTO. Go, call her. It is late.
The sun has set, and I shall have to rest
A little at Gradara,
And yet be at the gates
Of Pesaro before the third hour. Go,
Go you yourself and call her. She has gone
Back to her room, because Malatestino
Frightened her with his cruelty. Go you,
Comfort her, tell her not to be afraid
Of being left alone, and call her here.

(*He rises and puts his hand lightly on his brother's shoulder as
if to urge him.* PAOLO *goes towards the door.* GIOVANNI
*stands motionless, and follows him with murderous eyes. As
he goes out,* GIOVANNI *stretches out his hand as if to swear an
oath. Then he moves towards the table, and takes up the
cracked cup, wishing to hide it. He turns, sees the little barred
door still open, throws the cup into the darkness, and closes the
door. At the other door* FRANCESCA *appears by the side of*
PAOLO.)

FRANCESCA. Pardon me, my dear lord,
If I have left you hastily. You know
The reason.

GIANCIOTTO. My dear lady, I know well
The reason, and I am sorry
That you have had to suffer by the fault
Of this sad brother. And I go to see
Both to your peace and to his punishment,
For I intend to take him to our father,
For judgment at Gradara. He prepares
Already to set forth. Within a little
We shall have left the city.

FRANCESCA. He will bear
Ill-will against me, if you should accuse him
Before his father. Pardon him, I pray.
He is a boy.

GIANCIOTTO. Yet, lady, it is better,
For your sake, that he comes with me. I leave
Paolo with you. Trust Paolo. His Orabile
Will come to stay with you at Rimino,
And keep you company: he promises.
Often from Pesaro
I mean to send you messages, and hope
Often to have the like from Rimino.

FRANCESCA. Surely, my lord. You need not fear for me.

GIANCIOTTO. Put every trouble freely from your mind,
Let songs and music give you joy, and have
Beautiful robes, and lovely odours. Not
To Guido's daughter suits the spinning wheel.

I know it. And I say
My mother's saying but to make you smile.
You are not angry with me?

FRANCESCA. In your saying
There seems to lie secret rebuke for me,
My lord.

GIANCIOTTO. A good old saying, that was born
Within the dark walls of Verrucchio,
That now are grown too narrow to hem in
The Malatesti in our house today.
If any spin, they spin
Only the purple, and with golden distaffs.
Come to my arms, my most dear lady!

(FRANCESCA *goes up to him; he takes her in his arms and kisses*
her. PAOLO *stands silent in the doorway.*)

Now
I have to say farewell. Never so fair
You seemed to me, never so sweet. And yet
I leave you. (*He smoothes her hair with his hand; then looses her.*)
O, my brother,
Keep her in safety and heaven keep you both.
Come, and pledge faith with me.

(PAOLO *goes up to him, and they embrace.*)

Where is my gorget?

FRANCESCA. Here it is. (*She gives it to him.*)

GIANCIOTTO (*putting it on*). Paolo, buckle it for me.

(PAOLO *buckles it on.* FRANCESCA *hands him the basnet.*)

Do you remember, brother,
That night before the Mastra Tower, that bolt
Out of a crossbow? You,
Francesca, do you remember?
It was at just this hour.
Cignatta was killed then. Today Montagna
Joins him. 'Tis not a year.
The house is silent now; then, all the towers
Were crackling to the sky.

(FRANCESCA *takes the sword from the table and buckles his*
sword-belt.)

Francesca, do you remember?   Then you gave us
Wine, Scian wine, to drink.   We drank together
Out of one cup.   *(He is fully armed.)*
Now let me drink again!

FRANCESCA. One of the cups is missing.   There were two.
Where is the other?   *(She looks to see if it has fallen.)*

GIANCIOTTO. One will do for us
Still.   *(He pours out the wine and offers it to FRANCESCA.)*
And good luck God give you!

FRANCESCA. I cannot drink
This wine, my lord.   I am not used to it.

GIANCIOTTO. Drink as you drank then, and pass on the cup
That your kinsman may drink also, as he drank then.
            (FRANCESCA drinks and offers the cup to PAOLO, who takes it.)

PAOLO. Good luck to the Podestà of Pesaro!
            *(He drinks, throwing back his curled head.   Through the door
            is heard the voice of MALATESTINO, who throws open the
            door, and appears in full armour.   From the court is heard
            the sound of bugles.)*

MALATESTINO. Ready, Giovanni? Hark, the clarion!
To horse! To horse!
            (PAOLO goes up to him, and they embrace.)

ACT FIVE

*The room with the curtained alcove, the musicians' gallery, the lectern,
with the book closed.   Four waxen torches burn in the iron candlestick;
two tapers on the small table.   The compartments of the long window
are almost all open to the peaceful night air.   The pot of basil is on the
window-sill, and beside it is a gilt plate heaped with bunches of early
grapes.*

FRANCESCA *is seen through the half-drawn curtains of the alcove,
lying on the bed, on which she has laid herself without undressing.   The*
WOMEN, *who wear white fillets, are seated on low stools; they speak quietly,
so as not to disturb their mistress.   Near them, on a stool, are laid five
silver lamps, which have gone out.*

ADONELLA. She has fallen asleep.   She dreams.
            *(BIANCOFIORE rises and goes softly up to the alcove, looks, then
            turns, and goes back to her seat.)*

BIANCOFIORE. How beautiful she is!

ALTICHIARA. Summer is come; she grows
In beauty with the summer.

ALDA. Like ears of corn.

GARSENDA. And like
Poppies.

BIANCOFIORE. O, beautiful
Summer, go not away!
The nights begin to grow a little cool.
Do you feel the breeze?

ALDA. It comes
From the sea. Oh, the delight!
(*With her face to the window, she draws in a long breath.*)

ADONELLA. Lord Autumn comes our way
With grass and figs in his lap.

BIANCOFIORE. September! Grape and fig begin to droop.

ALTICHIARA (*pointing to the plate*). Here, Adonella, take
A bunch of grapes to strip.

ADONELLA. You are too greedy.

ALTICHIARA. Come, come, your mouth is watering for them.
(ADONELLA *takes a bunch of grapes from the plate, and goes
back to her seat, holding the bunch in the air, while the others
strip it of its grapes.*)

BIANCOFIORE. It is like sweet muscatel.

ALDA. Don't throw away the skin!

ALTICHIARA. It is all good to eat, kernel and skin.

GARSENDA. Here is a bitter kernel.

BIANCOFIORE. Grown on the shady side.

ADONELLA. How still it is!

ALDA. How tranquil!

GARSENDA. Listen! I hear a galley
Weigh anchor.

BIANCOFIORE. For tonight
Madonna has no singing.

ALTICHIARA. She is weary.

ALDA. Why does the prisoner
Cry out no more?

GARSENDA. Messer Malatestino has cut off
His head.

ALDA. Is that the truth?

GARSENDA. The truth; today, at Vespers.

ALDA. How do you know?

GARSENDA. Smaragdi told it me,
And had seen him, too,
Tie something huddled in a cloth to his saddle,
When, with Messer Giovanni
He mounted in the court.   It was the head,
The prisoner's head.

ADONELLA. Where do they carry it?

ALTICHIARA. To whom do they carry it?

BIANCOFIORE. Now they are riding.
By the seashore,
Under the stars,
They and the murdered
Head!

ADONELLA. Where will they have come?

ALDA. They should have come
To hell, and stayed there!

GARSENDA. One can breathe in the house
Now they are here no longer,
The lame man and the blind man!

ALTICHIARA. Hush! hush! let not Madonna
Hear you.

GARSENDA. She is hardly breathing.

ALDA. Messer Paolo
Is back again?

ALTICHIARA. Hush!   (FRANCESCA *groans in her sleep.*)

ADONELLA. She is wakening.

> (*She throws the grape-stalk out of the window.* BIANCOFIORE
> *again rises, and goes up to the alcove, and looks.*)

BIANCOFIORE. No,
She is not awake; she is crying in her sleep.

ADONELLA. She is dreaming.

ALDA. O Garsenda, does she know
The prisoner is not crying any more
Because they have cut his head off?

GARSENDA. Certainly
She knows.

BIANCOFIORE. Perhaps she is dreaming of it now.

ADONELLA. We must sit up tonight,
Who knows to what hour?

ALDA. Are you sleepy, Adonella?

ALTICHIARA. Simonetto, the fifer, is waiting on the stairs!

ADONELLA. Who waits for you, then? Suzzo, the falconer,
With lure of pretty leather?

ALDA. Hush! She is wakening.

BIANCOFIORE. And did it bleed, Garsenda?

GARSENDA. Bleed? What?

BIANCOFIORE. That bundle at the saddle-bow?

GARSENDA. I saw but dimly, for the court was dark
But this I know: Smaragdi had to wash
The pavement, there, in the hall.

BIANCOFIORE. Now they are nearing the Cattolica.

GARSENDA. God keep them far away, and let them never
Find their way back again!

BIANCOFIORE. Think of the frightened horse
Feeling the dead thing dangle in the night!

ADONELLA. How sweetly the sweet basil smells by night!

ALTICHIARA. How thick it grows; the pot
No longer holds it.

BIANCOFIORE. You know, Garsenda, tell us
The story of Lisabetta of Messina,
That loved a youth of Pisa, and how her brothers
Killed him in secret, and she found his body
And cut the head away
From off the shoulders, set it in a pot,
And earth with it, and planted
A sprig of basil plant,
And watered it with her tears,
And saw it blossom so, out of her weeping.
Tell us, Garsenda, very quietly
While we are waiting.

> (FRANCESCA *gives a deeper groan, and turns as if half stifled on the
> bed. The* WOMEN *shiver.*)

ALDA. Listen,
She is crying in her sleep. It is some bad dream.

GARSENDA. She is sleeping on her back; the nightmare weighs
Upon her breast.

ALTICHIARA. Shall we awake her?

BIANCOFIORE. Evil
It is too suddenly
To rouse the heart that sees.
How should we know
What truth she sees revealed?

ADONELLA. The Slave interprets all her dreams to her.

(FRANCESCA *utters a cry of terror, springs from the bed, and
seems in the act to fly from some savage pursuit, throwing out
her hands as if to unloose herself from some grasp.*)

FRANCESCA. No, no, it is not I, it is not I!
Ah, ah, they seize me with their teeth! Help! help!
They snatch my heart. Help, help!
Paolo!

(*She shudders, stops, and turns on herself, pale, and breathing
with difficulty, while her* WOMEN *surround her in consternation,
trying to comfort her.*)

GARSENDA. Madonna, Madonna, we are here, see, see,
We are here, Madonna.

ALTICHIARA. Do not be afraid!

ADONELLA. There is no one here; there is no one here but we,
Madonna. No one is harming you, Madonna.

FRANCESCA (*shivering*). What have I said? Did I call?
O God, what have I done?

ALDA. You have had some discomfortable dream,
Madonna.

GARSENDA. Now it is finished. We are here.
All's quiet.

FRANCESCA. Is it late?

BIANCOFIORE. The sweat is standing out upon your forehead.
(*She wipes it off.*)

FRANCESCA. Is it night yet? Garsenda,
Biancofiore, Alda, you are all in white.

GARSENDA. It might perhaps be four hours after midnight,
Madonna.

FRANCESCA. Have I slept so long? Smaragdi,

Where is Smaragdi?

She has not come back yet?

BIANCOFIORE. She has not come back.

FRANCESCA. Why has she not come back?

BIANCOFIORE. When did you send her,
Madonna?

FRANCESCA. Are you not mistaken? Sleep,
Perhaps, deceived you, and you did not see her
When she came in.

GARSENDA. Madonna,
No, none of us closed eyelid;
We watched beside you all the night.

ADONELLA. Perhaps
She has come back, and waits, as she is wont
Lying without the door.

FRANCESCA. Look out and see,
Adonella, see if she is there.

(ADONELLA *draws back the folds of the curtain, opens the door,
and looks out.*)

ADONELLA. Smaragdi!
Smaragdi! There is no answer.
No one is there. It is all dark.

FRANCESCA. But call,
Call her again.

ADONELLA. Smaragdi!

FRANCESCA. Take a light.

(GARSENDA *takes one of the lamps, lights it at a taper, and goes to
the door. She and her companion look around.*)

She should have been here now some time ago.
What harm can have befallen her? God knows what;
It can be no good thing.

BIANCOFIORE. You have not yet
Come quite out of the horror of the dream,
Madonna.

ALTICHIARA. Breathe the air, the night is fresh,
The night is still.

FRANCESCA. The moon
Is risen?

ALDA. It must be rising on the hills,
But there is yet no dawn upon the sea.

(ADONELLA *and* GARSENDA *re-enter. One of them puts out the lamp.*)

FRANCESCA (*anxiously*). Well? Is she there?

GARSENDA. Madonna, there is no one.

ADONELLA. Nothing but silence
And darkness everywhere; the whole house sleeps.

GARSENDA. We only saw... (*She hesitates.*)

FRANCESCA. You only saw... whom did you see?

GARSENDA (*hesitatingly*). Madonna,
Someone was there... someone was standing there,
Leaning against the wall...
Still as a statue... all alone... his girdle
Shining... Madonna, do not be afraid...
(*Goes near to her and lowers her voice.*)
It was Messer Paolo!

FRANCESCA (*startled*). O, why?

ADONELLA. Madonna
Will have her hair made ready for the night?

FRANCESCA. No, no, I am not sleepy. I will wait.

BIANCOFIORE. Her shoes unloosed?

ALDA. The perfumes?

FRANCESCA. I will wait
A little more. I am no longer sleepy.
I will wait until Smaragdi comes.

ALTICHIARA. Let me go
And seek her.

GARSENDA. The poor thing is tired perhaps,
At the day's end, and sleeps where she has dropped.
Perhaps she is lying now
Upon the stairs.

FRANCESCA. Go, go, and I will read
Till you return. Bring me a taper, Alda.
(*ALDA takes a taper and fixes it at the head of the reading-desk.*)
Go now. You are all in white!
The Summer is not dead?
When it was evening, did you see the swallows

Begin to fly away?
I was elsewhere,
I was looking on the hills,
When the sun set tonight.
They have not all flown yet, have they? But perhaps
Tomorrow all the other flocks will follow.
I will go up on the tower, to see them go,
And you will sing me a merry song men dance to,
As if 'twere the March calends. Have you still
The flight of swallows painted, as you had?

ALDA. Yes, Madonna.

FRANCESCA. Tomorrow at the dance
You will put on
Over these white
Dresses a vest of black.
You will be like
"The creature of delight."

BIANCOFIORE. Yes, Madonna.

FRANCESCA. Go, go!   (*She opens the book.*)
(*Each of the* WOMEN *takes her silver lamp, which swings from a
curved handle. First* ADONELLA *goes to the tall candlestick,
and, standing on tiptoe, lights her lamp at one of the torches.
She bows, and goes out, while* FRANCESCA *follows her with
her eyes.*)

Go, too, Adonella!   (GARSENDA *does the same.*)
And you, Garsenda.   (ALTICHIARA *does the same.*)
And you, too, Altichiara.   (ALDA *does the same.*)
And you, Alda.

(*The four have gone out, one by one.* BIANCOFIORE *remains, and
she also is about to light her lamp, but as she is shorter than the
others, she cannot reach the flame.*)

Oh, Biancofiore, what a little one!
You will not ever reach to light your lamp.
You are the gentlest of them. Little dove,
                                  (BIANCOFIORE *turns smiling.*)

Come!
(BIANCOFIORE *goes up to her.* FRANCESCA *caresses her hair.*)
It is all of gold. You are, I think,

A little like my sister; you remember her,
Samaritana?

BIANCOFIORE. Yes, indeed, Madonna.
Such sweetness cannot be forgot. I have her
Here, in my heart, with the angels.

FRANCESCA. She was sweet,
My sister; was she not sweet, Biancofiore?
Ah, if she were but here, if she might make
Her little bed beside my bed tonight!
If I might hear again
Her little naked feet run to the window,
If I might hear her run with naked feet,
My little dove, and say, and say to me:
"Francesca, now the morning-star is born,
And it has chased away the Pleiades!".

BIANCOFIORE. You weep, Madonna.

FRANCESCA. You tremble, Biancofiore.
She too was frightened of a sudden; I heard
Her heart beat; and she said to me: "O sister,
Listen to me: stay with me still, O stay
With me! we were born here:
Do not forsake me!"
And I said to her: "O take me,
And let me be with you,
And let one covering cover us!"

BIANCOFIORE. O Madonna,
Your words pierce through my heart,
What melancholy holds you
Still?

FRANCESCA. No, no, do not weep:
Gentle you are. But come, light your lamp here.

BIANCOFIORE. May I not stay with you? May I not sleep
Here, at the foot of the bed?

FRANCESCA. No, Biancofiore. Light your lamp, and go,
And God go with you. Now Samaritana,
It may be, is thinking of her sister.

(BIANCOFIORE *lights her lamp at the taper, and bends to kiss*
FRANCESCA's *hand.*)

Go,

Go, do not weep. Let all sad thoughts go by.
Tomorrow you shall sing to me. Now go.

(BIANCOFIORE *turns and walks slowly towards the door. As
she is going out,* FRANCESCA *gives way to her presentiment.*)

You are not going, Biancofiore?
BIANCOFIORE. No,

I will stay with you, Madonna. Let me stay
At least until Smaragdi has come back.
FRANCESCA (*hesitates an instant*). Go!
BIANCOFIORE. God keep you, Madonna.

(*She goes out, closing the door behind her. Left alone,* FRANCESCA
makes several steps towards the door; then stands still, listening.)

FRANCESCA. And let it be so if it is my fate.

(*Goes resolutely up to the door.*)

I will call him. (*Hesitates and draws back.*)

He is still there, and he stands
Leaning against the wall;
Still as a statue, all alone; his girdle
Shining in the shadow. Who said that to me?
Who was it? Was it not said long ago?
Within the helmet all the face like fire...

(*Visions pass before her soul in a flash.*)

He is silent, and the lances
Of the spearmen round him.
He stands, and the arrow whistles through his hair.
He is cleansed from the pollution of the guile.
He drains the long draught, throwing back his head.
Ah, now all's gone again!
The enemy holds fast
The secret and the sword.
"The executioner
I make me of your will."
But iron shall not divide the lips, but flame
Shall not divide the lips.

(*She wanders to and fro, wretched and feverish.*)

The utmost flame of fire shall not divide them.

(*She takes up the silver mirror and looks at herself in it.*)

O silence, and still water, sepulchre,
Pale sepulchre of my face!
What is this voice that says
I never was more beautiful than now?
"And in the solitude that was on fire
With your eyes, I have lived
With so swift energy,
Travailing secretly."...
One voice alone cries out
On the topmost of my heart,
And all the blood flies.... Ah!

> (*She starts, hearing a light knocking at the door. She puts down
> the mirror, blows out the taper with a breath, goes to the door,
> tottering, and calls, in a low voice.*)

Smaragdi! Smaragdi!

PAOLO (*voice heard*). Francesca!

> (*She flings the door open vehemently. With a craving as of thirst
> she throws herself into the arms of her lover.*)

FRANCESCA. Paolo! Paolo!

> (*He is dressed as at Vespers; his head is bare.*)

PAOLO. Life of my life, never was my desire
So ardent for you.   In my heart I felt
A dying down
Of the bright spirits that live within your eyes.
My forces ebbed away into the night,
Out of my breast, a flood
Terrible, clangorous,
And fear took hold upon my soul, as when
In that sealed hour,
You put me to the test, God witnessing,
The test of the arrow,
And raised me there whither although he wills it
No man returns by willing to return.
Is it not morning, is it not morning yet?
The stars have all gone down into your hair,
Scattered about the confines of the shades,
Where life may never find them!

> (*He kisses her hair passionately again and again.*)

FRANCESCA. Pardon me,
    Pardon me! Far away
    You come before me,
    Far off and silent,
    With fixed, dry eyeballs, as upon that day
    Between the inflexible lances of the fight.
    A hard sleep falling on me like a blow
    Scattered my soul
    As a stem breaks, and then I seemed to lie
    Lost on the stones. And then there came to me
    The dream that long while now
    I have seen in sleep, the strange
    Dream that has tortured me;
    And I was full of many terrors, full
    Of terrors; and my women
    Saw me, and how I trembled,
    And how I wept...
PAOLO. O, wept!
FRANCESCA. Pardon me, pardon me,
    Sweet friend! You have awakened me from sleep,
    Freed me from every anguish.
    It is not morning yet,
    The stars have not gone down into the sea,
    The summer is not over, and you are mine,
    And I, I am all yours,
    And this is perfect joy
    The passion of the ardour of our life.

                      (PAOLO *kisses her insatiably.*)

PAOLO. You shivered?
FRANCESCA. See, the door
    Is open, and there passes
    The breath of the night. Do you not feel it too?
    This is the hour,
    The hour of silence,
    That sheds the dew of night
    Upon the manes
    Of horses on the roads.
    But shut the door.   (PAOLO *shuts the door.*)

Paolo, did you see with your own eyes
The horsemen as they went away?

PAOLO. Yes, yes,
I watched them from the tower, for a long while
Until the last lance faded
Into the dark, and I could see no more.
Come, come, Francesca! Many hours of gladness
We have before us,
With the wild melody of unknown winds
And the swift ravishment of solitude
In fire, and the violent
River without a goal,
And the immortal thirst;
But now this hour that flies
Fills me with lust to live
A thousand lives,
In the quiver of the air that kisses you,
In the short breath of the sea,
In the fury of the world,
That not one thing
Of all the infinite things
That are in you
Lie hid from me,
And I die not before I have ploughed up
Out of your depths
And relished to its infinite root in you
My perfect joy. (*He draws her towards the cushions by the windows.*)

FRANCESCA. Kiss me upon my eyes, upon my brow,
Upon my cheeks, my throat,
So... so...
Stay, and my wrists, my fingers...
So... so... And take my soul and pour it out,
Because the breath of the night
Turns back my soul again
To things of long ago,
And the low voices of the night turn back
My soul to things that were,
And joys enjoyed are they that now weigh down

My heart, and as you were
I see you still, and not as you shall be,
My fair friend, my sweet friend.

PAOLO. I will carry you where all things are forgot,
And no more time made slave
Is lord of our desire.
Then shall the day and night
Be mingled even as one
Upon the earth as upon one sole pillow;
Then shall the hands of dawn
No more unclasp from one another's holding
The dusky arms and the white arms of them,
Nor yet untwist
The tangles of their hair and veins.

FRANCESCA. It says
Here in the book, here where you have not read:
"We have been one life; it were a seemly thing
That we be also one death."

PAOLO. Let the book
Be closed!

(*He rises, closes the book on the reading-desk, and blows out the taper.*)

And read in it no more. Not there
Our destiny is written, but in the stars,
That palpitate above
As your throat palpitates,
Your wrists, your brow,
Perhaps because they were your garland once,
Your necklet when you went
Burningly through the ways of heaven? From what
Vineyard of earth were these grapes gathered in?
They have the smell
Of drunkenness and honey,
They are like veins, they are swollen with delight,
Fruits of the night! The flaming feet of Love
Shall tread them in the winepress. Give me your mouth
Again! again!

(FRANCESCA *lies back on the cushions, forgetful of everything.*
All at once, in the dead silence, a violent shock is heard on the

door, as if someone hurled himself against it. The lovers start up in terror, and rise to their feet.)

THE VOICE OF GIANCIOTTO. Francesca, open! Francesca!

(FRANCESCA *is petrified with terror.* PAOLO *looks round the room, putting his hand to his dagger. He catches sight of the bolt of the trap-door.)*

PAOLO (*in a low voice*). Take heart, take heart, Francesca! I will get down

By the way of the trap-door.

Go, go, and open to him.

But do not tremble.

(*He lifts the trap-door. The door seems to quiver at the repeated blows.)*

THE VOICE OF GIANCIOTTO. Open, Francesca, open!

PAOLO. Open to him! Go now.

I wait beneath. If he but touches you

Cry out and I am with you.

Go boldly, do not tremble!

(*He begins to go down, while* FRANCESCA *in obedience to him goes to open the door, tottering.)*

THE VOICE OF GIANCIOTTO. Open! upon your life, Francesca, open!

(*The door being opened* GIANCIOTTO, *armed, and covered with dust, rushes furiously into the room, looking for his brother in every direction. Suddenly he catches sight of* PAOLO, *standing head and shoulders above the level of the floor, struggling to free himself from the bolt of the trap-door, which has caught in a corner of his cloak.* FRANCESCA *utters a piercing cry, while* GIANCIOTTO *falls upon his brother, seizing him by the hair, and forcing him to come up.)*

GIANCIOTTO. So, you are caught in a trap,

Traitor! They are good to have you by the hair,

Your ringlets!

FRANCESCA (*rushing forward*). Let him go!

Let him go! Me, take me!

(*The husband loosens his hold.* PAOLO *springs up on the other side of the trap-door, and unsheathes his dagger.* GIANCIOTTO, *drawing back, bares his sword, and rushes upon him with terrible force.* FRANCESCA *throws herself between the two men;*

but as her husband has leant all his weight on the blow, and is unable to draw back, her breast is pierced by the sword, she staggers, turns on herself, towards PAOLO, *who lets fall his dagger, and catches her in his arms.*)

FRANCESCA (*dying*). Ah, Paolo!

(GIANCIOTTO *pauses for an instant. He sees the woman clasped in the arms of her lover, who seals her expiring life with his lips. Mad with rage and sorrow, he pierces his brother's side with another deadly thrust. The two bodies sway to and fro for an instant without a sound. Then, still linked together, they fall at full length on the pavement.* GIANCIOTTO *stoops in silence, bends his knee with a painful effort, and, across the other knee, breaks his blood-stained sword.*)

THE END

THE CHERRY ORCHARD

A COMEDY IN FOUR ACTS

By ANTON CHEKHOV

Translated by CONSTANCE GARNETT

First performed at Moscow, January 17, 1904

ANTON CHEKHOV

ANTON CHEKHOV was born January 17, 1860, in Taganrog on the Sea of Azov. His grandfather was a serf. Educated first in his native town, he began in 1879 the study of medicine at the University of Moscow. During his college course he wrote comic sketches which he published widely, some under his own name and some under a pseudonym. These aided in his support until he took his degree in 1884. He was never active in the profession of medicine. Immediately upon his graduation he began to write plays. Extremely fecund as a writer of stories and sketches he was by no means so vigorous in his playwriting. He wrote in all only fourteen plays, of which two thirds were short pieces, dramatized versions of his literary sketches. His fame as a dramatist rests upon his five long plays of which four were written during the last eight years of his life. From 1891 to 1897 Chekhov lived on an estate near Moscow. Long a sufferer from tuberculosis he moved to the Crimea for his health in 1897. His career as a dramatist is associated with the Moscow Art Theater which first produced his plays with outstanding success, and by their aid entered into its period of greatest significance. Chekhov died in the Crimea July 2, 1904. While his plays are accepted throughout the world as the highest expression of the Russian dramatic genius of our period, they are not characteristic of the Russian theater today and are seldom produced in Soviet Russia.

THE CHERRY ORCHARD

By some critics Chekhov's *The Cherry Orchard* is held to be the supreme example for our time of what has been called a spiritual naturalism. By this is meant, it is presumed, that this play, along with the other four long plays upon which Chekhov's fame rests, seeks to do for the inner life of a social group what the other naturalists do for the outer life of action and environment. Such a judgment needs to be closely scrutinized. It is true that in a superficial sense Chekhov's method has many of the earmarks of naturalism. He holds his material objectively at arm's length. He does not elevate one character above another as do the writers of the plays of artifice. While supplying his play with sufficient action he does not manipulate it into a "theatrical" plot. The action proceeds with the inevitability and something of the indifference of events themselves. Above all he employs the clipped and broken speech of daily usage, depending upon suggestion, allusion, and overtone far more than upon outright expression in formulated phrasing. In all these respects Chekhov does display indeed the qualities of a naturalism of the highest order. And yet these qualities do not comprehend all his gifts, nor does their employment explain the peculiar effects which he gains in his plays, effects which are so individual to the man that they are the signs manual of his work. In our search for the source of these qualities we must look outside the limits of naturalism entirely. First it is to be noted that Chekhov's long plays are quite unlike the great mass of his other work, his sketches, narratives, and short plays. In this he is indeed the naturalist who permits characters and events to manage themselves. In the long plays the first quality we note is that of a vigorous creative management. The author is as much master of form as is the composer of a symphony. He holds everything under strict discipline. *The Cherry Orchard* is fashioned to the dictates of a rigorous artistry, an artistry that refines its materials beyond their own semblance. For the sources of such work as this we need not seek among the experiments of the naturalists even the most refined, the Goncourts for instance. We seek the sources among the most careful craftsmen of the literature of artifice.

Though he deals with the life of a changing Russia, Russian critics of today are insistent in stating that Chekhov is not a typical Russian. In this he is like another Russian with whose work Chekhov's long plays are to be compared. This is Turgenev. Like Turgenev, Chekhov in *The Cherry Orchard* views his action through a haze of nostalgia rigorously maintained. His action is dominated by pity, but a pity that is never particularized, and avoids partisan animus. He is also to be compared with one of his contemporaries, an artist of less intense conviction, Schnitzler, who in a mood of melancholy conceals an impulse of escape. The conclusion must be that though Chekhov has some of the qualities of naturalism his naturalism is only skin deep. Through the clairvoyance of an ailing and doomed spirit he built up an artistry as pure and detached as that of music. Like Maeterlinck's early plays *The Cherry Orchard* and its fellows demand new and purified orders of staging. Gorky tells us that one of Chekhov's contemporaries passed this judgment on his work, "Chekhov's plays should be staged as lyrical dramas." Perhaps no better summary could be made in as few words. *The Cherry Orchard*, written in 1904, was produced in the same year by the Moscow Art Theater. It was performed by the London Stage Society in 1911. As a part of the repertory of the Moscow Art Theater it was played in America in Russian in 1923–24. It has been often translated and frequently produced in this country.

CHARACTERS IN THE PLAY

MADAME RANEVSKY (LYUBOV ANDREYEVNA), *the owner of the Cherry Orchard.*

ANYA, *her daughter, aged seventeen.*

VARYA, *her adopted daughter, aged twenty-four.*

GAEV (LEONID ANDREYEVITCH), *brother of Madame Ranevsky.*

LOPAHIN (YERMOLAY ALEXEYEVITCH), *a merchant.*

TROFIMOV (PYOTR SERGEYEVITCH), *a student.*

SEMYONOV-PISHTCHIK, *a landowner.*

CHARLOTTA IVANOVNA, *a governess.*

EPIHODOV (SEMYON PANTALEYEVITCH), *a clerk.*

DUNYASHA, *a maid.*

FIRS, *an old valet, aged eighty-seven.*

YASHA, *a young valet.*

A VAGRANT.

THE STATION MASTER.

A POST-OFFICE CLERK.

VISITORS, SERVANTS.

The action takes place on the estate of MADAME RANEVSKY.

ACT I

A room, which has always been called the nursery. One of the doors leads into ANYA'S room. Dawn, sun rises during the scene. May, the cherry trees in flower, but it is cold in the garden with the frost of early morning. Windows closed.

(*Enter* DUNYASHA *with a candle and* LOPAHIN *with a book in his hand.*)

LOPAHIN. The train's in, thank God. What time is it?

DUNYASHA. Nearly two o'clock. (*Puts out the candle.*) It's daylight already.

LOPAHIN. The train's late! Two hours, at least. (*Yawns and stretches.*) I'm a pretty one; what a fool I've been. Came here on purpose to meet them at the station and dropped asleep.... Dozed off as I sat in the chair. It's annoying.... You might have waked me.

DUNYASHA. I thought you had gone. (*Listens.*) There, I do believe they're coming!

LOPAHIN (*listens*). No, what with the luggage and one thing and another. (*A pause.*) Lyubov Andreyevna has been abroad five years; I don't know what she is like now.... She's a splendid woman. A good-natured, kind-hearted woman. I remember when I was a lad of fifteen, my poor father — he used to keep a little shop here in the village in those days — gave me a punch in the face with his fist and made my nose bleed. We were in the yard here, I forget what we'd come about — he had had a drop. Lyubov Andreyevna — I can see her now — she was a slim young girl then — took me to wash my face, and then brought me into this very room, into the nursery. "Don't cry, little peasant," says she, "it will be well in time for your wedding day"... (*A pause.*) Little peasant.... My father was a peasant, it's true, but here am I in a white waistcoat and brown shoes, like a pig in a bun shop. Yes, I'm a rich man, but for all my money, come to think, a peasant I was, and a peasant I am. (*Turns over the pages of the book.*) I've been reading this book and I can't make head or tail of it. I fell asleep over it. (*A pause.*)

DUNYASHA. The dogs have been awake all night, they feel that the mistress is coming.

LOPAHIN. Why, what's the matter with you, Dunyasha?

DUNYASHA. My hands are all of a tremble. I feel as though I should faint.

LOPAHIN. You're a spoilt soft creature, Dunyasha. And dressed like a lady too, and your hair done up. That's not the thing. One must know one's place.

(*Enter* EPIHODOV *with a nosegay; he wears a pea-jacket and highly polished creaking topboots; he drops the nosegay as he comes in.*)

EPIHODOV (*picking up the nosegay*). Here! the gardener's sent this, says you're to put it in the dining-room.

(*Gives* DUNYASHA *the nosegay.*)

LOPAHIN. And bring me some kvass.

DUNYASHA. I will. (*Goes out.*)

EPIHODOV. It's chilly this morning, three degrees of frost, though the cherries are all in flower. I can't say much for our climate. (*Sighs.*) I can't. Our climate is not often propitious to the occasion. Yermolay Alexeyevitch, permit me to call your attention to the fact that I purchased myself a pair of boots the day before yesterday, and they creak, I venture to assure you, so that there's no tolerating them. What ought I to grease them with?

LOPAHIN. Oh, shut up! Don't bother me.

EPIHODOV. Every day some misfortune befalls me. I don't complain, I'm used to it, and I wear a smiling face.

(DUNYASHA *comes in, hands* LOPAHIN *the kvass.*)

EPIHODOV. I am going. (*Stumbles against a chair, which falls over.*) There! (*As though triumphant.*) There you see now, excuse the expression, an accident like that among others.... It's positively remarkable. (*Goes out.*)

DUNYASHA. Do you know, Yermolay Alexeyevitch, I must confess, Epihodov has made me a proposal.

LOPAHIN. Ah!

DUNYASHA. I'm sure I don't know.... He's a harmless fellow, but sometimes when he begins talking, there's no making anything of it. It's all very fine and expressive, only there's no understanding it. I've a sort of liking for him too. He loves me to distraction. He's an unfortunate man; every day there's something. They tease him about it — two and twenty misfortunes they call him.

LOPAHIN (*listening*). There! I do believe they're coming.

DUNYASHA. They are coming! What's the matter with me? ... I'm cold all over.

LOPAHIN. They really are coming. Let's go and meet them. Will she know me? It's five years since I saw her.

DUNYASHA (*in a flutter*). I shall drop this very minute.... Ah, I shall drop.

(*There is a sound of two carriages driving up to the house. Lo-PAHIN and DUNYASHA go out quickly. The stage is left empty. A noise is heard in the adjoining rooms. FIRS, who has driven to meet MADAME RANEVSKY, crosses the stage hurriedly leaning on a stick. He is wearing old-fashioned livery and a high hat. He says something to himself, but not a word can be distinguished. The noise behind the scenes goes on increasing. A voice: "Come, let's go in here."*)

(*Enter LYUBOV ANDREYEVNA, ANYA, and CHARLOTTA IVANOVNA with a pet dog on a chain, all in travelling dresses. VARYA in an out-door coat with a kerchief over her head, GAEV, SEMYONOV-PISHTCHIK, LOPAHIN, DUNYASHA with bag and parasol, servants with other articles. All walk across the room.*)

ANYA. Let's come in here. Do you remember what room this is, mamma?

LYUBOV (*joyfully, through her tears*). The nursery!

VARYA. How cold it is, my hands are numb. (*To LYUBOV ANDREYEVNA.*) Your rooms, the white room and the lavender one, are just the same as ever, mamma.

LYUBOV. My nursery, dear delightful room.... I used to sleep here when I was little... (*cries*). And here I am, like a little child... (*Kisses her brother and VARYA, and then her brother again.*) Varya's just the same as ever, like a nun. And I knew Dunyasha.

(*Kisses DUNYASHA.*)

GAEV. The train was two hours late. What do you think of that? Is that the way to do things?

CHARLOTTA (*to* PISHTCHIK). My dog eats nuts, too.

PISHTCHIK (*wonderingly*). Fancy that!

(*They all go out except* ANYA *and* DUNYASHA.)

DUNYASHA. We've been expecting you so long.

(*Takes* ANYA'S *hat and coat.*)

ANYA. I haven't slept for four nights on the journey. I feel dreadfully cold.

DUNYASHA. You set out in Lent, there was snow and frost, and now? My darling! (*Laughs and kisses her.*) I *have* missed you, my precious, my joy. I must tell you... I can't put it off a minute....

ANYA (*wearily*). What now?

DUNYASHA. Epihodov, the clerk, made me a proposal just after Easter.

ANYA. It's always the same thing with you... (*Straightening her hair.*) I've lost all my hairpins...

(*She is staggering from exhaustion.*)

DUNYASHA. I don't know what to think, really. He does love me, he does love me so!

ANYA (*looking towards her door, tenderly*). My own room, my windows just as though I had never gone away. I'm home! Tomorrow morning I shall get up and run into the garden.... Oh, if I could get to sleep! I haven't slept all the journey, I was so anxious and worried.

DUNYASHA. Pyotr Sergeyevitch came the day before yesterday.

ANYA (*joyfully*). Petya!

DUNYASHA. He's asleep in the bath house, he has settled in there. I'm afraid of being in their way, says he. (*Glancing at her watch.*) I was to have waked him, but Varvara Mihalovna told me not to. Don't you wake him, says she.

(*Enter* VARYA *with a bunch of keys at her waist.*)

VARYA. Dunyasha, coffee and make haste.... Mamma's asking for coffee.

DUNYASHA. This very minute. (*Goes out.*)

VARYA. Well, thank God, you've come. You're home again. (*Petting her.*) My little darling has come back! My precious beauty has come back again!

ANYA. I have had a time of it!

VARYA. I can fancy.

ANYA. We set off in Holy Week — it was so cold then, and all the way Charlotta would talk and show off her tricks. What did you want to burden me with Charlotta for?

VARYA. You couldn't have travelled all alone, darling. At seventeen!

ANYA. We got to Paris at last, it was cold there — snow. I speak French shockingly. Mamma lives on the fifth floor, I went up to her and there were a lot of French people, ladies, an old priest with a book. The place smelt of tobacco and so comfortless. I felt sorry, oh! so sorry for mamma all at once, I put my arms round her neck, and hugged her and wouldn't let her go. Mamma was as kind as she could be, and she cried....

VARYA (*through her tears*). Don't speak of it, don't speak of it!

ANYA. She had sold her villa at Mentone, she had nothing left, nothing. I hadn't a farthing left either, we only just had enough to get here. And mamma doesn't understand! When we had dinner at the stations, she always ordered the most expensive things and gave the waiters a whole rouble. Charlotta's just the same. Yasha too must have the same as we do; it's simply awful. You know Yasha is mamma's valet now, we brought him here with us.

VARYA. Yes, I've seen the young rascal.

ANYA. Well, tell me — have you paid the arrears on the mortgage?

VARYA. How could we get the money?

ANYA. Oh, dear! Oh, dear!

VARYA. In August the place will be sold.

ANYA. My goodness!

LOPAHIN (*peeps in at the door and moos like a cow*). Moo!

(*Disappears.*)

VARYA (*weeping*). There, that's what I could do to him.

(*Shakes her fist.*)

ANYA (*embracing* VARYA, *softly*). Varya, has he made you an offer? (VARYA *shakes her head.*) Why, but he loves you. Why is it you don't come to an understanding? What are you waiting for?

VARYA. I believe that there never will be anything between us. He has a lot to do, he has no time for me... and takes no notice of me. Bless the man, it makes me miserable to see him.... Everyone's talking of our being married, everyone's congratulating me, and all the while there's really nothing in it; it's all like a dream. (*In another tone.*) You have a new brooch like a bee.

ANYA (*mournfully*). Mamma bought it. (*Goes into her own room and in a light-hearted childish tone.*) And you know, in Paris I went up in a balloon!

VARYA. My darling's home again! My pretty is home again!

(DUNYASHA *returns with the coffee-pot and is making the coffee.*)

VARYA (*standing at the door*). All day long, darling, as I go about looking after the house, I keep dreaming all the time. If only we could marry you to a rich man, then I should feel more at rest. Then I would go off by myself on a pilgrimage to Kiev, to Moscow... and so I would spend my life going from one holy place to another.... I would go on and on.... What bliss!

ANYA. The birds are singing in the garden. What time is it?

VARYA. It must be nearly three. It's time you were asleep, darling. (*Going into* ANYA's *room.*) What bliss!

(YASHA *enters with a rug and a travelling bag.*)

YASHA (*crosses the stage, mincingly*). May one come in here, pray?

DUNYASHA. I shouldn't have known you, Yasha. How you have changed abroad.

YASHA. H'm!... And who are you?

DUNYASHA. When you went away, I was that high. (*Shows distance from floor.*) Dunyasha, Fyodor's daughter.... You don't remember me!

YASHA. H'm!... You're a peach!

(*Looks round and embraces her: she shrieks and drops a saucer. YASHA goes out hastily.*)

VARYA (*in the doorway, in a tone of vexation*). What now?

DUNYASHA (*through her tears*). I have broken a saucer.

VARYA. Well, that brings good luck.

ANYA (*coming out of her room*). We ought to prepare mamma: Petya is here.

VARYA. I told them not to wake him.

ANYA (*dreamily*). It's six years since father died. Then only a month later little brother Grisha was drowned in the river, such a pretty boy he was, only seven. It was more than mamma could bear, so she went away, went away without looking back. (*Shuddering.*) ... How well I understand her, if only she knew! (*A pause.*) And Petya Trofimov was Grisha's tutor, he may remind her.

(*Enter* FIRS: *he is wearing a pea-jacket and a white waistcoat.*)

FIRS (*goes up to the coffee-pot, anxiously*). The mistress will be served here. (*Puts on white gloves.*) Is the coffee ready? (*Sternly to* DUNYASHA.) Girl! Where's the cream?

DUNYASHA. Ah, mercy on us! (*Goes out quickly.*)

FIRS (*fussing round the coffee-pot*). Ech! you good-for-nothing! (*Muttering to himself.*) Come back from Paris. And the old master used to go to Paris too... horses all the way. (*Laughs.*)

VARYA. What is it, Firs?

FIRS. What is your pleasure? (*Gleefully.*) My lady has come home! I have lived to see her again! Now I can die.

(*Weeps with joy.*)

(*Enter* LYUBOV ANDREYEVNA, GAEV *and* SEMYONOV-PISHTCHIK; *the latter is in a short-waisted full coat of fine cloth, and full trousers.* GAEV, *as he comes in, makes a gesture with his arms and his whole body, as though he were playing billiards.*)

LYUBOV. How does it go? Let me remember. Cannon off the red!

GAEV. That's it — in off the white! Why, once, sister, we used to sleep together in this very room, and now I'm fifty-one, strange as it seems.

LOPAHIN. Yes, time flies.

GAEV. What do you say?

LOPAHIN. Time, I say, flies.

GAEV. What a smell of patchouli!

ANYA. I'm going to bed. Good-night, mamma.

(*Kisses her mother.*)

LYUBOV. My precious darling. (*Kisses her hands.*) Are you glad to be home? I can't believe it.

ANYA. Good-night, uncle.

GAEV (*kissing her face and hands*).   God bless you!   How like you
are to your mother!   (*To his sister.*)   At her age you were just
the same, Lyuba.

> (ANYA *shakes hands with* LOPAHIN *and* PISHTCHIK, *then goes
> out, shutting the door after her.*)

LYUBOV. She's quite worn out.

PISHTCHIK. Aye, it's a long journey, to be sure.

VARYA (*to* LOPAHIN *and* PISHTCHIK).   Well, gentlemen?   It's three
o'clock and time to say good-bye.

LYUBOV (*laughs*).   You're just the same as ever, Varya.   (*Draws
her to her and kisses her.*)   I'll just drink my coffee and then we
will all go and rest.   (FIRS *puts a cushion under her feet.*)   Thanks,
friend.   I am so fond of coffee, I drink it day and night.   Thanks,
dear old man.   (*Kisses* FIRS.)

VARYA. I'll just see whether all the things have been brought in.
                                                        (*Goes out.*)

LYUBOV. Can it really be me sitting here?   (*Laughs.*)   I want to
dance about and clap my hands.   (*Covers her face with her hands.*)
And I could drop asleep in a moment!   God knows I love my
country, I love it tenderly; I couldn't look out of the window in
the train, I kept crying so.   (*Through her tears.*)   But I must drink
my coffee, though.   Thank you, Firs, thanks, dear old man.
I'm so glad to find you still alive.

FIRS. The day before yesterday.

GAEV. He's rather deaf.

LOPAHIN. I have to set off for Harkov directly, at five o'clock....
It is annoying!   I wanted to have a look at you, and a little talk.
... You are just as splendid as ever.

PISHTCHIK (*breathing heavily*).   Handsomer, indeed.... Dressed in
Parisian style... completely bowled me over.

LOPAHIN. Your brother, Leonid Andreyevitch here, is always
saying that I'm a low-born knave, that I'm a money-grubber,
but I don't care one straw for that.   Let him talk.   Only I do
want you to believe in me as you used to.   I do want your
wonderful tender eyes to look at me as they used to in the old
days.   Merciful God!   My father was a serf of your father and
of your grandfather, but you — you — did so much for me

once, that I've forgotten all that; I love you as though you were my kin... more than my kin.

LYUBOV. I can't sit still, I simply can't... (*Jumps up and walks about in violent agitation.*) This happiness is too much for me.... You may laugh at me, I know I'm silly.... My own bookcase. (*Kisses the bookcase.*) My little table.

GAEV. Nurse died while you were away.

LYUBOV (*sits down and drinks coffee*). Yes, the Kingdom of Heaven be hers! You wrote me of her death.

GAEV. And Anastasy is dead. Squinting Petruchka has left me and is in service now with the police captain in the town.

(*Takes a box of caramels out of his pocket and sucks one.*)

PISHTCHIK. My daughter, Dashenka, wishes to be remembered to you.

LOPAHIN. I want to tell you something very pleasant and cheering. (*Glancing at his watch.*) I'm going directly... there's no time to say much... well, I can say it in a couple of words. I needn't tell you your cherry orchard is to be sold to pay your debts; the 22nd of August is the date fixed for the sale; but don't you worry, dearest lady, you may sleep in peace, there is a way of saving it.... This is what I propose. I beg your attention! Your estate is not twenty miles from the town, the railway runs close by it, and if the cherry orchard and the land along the river bank were cut up into building plots and then let on lease for summer villas, you would make an income of at least 25,000 roubles a year out of it.

GAEV. That's all rot, if you'll excuse me.

LYUBOV. I don't quite understand you, Yermolay Alexeyevitch.

LOPAHIN. You will get a rent of at least 25 roubles a year for a three-acre plot from summer visitors, and if you say the word now, I'll bet you what you like there won't be one square foot of ground vacant by the autumn, all the plots will be taken up. I congratulate you; in fact, you are saved. It's a perfect situation with that deep river. Only, of course, it must be cleared — all the old buildings, for example, must be removed, this house too, which is really good for nothing and the old cherry orchard must be cut down.

LYUBOV. Cut down? My dear fellow, forgive me, but you don't

know what you are talking about. If there is one thing interesting — remarkable indeed — in the whole province, it's just our cherry orchard.

LOPAHIN. The only thing remarkable about the orchard is that it's a very large one. There's a crop of cherries every alternate year, and then there's nothing to be done with them, no one buys them.

GAEV. This orchard is mentioned in the "Encyclopædia."

LOPAHIN (*glancing at his watch*). If we don't decide on something and don't take some steps, on the 22nd of August the cherry orchard and the whole estate too will be sold by auction. Make up your minds! There is no other way of saving it, I'll take my oath on that. No, No!

FIRS. In old days, forty or fifty years ago, they used to dry the cherries, soak them, pickle them, make jam too, and they used ——

GAEV. Be quiet, Firs.

FIRS. And they used to send the preserved cherries to Moscow and to Harkov by the waggon-load. That brought the money in! And the preserved cherries in those days were soft and juicy, sweet and fragrant.... They knew the way to do them then....

LYUBOV. And where is the recipe now?

FIRS. It's forgotten. Nobody remembers it.

PISHTCHIK (*to* LYUBOV ANDREYEVNA). What's it like in Paris? Did you eat frogs there?

LYUBOV. Oh, I ate crocodiles.

PISHTCHIK. Fancy that now!

LOPAHIN. There used to be only the gentlefolks and the peasants in the country, but now there are these summer visitors. All the towns, even the small ones, are surrounded nowadays by these summer villas. And one may say for sure, that in another twenty years there'll be many more of these people and that they'll be everywhere. At present the summer visitor only drinks tea in his verandah, but maybe he'll take to working his bit of land too, and then your cherry orchard would become happy, rich and prosperous....

GAEV (*indignant*). What rot!

(*Enter* VARYA *and* YASHA.)

VARYA. There are two telegrams for you, mamma. (*Takes out keys and opens an old-fashioned bookcase with a loud crack.*) Here they are.

LYUBOV. From Paris. (*Tears the telegrams, without reading them.*) I have done with Paris.

GAEV. Do you know, Lyuba, how old that bookcase is? Last week I pulled out the bottom drawer and there I found the date branded on it. The bookcase was made just a hundred years ago. What do you say to that? We might have celebrated its jubilee. Though it's an inanimate object, still it is a *book* case.

PISHTCHIK (*amazed*). A hundred years! Fancy that now.

GAEV. Yes.... It is a thing... (*Feeling the bookcase.*) Dear, honoured, bookcase! Hail to thee who for more than a hundred years hast served the pure ideals of good and justice; thy silent call to fruitful labour has never flagged in those hundred years, maintaining (*in tears*) in the generations of man, courage and faith in a brighter future and fostering in us ideals of good and social consciousness. (*A pause.*)

LOPAHIN. Yes....

LYUBOV. You are just the same as ever, Leonid.

GAEV (*a little embarrassed*). Cannon off the right into the pocket!

LOPAHIN (*looking at his watch*). Well, it's time I was off.

YASHA (*handing* LYUBOV ANDREYEVNA *medicine*). Perhaps you will take your pills now.

PISHTCHIK. You shouldn't take medicines, my dear madam... they do no harm and no good. Give them here... honoured lady. (*Takes the pill-box, pours the pills into the hollow of his hand, blows on them, puts them in his mouth and drinks off some kvass.*) There!

LYUBOV (*in alarm*). Why, you must be out of your mind!

PISHTCHIK. I have taken all the pills.

LOPAHIN. What a glutton! (*All laugh.*)

FIRS. His honour stayed with us in Easter week, ate a gallon and a half of cucumbers... (*Mutters.*)

LYUBOV. What is he saying?

VARYA. He has taken to muttering like that for the last three years. We are used to it.

YASHA. His declining years!

(CHARLOTTA IVANOVNA, *a very thin, lanky figure in a white dress with a lorgnette in her belt, walks across the stage.*)

LOPAHIN. I beg your pardon, Charlotta Ivanovna, I have not had time to greet you. (*Tries to kiss her hand.*)

CHARLOTTA (*pulling away her hand*). If I let you kiss my hand, you'll be wanting to kiss my elbow, and then my shoulder.

LOPAHIN. I've no luck today! (*All laugh.*) Charlotta Ivanovna, show us some tricks!

LYUBOV. Charlotta, do show us some tricks!

CHARLOTTA. I don't want to. I'm sleepy. (*Goes out.*)

LOPAHIN. In three weeks' time we shall meet again. (*Kisses* LYUBOV ANDREYEVNA'S *hand.*) Good-bye till then — I must go. (*To* GAEV.) Good-bye. (*Kisses* PISHTCHIK.) Good-bye. (*Gives his hand to* VARYA, *then to* FIRS *and* YASHA.) I don't want to go. (*To* LYUBOV ANDREYEVNA.) If you think over my plan for the villas and make up your mind, then let me know; I will lend you 50,000 roubles. Think of it seriously.

VARYA (*angrily*). Well, do go, for goodness sake.

LOPAHIN. I'm going, I'm going. (*Goes out.*)

GAEV. Low-born knave! I beg pardon, though... Varya is going to marry him, he's Varya's fiancé.

VARYA. Don't talk nonsense, uncle.

LYUBOV. Well, Varya, I shall be delighted. He's a good man.

PISHTCHIK. He is, one must acknowledge, a most worthy man. And my Dashenka... says too that... she says... various things. (*Snores, but at once wakes up.*) But all the same, honoured lady, could you oblige me... with a loan of 240 roubles... to pay the interest on my mortgage tomorrow?

VARYA (*dismayed*). No, no.

LYUBOV. I really haven't any money.

PISHTCHIK. It will turn up. (*Laughs.*) I never lose hope. I thought everything was over, I was a ruined man, and lo and behold — the railway passed through my land and... they paid me for it. And something else will turn up again, if not today, then tomorrow... Dashenka'll win two hundred thousand... she's got a lottery ticket.

LYUBOV. Well, we've finished our coffee, we can go to bed.

FIRS (*brushes* GAEV, *reprovingly*). You have got on the wrong trousers again! What am I to do with you?

VARYA (*softly*). Anya's asleep. (*Softly opens the window.*) Now the sun's risen, it's not a bit cold. Look, mamma, what exquisite trees! My goodness! And the air! The starlings are singing!

GAEV (*opens another window*). The orchard is all white. You've not forgotten it, Lyuba? That long avenue that runs straight, straight as an arrow, how it shines on a moonlight night. You remember? You've not forgotten?

LYUBOV (*looking out of the window into the garden*). Oh, my childhood, my innocence! It was in this nursery I used to sleep, from here I looked out into the orchard, happiness waked with me every morning and in those days the orchard was just the same, nothing has changed. (*Laughs with delight.*) All, all white! Oh, my orchard! After the dark gloomy autumn, and the cold winter; you are young again, and full of happiness, the heavenly angels have never left you.... If I could cast off the burden that weighs on my heart, if I could forget the past!

GAEV. H'm! and the orchard will be sold to pay our debts; it seems strange....

LYUBOV. See, our mother walking... all in white, down the avenue! (*Laughs with delight.*) It is she!

GAEV. Where?

VARYA. Oh, don't, mamma!

LYUBOV. There is no one. It was my fancy. On the right there, by the path to the arbour, there is a white tree bending like a woman....

(*Enter* TROFIMOV *wearing a shabby student's uniform and spectacles.*)

LYUBOV. What a ravishing orchard! White masses of blossom, blue sky....

TROFIMOV. Lyubov Andreyevna! (*She looks round at him.*) I will just pay my respects to you and then leave you at once. (*Kisses her hand warmly.*) I was told to wait until morning, but I haven't the patience to wait any longer....

(LYUBOV ANDREYEVNA *looks at him in perplexity.*)

VARYA (*through her tears*). This is Petya Trofimov.

TROFIMOV. Petya Trofimov, who was your Grisha's tutor.... Can I have changed so much?

(LYUBOV ANDREYEVNA *embraces him and weeps quietly.*)

GAEV (*in confusion*). There, there, Lyuba.

VARYA (*crying*). I told you, Petya, to wait till tomorrow.

LYUBOV. My Grisha... my boy... Grisha... my son!

VARYA. We can't help it, mamma, it is God's will.

TROFIMOV (*softly through his tears*). There... there.

LYUBOV (*weeping quietly*). My boy was lost... drowned. Why? Oh, why, dear Petya? (*More quietly.*) Anya is asleep in there, and I'm talking loudly... making this noise.... But, Petya? Why have you grown so ugly? Why do you look so old?

TROFIMOV. A peasant-woman in the train called me a mangy-looking gentleman.

LYUBOV. You were quite a boy then, a pretty little student, and now your hair's thin — and spectacles. Are you really a student still? (*Goes towards the door.*)

TROFIMOV. I seem likely to be a perpetual student.

LYUBOV (*kisses her brother, then* VARYA). Well, go to bed.... You are older too, Leonid.

PISHTCHIK (*follows her*). I suppose it's time we were asleep.... Ugh! my gout. I'm staying the night! Lyubov Andreyevna, my dear soul, if you could... tomorrow morning... 240 roubles.

GAEV. That's always his story.

PISHTCHIK. 240 roubles... to pay the interest on my mortgage.

LYUBOV. My dear man, I have no money.

PISHTCHIK. I'll pay it back, my dear... a trifling sum.

LYUBOV. Oh, well, Leonid will give it you.... You give him the money, Leonid.

GAEV. Me give it him! Let him wait till he gets it!

LYUBOV. It can't be helped, give it him. He needs it. He'll pay it back.

(LYUBOV ANDREYEVNA, TROFIMOV, PISHTCHIK *and* FIRS *go out.* GAEV, VARYA *and* YASHA *remain.*)

GAEV. Sister hasn't got out of the habit of flinging away her money. (*To* YASHA.) Get away, my good fellow, you smell of the hen-house.

YASHA (*with a grin*). And you, Leonid Andreyevitch, are just the same as ever.

GAEV. What's that? (*To* VARYA.) What did he say?

VARYA (*to* YASHA). Your mother has come from the village; she has been sitting in the servants' room since yesterday, waiting to see you.

YASHA. Oh, bother her!

VARYA. For shame!

YASHA. What's the hurry? She might just as well have come tomorrow. (*Goes out.*)

VARYA. Mamma's just the same as ever, she hasn't changed a bit. If she had her own way, she'd give away everything.

GAEV. Yes. (*A pause.*) If a great many remedies are suggested for some disease, it means that the disease is incurable. I keep thinking and racking my brains; I have many schemes, a great many, and that really means none. If we could only come in for a legacy from somebody, or marry our Anya to a very rich man, or we might go to Yaroslavl and try our luck with our old aunt, the Countess. She's very, very rich, you know.

VARYA (*weeps*). If God would help us.

GAEV. Don't blubber. Aunt's very rich, but she doesn't like us. First, sister married a lawyer instead of a nobleman...

(ANYA *appears in the doorway.*)

GAEV. And then her conduct, one can't call it virtuous. She is good, and kind, and nice, and I love her, but, however one allows for extenuating circumstances, there's no denying that she's an immoral woman. One feels it in her slightest gesture.

VARYA (*in a whisper*). Anya's in the doorway.

GAEV. What do you say? (*A pause.*) It's queer, there seems to be something wrong with my right eye. I don't see as well as I did. And on Thursday when I was in the district Court...

(*Enter* ANYA.)

VARYA. Why aren't you asleep, Anya?

ANYA. I can't get to sleep.

GAEV. My pet. (*Kisses* ANYA's *face and hands.*) My child. (*Weeps.*) You are not my niece, you are my angel, you are everything to me. Believe me, believe...

ANYA. I believe you, uncle. Everyone loves you and respects you... but, uncle dear, you must be silent... simply be silent.

What were you saying just now about my mother, about your own sister? What made you say that?

GAEV. Yes, yes... (*Puts his hand over his face.*) Really, that was awful! My God, save me! And today I made a speech to the bookcase... so stupid! And only when I had finished, I saw how stupid it was.

VARYA. It's true, uncle, you ought to keep quiet. Don't talk, that's all.

ANYA. If you could keep from talking, it would make things easier for you, too.

GAEV. I won't speak. (*Kisses* ANYA's *and* VARYA's *hands.*) I'll be silent. Only this is about business. On Thursday I was in the district Court; well, there was a large party of us there and we began talking of one thing and another, and this and that, and do you know, I believe that it will be possible to raise a loan on an I.O.U. to pay the arrears on the mortgage.

VARYA. If the Lord would help us!

GAEV. I'm going on Tuesday; I'll talk of it again. (*To* VARYA.) Don't blubber. (*To* ANYA.) Your mamma will talk to Lopahin; of course, he won't refuse her. And as soon as you're rested you shall go to Yaroslavl to the Countess, your great-aunt. So we shall all set to work in three directions at once, and the business is done. We shall pay off arrears, I'm convinced of it. (*Puts a caramel in his mouth.*) I swear on my honour, I swear by anything you like, the estate shan't be sold. (*Excitedly.*) By my own happiness, I swear it! Here's my hand on it, call me the basest, vilest of men, if I let it come to an auction! Upon my soul I swear it!

ANYA (*her equanimity has returned, she is quite happy*). How good you are, uncle, and how clever! (*Embraces her uncle.*) I'm at peace now! Quite at peace! I'm happy!

(*Enter* FIRS.)

FIRS (*reproachfully*). Leonid Andreyevitch, have you no fear of God? When are you going to bed?

GAEV. Directly, directly. You can go, Firs. I'll... yes, I will undress myself. Come, children, bye-bye. We'll go into details tomorrow, but now go to bed. (*Kisses* ANYA *and* VARYA.)

I'm a man of the eighties. They run down that period, but still I can say I have had to suffer not a little for my convictions in my life. It's not for nothing that the peasant loves me. One must know the peasant! One must know how…

ANYA. At it again, uncle!

VARYA. Uncle dear, you'd better be quiet!

FIRS (*angrily*). Leonid Andreyevitch!

GAEV. I'm coming. I'm coming. Go to bed. Potted the shot — there's a shot for you! A beauty!

(*Goes out*, FIRS *hobbling after him*.)

ANYA. My mind's at rest now. I don't want to go to Yaroslavl, I don't like my great-aunt, but still my mind's at rest. Thanks to uncle. (*Sits down*.)

VARYA. We must go to bed. I'm going. Something unpleasant happened while you were away. In the old servants' quarters there are only the old servants, as you know —Efimyushka, Polya and Yevstigney — and Karp too. They began letting stray people in to spend the night — I said nothing. But all at once I heard they had been spreading a report that I gave them nothing but pease pudding to eat. Out of stinginess, you know…. And it was all Yevstigney's doing…. Very well, I said to myself…. If that's how it is, I thought, wait a bit. I sent for Yevstigney… (*Yawns*.) He comes…. "How's this, Yevstigney," I said, "you could be such a fool as to?…" (*Looking at* ANYA.) Anitchka! (*A pause*.) She's asleep. (*Puts her arm round* ANYA.) Come to bed… come along! (*Leads her*.) My darling has fallen asleep! Come… (*They go*.)

(*Far away beyond the orchard a shepherd plays on a pipe*. TRO-FIMOV *crosses the stage and, seeing* VARYA *and* ANYA, *stands still*.)

VARYA. 'Sh! asleep, asleep. Come, my own.

ANYA (*softly, half asleep*). I'm so tired. Still those bells. Uncle… dear… mamma and uncle….

VARYA. Come, my own, come along. (*They go into* ANYA'S *room*.)

TROFIMOV (*tenderly*). My sunshine! My spring.

CURTAIN

ACT II

The open country.   An old shrine, long abandoned and fallen out of the perpendicular; near it a well, large stones that have apparently once been tombstones, and an old garden seat.   The road to GAEV's house is seen. On one side rise dark poplars; and there the cherry orchard begins.   In the distance a row of telegraph poles and far, far away on the horizon there is faintly outlined a great town, only visible in very fine clear weather.   It is near sunset.   CHARLOTTA, YASHA and DUNYASHA are sitting on the seat. EPIHODOV is standing near, playing something mournful on a guitar. All sit plunged in thought.   CHARLOTTA wears an old forage cap; she has taken a gun from her shoulder and is tightening the buckle on the strap.

CHARLOTTA (*musingly*).   I haven't a real passport of my own, and I don't know how old I am, and I always feel that I'm a young thing.   When I was a little girl, my father and mother used to travel about to fairs and give performances — very good ones. And I used to dance *salto-mortale* and all sorts of things.   And when papa and mamma died, a German lady took me and had me educated.   And so I grew up and became a governess. But where I came from, and who I am, I don't know…. Who my parents were, very likely they weren't married… I don't know.   (*Takes a cucumber out of her pocket and eats.*)   I know nothing at all.   (*A pause.*)   One wants to talk and has no one to talk to… I have nobody.

EPIHODOV (*plays on the guitar and sings*).   "What care I for the noisy world!   What care I for friends or foes!"   How agreeable it is to play on the mandoline!

DUNYASHA.   That's a guitar, not a mandoline.
                    (*Looks in a hand-mirror and powders herself.*)

EPIHODOV.   To a man mad with love, it's a mandoline.   (*Sings.*) "Were her heart but aglow with love's mutual flame."
                                        (*YASHA joins in.*)

CHARLOTTA.   How shockingly these people sing!   Foo!   Like jackals!

DUNYASHA (*to* YASHA).   What happiness, though, to visit foreign lands.

YASHA.   Ah, yes!   I rather agree with you there.
                              (*Yawns, then lights a cigar.*)

EPIHODOV. That's comprehensible. In foreign lands everything has long since reached full complexion.

YASHA. That's so, of course.

EPIHODOV. I'm a cultivated man, I read remarkable books of all sorts, but I can never make out the tendency I am myself precisely inclined for, whether to live or to shoot myself, speaking precisely, but nevertheless I always carry a revolver. Here it is… (*Shows revolver.*)

CHARLOTTA. I've had enough, and now I'm going. (*Puts on the gun.*) Epihodov, you're a very clever fellow, and a very terrible one too, all the women must be wild about you. Br-r-r! (*Goes.*) These clever fellows are all so stupid; there's not a creature for me to speak to…. Always alone, alone, nobody belonging to me … and who I am, and why I'm on earth, I don't know.

(*Walks away slowly.*)

EPIHODOV. Speaking precisely, not touching upon other subjects, I'm bound to admit about myself, that destiny behaves mercilessly to me, as a storm to a little boat. If, let us suppose, I am mistaken, then why did I wake up this morning, to quote an example, and look round, and there on my chest was a spider of fearful magnitude… like this. (*Shows with both hands.*) And then I take up a jug of kvass, to quench my thirst, and in it there is something in the highest degree unseemly of the nature of a cockroach. (*A pause.*) Have you read Buckle? (*A pause.*) I am desirous of troubling you, Dunyasha, with a couple of words.

DUNYASHA. Well, speak.

EPIHODOV. I should be desirous to speak with you alone. (*Sighs.*)

DUNYASHA (*embarrassed*). Well — only bring me my mantle first. It's by the cupboard. It's rather damp here.

EPIHODOV. Certainly. I will fetch it. Now I know what I must do with my revolver. (*Takes guitar and goes off playing on it.*)

YASHA. Two and twenty misfortunes! Between ourselves, he's a fool. (*Yawns.*)

DUNYASHA. God grant he doesn't shoot himself! (*A pause.*) I am so nervous, I'm always in a flutter. I was a little girl when I was taken into our lady's house, and now I have quite grown out of peasant ways, and my hands are white, as white as a lady's.

I'm such a delicate, sensitive creature, I'm afraid of everything. I'm so frightened. And if you deceive me, Yasha, I don't know what will become of my nerves.

YASHA (*kisses her*). You're a peach! Of course a girl must never forget herself; what I dislike more than anything is a girl being flighty in her behaviour.

DUNYASHA. I'm passionately in love with you, Yasha; you are a man of culture — you can give your opinion about anything.
(*A pause.*)

YASHA (*yawns*). Yes, that's so. My opinion is this: if a girl loves anyone, that means that she has no principles. (*A pause.*) It's pleasant smoking a cigar in the open air. (*Listens.*) Someone's coming this way... it's the gentlefolk. (DUNYASHA *embraces him impulsively.*) Go home, as though you had been to the river to bathe; go by that path, or else they'll meet you and suppose I have made an appointment with you here. That I can't endure.

DUNYASHA (*coughing softly*). The cigar has made my head ache...
(*Goes off.*)

(YASHA *remains sitting near the shrine.* Enter LYUBOV ANDREYEVNA, GAEV *and* LOPAHIN.)

LOPAHIN. You must make up your mind once for all — there's no time to lose. It's quite a simple question, you know. Will you consent to letting the land for building or not? One word in answer: Yes or no? Only one word!

LYUBOV. Who is smoking such horrible cigars here? (*Sits down.*)

GAEV. Now the railway line has been brought near, it's made things very convenient. (*Sits down.*) Here we have been over and lunched in town. Cannon off the white! I should like to go home and have a game.

LYUBOV. You have plenty of time.

LOPAHIN. Only one word! (*Beseechingly.*) Give me an answer!

GAEV (*yawning*). What do you say?

LYUBOV (*looks in her purse*). I had quite a lot of money here yesterday, and there's scarcely any left today. My poor Varya feeds us all on milk soup for the sake of economy; the old folks in the kitchen get nothing but pease pudding, while I waste my money in a senseless way. (*Drops purse, scattering gold pieces.*)   There, they have all fallen out!   (*Annoyed.*)

YASHA. Allow me, I'll soon pick them up.   (*Collects the coins.*)

LYUBOV. Pray do, Yasha.   And what did I go off to the town to lunch for?   Your restaurant's a wretched place with its music and the tablecloth smelling of soap.... Why drink so much, Leonid?   And eat so much?   And talk so much?   Today you talked a great deal again in the restaurant, and all so inappropriately.   About the era of the 'seventies, about the decadents.   And to whom?   Talking to waiters about decadents!

LOPAHIN. Yes.

GAEV (*waving his hand*).   I'm incorrigible; that's evident.   (*Irritably to* YASHA.)   Why is it you keep fidgeting about in front of us!

YASHA (*laughs*).   I can't help laughing when I hear your voice.

GAEV (*to his sister*).   Either I or he...

LYUBOV. Get along!   Go away, Yasha.

YASHA (*gives* LYUBOV ANDREYEVNA *her purse*).   Directly.   (*Hardly able to suppress his laughter.*)   This minute...   (*Goes off.*)

LOPAHIN. Deriganov, the millionaire, means to buy your estate. They say he is coming to the sale himself.

LYUBOV. Where did you hear that?

LOPAHIN. That's what they say in town.

GAEV. Our aunt in Yaroslavl has promised to send help; but when, and how much she will send, we don't know.

LOPAHIN. How much will she send?   A hundred thousand?   Two hundred?

LYUBOV. Oh, well!... Ten or fifteen thousand, and we must be thankful to get that.

LOPAHIN. Forgive me, but such reckless people as you are — such queer, unbusiness-like people — I never met in my life.   One tells you in plain Russian your estate is going to be sold, and you seem not to understand it.

LYUBOV. What are we to do?   Tell us what to do.

LOPAHIN. I do tell you every day.   Every day I say the same thing. You absolutely must let the cherry orchard and the land on building leases; and do it at once, as quick as may be — the auction's close upon us!   Do understand!   Once make up your mind to build villas, and you can raise as much money as you like, and then you are saved.

LYUBOV. Villas and summer visitors — forgive me saying so — it's so vulgar.

GAEV. There I perfectly agree with you.

LOPAHIN. I shall sob, or scream, or fall into a fit. I can't stand it! You drive me mad! (*To* GAEV.) You're an old woman!

GAEV. What do you say?

LOPAHIN. An old woman!   (*Gets up to go.*)

LYUBOV (*in dismay*). No, don't go! Do stay, my dear friend! Perhaps we shall think of something.

LOPAHIN. What is there to think of?

LYUBOV. Don't go, I entreat you! With you here it's more cheerful, anyway. (*A pause.*) I keep expecting something, as though the house were going to fall about our ears.

GAEV (*in profound dejection*). Potted the white! It fails — a kiss.

LYUBOV. We have been great sinners....

LOPAHIN. You have no sins to repent of.

GAEV (*puts a caramel in his mouth*). They say I've eaten up my property in caramels.   (*Laughs.*)

LYUBOV. Oh, my sins! I've always thrown my money away recklessly like a lunatic. I married a man who made nothing but debts. My husband died of champagne — he drank dreadfully. To my misery I loved another man, and immediately — it was my first punishment — the blow fell upon me, here, in the river ... my boy was drowned and I went abroad — went away for ever, never to return, not to see that river again... I shut my eyes, and fled, distracted, and *he* after me... pitilessly, brutally. I bought a villa at Mentone, for *he* fell ill there, and for three years I had no rest day or night. His illness wore me out, my soul was dried up. And last year, when my villa was sold to pay my debts, I went to Paris and there he robbed me of everything and abandoned me for another woman; and I tried to poison myself.... So stupid, so shameful!.... And suddenly I felt a yearning for Russia, for my country, for my little girl... (*Dries her tears.*) Lord, Lord, be merciful! Forgive my sins! Do not chastise me more! (*Takes a telegram out of her pocket.*) I got this today from Paris. He implores forgiveness, entreats me to

return. (*Tears up the telegram.*) I fancy there is music somewhere. (*Listens.*)

GAEV. That's our famous Jewish orchestra. You remember, four
violins, a flute and a double bass.

LYUBOV. That still in existence? We ought to send for them one
evening, and give a dance.

LOPAHIN (*listens*). I can't hear.... (*Hums softly.*) "For money
the Germans will turn a Russian into a Frenchman." (*Laughs.*)
I did see such a piece at the theatre yesterday! It was funny!

LYUBOV. And most likely there was nothing funny in it. You
shouldn't look at plays, you should look at yourselves a little
oftener. How grey your lives are! How much nonsense you
talk.

LOPAHIN. That's true. One may say honestly, we live a fool's life.
(*Pause.*) My father was a peasant, an idiot; he knew nothing
and taught me nothing, only beat me when he was drunk, and
always with his stick. In reality I am just such another blockhead and idiot. I've learnt nothing properly. I write a
wretched hand. I write so that I feel ashamed before folks, like
a pig.

LYUBOV. You ought to get married, my dear fellow.

LOPAHIN. Yes... that's true.

LYUBOV. You should marry our Varya, she's a good girl.

LOPAHIN. Yes.

LYUBOV. She's a good-natured girl, she's busy all day long, and
what's more, she loves you. And you have liked her for ever
so long.

LOPAHIN. Well? I'm not against it.... She's a good girl. (*Pause.*)

GAEV. I've been offered a place in the bank: 6,000 roubles a year.
Did you know?

LYUBOV. You would never do for that! You must stay as you are.

(*Enter* FIRS *with overcoat.*)

FIRS. Put it on, sir, it's damp.

GAEV (*putting it on*). You bother me, old fellow.

FIRS. You can't go on like this. You went away in the morning
without leaving word. (*Looks him over.*)

LYUBOV. You look older, Firs!

FIRS. What is your pleasure?

LOPAHIN. You look older, she said.

FIRS. I've had a long life. They were arranging my wedding before your papa was born.... (*Laughs.*) I was the head footman before the emancipation came. I wouldn't consent to be set free then; I stayed on with the old master... (*A pause.*) I remember what rejoicings they made and didn't know themselves what they were rejoicing over.

LOPAHIN. Those were fine old times. There was flogging anyway.

FIRS (*not hearing*). To be sure! The peasants knew their place, and the masters knew theirs; but now they're all at sixes and sevens, there's no making it out.

GAEV. Hold your tongue, Firs. I must go to town tomorrow. I have been promised an introduction to a general, who might let us have a loan.

LOPAHIN. You won't bring that off. And you won't pay your arrears, you may rest assured of that.

LYUBOV. That's all his nonsense. There is no such general.

(*Enter* TROFIMOV, ANYA *and* VARYA.)

GAEV. Here come our girls.

ANYA. There's mamma on the seat.

LYUBOV (*tenderly*). Come here, come along. My darlings! (*Embraces* ANYA *and* VARYA.) If you only knew how I love you both. Sit beside me, there, like that. (*All sit down.*)

LOPAHIN. Our perpetual student is always with the young ladies.

TROFIMOV. That's not your business.

LOPAHIN. He'll soon be fifty, and he's still a student.

TROFIMOV. Drop your idiotic jokes.

LOPAHIN. Why are you so cross, you queer fish?

TROFIMOV. Oh, don't persist!

LOPAHIN (*laughs*). Allow me to ask you what's your idea of me?

TROFIMOV. I'll tell you my idea of you, Yermolay Alexeyevitch: you are a rich man, you'll soon be a millionaire. Well, just as in the economy of nature a wild beast is of use, who devours everything that comes in his way, so you too have your use. (*All laugh.*)

VARYA. Better tell us something about the planets, Petya.

LYUBOV. No, let us go on with the conversation we had yesterday.

TROFIMOV. What was it about?

GAEV. About pride.

TROFIMOV. We had a long conversation yesterday, but we came to no conclusion. In pride, in your sense of it, there is something mystical. Perhaps you are right from your point of view; but if one looks at it simply, without subtlety, what sort of pride can there be, what sense is there in it, if man in his physiological formation is very imperfect, if in the immense majority of cases he is coarse, dull-witted, profoundly unhappy? One must give up glorification of self. One should work, and nothing else.

GAEV. One must die in any case.

TROFIMOV. Who knows? And what does it mean — dying? Perhaps man has a hundred senses, and only the five we know are lost at death, while the other ninety-five remain alive.

LYUBOV. How clever you are, Petya!

LOPAHIN (*ironically*). Fearfully clever!

TROFIMOV. Humanity progresses, perfecting its powers. Everything that is beyond its ken now will one day become familiar and comprehensible; only we must work, we must with all our powers aid the seeker after truth. Here among us in Russia the workers are few in number as yet. The vast majority of the intellectual people I know, seek nothing, do nothing, are not fit as yet for work of any kind. They call themselves intellectual, but they treat their servants as inferiors, behave to the peasants as though they were animals, learn little, read nothing seriously, do practically nothing, only talk about science and know very little about art. They are all serious people, they all have severe faces, they all talk of weighty matters and air their theories, and yet the vast majority of us — ninety-nine per cent — live like savages, at the least thing fly to blows and abuse, eat piggishly, sleep in filth and stuffiness, bugs everywhere, stench and damp and moral impurity. And it's clear all our fine talk is only to divert our attention and other people's. Show me where to find the crèches there's so much talk about, and the reading-rooms? They only exist in novels: in real life there are none of them. There is nothing but filth and vulgarity and Asiatic apathy. I fear and dislike very serious faces. I'm afraid of serious conversation. We should do better to be silent.

LOPAHIN. You know, I get up at five o'clock in the morning, and I work from morning to night; and I've money, my own and other people's, always passing through my hands, and I see what people are made of all round me. One has only to begin to do anything to see how few honest, decent people there are. Sometimes when I lie awake at night, I think: "Oh! Lord, thou hast given us immense forests, boundless plains, the widest horizons, and living here we ourselves ought really to be giants."

LYUBOV. You ask for giants! They are no good except in story-books; in real life they frighten us.

(EPIHODOV *advances in the background, playing on the guitar.*)

LYUBOV (*dreamily*). There goes Epihodov.

ANYA (*dreamily*). There goes Epihodov.

GAEV. The sun has set, my friends.

TROFIMOV. Yes.

GAEV (*not loudly, but, as it were, declaiming*). O nature, divine nature, thou art bright with eternal lustre, beautiful and indifferent! Thou, whom we call mother, thou dost unite within thee life and death! Thou dost give life and dost destroy!

VARYA (*in a tone of supplication*). Uncle!

ANYA. Uncle, you are at it again!

TROFIMOV. You'd much better be cannoning off the red!

GAEV. I'll hold my tongue, I will.

(*All sit plunged in thought. Perfect stillness. The only thing audible is the muttering of* FIRS. *Suddenly there is a sound in the distance, as it were from the sky — the sound of a breaking harp-string, mournfully dying away.*)

LYUBOV. What is that?

LOPAHIN. I don't know. Somewhere far away a bucket fallen and broken in the pits. But somewhere very far away.

GAEV. It might be a bird of some sort — such as a heron.

TROFIMOV. Or an owl.

LYUBOV (*shudders*). I don't know why, but it's horrid. (*A pause.*)

FIRS. It was the same before the calamity — the owl hooted and the samovar hissed all the time.

GAEV. Before what calamity?

FIRS. Before the emancipation. (*A pause.*)

LYUBOV. Come, my friends, let us be going; evening is falling. (*To* ANYA.) There are tears in your eyes. What is it, darling? (*Embraces her.*)

ANYA. Nothing, mamma; it's nothing.

TROFIMOV. There is somebody coming.

(*The wayfarer appears in a shabby white forage cap and an overcoat; he is slightly drunk.*)

WAYFARER. Allow me to inquire, can I get to the station this way?

GAEV. Yes. Go along that road.

WAYFARER. I thank you most feelingly. (*Coughing.*) The weather is superb. (*Declaims.*) My brother, my suffering brother!... Come out to the Volga! Whose groan do you hear?... (*To* VARYA.) Mademoiselle, vouchsafe a hungry Russian thirty kopeks. (VARYA *utters a shriek of alarm.*)

LOPAHIN (*angrily*). There's a right and a wrong way of doing everything!

LYUBOV (*hurriedly*). Here, take this. (*Looks in her purse.*) I've no silver. No matter — here's gold for you.

WAYFARER. I thank you most feelingly! (*Goes off.*) (*Laughter.*)

VARYA (*frightened*). I'm going home — I'm going... Oh, mamma, the servants have nothing to eat, and you gave him gold!

LYUBOV. There's no doing anything with me. I'm so silly! When we get home, I'll give you all I possess. Yermolay Alexeyevitch, you will lend me some more!...

LOPAHIN. I will.

LYUBOV. Come, friends, it's time to be going. And Varya, we have made a match of it for you. I congratulate you.

VARYA (*through her tears*). Mamma, that's not a joking matter.

LOPAHIN. "Ophelia, get thee to a nunnery!"

GAEV. My hands are trembling; it's a long while since I had a game of billiards.

LOPAHIN. "Ophelia! Nymph, in thy orisons be all my sins remember'd."

LYUBOV. Come, it will soon be supper-time.

VARYA. How he frightened me! My heart's simply throbbing.

LOPAHIN. Let me remind you, ladies and gentlemen: on the 22nd of August the cherry orchard will be sold. Think about that! Think about it! (*All go off, except* TROFIMOV *and* ANYA.)

ANYA (*laughing*). I'm grateful to the wayfarer! He frightened Varya and we are left alone.

TROFIMOV. Varya's afraid we shall fall in love with each other, and for days together she won't leave us. With her narrow brain she can't grasp that we are above love. To eliminate the petty and transitory which hinders us from being free and happy — that is the aim and meaning of our life. Forward! We go forward irresistibly towards the bright star that shines yonder in the distance. Forward! Do not lag behind, friends.

ANYA (*claps her hands*). How well you speak! (*A pause.*) It is divine here today.

TROFIMOV. Yes, it's glorious weather.

ANYA. Somehow, Petya, you've made me so that I don't love the cherry orchard as I used to. I used to love it so dearly. I used to think that there was no spot on earth like our garden.

TROFIMOV. All Russia is our garden. The earth is great and beautiful — there are many beautiful places in it. (*A pause.*) Think only, Anya, your grandfather, and great-grandfather, and all your ancestors were slave-owners — the owners of living souls — and from every cherry in the orchard, from every leaf, from every trunk there are human creatures looking at you. Cannot you hear their voices? Oh, it is awful! Your orchard is a fearful thing, and when in the evening or at night one walks about the orchard, the old bark on the trees glimmers dimly in the dusk, and the old cherry trees seem to be dreaming of centuries gone by and tortured by fearful visions. Yes! We are at least two hundred years behind, we have really gained nothing yet, we have no definite attitude to the past, we do nothing but theorise or complain of depression or drink vodka. It is clear that to begin to live in the present we must first expiate our past, we must break with it; and we can expiate it only by suffering, by extraordinary unceasing labour. Understand that, Anya.

ANYA. The house we live in has long ceased to be our own, and I shall leave it, I give you my word.

TROFIMOV. If you have the house keys, fling them into the well and go away. Be free as the wind.

ANYA (*in ecstasy*). How beautifully you said that!

TROFIMOV. Believe me, Anya, believe me! I am not thirty yet, I am young, I am still a student, but I have gone through so much already! As soon as winter comes I am hungry, sick, careworn, poor as a beggar, and what ups and downs of fortune have I not known! And my soul was always, every minute, day and night, full of inexplicable forebodings. I have a foreboding of happiness, Anya. I see glimpses of it already.

ANYA (*pensively*). The moon is rising.

(EPIHODOV *is heard playing still the same mournful song on the guitar. The moon rises. Somewhere near the poplars* VARYA *is looking for* ANYA *and calling* "Anya! where are you?")

TROFIMOV. Yes, the moon is rising. (*A pause.*) Here is happiness — here it comes! It is coming nearer and nearer; already I can hear its footsteps. And if we never see it — if we may never know it — what does it matter? Others will see it after us.

VARYA'S VOICE. Anya! Where are you?

TROFIMOV. That Varya again! (*Angrily.*) It's revolting!

ANYA. Well, let's go down to the river. It's lovely there.

TROFIMOV. Yes, let's go. (*They go.*)

VARYA'S VOICE. Anya! Anya!

CURTAIN

ACT III

A drawing-room divided by an arch from a larger drawing-room. A chandelier burning. The Jewish orchestra, the same that was mentioned in Act II, is heard playing in the ante-room. It is evening. In the larger drawing-room they are dancing the grand chain. The voice of SEMYONOV-PISHTCHIK: "Promenade à une paire!" *Then enter the drawing-room in couples first* PISHTCHIK *and* CHARLOTTA IVANOVNA, *then* TROFIMOV *and* LYUBOV ANDREYEVNA, *thirdly* ANYA *with the Post-Office Clerk, fourthly* VARYA *with the Station Master, and other guests.* VARYA *is quietly weeping and wiping away her tears as she dances. In the last*

couple is DUNYASHA. *They move across the drawing-room.* PISHTCHIK
shouts: "Grand rond, balancez!" *and* "Les Cavaliers à genou et
remerciez vos dames."

(FIRS *in a swallow-tail coat brings in seltzer water on a tray.*
PISHTCHIK *and* TROFIMOV *enter the drawing-room.*)

PISHTCHIK. I am a full-blooded man; I have already had two
strokes. Dancing's hard work for me, but as they say, if you're
in the pack, you must bark with the rest. I'm as strong, I may
say, as a horse. My parent, who would have his joke — may
the Kingdom of Heaven be his! — used to say about our origin
that the ancient stock of the Semyonov-Pishtchiks was derived
from the very horse that Caligula made a member of the senate.
(*Sits down.*) But I've no money, that's where the mischief is.
A hungry dog believes in nothing but meat... (*Snores, but at once
wakes up.*) That's like me... I can think of nothing but money.

TROFIMOV. There really is something horsy about your appearance.

PISHTCHIK. Well... a horse is a fine beast... a horse can be sold.

(*There is the sound of billiards being played in an adjoining room.*
VARYA *appears in the arch leading to the larger drawing-room.*)

TROFIMOV (*teasing*). Madame Lopahin! Madame Lopahin!

VARYA (*angrily*). Mangy-looking gentleman!

TROFIMOV. Yes, I am a mangy-looking gentleman, and I'm proud
of it!

VARYA (*pondering bitterly*). Here we have hired musicians and
nothing to pay them! (*Goes out.*)

TROFIMOV (*to* PISHTCHIK). If the energy you have wasted during
your lifetime in trying to find the money to pay your interest,
had gone to something else, you might in the end have turned
the world upside down.

PISHTCHIK. Nietzsche, the philosopher, a very great and celebrated
man... of enormous intellect... says in his works, that one can
make forged bank-notes.

TROFIMOV. Why, have you read Nietzsche?

PISHTCHIK. What next... Dashenka told me.... And now I am in
such a position, I might just as well forge bank-notes. The day
after tomorrow I must pay 310 roubles — 130 I have procured.
(*Feels in his pockets, in alarm.*) The money's gone! I have lost

my money! (*Through his tears.*) Where's the money? (*Gleefully.*) Why, here it is behind the lining.... It has made me hot all over.

(*Enter* LYUBOV ANDREYEVNA *and* CHARLOTTA IVANOVNA.)

LYUBOV (*hums the Lezginka*). Why is Leonid so long? What can he be doing in town? (*To* DUNYASHA.) Offer the musicians some tea.

TROFIMOV. The sale hasn't taken place, most likely.

LYUBOV. It's the wrong time to have the orchestra, and the wrong time to give a dance. Well, never mind.

(*Sits down and hums softly.*)

CHARLOTTA (*gives* PISHTCHIK *a pack of cards*). Here's a pack of cards. Think of any card you like.

PISHTCHIK. I've thought of one.

CHARLOTTA. Shuffle the pack now. That's right. Give it here, my dear Mr. Pishtchik. Ein, zwei, drei — now look, it's in your breast pocket.

PISHTCHIK (*taking a card out of his breast pocket*). The eight of spades! Perfectly right! (*Wonderingly.*) Fancy that now!

CHARLOTTA (*holding pack of cards in her hands, to* TROFIMOV). Tell me quickly which is the top card.

TROFIMOV. Well, the queen of spades.

CHARLOTTA. It is! (*To* PISHTCHIK.) Well, which card is uppermost?

PISHTCHIK. The ace of hearts.

CHARLOTTA. It is! (*Claps her hands, pack of cards disappears.*) Ah! what lovely weather it is today!

(*A mysterious feminine voice which seems coming out of the floor answers her.* "Oh, yes, it's magnificent weather, madam.")

CHARLOTTA. You are my perfect ideal.

VOICE. And I greatly admire you too, madam.

STATION MASTER (*applauding*). The lady ventriloquist — bravo!

PISHTCHIK (*wonderingly*). Fancy that now! Most enchanting Charlotta Ivanovna. I'm simply in love with you.

CHARLOTTA. In love? (*Shrugging shoulders.*) What do you know of love, guter Mensch, aber schlechter Musikant.

TROFIMOV (*pats* PISHTCHIK *on the shoulder*). You dear old horse....

CHARLOTTA. Attention, please! Another trick! (*Takes a travelling rug from a chair.*) Here's a very good rug; I want to sell it. (*Shaking it out.*) Doesn't anyone want to buy it?

PISHTCHIK (*wonderingly*). Fancy that!

CHARLOTTA. Ein, zwei, drei!

> (*Quickly picks up rug she has dropped; behind the rug stands* ANYA; *she makes a curtsey, runs to her mother, embraces her and runs back into the larger drawing-room amidst general enthusiasm.*)

LYUBOV (*applauds*). Bravo! Bravo!

CHARLOTTA. Now again! Ein, zwei, drei!

> (*Lifts up the rug; behind the rug stands* VARYA, *bowing.*)

PISHTCHIK (*wonderingly*). Fancy that now!

CHARLOTTA. That's the end.

> (*Throws the rug at* PISHTCHIK, *makes a curtsey, runs into the larger drawing-room.*)

PISHTCHIK (*hurries after her*). Mischievous creature! Fancy!

(*Goes out.*)

LYUBOV. And still Leonid doesn't come. I can't understand what he's doing in the town so long! Why, everything must be over by now. The estate is sold, or the sale has not taken place. Why keep us so long in suspense?

VARYA (*trying to console her*). Uncle's bought it. I feel sure of that.

TROFIMOV (*ironically*). Oh, yes!

VARYA. Great-aunt sent him an authorisation to buy it in her name, and transfer the debt. She's doing it for Anya's sake, and I'm sure God will be merciful. Uncle will buy it.

LYUBOV. My aunt in Yaroslavl sent fifteen thousand to buy the estate in her name, she doesn't trust us — but that's not enough even to pay the arrears. (*Hides her face in her hands.*) My fate is being sealed today, my fate...

TROFIMOV (*teasing* VARYA). Madame Lopahin.

VARYA (*angrily*). Perpetual student! Twice already you've been sent down from the University.

LYUBOV. Why are you angry, Varya? He's teasing you about Lopahin. Well, what of that? Marry Lopahin if you like, he's a good man, and interesting; if you don't want to, don't! Nobody compels you, darling.

VARYA. I must tell you plainly, mamma, I look at the matter seriously; he's a good man, I like him.

LYUBOV. Well, marry him. I can't see what you're waiting for.

VARYA. Mamma. I can't make him an offer myself. For the last two years, everyone's been talking to me about him. Everyone talks; but he says nothing or else makes a joke. I see what it means. He's growing rich, he's absorbed in business, he has no thoughts for me. If I had money, were it ever so little, if I had only a hundred roubles, I'd throw everything up and go far away. I would go into a nunnery.

TROFIMOV. What bliss!

VARYA (to TROFIMOV). A student ought to have sense! (In a soft tone with tears.) How ugly you've grown, Petya! How old you look! (To LYUBOV ANDREYEVNA, no longer crying.) But I can't do without work, mamma; I must have something to do every minute.

(Enter YASHA.)

YASHA (hardly restraining his laughter). Epihodov has broken a billiard cue! (Goes out.)

VARYA. What is Epihodov doing here? Who gave him leave to play billiards? I can't make these people out. (Goes out.)

LYUBOV. Don't tease her, Petya. You see she has grief enough without that.

TROFIMOV. She is so very officious, meddling in what's not her business. All the summer she's given Anya and me no peace. She's afraid of a love affair between us. What's it to do with her? Besides, I have given no grounds for it. Such triviality is not in my line. We are above love!

LYUBOV. And I suppose I am beneath love. (Very uneasily.) Why is it Leonid's not here? If only I could know whether the estate is sold or not! It seems such an incredible calamity that I really don't know what to think. I am distracted... I shall scream in a minute... I shall do something stupid. Save me, Petya, tell me something, talk to me!

TROFIMOV. What does it matter whether the estate is sold today or not? That's all done with long ago. There's no turning back, the path is overgrown. Don't worry yourself, dear Lyubov

Andreyevna. You mustn't deceive yourself; for once in your life you must face the truth!

LYUBOV. What truth? You see where the truth lies, but I seem to have lost my sight, I see nothing. You settle every great problem so boldly, but tell me, my dear boy, isn't it because you're young — because you haven't yet understood one of your problems through suffering? You look forward boldly, and isn't it that you don't see and don't expect anything dreadful because life is still hidden from your young eyes? You're bolder, more honest, deeper than we are, but think, be just a little magnanimous, have pity on me. I was born here, you know, my father and mother lived here, my grandfather lived here, I love this house. I can't conceive of life without the cherry orchard, and if it really must be sold, then sell me with the orchard. (*Embraces* TROFIMOV, *kisses him on the forehead.*) My boy was drowned here. (*Weeps.*) Pity me, my dear kind fellow.

TROFIMOV. You know I feel for you with all my heart.

LYUBOV. But that should have been said differently, so differently. (*Takes out her handkerchief, telegram falls on the floor.*) My heart is so heavy today. It's so noisy here, my soul is quivering at every sound, I'm shuddering all over, but I can't go away; I'm afraid to be quiet and alone. Don't be hard on me, Petya... I love you as though you were one of ourselves. I would gladly let you marry Anya — I swear I would — only, my dear boy, you must take your degree, you do nothing — you're simply tossed by fate from place to place. That's so strange. It is, isn't it? And you must do something with your beard to make it grow somehow. (*Laughs.*) You look so funny!

TROFIMOV (*picks up the telegram*). I've no wish to be a beauty.

LYUBOV. That's a telegram from Paris. I get one every day. One yesterday and one today. That savage creature is ill again, he's in trouble again. He begs forgiveness, beseeches me to go, and really I ought to go to Paris to see him. You look shocked, Petya. What am I to do, my dear boy, what am I to do? He is ill, he is alone and unhappy, and who'll look after him, who'll keep him from doing the wrong thing, who'll give him his medicine at the right time? And why hide it or be silent?

I love him, that's clear. I love him! I love him! He's a mill-stone about my neck, I'm going to the bottom with him, but I love that stone and can't live without it. (*Presses* TROFIMOV's *hand.*) Don't think ill of me, Petya, don't tell me anything, don't tell me....

TROFIMOV (*through his tears*). For God's sake forgive my frankness: why, he robbed you!

LYUBOV. No! No! No! You mustn't speak like that.

(*Covers her ears.*)

TROFIMOV. He is a wretch! You're the only person that doesn't know it! He's a worthless creature! A despicable wretch!

LYUBOV (*getting angry, but speaking with restraint*). You're twenty-six or twenty-seven years old, but you're still a schoolboy.

TROFIMOV. Possibly.

LYUBOV. You should be a man at your age! You should under-stand what love means! And you ought to be in love yourself. You ought to fall in love! (*Angrily.*) Yes, yes, and it's no purity in you, you're simply a prude, a comic fool, a freak.

TROFIMOV (*in horror*). The things she's saying!

LYUBOV. I am above love! You're not above love, but simply as our Firs here says, "You are a good-for-nothing." At your age not to have a mistress!

TROFIMOV (*in horror*). This is awful! The things she is saying! (*Goes rapidly into the larger drawing-room clutching his head.*) This is awful! I can't stand it! I'm going. (*Goes off, but at once returns.*) All is over between us! (*Goes off into the ante-room.*)

LYUBOV (*shouts after him*). Petya! Wait a minute! You funny creature! I was joking! Petya!

(*There is a sound of somebody running quickly downstairs and suddenly falling with a crash. ANYA and VARYA scream, but there is a sound of laughter at once.*)

LYUBOV. What has happened?

(ANYA *runs in.*)

ANYA (*laughing*). Petya's fallen downstairs! (*Runs out.*)

LYUBOV. What a queer fellow that Petya is!

(*The Station Master stands in the middle of the larger room and reads "The Magdalene," by Alexey Tolstoy. They listen to him, but before he has recited many lines strains of a waltz are heard from the ante-room and the reading is broken off. All dance.* TROFIMOV, ANYA, VARYA *and* LYUBOV ANDREYEVNA *come in from the ante-room.*)

LYUBOV. Come, Petya — come, pure heart! I beg your pardon. Let's have a dance! *(Dances with* PETYA.)

(ANYA *and* VARYA *dance.* FIRS *comes in, puts his stick down near the side door.* YASHA *also comes into the drawing-room and looks on at the dancing.*)

YASHA. What is it, old man?

FIRS. I don't feel well. In old days we used to have generals, barons and admirals dancing at our balls, and now we send for the post-office clerk and the station master and even they're not overanxious to come. I am getting feeble. The old master, the grandfather, used to give sealing-wax for all complaints. I have been taking sealing-wax for twenty years or more. Perhaps that's what's kept me alive.

YASHA. You bore me, old man! *(Yawns.)* It's time you were done with.

FIRS. Ach, you're a good-for-nothing! *(Mutters.)*

(TROFIMOV *and* LYUBOV ANDREYEVNA *dance in larger room and then on to the stage.*)

LYUBOV. *Merci.* I'll sit down a little. *(Sits down.)* I'm tired.

(Enter ANYA.)

ANYA *(excitedly).* There's a man in the kitchen has been saying that the cherry orchard's been sold today.

LYUBOV. Sold to whom?

ANYA. He didn't say to whom. He's gone away.

(She dances with TROFIMOV, *and they go off into the larger room.*)

YASHA. There was an old man gossiping there, a stranger.

FIRS. Leonid Andreyevitch isn't here yet, he hasn't come back. He has his light overcoat on, *demi-saison*, he'll catch cold for sure. Ach! Foolish young things! !

LYUBOV. I feel as though I should die. Go, Yasha, find out to whom it has been sold.

YASHA. But he went away long ago, the old chap. *(Laughs.)*

LYUBOV *(with slight vexation).* What are you laughing at? What are you pleased at?

YASHA. Epihodov is so funny. He's a silly fellow, two and twenty misfortunes.

LYUBOV. Firs, if the estate is sold, where will you go?

FIRS. Where you bid me, there I'll go.

LYUBOV. Why do you look like that? Are you ill? You ought to be in bed.

FIRS. Yes. (*Ironically.*) Me go to bed and who's to wait here? Who's to see to things without me? I'm the only one in all the house.

YASHA (*to* LYUBOV ANDREYEVNA). Lyubov Andreyevna, permit me to make a request of you; if you go back to Paris again, be so kind as to take me with you. It's positively impossible for me to stay here. (*Looking about him; in an undertone.*) There's no need to say it, you see for yourself — an uncivilised country, the people have no morals, and then the dullness! The food in the kitchen's abominable, and then Firs runs after one muttering all sorts of unsuitable words. Take me with you, please do!

(*Enter* PISHTCHIK.)

PISHTCHIK. Allow me to ask you for a waltz, my dear lady. (LYUBOV ANDREYEVNA *goes with him.*) Enchanting lady, I really must borrow of you just 180 roubles (*dances*), only 180 roubles.
(*They pass into the larger room.*)

YASHA (*hums softly*). "Knowest thou my soul's emotion."
(*In the larger drawing-room, a figure in a gray top hat and in check trousers is gesticulating and jumping about.* Shouts of "Bravo, Charlotta Ivanovna.")

DUNYASHA (*she has stopped to powder herself*). My young lady tells me to dance. There are plenty of gentlemen, and two few ladies, but dancing makes me giddy and makes my heart beat. Firs, the post-office clerk said something to me just now that quite took my breath away. (*Music becomes more subdued.*)

FIRS. What did he say to you?

DUNYASHA. He said I was like a flower.

YASHA (*yawns*). What ignorance! (*Goes out.*)

DUNYASHA. Like a flower. I am a girl of such delicate feelings, I am awfully fond of soft speeches.

FIRS. Your head's being turned.

(Enter EPIHODOV.)

EPIHODOV. You have no desire to see me, Dunyasha. I might be an insect. *(Sighs.)* Ah! life!

DUNYASHA. What is it you want?

EPIHODOV. Undoubtedly you may be right. *(Sighs.)* But of course, if one looks at it from that point of view, if I may so express myself, you have, excuse my plain speaking, reduced me to a complete state of mind. I know my destiny. Every day some misfortune befalls me and I have long ago grown accustomed to it, so that I look upon my fate with a smile. You gave me your word, and though I ——

DUNYASHA. Let us have a talk later, I entreat you, but now leave me in peace, for I am lost in reverie. *(Plays with her fan.)*

EPIHODOV. I have a misfortune every day, and if I may venture to express myself, I merely smile at it, I even laugh.

(VARYA *enters from the larger drawing-room.*)

VARYA. You still have not gone, Epihodov. What a disrespectful creature you are, really! *(To* DUNYASHA.) Go along, Dunyasha! *(To* EPIHODOV.) First you play billiards and break the cue, then you go wandering about the drawing-room like a visitor!

EPIHODOV. You really cannot, if I may so express myself, call me to account like this.

VARYA. I'm not calling you to account, I'm speaking to you. You do nothing but wander from place to place and don't do your work. We keep you as a counting-house clerk, but what use you are I can't say.

EPIHODOV *(offended).* Whether I work or whether I walk, whether I eat or whether I play billiards, is a matter to be judged by persons of understanding and my elders.

VARYA. You dare to tell me that! *(Firing up.)* You dare! You mean to say I've no understanding. Begone from here! This minute!

EPIHODOV *(intimidated).* I beg you to express yourself with delicacy.

VARYA *(beside herself with anger).* This moment! get out! away! *(He goes toward the door, she following him.)* Two and twenty

misfortunes! Take yourself off! Don't let me set eyes on you!
(EPIHODOV *has gone out, behind the door his voice,* "I shall lodge
a complaint against you.") What! You're coming back?
(*Snatches up the stick* FIRS *has put down near the door.*) Come!
Come! Come! I'll show you! What! you're coming? Then
take that!

(*She swings the stick, at the very moment that* LOPAHIN *comes in.*)

LOPAHIN. Very much obliged to you!

VARYA (*angrily and ironically*). I beg your pardon!

LOPAHIN. Not at all! I humbly thank you for your kind reception!

VARYA. No need of thanks for it. (*Moves away, then looks round and
asks softly.*) I haven't hurt you?

LOPAHIN. Oh, no! Not at all! There's an immense bump
coming up, though!

VOICES FROM LARGER ROOM. Lopahin has come! Yermolay
Alexeyevitch!

PISHTCHIK. What do I see and hear? (*Kisses* LOPAHIN.) There's
a whiff of cognac about you, my dear soul, and we're making
merry here too!

(*Enter* LYUBOV ANDREYEVNA.)

LYUBOV. Is it you, Yermolay Alexeyevitch? Why have you been
so long? Where's Leonid?

LOPAHIN. Leonid Andreyevitch arrived with me. He is coming.

LYUBOV (*in agitation*). Well! Well! Was there a sale? Speak!

LOPAHIN (*embarrassed, afraid of betraying his joy*). The sale was over
at four o'clock. We missed our train — had to wait till half-
past nine. (*Sighing heavily.*) Ugh! I feel a little giddy.

(*Enter* GAEV. *In his right hand he has purchases, with his left hand he
is wiping away his tears.*)

LYUBOV. Well, Leonid? What news? (*Impatiently, with tears.*)
Make haste, for God's sake!

GAEV (*makes her no answer, simply waves his hand. To* FIRS, *weeping*).
Here, take them; there's anchovies, Kertch herrings. I have
eaten nothing all day. What I have been through! (*Door into
the billiard room is open. There is heard a knocking of balls and the*

voice of YASHA *saying* "Eighty-seven." GAEV'S *expression changes, he leaves off weeping.*) I am fearfully tired. Firs, come and help me change my things.

(*Goes to his own room across the larger drawing-room.*)

PISHTCHIK. How about the sale? Tell us, do!

LYUBOV. Is the cherry orchard sold?

LOPAHIN. It is sold.

LYUBOV. Who has bought it?

LOPAHIN. I have bought it.

(*A pause.* LYUBOV *is crushed; she would fall down if she were not standing near a chair and table.*)

(VARYA *takes keys from her waist-band, flings them on the floor in middle of drawing-room and goes out.*)

LOPAHIN. I have bought it! Wait a bit, ladies and gentlemen, pray. My head's a bit muddled, I can't speak. (*Laughs.*) We came to the auction. Deriganov was there already. Leonid Andreyevitch only had 15,000 and Deriganov bid 30,000, besides the arrears, straight off. I saw how the land lay. I bid against him. I bid 40,000, he bid 45,000, I said 55, and so he went on, adding 5 thousands and I adding 10. Well... So it ended. I bid 90, and it was knocked down to me. Now the cherry orchard's mine! Mine! (*Chuckles.*) My God, the cherry orchard's mine! Tell me that I'm drunk, that I'm out of my mind, that it's all a dream. (*Stamps with his feet.*) Don't laugh at me! If my father and my grandfather could rise from their graves and see all that has happened! How their Yermolay, ignorant, beaten Yermolay, who used to run about barefoot in winter, how that very Yermolay has bought the finest estate in the world! I have bought the estate where my father and grandfather were slaves, where they weren't even admitted into the kitchen. I am asleep, I am dreaming! It is all fancy, it is the work of your imagination plunged in the darkness of ignorance. (*Picks up keys, smiling fondly.*) She threw away the keys; she means to show she's not the housewife now. (*Jingles the keys.*) Well, no matter. (*The orchestra is heard tuning up.*) Hey, musicians! Play! I want to hear you. Come, all of you, and look how Yermolay Lopahin will take the axe to the cherry orchard, how the trees will fall to the ground! We will build houses on it and our grandsons and great-grandsons will see a new life springing up there. Music! Play up!

(*Music begins to play.* LYUBOV ANDREYEVNA *has sunk into a chair and is weeping bitterly.*)

LOPAHIN (*reproachfully*). Why, why didn't you listen to me? My poor friend! Dear lady, there's no turning back now. (*With tears.*) Oh, if all this could be over, oh, if our miserable disjointed life could somehow soon be changed!

PISHTCHIK (*takes him by the arm, in an undertone*). She's weeping, let us go and leave her alone. Come.

(*Takes him by the arm and leads him into the larger drawing-room.*)

LOPAHIN. What's that? Musicians, play up! All must be as I wish it. (*With irony.*) Here comes the new master, the owner of the cherry orchard! (*Accidentally tips over a little table, almost upsetting the candelabra.*) I can pay for everything!

(*Goes out with* PISHTCHIK. *No one remains on the stage or in the larger drawing-room except* LYUBOV, *who sits huddled up, weeping bitterly. The music plays softly.* ANYA *and* TROFIMOV *come in quickly.* ANYA *goes up to her mother and falls on her knees before her.* TROFIMOV *stands at the entrance to the larger drawing-room.*)

ANYA. Mamma! Mamma, you're crying, dear, kind, good mamma! My precious! I love you! I bless you! The cherry orchard is sold, it is gone, that's true, that's true! But don't weep, mamma! Life is still before you, you have still your good, pure heart! Let us go, let us go, darling, away from here! We will make a new garden, more splendid than this one; you will see it, you will understand. And joy, quiet, deep joy, will sink into your soul like the sun at evening! And you will smile, mamma! Come, darling, let us go!

CURTAIN

ACT IV

SCENE: *Same as in First Act. There are neither curtains on the windows nor pictures on the walls: only a little furniture remains piled up in a corner as if for sale. There is a sense of desolation; near the outer door and in the background of the scene are packed trunks, travelling bags, etc. On the left the door is open, and from here the voices of* VARYA *and* ANYA *are audible.* LOPAHIN *is standing waiting.* YASHA *is holding a tray with glasses full of champagne. In front of the stage* EPIHODOV *is tying up a box. In the background behind the scene a hum of talk from the peasants who have come to say good-bye. The voice of* GAEV: *"Thanks, brothers, thanks!"*

YASHA. The peasants have come to say good-bye. In my opinion, Yermolay Alexeyevitch, the peasants are good-natured, but they don't know much about things.

 (*The hum of talk dies away. Enter across front of stage* LYUBOV ANDREYEVNA *and* GAEV. *She is not weeping, but is pale; her face is quivering — she cannot speak.*)

GAEV. You gave them your purse, Lyuba. That won't do — that won't do!

LYUBOV. I couldn't help it! I couldn't help it! (*Both go out.*)

LOPAHIN (*in the doorway, calls after them*). You will take a glass at parting? Please do. I didn't think to bring any from the town, and at the station I could only get one bottle. Please take a glass. (*A pause.*) What? You don't care for any? (*Comes away from the door.*) If I'd known, I wouldn't have bought it. Well, and I'm not going to drink it. (YASHA *carefully sets the tray down on a chair.*) You have a glass, Yasha, anyway.

YASHA. Good luck to the travellers, and luck to those that stay behind! (*Drinks.*) This champagne isn't the real thing, I can assure you.

LOPAHIN. It cost eight roubles the bottle. (*A pause.*) It's devilish cold here.

YASHA. They haven't heated the stove today — it's all the same since we're going. (*Laughs.*)

LOPAHIN. What are you laughing for?

YASHA. For pleasure.

LOPAHIN. Though it's October, it's as still and sunny as though it

were summer. It's just right for building! (*Looks at his watch;
says in doorway.*) Take note, ladies and gentlemen, the train
goes in forty-seven minutes; so you ought to start for the station
in twenty minutes. You must hurry up!

(TROFIMOV *comes in from out of doors wearing a great-coat.*)

TROFIMOV. I think it must be time to start, the horses are ready.
The devil only knows what's become of my goloshes; they're
lost. (*In the doorway.*) Anya! My goloshes aren't here. I can't
find them.

LOPAHIN. And I'm getting off to Harkov. I am going in the same
train with you. I'm spending all the winter at Harkov. I've
been wasting all my time gossiping with you and fretting with
no work to do. I can't get on without work. I don't know
what to do with my hands, they flap about so queerly, as if they
didn't belong to me.

TROFIMOV. Well, we're just going away, and you will take up your
profitable labours again.

LOPAHIN. Do take a glass.

TROFIMOV. No, thanks.

LOPAHIN. Then you're going to Moscow now?

TROFIMOV. Yes. I shall see them as far as the town, and tomorrow
I shall go on to Moscow.

LOPAHIN. Yes, I daresay, the professors aren't giving any lectures,
they're waiting for your arrival.

TROFIMOV. That's not your business.

LOPAHIN. How many years have you been at the University?

TROFIMOV. Do think of something newer than that — that's stale
and flat. (*Hunts for goloshes.*) You know we shall most likely
never see each other again, so let me give you one piece of advice
at parting: don't wave your arms about — get out of the habit.
And another thing, building villas, reckoning up that the summer
visitors will in time become independent farmers — reckoning
like that, that's not the thing to do either. After all, I am fond
of you: you have fine delicate fingers like an artist, you've a fine
delicate soul.

LOPAHIN (*embraces him.*) Good-bye, my dear fellow. Thanks for
everything. Let me give you money for the journey, if you need
it.

TROFIMOV. What for? I don't need it.

LOPAHIN. Why, you haven't got a halfpenny.

TROFIMOV. Yes, I have, thank you. I got some money for a translation. Here it is in my pocket (*anxiously*), but where can my goloshes be!

VARYA (*from the next room*). Take the nasty things!

(*Flings a pair of goloshes on to the stage.*)

TROFIMOV. Why are you so cross, Varya? h'm!... but those aren't my goloshes.

LOPAHIN. I sowed three thousand acres with poppies in the spring, and now I have cleared forty thousand profit. And when my poppies were in flower, wasn't it a picture! So here, as I say, I made forty thousand, and I'm offering you a loan because I can afford to. Why turn up your nose? I am a peasant — I speak bluntly.

TROFIMOV. Your father was a peasant, mine was a chemist — and that proves absolutely nothing whatever. (LOPAHIN *takes out his pocket-book.*) Stop that — stop that. If you were to offer me two hundred thousand I wouldn't take it. I am an independent man, and everything that all of you, rich and poor alike, prize so highly and hold so dear, hasn't the slightest power over me — it's like so much fluff fluttering in the air. I can get on without you. I can pass by you. I am strong and proud. Humanity is advancing towards the highest truth, the highest happiness, which is possible on earth, and I am in the front ranks.

LOPAHIN. Will you get there?

TROFIMOV. I shall get there. (*A pause.*) I shall get there, or I shall show others the way to get there.

(*In the distance is heard the stroke of an axe on a tree.*)

LOPAHIN. Good-bye, my dear fellow; it's time to be off. We turn up our noses at one another, but life is passing all the while. When I am working hard without resting, then my mind is more at ease, and it seems to me as though I too know what I exist for; but how many people there are in Russia, my dear boy, who exist, one doesn't know what for. Well, it doesn't matter. That's not what keeps things spinning. They tell me Leonid Andreyevitch has taken a situation. He is going to be a clerk at the bank — 6,000 roubles a year. Only, of course, he won't stick to it — he's too lazy.

ANYA (*in the doorway*). Mamma begs you not to let them chop down the orchard until she's gone.

TROFIMOV. Yes, really, you might have the tact. (*Walks out across the front of the stage.*)

LOPAHIN. I'll see to it! I'll see to it! Stupid fellows! (*Goes out after him.*)

ANYA. Has Firs been taken to the hospital?

YASHA. I told them this morning. No doubt they have taken him.

ANYA (*to* EPIHODOV, *who passes across the drawing-room*). Semyon Pantaleyevitch, inquire, please, if Firs has been taken to the hospital.

YASHA (*in a tone of offence*). I told Yegor this morning — why ask a dozen times?

EPIHODOV. Firs is advanced in years. It's my conclusive opinion no treatment would do him good; it's time he was gathered to his fathers. And I can only envy him. (*Puts a trunk down on a cardboard hat-box and crushes it.*) There, now, of course — I knew it would be so.

YASHA (*jeeringly*). Two and twenty misfortunes!

VARYA (*through the door*). Has Firs been taken to the hospital?

ANYA. Yes.

VARYA. Why wasn't the note for the doctor taken too?

ANYA. Oh, then, we must send it after them. (*Goes out.*)

VARYA (*from the adjoining room*). Where's Yasha? Tell him his mother's come to say good-bye to him.

YASHA (*waves his hand*). They put me out of all patience! (DUNYASHA *has all this time been busy about the luggage. Now, when* YASHA *is left alone, she goes up to him.*)

DUNYASHA. You might just give me one look, Yasha. You're going away. You're leaving me. (*Weeps and throws herself on his neck.*)

YASHA. What are you crying for? (*Drinks the champagne.*) In six days I shall be in Paris again. Tomorrow we shall get into the express train and roll away in a flash. I can scarcely believe it! *Vive la France!* It doesn't suit me here — it's not the life for me; there's no doing anything. I have seen enough of the

ignorance here. I have had enough of it. (*Drinks champagne.*)
What are you crying for? Behave yourself properly, and then
you won't cry.

DUNYASHA (*powders her face, looking in a pocket-mirror*). Do send me
a letter from Paris. You know how I loved you, Yasha — how
I loved you! I am a tender creature, Yasha.

YASHA. Here they are coming!

(*Busies himself about the trunks, humming softly.*)

(*Enter* LYUBOV ANDREYEVNA, GAEV, ANYA *and* CHARLOTTA
IVANOVNA.)

GAEV. We ought to be off. There's not much time now. (*Looking
at* YASHA.) What a smell of herrings!

LYUBOV. In ten minutes we must get into the carriage. (*Casts
a look about the room.*) Farewell, dear house, dear old home of
our fathers! Winter will pass and spring will come, and then
you will be no more; they will tear you down! How much those
walls have seen! (*Kisses her daughter passionately.*) My treasure,
how bright you look! Your eyes are sparkling like diamonds!
Are you glad? Very glad?

ANYA. Very glad! A new life is beginning, mamma.

GAEV. Yes, really, everything is all right now. Before the cherry
orchard was sold, we were all worried and wretched, but afterwards, when once the question was settled conclusively, ir-
revocably, we all felt calm and even cheerful. I am a bank clerk
now — I am a financier — cannon off the red. And you, Lyuba,
after all, you are looking better; there's no question of that.

LYUBOV. Yes. My nerves are better, that's true. (*Her hat and
coat are handed to her.*) I'm sleeping well. Carry out my things,
Yasha. It's time. (*To* ANYA.) My darling, we shall soon see
each other again. I am going to Paris. I can live there on the
money your Yaroslavl auntie sent us to buy the estate with —
hurrah for auntie! — but that money won't last long.

ANYA. You'll come back soon, mamma, won't you? I'll be working up for my examination in the high school, and when I have
passed that, I shall set to work and be a help to you. We will
read all sorts of things together, mamma, won't we? (*Kisses
her mother's hands.*) We will read in the autumn evenings. We'll

read lots of books, and a new wonderful world will open out before us. (*Dreamily.*) Mamma, come soon.

LYUBOV. I shall come, my precious treasure. (*Embraces her.*)

(*Enter* LOPAHIN. CHARLOTTA *softly hums a song.*)

GAEV. Charlotta's happy; she's singing!

CHARLOTTA (*picks up a bundle like a swaddled baby*). Bye, bye, my baby. (*A baby is heard crying:* "*Ooah! ooah!*") Hush, hush, my pretty boy! (*Ooah! ooah!*) Poor little thing! (*Throws the bundle back.*) You must please find me a situation. I can't go on like this.

LOPAHIN. We'll find you one, Charlotta Ivanovna. Don't you worry yourself.

GAEV. Everyone's leaving us. Varya's going away. We have become of no use all at once.

CHARLOTTA. There's nowhere for me to be in the town. I must go away. (*Hums.*) What care I...

(*Enter* PISHTCHIK.)

LOPAHIN. The freak of nature!

PISHTCHIK (*gasping*). Oh!... let me get my breath.... I'm worn out... my most honoured... Give me some water.

GAEV. Want some money, I suppose? Your humble servant! I'll go out of the way of temptation. (*Goes out.*)

PISHTCHIK. It's a long while since I have been to see you... dearest lady. (*To* LOPAHIN.) You are here... glad to see you... a man of immense intellect... take... here (*gives* LOPAHIN) 400 roubles. That leaves me owing 840.

LOPAHIN (*shrugging his shoulders in amazement*). It's like a dream. Where did you get it?

PISHTCHIK. Wait a bit... I'm hot... a most extraordinary occurrence! Some Englishmen came along and found in my land some sort of white clay. (*To* LYUBOV ANDREYEVNA.) And 400 for you... most lovely... wonderful. (*Gives money.*) The rest later. (*Sips water.*) A young man in the train was telling me just now that a great philosopher advises jumping off a housetop. "Jump!" says he; "the whole gist of the problem lies in that." (*Wonderingly.*) Fancy that, now! Water, please!

LOPAHIN. What Englishmen?

PISHTCHIK. I have made over to them the rights to dig the clay for twenty-four years... and now, excuse me... I can't stay... I must be trotting on. I'm going to Znoikovo... to Kardamanovo.... I'm in debt all round. (*Sips*.)... To your very good health!... I'll come in on Thursday.

LYUBOV. We are just off to the town, and tomorrow I start for abroad.

PISHTCHIK. What! (*In agitation*.) Why to the town? Oh, I see the furniture... the boxes. No matter... (*Through his tears*)... no matter... men of enormous intellect... these Englishmen.... Never mind... be happy. God will succour you... no matter... everything in this world must have an end. (*Kisses* LYUBOV ANDREYEVNA's *hand*.) If the rumour reaches you that my end has come, think of this... old horse, and say: "There once was such a man in the world... Semyonov-Pishtchik... the Kingdom of Heaven be his!"... most extraordinary weather... yes. (*Goes out in violent agitation, but at once returns and says in the doorway*.) Dashenka wishes to be remembered to you.   (*Goes out*.)

LYUBOV. Now we can start. I leave with two cares in my heart. The first is leaving Firs ill. (*Looking at her watch*.) We have still five minutes.

ANYA. Mamma, Firs has been taken to the hospital. Yasha sent him off this morning.

LYUBOV. My other anxiety is Varya. She is used to getting up early and working; and now, without work, she's like a fish out of water. She is thin and pale, and she's crying, poor dear! (*A pause*.) You are well aware, Yermolay Alexeyevitch, I dreamed of marrying her to you, and everything to show that you would get married. (*Whispers to* ANYA *and motions to* CHARLOTTA *and both go out*.) She loves you — she suits you. And I don't know — I don't know why it is you seem, as it were, to avoid each other. I can't understand it!

LOPAHIN. I don't understand it myself, I confess. It's queer somehow, altogether. If there's still time, I'm ready now at once. Let's settle it straight off, and go ahead; but without you, I feel I shan't make her an offer.

LYUBOV. That's excellent. Why, a single moment's all that's necessary. I'll call her at once.

LOPAHIN. And there's champagne all ready too. (*Looking into the glasses.*) Empty! Someone's emptied them already. (YASHA *coughs.*) I call that greedy.

LYUBOV (*eagerly*). Capital! We will go out. Yasha, *allez!* I'll call her in. (*At the door.*) Varya, leave all that; come here. Come along! (*Goes out with* YASHA.)

LOPAHIN (*looking at his watch*). Yes.

> (*A pause. Behind the door, smothered laughter and whispering, and, at last, enter* VARYA.)

VARYA (*looking a long while over the things*). It is strange, I can't find it anywhere.

LOPAHIN. What are you looking for?

VARYA. I packed it myself, and I can't remember. (*A pause.*)

LOPAHIN. Where are you going now, Varvara Mihailova?

VARYA. I? To the Ragulins. I have arranged to go to them to look after the house — as a housekeeper.

LOPAHIN. That's in Yashnovo? It'll be seventy miles away. (*A pause.*) So this is the end of life in this house!

VARYA (*looking among the things*). Where is it? Perhaps I put it in the trunk. Yes, life in this house is over — there will be no more of it.

LOPAHIN. And I'm just off to Harkov — by this next train. I've a lot of business there. I'm leaving Epihodov here, and I've taken him on.

VARYA. Really!

LOPAHIN. This time last year we had snow already, if you remember; but now it's so fine and sunny. Though it's cold, to be sure — three degrees of frost.

VARYA. I haven't looked. (*A pause.*) And besides, our thermometer's broken. (*A pause.*)

> (*Voice at the door from the yard:* "Yermolay Alexeyevitch!")

LOPAHIN (*as though he had long been expecting this summons*). This minute!

> (LOPAHIN *goes out quickly.* VARYA *sitting on the floor and laying her head on a bag full of clothes, sobs quietly. The door opens.* LYUBOV ANDREYEVNA *comes in cautiously.*)

LYUBOV. Well? (*A pause.*) We must be going.

VARYA (*has wiped her eyes and is no longer crying*). Yes, mamma, it's time to start. I shall have time to get to the Ragulins today, if only you're not late for the train.

LYUBOV (*in the doorway*). Anya, put your things on.

(*Enter* ANYA, *then* GAEV *and* CHARLOTTA IVANOVNA. GAEV *has on a warm coat with a hood. Servants and cabmen come in.* EPIHODOV *bustles about the luggage.*)

LYUBOV. Now we can start on our travels.

ANYA (*joyfully*). On our travels!

GAEV. My friends — my dear, my precious friends! Leaving this house for ever, can I be silent? Can I refrain from giving utterance at leave-taking to those emotions which now flood all my being?

ANYA (*supplicatingly*). Uncle!

VARYA. Uncle, you mustn't!

GAEV (*dejectedly*). Cannon and into the pocket... I'll be quiet....

(*Enter* TROFIMOV *and afterwards* LOPAHIN.)

TROFIMOV. Well, ladies and gentlemen, we must start.

LOPAHIN. Epihodov, my coat!

LYUBOV. I'll stay just one minute. It seems as though I have never seen before what the walls, what the ceilings in this house were like, and now I look at them with greediness, with such tender love.

GAEV. I remember when I was six years old sitting in that window on Trinity Day watching my father going to church.

LYUBOV. Have all the things been taken?

LOPAHIN. I think all. (*Putting on overcoat, to* EPIHODOV.) You, Epihodov, mind you see everything is right.

EPIHODOV (*in a husky voice*). Don't you trouble, Yermolay Alexeyevitch.

LOPAHIN. Why, what's wrong with your voice?

EPIHODOV. I've just had a drink of water, and I choked over something.

YASHA (*contemptuously*). The ignorance!

LYUBOV. We are going — and not a soul will be left here.

LOPAHIN. Not till the spring.

VARYA (*pulls a parasol out of a bundle, as though about to hit someone with it.* LOPAHIN *makes a gesture as though alarmed).* What is it? I didn't mean anything.

TROFIMOV. Ladies and gentlemen, let us get into the carriage. It's time. The train will be in directly.

VARYA. Petya, here they are, your goloshes, by that box. (*With tears.*) And what dirty old things they are!

TROFIMOV (*putting on his goloshes*). Let us go, friends!

GAEV (*greatly agitated, afraid of weeping*). The train — the station! Double baulk, ah!

LYUBOV. Let us go!

LOPAHIN. Are we all here? (*Locks the side-door on left.*) The things are all here. We must lock up. Let us go!

ANYA. Good-bye, home! Good-bye to the old life!

TROFIMOV. Welcome to the new life!

(TROFIMOV *goes out with* ANYA. VARYA *looks round the room and goes out slowly.* YASHA *and* CHARLOTTA IVANOVNA, *with her dog, go out.*)

LOPAHIN. Till the spring, then! Come, friends, till we meet!

(*Goes out.*)

(LYUBOV ANDREYEVNA *and* GAEV *remain alone. As though they had been waiting for this, they throw themselves on each other's necks, and break into subdued smothered sobbing, afraid of being overheard.*)

GAEV (*in despair*). Sister, my sister!

LYUBOV. Oh, my orchard! — my sweet, beautiful orchard! My life, my youth, my happiness, good-bye! good-bye!

VOICE OF ANYA (*calling gaily*). Mamma!

VOICE OF TROFIMOV (*gaily, excitedly*). Aa — oo!

LYUBOV. One last look at the walls, at the windows. My dear mother loved to walk about this room.

GAEV. Sister, sister!

VOICE OF ANYA. Mamma!

VOICE OF TROFIMOV. Aa — oo!

LYUBOV. We are coming. (*They go out.*)

(*The stage is empty. There is the sound of the doors being locked up, then of the carriages driving away. There is silence. In the stillness there is the dull stroke of an axe in a tree, clanging with a mournful lonely sound. Footsteps are heard.* FIRS

appears in the doorway on the right.   He is dressed as always —
in a pea-jacket and white waistcoat, with slippers on his feet.
He is ill.)

FIRS (*goes up to the doors, and tries the handles*).   Locked!   They have
gone... (*Sits down on sofa.*)   They have forgotten me....   Never
mind...   I'll sit here a bit....   I'll be bound Leonid Andreyevitch
hasn't put his fur coat on and has gone off in his thin overcoat.
(*Sighs anxiously.*)   I didn't see after him....   These young people
... (*Mutters something that can't be distinguished.*)   Life has slipped
by as though I hadn't lived.   (*Lies down.*)   I'll lie down a bit....
There's no strength in you, nothing left you — all gone!   Ech!
I'm good for nothing.   (*Lies motionless.*)

(*A sound is heard that seems to come from the sky, like a breaking*
harp-string, dying away mournfully.   All is still again, and
there is heard nothing but the strokes of the axe far away in the
orchard.)

CURTAIN

A BRIGHT MORNING

A COMEDY IN ONE ACT

By SERAFIN and JOAQUIN ALVAREZ QUINTERO

*Translated from the Spanish by CARLOS C. CASTILLO
and E. L. OVERMAN*

THE BROTHERS ALVAREZ QUINTERO
SERAFIN, 1871–
JOAQUIN, 1873–

THE brothers Alvarez Quintero were born in Utrera and lived until 1888 in Seville. Their first farce *Love and Fencing* was produced before the elder was seventeen years old. Their second farce was acted at the Teatro Español in Madrid. In 1898 their position was assured by the success of *La buena Sombra*, a farce with music. Their most notable play is perhaps *Las Flores* (1901); their most successful and typical play is *Malvaloca*. They have written more than a hundred and fifty plays of all types. Many of these belong to the class of *género chico*, or little dramas. These are flimsy fragments of graceful imagination sometimes taken from the simple life of the common people in rural districts of Andalusia, sometimes from the folk or upper circles of Madrid. Many have paid tribute to Seville, offering "a handful of its wit, a piece of its streets, a corner of its houses, a flower of its flowers." With Jacinto Benavente, Gregorio Martínez Sierra, Manuel Linares Rivas, the brothers Alvarez Quintero represent the fecund genius of the modern Spanish theater at its best.

A BRIGHT MORNING

THE contemporary Spanish theater is a world in itself. Endowed with playwrights of fecundity and unfailing theatrical gifts, serving an audience that is tireless in demanding something new, the theatrical seasons in the great cities are a procession of new pieces of wit and skill, frequently of theatrical passion, which live but a few short weeks and then are not seen again. With all the theatrical mastery of the Spanish genius, few plays find their way across the border. Perhaps this is because of a certain butterfly quality in Spanish drama. In 1868, a year of revolution, the Teatro de Recreo at Madrid began the presentation of graceful little one-hour pieces, compounds of sentiment and humor, sometimes with music. This type of play became the vogue, and has been for some time perhaps the most typical form of the Spanish theater. Fabrics of theatrical artifice, the artifice is so playful, the plays are so short and simple, that though they are spun in the study they lack all taint of the artificial, and achieve now and then a veritable representative quality. Classed under the general head of *género chico*, no fewer than twenty theaters in Madrid have been known to be open at once for their presentation. They pass by different names of *zarzuelas, revistas líricas, sainetes, entremeses*. Now and then the forms tend to become debased with punning and topical allusions. Among the writers who have never debased their product are the brothers Alvarez Quintero, the authors of *A Bright Morning*. *Mañana de Sol* was produced for the first time in the Teatro Lara, Madrid, February 23, 1905. Under the title of *A Sunny Morning*, it was played at the Neighborhood Playhouse in New York in 1922. The present translation was published in *Poet Lore* in 1916.

PERSONS

Doña Laura
Petra
Don Gonzalo
Juanito

SCENE

A lonely place on a public promenade in Madrid. A bench at the left. A mild autumn morning. Bright sunshine.

DOÑA LAURA *and* PETRA *enter at right.* DOÑA LAURA *is a little woman seventy years old, but her mind is quick and alert. She is neatly dressed, her hair is very white, and her hands show refinement and care. She leans on the arm of* PETRA, *her servant, and carries an umbrella, which she uses as a staff.*

DOÑA LAURA. Thank God, we are here at last. I was afraid someone might be occupying the bench. What a cheerful little morning it is!

PETRA. The sun burns.

DOÑA LAURA. And you are only twenty years old? (*She sits on the bench.*) Today I am more tired than usual. (*Pause. She looks at* PETRA, *who seems impatient.*) Go, if you wish to chat with your guard.

PETRA. He is not my guard. He watches the garden.

DOÑA LAURA. He belongs to you more than to the garden. Look for him, but do not go far away.

PETRA. There he is, waiting for me.

DOÑA LAURA. You may talk to him for ten minutes. Come back at once when the time is up.

PETRA. Very well, Señora.

DOÑA LAURA (*stopping her*). But listen!

PETRA. What is it?

DOÑA LAURA. You are carrying away the bread-crumbs.

PETRA. Indeed, I wasn't thinking.

DOÑA LAURA. Your mind was on the cockade of the guard.

PETRA. Here they are.

　　　　　　　(*Hands her a little package, and leaves at left.*)

DOÑA LAURA. Good-bye. (*She looks toward the trees at left.*) The little rascals are coming. How well they know when I arrive! (*She rises, walks toward the right and throws three small handfuls to the rear.*) One for the boldest, one for the greediest and one for the dearest, the little ones.   Ah.   (*She returns to the bench and from it watches the birds as they eat.*)   You are always the first to come down!   Always the same; I know you, Big Head!   You are like my administrator — large head and drooping mouth. There comes another, and now a third, and now two together and still another.   Three more — that little one yonder is coming nearer, too.   There goes one up to the branch with his bread-crumb.   He is a philosopher.   But what a flock!   Where do they all come from?   How fast the news must spread!   Hum, Hum!   Some of them must come even from the Guindalera. Hum, Hum!   Come, do not fight!   There is enough for all. I will bring some more tomorrow.

(*Enter* Don Gonzalo *and* Juanito *to left.   Don Gonzalo *is an old irritable man, a contemporary of* Doña Laura; *drags his feet as he walks.   He comes in a bad humor; leans on the arm of* Juanito, *his servant.*)

DON GONZALO.   Vagrants!   Worse than vagrants — they should be saying mass in church.

JUANITO.   You may sit here; there is only a lady here.

(Doña Laura *turns round and listens.*)

DON GONZALO.   I don't care to, Juanito.   I wish to sit on a bench alone.

JUANITO.   But there is none.

DON GONZALO.   That one there is mine!

JUANITO.   Three priests are sitting on it.

DON GONZALO.   Let them get up.   Are they getting up?

JUANITO.   Indeed, they are not.   They are still talking.

DON GONZALO.   They seem to be glued to the bench.   When a priest settles himself no one can budge him.   Come this way, Juanito, come.

(*He goes resolutely toward the right, and* Juanito *follows.*)

DOÑA LAURA (*indignantly*).   Heavens, man!

DON GONZALO (*turning*).   Did you address me?

DOÑA LAURA.   Yes, Señor, I referred to you.

DON GONZALO.   What is the matter?

DOÑA LAURA.   You have frightened the sparrows away!   They were eating bread-crumbs.

DON GONZALO. What have I to do with the sparrows?

DOÑA LAURA. I have something to do with them!

DON GONZALO. This is a public place.

DOÑA LAURA. Then do not complain because the priests have taken your bench.

DON GONZALO. Señora, we have never met each other. How dare you take the liberty of addressing me! Follow me, Juanito! *(Exeunt right.)*

DOÑA LAURA. A fiendish old man! Impertinence seems to come with old age. *(Pause.)* I am glad! They have also taken that bench away from him! There! It serves him right for frightening my little birds! He is furious! Yes, yes; search and search! Unless you sit on your own hat you will not find a place. Poor creature! He is wiping his brow! Here he comes! He raises more dust with his feet than a cab!

DON GONZALO *(returning from the direction he went, and walking toward the left)*. Have the priests gone yet, Juanito?

JUANITO. Don't dream of such a thing, Señor! They are still there.

DON GONZALO. For the sake of... *(Looks around in perplexity.)* The city officials do not provide enough benches for these bright mornings. Well, I suppose I must share that of the old woman. *(He sits muttering at the end of DOÑA LAURA's bench, and looks at DOÑA LAURA indignantly.)* Good morning.

DOÑA LAURA. Hello! you here?

DON GONZALO. I insist we have not met each other.

DOÑA LAURA. I answer since you greet me.

DON GONZALO. To my greeting, you should have answered, "Good morning." That is what you should have done.

DOÑA LAURA. And you should have asked my permission to sit on this bench — it is mine.

DON GONZALO. The benches here belong to nobody.

DOÑA LAURA. Didn't you say the priests' bench was yours?

DON GONZALO. Well, well, well! We have said enough. *(Between his teeth.)* Feeble minded old woman! She ought to be darning instead of being here!

DOÑA LAURA. You need not grumble. I will not go.

DON GONZALO *(dusting his boots with his handkerchief)*. Sprinkling would not come amiss either!

DOÑA LAURA. How strange that one should dust his boots with his handkerchief!

DON GONZALO. What?

DOÑA LAURA. Perhaps you use a brush for your nose?

DON GONZALO. What? Señora, what right have you ——

DOÑA LAURA. The right of a neighbor.

DON GONZALO (*abruptly*). Here Juanito, give me my book. I will listen to no more nonsense.

DOÑA LAURA. You are very kind.

DON GONZALO. If you were not so meddlesome.

DOÑA LAURA. A weakness of mine, is that I say all I think.

DON GONZALO. That of speaking more than is proper! Give me the book, Juanito.

JUANITO. Here it is, Señor.

> (*Takes a book from his pocket, and hands it to him. Paces the stage, moves farther away, and disappears, at right.* DON GONZALO, *still looking angrily at* DOÑA LAURA, *puts on a pair of antique spectacles; takes a large lens from his pocket and with the aid of these prepares to read.*)

DOÑA LAURA. You should next take out a telescope.

DON GONZALO. See here!

DOÑA LAURA. Your eyes must be excellent.

DON GONZALO. About four times as good as yours.

DOÑA LAURA. Indeed, it seems so!

DON GONZALO. A few hares and partridges could bear me witness.

DOÑA LAURA. Are you a hunter?

DON GONZALO. I have been and even now ——

DOÑA LAURA. Indeed? So?

DON GONZALO. Yes, Señora. Every Sunday I take my shot gun and dog and go to one of my farms near Aravaca — to kill time, you know.

DOÑA LAURA. Yes, time — that's all you can kill.

DON GONZALO. You think so? I could show you a boar's head, which I have in my office.

DOÑA LAURA. Indeed, and I could show you the skin of a tiger which I have in my parlor. Such an argument!

DON GONZALO. Well, Señora, let me read. I have no desire to talk longer.

DOÑA LAURA. Then keep still yourself. That ought to suit you.

DON GONZALO. I will take a pinch of snuff first. (*He takes out a snuff box.*) Will you have some? Do you like it?

DOÑA LAURA. That depends — is it of good quality?

DON GONZALO. There is none better. You will like it.

DOÑA LAURA. It clears one's head.

DON GONZALO. It does.

DOÑA LAURA. Does it make you sneeze?

DON GONZALO. Yes, Señora, three times.

DOÑA LAURA. And me three times, too. What a coincidence! (*After they take snuff they sneeze alternately.*) Ca-choo!

DON GONZALO. Ca-choo, oo!

DOÑA LAURA. Ca-choo!

DON GONZALO. Ca-choo!

DOÑA LAURA. Ca-choo!

DON GONZALO. Ca-choo!

DOÑA LAURA. Health!

DON GONZALO. Thank you, may it do you good.

DOÑA LAURA. And you. (*Aside.*) The snuff has reconciled us.

DON GONZALO. You will excuse me if I read aloud?

DOÑA LAURA. Read as you wish. It will not disturb me.

DON GONZALO. (*Reading.*)

"Though only sad withal
Love is best of all."

This is from Campoamor, from Campoamor.

DOÑA LAURA. Oh!

GONZALO. (*Reading.*)

"Daughters whose mothers once I loved
Now kiss me as they would an image."

These are Humoradas!

DOÑA LAURA. Yes indeed, Humoradas!

DON GONZALO. I prefer the Doloras.

DOÑA LAURA. I do, too.

DON GONZALO. There are some of them in this volume. (*He looks for them and then reads.*) Listen to this.

"Two decades pass; and he returns —"

DOÑA LAURA. It drives me wild to see you with those spectacles.

DON GONZALO. Do you, perchance, read without glasses?

DOÑA LAURA. Certainly.

DON GONZALO. At your age? I take the liberty of doubting it.

DOÑA LAURA. Give me the book. (*She takes it from him and reads.*) Listen to this.

> "Two decades pass; and he returns.
>   They, into each other's faces look and cry;
>   'Great God! can this be she!
>   Good God! can this be he!'" (*Returns book.*)

DON GONZALO. You have enviable eyesight indeed.

DOÑA LAURA (*aside*). When I know the poem by heart!

DON GONZALO. I am very fond of good poetry and even composed some verses in my youth.

DOÑA LAURA. Good ones?

DON GONZALO. They were of all kinds. I was a friend of Espronceda, and Zorrilla, and Becquer. I knew Zorrilla in America.

DOÑA LAURA. Have you been in America?

DON GONZALO. Several times. The first time when I was six years old.

DOÑA LAURA. Columbus took you in a caravel, did he not?

DON GONZALO. Not so fast, not so fast; I am old but I did not know the Catholic kings. (*Laughing.*)

DOÑA LAURA. Ha, ha.

DON GONZALO. I was also a great friend of Campoamor. We met in Valencia. I am a Valencian.

DOÑA LAURA. Yes?

DON GONZALO. I was raised there and spent my early youth there. Are you acquainted with that region?

DOÑA LAURA. Yes, Señor. Near Valencia, two or three leagues away, there was a farm house, which will remember me still, if it is there. In it I spent a few seasons many, many years ago. It was near the sea, concealed by orange and lemon trees. They called it — what did they call it? Maricella.

DON GONZALO. Maricella?

DOÑA LAURA. Maricella. Does the name sound familiar to you?

DON GONZALO. I should say so! If my memory serves me right — years enfeeble one's mind! — there lived the most beautiful woman I ever saw — and I have seen many in my life! Wait a moment, let me see. Her name was Laura. I do not remember her surname. (*Trying to remember.*) Laura, Laura — Laura Llorente!

DOÑA LAURA. Laura Llorente!

DON GONZALO. What? (*They look at each other searchingly.*)

DOÑA LAURA. Nothing. You recall to memory, my most beloved friend.

DON GONZALO. What a coincidence!

DOÑA LAURA. An unusual coincidence, indeed. *The Silver Girl.*

DON GONZALO. *The Silver Girl!* That was what the gardeners and fishermen called her. Would you believe it? I can see her now in that little window with the blue tassels. Do you remember that window?

DOÑA LAURA. I do. That was her room. I do remember.

DON GONZALO. She spent hours and hours, at the window — in my youth, I say.

DOÑA LAURA. And in mine also. (*Sighing.*)

DON GONZALO. She was perfect, perfect; fair as snow; very black hair; black eyes, soft and tender; and from her brow radiated light. Her body was fine and slender, with gentle curves.

"What sovereign grace and line,
Moulds God in human form divine."

It was a dream, just a dream.

DOÑA LAURA (*aside*). If you knew she was by your side, you would see what dreams are worth. (*To* DON GONZALO.) I loved her very dearly, with all my heart. She was very unhappy. She had some sad love affairs.

DON GONZALO. Very sad. (*They look at each other again.*)

DOÑA LAURA. Do you know that?

DON GONZALO. Yes.

DOÑA LAURA (*aside*). O what Providence permits us! This man is he!

DON GONZALO. Precisely. The gallant lover — if we refer to the same case ——

DOÑA LAURA. To the one of the duel?

DON GONZALO. Exactly — the one of the duel. The gallant was — was a relative of mine, a boy to whom I gave all my affection.

DOÑA LAURA. A relative! She told me in one of the last letters the story of that most romantic love affair.

DON GONZALO. Platonic love. They never spoke to each other about love.

DOÑA LAURA. Your relative passed on horseback, every morning, through the little path among the rose bushes, and threw her a bouquet, which she was always at the window to receive.

DON GONZALO. And then in the afternoon the gallant rider passed again and received a bouquet, which she threw to him in return. Did he not?

DOÑA LAURA. That is true. They wished her to marry a merchant. A nobody, with no more titles than love.

DON GONZALO. And on a certain night, as my relative was walking about the grounds to hear her sing, that man suddenly appeared.

DOÑA LAURA. And provoked your relative.

DON GONZALO. And they quarreled.

DOÑA LAURA. And there was a duel.

DON GONZALO. At daybreak at the seashore. There the challenger was left, mortally wounded. My relative was first obliged to hide himself and then to flee.

DOÑA LAURA. You know the story in detail.

DON GONZALO. And you, too.

DOÑA LAURA. I have already said that she told it to me.

DON GONZALO. And my relative to me. (Aside.) This woman is Laura! What strange things God brings about!

DOÑA LAURA (aside). He does not suspect who I am. Why should I tell him? Let him cherish his dream.

DON GONZALO (aside). She does not suspect that she is speaking to the gallant himself. How could she guess? I will not tell her. (Pause.)

DOÑA LAURA. And was it you, perchance, who advised your relative to forget Laura? (Aside.) Now what?

DON GONZALO. I, when my relative did not forget her for a single second?

DOÑA LAURA. How then can his conduct be explained?

DON GONZALO. Do you know? Listen Señora; the youth first took refuge in my house, as he was afraid of the consequences of a duel with a man so esteemed there. Then he went to Sevilla, and afterward to Madrid. He wrote I don't know how many letters to Laura, some of them in verse. I bear witness to this; but there is no doubt that her parents intercepted the letters, since Laura did not answer. Then Gonzalo in disappointment and despair, enlisted with the army in Africa, and there in a trench met his fate, embracing the flag of Spain, and repeating the name of his love: Laura, Laura, Laura.

DOÑA LAURA (aside). Such a liar!

DON GONZALO (aside). I could not have been killed in a more romantic manner.

DOÑA LAURA. You must have regretted that misfortune to the bottom of your soul.

DON GONZALO. The same as if I had been the victim. But then who can tell that the ungrateful Laura was not chasing butterflies in her garden within two months after the duel, indifferent to everything.

DOÑA LAURA. O no, Señor, no!

DON GONZALO. That is the nature of woman.

DOÑA LAURA. Although that be the nature of woman, the *Silver Girl* was different. My friend looked for news day after day — a month passed and then a year, but no letter ever came. One evening at sunset, when the first star was about to appear, she was seen by someone as she walked resolutely toward the sea-shore — to that place where the chosen of her heart had risked his life. There she inscribed his name on the sand, and then seated herself on a rock, and fixed her gaze on the horizon. The waves murmured their eternal monologue, and covered little by little, the rock on which she sat. Do you wish to know the rest? The tide continued to ascend, and carried her away.

DON GONZALO. Heavens!

DOÑA LAURA. The fishermen along the shore say that for a long time the waves could not efface the inscription from the sand. (*Aside.*) You can't beat me when it comes to a poetic climax.

DON GONZALO (aside). She lies even better than I! (*Pause.*)

DOÑA LAURA. Poor Laura!

DON GONZALO. Poor Gonzalo!

DOÑA LAURA (*aside*). I won't tell him that two years afterward, I married a brewer.

DON GONZALO (*aside*). I shall never let her know that I eloped to Paris with a dancer three months later.

DOÑA LAURA. Isn't it remarkable how chance has brought us together, and how an old adventure has caused us to talk to each other as though we were old friends?

DON GONZALO. Yes, in spite of our having begun by quarreling.

DOÑA LAURA. That was because you frightened the sparrows.

DON GONZALO. I was in an ugly mood.

DOÑA LAURA. Yes, indeed, I saw that you were. Will you come here again tomorrow?

DON GONZALO. Most assuredly, if the sun is shining. I will not only be careful not to frighten the sparrows, but will also bring them some bread-crumbs.

DOÑA LAURA. Many thanks, Señor. They are good folks and deserve all they receive. By the way, I don't know where my maid is. (*She arises.*) What time is it now?

DON GONZALO (*getting up*). Almost twelve. And that rascal Juanito! (*He goes toward the right.*)

DOÑA LAURA (*from the left looking toward the rear of the stage*). There she is with her guard. (*She beckons with her hand for her to come.*)

DON GONZALO (*looking intently at* DOÑA LAURA). (*Aside.*) No, I will not tell her who I am. I have become such a scarecrow! Let her remember forever the gallant as he used to gallop past and fling bouquets to her in the window, with the little blue tassels.

DOÑA LAURA. How hard it is for her to leave him! Here she comes.

DON GONZALO. Juanito — where can he be anyway? Perhaps he is absorbed in conversation with some maid servant. (*He looks first to the right and then motions as* DOÑA LAURA *has done.*) The devil of a boy!

DOÑA LAURA (*watching the old man attentively*). (*Aside.*) No, I will not tell him who I am. I look like an old witch now. It is better to let him remember always, the black-eyed girl who used to throw flowers to him from her window as he passed along the little path between the rose bushes.

*(JUANITO enters at the right, and PETRA at the left, PETRA
carries a bunch of violets.)*

Come, woman, I thought you would never return.

DON GONZALO. Heavens! Juanito, it is very late.

PETRA. My lover gave me these flowers to give you.

DOÑA LAURA. How kind of him. I appreciate them very much.
(As she takes them, one or two fall.) They are very beautiful.

DON GONZALO *(about to depart)*. My Señora, this has been a very
great honor — a very great pleasure ——

DOÑA LAURA *(about to go)*. And it has been a great satisfaction to
me.

DON GONZALO. Till tomorrow?

DOÑA LAURA. Till tomorrow.

DON GONZALO. If the sun is shining ——

DOÑA LAURA. If the sun is shining, will you go to your own bench?

DON GONZALO. No, Señora, I will come to this one.

DOÑA LAURA. This bench is always yours. *(They laugh.)*

DON GONZALO. And I repeat that I will bring some bread-crumbs
for the sparrows. *(They laugh again.)*

DOÑA LAURA. Till tomorrow.

DON GONZALO. Till tomorrow.

*(DOÑA LAURA walks with PETRA toward the right. DON
GONZALO before leaving with JUANITO at the left, trembling
and with great effort stoops to gather the fallen violets. DOÑA
LAURA turns in a natural way and looks at him.)*

JUANITO. What are you doing, Señor?

DON GONZALO. Wait, wait!

DOÑA LAURA *(aside)*. Now I know it is he.

DON GONZALO *(aside)*. I am certain it is she.

(They bow to each other again.)

DOÑA LAURA *(aside)*. "Good God! can this be he?" ——

DON GONZALO *(aside)*. "Great God! can this be she?"——

*(They depart each leaning on the arm of his servant. DON
GONZALO smiles as though he were passing along the little path
between the rose bushes, and DOÑA LAURA as though she were
at the window with the little blue tassels.)*

CURTAIN

LILIOM

A LEGEND IN SEVEN SCENES
AND A PROLOGUE

By FERENC MOLNAR

English text by BENJAMIN F. GLAZER

FERENC MOLNAR

To THE world at large Ferenc Molnar is the typical figure of the post-war literary life of Hungary. As journalist, short-story writer, playwright he can turn his hand with exquisite skill to the fashioning of commodities for sale to foreign peoples. This does not mean that he lacks sincerity, or that he fails in grasp of the deeper strains of life experience. He has both these qualities. Many other Hungarian writers have them to an equal or a greater degree. But they lack the indispensable quality that Molnar possesses, namely, an elfin grace of imagination, a festive fancy, that gives everything he writes a pattern as of something new and strange. Remove this quality from Molnar and he would be indeed second or third rate. After much using, the quality itself seems to be failing the hand of the craftsman. It never again achieved the perfection of grace and surprise that it reached in *Liliom*. *Liliom* has been called a play of fantasy. What is a fantastic play? It is at bottom a drama of artifice in which the materials of real life are handled with an expert playfulness. Two things are essential in the artifice of fantasy, a complete logic in details, a complete lack of logic in their sequence. Among the masters of this type of artifice few take higher rank than Molnar. But in the veritable professionalism of his craftsmanship he takes a position well below the supreme master of illogic, Lewis Carroll, and even in some respects below Barrie. Molnar was born January 12, 1878, at Budapest, the son of a merchant. He attended college at Budapest and Geneva. He early established himself as a writer of graceful sketches for the newspapers. He has written something like twenty plays, many of which have been produced in the theaters of Europe and America. Among other Hungarian writers who have obtained a kind of vogue in a fashion similar to that of Molnar are Melchior Lengyel, Ernst Vajda, Imre Földes, Ferenc Herzeg, and Andor Gabor.

As HAS been remarked fantasy is a form of sophisticated playfulness. It is therefore essentially a form of artifice. One should not be misled regarding the artifice of such a play as *Liliom* by the fact that it begins with an exquisite and disarming naturalism. The naturalism is designed to be disarming. Nor should one be misled by the fact that there are in the play heartrending strains of tenderness and human feeling. There is nothing inappropriate in the mingling of deep feeling with free fancy. After many years of naturalism it has now become clear that a structure rigorously constrained within the limits of observation is itself a barrier to the evocation either of full-grown character or of a sentiment that purifies itself in complete expression. So it is that in such fantasies as those of Barrie and Molnar, products of artifice though they may be, we find vehicles for the expression of the purest feeling in contemporary drama. *Liliom* (meaning *The Lily*) was written by Molnar in 1909 and produced in December of that year in Budapest. At its first production its reception was not notably warm. In fact it is characteristic of the so-called "Hungarian" school of playwriting led by Molnar that its chief successes are obtained abroad. The game of playful *nuances* lacks the novelty for the Hungarian that it has for the audience of western Europe and America. At its second performance some years later, it was, however, received with enthusiasm. It was translated into French by Mme. de Comminge and M. Adorjan; and was produced as *The Daisy* in London in September, 1920. In April of the same year it was produced by the Theater Guild in New York in the translation here printed, with Eva Le Gallienne in the part of Julie. In 1926 the play was produced in London; in 1923 in Paris. The play also had a place in the repertory of the Civic Repertory Theater in New York.

SYNOPSIS OF SCENES

PROLOGUE, *an amusement park on the outskirts of Budapest*
FIRST SCENE, *a lonely place in the park*
SECOND SCENE, *the photographic studio of the* HOLLUNDERS
THIRD SCENE, *same as scene two*
FOURTH SCENE, *a railroad embankment outside the city*
FIFTH SCENE, *same as scene two*
SIXTH SCENE, *a courtroom in the beyond*
SEVENTH SCENE, JULIE'S *garden*

There are intermissions only after the second and fifth scenes.

CAST OF CHARACTERS

LILIOM
JULIE
MARIE
MRS. MUSKAT
LOUISE
MRS. HOLLUNDER
FICSUR
YOUNG HOLLUNDER
WOLF BEIFELD
THE CARPENTER
LINZMAN
THE DOCTOR
THE MAGISTRATE
TWO MOUNTED POLICEMEN
TWO PLAINCLOTHES POLICEMEN
TWO HEAVENLY POLICEMEN
THE RICHLY DRESSED MAN
THE POORLY DRESSED MAN
THE GUARD
A SUBURBAN POLICEMAN

THE PROLOGUE

An amusement park on the outskirts of Budapest on a late afternoon in Spring. Barkers stand before the booths of the sideshows haranguing the passing crowd. The strident music of a calliope is heard; laughter, shouts, the scuffle of feet, the signal bells of a merry-go-round.

The merry-go-round is at center. LILIOM *stands at the entrance, a cigarette in his mouth, coaxing the people in. The girls regard him with idolizing glances and screech with pleasure as he playfully pushes them through entrance. Now and then some girl's escort resents the familiarity, whereupon* LILIOM'S *demeanor becomes ugly and menacing, and the cowed escort slinks through the entrance behind his girl or contents himself with a muttered resentful comment.*

One girl hands LILIOM *a red carnation; he rewards her with a bow and a smile. When the soldier who accompanies her protests,* LILIOM *cows him with a fierce glance and a threatening gesture.* MARIE *and* JULIE *come out of the crowd and* LILIOM *favors them with particular notice as they pass into the merry-go-round.*

MRS. MUSKAT *comes out of the merry-go-round, bringing* LILIOM *coffee and rolls.* LILIOM *mounts the barker's stand at the entrance, where he is elevated over everyone on the stage. Here he begins his harangue. Everybody turns toward him. The other booths are gradually deserted. The tumult makes it impossible for the audience to hear what he is saying, but every now and then some witticism of his provokes a storm of laughter which is audible above the din. Many people enter the merry-go-round. Here and there one catches a phrase "Room for one more on the zebra's back," "Which of you ladies?" "Ten heller for adults, five for children," "Step right up ——"*

It is growing darker. A lamplighter crosses the stage, and begins unperturbedly lighting the colored gas-lamps. The whistle of a distant locomotive is heard. Suddenly the tumult ceases, the lights go out, and the curtain falls in darkness.

END OF PROLOGUE

SCENE I

*A lonely place in the park, half hidden by trees and shrubbery. Under
a flowering acacia tree stands a painted wooden bench. From the distance,
faintly, comes the tumult of the amusement park. It is the sunset of the
same day.*

When the curtain rises the stage is empty.

(MARIE *enters quickly, pauses at center, and looks back.*)

MARIE. Julie, Julie! (*There is no answer.*) Do you hear me,
Julie? Let her be! Come on. Let her be. (*Starts to go back.*)

(JULIE *enters, looks back angrily.*)

JULIE. Did you ever hear of such a thing? What's the matter
with the woman anyway?

MARIE (*looking back again*). Here she comes again.

JULIE. Let her come. I didn't do anything to her. All of a
sudden she comes up to me and begins to raise a row.

MARIE. Here she is. Come on, let's run.   (*Tries to urge her off.*)

JULIE. Run? I should say not. What would I want to run for?
I'm not afraid of her.

MARIE. Oh, come on. She'll only start a fight.

JULIE. I'm going to stay right here. Let her *start* a fight.

MRS. MUSKAT (*entering*). What do you want to run away for?
(*To* JULIE.) Don't worry. I won't eat you. But there's one
thing I want to tell you, my dear. Don't let me catch you in
my carousel again. I stand for a whole lot, I have to in my
business. It makes no difference to me whether my customers are ladies or the likes of you — as long as they pay
their money. But when a girl misbehaves herself on my
carousel — out she goes. Do you understand?

JULIE. Are you talking to me?

MRS. MUSKAT. Yes, you! You — chambermaid, you! In my
carousel ——

JULIE. Who did anything in your old carousel? I paid my fare
and took my seat and never said a word, except to my friend
here.

MARIE. No, she never opened her mouth. Liliom came over
to her of his own accord.

MRS. MUSKAT. It's all the same. I'm not going to get in trouble
with the police, and lose my license on account of you — you
shabby kitchen maid!

JULIE. Shabby yourself.

MRS. MUSKAT. You stay out of my carousel! Letting my barker
fool with you! Aren't you ashamed of yourself?

JULIE. What? What did you say?

MRS. MUSKAT. I suppose you think I have no eyes in my head.
I see everything that goes on in my carousel. During the
whole ride she let Liliom fool with her — the shameless hussy!

JULIE. He did not fool with me! I don't let any man fool with me!

MRS. MUSKAT. He leaned against you all through the ride!

JULIE. He leaned against the panther. He always leans against
something, doesn't he? Everybody leans where he wants.
I couldn't tell him not to lean, if he always leans, could I?
But he didn't lay a hand on me.

MRS. MUSKAT. Oh, didn't he? And I suppose he didn't put
his hand around your waist, either?

MARIE. And if he did? What of it?

MRS. MUSKAT. You hold your tongue! No one's asking you — just
you keep out of it.

JULIE. He put his arm around my waist — just the same as he
does to all the girls. He always does that.

MRS. MUSKAT. I'll teach him not to do it any more, my dear. No
carryings on in my carousel! If you are looking for that sort
of thing, you'd better go to the circus! You'll find lots of
soldiers there to carry on with!

JULIE. You keep your soldiers for yourself!

MARIE. Soldiers! As if we wanted soldiers!

MRS. MUSKAT. Well, I only want to tell you this, my dear, so that
we understand each other perfectly. If you ever stick your
nose in my carousel again, you'll wish you hadn't! I'm not
going to lose my license on account of the likes of you! People
who don't know how to behave, have got to stay out!

JULIE. You're wasting your breath. If I feel like riding on your
carousel I'll pay my ten heller and I'll ride. I'd like to see
anyone try to stop me!

MRS. MUSKAT. Just come and try it, my dear — just come and try it.

MARIE. We'll see what'll happen.

MRS. MUSKAT. Yes, you will see something happen that never happened before in this park.

JULIE. Perhaps you think you could throw me out!

MRS. MUSKAT. I'm sure of it, my dear.

JULIE. And suppose I'm stronger than you?

MRS. MUSKAT. I'd think twice before I'd dirty my hands on a common servant girl. I'll have Liliom throw you out. He knows how to handle your kind.

JULIE. You think Liliom would throw me out.

MRS. MUSKAT. Yes, my dear, so fast that you won't know what happened to you!

JULIE. He'd throw me ——

(*Stops suddenly, for* MRS. MUSKAT *has turned away. Both look off stage until* LILIOM *enters, surrounded by four giggling servant girls.*)

LILIOM. Go away! Stop following me, or I'll smack your face!

A LITTLE SERVANT GIRL. Well, give me back my handkerchief.

LILIOM. Go on now ——

THE FOUR SERVANT GIRLS (*simultaneously*). What do you think of him? — My handkerchief! — Give it back to her! — That's a nice thing to do!

THE LITTLE SERVANT GIRL (*to* MRS. MUSKAT). Please, lady, make him ——

MRS. MUSKAT. Oh, shut up!

LILIOM. Will you get out of here?

(*Makes a threatening gesture — the* FOUR SERVANT GIRLS *exit in voluble but fearful haste.*)

MRS. MUSKAT. What have you been doing now?

LILIOM. None of your business. (*Glances at* JULIE.) Have you been starting with her again?

JULIE. Mister Liliom, please ——

LILIOM (*steps threateningly toward her*). Don't yell!

JULIE (*timidly*). I didn't yell.

LILIOM. Well, don't. (*To* MRS. MUSKAT.) What's the matter? What has she done to you?

MRS. MUSKAT. What has she done? She's been impudent to me.

JULIE (*timidly*). Mister Liliom, if she's willing to say that she hasn't discharged you ——

LILIOM. You keep out of this.

JULIE (*timidly*). I don't want this to happen on account of me.

LILIOM (*to* MRS. MUSKAT, *pointing to* JULIE). Apologize to her!

MARIE. A-ha!

MRS. MUSKAT. Apologize? To who?

LILIOM. To this little pigeon. Well — are you going to do it?

MRS. MUSKAT. If you give me this whole park on a silver plate, and all the gold of the Rothschilds on top of it — I'd — I'd —— Let her dare to come into my carousel again and she'll get thrown out so hard that she'll see stars in daylight!

LILIOM. In that case, dear lady (*takes off his cap with a flourish*) you are respectfully requested to get out o' here as fast as your legs will carry you — I never beat up a woman yet — except that Holzer woman who I sent to the hospital for three weeks — but — if you don't get out o' here, this minute, and let this little squab be, I'll give you the prettiest slap in the jaw you ever had in your life.

MRS. MUSKAT. Very good, my son. Now you *can* go to the devil. Good-bye. You're discharged, and you needn't try to come back, either.   (*She exits. It is beginning to grow dark.*)

MARIE (*with grave concern*). Mister Liliom ——

LILIOM. Don't you pity me or I'll give *you* a slap in the jaw. (*To* JULIE.) And don't you pity me, either.

JULIE (*in alarm*). I don't pity you, Mister Liliom.

LILIOM. You're a liar, you *are* pitying me. I can see it in your face. You're thinking, now that Madame Muskat has thrown him out, Liliom will have to go begging. Huh! Look at me. I'm big enough to get along without a Madame Muskat. I have been thrown out of better jobs than hers.

JULIE. What will you do now, Mister Liliom?

LILIOM. Now? First of all, I'll go and get myself — a glass of beer. You see, when something happens to annoy me, I always drink a glass of beer.

JULIE. Then you *are* annoyed about losing your job.

LILIOM. No, only about where I'm going to get the beer.

MARIE. Well — eh ——

LILIOM. Well — eh — what?

MARIE. Well — eh — are you going to stay with us, Mister Liliom?

LILIOM. Will you pay for the beer? (MARIE *looks doubtful; he turns to* JULIE.) Will you? (*She does not answer.*) How much money have you got?

JULIE (*bashfully*). Eight heller.

LILIOM. And you? (MARIE *casts down her eyes and does not reply.* LILIOM *continues sternly.*) I asked you how much you've got? (MARIE *begins to weep softly.*) I understand. Well, you needn't cry about it. You girls stay here, while I go back to the carousel and get my clothes and things. And when I come back, we'll go to the Hungarian beer-garden. It's all right, I'll pay. Keep your money.

(*He exits.* MARIE *and* JULIE *stand silent, watching him until he has gone.*)

MARIE. Are you sorry for him?

JULIE. Are you?

MARIE. Yes, a little. Why are you looking after him in that funny way?

JULIE (*sits down*). Nothing — except I'm sorry he lost his job.

MARIE (*with a touch of pride*). It was on our account he lost his job. Because he's fallen in love with you.

JULIE. He hasn't at all.

MARIE (*confidently*). Oh, yes! he is in love with you. (*Hesitantly, romantically.*) There is someone in love with me, too.

JULIE. There is? Who?

MARIE. I — I never mentioned it before, because you hadn't a lover of your own — but now you have — and I'm free to speak. (*Very grandiloquently.*) My heart has found its mate.

JULIE. You're only making it up.

MARIE. No, it's true — my heart's true love ——

JULIE. Who? Who is he?

MARIE. A soldier.

JULIE. What kind of a soldier?

MARIE. I don't know. Just a soldier. Are there different kinds?

JULIE. Many different kinds. There are hussars, artillerymen, engineers, infantry — that's the kind that walks — and ——

MARIE. How can you tell which is which?

JULIE. By their uniforms.

MARIE (*after trying to puzzle it out*). The conductors on the street cars — are they soldiers?

JULIE. Certainly not. They're conductors.

MARIE. Well, they have uniforms.

JULIE. But they don't carry swords or guns.

MARIE. Oh! (*Thinks it over again; then.*) Well, policemen — are they?

JULIE (*with a touch of exasperation*). Are they what?

MARIE. Soldiers.

JULIE. Certainly not. They're just policemen.

MARIE (*triumphantly*). But they have uniforms — and they carry weapons, too.

JULIE. You're just as dumb as you can be. You don't go by their uniforms.

MARIE. But you said ——

JULIE. No, I didn't. A letter-carrier wears a uniform, too, but that doesn't make him a soldier.

MARIE. But if he carried a gun or a sword, would he be ——

JULIE. No, he'd still be a letter-carrier. You can't go by guns or swords, either.

MARIE. Well, if you don't go by the uniforms or the weapons, what *do* you go by?

JULIE. By —— (*Tries to put it into words; fails; then breaks off suddenly.*) Oh, you'll get to know when you've lived in the city long enough. You're nothing but a country girl. When you've lived in the city a year, like I have, you'll know all about it.

MARIE (*half angrily*). Well, how *do* you know when *you* see a real soldier?

JULIE. By one thing.

MARIE. What?

JULIE. One thing —— (*She pauses.* MARIE *starts to cry.*) Oh, what are you crying about?

MARIE. Because you're making fun of me.... You're a city girl, and I'm just fresh from the country... and how am I expected to know a soldier when I see one?... You, you ought to tell me, instead of making fun of me ——

JULIE. All right. Listen then, cry-baby. There's only one way to tell a soldier: by his salute! That's the only way.

MARIE (*joyfully; with a sigh of relief*). Ah — that's good.

JULIE. What?

MARIE. I say — it's all right then — because Wolf — Wolf —— (JULIE *laughs derisively*.) Wolf — that's his name.

(*She weeps again.*)

JULIE. Crying again? What now?

MARIE. You're making fun of me again.

JULIE. I'm not. But when you say, "Wolf—Wolf—" like that, I have to laugh, don't I? (*Archly.*) What's his name again?

MARIE. I won't tell you.

JULIE. All right. If you won't say it, then he's no soldier.

MARIE. I'll say it.

JULIE. Go on.

MARIE. No, I won't. (*She weeps again.*)

JULIE. Then he's not a soldier. I guess he's a letter-carrier ——

MARIE. No — no — I'd rather say it.

JULIE. Well, then.

MARIE (*giggling*). But you mustn't look at me. You look the other way, and I'll say it. (JULIE *looks away*. MARIE *can hardly restrain her own laughter*.) Wolf! (*She laughs.*) That's his real name. Wolf, Wolf, Soldier — Wolf!

JULIE. What kind of a uniform does he wear?

MARIE. Red.

JULIE. Red trousers?

MARIE. No.

JULIE. Red coat?

MARIE. No.

JULIE. What then?

MARIE (*triumphantly*). His cap!

JULIE (*after a long pause*). He's just a porter, you dunce. Red cap... that's a porter — and he doesn't carry a gun or a sword, either.

MARIE (*triumphantly*). But he salutes. You said yourself that was the only way to tell a soldier ——

JULIE. He doesn't salute at all. He only greets people ——

MARIE. He salutes me.... And if his name *is* Wolf, that doesn't

prove he ain't a soldier — he salutes, and he wears a red cap
and he stands on guard all day long outside a big building ——

JULIE. What does he do there?

MARIE (*seriously*). He spits.

JULIE (*with contempt*). He's nothing — nothing but a common
porter.

MARIE. What's Liliom?

JULIE (*indignantly*). Why speak of him? What has he to do with
me?

MARIE. The same as Wolf has to do with me. If you can talk to
me like that about Wolf, I can talk to you about Liliom.

JULIE. He's nothing to me. He puts his arm around me in the
carousel. I couldn't tell him not to put his arm around me
after he had done it, could I?

MARIE. I suppose you didn't like him to do it?

JULIE. No.

MARIE. Then why are you waiting for him? Why don't you go
home?

JULIE. Why — eh — he *said* we were to wait for him.

(LILIOM *enters. There is a long silence.*)

LILIOM. Are you still here? What are you waiting for?

MARIE. You told us to wait.

LILIOM. Must you always interfere? No one is talking to you.

MARIE. You asked us — why we ——

LILIOM. Will you keep your mouth shut? What do you suppose
I want with two of you? I meant that one of you was to wait.
The other can go home.

MARIE. All right.

JULIE. All right. (*Neither starts to go.*)

LILIOM. One of you goes home. (*To* MARIE.) Where do you
work?

MARIE. At the Breiers', Damjanovitsch Street, Number 20.

LILIOM. And you?

JULIE. I work there, too.

LILIOM. Well, one of you goes home. Which of you wants to
stay? (*There is no answer.*) Come on, speak up, which of you
stays?

MARIE (*officiously*). She'll lose her job if she stays.

LILIOM. Who will?

MARIE. Julie. She has to be back by seven o'clock.

LILIOM. Is that true? Will they discharge you if you're not back on time?

JULIE. Yes.

LILIOM. Well, wasn't I discharged?

JULIE. Yes — you were discharged, too.

MARIE. Julie, shall I go?

JULIE. I — can't tell you what to do.

MARIE. All right — stay if you like.

LILIOM. You'll be discharged if you do?

MARIE. Shall I go, Julie?

JULIE (*embarrassed*). Why do you keep asking me that?

MARIE. You know best what to do.

JULIE (*profoundly moved; slowly*). It's all right, Marie, you can go home.

MARIE (*exits reluctantly, but comes back, and says uncertainly*). Goodnight.

> (*She waits a moment to see if* JULIE *will follow her.* JULIE *does not move.* MARIE *exits. Meantime it has grown quite dark. During the following scene the gas-lamps far in the distance are lighted one by one.* LILIOM *and* JULIE *sit on the bench. From afar, very faintly, comes the music of a calliope. But the music is intermittently heard; now it breaks off, now it resumes again, as if it came down on a fitful wind. Blending with it are the sounds of human voices, now loud, now soft; the blare of a toy trumpet; the confused noises of the show booths. It grows progressively darker until the end of the scene. There is no moonlight. The spring iridescence glows in the deep blue sky.*)

LILIOM. Now we're both discharged. (*She does not answer. From now on they speak gradually lower and lower until the end of the scene, which is played almost in whispers. Whistles softly, then.*) Have you had your supper?

JULIE. No.

LILIOM. Want to go eat something at the Garden?

JULIE. No.

LILIOM. Anywhere else?

JULIE. No.

LILIOM (*whistles softly, then*). You don't come to this park very often, do you? I've only seen you three times. Been here oftener than that?

JULIE. Oh, yes.

LILIOM. Did you see me?

JULIE. Yes.

LILIOM. And did you know I was Liliom?

JULIE. They told me.

LILIOM (*whistles softly, then*). Have you got a sweetheart?

JULIE. No.

LILIOM. Don't lie to me.

JULIE. I haven't. If I had, I'd tell you. I've never had one.

LILIOM. What an awful liar you are. I've got a good mind to go away and leave you here.

JULIE. I've never had one.

LILIOM. Tell that to someone else.

JULIE (*reproachfully*). Why do you insist I have?

LILIOM. Because you stayed here with me the first time I asked you to. You know your way around, you do.

JULIE. No, I don't, Mister Liliom.

LILIOM. I suppose you'll tell me you don't know why you're sitting here — like this, in the dark, alone with me —— You wouldn't 'a' stayed so quick, if you hadn't done it before — with some soldier, maybe. This isn't the first time. You wouldn't have been so ready to stay if it was — what *did* you stay for, anyhow?

JULIE. So you wouldn't be left alone.

LILIOM. Alone! God, you're dumb! I don't need to be alone. I can have all the girls I want. Not only servant girls like you, but cooks and governesses, even French girls. I could have twenty of them if I wanted to.

JULIE. I know, Mister Liliom.

LILIOM. What do you know?

JULIE. That all the girls are in love with you. But that's not why *I* stayed. I stayed because you've been so good to me.

LILIOM. Well, then you can go home.

JULIE. I don't want to go home now.

LILIOM. And what if I go away and leave you sitting here?

JULIE. If you did, I wouldn't go home.

LILIOM. Do you know what you remind me of? A sweetheart I had once — I'll tell you how I met her —— One night, at closing time, we had put out the lights in the carousel, and just as I was ——

(*He is interrupted by the entrance of two plainclothes policemen. They take their stations on either side of the bench. They are police, searching the park for vagabonds.*)

FIRST POLICEMAN. What are you doing there?

LILIOM. Me?

SECOND POLICEMAN. Stand up when you're spoken to!

                              (*He taps* LILIOM *imperatively on the shoulder.*)

FIRST POLICEMAN. What's your name?

LILIOM. Andreas Zavoczki.   (JULIE *begins to weep softly.*)

SECOND POLICEMAN. Stop your bawling. We're not goin' to eat you. We are only making our rounds.

FIRST POLICEMAN. See that he doesn't get away. (THE SECOND POLICEMAN *steps closer to* LILIOM.) What's your business?

LILIOM. Barker and bouncer.

SECOND POLICEMAN. They call him Liliom, Chief. We've had him up a couple of times.

FIRST POLICEMAN. So that's who you are! Who do you work for now?

LILIOM. I work for the widow Muskat.

FIRST POLICEMAN. What are you hanging around here for?

LILIOM. We're just sitting here — me and this girl.

FIRST POLICEMAN. Your sweetheart?

LILIOM. No.

FIRST POLICEMAN (*to* JULIE). And who are you?

JULIE. Julie Zeller.

FIRST POLICEMAN. Servant girl?

JULIE. Maid of All Work for Mister Georg Breier, Number Twenty Damjanovitsch Street.

FIRST POLICEMAN. Show your hands.

SECOND POLICEMAN (*after examining* JULIE's *hand*). Servant girl.

FIRST POLICEMAN. Why aren't you at home? What are you doing out here with him?

JULIE. This is my day out, sir.

FIRST POLICEMAN. It would be better for you if you didn't spend it sitting around with a fellow like this.

SECOND POLICEMAN. They'll be disappearing in the bushes as soon as we turn our backs.

FIRST POLICEMAN. He's only after your money. We know this fine fellow. He picks up you silly servant girls and takes what money you have. Tomorrow you'll probably be coming around to report him. If you do, I'll throw you out.

JULIE. I haven't any money, sir.

FIRST POLICEMAN. Do you hear that, Liliom?

LILIOM. I'm not looking for her money.

SECOND POLICEMAN (*nudging him warningly*). Keep your mouth shut.

FIRST POLICEMAN. It is my duty to warn you, my child, what kind of company you're in. He makes a specialty of servant girls. That's why he works in a carousel. He gets hold of a girl, promises to marry her, then he takes her money and her ring.

JULIE. But I haven't got a ring.

SECOND POLICEMAN. You're not to talk unless you're asked a question.

FIRST POLICEMAN. You be thankful that I'm warning you. It's nothing to me what you do. I'm not your father, thank God. But I'm telling you what kind of a fellow he is. By tomorrow morning you'll be coming around to us to report him. Now you be sensible and go home. You needn't be afraid of him. This officer will take you home if you're afraid.

JULIE. Do I *have* to go?

FIRST POLICEMAN. No, you don't *have* to go.

JULIE. Then I'll stay, sir.

FIRST POLICEMAN. Well, you've been warned.

JULIE. Yes, sir. Thank you, sir.

FIRST POLICEMAN. Come on, Berkovics.

(*The* POLICEMEN *exit.* JULIE *and* LILIOM *sit on the bench again. There is a brief pause.*)

JULIE. Well, and what then?

LILIOM (*fails to understand*). Huh?

JULIE. You were beginning to tell me a story.

LILIOM. Me?

JULIE. Yes, about a sweetheart. You said, one night, just as they were putting out the lights of the carousel —— That's as far as you got.

LILIOM. Oh, yes, yes, just as the lights were going out, someone came along — a little girl with a big shawl — you know —— She came — eh — from —— Say — tell me — ain't you — that is, ain't you at all — afraid of me? The officer told you what kind of a fellow I am — and that I'd take your money away from you ——

JULIE. You couldn't take it away — I haven't got any. But if I had — I'd — I'd give it to you — I'd give it all to you.

LILIOM. You would?

JULIE. If you asked me for it.

LILIOM. Have you ever had a fellow you gave money to?

JULIE. No.

LILIOM. Haven't you ever had a sweetheart?

JULIE. No.

LILIOM. Someone you used to go walking with. You've had one like that?

JULIE. Yes.

LILIOM. A soldier?

JULIE. He came from the same village I did.

LILIOM. That's what all the soldiers say. Where *do* you come from, anyway?

JULIE. Not far from here.   (*There is a pause.*)

LILIOM. Were you in love with him?

JULIE. Why do you keep asking me that all the time, Mister Liliom? I wasn't in love with him. We only went walking together.

LILIOM. Where did you walk?

JULIE. In the park.

LILIOM. And your virtue? Where did you lose that?

JULIE. I haven't got any virtue.

LILIOM. Well, you had once.

JULIE. No, I never had. I'm a respectable girl.

LILIOM. Yes, but you gave the soldier something.

JULIE. Why do you question me like that, Mister Liliom?

LILIOM. Did you give him something?

JULIE. You have to. But I didn't love him.

LILIOM. Do you love me?

JULIE. No, Mister Liliom.

LILIOM. Then why do you stay here with me?

JULIE. Um — nothing.

(*There is a pause. The music from afar is plainly heard.*)

LILIOM. Want to dance?

JULIE. No. I have to be very careful.

LILIOM. Of what?

JULIE. My — character.

LILIOM. Why?

JULIE. Because I'm never going to marry. If I was going to marry, it would be different. Then I wouldn't need to worry so much about my character. It doesn't make any difference if you're married. But I shan't marry — and that's why I've got to take care to be a respectable girl.

LILIOM. Suppose I were to say to you — I'll marry you.

JULIE. You?

LILIOM. That frightens you, doesn't it? You're thinking of what the officer said and you're afraid.

JULIE. No, I'm not, Mister Liliom. I don't pay any attention to what he said.

LILIOM. But you wouldn't dare to marry anyone like me, would you?

JULIE. I know that — that — if I loved anyone — it wouldn't make any difference to me what he — even if I died for it.

LILIOM. But you wouldn't marry a rough guy like me — that is — eh — if you loved me ——

JULIE. Yes, I would — if I loved you, Mister Liliom.

(*There is a pause.*)

LILIOM (*whispers*). Well — you just said — didn't you? — that you don't love me. Well, why don't you go home then?

JULIE. It's too late now, they'd all be asleep.

LILIOM. Locked out?

JULIE. Certainly. (*They are silent awhile.*)

LILIOM. I think — that even a lowdown good-for-nothing — can make a man of himself.

JULIE. Certainly.

> (*They are silent again. A lamplighter crosses the stage, lights the lamp over the bench, and exits.*)

LILIOM. Are you hungry?

JULIE. No.   (*Another pause.*)

LILIOM. Suppose — you had some money — and I took it from you?

JULIE. Then you could take it, that's all.

LILIOM (*after another brief silence*). All I have to do — is go back to her — that Muskat woman — she'll be glad to get me back — then I'd be earning my wages again.

> (*She is silent. The twilight folds darker about them.*)

JULIE (*very softly*). Don't go back — to her ——   (*Pause.*)

LILIOM. There are a lot of acacia trees around here.   (*Pause.*)

JULIE. Don't go back to her —— .   (*Pause.*)

LILIOM. She'd take me back the minute I asked her. I know why — she knows, too ——   (*Pause.*)

JULIE. I can smell them, too — acacia blossoms ——

> (*There is a pause. Some blossoms drift down from the tree-top to the bench. LILIOM picks one up and smells it.*)

LILIOM. White acacias!

JULIE (*after a brief pause*). The wind brings them down.

> (*They are silent. There is a long pause before*

THE CURTAIN FALLS

SCENE II

A photographer's "studio," operated by the HOLLUNDERS, *on the fringe of the park. It is a dilapidated hovel. The general entrance is back left. Back right there is a window with a sofa before it. The outlook is on the amusement park with perhaps a small Ferris wheel or the scaffolding of a "scenic-railway" in the background.*

The door to the kitchen is up left and a black-curtained entrance to the dark-room is down left. Just in front of the dark-room stands the camera on its tripod. Against the back wall, between the door and window, stands the inevitable photographer's background-screen, ready to be wheeled into place.

It is forenoon. When the curtain rises, MARIE *and* JULIE *are discovered.*

MARIE. And *he* beat up Hollinger?

JULIE. Yes, he gave him an awful licking.

MARIE. But Hollinger is bigger than he is.

JULIE. He licked him just the same. It isn't size that counts, you know, it's cleverness. And Liliom's awful quick.

MARIE. And then he was arrested?

JULIE. Yes, they arrested him, but they let him go the next day. That makes twice in the two months we've been living here that Liliom's been arrested and let go again.

MARIE. Why do they let him go?

JULIE. Because he is innocent.

(MOTHER HOLLUNDER, *a very old woman, sharp-tongued, but in reality quite warm-hearted beneath her formidable exterior, enters at back carrying a few sticks of firewood, and scolding, half to herself.*)

MOTHER HOLLUNDER. Always wanting something, but never willing to work for it. He won't work, and he won't steal, but he'll use up a poor old widow's last bit of firewood. He'll do that cheerfully enough! A big, strong lout like that lying around all day resting his lazy bones! He ought to be ashamed to look decent people in the face.

JULIE. I'm sorry, Mother Hollunder...

MOTHER HOLLUNDER. Sorry! Better be sorry the lazy good-for-nothing ain't in jail where he belongs instead of in the way of honest, hard-working people. (*She exits into the kitchen.*)

MARIE. Who's that?

JULIE. Mrs. Hollunder — my aunt. This is her (*with a sweeping gesture that takes in the camera, dark-room and screen*) studio. She lets us live here for nothing.

MARIE. What's she fetching the wood for?

JULIE. She brings us everything we need. If it weren't for her I don't know what would become of us. She's a good-hearted soul even if her tongue is sharp. (*There is a pause.*)

MARIE (*shyly*). Do you know — I've found out. He's not a soldier.

JULIE. Do you still see him?

MARIE. Oh, yes.

JULIE. Often?

MARIE. Very often. He's asked me ——

JULIE. To marry you?

MARIE. To marry me.

JULIE. You see — that proves he isn't a soldier.

(*There is another pause.*)

MARIE (*abashed, yet a bit boastfully*). Do you know what I'm doing — I'm flirting with him.

JULIE. Flirting?

MARIE. Yes. He asks me to go to the park — and I say I can't go. Then he coaxes me, and promises me a new scarf for my head if I go. But I don't go — even then... So then he walks all the way home with me — and I bid him good-night at the door.

JULIE. Is that what you call flirting?

MARIE. Um-hm! It's sinful, but it's so *thrilling*.

JULIE. Do you ever quarrel?

MARIE (*grandly*). Only when our Passionate Love surges up.

JULIE. Your passionate love?

MARIE. Yes... He takes my hand and we walk along together. Then he wants to swing hands, but I won't let him. I say: "Don't swing my hand"; and he says, "Don't be so stubborn." And then he tries to swing my hand again, but still I don't let him. And for a long time I don't let him — until in the end I let him. Then we walk along swinging hands — up and down, up and down — just like this. *That* is Passionate Love. It's sinful, but it's awfully *thrilling*.

JULIE. You're happy, aren't you?

MARIE. Happier than — anything —— But the most beautiful thing on earth is Ideal Love.

JULIE. What kind is that?

MARIE. Daylight comes about three in the morning this time of the year. When we've been up that long we're all through with flirting and Passionate Love — and then our Ideal Love comes to the surface. It comes like this: I'll be sitting on the bench and Wolf, he holds my hand tight — and he puts his cheek against my cheek and we don't talk... we just sit there very quiet... And after a while he gets sleepy, and his head sinks down, and he falls asleep... but even in his sleep he holds tight to my hand. And I — I sit perfectly still just looking around me and taking long, deep breaths — for by that time it's morning and the trees and flowers are fresh with dew. But Wolf doesn't smell anything because he's so fast asleep. And I get awfully sleepy myself, but I don't sleep. And we sit like that for a long time. That is Ideal Love ——

(*There is a long pause.*)

JULIE (*regretfully; uneasily*). He went out last night and he hasn't come home yet.

MARIE. Here are sixteen Kreuzer. It was supposed to be carfare to take my young lady to the conservatory — eight there and eight back — but I made her walk. Here — save it with the rest.

JULIE. This makes three gulden, forty-six.

MARIE. Three gulden, forty-six.

JULIE. He won't work at all.

MARIE. Too lazy?

JULIE. No. He never learned a trade, you see, and he can't just go and be a day-laborer — so he just does nothing.

MARIE. That ain't right.

JULIE. No. Have the Breiers got a new maid yet?

MARIE. They've had three since you left. You know, Wolf's going to take a new job. He's going to work for the city. He'll get rent free, too.

JULIE. He won't go back to work at the carousel either. I ask him why, but he won't tell me —— Last Monday he hit me.

MARIE. Did you hit him back?

JULIE. No.

MARIE. Why don't you leave him?

JULIE. I don't want to.

MARIE. I would. I'd leave him. (*There is a strained silence.*)

MOTHER HOLLUNDER (*enters, carrying a pot of water; muttering aloud*). He can play cards, all right. He can fight, too; and take money from poor servant girls. And the police turn their heads the other way —— The carpenter was here.

JULIE. Is that water for the soup?

MOTHER HOLLUNDER. The carpenter was here. There's a *man* for you! Dark, handsome, lots of hair, a respectable widower with two children — and money, and a good paying business.

JULIE (*to* MARIE). It's three gulden sixty-six, not forty-six.

MARIE. Yes, that's what I make it — sixty-six.

MOTHER HOLLUNDER. He wants to take her out of this and marry her. This is the fifth time he's been here. He has two children, but ——

JULIE. Please don't bother, Aunt Hollunder, I'll get the water myself.

MOTHER HOLLUNDER. He's waiting outside now.

JULIE. Send him away.

MOTHER HOLLUNDER. He'll only come back again — and first thing you know that vagabond will get jealous and there'll be a fight. (*Goes out, muttering.*) Oh, he's ready enough to fight, he is. Strike a poor little girl like that! Ought to be ashamed of himself! And the police just let him go on doing as he pleases. (*Still scolding, she exits at back.*)

MARIE. A carpenter wants to marry you?

JULIE. Yes.

MARIE. Why don't you?

JULIE. Because ——

MARIE. Liliom doesn't support you, and he beats you — he thinks he can do whatever he likes just because he's Liliom. He's a bad one.

JULIE. He's not really bad.

MARIE. That night you sat on the bench together — he was gentle then.

JULIE. Yes, he was gentle.

MARIE. And afterwards he got wild again.

JULIE. Afterwards he got wild — sometimes. But that night on the bench... he was gentle. He's gentle now, sometimes, very gentle. After supper, when he stands there and listens to the music of the carousel, something comes over him — and he is gentle.

MARIE. Does he say anything?

JULIE. He doesn't say anything. He gets thoughtful and very quiet, and his big eyes stare straight ahead of him.

MARIE. Into your eyes?

JULIE. Not exactly. He's unhappy because he isn't working. That's really why he hit me on Monday.

MARIE. That's a fine reason for hitting you! Beats his wife because he isn't working, the ruffian!

JULIE. It preys on his mind ——

MARIE. Did he hurt you?

JULIE (*very eagerly*). Oh, no.

MRS. MUSKAT (*enters haughtily*). Good-morning. Is Liliom home?

JULIE. No.

MRS. MUSKAT. Gone out?

JULIE. He hasn't come home yet.

MRS. MUSKAT. I'll wait for him. (*She sits down.*)

MARIE. You've got a lot of gall — to come here.

MRS MUSKAT. Are you the lady of the house, my dear? Better look out or you'll get a slap in the mouth.

MARIE. How dare you set foot in Julie's house?

MRS. MUSKAT (*to* JULIE). Pay no attention to her, my child. You know what brings me here. That vagabond, that good-for-nothing, I've come to give him his bread and butter back.

MARIE. He's not dependent on you for his bread.

MRS. MUSKAT (*to* JULIE). Just ignore her, my child. She's just ignorant.

MARIE (*going*). Good-bye.

JULIE. Good-bye.

MARIE (*in the doorway, calling back*). Sixty-six.

JULIE. Yes, sixty-six.

MARIE. Good-bye. (*She exits.* JULIE *starts to go toward the kitchen.*)

MRS. MUSKAT. I paid him a krone a day, and on Sunday a gulden. And he got all the beer and cigars he wanted from the customers. (JULIE *pauses on the threshold, but does not answer.*) And he'd rather starve than beg my pardon. Well, I don't insist on that. I'll take him back without it. (JULIE *does not answer.*) The fact is the people ask for him — and, you see, I've got to consider business first. It's nothing to me if he starves. I wouldn't be here at all, if it wasn't for business ——

(She pauses, for LILIOM *and* FICSUR *have entered.)*

JULIE. Mrs. Muskat is here.

LILIOM. I see she is.

JULIE. You might say good-morning.

LILIOM. What for? And what do *you* want, anyhow?

JULIE. I don't want anything.

LILIOM. Then keep your mouth shut. Next thing you'll be starting to nag again about my being out all night and out of work and living on your relations ——

JULIE. I'm not saying anything.

LILIOM. But it's all on the tip of your tongue — I know you — now don't start or you'll get another.

> *(He paces angrily up and down. They are all a bit afraid of him, and shrink and look away as he passes them. FICSUR shambles from place to place, his eyes cast down as if he were searching for something on the floor.)*

MRS. MUSKAT *(suddenly, to* FICSUR). You're always dragging him out to play cards and drink with you. I'll have you locked up, I will.

FICSUR. I don't want to talk to you. You're too common.

> *(He goes out by the door at back and lingers there in plain view. There is a pause.)*

JULIE. Mrs. Muskat is here.

LILIOM. Well, why doesn't she open her mouth, if she has anything to say?

MRS. MUSKAT. Why do you go around with this man, Ficsur? He'll get you mixed up in one of his robberies first thing you know.

LILIOM. What's it to you who I go with? I do what I please. What do you want?

MRS. MUSKAT. You know what I want.

LILIOM. No, I don't.

MRS. MUSKAT. What do you suppose I want? Think I've come just to pay a social call?

LILIOM. Do I owe you anything?

MRS. MUSKAT. Yes, you do — but that's not what I came for. You're a fine one to come to for money! You earn so much these days! You know very well what I'm here for.

LILIOM. You've got Hollinger at the carousel, haven't you?

MRS. MUSKAT. Sure I have.

LILIOM. Well, what else do you want? He's as good as I am.

MRS. MUSKAT. You're quite right, my boy. He's every bit as good as you are. I'd not dream of letting him go. But one isn't enough any more. There's work enough for two ——

LILIOM. One was enough when *I* was there.

MRS. MUSKAT. Well, I might let Hollinger go ——

LILIOM. Why let him go, if he's so good?

MRS. MUSKAT (*shrugs her shoulders*). Yes, he's good.

(*Not once until now has she looked at* LILIOM.)

LILIOM (*to* JULIE). Ask your aunt if I can have a cup of coffee. (JULIE *exits into the kitchen.*) So Hollinger is good, is he?

MRS. MUSKAT (*crosses to him and looks him in the face*). Why don't you stay home and sleep at night? You're a sight to look at.

LILIOM. He's good, is he?

MRS. MUSKAT. Push your hair back from your forehead.

LILIOM. Let my hair be. It's nothing to you.

MRS. MUSKAT. All right. But if I'd told you to let it hang down over your eyes you'd have pushed it back — I hear you've been beating her, this — this ——

LILIOM. None of your business.

MRS. MUSKAT. You're a fine fellow! Beating a skinny little thing like that! If you're tired of her, leave her, but there's no use beating the poor ——

LILIOM. Leave her, eh? You'd like that, wouldn't you?

MRS. MUSKAT. Don't flatter yourself. (*Quite embarrassed.*) Serves me right, too. If I had any sense I wouldn't have run after you —— My God, the things one must do for the sake of business! If I could only sell the carousel I wouldn't be sitting here.... Come, Liliom, if you have any sense, you'll come back. I'll pay you well.

LILIOM. The carousel is crowded just the same... *without me?*

MRS. MUSKAT. Crowded, yes — but it's not the same.

LILIOM. Then you admit that you *do* miss me.

MRS. MUSKAT. Miss you? Not I. But the silly girls miss you. They're always asking for you. Well, are you going to be sensible and come back?

LILIOM. And leave — her?

MRS. MUSKAT. You beat her, don't you?

LILIOM. No, I don't beat her. What's all this damn fool talk about beating her? I hit her once — that was all — and now the whole city seems to be talking about it. You don't call that beating her, do you?

MRS. MUSKAT. All right, all right. I take it back. I don't want to get mixed up in it.

LILIOM. Beating her! As if I'd beat her ——

MRS. MUSKAT. I can't make out why you're so concerned about her. You've been married to her two months — it's plain to see that you're sick of it — and out there is the carousel — and the show booths — and money — and you'd throw it all away. For what? Heavens, how can anyone be such a fool? (*Looks at him appraisingly.*) Where have you been all night? You look awful.

LILIOM. It's no business of yours.

MRS. MUSKAT. You never used to look like that. This life is telling on you. (*Pauses.*) Do you know — I've got a new organ.

LILIOM (*softly*). I know.

MRS. MUSKAT. How did you know?

LILIOM. You can hear it — from here.

MRS. MUSKAT. It's a good one, eh?

LILIOM (*wistfully*). Very good. Fine. It roars and snorts — so fine.

MRS. MUSKAT. You should hear it close by — it's heavenly. Even the carousel seems to know... it goes quicker. I got rid of those two horses — you know, the ones with the broken ears?

LILIOM. What have you put in their place?

MRS. MUSKAT. Guess.

LILIOM. Zebras?

MRS. MUSKAT. No — an automobile.

LILIOM (*transported*). An automobile ——

MRS. MUSKAT. Yes. If you've got any sense you'll come back. What good are you doing here? Out there is your *art*, the only thing you're fit for. You are an artist, not a respectable married man.

LILIOM. *Leave* her — this little ——

MRS. MUSKAT. She'll be better off. She'll go back and be a servant girl again. As for you — you're an artist and you belong among artists. All the beer you want, cigars, a krone a day and a gulden on Sunday, and the girls, Liliom, the girls — I've always treated you right, haven't I? I bought you a watch, and ——

LILIOM. She's not that kind. She'd never be a servant girl again.

MRS. MUSKAT. I suppose you think she'd kill herself. Don't worry. Heavens, if every girl was to commit suicide just because her —— (Finishes with a gesture.)

LILIOM (stares at her a moment, considering, then with sudden, smiling animation). So the people don't like Hollinger?

MRS. MUSKAT. You know very well they don't, you rascal.

LILIOM. Well ——

MRS. MUSKAT. You've always been happy at the carousel. It's a great life — pretty girls and beer and cigars and music — a great life and an easy one. I'll tell you what — come back and I'll give you a ring that used to belong to my dear departed husband. Well, will you come?

LILIOM. She's not that kind. She'd never be a servant girl again. But — but — for my part — if I decide — that needn't make any difference. I can go on living with her even if I do go back to my art ——

MRS. MUSKAT. My God!

LILIOM. What's the matter?

MRS. MUSKAT. Who ever heard of a married man — I suppose you think all girls would be pleased to know that you were running home to your wife every night. It's ridiculous! When the people found out they'd laugh themselves sick ——

LILIOM. I know what you want.

MRS. MUSKAT (refuses to meet his gaze). You flatter yourself.

LILIOM. You'll give me that ring, too?

MRS. MUSKAT (pushes the hair back from his forehead). Yes.

LILIOM. I'm not happy in this house.

MRS. MUSKAT (still stroking his hair). Nobody takes care of you.

(*They are silent. JULIE enters, carrying a cup of coffee. MRS. MUSKAT removes her hand from LILIOM's head. There is a pause.*)

LILIOM. Do you want anything?

JULIE. No.   (*There is a pause. She exits slowly into the kitchen.*)

MRS. MUSKAT. The old woman says there is a carpenter, a widower, who ——

LILIOM. I know — I know ——

JULIE (*re-entering*). Liliom, before I forget, I have something to tell you.

LILIOM. All right.

JULIE. I've been wanting to tell you — in fact, I was going to tell you yesterday ——

LILIOM. Go ahead.

JULIE. But I must tell you alone — if you'll come in — it will only take a minute.

LILIOM. Don't you see I'm busy now? Here I am talking business and you interrupt with ——

JULIE. It'll only take a minute.

LILIOM. Get out of here, or ——

JULIE. But I tell you it will only take a minute ——

LILIOM. Will you get out of here?

JULIE (*courageously*). No.

LILIOM (*rising*). What's that!

JULIE. No.

MRS. MUSKAT (*rises, too*). Now don't start fighting. I'll go out and look at the photographs in the show case a while and come back later for your answer.   (*She exits at back.*)

JULIE. You can hit me again if you like — don't look at me like that. I'm not afraid of you.... I'm not afraid of anyone. I told you I had something to tell you.

LILIOM. Well, out with it — quick.

JULIE. I can't tell you so quick. Why don't you drink your coffee?

LILIOM. Is that what you wanted to tell me?

JULIE. No. By the time you've drunk your coffee I'll have told you.

LILIOM (*gets the coffee and sips it*). Well?

JULIE. Yesterday my head ached — and you asked me ——

LILIOM. Yes ——

JULIE. Well — you see — that's what it is ——

LILIOM. Are you sick?

JULIE. No.... But you wanted to know what my headaches came from — and you said I seemed — changed.

LILIOM. Did I? I guess I meant the carpenter.

JULIE. I've been — what? The carpenter? No. It's something entirely different — it's awful hard to tell — but you'll have to know sooner or later — I'm not a bit — scared — because it's a perfectly natural thing ——

LILIOM (*puts the coffee cup on the table*). What?

JULIE. When — when a man and woman — live together ——

LILIOM. Yes.

JULIE. I'm going to have a baby.

    (*She exits swiftly at back. There is a pause. FICSUR appears at the open window and looks in.*)

LILIOM. Ficsur! (FICSUR *sticks his head in.*) Say, Ficsur — Julie is going to have a baby.

FICSUR. Yes? What of it?

LILIOM. Nothing. (*Suddenly.*) Get out of here.

    (FICSUR's *head is quickly withdrawn.*)

(MRS. MUSKAT *re-enters.*)

MRS. MUSKAT. Has she gone?

LILIOM. Yes.

MRS. MUSKAT. I might as well give you ten kronen in advance. (*Opens her purse.* LILIOM *takes up his coffee cup.*) Here you are. (*She proffers some coins.* LILIOM *ignores her.*) Why don't you take it?

LILIOM (*very nonchalantly, his cup poised, ready to drink*). Go home, Mrs. Muskat.

MRS. MUSKAT. What's the matter with you?

LILIOM. Go home (*sips his coffee*) and let me finish my coffee in peace. Don't you see I'm at breakfast?

MRS. MUSKAT. Have you gone crazy?

LILIOM. Will you get out of here? (*Turns to her threateningly.*)

MRS. MUSKAT (*restoring the coins to her purse*). I'll never speak to you again as long as you live.

LILIOM. That worries me a lot.

MRS. MUSKAT. Good-bye!

LILIOM. Good-bye. (*As she exits, he calls.*) Ficsur! (FICSUR *enters.*) Tell me, Ficsur. You said you knew a way to get a whole lot of money ——

FICSUR. Sure I do.

LILIOM. How much?

FICSUR. More than you ever had in your life before. You leave it to an old hand like me.

MOTHER HOLLUNDER (*enters from the kitchen*). In the morning he must have his coffee, and at noon his soup, and in the evening coffee again — and plenty of firewood — and I'm expected to furnish it all. Give me back my cup and saucer.

    (*The show booths of the amusement park have opened for business. The familiar noises begin to sound; clear above them all, but far in the distance, sounds the organ of the carousel.*)

LILIOM. Now, Aunt Hollunder.

    (*From now until the fall of the curtain it is apparent that the sound of the organ makes him more and more uneasy.*)

MOTHER HOLLUNDER. And you, you vagabond, get out of here this minute or I'll call my son ——

FICSUR. I have nothing to do with the likes of him. He's too common.   (*But he slinks out at back.*)

LILIOM. Aunt Hollunder!

MOTHER HOLLUNDER. What now?

LILIOM. When your son was born — when you brought him into the world ——

MOTHER HOLLUNDER. Well?

LILIOM. Nothing.

MOTHER HOLLUNDER (*muttering as she exits*). Sleep it off, you good-for-nothing lout. Drink and play cards all night long — that's all you know how to do — and take the bread out of poor people's mouths — you can do that, too.   (*She exits.*)

LILIOM. Ficsur!

FICSUR (*at the window*). Julie's going to have a baby. You told me before.

LILIOM. This scheme — about the cashier of the leather factory — there's money in it ——

FICSUR. Lots of money — but — it takes two to pull it off.

LILIOM (*meditatively*). Yes. (*Uneasily.*) All right, Ficsur. Go away — and come back later.

> (FICSUR *vanishes. The organ in the distant carousel drones incessantly.* LILIOM *listens awhile, then goes to the door and calls.*)

LILIOM. Aunt Hollunder! (*With naïve joy.*) Julie's going to have a baby. (*Then he goes to the window, jumps on the sofa, looks out. Suddenly, in a voice that overtops the droning of the organ, he shouts as if addressing the far-off carousel.*) I'm going to be a father.

JULIE (*enters from the kitchen*). Liliom! What's the matter? What's happened?

LILIOM (*coming down from the sofa*). Nothing.

> (*Throws himself on the sofa, buries his face in the cushion.* JULIE *watches him a moment, comes over to him and covers him with a shawl. Then she goes on tiptoe to the door at back and remains standing in the doorway, looking out and listening to the droning of the organ.*)

THE CURTAIN FALLS

SCENE III

The setting is the same, later that afternoon. LILIOM *is sitting opposite* FICSUR, *who is teaching him a song.* JULIE *hovers in the background, engaged in some household task.*

FICSUR. Listen, now. Here's the third verse. (*Sings hoarsely.*)

> "Look out, look out, my pretty lad,
> The damn police are on your trail;
> The nicest girl you ever had
> Has now commenced to weep and wail:
> Look out, here comes the damn police,
> The damn police, —
> The damn police,
> Look out, here comes the damn police,
> They'll get you every time."

LILIOM (*sings*).

> "Look out, look out, my pretty lad,
> The damn police ——"

FICSUR, LILIOM (*sing together*).

> "*are on your trail;*
> *The nicest girl you ever had*
> *Has now commenced to weep and wail.*"

LILIOM (*alone*).

> "*Look out, here comes the damn police,*
> *The damn police,*
> *The damn police* ——"

(JULIE, *troubled and uneasy, looks from one to the other, then exits into the kitchen.*)

FICSUR (*when she has gone, comes quickly over to* LILIOM *and speaks furtively*). As you go down Franzen Street you come to the railroad embankment. Beyond that — all the way to the leather factory — there's not a thing in sight, not even a watchman's hut.

LILIOM. And does he always come that way?

FICSUR. Yes. Not along the embankment, but down below along the path across the fields. Since last year he's been going alone. Before that he always used to have someone with him.

LILIOM. Every Saturday?

FICSUR. Every Saturday.

LILIOM. And the money? Where does he keep it?

FICSUR. In a leather bag. The whole week's pay for the workmen at the factory.

LILIOM. Much?

FICSUR. Sixteen thousand kronen. Quite a haul, what?

LILIOM. What's his name?

FICSUR. Linzman. He's a Jew.

LILIOM. The cashier?

FICSUR. Yes — but when he gets a knife between his ribs — or if I smash his skull for him — he won't be a cashier any more.

LILIOM. Does he have to be killed?

FICSUR. No, he doesn't *have* to be. He can give up the money *without* being killed — but most of these cashiers are peculiar — they'd rather be killed.

(JULIE *re-enters, pretends to get something on the other side of the room, then exits at back. During the ensuing dialogue she keeps coming in and out in the same way, showing plainly that she is suspicious and anxious. She attempts to overhear what they are saying and, in spite of their caution, does catch a word here and there, which adds to her disquiet. FICSUR, catching sight of her, abruptly changes the conversation.*)

FICSUR. And the next verse is:

> "*And when you're in the prison cell*
> *They'll feed you bread and water.*"

FICSUR AND LILIOM (*sing together*).

> "*They'll make your little sweetheart tell*
> *Them all the things you brought her.*
> *Look out, here comes the damn police,*
> *The damn police,*
> *The damn police.*
> *Look out, here comes the damn police*
> *They'll get you every time.*"

LILIOM (*sings alone*).

> "*And when you're in the prison cell*
> *They'll feed you bread and water* ——"

(*Breaks off, as* JULIE *exits.*)

And when it's done, do we start right off for America?

FICSUR. No.

LILIOM. What then?

FICSUR. We bury the money for six months. That's the usual time. And after the sixth month we dig it up again.

LILIOM. And then?

FICSUR. Then you go on living just as usual for six months more — you don't touch a heller of the money.

LILIOM. In six months the baby will be born.

FICSUR. Then we'll take the baby with us, too. Three months before the time you'll go to work so as to be able to say you saved up your wages to get to America.

LILIOM. Which of us goes up and talks to him?

FICSUR. One of us talks to him with his mouth and the other talks with his knife. Depends on which you'd rather do. I'll tell you what — you talk to him with your mouth.

LILIOM. Do you hear that?

FICSUR. What?

LILIOM. Outside... like the rattle of swords. (FICSUR *listens. After a pause,* LILIOM *continues.*) What do I say to him?

FICSUR. You say good-evening to him and: "Excuse me, sir; can you tell me the time?"

LILIOM. And then what?

FICSUR. By that time I'll have stuck him — and then you take *your* knife —— (*He stops as a* POLICEMAN *enters at back.*)

POLICEMAN. Good-day!

FICSUR, LILIOM (*in unison*). Good-day!

FICSUR (*calling toward the kitchen*). Hey, photographer, come out.... Here's a customer.

> (*There is a pause. The* POLICEMAN *waits.* FICSUR *sings softly.*)
>> "*And when you're in the prison cell*
>> *They'll feed you bread and water,*
>> *They'll make your little sweetheart tell*"

LILIOM, FICSUR (*sing together, low*).
>> "*Them all the things you brought her.*
>> *Look out, here comes the* ——"

(*They hum the rest so as not to let the* POLICEMAN *hear the words "the damn police." As they sing,* MRS. HOLLUNDER *and her son enter.*)

POLICEMAN. Do you make cabinet photographs?

YOUNG HOLLUNDER. Certainly, sir. (*Points to a rack of photographs on the wall.*) Take your choice, sir. Would you like one full length?

POLICEMAN. Yes, full length.

(MOTHER HOLLUNDER *pushes out the camera while her son poses the* POLICEMAN, *runs from him to the camera and back again, now altering the pose, now ducking under the black cloth and pushing the camera nearer. Meanwhile* MOTHER HOLLUNDER *has fetched a plate from the dark-room and thrust it in the camera. While this is going on,* LILIOM *and* FICSUR, *their heads together, speak in very low tones.*)

LILIOM. Belong around here?

FICSUR. Not around here.

LILIÓM. Where, then?

FICSUR. Suburban. (*There is a pause.*)

LILIOM (*bursts out suddenly in a rather grotesquely childish and over-strained lament*). O God, what a dirty life I'm leading — God, God!

FICSUR (*reassuring him benevolently*). Over in America it will be better, all right.

LILIOM. What's over there?

FICSUR (*virtuously*). Factories... industries ——

YOUNG HOLLUNDER (*to the* POLICEMAN). Now, quite still, please. One, two, three. (*Deftly removes the cover of the lens and in a few seconds restores it.*) Thank you.

MOTHER HOLLUNDER. The picture will be ready in five minutes.

POLICEMAN. Good. I'll come back in five minutes. How much do I owe you?

YOUNG HOLLUNDER (*with exaggerated deference*). You don't need to pay in advance, Mr. Commissioner.

(*The* POLICEMAN *salutes condescendingly and exits at back.* MOTHER HOLLUNDER *carries the plate into the dark-room.* YOUNG HOLLUNDER, *after pushing the camera back in place, follows her.*)

MOTHER HOLLUNDER (*muttering angrily as she passes* FICSUR *and* LILIOM). You hang around and dirty the whole place up! Why don't you go take a walk? Things are going so well with you that you have to sing, eh? (*Confronting* FICSUR *suddenly.*) Weren't you frightened sick when you saw the policeman?

FICSUR (*with loathing*). Go 'way, or I'll step on you.

(*She exits into the dark-room.*)

LILIOM. They like Hollinger at the carousel?

FICSUR. I should say they do.

LILIOM. Did you see the Muskat woman, too?

FICSUR. Sure. She takes care of Hollinger's hair.

LILIOM. Combs his hair?

FICSUR. She fixes him all up.

LILIOM. Let her fix him all she likes.

FICSUR (*urging him toward the kitchen door*). Go on. Now's your chance.

LILIOM. What for?

FICSUR. To get the knife.

LILIOM. What knife?

FICSUR. The kitchen knife. I've got a pocket-knife, but if he shows fight, we'll let him have the big knife.

LILIOM. What for? If he gets ugly, I'll bat him one over the head that'll make him squint for the rest of his life.

FICSUR. You've got to have something on you. You can't slit his throat with a bat over the head.

LILIOM. Must his throat be slit?

FICSUR. No, it *mustn't*. But if he asks for it. (*There is a pause.*) You'd like to sail on the big steamer, wouldn't you? And you want to see the factories over there, don't you? But you're not willing to inconvenience yourself a little for them.

LILIOM. If I take the knife, Julie will see me.

FICSUR. Take it so she won't see you.

LILIOM (*advances a few paces toward the kitchen. The* POLICEMAN *enters at back.* LILIOM *knocks on the door of the dark-room*). Here's the policeman!

MOTHER HOLLUNDER (*coming out*). One minute more, please. Just a minute.

    (*She re-enters the dark-room.* LILIOM *hesitates a moment, then exits into the kitchen. The* POLICEMAN *scrutinizes* FICSUR *mockingly.*)

FICSUR (*returns his stare, walks a few paces toward him, then deliberately turns his back. Suddenly he wheels around, points at the* POLICEMAN *and addresses him in a teasing, childish tone*). Christiana Street at the corner of Retti!

POLICEMAN (*amazed, self-conscious*). How do you know that?

FICSUR. I used to practice my profession in that neighborhood.

POLICEMAN. What is your profession?

FICSUR. Professor of pianola ——

    (*The* POLICEMAN *glares, aware that the man is joking with him, twirls his moustache indignantly.* YOUNG HOLLUNDER *comes out of the dark-room and gives him the finished pictures.*)

YOUNG HOLLUNDER. Here you are, sir.

    (*The* POLICEMAN *examines the photographs, pays for them, starts to go, stops, glares at* FICSUR *and exits. When he is gone,* FICSUR *goes to the doorway and looks out after him.* YOUNG HOLLUNDER *exits.* LILIOM *re-enters, buttoning his coat.*)

FICSUR (*turns, sees* LILIOM). What are you staring at?

LILIOM. I'm not staring.

FICSUR. What then are you doing?

LILIOM. I'm thinking it over.

FICSUR (*comes very close to him*). Tell me, then — what will you say to him?

LILIOM (*unsteadily*). I'll say — "Good-evening — Excuse me, sir — Can you tell me the time?" And suppose he answers me, what do I say to him?

FICSUR. He won't answer you.

LILIOM. Don't you think so?

FICSUR. No. (*Feeling for the knife under* LILIOM'S *coat.*) Where is it? Where did you put it?

LILIOM (*stonily*). Left side.

FICSUR. That's right — over your heart. (*Feels it.*) Ah — there it is — there — there's the blade — quite a big fellow, isn't it — ah, here it begins to get narrower. (*Reaches the tip of the knife.*) And here is its eye — that's what it sees with. (JULIE *enters from the kitchen, passes them slowly, watching them in silent terror, then stops.* FICSUR *nudges* LILIOM.) Sing, come on, sing!

LILIOM (*in a quavering voice*). "*Look out for the damn police.*"

FICSUR (*joining in, cheerily, loudly, marking time with the swaying of his body*). "*Look out, look out, my pretty lad.*"

LILIOM. "*— look out, my pretty lad.*"

(JULIE *goes out at back.* LILIOM'S *glance follows her. When she has gone, he turns to* FICSUR.)

LILIOM. At night — in my dreams — if his ghost comes back — what will I do then?

FICSUR. His ghost won't never come back.

LILIOM. Why not?

FICSUR. A Jew's ghost don't come back.

LILIOM. Well, then — afterwards ——

FICSUR (*impatiently*). What do you mean — afterwards?

LILIOM. In the next world — when I come up before the Lord God — what'll I say then?

FICSUR. The likes of you will never come up before Him.

LILIOM. Why not?

FICSUR. Have you ever come up before the high court?

LILIOM. No.

FICSUR. Our kind comes up before the police magistrate — and the highest we *ever* get is the criminal court.

LILIOM. Will it be the same in the next world?

FICSUR. Just the same. We'll come up before a police magistrate, same as we did in this world.

LILIOM. A police magistrate?

FICSUR. Sure. For the rich folks — the Heavenly Court. For us poor people — only a police magistrate. For the rich folks — fine music and angels. For us ——

LILIOM. For us?

FICSUR. For us, my son, there's only justice. In the next world there'll be lots of justice, yes, nothing but justice. And where there's justice, there must be police magistrates; and where there're police magistrates, people like us get ——

LILIOM (*interrupting*). Good-evening. Excuse me, sir, can you tell me the time? (*Lays his hand over his heart.*)

FICSUR. What do you put your hand there for?

LILIOM. My heart is jumping — under the knife.

FICSUR. Put it on the other side, then. (*Looks out at the sky.*) It's time we started — we'll walk slow ——

LILIOM. It's too early.

FICSUR. Come on.

(*As they are about to go,* JULIE *appears in the doorway at back, obstructing the way.*)

JULIE. Where are you going with him?

LILIOM. Where am I going with him?

JULIE. Stay home.

LILIOM. No.

JULIE. Stay home. It's going to rain soon, and you'll get wet.

FICSUR. It won't rain.

JULIE. How do you know?

FICSUR. I always get notice in advance.

JULIE. Stay home. This evening the carpenter's coming. I've asked him to give you work.

LILIOM. I'm not a carpenter.

JULIE (*more and more anxious, though she tries to conceal it*). Stay home.

Marie's coming with her intended to have their picture taken. She wants to introduce us to her intended husband.

LILIOM. I've seen enough intended husbands ——

JULIE. Stay home. Marie's bringing some money, and I'll give it all to you.

LILIOM (*approaching the door*). I'm going — for a walk — with Ficsur. We'll be right back.

JULIE (*forcing a smile to keep back her tears*). If you stay home, I'll get you a glass of beer — or wine, if you prefer.

FICSUR. Coming or not?

JULIE. I'm not angry with you any more for hitting me.

LILIOM (*gruffly, but his gruffness is simulated to hide the fact that he cannot bear the sight of her suffering*). Stand out of the way — or I'll ——· (*He clenches his fist.*) Let me out!

JULIE (*trembling*). What have you got under your coat?

LILIOM (*produces from his pocket a greasy pack of cards*). Cards.

JULIE (*trembling, speaks very low*). What's under your coat?

LILIOM. Let me out!

JULIE (*obstructing the way. Speaks quickly, eagerly, in a last effort to detain him*). Marie's intended knows about a place for a married couple without children to be caretakers of a house on Arader Street. Rent free, a kitchen of your own, and the privilege of keeping chickens ——

LILIOM. Get out of the way!

> (JULIE *stands aside.* LILIOM *exits.* FICSUR *follows him.* JULIE *remains standing meditatively in the doorway.* MOTHER HOLLUNDER *comes out of the kitchen.*)

MOTHER HOLLUNDER. I can't find my kitchen knife anywhere. Have you seen anything of it?

JULIE (*horrified*). No.

MOTHER HOLLUNDER. It was on the kitchen table just a few minutes ago. No one was in there except Liliom.

JULIE. He didn't take it.

MOTHER HOLLUNDER. No one else was in there.

JULIE. What would Liliom want with a kitchen knife?

MOTHER HOLLUNDER. He'd sell it and spend the money on drink.

JULIE. It just so happens — see how unjust you are to him — it just so happens that I went through all of Liliom's pockets just now — I wanted to see if he had any money on him. But he had nothing but a pack of cards.

MOTHER HOLLUNDER (*returns to the kitchen, grumbling*). Cards in his pocket — cards! The fine gentlemen have evidently gone off to their club to play a little game.

    (*She exits. After a pause* MARIE, *happy and beaming, appears in the doorway at back, and enters, followed by* WOLF.)

MARIE. Here we are! (*She takes* WOLF *by the hand and leads him, grinning shyly, to* JULIE, *who has turned at her call.*) Hello!

JULIE. Hello.

MARIE. Well, we're here.

JULIE. Yes.

WOLF (*bows awkwardly and extends his hand*). My name is Wolf Beifeld.

JULIE. My name is Julie Zeller.

    (*They shake hands. There is an embarrassed silence. Then, to relieve the situation,* WOLF *takes* JULIE's *hand again and shakes it vigorously.*)

MARIE. Well — this is Wolf.

WOLF. Yes.

JULIE. Yes. (*Another awkward silence.*)

MARIE. Where is Liliom?

WOLF. Yes, where is your husband?

JULIE. He's out.

MARIE. Where?

JULIE. Just for a walk.

MARIE. Is he?

JULIE. Yes.

WOLF. Oh! (*Another silence.*)

MARIE. Wolf's got a new place. After the first of the month he won't have to stand outside any more. He's going to work in a club after the first of the month.

WOLF (*apologetically*). She don't know yet how to explain these things just right — hehehe —— Beginning the first I'm to be second steward at the Burger Club — a good job, if one conducts oneself properly.

JULIE. Yes?

WOLF. The pay — is quite good — but the main thing is the tips.

When they play cards there's always a bit for the steward. The tips, I may say, amount to twenty, even thirty kronen every night.

MARIE. Yes.

WOLF. We've rented two rooms for ourselves to start with — and if things go well ——

MARIE. Then we'll buy a house in the country.

WOLF. If one only tends to business and keeps honest. Of course, in the country we'll miss the city life, but if the good Lord sends us children — it's much healthier for children in the country. (*There is a brief pause.*)

MARIE. Wolf's nice looking, isn't he?

JULIE. Yes.

MARIE. And he's a good boy, Wolf.

JULIE. Yes.

MARIE. The only thing is — he's a Jew.

JULIE. Oh, well, you can get used to that.

MARIE. Well, aren't you going to wish us luck?

JULIE. Of course I do. (*She embraces* MARIE.)

MARIE. And aren't you going to kiss Wolf, too?

JULIE. Him, too.

> (*She embraces* WOLF, *remains quite still a moment, her head resting on his shoulder.*)

WOLF. Why are you crying, my dear Mrs. ——

> (*He looks questioningly at* MARIE *over* JULIE'S *shoulder.*)

MARIE. Because she has such a good heart.

> (*She becomes sentimental, too.*)

WOLF (*touched*). We thank you for your heartfelt sympathy ——

> (*He cannot restrain his own tears. There is a pause before* MOTHER HOLLUNDER *and her son enter.* YOUNG HOLLUNDER *immediately busies himself with the camera.*)

MOTHER HOLLUNDER. Now if you don't mind, we'll do it right away, before it gets too dark. (*She leads* MARIE *and* WOLF *into position before the background-screen. Here they immediately fall into an awkward pose, smiling mechanically.*) Full length?

MARIE. Please. Both figures full length.

MOTHER HOLLUNDER. Bride and groom?

MARIE. Yes.

MOTHER HOLLUNDER, YOUNG HOLLUNDER (*speak in unison, in loud professionally expressionless tones*). The lady looks at the gentleman and the gentleman looks straight into the camera.

MOTHER HOLLUNDER (*poses first* MARIE, *then* WOLF). Now, if you please.

YOUNG HOLLUNDER (*who has crept under the black cloth, calls in muffled tones*). That's good — that's very good!

MARIE (*stonily rigid, but very happy, trying to speak without altering her expression*). Julie, dear, do we look all right?

JULIE. Yes, dear.

YOUNG HOLLUNDER. Now, if you please, hold still. I'll count up to three, and then you must hold perfectly still. (*Grasps the cover of the lens and calls threateningly.*) One — two — three!

   (*He removes the cover; there is utter silence. But as he speaks the word "one" there is heard, very faintly in the distance, the refrain of the thieves' song which* FICSUR *and* LILIOM *have been singing. The refrain continues until the fall of the curtain. As he speaks the word "three" everybody is perfectly rigid save* JULIE, *who lets her head sink slowly to the table. The distant refrain dies out.*)

THE CURTAIN FALLS

SCENE IV

   In the fields on the outskirts of the city. At back a railroad embankment crosses the stage obliquely. At center of the embankment stands a red and white signal flag, and near it a little red signal lamp which is not yet lighted. Here also a wooden stairway leads up to the embankment.

   At the foot of the embankment to the right is a pile of used railroad ties. In the background a telegraph pole, beyond it a view of trees, fences and fields; still further back a factory building and a cluster of little dwellings.

   It is six o'clock of the same afternoon. Dusk has begun to fall.

   LILIOM *and* FICSUR *are discovered on the stairway looking after the train which has just passed.*

LILIOM. Can you still hear it snort?

FICSUR. Listen! (*They watch the vanishing train.*)

LILIOM. If you put your ear on the tracks you can hear it go all the way to Vienna.

FICSUR. Huh!

LILIOM. The one that just puffed past us — it goes all the way to Vienna.

FICSUR. No further?

LILIOM. Yes — further, too. (*There is a pause.*)

FICSUR. It must be near six. (*As* LILIOM *ascends the steps.*) Where are you going?

LILIOM. Don't be afraid. I'm not giving you the slip.

FICSUR. Why should you give me the slip? That cashier has sixteen thousand kronen on him. Just be patient till he comes, then you can talk to him, nice and polite.

LILIOM. I say, "Good-evening — excuse me, sir; what time is it?"

FICSUR. Then he tells you what time it is.

LILIOM. Suppose he don't come?

FICSUR (*coming down the steps*). Nonsense! He's got to come. He pays off the workmen every Saturday. And this is Saturday, ain't it? (LILIOM *has ascended to the top of the stairway and is gazing along the tracks.*) What are you looking at up there?

LILIOM. The tracks go on and on — there's no end to them.

FICSUR. What's that to stare about?

LILIOM. Nothing — only I always look after the train. When you stand down there at night it snorts past you, and spits down.

FICSUR. Spits?

LILIOM. Yes, the engine. It spits down. And then the whole train rattles past and away — and you stand there — spat on — but it draws your eyes along with it.

FICSUR. Draws your eyes along?

LILIOM. Yes — whether you want to or not, you've got to look after it — as long as the tiniest bit of it is in sight.

FICSUR. Swell people sit in it.

LILIOM. And read newspapers.

FICSUR. And smoke cigars.

LILIOM. And inhale the smoke. (*There is a short silence.*)

FICSUR. Is he coming?

LILIOM. Not yet. (*Silence again.* LILIOM *comes down, speaks low, confidentially.*) Do you hear the telegraph wires?

FICSUR. I hear them when the wind blows.

LILIOM. Even when the wind doesn't blow you can hear them
humming, humming —— People talk through them.

FICSUR. Who?

LILIOM. Jews.

FICSUR. No — they telegraph.

LILIOM. They talk through them and from some other place
they get answered. And it all goes through the iron strings —
that's why they hum like that — they hum-m ——

FICSUR. What do they hum?

LILIOM. They hum! ninety-nine, ninety-nine. Just listen.

FICSUR. What for?

LILIOM. That sparrow's listening, too. He's cocked one eye and
looks at me as if to say: "I'd like to know what they're talking
about."

FICSUR. You're looking at a bird?

LILIOM. He's looking at me, too.

FICSUR. Listen, you're sick. There's something the matter with
you. Do you know what it is? Money. That bird has no
money, either; that's why he cocks his eye.

LILIOM. Maybe.

FICSUR. Whoever has money don't cock his eye.

LILIOM. What then does he do?

FICSUR. He does most anything he wants. But nobody works
unless he has money. We'll soon have money ourselves.

LILIOM. I say, "Good-evening. Excuse me, sir, can you tell me
what time it is!"

FICSUR. He's not coming yet. Got the cards? (LILIOM *gives him
the pack of cards*.) Got any money?

LILIOM (*takes some coins from his trousers pocket and counts*). Eleven.

FISCUR (*sits astride on the pile of ties and looks off left*). All right — eleven.

LILIOM (*sitting astride on the ties facing him*). Put it up.

FICSUR (*puts the money on the ties; rapidly shuffles the cards*). We'll
play twenty-one. I'll bank.   (*He deals deftly.*)

LILIOM (*looks at his card*). Good. I'll bet the bank.

FICSUR. Must have an ace!   (*Deals him a second card.*)

LILIOM. Another one. (*He gets another card.*) Another. (*Gets
still another.*) Over. (*Throws down his cards.* FICSUR *gathers in
the money.*) Come on!

FICSUR. Come on what! Got no more money, have you?

LILIOM. No.

FICSUR. Then the game's over — unless you want to ——

LILIOM. What?

FICSUR. Play on credit.

LILIOM. You'll trust me?

FICSUR. No — but — I'll deduct it.

LILIOM. Deduct it from what?

FICSUR. From your share of the money. If *you* win you deduct from my share.

LILIOM (*looks over his shoulder to see if the cashier is coming; nervous and ashamed*). All right. How much is bank?

FICSUR. That cashier is bringing us sixteen thousand kronen. Eight thousand of that is mine. Well, then, the bank is eight thousand.

LILIOM. Good.

FICSUR. Whoever has the most luck will have the most money.

(*He deals.*)

LILIOM. Six hundred kronen. (FICSUR *gives him another card.*) Enough.

FICSUR (*laying out his own cards*). Twenty-one. (*He shuffles rapidly.*)

LILIOM (*moves excitedly nearer to* FICSUR). Well, then, double or nothing.

FICSUR (*dealing*). Double or nothing.

LILIOM (*gets a card*). Enough.

FICSUR (*laying out his own cards*). Twenty-one. (*Shuffles rapidly again.*)

LILIOM (*in alarm*). You're not — cheating?

FICSUR. Me? Do I look like a cheat? (*Deals the cards again.*)

LILIOM (*glances nervously over his shoulder*). A thousand.

FICSUR (*nonchalantly*). Kronen?

LILIOM. Kronen. (*He gets a card.*) Another one. (*Gets another card.*) Over again!

(*Like an inexperienced gambler who is losing heavily,* LILIOM *is very nervous. He plays dazedly, wildly, irrationally. From now on it is apparent that his only thought is to win his money back.*)

FICSUR. That makes twelve hundred you owe.

LILIOM. Double or nothing. (*He gets a card. He is greatly excited.*) Another one. (*Gets another card.*) Another.

(*Throws down three cards.*)

FICSUR (*bends over and adds up the sum on the ground*). Ten — fourteen — twenty-three—— You owe two thousand, four hundred.

LILIOM. Now what?

FICSUR (*takes a card out of the deck and gives it to him*). Here's the red ace. You can play double or nothing again.

LILIOM (*eagerly*). Good. (*Gets another card.*) Enough.

FICSUR (*turns up his own cards*). Nineteen.

LILIOM. You win again. (*Almost imploring.*) Give me an ace again. Give me the green one. (*Takes a card.*) Double or nothing.

FICSUR. Not any more.

LILIOM. Why not?

FICSUR. Because if you lose you won't be able to pay. Double would be nine thousand six hundred. And you've only got eight thousand altogether.

LILIOM (*greatly excited*). That — that — I call that — a dirty trick!

FICSUR. Three thousand, two hundred. That's all you can put up.

LILIOM (*eagerly*). All right, then — three thousand, two hundred. (FICSUR *deals him a card.*) Enough.

FICSUR. I've got an ace myself. Now we'll have to take our time and squeeze 'em. (LILIOM *pushes closer to him as he takes up his cards and slowly, intently unfolds them.*) Twenty-one.

(*He quickly puts the cards in his pocket. There is a pause.*)

LILIOM. Now — now — I'll tell you now — you're a crook, a low-down ——

(*Now* LINZMAN *enters at right. He is a strong, robust, red-bearded Jew about forty years of age. At his side he carries a leather bag slung by a strap from his shoulder.* FICSUR *coughs warningly, moves to the right between* LINZMAN *and the embankment, pauses just behind* LINZMAN *and follows him.*)

LILIOM (*stands bewildered a few paces to the left of the railroad ties. He finds himself facing* LINZMAN. *Trembling in every limb*). Good-evening. Excuse me, sir, can you tell me the time?

(FICSUR *springs silently at* LINZMAN, *the little knife in his right hand. But* LINZMAN *catches* FICSUR's *right hand with his own left and forces* FICSUR *to his knees. Simultaneously* LINZMAN *thrusts his right hand into his coat pocket and produces a re-*

volver which he points at LILIOM'S *breast.* LILIOM *is standing two paces away from the revolver. There is a long pause.*)

LINZMAN (*in a low, even voice*). It is twenty-five minutes past six. (*Pauses, looks ironically down at* FICSUR.) It's lucky I grabbed the hand with the knife instead of the other one. (*Pauses again, looks appraisingly from one to the other.*) Two fine birds! (*To* FICSUR.) I should live so — Rothschild has more luck than you. (*To* LILIOM.) I'd advise you to keep nice and quiet. If you make one move, you'll get two bullets in you. Just look into the barrel. You'll see some little things in there made of lead.

FICSUR. Let me go. I didn't do anything.

LINZMAN (*mockingly shakes the hand which still holds the knife*). And this? What do you call this? Oh, yes, I know. You thought I had an apple in my pocket, and you wanted to peel it. That's it. Forgive me for my error. I beg your pardon, sir.

LILIOM. But I — I ——

LINZMAN. Yes, my son, I know. It's so simple. You only asked what time it is. Well, it's twenty-five minutes after six.

FICSUR. Let us go, honorable sir. We didn't do anything to you.

LINZMAN. In the first place, my son, I'm not an honorable sir. In the second place, for the same money, you could have said Your Excellency. But in the third place you'll find it very hard to beg off by flattering me.

LILIOM. But I — *I* really didn't do anything to you.

LINZMAN. Look behind you, my boy. Don't be afraid. Look behind you, but don't run away or I'll have to shoot you down. (LILIOM *turns his head slowly around.*) Who's coming up there?

LILIOM (*looking at* LINZMAN). Policemen.

LINZMAN (*to* FICSUR). You hold still, or —— (*To* LILIOM *teasingly.*) How many policemen are there?

LILIOM (*his eyes cast down*). Two.

LINZMAN. And what are the policemen sitting on?

LILIOM. Horses.

LINZMAN. And which can run faster, a horse or a man?

LILIOM. A horse.

LINZMAN. There, you see. It would be hard to get away now. (*Laughs.*) I never saw such an unlucky pair of highway robbers. I can't imagine worse luck. Just today I had to put a pistol in my pocket. And even if I hadn't — old Linzman is a match for four like you. But even that isn't all. Did you happen to notice, you oxen, what direction I came from? From the factory, didn't I? When I *went* there I had a nice bit of money with me. Sixteen thousand crowns! But now — not a heller. (*Calls off left.*) Hey, come quicker, will you? This fellow is pulling pretty strong. (*Ficsur frees himself with a mighty wrench and darts rapidly off. As Linzman aims his pistol at the vanishing Ficsur, Liliom runs up the steps to the embankment. Linzman hesitates, perceives that Liliom is the better target, points the pistol at him.*) Stop, or I'll shoot! (*Calls off left to the Police-men.*) Why don't you come down off your horses? (*His pistol is leveled at Liliom, who stands on the embankment, facing the audience. From the left on the embankment a Policeman appears, revolver in hand.*)

FIRST POLICEMAN. Stop!

LINZMAN. Well, my boy, do you still want to know what time it is? From ten to twelve years in prison!

LILIOM. You won't get me! (*Linzman laughs derisively. Liliom is now three or four paces from the Policeman and equally distant from Linzman. His face is uplifted to the sky. He bursts into laughter, half defiant, half self-pitying, and takes the kitchen knife from under his coat.*) Julie ——

> (*The ring of farewell is in the word. He turns sideways, thrusts the knife deep in his breast, sways, falls and rolls down the far side of the embankment. There is a long pause. From the left up on the embankment come the Two Policemen.*)

LINZMAN. What's the matter? (*The First Policeman comes along the embankment as far as the steps, looks down in the opposite side, then climbs down at about the spot where Liliom disappeared. Linzman and the other Policeman mount the embankment and look down on him.*) Stabbed himself?

VOICE OF FIRST POLICEMAN. Yes — and he seems to have made a thorough job of it.

LINZMAN (*excitedly to the Second Policeman*). I'll go and telephone to the hospital. (*He runs down the steps and exits at left.*)

SECOND POLICEMAN. Go to Eisler's grocery store and telephone to the factory from there. They've a doctor there, too. (*Calling down to the other* POLICEMAN.) I'm going to tie up the horses.

(*Comes down the steps and exits at left. The stage is empty. There is a pause. The little red signal lamp is lit.*)

VOICE OF FIRST POLICEMAN. Hey, Stephan!

VOICE OF SECOND POLICEMAN. What?

VOICE OF FIRST POLICEMAN. Shall I pull the knife out of his chest?

VOICE OF SECOND POLICEMAN. Better not, or he may bleed to death.

(*There is a pause.*)

VOICE OF FIRST POLICEMAN. Stephan!

VOICE OF SECOND POLICEMAN. Yes.

VOICE OF FIRST POLICEMAN. Lot of mosquitoes around here.

VOICE OF SECOND POLICEMAN. Yes.

VOICE OF FIRST POLICEMAN. Got a cigar?

VOICE OF SECOND POLICEMAN. No.

(*There is a pause. The* FIRST POLICEMAN *appears over the opposite side of the embankment.*)

FIRST POLICEMAN. A lot of good the new pay-schedule's done us — made things worse than they used to be — we *get* more but we *have* less than we ever had. If the Government could be made to realize that. It's a thankless job at best. You work hard year after year, you get gray in the service, and slowly you die — yes.

SECOND POLICEMAN. That's right.

FIRST POLICEMAN. Yes.

(*In the distance is heard the bell of the signal tower.*)

THE CURTAIN FALLS

SCENE V

The photographic "studio" a half hour later that same evening.

MOTHER HOLLUNDER, *her son,* MARIE *and* WOLF *stand in a group back right, their heads togther.* JULIE *stands apart from them, a few paces to the left.*

YOUNG HOLLUNDER (*who has just come in, tells his story excitedly*). They're bringing him now. Two workmen from the factory are carrying him on a stretcher.

WOLF. Where is the doctor?

YOUNG HOLLUNDER. A policeman telephoned to headquarters. The police-surgeon ought to be here any minute.

MARIE. Maybe they'll pull him through after all.

YOUNG HOLLUNDER. He stabbed himself too deep in his chest. But he's still breathing. He can still talk, too, but very faintly. At first he lay there unconscious, but when they put him on the stretcher he came to.

WOLF. That was from the shaking.

MARIE. We'd better make room.

(*They make room. Two workmen carry in* LILIOM *on a stretcher which has four legs and stands about as high as a bed. They put the stretcher at left directly in front of the sofa, so that the head is at right and the foot at left. Then they unobtrusively join the group at the door. Later, they go out.* JULIE *is standing at the side of the stretcher, where, without moving, she can see* LILIOM'S *face. The others crowd emotionally together near the door. The* FIRST POLICEMAN *enters.*)

FIRST POLICEMAN. Are you his wife?

JULIE. Yes.

FIRST POLICEMAN. The doctor at the factory who bandaged him up forbade us to take him to the hospital.— Dangerous to move him that far. What he needs now is rest. Just let him be until the police-surgeon comes. (*To the group near the door.*) He's not to be disturbed.

(*They make way for him. He exits. There is a pause.*)

WOLF (*gently urging the others out*). Please — it's best if we all get out of here now. We'll only be in the way.

MARIE (*to* JULIE). Julie, what do you think? (JULIE *looks at her without answering.*) Julie, can I do anything to help? (JULIE *does not answer.*) We'll be just outside on the bench if you want us.

(MOTHER HOLLUNDER *and her son have gone out when first requested. Now* MARIE *and* WOLF *exit, too.* JULIE *sits on the edge of the stretcher and looks at* LILIOM. *He stretches his hand out to her. She clasps it. It is not quite dark yet. Both of them can still be plainly seen.*)

LILIOM (*raises himself with difficulty; speaks lightly at first, but later*

soberly, defiantly). Little — Julie — there's something — I want
to tell you — like when you go to a restaurant — and you've
finished eating — and it's time — to pay — then you have to
count up everything — everything you owe — well — I beat
you — not because I was mad at you — no — only because
I can't bear to see anyone crying. You always cried — on
my account — and, well, you see — I never learned a trade —
what kind of a caretaker would I make? But anyhow — I
wasn't going back to the carousel to fool with the girls. No,
I spit on them all — understand?

JULIE. Yes.

LILIOM. And — as for Hollinger — he's good enough — Mrs.
Muskat can get along all right with him. The jokes he tells
are mine — and the people laugh when he tells them — but
I don't care. — I didn't give you anything — no home — not
even the food you ate — but you don't understand. — It's true
I'm not much good — but I couldn't be a caretaker — and so
I thought maybe it would be better over there — in America —
do you see?

JULIE. Yes.

LILIOM. I'm not asking — forgiveness — I don't do that — I
don't. Tell the baby — if you like.

JULIE. Yes.

LILIOM. Tell the baby — I wasn't much good — but tell him —
if you ever talk about me — tell him — I thought — perhaps —
over in America — but that's no affair of yours. I'm not
asking forgiveness. For my part the police can come now. —
If it's a boy — if it's a girl. — Perhaps I'll see the Lord God
today. — Do you think I'll see Him?

JULIE. Yes.

LILIOM. I'm not afraid — of the police. Up There — if they'll
only let me come up in front of the Lord God Himself — not
like down here where an officer stops you at the door. If
the carpenter asks you — yes — be his wife — marry him.
And the child — tell him he's his father. — He'll believe you —
won't he?

JULIE. Yes.

LILIOM. When I beat you — I was right. — You mustn't always

think — you mustn't always be right.— Liliom can be right once, too.— It's all the same to me who was right.— It's so dumb. Nobody's right — but they all think they are right. — A lot they know!

JULIE. Yes.

LILIOM. Julie — come — hold my hand tight.

JULIE. I'm holding it tight — all the time.

LILIOM. Tighter, still tighter — I'm going —— (*Pauses.*) Julie ——

JULIE. Good-bye.

> (LILIOM *sinks slowly back and dies.* JULIE *frees her hand.* The DOCTOR *enters with the* FIRST POLICEMAN.)

DOCTOR. Good-evening. His wife?

JULIE. Yes, sir.

(*Behind the* DOCTOR *and* POLICEMAN *enter* MARIE, WOLF, MOTHER HOLLUNDER, YOUNG HOLLUNDER *and* MRS. MUSKAT. *They remain respectfully at the doorway. The* DOCTOR *bends over* LILIOM *and examines him.*)

DOCTOR. A light, if you please. (JULIE *fetches a burning candle from the dark-room. The* DOCTOR *examines* LILIOM *briefly in the candle-light, then turns suddenly away.*) Have you pen and ink?

WOLF (*proffering a pen*). A fountain-pen — American ——

DOCTOR (*takes a printed form from his pocket; speaks as he writes out the death-certificate at the little table*). My poor woman, your husband is dead — there's nothing to be done for him — the good God will help him now — I'll leave this certificate with you. You will give it to the people from the hospital when they come — I'll arrange for the body to be removed at once. (*Rises.*) Please give me a towel and soap.

POLICEMAN. I've got them for you out here, sir.

> (*Points to door at back.*)

DOCTOR. God be with you, my good woman.

JULIE. Thank you, sir.

> (*The* DOCTOR *and* POLICEMAN *exit. The others slowly draw nearer.*)

MARIE. Poor Julie. May he rest in peace, poor man, but as

for you — please don't be angry with me for saying it — but you're better off this way.

MOTHER HOLLUNDER. He is better off, the poor fellow, and so are you.

MARIE. Much better, Julie... you are young... and one of these days some good man will come along. Am I right?

WOLF. She's right.

MARIE. Julie, tell me, am I right?

JULIE. You are right, dear; you are very good.

YOUNG HOLLUNDER. There's a good man — the carpenter. Oh, I can speak of it now. He comes here every day on some excuse or other — and he never fails to ask for you.

MARIE. A widower — with two children.

MOTHER HOLLUNDER. He's better off, poor fellow — and so are you. He was a bad man.

MARIE. He wasn't good-hearted. Was he, Wolf?

WOLF. No, I must say, he really wasn't. No, Liliom wasn't a good man. A good man doesn't strike a woman.

MARIE. Am I right? Tell me, Julie, am I right?

JULIE. You are right, dear.

YOUNG HOLLUNDER. It's really a good thing for her it happened.

MOTHER HOLLUNDER. He's better off — and so is she.

WOLF. Now you have your freedom again. How old are you?

JULIE. Eighteen.

WOLF. Eighteen. A mere child! Am I right?

JULIE. You are right, Wolf. You are kind.

YOUNG HOLLUNDER. Lucky for you it happened, isn't it?

JULIE. Yes.

YOUNG HOLLUNDER. All you had before was bad luck. If it weren't for my mother you wouldn't have had a roof over your head or a bite to eat — and now Autumn's coming and Winter. You couldn't have lived in this shack in the Winter time, could you?

MARIE. Certainly not! You'd have frozen like the birds in the fields. Am I right, Julie?

JULIE. Yes, Marie.

MARIE. A year from now you will have forgotten all about him, won't you?

JULIE. You are right, Marie.

WOLF. If you need anything, count on us. We'll go now. But tomorrow morning we'll be back. Come, Marie. God be with you. (*Offers* JULIE *his hand.*)

JULIE. God be with you.

MARIE (*embraces* JULIE, *weeping*). It's the best thing that could have happened to you, Julie, the best thing.

JULIE. Don't cry, Marie. (MARIE *and* WOLF *exit.*)

MOTHER HOLLUNDER. I'll make a little black coffee. You haven't had a thing to eat today. Then you'll come home with us.

(MOTHER HOLLUNDER *and her son exit.* MRS. MUSKAT *comes over to* JULIE.)

MRS. MUSKAT. Would you mind if I — looked at him?

JULIE. He used to work for you.

MRS. MUSKAT (*contemplates the body; turns to* JULIE). Won't you make up with me?

JULIE. I wasn't angry with you.

MRS. MUSKAT. But you were. Let's make it up.

JULIE (*raising her voice eagerly, almost triumphantly*). I've nothing to make up with *you*.

MRS. MUSKAT. But I have with you. Everyone says hard things against the poor dead boy — except us two. You don't say he was bad.

JULIE (*raising her voice yet higher, this time on a defiant, wholly triumphant note*). Yes, I *do*.

MRS. MUSKAT. I understand, my child. But he beat me, too. What does that matter? I've forgotten it.

JULIE (*from now on answers her coldly, dryly, without looking at her*). That's your own affair.

MRS. MUSKAT. If I can help you in any way ——

JULIE. There's nothing I need.

MRS. MUSKAT. I still owe him two kronen, back pay.

JULIE. You should have paid him.

MRS. MUSKAT. Now that the poor fellow is dead I thought perhaps it would be the same if I paid you.

JULIE. I've nothing to do with it.

MRS. MUSKAT. All right. Please don't think I'm trying to force myself on you. I stayed because we two are the only ones on earth who loved him. That's why I thought we ought to stick together.

JULIE. No, thank you.

MRS. MUSKAT. Then you couldn't have loved him as I did.

JULIE. No.

MRS. MUSKAT. I loved him better.

JULIE. Yes.

MRS. MUSKAT. Good-bye.

JULIE. Good-bye. (MRS. MUSKAT *exits.* JULIE *puts the candle on the table near* LILIOM'S *head, sits on the edge of the stretcher, looks into the dead man's face and caresses it tenderly.*) Sleep, Liliom, sleep — it's no business of hers — I never even told you — but now I'll tell you — now I'll tell you — you bad, quick-tempered, rough, unhappy, wicked — *dear* boy — sleep peacefully, Liliom — they can't understand how I feel — I can't even explain to you — not even to you — how I feel — you'd only laugh at me — but you can't hear me any more. (*Between tender motherliness and reproach, yet with great love in her voice.*) It was wicked of you to beat me — on the breast and on the head and face — but you're gone now. — You treated me badly — that was wicked of you — but sleep peacefully, Liliom — you bad, bad boy, you — I love you — I never told you before — I was ashamed — but now I've told you — I love you. Liliom — sleep — my boy — sleep.

(*She rises, gets a Bible, sits down near the candle and reads softly to herself, so that not the words but an inarticulate murmur is heard. The* CARPENTER *enters at back.*)

CARPENTER (*stands near the door; in the dimness of the room he can scarcely be seen*). Miss Julie ——

JULIE (*without alarm*). Who is that?

CARPENTER (*very slowly*). The carpenter.

JULIE. What does the carpenter want?

CARPENTER. Can I be of help to you in any way? Shall I stay here with you?

JULIE (*gratefully, but firmly*). Don't stay, carpenter.

CARPENTER. Shall I come back tomorrow?

JULIE. Not tomorrow, either.

CARPENTER. Don't be offended, Miss Julie, but I'd like to know —
you see, I'm not a young man any more — I have two children
— and if I'm to come back any more — I'd like to know — if
there's any use ——

JULIE. No use, carpenter.

CARPENTER (*as he exits*). God be with you.

(JULIE *resumes her reading.* FICSUR *enters, slinks furtively sideways to
the stretcher, looks at* LILIOM, *shakes his head.* JULIE *looks up
from her reading.* FICSUR *takes fright, slinks away from the
stretcher, sits down at right, biting his nails.* JULIE *rises.* FICSUR
*rises, too, and looks at her half fearfully. With her piercing glance
upon him he slinks to the doorway at back, where he pauses and speaks.*)

FICSUR. The old woman asked me to tell you that coffee is ready,
and you are to come in.

(JULIE *goes to the kitchen door.* FICSUR *withdraws until she has
closed the door behind her. Then he reappears in the doorway,
stands on tiptoes, looks at* LILIOM, *then exits. Now the body lies
alone. After a brief silence music is heard, distant at first,
but gradually coming nearer. It is very much like the music
of the carousel, but slower, graver, more exalted. The melody,
too, is the same, yet the tempo is altered and contrapuntal measures of the thieves' song are intertwined in it. Two men in
black, with heavy sticks, soft black hats and black gloves,
appear in the doorway at back and stride slowly into the room.
Their faces are beardless, marble white, grave and benign.
One stops in front of the stretcher, the other a pace to the right.
From above a dim violet light illuminates their faces.*)

THE FIRST (*to* LILIOM). Rise and come with us.

THE SECOND (*politely*). You're under arrest.

THE FIRST (*somewhat louder, but always in a gentle, low, resonant voice*).
Do you hear? Rise. Don't you hear?

THE SECOND. We are the police.

THE FIRST (*bends down, touches* LILIOM's *shoulder*). Get up and come
with us. (LILIOM *slowly sits up.*)

THE SECOND. Come along.

THE FIRST (*paternally*). These people suppose that when they die
all their difficulties are solved for them.

THE SECOND (*raising his voice sternly*). That simply by thrusting a knife in your heart and making it stop beating you can leave your wife behind with a child in her womb ——

THE FIRST. It is not as simple as that.

THE SECOND. Such things are not settled so easily.

THE FIRST. Come along. You will have to give an account of yourself. (*As both bow their heads, he continues softly.*) We are God's police. (*An expression of glad relief lights upon* LILIOM's *face. He rises from the stretcher.*) Come.

THE SECOND. You mortals don't get off quite as easy as that.

THE FIRST (*softly*). Come. (LILIOM *starts to walk ahead of them, then stops and looks at them.*) The end is not as abrupt as that. Your name is still spoken. Your face is still remembered. And what you said, and what you did, and what you failed to do — these are still remembered. Remembered, too, are the manner of your glance, the ring of your voice, the clasp of your hand and how your step sounded — as long as one is left who remembers you, so long is the matter unended. Before the end there is much to be undone. Until you are quite forgotten, my son, you will not be finished with the earth — even though you *are* dead.

THE SECOND (*very gently*). Come.

> (*The music begins again. All three exit at back,* LILIOM *leading, the others following. The stage is empty and quite dark save for the candle which burns by the stretcher, on which, in the shadows, the covers are so arranged that one cannot quite be sure that a body is not still lying. The music dies out in the distance as if it had followed* LILIOM *and the two* POLICEMEN. *The candle flickers and goes out. There is a brief interval of silence and total darkness before*

THE CURTAIN FALLS

SCENE VI

In the Beyond. A whitewashed courtroom. There is a green-topped table; behind it a bench. Back center is a door with a bell over it. Next to this door is a window through which can be seen a vista of rose-tinted clouds.

Down right there is a grated iron door. Down left another door.

Two men are on the bench when the curtain rises. One is richly, the other poorly dressed.

From a great distance is heard a fanfare of trumpets playing the refrain of the thieves' song in slow, altered tempo.

Passing the window at back appear LILIOM *and the two* POLICEMEN. *The bell rings.*

An old GUARD *enters at right. He is bald and has a long white beard. He wears the conventional police uniform.*

He goes to the door at back, opens it, exchanges silent greetings with the two POLICEMEN *and closes the door again.*

LILIOM *looks wonderingly around.*

THE FIRST (*to the old* GUARD). Announce us.

(*The* GUARD *exits at left.*)

LILIOM. Is this it?

THE SECOND. Yes, my son.

LILIOM. This is the police court?

THE SECOND. Yes, my son. The part for suicide cases.

LILIOM. And what happens here?

THE FIRST. Here justice is done. Sit down.

(LILIOM *sits next to the two men. The two* POLICEMEN *stand silent near the table.*)

THE RICHLY DRESSED MAN (*whispers*). Suicide, too?

LILIOM. Yes.

THE RICHLY DRESSED MAN (*points to* THE POORLY DRESSED MAN). So's he. (*Introducing himself.*) My name is Reich.

THE POORLY DRESSED MAN (*whispers, too*). My name is Stephan Kadar. (LILIOM *only looks at them.*)

THE POORLY DRESSED MAN. And you? What's your name?

LILIOM. None of your business. (*Both move a bit away from him.*)

THE POORLY DRESSED MAN. I did it by jumping out of a window.

THE RICHLY DRESSED MAN. I did it with a pistol — and you?

LILIOM. With a knife. (*They move a bit further away from him.*)

THE RICHLY DRESSED MAN. A pistol is cleaner.

LILIOM. If I had the price of a pistol ——

THE SECOND. Silence!

(*The* POLICE MAGISTRATE *enters. He has a long white beard, is bald, but only in profile can be seen on his head a single tuft of snow-white hair.* THE GUARD *re-enters behind him and sits on the bench with the dead men. As* THE MAGISTRATE *enters, all rise, except* LILIOM, *who remains surlily seated. When* THE MAGISTRATE *sits down, so do the others.*

THE GUARD. Yesterday's cases, your honor. The numbers are entered in the docket.

THE MAGISTRATE. Number 16,472.

THE FIRST (*looks in his notebook, beckons* THE RICHLY DRESSED MAN) Stand up, please.   (THE RICHLY DRESSED MAN *rises.*)

THE MAGISTRATE. Your name?

THE RICHLY DRESSED MAN. Doctor Reich.

THE MAGISTRATE. Age?

THE RICHLY DRESSED MAN. Forty-two, married, Jew.

THE MAGISTRATE (*with a gesture of dismissal*). Religion does not interest us here — why did you kill yourself?

THE RICHLY DRESSED MAN. On account of debts.

THE MAGISTRATE. What good did you do on earth?

THE RICHLY DRESSED MAN. I was a lawyer ——

THE MAGISTRATE (*coughs significantly*). Yes — we'll discuss that later. For the present I shall only ask you: Would you like to go back to earth once more before sunrise? I advise you that you have the right to go if you choose. Do you understand?

THE RICHLY DRESSED MAN. Yes, sir.

THE MAGISTRATE. He who takes his life is apt, in his haste and his excitement, to forget something. Is there anything important down there you have left undone? Something to tell someone? Something to undo?

THE RICHLY DRESSED MAN. My debts ——

THE MAGISTRATE. They do not matter here. Here we are concerned only with the affairs of the soul.

THE RICHLY DRESSED MAN. Then — if you please — when I left — the house — my youngest son, Oscar — was asleep. I didn't trust myself to wake him — and bid him good-bye. I would have liked — to kiss him good-bye.

THE MAGISTRATE (*to* THE SECOND). You will take Dr. Reich back and let him kiss his son Oscar.

THE SECOND. Come with me, please.

THE RICHLY DRESSED MAN (*to* THE MAGISTRATE). I thank you.

> (*He bows and exits at back with* THE SECOND.)

THE MAGISTRATE (*after making an entry in the docket*). Number 16,473.

THE FIRST (*looks in his notebook, then beckons* LILIOM). Stand up.

LILIOM. You said *please* to him.   (*He rises.*)

THE MAGISTRATE. Your name?

LILIOM. Liliom.

THE MAGISTRATE. Isn't that your nickname?

LILIOM. Yes.

THE MAGISTRATE. What is your right name?

LILIOM. Andreas.

THE MAGISTRATE. And your last name?

LILIOM. Zavocki — after my mother.

THE MAGISTRATE. Your age?

LILIOM. Twenty-four.

THE MAGISTRATE. What good did *you* do on earth? (LILIOM *is silent.*) Why did you take your life? (LILIOM *does not answer.* THE MAGISTRATE *addresses* THE FIRST.) Take that knife away from him. (THE FIRST *does so.*) It will be returned to you, if you go back to earth.

LILIOM. Do I go back to earth again?

THE MAGISTRATE. Just answer my questions.

LILIOM. I wasn't answering then, I was asking if ——

THE MAGISTRATE. You don't ask questions here. You only answer. Only answer, Andreas Zavocki! I ask you whether there is anything on earth you neglected to accomplish? Anything down there you would like to do?

LILIOM. Yes.

THE MAGISTRATE. What is it?

LILIOM. I'd like to break Ficsur's head for him.

THE MAGISTRATE. Punishment is our office. Is there nothing else on earth you'd like to do?

LILIOM. I don't know — I guess, as long as I'm here, I'll not go back.

THE MAGISTRATE (*to* THE FIRST). Note that. He waives his right. (LILIOM *starts back to the bench.*) Stay where you are. You are aware that you left your wife without food or shelter?

LILIOM. Yes.

THE MAGISTRATE. Don't you regret it?

LILIOM. No.

THE MAGISTRATE. You are aware that your wife is pregnant, and that in six months a child will be born?

LILIOM. I know.

THE MAGISTRATE. And that the child, too, will be without food or shelter? Do you regret that?

LILIOM. As long as I won't be there, what's it got to do with me?

THE MAGISTRATE. Don't try to deceive us, Andreas Zavocki. We see through you as through a pane of glass.

LILIOM. If you see so much, what do you want to ask me for? Why don't you let me rest — in peace?

THE MAGISTRATE. First you must earn your rest.

LILIOM. I want — only — to sleep.

THE MAGISTRATE. Your obstinacy won't help you. Here patience is endless as time. We can wait.

LILIOM. Can I ask something — I'd like to know — if Your Honor will tell me — whether the baby will be a boy or a girl.

THE MAGISTRATE. You shall see that for yourself.

LILIOM (*excitedly*). I'll see the baby?

THE MAGISTRATE. When you do it won't be a baby any more. But we haven't reached that question yet.

LILIOM. I'll see it?

THE MAGISTRATE. Again I ask you: Do you not regret that you deserted your wife and child; that you were a bad husband, a bad father?

LILIOM. A bad husband?

THE MAGISTRATE. Yes.

LILIOM. And a bad father?

THE MAGISTRATE. That, too.

LILIOM. I couldn't get work — and I couldn't bear to see Julie — all the time — all the time ——

THE MAGISTRATE. Weeping! Why are you ashamed to say it? You couldn't bear to see her weeping. Why are you afraid of that word? And why are you ashamed that you loved her?

LILIOM (*shrugs his shoulders*). Who's ashamed? But I couldn't bear to see her — and that's why I was bad to her. You see, it wouldn't do to go back to the carousel — and Ficsur came along with his talk about — that other thing — and all of a sudden it happened, I don't know how. The police and the Jew with the pistol — and there I stood — and I'd lost the money playing cards — and I didn't want to be put in prison. (*Demanding justification.*) Maybe I was wrong not to go out and steal when there was nothing to eat in the house? Should I have gone out to steal for Julie?

THE MAGISTRATE (*emphatically*). Yes.

LILIOM (*after an astounded pause*). The police down there never said that.

THE MAGISTRATE. You beat that poor, frail girl; you beat her because she loved you. How could you do that?

LILIOM. We argued with each other — she said this and I said that — and because she was right I couldn't answer her — and I got mad — and the anger rose up in me — until it reached here (*points to his throat*) and then I beat her.

THE MAGISTRATE. Are you sorry?

LILIOM (*shakes his head, but cannot utter the word "no"; continues softly*). When I touched her slender throat — then — if you like — you might say —— (*Falters, looks embarrassed at* THE MAGISTRATE.)

THE MAGISTRATE (*confidently expectant*). Are you sorry?

LILIOM (*with a stare*). I'm not sorry for anything.

THE MAGISTRATE. Liliom, Liliom, it will be difficult to help you.

LILIOM. I'm not asking any help.

THE MAGISTRATE. You were offered employment as a caretaker on Arader Street. (*To* THE FIRST.) Where is that entered?

THE FIRST. In the small docket.

(*Hands him the open book.* THE MAGISTRATE *looks in it.*)

THE MAGISTRATE. Rooms, kitchen, quarterly wages, the privilege of keeping poultry. Why didn't you accept it?

LILIOM. I'm not a caretaker. I'm no good at caretaking. To be a caretaker — you have to be a caretaker ——

THE MAGISTRATE. If I said to you now: Liliom, go back on your stretcher. Tomorrow morning you will arise alive and well again. Would you be a caretaker then?

LILIOM. No.

THE MAGISTRATE. Why not?

LILIOM. Because — because that's just why I died.

THE MAGISTRATE. That is not true, my son. You died because you loved little Julie and the child she is bearing under her heart.

LILIOM. No.

THE MAGISTRATE. Look me in the eye.

LILIOM (*looks him in the eye*). No.

THE MAGISTRATE (*stroking his beard*). Liliom, Liliom, if it were not for our Heavenly patience —— Go back to your seat. Number 16,474.

THE FIRST (*looks in his notebook*). Stephan Kadar.

(THE POORLY DRESSED MAN *rises*.)

THE MAGISTRATE. You came out today?

THE POORLY DRESSED MAN. Today.

THE MAGISTRATE (*indicating the crimson sea of clouds*). How long were you in there?

THE POORLY DRESSED MAN. Thirteen years.

THE MAGISTRATE. Officer, you went to earth with him?

THE FIRST. Yes, sir.

THE MAGISTRATE. Stephan Kadar, after thirteen years of purification by fire you returned to earth to give proof that your soul had been burned clean. What good deed did you perform?

THE POORLY DRESSED MAN. When I came to the village and looked in the window of our cottage I saw my poor little orphans sleeping peacefully. But it was raining and the rain beat into the room through a hole in the roof. So I went and fixed the roof so it wouldn't rain in any more. My hammering woke them up and they were afraid. But their mother came in to them and comforted them. She said to them: "Don't cry! It's your poor, dear father hammering up there. He's come back from the other world to fix the roof for us."

THE MAGISTRATE. Officer?

THE FIRST. That's what happened.

THE MAGISTRATE. Stephan Kadar, you have done a good deed. What you did will be written in books to gladden the hearts of children who read them. (*Indicates the door at left.*) The door is open to you. The eternal light awaits you. (THE FIRST *escorts* THE POORLY DRESSED MAN *out at left with great deference.*) Liliom! (LILIOM *rises.*) You have heard?

LILIOM. Yes.

THE MAGISTRATE. When this man first appeared before us he was as stubborn as you. But now he has purified himself and withstood the test. He has done a good deed.

LILIOM. What's he done, anyhow? Any roofer can fix a roof. It's much harder to be a barker in an amusement park.

THE MAGISTRATE. Liliom, you shall remain for sixteen years in the crimson fire until your child is full grown. By that time your pride and your stubbornness will have been burnt out of you. And when your daughter ——

LILIOM. My daughter!

THE MAGISTRATE. When your daughter has reached the age of sixteen ——

(LILIOM *bows his head, covers his eyes with his hands, and to keep from weeping laughs defiantly, sadly.*)

THE MAGISTRATE. When your daughter has reached the age of sixteen you will be sent for one day back to earth.

LILIOM. Me?

THE MAGISTRATE. Yes — just as you may have read in the legends of how the dead reappear on earth for a time.

LILIOM. I never believed them.

THE MAGISTRATE. Now you see they are true. You will go back to earth one day to show how far the purification of your soul has progressed.

LILIOM. Then I must show what I can do — like when you apply for a job — as a coachman?

THE MAGISTRATE. Yes — it is a test.

LILIOM. And will I be told what I have to do?

THE MAGISTRATE. No.

LILIOM. How will I know, then?

THE MAGISTRATE. You must decide that for yourself. That's what you burn sixteen years for. And if you do something good, something splendid for your child, then ——

LILIOM (*laughs sadly*). Then? (*All stand up and bow their heads reverently. There is a pause.*) Then?

THE MAGISTRATE. Now I'll bid you farewell, Liliom. Sixteen years and a day shall pass before I see you again. When you have returned from earth you will come up before me again.

Take heed and think well of some good deed to do for your child. On that will depend which door shall be opened to you up here. Now go, Liliom.

(*He exits at left.* THE GUARD *stands at attention. There is a pause.*)

THE FIRST (*approaches* LILIOM). Come along, my son.

(*He goes to the door at right; pulls open the bolt and waits.*)

LILIOM (*to the old* GUARD, *softly*). Say, officer.

THE GUARD. What do you want?

LILIOM. Please — can I get — have you got ——?

THE GUARD. What?

LILIOM (*whispers*). A cigarette?

(*The old* GUARD *stares at him, goes a few paces to the left, shakes his head disapprovingly. Then his expression softens. He takes a cigarette from his pocket and, crossing to* LILIOM — *who has gone over to the door at right — gives him the cigarette.* THE FIRST *throws open the door. An intense rose-colored light streams in. The glow of it is so strong that it blinds* LILIOM *and he takes a step backward and bows his head and covers his eyes with his hand before he steps forward into the light.*)

THE CURTAIN FALLS

SCENE VII

Sixteen years later. A small, tumbledown house on a bare, unenclosed plot of ground. Before the house is a tiny garden enclosed by a hip-high hedge.

At back a wooden fence crosses the stage; in the center of it is a door large enough to admit a wagon. Beyond the fence is a view of a suburban street which blends into a broad vista of tilled fields.

It is a bright Sunday in Spring.

In the garden a table for two is laid.

JULIE, *her daughter* LOUISE, WOLF *and* MARIE *are discovered in the garden.* WOLF *is prosperously dressed,* MARIE *somewhat elaborately, with a huge hat.*

JULIE. You could stay for lunch.

MARIE. Impossible, dear. Since he became the proprietor of

the Café Sorrento, Wolf simply has to be there all the time.

JULIE. But you needn't stay there all day, too.

MARIE. Oh, yes. I sit near the cashier's cage, read the papers, keep an eye on the waiters and drink in the bustle and excitement of the great city.

JULIE. And what about the children?

MARIE. You know what modern families are like. Parents scarcely ever see their children these days. The four girls are with their governess, the three boys with their tutor.

LOUISE. Auntie, dear, do stay and eat with us.

MARIE (*importantly*). Impossible today, dear child, impossible. Perhaps some other time. Come, Mr. Beifeld.

JULIE. Since when do you call your husband mister?

WOLF. I'd rather she did, dear lady. When we used to be very familiar we quarreled all the time. Now we are formal with each other and get along like society folk. I kiss your hand, dear lady.

JULIE. Good-bye, Wolf.

MARIE. Adieu, my dear. (*They embrace.*) Adieu, my dear child.

LOUISE. Good-bye, Aunt Marie. Good-bye, Uncle Wolf.

(WOLF *and* MARIE *exit.*)

JULIE. You can get the soup now, Louise, dear.

(LOUISE *goes into the house and re-enters with the soup. They sit at the table.*)

LOUISE. Mother, is it true we're not going to work at the jute factory any more?

JULIE. Yes, dear.

LOUISE. Where then?

JULIE. Uncle Wolf has gotten us a place in a big establishment where they make all kinds of fittings for cafés. We're to make big curtains, you know, the kind they hang in the windows, with lettering on them.

LOUISE. It'll be nicer there than at the jute factory.

JULIE. Yes, dear. The work isn't as dirty and pays better, too. A poor widow like your mother is lucky to get it.

(*They eat.* LILIOM *and the two* HEAVENLY POLICEMEN *appear in the big doorway at back. The* POLICEMEN *pass slowly by.* LILIOM *stands there alone a moment, then comes slowly down and pauses at the opening of the hedge. He is dressed as he was on the day of his death. He is very pale, but otherwise unaltered.* JULIE, *at the table, has her back to him.* LOUISE *sits facing the audience.*)

LILIOM. Good-day.

LOUISE. Good-day.

JULIE. Another beggar! What is it you want, my poor man?

LILIOM. Nothing.

JULIE. We have no money to give, but if you care for a plate of soup —— (LOUISE *goes into the house.*) Have you come far today?

LILIOM. Yes — very far.

JULIE. Are you tired?

LILIOM. Very tired.

JULIE. Over there at the gate is a stone. Sit down and rest. My daughter is bringing you the soup.

(LOUISE *comes out of the house.*)

LILIOM. Is that your daughter?

JULIE. Yes.

LILIOM (*to* LOUISE). You are the daughter?

LOUISE. Yes, sir.

LILIOM. A fine, healthy girl.

(*Takes the soup plate from her with one hand, while with the other he touches her arm.* LOUISE *draws back quickly.*)

LOUISE (*crosses to* JULIE). Mother!

JULIE. What, my child?

LOUISE. The man tried to take me by the arm.

JULIE. Nonsense! You only imagined it, dear. The poor, hungry man has other things to think about than fooling with young girls. Sit down and eat your soup. (*They eat.*)

LILIOM (*eats, too, but keeps looking at them*). You work at the factory, eh?

JULIE. Yes.

LILIOM. Your daughter, too?

LOUISE. Yes.

LILIOM. And your husband?

JULIE (*after a pause*). I have no husband. I'm a widow.

LILIOM. A widow?

JULIE. Yes.

LILIOM. Your husband — I suppose he's been dead a long time. (JULIE *does not answer.*) I say — has your husband been dead a long time?

JULIE. A long time.

LILIOM. What did he die of?   (JULIE *is silent.*)

LOUISE. No one knows. He went to America to work and he died there — in the hospital. Poor father, I never knew him.

LILIOM. He went to America?

LOUISE. Yes, before I was born.

LILIOM. To America?

JULIE. Why do you ask so many questions? Did you know him, perhaps?

LILIOM (*puts the plate down*). Heaven knows! I've known so many people. Maybe I knew him, too.

JULIE. Well, if you knew him, leave him and us in peace with your questions. He went to America and died there. That's all there is to tell.

LILIOM. All right. All right. Don't be angry with me. I didn't mean any harm.   (*There is a pause.*)

LOUISE. My father was a very handsome man.

JULIE. Don't talk so much.

LOUISE. Did I say anything ——?

LILIOM. Surely the little orphan can say that about her father.

LOUISE. My father could juggle so beautifully with three ivory balls that people used to advise him to go on the stage.

JULIE. Who told you that?

LOUISE. Uncle Wolf.

LILIOM. Who is that?

LOUISE. Mr. Wolf Beifeld, who owns the Café Sorrento.

LILIOM. The one who used to be a porter?

JULIE (*astonished*). Do you know him, too? It seems that you know all Budapest.

LILIOM. Wolf Beifeld is a long way from being all Budapest. But I do know a lot of people. Why shouldn't I know Wolf Beifeld?

LOUISE. He was a friend of my father.

JULIE. He was not his friend. No one was.

LILIOM. You speak of your husband so sternly.

JULIE. What's that to you? Doesn't it suit you? I can speak of my husband any way I like. It's nobody's business but mine.

LILIOM. Certainly, certainly — it's your own business.

(Takes up his soup plate again. All three eat.)

LOUISE (*to* JULIE). Perhaps he knew father, too.

JULIE. Ask him, if you like.

LOUISE (*crosses to* LILIOM. *He stands up*). Did you know my father?

(LILIOM *nods.* LOUISE *addresses her mother.*) Yes, he knew him.

JULIE (*rises*). You knew Andreas Zavocki?

LILIOM. Liliom? Yes.

LOUISE. Was he really a very handsome man?

LILIOM. I wouldn't exactly say handsome.

LOUISE (*confidently*). But he was an awfully good man, wasn't he?

LILIOM. He wasn't so good, either. As far as I know he was what they called a clown, a barker in a carousel.

LOUISE (*pleased*). Did he tell funny jokes?

LILIOM. Lots of 'em. And he sang funny songs, too.

LOUISE. In the carousel?

LILIOM. Yes — but he was something of a bully, too. He'd fight anyone. He even hit your dear little mother.

JULIE. That's a lie.

LILIOM. It's true.

JULIE. Aren't you ashamed to tell the child such awful things about her father? Get out of here, you shameless liar. Eats our soup and our bread and has the impudence to slander our dead!

LILIOM. I didn't mean — I ——

JULIE. What right have you to tell lies to the child? Take that plate, Louise, and let him be on his way. If he wasn't such a hungry-looking beggar, I'd put him out myself.

(LOUISE *takes the plate out of his hand.*)

LILIOM. So he didn't hit you?

JULIE. No, never. He was always good to me.

LOUISE (*whispers*). Did he tell funny stories, too?

LILIOM. Yes, and *such* funny ones.

JULIE. Don't speak to him any more. In God's name, go.

LOUISE. In God's name.

> (JULIE *resumes her seat at the table and eats.*)

LILIOM. If you please, Miss — I have a pack of cards in my pocket. And if you like, I'll show you some tricks that'll make you split your sides laughing. (LOUISE *holds* LILIOM'S *plate in her left hand. With her right she reaches out and holds the garden gate shut.*) Let me in, just a little way, Miss, and I'll do the tricks for you.

LOUISE. Go, in God's name, and let us be. Why are you making those ugly faces?

LILIOM. Don't chase me away, Miss; let me come in for just a minute — just for a minute — just long enough to let me show you something pretty, something wonderful. (*Opens the gate.*) Miss, I've something to give you.

> (*Takes from his pocket a big red handkerchief in which is wrapped a glittering star from Heaven. He looks furtively about him to make sure that the* POLICE *are not watching.*)

LOUISE. What's that?

LILIOM. Pst! A star!

> (*With a gesture he indicates that he has stolen it out of the sky.*)

JULIE (*sternly*). Don't take anything from him. He's probably stolen it somewhere. (*To* LILIOM.) In God's name, be off with you.

LOUISE. Yes, be off with you. Be off. (*She slams the gate.*)

LILIOM. Miss — please, Miss — I've got to do something good — or — do something good — a good deed ——

LOUISE (*pointing with her right hand*). That's the way out.

LILIOM. Miss ——

LOUISE. Get out!

LILIOM. Miss!

> (*Looks up at her suddenly and slaps her extended hand, so that the slap resounds loudly.*)

LOUISE. Mother!

> (*Looks dazedly at* LILIOM, *who bows his head dismayed, forlorn.* JULIE *rises and looks at* LILIOM *in astonishment. There is a long pause.*)

JULIE (*comes over to them slowly*). What's the matter here?

LOUISE (*bewildered, does not take her eyes off* LILIOM). Mother — the man — he hit me — on the hand — hard — I heard the sound of it — but it didn't hurt — mother — it didn't hurt — it was like a caress — as if he had just touched my hand tenderly.

> (*She hides behind* JULIE. LILIOM *sulkily raises his head and looks at* JULIE.)

JULIE (*softly*). Go, my child. Go into the house. Go.

LOUISE (*going*). But mother — I'm afraid — it sounded so loud —— (*Weepingly.*) And it didn't hurt at all — just as if he'd — kissed my hand instead — mother! (*She hides her face.*)

JULIE. Go in, my child, go in.

> (LOUISE *goes slowly into the house.* JULIE *watches her until she has disappeared, then turns slowly to* LILIOM.)

JULIE. You struck my child.

LILIOM. Yes — I struck her.

JULIE. Is that what you came for, to strike my child?

LILIOM. No — I didn't come for that — but I did strike her — and now I'm going back.

JULIE. In the name of the Lord Jesus, who are you?

LILIOM (*simply*). A poor, tired beggar who came a long way and who was hungry. And I took your soup and bread and I struck your child. Are you angry with me?

JULIE (*her hand on her heart; fearfully, wonderingly*). Jesus protect me — I don't understand it — I'm *not* angry — not angry at all ——

> (LILIOM *goes to the doorway and leans against the doorpost, his back to the audience.* JULIE *goes to the table and sits.*)

JULIE. Louise! (LOUISE *comes out of the house.*) Sit down, dear, we'll finish eating.

LOUISE. Has he gone?

JULIE. Yes. (*They are both seated at the table.* LOUISE, *her head in her hands, is staring into space.*) Why don't you eat, dear?

LOUISE. What has happened, mother?

JULIE. Nothing, my child.

> (*The* HEAVENLY POLICEMEN *appear outside.* LILIOM *walks slowly off at left. The* FIRST POLICEMAN *makes a deploring gesture. Both shake their heads deploringly and follow* LILIOM *slowly off at left.*)

LOUISE. Mother, dear, why won't you tell me?

JULIE. What is there to tell you, child? Nothing has happened.

We were peacefully eating, and a beggar came who talked of bygone days, and then I thought of your father.

LOUISE. My father?

JULIE. Your father — Liliom.   (*There is a pause.*)

LOUISE. Mother — tell me — has it ever happened to you — has anyone ever hit you — without hurting you in the least?

JULIE. Yes, my child. It has happened to me, too.

                              (*There is a pause.*)

LOUISE. Is it possible for someone to hit you — hard like that — real loud and hard — and not hurt you at all?

JULIE. It is possible, dear — that someone may beat you and beat you and beat you — and not hurt you at all.——

> (*There is a pause. Nearby an organ-grinder has stopped. The music of his organ begins.*)

THE CURTAIN FALLS

THE TIDINGS BROUGHT TO MARY

(L'ANNONCE FAITE À MARIE)

By PAUL CLAUDEL

Translated from the French by LOUISE MORGAN SILL

PAUL CLAUDEL

PAUL LOUIS CHARLES MARIE CLAUDEL, poet, essayist, dramatist, and diplomat, was born August 6, 1868, at Villeneuve-sur-Fère-en-Tardenois, Aisne, Picardy. He has had three careers which on the surface he has kept clear and distinct. In their deeper springs these careers combine in one of the most profound spirits and most influential personalities of our time. The career that stands nearest to the world is that of the man of diplomacy who has represented his country in far places. Claudel was educated at a Paris Lycée and at the École des Sciences Politiques. He began his career by serving in consulates in Berlin and New York. He was then sent to Tientsin, China, where he imbibed that insight into the East out of which came *La Connaissance de l'Est* and the Chinese tragedy, *Le Repos du Septième Jour*. Later he served in the consular service at Prague, Frankfort, and Hamburg. Transferred to the diplomatic service he was Minister to Brazil, Ambassador to Japan and to the United States. Such is his external career. The other two careers tend to merge. The one is that of the playwright who has hewed an absolutely new path in modern playwriting, who in his technical forms takes nothing from either naturalism or romanticism, and goes back for his inspiration to the forms of the Middle Ages. By no means all of Claudel's plays are religious mysteries. While in the United States he wrote the problem play *L'Échange*; his Miracle play *Christmas Eve, 1914*, is a war drama that will probably outlive most of the plays produced by the Great War; he has written a play on Christopher Columbus, and another on the events of 1815. Nevertheless Claudel as a playwright cannot be understood apart from Claudel the philosopher and the religious and ecclesiastical statesman. Claudel's deep spiritual faith has at the same time an æsthetic and an evangelical side. He is at once influenced by Arthur Rimbaud, William James, Bergson, and the Fathers of the Church. He is today a leader in the Catholic movement in literature, art, and affairs. His dramas have been called "poetic arsenals against the modern world." As such they have had a strong influence on many of the new writers of France — Jules Romains, Georges Duhamel, Jacques Rivière as well as Charles Vildrac, Denys Amiel, and André Obey. Claudel's plays have never entered actively into the commercial-professional field. Nevertheless they have made their mark in spite of the fact that the author's methods of publication are confusing. He publishes his plays in successive versions and in out-of-the-way places. He makes no effort to bring them to the attention of a scoffing world. He has permitted himself to rest under a charge of other-worldliness that quite misrepresents his nature and gifts. André Gide sums up his position fairly when he says: "At present there are two kinds of plays: the one kind is not played but it is important; the other is played but it is without importance. Claudel's plays are more important than all the works of Donnay and Capus."

THE TIDINGS BROUGHT TO MARY

PAUL CLAUDEL writes alike plays of love, passion, and mystical adoration. *La jeune fille Violaine,* which was the early form of *L'Annonce faite à Marie,* is a tale of religious ecstasy and religious devotion. *L'Otage* was a historical drama of 1815. *Le Repos du Septième Jour* deals with the visit of the Emperor of China to Hell. *L'Échange* and *Le Partage du Midi* are love dramas of mediæval passion. *The Tidings Brought to Mary* and its earlier form, *The Young Maiden Violaine,* deal with a theme which has been in the author's mind throughout his life as an author. The earlier form written first in 1892, was not printed until 1926. Meanwhile, however, revised versions under the same title had been variously printed in 1900, in *L'Arbre* in 1901, and in *Théâtre* in 1911–12. Finally in 1912 the full form of *L'Annonce faite à Marie* was performed at Paris. Claudel himself calls this play a Mystery. As such it associates itself immediately with the sacred plays of the Middle Ages, performed in the churches and based upon the legends of Christianity. Not all these plays are based on the stories of the New Testament. As time went on, there grew up cycles of stories which have in all times served as the fables of plays for either sacred or profane production. Many authors, among them Claudel, have not hesitated to employ their own imaginations, to add details, and even to create new fables. The style in which Claudel writes is not the least interesting feature of his work. While reaching sublime heights, it is flexible and adapts itself closely to the purposes of production. This play was first produced by the Théâtre l'Œuvre at the Salle Malakoff, Paris, December 24, 1912. In published form it appeared first in the *Nouvelle Revue Française* in 1912. Thereafter it was produced in Germany and Russia and, in 1917, in London. The author issued revised editions of the play in 1917 and 1929. The translation by Louise Morgan Sill was published in London and New Haven in 1916. It was produced by the New York Theater Guild, December 25, 1922.

CHARACTERS

ANNE VERCORS
ELISABETH, *his wife*
VIOLAINE, *his elder daughter*
MARA, *his younger daughter*
PIERRE DE CRAON
JACQUES HURY
THE MAYOR OF CHEVOCHE
WORKMEN
AN APPRENTICE
COUNTRYWOMEN
A NUN

The action takes place in France some time in the Middle Ages

WORKMAN

AN APPRENTICE

COUNTRYWOMAN

PROLOGUE

The barn at Combernon. It is a lofty edifice, with square pillars that support a vaulted roof. It is empty except for the right wing, which is still filled with straw; and straws are scattered about on the floor, which is of well-trampled earth. At the back is a large double door in the thick wall, with complicated bars and bolts. On the valves of the door are painted rude images of St. Peter and St. Paul, one holding the keys, the other the sword. The scene is lighted by a large yellow wax candle in an iron socket fastened to one of the pillars.

The scenes of the drama take place at the close of the Middle Ages, seen conventionally, as mediæval poets might have imagined classic antiquity.

The time is night, merging into the hours of dawn.

Enter, on a heavy horse, a man wearing a black cloak, and with a leathern bag on the horse's croup behind him, PIERRE DE CRAON. *His gigantic shadow moves across the wall, the floor, the pillars.*

Suddenly, from behind a pillar, VIOLAINE *steps out to meet him. She is tall and slender, and her feet are bare. Her gown is of coarse woollen stuff, and upon her head is a linen coif at once peasant-like and monastic.*

VIOLAINE (*laughingly raising her hands toward him, with the forefingers crossed*). Halt, my lord cavalier! Dismount!

PIERRE DE CRAON. Violaine! (*He gets off the horse.*)

VIOLAINE. Softly, Master Pierre! Is that the way one leaves the house, like a thief without an honest greeting to the ladies?

PIERRE DE CRAON. Violaine, take yourself off. It is the dead of night, and we are here alone, the two of us.

And you know that I am not such a very safe man.

VIOLAINE. I am not afraid of you, mason! A man is not wicked merely because he wants to be!

And a man doesn't do with me just as he wills!

Poor Pierre! You did not even succeed in killing me

With your wretched knife! Nothing but a little snick on my arm which nobody has seen.

PIERRE DE CRAON. Violaine, you must forgive me.

VIOLAINE. It is for that I came.

PIERRE DE CRAON. You are the first woman I ever laid hands on.

The devil, who always seizes his chance, took possession of me.

VIOLAINE. But you found me stronger than him.

PIERRE DE CRAON. Violaine, I am even more dangerous now than I was then.

VIOLAINE. Must we then fight once more?

PIERRE DE CRAON. Even my very presence here is baleful.

(*Silence.*)

VIOLAINE. I don't know what you mean.

PIERRE DE CRAON. Had I not my work? Stones enough to choose and gather, wood enough to join, and metals to melt and mould.

My own work, that suddenly I should lay an impious and lustful hand on the work of another, a living being?

VIOLAINE. In my father's house, the house of your host! Lord! what would they have said if they had known? But I concealed it well.

And they all take you for a sincere and blameless man, just as they did before.

PIERRE DE CRAON. Under appearances, God judges the heart.

VIOLAINE. We three then will guard the secret.

PIERRE DE CRAON. Violaine!

VIOLAINE. Master Pierre?

PIERRE DE CRAON. Stand there near the candle that I may see you well.

(*She stands, smiling, under the candle. He looks a long while at her.*)

VIOLAINE. Have you looked at me long enough?

PIERRE DE CRAON. Who are you, young girl, and what part in you has God reserved to himself?

That the hand which touches you with fleshly desire should in that same instant be thus

Withered, as if it had approached too near the mystery of his dwelling-place?

VIOLAINE. What has happened to you, then, since last year?

PIERRE DE CRAON. The very next day after that one you remember...

VIOLAINE. Well ——?

PIERRE DE CRAON. I discovered in my side the horrible scourge.

VIOLAINE. The scourge, you say? What scourge?

PIERRE DE CRAON. Leprosy, the same we read of in the book of Moses.

VIOLAINE. What is leprosy?

PIERRE DE CRAON. Have you never heard of the woman who lived alone among the rocks of the Gèyn?

Veiled from head to foot, and with a rattle in her hand?

VIOLAINE. That malady, Master Pierre?

PIERRE DE CRAON. Such a scourge it is

That he who has it in its most malicious form

Must be set apart at once,

For there is no living man so healthy that leprosy cannot taint him.

VIOLAINE. Why, then, are you still at liberty among us?

PIERRE DE CRAON. The Bishop gave me a dispensation, and you must know how few people I see,

Except my workmen to give them orders, and my malady is as yet secret and concealed.

And, were I not there, who would give away those newborn churches whom God has confided to my care, on their wedding day?

VIOLAINE. Is that why nobody has seen you this time at Combernon?

PIERRE DE CRAON. I could not avoid returning here,

Because it is my duty to open the side of Monsanvierge

And to unseal the wall for each new flight of doves that seek entrance into the high Ark whose gates may only open toward heaven!

And this time we led to the altar an illustrious victim, a solemn censer,

The Queen herself, mother of the King, ascending in her own person,

For her son deprived of his kingdom.

And now I return to Rheims.

VIOLAINE. Maker of doors, let me open this one for you.

PIERRE DE CRAON. Was there no one else at the farm to do me this service?

VIOLAINE. The servant likes to sleep, and willingly gave me the keys.

PIERRE DE CRAON. Have you no fear or horror of the leper?

VIOLAINE. There is God, He knows how to protect me.

PIERRE DE CRAON. Give me the key, then.

VIOLAINE. No. Let me. You do not understand the working of these old doors.

Indeed! Do you take me for a dainty damsel

Whose taper fingers are used to nothing rougher than the spur, light as the bone of a bird, that arms the heel of her new knight?

You shall see!

(*She turns the keys in the two grinding locks and draws the bolts.*)

PIERRE DE CRAON. This iron is very rusty.

VIOLAINE. The door is no longer used. But the road is shorter this way. (*She strains at the bar.*)

I have opened the door!

PIERRE DE CRAON. What could resist such an assailant?

What a dust! the old valve from top to bottom creaks and moves,

The black spiders run away, the old nests crumble, and the door at last opens from the centre.

(*The door opens; through the darkness can be seen the meadows and the harvest. A feeble glimmer in the east.*)

VIOLAINE. This little rain has done everybody good.

PIERRE DE CRAON. The dust in the road will be well laid.

VIOLAINE (*in a low voice, affectionately*). Peace to you, Pierre!

(*Silence. And, suddenly, sonorous and clear and very high in the heaven, the first tolling of the Angelus. PIERRE takes off his hat, and both make the sign of the cross.*)

VIOLAINE (*her hands clasped and her face raised to heaven, in a voice beautifully clear and touching*). REGINA CÆLI, LÆTARE, ALLELUIA! (*Second tolling.*)

PIERRE DE CRAON (*in a hollow voice*). QUIA QUEM MERUISTI PORTARE, ALLELUIA! (*Third tolling.*)

VIOLAINE. RESURREXIT SICUT DIXIT, ALLELUIA!

PIERRE DE CRAON. ORA PRO NOBIS DEUM. (*Pause.*)

VIOLAINE. GAUDE ET LÆTARE, VIRGO MARIA, ALLELUIA!

PIERRE DE CRAON. QUIA RESURREXIT DOMINUS VERE, ALLELUIA!

(*Peal of the Angelus.*)

PIERRE DE CRAON (*very low*). OREMUS. DEUS QUI PER RESURREC-
    TIONEM FILII TUI DOMINI NOSTRI JESU CRISTI MUNDUM
    LÆTIFICARE DIGNATUS ES, PRÆSTA, QUÆSUMUS, UT PER EJUS
    GENITRICEM VIRGINEM MARIAM PERPETUÆ CAPIAMUS GAUDIA
    VITÆ. PER EUNDEM DOMINUM NOSTRUM JESUM CHRISTUM
    QUI TECUM VIVIT ET REGNAT IN UNITATE SPIRITUS SANCTI
    DEUS PER OMNIA SÆCULA SÆCULORUM.

VIOLAINE. Amen.   (*Both cross themselves.*)

PIERRE DE CRAON. How early the Angelus rings!

VIOLAINE. They say matins up there at midnight like the Carthu-
    sians.

PIERRE DE CRAON. I shall be at Rheims this evening.

VIOLAINE. Know you well the road?

    First along this hedge,

    And then by that low house in the grove of elder bushes, under
      which you will see five or six beehives.

    And a hundred paces further on you reach the King's Highway.
                                (*A pause.*)

PIERRE DE CRAON. PAX TIBI.

    How all creation seems to rest with God in a profound mystery!

    That which was hidden grows visible again with Him, and I feel
      on my face a breath as fresh as roses.

    Praise thy God, blessed earth, in tears and darkness!

    The fruit is for man, but the flower is for God and the sweet
      fragrance of all things born.

    Thus the virtue of the holy soul that is hidden is subtly revealed,
      as the mint leaf by its odour.

    Violaine, who have opened the door for me, farewell!

    I shall never return again to you.

    O young tree of the knowledge of Good and Evil, behold how
      my dissolution begins because I have laid my hands upon
      you,

    And already my soul and body are being divided, as the wine
      in the vat from the crushed grape! What matters it? I
      had no need of woman.

    I have never possessed a corruptible woman.

    The man who in his heart has preferred God, sees when he dies
      his guardian Angel.

The time will soon come when another door opens,

When he who in this life has pleased but few, having finished
his work, falls asleep in the arms of the eternal Bird:

When through translucent walls looms on all sides the sombre
Paradise,

And the censers of the night mingle their scent with the odour of
the noisome wick as it sputters out.

VIOLAINE. Pierre de Craon, I know that you do not expect to hear
from me any false sighs, "Poor fellows!" or "Poor Pierres."

Because to him who suffers the consolation of a joyous comforter
is not of much worth, for his anguish is not to us what it is
to him.

Suffer with our Lord.

But know that your evil act is forgotten

So far as it concerns me, and that I am at peace with you,

And that I do not scorn or abhor you because you are stricken
with the pest and malady,

But I shall treat you like a healthy man, and like Pierre de Craon,
our old friend, whom I respect and love and fear.

What I say to you is true.

PIERRE DE CRAON. Thank you, Violaine.

VIOLAINE. And now I have something to ask you.

PIERRE DE CRAON. Speak.

VIOLAINE. What is this beautiful story that my father has told us?
What is this "Justice" that you are building at Rheims, and
that will be more beautiful than Saint-Rémy and Notre-
Dame?

PIERRE DE CRAON. It is the church which the guilds of Rheims
gave me to build on the site of the old Parc-aux-Ouilles,[1]

There where the old Marc-de-l'Evêque [2] was burned down
yesteryear.

Firstly, as a thank-offering to God for seven fat summers while
distress reigned everywhere else in the kingdom,

For abundant grain and fruit, for cheap and beautiful wool,

For cloth and parchment profitably sold to the merchants of
Paris and Germany.

---

[1] Sheep-fold.   [2] The bishop's still.

Secondly, for the liberties acquired, the privileges conferred by
our Lord the King,

The old order issued against us by Bishops Felix II and Abondant
de Cramail

Rescinded by the Pope,

And all that by the aid of the bright sword and Champenois
coins.

For such is the Christian commonwealth, without servile fear,

But that each should have his right, according to justice, in
marvellous diversity,

That charity may be fulfilled.

VIOLAINE. But of which King and of which Pope do you speak?
For there are two, and one does not know which is the good
one.

PIERRE DE CRAON. The good one is he who is good to us.

VIOLAINE. You do not speak rightly.

PIERRE DE CRAON. Forgive me. I am only an ignorant man.

VIOLAINE. And whence comes this name given to the new parish?

PIERRE DE CRAON. Have you never heard of Saint Justice who was
martyred in an anise field in the time of the Emperor Julian?

(The anise seeds which they put in our gingerbread at the
Easter fair.)

As we were trying to divert the waters of a subterranean spring,
to make way for our foundations,

We discovered her tomb, with this inscription on a slab of stone,
broken in two: JUSTITIA ANCILLA DOMINI IN PACE.

The fragile little skull was broken like a nut — she was a child
of eight years —

And a few milk teeth still adhere to the jaw.

For which all Rheims is filled with admiration, and many signs
and miracles follow the body

Which we have laid in a chapel, to await the completion of our
work.

But under the great foundation stone we have left, like seed, the
little teeth.

VIOLAINE. What a beautiful story! And father also told us that
all the ladies of Rheims give their jewels for the building
of the Justice.

PIERRE DE CRAON. We have a great heap of them, and many
Jews around them like flies.

(VIOLAINE *has been looking down and turning hesitatingly a massive gold ring which she wears on her fourth finger.*)

PIERRE DE CRAON. What ring is that, Violaine?

VIOLAINE. A ring that Jacques gave me.   (*Silence.*)

PIERRE DE CRAON. I congratulate you.

(*She holds out the ring to him.*)

VIOLAINE. It is not yet settled.   My father has said nothing.

Well!   That is what I wanted to tell you.

Take my beautiful ring, which is all I have, and Jacques gave
it to me secretly.

PIERRE DE CRAON. But I do not want it!

VIOLAINE. Take it quickly, or I shall no longer have the strength
to part with it.   (*He takes the ring.*)

PIERRE DE CRAON. What will your betrothed say?

VIOLAINE. He is not really my betrothed yet.

The loss of a ring does not change the heart.   He knows me.
He will give me another of silver.   This one was too fine
for me.

PIERRE DE CRAON (*examining it*).   It is of vegetable gold which, in
former times, they knew how to make with an alloy of honey.

It is as supple as wax, and nothing can break it.

VIOLAINE. Jacques turned it up in the ground when he was ploughing, in a place where they sometimes find old swords turned
quite green, and pretty bits of glass.

I was afraid to wear such a pagan thing, which belongs to the
dead.

PIERRE DE CRAON. I accept this pure gold.

VIOLAINE. And kiss my sister Justice for me.

PIERRE DE CRAON (*looking suddenly at her, as if struck with an idea*).
Is that all you have to give me for her? a bit of gold taken
off your finger?

VIOLAINE. Will that not be enough to pay for one little stone?

PIERRE DE CRAON. But Justice is a large stone herself.

VIOLAINE (*laughing*).   I am not from the same quarry.

PIERRE DE CRAON. The stone needed for the base is not the stone
needed for the pinnacle.

VIOLAINE. Then, if I am a stone, may it be that useful one that grinds the corn, coupled to the twin millstone.

PIERRE DE CRAON. And Justitia also was only a humble little girl at her mother's side,

Until the moment God called her to the confession of faith.

VIOLAINE. But nobody wishes me ill! Is it necessary that I should go preach the Gospel to the Saracens?

PIERRE DE CRAON. It is not for the stone to choose its own place, but for the Master of the Work who chose the stone.

VIOLAINE. Then praised be God who has given me mine now, and I have no longer to seek it. And I ask him for no other.

I am Violaine, I am eighteen years old, my father's name is Anne Vercors, my mother's name is Elisabeth,

My sister's name is Mara, my betrothed is named Jacques. There, that is all, there is nothing more to know.

Everything is perfectly clear, all is arranged beforehand, and I am very glad.

I am free, I have nothing to trouble me; another will lead me, the poor man, and he knows everything that there is to do.

Sower of steeples, come to Combernon! we will give you stone and wood, but you shall not have the daughter of the house!

And, besides, is this not already the house of God, the land of God, the service of God?

Have we not charge over lonely Monsanvierge, which we must feed and guard, providing it with bread, wine, and wax,

Being a dependency of this lonely eyrie of angels with half-spread wings?

Thus, as the great lords have their dovecot, we too have ours, which is known from a great distance away.

PIERRE DE CRAON. One day as I went through the forest of Fisme, I heard two beautiful oak trees talking together,

Praising God for making them immovable on the spot where they were born.

Now one of them, in the prow of an ocean raft, makes war upon the Turks,

The other, felled under my care, supports Jehanne, the good bell in the tower of Laon, whose voice is heard ten leagues away.

Young girl, in my craft one does not keep one's eyes in one's pocket.

I know the good stone under the juniper trees, and the good
    wood like a master woodpecker;

In the same way, men and women.

VIOLAINE. But not girls, Master Pierre! That is too subtle for you.
    And in the first place, there is nothing at all to know.

PIERRE DE CRAON (*in a low voice*). You love him dearly, Violaine?

VIOLAINE (*lowering her eyes*). That is a great mystery between us
    two.

PIERRE DE CRAON. Blessed be thou in thy pure heart!

Holiness is not to get oneself stoned by the Turks, or to kiss
    a leper on the mouth,

But to obey promptly God's commands.
    Whether it be

To stay where we are, or to ascend higher.

VIOLAINE. Ah, how beautiful the world is, and how happy I am!

PIERRE DE CRAON (*speaking low*). Ah, how beautiful the world is,
    and how unhappy I am!

VIOLAINE (*pointing to the sky*). Man of the city, listen! (*Pause.*)
    Do you hear high up there that little soul singing?

PIERRE DE CRAON. It is the lark!

VIOLAINE. It is the lark, alleluia! The lark of the Christian earth,
    alleluia, alleluia!

Do you hear it cry four times, he! he! he! he! higher, higher!

Do you see it, the eager little cross, with its wings spread, like the
    seraphim who have only wings and no feet, singing shrilly
    before the throne of God?

PIERRE DE CRAON. I hear it.

And it is thus I heard it once at dawn, on the day we dedicated
    my daughter Notre-Dame de la Couture,

And a golden point gleamed at the topmost pinnacle of this great
    thing I had made, like a star new-born!

VIOLAINE. Pierre de Craon, if you had done with me as you would,
    Would you be more happy now because of that, or I more
    beautiful?

PIERRE DE CRAON. No, Violaine.

VIOLAINE. And would I still be the same Violaine whom you
    loved?

PIERRE DE CRAON. No, not she, but another.

VIOLAINE. And which is better, Pierre,

That I share my joy with you, or that I share your pain?

PIERRE DE CRAON. Sing far up in the highest heaven, lark of France!

VIOLAINE. Forgive me, for I am too happy, because he whom I love

Loves me, and I am sure of him, and I know he loves me, and all is equal between us.

And because God made me to be happy and not for evil nor any sorrow.

PIERRE DE CRAON. Mount to heaven in a single flight!

As for me, to ascend a little I must have the whole of a cathedral, with its deep foundations.

VIOLAINE. And tell me that you forgive Jacques for marrying me.

PIERRE DE CRAON. No, I do not forgive him.

VIOLAINE. Hatred does you no good, Pierre, and makes me grieve.

PIERRE DE CRAON. It is you who make me speak.

Why do you force me to show the ugly wound that no one sees?

Let me go, and ask me nothing more. We shall not see each other any more.

All the same, I carry away his ring!

VIOLAINE. Leave your hatred in its place, and I will give it back to you when you have need of it.

PIERRE DE CRAON. But besides, Violaine, I am very wretched.

It is hard to be a leper, to bear this shameful wound, knowing that there is no cure and that there is no help for it,

But that each day it spreads and bites deeper; and to be alone and to suffer one's own poison, to feel oneself alive in corruption,

Not only to taste death once, aye, ten times, but to miss nothing, even to the end, of the horrible alchemy of the tomb!

It is you who have brought this evil upon me by your beauty, for before I saw you I was pure and happy, .

My heart lost in my work and ideas, under another's command.

And now that I command in my turn, and draw the plans,

Behold, you turn your face toward me with that poisonous smile.

VIOLAINE. The poison was not in me, Pierre!

PIERRE DE CRAON. I know it, it was in me, and it is still there, and this sick flesh has not cured the tainted soul!

O little soul, was it possible that I should see you and not love you?

VIOLAINE. And certainly you have shown that you love me.

PIERRE DE CRAON. It is my fault if the fruit hangs on the branch? And who is he who loves and does not desire all?

VIOLAINE. And that is why you tried to destroy me?

PIERRE DE CRAON. Man, cruelly injured, has his infernal shades, too, like woman.

VIOLAINE. In what have I failed you?

PIERRE DE CRAON. O image of eternal Beauty, thou art not for me!

VIOLAINE. I am not an image!

That is not the way to speak!

PIERRE DE CRAON. Another takes from you that which was for me.

VIOLAINE. The image remains.

PIERRE DE CRAON. Another takes Violaine from me, and leaves me this tainted flesh and this consumed mind.

VIOLAINE. Be a man, Pierre! Be worthy of the flame which consumes you!

And if one must be consumed, let it be like the Paschal-candle, flaming on its golden candelabrum in the midst of the choir for the glory of all the Church!

PIERRE DE CRAON. So many sublime pinnacles! But shall I never see the roof of my own little house under the trees?

So many belfries whose circling shadows write the hour for all the city! But shall I never design an oven, and the room for the children?

VIOLAINE. It was not for me to take for myself alone what belongs to all.

PIERRE DE CRAON. When will the wedding be, Violaine?

VIOLAINE. At Michaelmas, I suppose, when the harvest is done.

PIERRE DE CRAON. On that day, when the bells of Monsanvierge have spoken and are silent, listen well and you will hear me answer them far away at Rheims.

VIOLAINE. Who takes care of you there?

PIERRE DE CRAON. I have always lived like a workman; it is enough for me if I have a bunch of straw between two stones, a leathern coat, and a little bacon on my bread.

VIOLAINE. Poor Pierre!

PIERRE DE CRAON. I am not to be pitied for that; we are set apart. I do not live as other men, as I am always under the ground with the foundations, or in the sky with the belfry.

VIOLAINE. Well! We could never have lived together! My head swims if I only go up to the hayloft.

PIERRE DE CRAON. This church alone will be my wife, drawn from my side like an Eve of stone, in the slumber of pain.

May I soon feel my great structure rising under me, and lay my hand on this indestructible thing I have made, whose parts hold firmly together, this solid work which I have constructed of strong stone that the Holy Sacrament may be placed there, my work that God inhabits!

I shall never come down again! It is I at whom they point, that group of young girls with arms interlaced, on the chequered pavement a hundred feet below!

VIOLAINE. You must come down. Who knows but I shall have need of you some day?

PIERRE DE CRAON. Farewell, Violaine, my soul, I shall never see you again!

VIOLAINE. Who knows that you will never see me again?

PIERRE DE CRAON. Farewell, Violaine!

How many things I have already done! How many things remain for me to do, how much building up of habitations!

Darkness, with God.

Not the hours of the office in a breviary, but the real hours of a cathedral, where the sun brings light and shade successfully to every part.

I take away your ring,

And of its little circle I will make golden seed!

"God caused the deluge to cease," as says the baptismal psalm,

And I, between the walls of the Justice, shall imprison the gold of the dawn!

The light of day changes, but not that which I shall distil under those arches,

Like the light of the human soul, that the Host may dwell in the midst of it.

The soul of Violaine, my child, in whom my heart delights.

There are churches like pits, and others which are like furnaces,
And others so delicately put together, adjusted with such art,
    that they seem as if they would ring like a bell under a
    finger-tap.
But that which I am going to build will lie under its own shadow
    like condensed gold, and like a pyx full of manna!

VIOLAINE. O Master Pierre, what a beautiful stained-glass window
    you gave to the monks of Clinchy!

PIERRE DE CRAON. The staining of glass is not my art, though
    I know something of it.
But, before the glass is made, the architect, by his knowledge of
    arrangement, makes the stone framework like a filter in the
    waves of God's Light,
And gives to the whole edifice its individual lustre, as to a pearl.

            (MARA VERCORS *enters and watches them without being seen.*)

And now farewell! The sun is risen, and I ought already to be
    far on my road.

VIOLAINE. Farewell, Pierre!

PIERRE DE CRAON. Farewell, Violaine!

VIOLAINE. Poor Pierre!

> (*She looks at him with eyes full of tears, hesitates, and offers him her
>   hand.   He seizes it, and while he holds it between his own she
>   leans towards him and kisses him on the face.*)

> (MARA *makes a gesture of surprise and goes out.*)

> (PIERRE DE CRAON *and* VIOLAINE *go out by the different doors.*)

ACT ONE

SCENE ONE

*The kitchen of Combernon, a spacious room having a great fireplace with
an emblazoned mantel; in the middle of the room a long table and all the
domestic utensils, as in a picture by Breughel.* THE MOTHER, *stooping
before the hearth, tries to revive the fire.* ANNE VERCORS, *standing,
looks at her.   He is a tall and strong man of sixty years, with a full blond
beard streaked with much white.*

THE MOTHER (*without turning around*). Why do you look at me like
    that?

ANNE VERCORS (*thinking*). The end, already! It is like coming
    to the last page in a picture book.

"When the night had passed, the woman having revived the
    household fire...," and the humble and touching story is
    finished.

It is as if I were no longer here. There she is, before my eyes, yet
    seeming already like something only remembered. (*Aloud.*)

O wife, it is a month since we were married

With a ring which is shaped like *Oui,*

A month of which each day is a year.

And for a long time you were fruitless

Like a tree which gives nothing but shade.

And one day we looked at each other

And it was the middle of our life,

Elisabeth! and I saw the first wrinkles on thy forehead and
    around thine eyes.

And, as on our wedding day,

We clasped and embraced each other, no longer with lightness
    of heart,

But with the tenderness and compassion and piety of our mutual
    trust.

And between us was our child and the modesty

Of this sweet narcissus, Violaine.

And then the second was born to us,

Mara the black. Another daughter, and not a son. (*Pause.*)

Well now, say what you have to say, for I know

When you begin speaking without looking at you, saying some-
    thing and nothing. Come now!

THE MOTHER. You know well that one can tell you nothing. You
    are never there, and I must even catch you to sew on a but-
    ton.

And you do not listen to one, but like a watchdog you watch,

Only attentive to the noises of the door.

But men never understand anything.

ANNE VERCORS. Now the little girls are grown up.

THE MOTHER. They? No.

ANNE VERCORS. To whom are we going to marry them all?

THE MOTHER. Marry them, Anne, say you? We have plenty of
    time to think of that.

ANNE VERCORS. Oh, deceit of woman! Tell me! When think you
    anything

But first you do not say just the contrary; maliciousness! I know
    thee.

THE MOTHER. I won't say anything more.

ANNE VERCORS. Jacques Hury.

THE MOTHER. Well?

ANNE VERCORS. There. I will give him Violaine...

And he will take the place of the son I have not had. He is an
    upright and industrious man.

I have known him since he was a little lad, and his mother gave
    him to us. It is I who have taught him everything,

Grain, cattle, servants, arms, tools, our neighbours, our betters,
    custom — God —

The weather, the nature of this ancient soil,

How to reflect before speaking.

I have seen him develop into a man while he was looking at me
    and the beard grow around his kind face,

As he is now, straight-backed and tight like the ears of the barley.

And he was never one of those who contradict, but who reflect,
    like the earth which receives all kinds of grain.

And that which is false, not taking root, dies;

And so, one may not say that he believes in truth, but rather
    that it grows within him, having found nourishment.

THE MOTHER. How do you know, if they love each other or not?

ANNE VERCORS. Violaine

Will do what I tell her.

As for him, I know that he loves her, and you too know it.

Yet the blockhead dares not speak to me. But I will give her to
    him if he wants her. So shall it be.

THE MOTHER. Yes.

No doubt that is as it should be.

ANNE VERCORS. Have you nothing more to say?

THE MOTHER. What, then?

ANNE VERCORS. Very well, I will go seek him.

THE MOTHER. What, seek him? Anne!

ANNE VERCORS. I want everything to be settled at once. I will tell
    you why presently.

THE MOTHER. What have you to tell me? — Anne, listen a moment. ... I fear....

ANNE VERCORS. Well?

THE MOTHER. Mara

Slept in my room this winter, while you were ill, and we talked at night in our beds.

Surely he is an honest lad, and I love him like my own child, almost.

He has no property, that is true, but he is a good ploughman, and comes of a good family.

We could give them

Our Demi-muids farm with the lower fields which are too far away for us. — I, too, wanted to speak to you of him.

ANNE VERCORS. Well?

THE MOTHER. Well, nothing.

No doubt Violaine is the eldest.

ANNE VERCORS. Come, come, what then?

THE MOTHER. What then? How do you know surely that he loves her? — Our old friend, Master Pierre (Why did he keep away from us this time without seeing anybody?),

You saw him last year when he came,

And how he looked at her while she served us. —

Certainly he has no land, but he earns much money.

— And she, while he spoke,

How she listened to him, with her eyes wide open like a child's,

Forgetting to pour the drink for us, so that I had to scold her!

— And Mara, you know her. You know how hard-headed she is!

If she has a notion then

That she will marry Jacques — heigh-ho! She is hard as iron. I don't know! Perhaps it would be better...

ANNE VERCORS. What is all this nonsense?

THE MOTHER. Very well! Very well! we can talk like that. You must not get angry.

ANNE VERCORS. It is my will.

Jacques shall marry Violaine.

THE MOTHER. Well! he shall marry her, then.

ANNE VERCORS. And now, mother, I have something else to tell you, poor old woman! I am going away.

THE MOTHER. You are going away? You are going away, old
man? What is that you say?

ANNE VERCORS. That is why Jacques must marry Violaine without
delay, and take my place here.

THE MOTHER. Lord! You are going away! You mean it? And
where are you going?

ANNE VERCORS (*pointing vaguely toward the south*). Down there.

THE MOTHER. To Château?

ANNE VERCORS. Farther than Château.

THE MOTHER (*lowering her voice*). To Bourges, to the other King?

ANNE VERCORS. To the Kings of Kings, to Jerusalem.

THE MOTHER. Lord!   (*She sits down.*)
    Is it because France is not good enough for you?

ANNE VERCORS. There is too much sorrow in France.

THE MOTHER. But we are very comfortable here and nobody
troubles Rheims.

ANNE VERCORS. That is it.

THE MOTHER. That is what?

ANNE VERCORS. The very thing; we are too happy,
    And the others not happy enough.

THE MOTHER. Anne, that is not our fault.

ANNE VERCORS. It is not theirs, either.

THE MOTHER. I don't know. I know that you are there and that
I have two children.

ANNE VERCORS. But you see, surely, that everything is upset and
put out of its right place, and everybody seeks distractedly
to find where that place is.

And the smoke we see sometimes in the distance is not merely
the smoke of burning straw.

And these crowds of poor people who come to us from every side.

There is no longer a King reigning over France, according to the
prediction of the prophet.[1]

"[1] For, behold the Lord, the Lord of hosts, doth take away from
Jerusalem and from Judah, the stay and the staff, the whole stay of
bread, and the whole stay of water.

"[2] The mighty man, and the man of war, the judge, and the prophet,
and the prudent, and the ancient.

"[3] The captain of fifty, and the honourable man, and the counsellor,
and the cunning artificer, and the eloquent orator.

"[4] And I will give children to be their princes, and babes shall rule
over them." — Isaiah iii, 1–5.

THE MOTHER. That is what you read to us the other day?

ANNE VERCORS. In the place of the King we have two children.

The English one, in his island,

And the other one, so little that among the reeds of the Loire he cannot be seen.

In place of the Pope we have three Popes, and instead of Rome, I don't know what council or other in Switzerland.

All is struggling and moving,

Having no longer any counterweight to steady it.

THE MOTHER. And you, also, where do you want to go?

ANNE VERCORS. I can no longer stay here.

THE MOTHER. Anne, have I done anything to grieve you?

ANNE VERCORS. No, my Elisabeth.

THE MOTHER. Here you abandon me in my old age.

ANNE VERCORS. Give me leave to go, yourself.

THE MOTHER. You do not love me any more and you are no longer happy with me.

ANNE VERCORS. I am weary of being happy.

THE MOTHER. Scorn not the gift which God has given you.

ANNE VERCORS. God be praised who has overwhelmed me with his goodness!

For these thirty years now I have held this sacred fief from my father, and God has sent rain on my furrows.

For ten years there has not been one hour of my work

That he has not repaid four times over and more,

As if it were not his will to keep open his account with me, or leave anything owing.

All else perished, yet I was spared;

So that I shall appear before him empty and without a claim, among those who have received their reward.

THE MOTHER. It is enough to have a grateful heart.

ANNE VERCORS. But I am not satisfied with his benefits,

And because I have received them, shall I leave the greater good to others?

THE MOTHER. I do not understand you.

ANNE VERCORS. Which receives more, the full or the empty vessel?

And which has need of the most water, the cistern or the spring?

THE MOTHER. Ours is nearly dried up by this long hot summer.

ANNE VERCORS. Such has been the evil of this world, that each has
    wanted to enjoy his own as if it had been created for him,
And not at all as if he had received it by the will of God,
The lord his estate, the father his children,
The King his Kingdom and the scholar his rank.
That is why God has taken away from them all these things
    which can be taken away,
And has sent to each man deliverance and fasting.
And why is the portion of others not mine also?
THE MOTHER. You have your duty here with us.
ANNE VERCORS. Not if you will absolve me from it.
THE MOTHER. I will not absolve you.
ANNE VERCORS. You see that what I had to do is done.
The two children are reared, and Jacques is there to take my
    place.
THE MOTHER. Who calls you far away from us?
ANNE VERCORS (smiling). An angel blowing a trumpet.
THE MOTHER. What trumpet?
ANNE VERCORS. The soundless trumpet that is heard by all.
The trumpet that calls all men from time to time that the por-
    tions may be distributed afresh.
The trumpet in the valley of Jehosaphat before it has made
    a sound,
That of Bethlehem when Augustus numbered the people.
The trumpet of the Assumption, when the apostles were as-
    sembled.
The voice which takes the place of the Word when the Chief no
    longer speaks
To the body that seeks union with him.
THE MOTHER. Jerusalem is so far away!
ANNE VERCORS. Paradise is still farther.
THE MOTHER. God in the tabernacle is with us even here.
ANNE VERCORS. But not that great hole in the earth.
THE MOTHER. What hole?
ANNE VERCORS. That the Cross made when it was set there.
Behold how it draws everything to itself.
There is the stitch which cannot be undone, the knot which
    cannot be untied,

The heritage of all, the interior boundary stone that can never
be uprooted,

The centre and the navel of the world, the element by which all
humanity is held together.

THE MOTHER. What can one pilgrim alone do?

ANNE VERCORS. I am not alone! A great multitude rejoice and
depart with me!

The multitude of all my dead,

Those souls, one above the other, of whom nothing is left now
but the tombstones, all those stones baptized with me who
claim their rightful place in the structure!

And as it is true that the Christian is never alone, but is in communion with all his brothers,

The whole kingdom is with me, invoking, and drawing near to
the Seat of God, taking anew its course toward him,

And I am its deputy and I carry it with me

To lay it once again upon the eternal Pattern.

THE MOTHER. Who knows but that we shall need you here?

ANNE VERCORS. Who knows but that I am needed elsewhere?

Everything is shaking; who knows but that I obstruct God's
plan by remaining here

Where the need there was of me is past?

THE MOTHER. I know you are an inflexible man.

ANNE VERCORS (*tenderly, changing his voice*). To me you are always
young and beautiful, and very great is the love I feel for
my black-haired sweet Elisabeth.

THE MOTHER. My hair is grey! —

ANNE VERCORS. Say yes, Elisabeth....

THE MOTHER. Anne, you have not left me in all these thirty years.
What will become of me without my chief and my companion?

ANNE VERCORS.... The yes which will separate us now, very low,

As round as the oui that formerly made us one.   (*Silence.*)

THE MOTHER (*speaking very low*). Yes, Anne.

ANNE VERCORS. Have patience, Zabillet! I shall soon return.

Can you not have faith in me a little while, though I am not here!

Soon will come another separation.

Come, put food for two days in a bag. It is time I was off.

THE MOTHER. What? Today, even today?

ANNE VERCORS. Even today.

(Her head droops and she does not move.   He takes her in his arms but she does not respond.)

Farewell, Elisabeth.

THE MOTHER. Alas, old man, I shall never see you again.

ANNE VERCORS. And now I must seek Jacques.

SCENE TWO

(Enter MARA.)

MARA TO THE MOTHER. Go, and tell him she is not to marry him.

THE MOTHER. Mara! How is this? You were there?

MARA. Go, I tell you, and tell him she is not to marry him.

THE MOTHER. What she? What he? What do you know of her marrying him?

MARA. I was there. I heard it all.

THE MOTHER. Very well, my child! Your father wishes it. You have seen I did what I could, and his mind is not changed.

MARA. Go and tell him that she is not to marry him, or I will kill myself!

THE MOTHER. Mara!

MARA. I will hang myself in the woodhouse, there where we found the cat hung.

THE MOTHER. Mara! Wicked girl!

MARA. There again she has taken him away from me! Now she has taken him away!.... It was always I who was to be his wife, and not she. She knows very well it is I.

THE MOTHER. She is the eldest.

MARA. What does that matter?

THE MOTHER. It is your father who wishes it.

MARA. I don't care.

THE MOTHER. Jacques Hury Loves her.

MARA. That is not true! I know well enough that you do not love me!

You have always loved her best! Oh, when you talk of your
Violaine it is like talking of sugar,

It is like sucking a cherry just when you are about to spit out the
stone!

But Mara the magpie! She is as hard as iron, she is as sour as the
wild cherry!

Added to that, there's always the talk of your Violaine being so
beautiful!

And behold, she is now to have Combernon!

What does she know how to do, the ferret? which of us two can
drive the cart?

She thinks herself like Saint Onzemillevierges!

But, as for me, I am Mara Vercors, who hates injustice and
deceit,

Mara who speaks the truth, and it is that which makes the
servants angry!

Let them be angry! I scorn them. Not one of the women dares
stir in my presence, the hypocrites! Everything goes as
smoothly as at the mill.

— And yet everything is for her and nothing for me.

THE MOTHER. You will have your share.

MARA. Aye, truly! The sandy ground up yonder! ooze and mud
that it needs five oxen to plough! the bad ground of Chinchy.

THE MOTHER. It brings in good profit all the same.

MARA. Surely.

Long-rooted reeds and cow-wheat, senna, and mullein!

I shall have enough to make my herb-tea.

THE MOTHER. Bad girl; you know well enough that is not true!

You know well no wrong is done you!

But you have always been wicked! When you were little

You would not cry when you were beaten.

Tell me, you black-skinned child, you ugly one!

Is she not the eldest?

What have you against her?

Jealous girl! Yet she has always done what you wish.

Very well! She will be married first, and you will be married,
you also, afterwards!

And it is too late to do differently, anyhow, because your father
is going away — oh, how sad I am!

He has gone to speak to Violaine and he will look for
   Jacques.

MARA. That's true! Go at once! Go, go at once!

THE MOTHER. Go where?

MARA. Mother, come now! You know well I am the one. Tell
   him she is not to marry him, *maman*!

THE MOTHER. Surely I shall do no such thing.

MARA. Only tell him what I have said. Tell him that I will kill
   myself. Do you understand?   (*She looks fixedly at her.*)

THE MOTHER. Ha!

MARA. Do you believe I will not do it?

THE MOTHER. Alack, I know you would!

MARA. Go then!

THE MOTHER. O

Obstinate!

MARA. You have nothing to do with it.

Only to repeat to him just what I have said.

THE MOTHER. And he — how do you know he will be willing to
   marry you?

MARA. Certainly he will not.

THE MOTHER. Well....

MARA. Well?

THE MOTHER. Don't think that I shall advise him to do your will! —
   on the contrary!

I will only tell him what you have said. It is very sure

That she will not be so silly as to give in to you, if she will listen
   to me.

MARA. Perhaps. — Go. — Do as I say.   (*She goes out.*)

Scene Three

(*Enter* ANNE VERCORS *and* JACQUES HURY, *afterwards* VIOLAINE,
   and then the farm labourers and servants.)

ANNE VERCORS (*stopping*). Heh! what is that thou tell'st me?

JACQUES HURY. Just as I say! This time I took him in the act, with
   the pruning-hook in his hand!

I came up softly behind him and all of a sudden

Flac! I threw myself full length on him,

As you throw yourself on a hare in her hole at harvest
And there beside him was a bunch of twenty young poplars, the
ones you set such store by!

ANNE VERCORS. Why did he not come to me? I should have given
him the wood he needed.

JACQUES HURY. The wood he needs is the handle of my whip!

It is not need but wickedness, the idea of doing wrong!

These ne'er-do-wells from Chevoche are always ready to do
anything

Out of bravado, and to defy people!

But as to that man, I will cut off his ears with my little knife!

ANNE VERCORS. No.

JACQUES HURY. At least let me tie him by his wrists to the harrow,
before the big gate,

With his face turned against the teeth; with Faraud the dog to
watch him.

ANNE VERCORS. Not that either.

JACQUES HURY. What is to be done then?

ANNE VERCORS. Send him home.

JACQUES HURY. With his bundle of wood?

ANNE VERCORS. And with another that thou wilt give him.

JACQUES HURY. Father, that is not right.

ANNE VERCORS. Thou canst tie his faggot around, that he may not
lose any of it.

That will help him in crossing the ford at Saponay.

JACQUES HURY. It is not well to be lax about one's rights.

ANNE VERCORS. I know it, it is not well!

Jacques, behold how lazy and old I am, weary of fighting and
defending.

Once I was harsh like thee.

There is a time to take and a time to let take.

The budding tree must be protected, but the tree where the fruit
hangs do not trouble thyself about.

Let us be unjust in very little, lest God be unjust to me in much.

— And besides, thou wilt do now as thou wilt, for thou art placed
over Combernon in my stead.

JACQUES HURY. What do you say?

THE MOTHER. He is going a pilgrim to Jerusalem.

JACQUES HURY. Jerusalem?

ANNE VERCORS. It is true. I start this very moment.

JACQUES HURY. What? What does that mean?

ANNE VERCORS. Thou hast heard very well.

JACQUES HURY. Thou wilt leave us like that, when the work is at its heaviest?

ANNE VERCORS. It is not necessary to have two masters at Combernon.

JACQUES HURY. My father, I am only your son!

ANNE VERCORS. Thou wilt be the father here, in my stead.

JACQUES HURY. I do not understand you.

ANNE VERCORS. I am going away. Take Combernon from me
As I took it from my father, and he from his,
And Radulphe the Frank, first of our line, from Saint Rémy de Rheims,
Who from Genevieve of Paris received this land, pagan and bristling with seedlings and wild thorns.
Radulphe and his children made it Christian by iron and by fire
And laid it naked and broken under the waters of baptism.
Hill and plain scored they with equal furrows,
As an industrious scholar copies line after line the word of God.
And they began to build Monsanvierge on the mountain, in that place where Evil was worshipped,
(And at first there was naught but a cabin made of logs and reeds, whose door the Bishop came to seal,
And two holy recluses were left to guard it),
And at the mountain's base, Combernon, a dwelling armed and provisioned.
Thus this land is free that we hold from St. Rémy in heaven, paying tithes up there to this flight, one moment stayed, of murmuring doves.
For everything is of God, and those who live in Him reap without ceasing the fruits of their works,
Which pass and come back to us again in their time in magnificent succession:
As over the various harvests every day in summer float those great clouds that drift toward Germany.
The cattle here are never sick, the udders and the wells are never dry; the grain is as solid as gold, the straw as firm as iron.

And for defence against pillagers we have arms, and the walls of
Combernon, and the King, our neighbour.

Gather this harvest that I have sown, as in the past I myself
have filled again the furrows my father ploughed.

O joyful work of the farmer, for which the sun is as bright as our
glistening ox, and the rain is our banker, and God works
with us every day, making of everything the best!

Others look to men for their rewards, but we receive ours straight
from heaven itself,

A hundred for one, the full ear for a seed, and the tree for a nut.

For such is the justice of God to us, and the measure with which
He repays us.

The earth cleaves to the sky, the body to the spirit, all things
that He has created are in communion, all have need of
one another.

Take the handles of the plough in my stead, that the earth may
bring forth bread as God Himself has wished.

Give food to all creatures, men and animals, to spirits and bodies,
and to immortal souls.

You, women, labourers, look! Behold the son
I have chosen, Jacques! I am going away and he stays in my
place. Obey him.

JACQUES HURY. May it be done according to your will.

ANNE VERCORS. Violaine!

My child, first born instead of the son I have not had!

Heir of my name in whom I too shall be given to another!

Violaine, when thou shalt have a husband, do not scorn the love
of thy father.

For thou canst not give back to a father what he has given thee,
when thou wouldst.

Between husband and wife everything is equal; what they do
not know they accept, one from the other, with faith.

This is the mutual religion, this is the servitude through which
the wife's breast grows large with milk!

But the father, seeing his children separate from him, recognizes
what was once within himself. My daughter, know thy
father!

A Father's love

Asks no return, and the child has no need either to win or merit
  it:

As it was his before the beginning, so it remains

His blessing and his inheritance, his help, his honour, his right,
  his justification!

My soul is never divided from the soul I have transmitted.

What I have given can never be given back.   Only know, O my
  child, that I am thy father!

And of my issue there is no male.   Only women have I brought
  into the world.

Nothing but that thing in us which gives and which is given.

— And now the hour of parting is come.

VIOLAINE. Father!   Do not say such a cruel thing!

ANNE VERCORS. Jacques, you are the man whom I love.   Take her!
      I give you my daughter, Violaine.   Take my name from her.

Love her, for she is as pure as gold.

All the days of thy life, like bread, of which one never tires.

She is simple and obedient, sensitive and reserved.

Do not cause her any sorrow, and give her only kindness.

Everything here is thine, except what will be given to Mara, in
  accordance with my plan.

JACQUES HURY. What, my father, your daughter, your property...

ANNE VERCORS. I give you all at once, as all is mine.

JACQUES HURY. But who knows if she still cares for me?

ANNE VERCORS. Who knows?

      (VIOLAINE *looks at* JACQUES *and forms* "*Yes*" *with her lips,
      without speaking*.)

JACQUES HURY. You care for me, Violaine?

VIOLAINE. My father wishes it.

JACQUES HURY. You wish it too?

VIOLAINE. I wish it too.

JACQUES HURY. Violaine!

  How shall we get on together?

VIOLAINE. Consider well while there is yet time!

JACQUES HURY. Then I take you by God's command, and I will
      nevermore let you go.   (*He takes her by both hands.*)

  I have you and hold you, your hand and the arm with it, and all
    that comes with the arm.

Parents, your daughter is no longer yours! She is mine only!

ANNE VERCORS. Well, they are married; it is done!
What say you, mother?

THE MOTHER. I am very glad! *(She weeps.)*

ANNE VERCORS. She weeps, my wife!

There! that is how they take our children from us and we shall be left alone,

The old woman who lives on a little milk and a small bit of cake,

And the old man with his ears full of white hairs like the heart of an artichoke.

— Let them make ready the wedding-dress!

— Children, I shall not be at your wedding.

VIOLAINE. What, father!

THE MOTHER. Anne!

ANNE VERCORS. I am going. Now.

VIOLAINE. O father! before we are married.

ANNE VERCORS. It must be. Your mother will explain all to you.

(Enter MARA.)

THE MOTHER. How long shall you stay over there?

ANNE VERCORS. I do not know. It may be but a short time.

I shall soon be coming back. *(Silence.)*

VOICE OF A CHILD *(in the distance)*. Oriole, oriole! all alone!

Who eats the wild cherry and throws out the stone!

ANNE VERCORS. The oriole, rosy and golden, whistles in the heart of the tree.

What does he say? that after these long days of heat

The rain last night was like a shower of gold falling upon the earth.

What does he say? he says it is good weather for ploughing.

What more does he say? that the weather is fine, that God is great, and that it is still two hours of noon.

What more does the little bird say?

That it is time for the old man to go

Elsewhere, and leave the world to itself.

— Jacques, I leave to you all my property — protect these women.

JACQUES HURY. What, are you really going?

ANNE VERCORS. I believe he has heard nothing.

JACQUES HURY. Like that, right away?

ANNE VERCORS. The hour is come.

THE MOTHER. You will not go without first eating?

> (*During this time the women servants have prepared the table for the farm meal.*)

ANNE VERCORS (*to a woman servant*). Ho! my bag, my hat!
Bring my shoes! bring my cloak!
I have not time enough to share this meal with you.

THE MOTHER. Anne! How long wilt thou stay over there? One
> year, two years? More than two years?

ANNE VERCORS. One year. Two years. Yes, that is it.
Put on my shoes.

> (THE MOTHER *kneels before him and puts on his shoes.*)

For the first time I leave thee, O house!
Combernon, lofty dwelling!
Watch faithfully over it all! Jacques will be here in my stead.
There is the hearth where there is always fire, there is the long
> table where I give food to my people.
All take your places! Just once more I will cut the bread....

> (*He seats himself at the head of the long table, with* THE MOTHER
> *at his right. All the men and women servants stand, each at his
> place. He takes the bread, making the sign of the cross above it
> with the knife, and cuts it; and gives it to* VIOLAINE *and* MARA
> *to pass. The last piece he keeps himself. Then he turns solemnly
> toward* THE MOTHER *and opens his arms.*)

Farewell, Elisabeth!

THE MOTHER (*weeping in his arms*). Thou wilt never see me more.

ANNE VERCORS (*in a lower tone*). Farewell, Elisabeth.

> (*He turns toward* MARA, *looks gravely at her for a long time, and
> then holds out his hand to her.*)

Farewell, Mara! be virtuous.

MARA (*kissing his hand*). Farewell, father!

> (*Silence.* ANNE VERCORS *stands, looking before him as if he did
> not see* VIOLAINE, *who stands full of agitation at his side. At
> last he turns slightly toward her, and she puts her arms around his
> neck, sobbing, with her face against his breast.*)

ANNE VERCORS (*to the men servants, as if he noticed nothing*). Farewell, all!

I have always dealt justly by you. If anyone denies this, he lies.

I am not like other masters. But I praise when praise is due, and I reprove when reproof is due.

Now that I am going away, do your duty as if I were there.

For I shall return. I shall return some time when you do not expect me.   (*He shakes hands with them all.*)

Let my horse be brought!

 (*Silence. He leans toward* VIOLAINE, *who continues to embrace him.*)

What is it, little child?

You have exchanged a husband for thy father.

VIOLAINE. Alas! Father! Alas!

 (*He removes her hands gently from around his neck.*)

THE MOTHER. Tell me when will you return.

ANNE VERCORS. I cannot tell.

Perhaps it will be in the morning, perhaps at mid-day, when you are eating.

And perhaps, awaking some night, you will hear my step on the road.

Farewell!   (*He goes.*)

ACT TWO

SCENE ONE

A fortnight later. The beginning of July. Noon.

A large orchard planted with regular rows of round trees. Higher, and a little withdrawn, the wall and towers and long buildings with tiled roofs of Combernon. Then, the side of the hill, which rises abruptly, and on its summit the massive stone arch of Monsanvierge, without door or window, with its five towers like those of the Cathedral of Laon, and in its side the great white scar made for the recent entrance of the Queen Mother of France.

Everything vibrates under an ardent sun.

(A woman's voice on high, from the height of the highest tower of Monsanvierge.)

SALVE REGINA MATER MISERICORDIAE

VITA DULCEDO ET SPES NOSTRA SALVE

AD TE CLAMAMUS EXULES FILII HEVAE

AD TE SUSPIRAMUS GEMENTES ET FLENTES IN HAC LACRYMARUM
VALLE EIA ERGO ADVOCATA NOSTRA ILLOS TUOS MISERICORDES
OCULOS AD NOS CONVERTE

ET JESUM BENEDICTUM FRUCTUS VENTRIS TUI NOBIS POST HOC
EXILIUM OSTENDE

O CLEMENS

O PIA

O DULCIS VIRGO MARIA

(Long pause during which the stage remains empty.)

(Enter THE MOTHER and MARA.)

MARA. What did she say?

THE MOTHER. I drew her out as we talked, without seeming to.
You see how she has lost her gay spirits these last few days.

MARA. She never talks much.

THE MOTHER. But she does not laugh any more.
That troubles me.
Perhaps it is because Jacquin is away, but he returns today.
— And her father too is gone.

MARA. That is all thou saidst to her?

THE MOTHER. That is what I said to her, and the rest of it without
changing a word, just as you said it to me: Jacquin and you:
that you love him and all.

And I added, and I said it over two or three times, that this time
she must not be foolish, and not resist at all,

Or break off the marriage, which is as good as made, against the
father's will.

What would people think of it?

MARA. And what did she answer?

THE MOTHER. She began to laugh, and I, I began to cry.

MARA. I will make her laugh!

THE MOTHER. It was not the laughter I love of my little girl, and
I began to cry.

And I said, "No, no, Violaine, my child!" not knowing any
longer what I said.

But she, without speaking, made a sign with her hand that she
wanted to be alone.

Ah! what misery we have with our children!

MARA. Hush!

THE MOTHER. What is it?

I am sorry for what I have done.

MARA. Well! Do you see her down there in the paddock? She is
walking behind the trees.

Now she is out of sight.

(*Silence. From behind the scene is heard the blast of a horn.*)

THE MOTHER. There is Jacquin come back. I know the sound of
his horn.

MARA. Let us go further off. (*They move off.*)

SCENE TWO

(*Enter* JACQUES HURY.)

JACQUES HURY (*looking all around*). I don't see her.

And yet she sent word

That she wanted to see me this morning,

Here.

(*Enter* MARA. *She advances to* JACQUES, *and at six paces before
him drops a ceremonious courtesy.*)

JACQUES HURY. Good morning, Mara.

MARA. My lord, your servant!

JACQUES HURY. What is this foolery?

MARA. Do I not owe you respect? Are you not the master here,
dependent only upon God, like the King of France himself
and the Emperor Charlemagne?

JACQUES HURY. Jest if you like, but it is true all the same! Yes,
Mara, it is glorious! Dear sister, I am too happy!

MARA. I am not your *dear* sister! I am your servant because
I must be.

Man of Braine! son of a serf! I am not your sister; you are not of
our blood!

JACQUES HURY. I am the husband of Violaine.

MARA. You are not that yet.

JACQUES HURY. I shall be tomorrow.

MARA. Who knows?

JACQUES HURY. Mara, I have thought deeply about it,

And I believe you have only dreamed that story you told me the other day.

MARA. What story?

JACQUES HURY. Don't pretend not to know.

That story about the mason, that secret kiss at dawn.

MARA. It is possible. I did not see well. Yet I have good eyes.

JACQUES HURY. And it has been whispered to me that the man is a leper!

MARA. I do not love you, Jacques.

But you have the right to know all. All must be pure and clear at Monsanvierge, which is held up like a monstrance before all the kingdom.

JACQUES HURY. All that will be explained in a moment.

MARA. You are clever and nothing can escape you.

JACQUES HURY. I see at any rate that you don't love me.

MARA. There! there! What did I say? what did I say?

JACQUES HURY. Everybody here is not of your mind.

MARA. You speak of Violaine? I blush for that little girl.

It is shameful to give oneself like that,

Soul, body, heart, skin, the outside, the inside, and the root.

JACQUES HURY. I know that she belongs entirely to me.

MARA. Yes.

How grandly he speaks! how sure he is of the things that belong to him! Brainard of Braine!

Only those things belong to one that one has made, or taken, or earned.

JACQUES HURY. But, Mara, I like you, and I have nothing against you.

MARA. Without doubt — like all the rest of the things here?

JACQUES HURY. It is no fault of mine that you are not a man, and that I take your property from you!

MARA. How proud and satisfied he is! Look at him, he can hardly keep from laughing!

There now! don't do yourself harm! Laugh!   (*He laughs.*)

I know your face well, Jacques.

JACQUES HURY. You are angry because you cannot make me unhappy.

MARA. Like the other day while the father was talking,

When one of your eyes smiled and the other wept — without
tears.

JACQUES HURY. Am I not master of a fine estate?

MARA. And the father was old, wasn't he?   You know a thing or
two more than he does?

JACQUES HURY. To each man his day.

MARA. That is true, Jacques, you are a tall and handsome young
man.

See him, how he blushes.

JACQUES HURY. Don't torment me.

MARA. All the same, it is a pity!

JACQUES HURY. What is a pity?

MARA. Farewell, husband of Violaine! 'Farewell, master of
Monsanvierge — ah — ah!

JACQUES HURY. I will show you that so I am.

MARA. Then understand the spirit of this place, Brainard of Braine!

He thinks that everything is his, like a peasant; you will be
shown the contrary!

Like a peasant who sees nothing higher than himself as he stands
in the midst of his flat little field!

But Monsanvierge belongs to God, and the master of Monsanvierge is God's man, who has nothing

For himself, having received everything for another.

That is the lesson passed on here from father to son.   There is no
higher position than ours.

Take on the spirit of your masters, peasant!

(*She makes as if to go and turns back.*)

Ah!

Violaine, when I met her,

Gave me a message for you.

JACQUES HURY. Why did you not say so sooner?

MARA. She is waiting for you near the fountain.

SCENE THREE

*The fountain of the Adoue.   It is a large square orifice cut in a vertical
wall, built of blocks of limestone.   A thin stream of water drips from it
with a melancholy sound.   Thank-offerings of crosses made of straw and
bouquets of faded flowers are hung on the wall.*

The fountain is surrounded with luxurious trees, and with a bower of rose-bushes whose abundant blossoms thickly star the green foliage.

JACQUES HURY (*he looks at* VIOLAINE *who comes along the winding path. She is all golden, and glows brilliantly at moments when the sun falls upon her between the leaves*). O my betrothed among the flowery branches, hail!

(VIOLAINE *enters and stands before him. She is clothed in a linen gown with a kind of dalmatic of cloth-of-gold decorated with large red and blue flowers. Her head is crowned with a diadem of enamel and gold.*)

Violaine, how beautiful you are!

VIOLAINE. Jacques! Good morning, Jacques! Ah, how long you stayed down there!

JACQUES HURY. I had to get rid of everything, and sell, in order to be perfectly free.

To be the man of Monsanvierge only and yours.

— What is this wonderful dress?

VIOLAINE. I wore it for you. I had spoken to you about it. Do you not recognize it?

It is the habit of the nuns of Monsanvierge, except only the maniple, the habit they wear in the choir,

The deacon's dalmatic which they have the privilege of wearing, something priestly, as they themselves are holy sacrifices,

And the women of Combernon have the right to wear it twice:

First, on the day of their betrothal,

Secondly, on the day of their death.

JACQUES HURY. It is really true, then, that this is the day of our betrothal, Violaine?

VIOLAINE. Jacques, there is yet time, we are not married yet!

If you have only wanted to please my father there is still time to withdraw; it concerns no one but us. Say but a word, and I would not want you any more, Jacques.

For nothing has yet been put in writing, and I do not know if I still please you.

JACQUES HURY. How beautiful you are, Violaine!

And how beautiful is the world of which you are the portion reserved for me.

VIOLAINE. It is you, Jacques, who are all that is best in the world.

JACQUES HURY. Is it true that you are willing to belong to me?

VIOLAINE. Yes, it is true! good morning, my beloved! I am yours.

JACQUES HURY. Good morning, my wife! Good morning, sweet Violaine!

VIOLAINE. These are good things to hear, Jacques!

JACQUES HURY. You must always be there! Tell me that you will always be the same, the angel who is sent to me!

VIOLAINE. For evermore all that is mine shall always be yours.

JACQUES HURY. And as for me, Violaine....

VIOLAINE. Say nothing. I ask you nothing. You are there, and that is enough for me. Good morning, Jacques!

Ah, how beautiful this hour is, and I ask for nothing more.

JACQUES HURY. Tomorrow will be still more beautiful!

VIOLAINE. Tomorrow I shall have taken off my gorgeous robe.

JACQUES HURY. But you will be so near to me that I shall no longer be able to see you.

VIOLAINE. Very near to you indeed!

JACQUES HURY. Your place is ready.

Violaine, what a solitary spot this is, and how secretly I am here with you!

VIOLAINE (in a low tone). Your heart is enough.

Go to, I am with you, and say not a word more.

JACQUES HURY. But tomorrow, before everybody,

I will take this Queen in my arms.

VIOLAINE. Take her, and do not let her go.

Ah, take your little one with you so that they can never find her, and never do her any harm!

JACQUES HURY. And you will not regret then the linen and the gold?

VIOLAINE. Was I wrong to make myself beautiful for one poor little hour?

JACQUES HURY. No, my beautiful lily, I can never tire of looking at you in your glory!

VIOLAINE. O Jacques! tell me again that you think me beautiful!

JACQUES HURY. Yes, Violaine!

VIOLAINE. The most beautiful of all, and the other women are nothing to you?

JACQUES HURY. Yes, Violaine.

VIOLAINE. And that you love me only, as the tenderest husband loves the poor creature who has given herself to him?

JACQUES HURY. Yes, Violaine.

VIOLAINE. Who gives herself to him with all her heart, Jacques, believe me, and holds nothing back.

JACQUES HURY. And you, Violaine, do you not believe me then?

VIOLAINE. I believe you, I believe you, Jacques!

I believe in you! I have confidence in you, my darling!

JACQUES HURY. Why, then, do you seem troubled and frightened? Show me your left hand.   (*She shows it.*)

My ring is gone.

VIOLAINE. I will explain that to you presently, you will be satisfied.

JACQUES HURY. I am satisfied, Violaine. I have faith in you.

VIOLAINE. I am more than a ring, Jacques. I am a great treasure.

JACQUES HURY. Yes, Violaine.

VIOLAINE. Ah, if I give myself to you,

Will you not know how to save your little one who loves you?

JACQUES HURY. There you are doubting me again.

VIOLAINE. Jacques! After all I do no harm in loving you. It is God's will, and my father's.

It is you who have charge of me! And who knows if you will not know perfectly how to defend and save me?

It is enough that I give myself entirely to you.

The rest is your affair, and no longer mine.

JACQUES HURY. And is it like this you give yourself to me, my flower-o'-the-sun?

VIOLAINE. Yes, Jacques.

JACQUES HURY. Who then can take you out of my arms?

VIOLAINE. Ah, how big the world is, and how alone we are!

JACQUES HURY. Poor child! I know that your father is gone.

And I too no longer have anyone with me to tell me what should be done, and what is good or ill.

You must help me, Violaine, as I love you.

VIOLAINE. My father has abandoned me.

JACQUES HURY. But I remain to you, Violaine.

VIOLAINE. Neither my mother nor my sister love me, though I have done them no wrong.

And nothing is left to me but this tall, terrible man whom I do not know.

(*He tries to take her in his arms. She pushes him away quickly.*)

Do not touch me, Jacques!

JACQUES HURY. Am I then a leper?

VIOLAINE. Jacques, I want to speak to you — ah, but it is hard!

Do not fail me, who now have only you!

JACQUES HURY. Who would do you harm?

VIOLAINE. Know what you do in taking me for your wife!

Let me speak to you very humbly, my lord Jacques,

Who are about to receive my soul and my body from the hands of God according to his command, and my father's who made them.

And know the dowry I bring to you which is not like those of other women,

But this holy mountain wrapped in prayer day and night before God, like an altar smoking always,

And this lamp whose light is never suffered to go out, and whose oil it is our duty to replenish.

And no man is witness to our marriage, but that Lord whose fief we alone hold,

Who is the Omnipotent, the God of the Armies.

And it is not the sun of July that lights us, but the light of his countenance.

To the holy be the holy things! Who knows if our heart be pure?

Never until now has a male been lacking to our race, and always the sacred place has been handed down from father to son,

And behold, for the first time it falls into the hands of a woman, and becomes with her the object of desire.

JACQUES HURY. Violaine — no: I am not a scholar nor a monk nor a saint.

I am not the lay-servant of Monsanvierge, nor the keeper of its turning-box.

I have a duty and I will perform it,

Which is to feed these murmuring birds,

And to fill each morning the basket they lower from the sky.

That is written down. That is right.

I have understood that, and I have fixed it in my head, and you must not ask any more of me.

You must not ask me to understand what is above me, and why, these holy women have imprisoned themselves up there in that pigeon-house.

To the heavenly be heaven, and the earth to the earthly.

For the wheat will not grow by itself, and a good ploughman is necessary.

And I can say without boasting that such I am, and no one can teach me that, not even your father himself perhaps,

For he was old and set in his ways.

To each one his own place, and that is justice.

And your father, in giving you to me,

Together with Monsanvierge, knew what he was doing, and that was just.

VIOLAINE. But Jacques, I do not love you because it is just.

And even if it were not just, I would love you the same, and more.

JACQUES HURY. I do not understand you, Violaine.

VIOLAINE. Jacques, do not make me speak! You love me so much, and I can only do you harm.

Let me alone! there cannot be justice between us two! but only faith and charity. Go away from me while there is yet time.

JACQUES HURY. I do not understand, Violaine.

VIOLAINE. My beloved, do not force me to tell you my great secret.

JACQUES HURY. A great secret, Violaine?

VIOLAINE. So great that all is over, and you will not ask to marry me any more.

JACQUES HURY. I do not understand you.

VIOLAINE. Am I not beautiful enough just now, Jacques? What more do you ask of me?

What does one ask of a flower

Except to be beautiful and fragrant for a moment, poor flower, and then — the end.

The flower's life is short, but the joy it 'has given for a minute

Is not of those things which have a beginning and an end.

Am I not beautiful enough? Is something lacking? Ah! I see thine eyes, my beloved! Is there anything in thee at this moment that does not love me, and that doubts me?

Is my soul not enough? Take it, and I am still here, and absorb to its depths that which is all thine!

To die requires but a moment, and to die in each other would
    not annihilate us more than love, and does one need to live
      when one is dead?

What more wouldst thou do with me?   Fly, take thyself away!
    Why dost thou wish to marry me?   Why dost thou wish
To take for thyself what belongs only to God?

The hand of God is upon us, and thou canst not defend me!

O Jacques, we shall never be husband and wife in this world!

JACQUES HURY. Violaine, what are these strange words, so tender,
      so bitter?   By what threatening and gloomy paths are you
      leading me?

I believe you wish to put me to the proof, and to triumph over
    me, who am but a simple and rough man.

Ah! Violaine, how beautiful you are like this! and yet I am afraid,
    and I see you in clothing that terrifies me!

For this is not a woman's dress, but the robe of one who offers
    the sacrifice at the altar,

Of him who waits upon the priest, leaving the side uncovered
    and the arms free!

Ah, I see, it is the spirit of Monsanvierge which lives in you, the
    supreme flower outside of this sealed garden!

Ah, do not turn to me that face which is no longer of this world!
    that is no longer my dear Violaine.

There are enough angels to serve the mass in heaven!

Have pity on me, who am only a man without wings, who re-
    joiced in this companion God had given me, and that I
      should hear her sigh with her head resting on my shoulder!

Sweet bird! the sky is beautiful, but it is beautiful too to be taken
    captive!

And the sky is beautiful! but this is a beautiful thing too, and
    even worthy of God, the heart of a man that can be filled,
    leaving no part empty.

Do not torment me by depriving me of your face!

And no doubt I am a dull and ugly man,

But I love you, my angel, my queen, my darling!

VIOLAINE. So I have warned you in vain, and you want to take me
    for your wife, and you will not give up your plan?

JACQUES HURY. Yes, Violaine.

VIOLAINE. When a man takes a woman for his wife they are then
    one soul in one body, and nothing will ever separate them.

JACQUES HURY. Yes, Violaine.

VIOLAINE. You wish it!

  Then it is not right that I should reserve anything, or keep to
    myself any longer

  This great, this unspeakable secret.

JACQUES HURY. Again this secret, Violaine?

VIOLAINE. So great, truly, Jacques,

  That your heart will be saturated with it,

  And you will ask nothing more of me,

  And that we shall never be torn apart from each other.

  A secret so deep

  That neither life, Jacques, nor hell, nor Heaven itself

  Will ever end it, or will ever end this

  Moment in which I have revealed it, here in the burning

  Heat of this terrible sun which almost prevents us from seeing
    each other!

JACQUES HURY. Speak, then!

VIOLAINE. But tell me first once more that you love me.

JACQUES HURY. I love you!

VIOLAINE. And that I am your wife and your only love?

JACQUES HURY. My wife, my only love.

VIOLAINE. Tell me, Jacques: neither my face nor my soul has
    sufficed thee, and that is not enough?

  And have you been misled by my proud words? Then learn of
    the fire which consumes me!

  Know this flesh which you have loved so much!

  Come nearer to me.   (*He comes nearer.*)

  Nearer! nearer still! close against my side. Sit down on that
    bench.   (*Silence.*)

  And give me your knife.

      (*He gives her his knife. She cuts the linen of her gown, at her side
      upon the heart, under the left breast, and leaning towards him she
      opens the slit with her hands and shows him the flesh where the
      first spot of leprosy has appeared. Silence.*)

JACQUES HURY (*slightly turning away his face*). Give me the knife.

      (*She gives it to him. Silence. Then Jacques moves a few steps*

*away from her, half turning his back, and he does not look at her
again until the end of the Act.)*

JACQUES HURY. Violaine, I am not mistaken? What is this silver
flower emblazoned on your flesh?

VIOLAINE. You are not mistaken.

JACQUES HURY. It is the malady? it is the malady, Violaine?

VIOLAINE. Yes, Jacques.

JACQUES HURY. Leprosy!

VIOLAINE. Surely you are hard to convince. And you had to see
it to believe.

JACQUES HURY. And which leprosy is the most hideous,
That of the soul or that of the body?

VIOLAINE. I cannot say as to the other. I only know that of the
body, which is bad enough.

JACQUES HURY. No, you know not the other, reprobate?

VIOLAINE. I am not a reprobate.

JACQUES HURY. Infamous woman, reprobate,
Infamous in your soul and in your flesh!

VIOLAINE. So you do not ask any more to marry me, Jacques?

JACQUES HURY. Scoff no more, child of the devil!

VIOLAINE. Such is that great love you had for me.

JACQUES HURY. Such is this lily that I had chosen.

VIOLAINE. Such is the man who takes the place of my father.

JACQUES HURY. Such is the angel that God had sent me.

VIOLAINE. Ah, who will tear us apart from each other? I love you,
Jacques, and you will defend me, and I know that in thy
arms I have nothing to fear.

JACQUES HURY. Do not mock thyself with these horrible words!

VIOLAINE. Tell me,
Have I broken my word? My soul was not enough for thee?
Have you enough now of my flesh?
Will you forget henceforth your Violaine, and the heart she
revealed to thee?

JACQUES HURY. Go farther away from me!

VIOLAINE. Go to, I am far enough away, Jacques; you have nothing
to fear.

JACQUES HURY. Yes, yes.
Further than you were from that measled pig of yours!

That maker of bones whereon the flesh rots!

VIOLAINE. Is it of Pierre de Craon that you speak?

JACQUES HURY. It is of him I speak, him you kissed on the mouth.

VIOLAINE. And who has told you that?

JACQUES HURY. Mara saw you with her own eyes.

And she has told me all, as it was her duty to do,

And I, fool that I was, did not believe it!

Come, confess it! confess it then!   It is true!   Say that it is true!

VIOLAINE. It is true, Jacques.

Mara always speaks the truth.

JACQUES HURY. And it is true that you kissed him on the face?

VIOLAINE. It is true.

JACQUES HURY. O damned one! are the flames of hell so savory that
        you have thus lusted after them while you were still alive?

VIOLAINE (*speaking very low*). No, not damned.

But sweet, sweet Violaine! sweet, sweet Violaine!

JACQUES HURY. And you do not deny that this man had you and
        possessed you?

VIOLAINE. I deny nothing, Jacques.

JACQUES HURY. But I love you still, Violaine!

Ah, this is too cruel!

Tell me something, even if you have nothing to say, and I will
        believe it!   Speak, I beg you! tell me it is not true!

VIOLAINE. I cannot turn all black in a minute, Jacques; but in
        a few months, a few months more,

You will not recognize me any longer.

JACQUES HURY. Tell me that all this is not true.

VIOLAINE. Mara always speaks the truth, and then there is that
        flower upon my body that you have seen.

JACQUES HURY. Farewell, Violaine.

VIOLAINE. Farewell, Jacques.

JACQUES HURY. Tell me, what shall you do, wretched woman?

VIOLAINE. Take off this robe.   Leave this house.

Fulfill the law.   Show myself to the priest.

Go to...

JACQUES HURY. Well?

VIOLAINE.... the place set apart for people like me.

The lazar-house of the Géyn, over there.

JACQUES HURY. When?

VIOLAINE. Today — this very evening. (*Long silence.*)
There is nothing else to be done.

JACQUES HURY. We must avoid any scandal.
Go, take off your robe and put on a travelling dress, and I will
tell you what it is right to do. (*They go out.*)

SCENE FOUR

The kitchen at Combernon, as in Act I

THE MOTHER. Every day the weather is fine. It has not rained for
eight days. (*She listens.*)
Now and then I hear the bells of Arcy.
Dong! Dong!
How warm it is, and how large everything looks!
What is Violaine doing? and Jacques? What have they to talk
about so long?
I am sorry for what I said to her. (*She sighs.*)
And what is the crazy old man doing? Where is he now?
Ah! (*She bows her head.*)

MARA (*entering quickly*). They are coming here. I think the
marriage is broken off. Do you hear me?
Be silent,
And say nothing.

THE MOTHER. What?
O wicked girl! wretch! You have got what you wished for!

MARA. Let it alone. It is only for a moment.
There was no other way
It could be done. So, now it is I
He must marry and not she. It will be better for her like that.
It must be thus. Do you hear?
Be silent!

THE MOTHER. Who told you that?

MARA. Was there need for me to be told? I saw it all in their faces.
I came upon them all warm. I understood everything in no
time at all.
And Jacques, poor fellow, I pity him.

THE MOTHER. I am sorry for what I said!

MARA. You have said nothing; you know nothing — be silent!

And if they say anything to you, no matter what they tell you,

Agree with them, do everything they wish. There is nothing
more to do.

THE MOTHER. I hope all is for the best.

SCENE FIVE

(*Enter* JACQUES HURY, *then* VIOLAINE *all in black, dressed as
for a journey.*)

THE MOTHER. What is the matter, Jacques? What is the matter,
Violaine?

Why have you put on this dress, as if you were going away?

VIOLAINE. I, too, am going away.

THE MOTHER. Going away? You going away, too? Jacques!
what has happened between you?

JACQUES HURY. Nothing has happened.

But you know that I went to see my mother at Braine, and have
only just returned.

THE MOTHER. Well?

JACQUES HURY. You know, she is old and feeble.

She says she wishes to see and bless

Her daughter-in-law before she dies.

THE MOTHER. Can she not come to the wedding?

JACQUES HURY. She is ill, she cannot wait.

And this harvest time, too, when there is so much to be done

Is not the time to be married.

We have just been talking about it, Violaine and I, just now, very
pleasantly,

And we have decided that it is best to wait till

The autumn.

Until then she will stay at Braine with my mother.

THE MOTHER. Is this your wish, Violaine?

VIOLAINE. Yes, mother.

THE MOTHER. But what! Do you wish to go away this very day?

VIOLAINE. This very evening.

JACQUES HURY. I shall go with her.

Time is short and work pressing in this month of hay and
harvest. I have already stayed away too long.

THE MOTHER. Stay, Violaine! Do not go away from us, thou too!

VIOLAINE. It is only for a short time, mother!

THE MOTHER. A short time, you promise?

JACQUES HURY. A short time, and when autumn comes

Here she will be with us again, never to go away any more.

THE MOTHER. Ah, Jacques! Why do you let her go away?

JACQUES HURY. Do you think it is not hard for me?

MARA. Mother, what they both say is reasonable.

THE MOTHER. It is hard to see my child leave me.

VIOLAINE. Do not be sad, mother!

What does it matter that we should wait a few days?

It is only a little time to pass.

Am I not sure of your affection? and of Mara's? and of Jacques', my betrothed?

Is it not so, Jacques? He is mine as I am his, and nothing can separate us? Look at me, dear Jacques. See how he weeps to see me go away!

This is not the time for weeping, mother! am I not young and beautiful and loved by everybody?

My father has gone away, it is true, but he has left me the tenderest of husbands, the friend who will never forsake me.

So it is not the time to weep, but to rejoice.

Ah, dear mother, how beautiful life is, and how happy I am!

MARA. And you, Jacques, what do you say? You do not look very happy.

JACQUES HURY. Is it not natural that I should be sad?

MARA. Come! it is only a separation for a few months!

JACQUES HURY. Too long for my heart.

MARA. Listen, Violaine, how well he said that!

And how is this, my sister, you so sad too? Smile at me with that charming mouth! Raise those blue eyes that our father loved so much. See Jacques! Look at your wife and see how beautiful she is when she smiles!

She will not be taken away from you! who would be sad who has a little sun like this to shine in his home?

Love her well for us, cruel man! Tell her to be brave!

JACQUES HURY. Courage, Violaine!

You have not lost me; we are not lost to each other!

You see that I do not doubt your love; but do you doubt mine?

Do I doubt you, Violaine? Do I not love you, Violaine? Am I not sure of you, Violaine?

I have talked about you to my mother, and you may imagine how happy she will be to see you.

It is hard to leave the house of your parents.

But where you are going you will have a safe shelter where no one can break in.

Neither your love nor your innocence, dear Violaine, has anything to fear.

THE MOTHER. These are very loving words,

And yet there is something in them, and in what you said to me, my child,

I don't know what — something strange which does not please me.

MARA. I see nothing strange, mother.

THE MOTHER. Violaine! If I hurt you just now, my child, Forget what I said.

VIOLAINE. You have not hurt me.

THE MOTHER. Then let me embrace you.

(*She opens her arms to her.*)

VIOLAINE. No, mother.

THE MOTHER. What?

VIOLAINE. No.

MARA. Violaine, that is wrong! Do you fear to have us touch thee? Why do you treat us thus, like lepers?

VIOLAINE. I have made a vow.

MARA. What vow?

VIOLAINE. That nobody shall touch me.

MARA. Until you return here? (*Silence. She lowers her head.*)

JACQUES HURY. Let her alone. You see she is troubled.

THE MOTHER. Go away for a moment. (*They move away.*)

Farewell, Violaine!

You will not deceive me, my child; you will not deceive the mother who bore thee.

What I have said to you is hard; but look at me, I am full of trouble, and I am old.

You — you are young, and you will forget.

My man is gone, and now here is my child turning away from me.

One's own sorrow is nothing, but the sorrow one has caused to others

Makes bitter the bread in the mouth.

Think of that, my sacrificed lamb, and say to yourself: Thus I have caused sorrow to no one.

I counselled thee as I thought for the best.   Don't bear malice, Violaine!   Save your sister.   Must she be left to be ruined?

And God will be with you, who is your recompense.

That is all.   You will never see my old face again.   May God be with thee!

And you do not wish to kiss me, but I can at least give you my blessing, sweet, sweet Violaine!

VIOLAINE.   Yes, mother! yes, mother!

(*She kneels, and* THE MOTHER *makes the sign of the cross above her.*)

JACQUES (*returning*).   Come, Violaine, it is time to go.

MARA.   Go and pray for us.

VIOLAINE (*calling*).   I give you my dresses, Mara, and all my things! Have no fear of them; you know that I have not touched them. I did not go into that room.

— Ah, ah! my poor wedding-dress that was so pretty!

(*She stretches out her arms as if to find support.   All remain at a distance from her.   She goes out tottering, followed by* JACQUES.)

ACT THREE

SCENE ONE

Chevoche.   A large forest sparsely grown with lofty oaks and birches, with an undergrowth of pines, firs, and a few holly trees.   A wide straight road has just been cut through the woods to the horizon.   Workmen are removing the last stumps of trees and preparing the roadway.   There is a camp at one side, with huts made of faggots, a pot over a camp-fire, etc. The camp lies in a sand-pit, where a few workmen are engaged in loading a cart with a fine white sand.   An apprentice of PIERRE DE CRAON, *squatting among the dry gorse bushes, oversees the work.   On either side of the new road stand two colossi made of faggots, with collars and smocks of white cloth, each with a red cross on its breast. A barrel forms the head of each colossus, with its edge cut into saw-teeth to simulate a crown, and a sort of face roughly painted on it in red. A long trumpet is fitted to the bunghole, and held in place by a board as if by an arm.*

It is the end of the day. There is snow on the ground and in the sky. It is Christmas Eve.

THE MAYOR OF CHEVOCHE. There. Now the King can come.

A WORKMAN. 'A can coom an' a' likes. We've done our part well.

THE MAYOR (*looking around with satisfaction*). It's mighty beautiful!
> Fact is, it can hold everybody, as many as there are, men, women, and tiny children.

And to think 'twas the worst part, with all these bad weeds and these briars, and the marsh.

It ain't the wise ones of Bruyères can teach us anything.

A WORKMAN. Their road has a beard, and teeth too, wi' all those stumps they's left us!   (*They laugh.*)

THE APPRENTICE (*pedantically, in a voice frightfully sharp and shrill*).
> Vox clamantis in deserto: Parate vias Domini et erunt prava in directa et aspera in vias planas.

It is true you have done your work well. I congratulate you, good people. It is like the road at Corpus Christi.

> (*Pointing to the Giants.*)

And who, gentlemen, are these two beautiful and reverend persons?

A WORKMAN. Beant they handsome? It was fathe' Vincent, the old drunkard, thet made 'em.

'A said it's th' great King of Abyssinia an' his wife Bellotte.

THE APPRENTICE. For my part I thought they were Gog and Magog.

THE MAYOR. 'Tis the two Angels of Chevoche who come to salute the King their lord.

They'll be set a-fire when 'a passes.

Listen!   (*All listen.*)

A WORKMAN. Oh, no, that beant him yet. We'd hear the bells o' Bruyères a-ringin'.

ANOTHER. 'A won't be here afore midnight. 'A supped at Fisme.

ANOTHER. 'Tis a good place to see from, here.

I shallna budge.

ANOTHER. Hast 'a eat, Perrot? I've on'y a mossel o' bread, all froze.

THE MAYOR. Don't be afraid. The's a quarter o' pork in the pot and some big sausages, and the roebuck we killed,

And three ells o' blood-sausages, and apples, and a good little keg of Marne wine.

THE APPRENTICE. I stay with you.

A WOMAN. And there's a good little Christmas for you.

THE APPRENTICE. It was on Christmas Day that King Clovis was baptized at Rheims.

ANOTHER WOMAN. 'Tis Christmas Day that oor King Charles comes back to get hi'self crowned.

ANOTHER. 'Tis a village girl, sent by God, Who brings him back to his own.

ANOTHER. Jeanne, they call her!

ANOTHER. The Maid!

ANOTHER. Who was born on Twelfth Night!

ANOTHER. Who drove the English away from Orleans when they besieged it!

ANOTHER WORKMAN. And who's goin' to drive 'em out of France too, all of 'em! Amen.

ANOTHER WORKMAN (humming). Noel!   Cock-a-doodle-do! Noel!   Noel come again!   Rrr! how cauld it be!

(He wraps himself closer in his cloak.)

A WOMAN. Mus' look well t' see if the's a little man all in red clothes by th' King. That's her.

ANOTHER WOMAN. On a tall black horse.

THE FIRST WOMAN. On'y six months agone her was keepin' her father's cows.

ANOTHER WOMAN. And now her carries a banner where Jesus is in writin'.

A WORKMAN. An' that the English run away before like mice.

ANOTHER WORKMAN. Let the wicked Bourguignons o' Saponay beware!

ANOTHER WORKMAN. They'll be at Rheims at the break o' day.

ANOTHER WORKMAN. What be they doin', those down there?

THE APPRENTICE. The two bells of the Cathedral, Baudon and Baude, will be rung at the Gloria at midnight, and they will never stop swinging and clanging until the French come.

Everybody will keep a lighted candle in his house until morning.

They expect the King to be there for the Mass at dawn, which is "Lux fulgebit."

All the clergy will go out to meet him, three hundred priests and the Archbishop in copes of gold, and the monks, the Mayor and the vestry.

All that will be very beautiful on the snow, in the bright merry sunshine, with all the people singing "Noel"!

And they say that the King intends to get down from his horse, and enter his good city riding upon an ass, like our Lord.

THE MAYOR. How comes it that you did not stay down there?

THE APPRENTICE. Master Pierre de Craon sent me here to get sand.

THE MAYOR. What! He busies himself about sand at such a time?

THE APPRENTICE. He says there is not much time.

THE MAYOR. But how could he employ himself better than in making this road, as we do?

THE APPRENTICE. He says that his work is not to make roads for the King, but a dwelling for God.

THE MAYOR. Of what use would Rheims be if the King could not reach it?

THE APPRENTICE. But what use would the road be if there is no church at the end of it?

THE MAYOR. He is not a good Frenchman.

THE APPRENTICE. He says that he knows nothing but his work. If anybody talks politics to us, we blacken his nose with the bottom of the frying-pan.

THE MAYOR. He has not even been able to finish his Justice, though 'tis ten years they've been working on it.

THE APPRENTICE. On the contrary! All the stone is polished and the woodwork is in place; it's only the spire that has not yet done growing.

THE MAYOR. They never work on it.

THE APPRENTICE. The master is preparing the glass for his windows now, and that is why he sends us here for sand;

Though that is not his craft.

All winter he has worked among his furnaces.

To make light, my poor people, is more difficult than to make
    gold,
To breathe on this heavy matter and make it transparent,
    "according as our bodies of mud shall be changed into
    bodies of glory,"
As Saint Paul said.
And he says that he must find for each colour
The mother-colour itself, just as God himself made it.
That is why, into his great clean vessels, full of shining water,
    he pours jacinth, ultra-marine, rich gold, vermilion,
And he watches these beautiful rose-coloured liquids to see
    what happens to them in the sunshine, and by virtue of
    the grace of God, and how they mingle and bloom in the
    matrass.
And he says there is not one colour which he cannot make out
    of his own knowledge alone,
As his body makes red and blue.
Because he wishes the Justice of Rheims to shine like the morning
    on the day of her nuptials.

THE MAYOR. They say he has leprosy.

THE APPRENTICE. That is not true! I saw him naked last summer.
    While he bathed in the Aisne at Soissons. I know what I say!
    His flesh is as healthy as a child's.

THE MAYOR. It is queer, all the same. Why did he keep himself
    hidden so long?

THE APPRENTICE. That is a lie.

THE MAYOR. I know, I am older than you. You mustn't get
    angry, little man. It doesn't matter if he be sick in the
    body.
    It isn't with his body he works.

THE APPRENTICE. Better not let him hear you say that! I re-
    member how he punished one of us because he stayed all the
    time in his corner, drawing:
    He sent him up on the scaffolding to serve the masons all day
    and pass them their hods and their stones,
    Saying that by the end of the day he would know two things
    better than he could learn them by rule and design: the
    weight a man can carry and the height of his body.

And as the grace of God multiplies each of our good deeds,

So he taught us about what he calls "the shekel of the Temple,"
and this dwelling of God of which each man who does all
that his body is capable of doing is like a secret foundation;

What means the thumb, and the hand, and the arm's length, and
the spread of both our arms, and the arm extended, and
the circle it makes,

And the foot and the step;

And how all these things are never the same.

Do you think Father Noah was indifferent to the body when he
built the ark? and are these things of no account:

The number of paces from the door to the altar, and the height
the eye may be lifted to, and the number of souls the two
sides of the Church may hold all at the same time?

For the heathen artist made everything from the outside, but
we make all from within, like the bees,

And as the soul does for the body: nothing is lifeless, everything
lives,

Everything gives thanks in action.

THE MAYOR. The little man talks well.

A WORKMAN. Hear him, like a magpie, all full of his master's words.

THE APPRENTICE. Speak with respect of Pierre de Craon!

THE MAYOR. 'Tis true he's a burgher of Rheims, and they call him
Master of the Compass.

As they used to call Messire Loys

The Master of the Rule.

ANOTHER. Throw some wood on the fire,

Perrot. Look, it's beginning to snow.

*(It snows. Night has come. Enter MARA dressed in black,
carrying a bundle under her cloak.)*

MARA. Are these the people of Chevoche?

THE MAYOR. 'Tis ourselves.

MARA. Praised be Jesus Christ.

THE MAYOR. Amen!

MARA. Is it around here I'll find the little cell of the Géyn?

THE MAYOR. Where the leper woman lives?

MARA. Yes.

THE MAYOR. Not exactly here, but close by.

ANOTHER. You want to see the leper woman?

MARA. Yes.

A MAN. She can't be seen; she always wears a veil over her face, as it's ordered.

ANOTHER. And well ordered! it isn't myself as wants to see her.

MARA. It's a long time you've had her?

A MAN. A'most eight years, and we'd like it well not to have her at all.

MARA. Is that because she has done harm?

A MAN. No, but all t'same it's unlucky to have these varmint kind of folk near by.

THE MAYOR. And then, 'tis the parish that feeds her.

A MAN. By the way, I bet they've forgot to take her her bite to eat for three days, with all these doings about the road!

A WOMAN. And what do you want o' this woman?

(MARA *makes no reply, but stands, looking at the fire.*)

A WOMAN. A person would say it's a child you're a-holdin' in your arms?

ANOTHER WOMAN. It's a fearsome cold to take out little children at such an hour.

MARA. It is not cold.

(*Silence. There is heard from the darkness under the trees, the sound of a wooden rattle.*)

AN OLD WOMAN. Wait! there's her! there's her click-click! Holy Virgin! what a pity her ain't dead!

A WOMAN. 'A comes to ask for her food. No fear her'll forget that!

A MAN. What a plague 'tis to feed such varmint.

ANOTHER. Toss her somethin'. She mustn't come anigh to us. First thing you know she'd give us the poison.

ANOTHER. No meat, Perrot! It's fast day, it's Christmas Eve!

(*They laugh.*)

Throw her this mossel o' bread that's froze. Good enough for the like o' her!

A MAN (*calling*). Heigh, No-face! Heigh, Jeanne, I say, hallo, rotting one!

(*The black form of the leper woman is seen on the snow.* MARA *looks at her.*)

Catch it!

> (*He throws her swiftly a piece of bread.   She stoops and picks it up
> and goes away.   MARA follows her.*)

A MAN. Where is it she's going?

ANOTHER. Here, woman! hallo! where be you going, what be you
doing?   (*MARA and THE WOMAN go farther away.*)

SCENE TWO

*They disappear within the forest, leaving their tracks upon the snow.
The night brightens.   The brilliant moon, surrounded by an immense
halo, lights up a hillock covered with heather and white sand.   Enormous
sandstone rocks, fantastically formed, rise here and there like beasts belonging to the fossil ages, like inexplicable monuments or idols with deformed
heads and limbs.   And the leper woman conducts MARA to the cave where
she lives, a kind of low cavern in which it is impossible to stand upright.
The back of the cave is closed, leaving only an opening for the smoke.*

SCENE THREE

VIOLAINE. Who is this

That does not fear to walk with the leper woman?

You must know that it is dangerous to be near her, and her
breath is deadly.

MARA. It is I, Violaine.

VIOLAINE. O voice, so long unheard! Is it you, mother?

MARA. It is I, Violaine.

VIOLAINE. It is your voice and another.

Let me light this fire, for it is very cold.   And this torch, too.

> (*She lights a fire of turf and heather by means of live embers which
> she takes from a pot, and then the torch.*)

MARA. It is I, Violaine; Mara, your sister.

VIOLAINE. Dear sister, hail! How good of you to come! But do
you not fear me?

MARA. I fear nothing in this world.

VIOLAINE. How much your voice has become like *Maman's!*

MARA. Violaine, our dear mother is no more.   (*Silence.*)

VIOLAINE. When did she die?

MARA. In that same month after your departure.

VIOLAINE. Knowing nothing?

MARA. I do not know.

VIOLAINE. Poor *Maman*!

May God have thy soul in his keeping!

MARA. And our father has not yet come back.

VIOLAINE. And you two?

MARA. It is well with us.

VIOLAINE. Everything at home is as you wish it?

MARA. Everything is well.

VIOLAINE. I know it could not be otherwise

With Jacques and you.

MARA. You should see what we have done! We have three more

ploughs.

You would not recognize Combernon.

And we are going to pull down those old walls,

Now that the King has come back.

VIOLAINE. And are you happy together, Mara?

MARA. Yes. We are happy. He loves me

As I love him.

VIOLAINE. God be praised.

MARA. Violaine!

You do not see what I hold in my arms?

VIOLAINE. I cannot see.

MARA. Lift your veil, then.

VIOLAINE. Under that I have another.

MARA. You cannot see any more?

VIOLAINE. I have no longer any eyes.

The soul lives alone in the ruined body.

MARA. Blind!

How then are you able to walk so straight?

VIOLAINE. I hear.

MARA. What do you hear?

VIOLAINE. I hear all things exist with me.

MARA (*significantly*). And I, Violaine, do you hear me?

VIOLAINE. God has given me the same intelligence

Which He has given to us all.

MARA. Do you hear me, Violaine?

VIOLAINE. Ah, poor Mara!

MARA. Do you hear me, Violaine?

VIOLAINE. What would you have of me, dear sister?

MARA. To join you in praise of this God who has struck you with the pestilence.

VIOLAINE. Then let us praise Him, on this Eve of His Nativity.

MARA. It is easy to be a saint when leprosy helps us.

VIOLAINE. I do not know, not being one.

MARA. We must turn to God when everything else is gone.

VIOLAINE. He at least will not fail us.

MARA (softly). Perhaps, who knows? Violaine, tell me!

VIOLAINE. Life fails, but not the death where I now live.

MARA. Heretic! are you sure, then, of your salvation?

VIOLAINE. I am sure of the goodness of Him who has provided for everything.

MARA. We see His first instalment.

VIOLAINE. I have faith in God who has ordained my destiny.

MARA. What do you know of Him who is invisible, who is never manifest?

VIOLAINE. He is not more invisible to me now than all the rest.

MARA (ironically). He is with you, little dove, and He loves you!

VIOLAINE. As with all who are wretched, Himself with me.

MARA. Surely how very great is His love!

VIOLAINE. As the love of the fire for the wood it flames above.

MARA. He has cruelly punished you.

VIOLAINE. Not more than it was due to me.

MARA. And already, he to whom you had submitted your body has forgotten you?

VIOLAINE. I have not submitted my body!

MARA. Sweet Violaine! lying Violaine! Did I not see you tenderly kiss Pierre de Craon the morning of that beautiful day in June?

VIOLAINE. You saw all, and there was nothing else.

MARA. Why, then, did you kiss him so feelingly?

VIOLAINE. The poor man was a leper, and I, I was so happy that day!

MARA. In all innocence, wasn't it?

VIOLAINE. Like a little girl who kisses a poor little boy.

MARA. Ought I to believe that, Violaine?

VIOLAINE. It is true.

MARA. Don't say, too, that it was of your own will you abandoned
  Jacques to me?

VIOLAINE. No, not of my own will. I loved him! I am not so
  good as that.

MARA. Ought he to have loved you the same, though you were
  a leper?

VIOLAINE. I did not expect it.

MARA. Who would love a leper woman?

VIOLAINE. My heart is pure!

MARA. But what did Jacques know of that? He believes you guilty.

VIOLAINE. Our mother had told me that you loved him.

MARA. Don't say it was she who made you a leper.

VIOLAINE. God in His goodness warned me.

MARA. So that when our mother spoke to you...

VIOLAINE. It was His voice that I heard.

MARA. But why allow yourself to seem guilty?

VIOLAINE. Should I have done nothing, then, on my part?
  Poor Jacquin! Was it necessary to leave him still regretting
  me?

MARA. Say that you did not love him at all.

VIOLAINE. I did not love him, Mara.

MARA. But I would never have let him go like that.

VIOLAINE. Was it I who let him go?

MARA. It would have killed me.

VIOLAINE. And am I living?

MARA. Now I am happy with him.

VIOLAINE. Peace be unto you!

MARA. And I have given him a child, Violaine! a dear little girl.
  A sweet little girl.

VIOLAINE. Peace be unto you!

MARA. Our happiness is great. But yours is greater, with God.

VIOLAINE. And I too knew what happiness was eight years ago,
  and my heart was ravished with it.
  So much, that I madly asked God — ah! — that it might last
  for ever!
  And God heard me in a strange manner! Will my leprosy ever
  be cured? No, no, as long as there remains a particle of
  my flesh to be devoured.

Will the love in my heart be cured? Never, as long as my
    immortal soul lives to nourish it.

Does your husband understand you, Mara?

MARA. What man understands a woman?

VIOLAINE. Happy is she who can be known, heart and soul, who
    can give herself utterly.

Jacques — what would he have done with all that I could have
    given him?

MARA. You have transferred your faith to Another?

VIOLAINE. Love has ended in pain, and pain has ended in love.

The wood we set on fire gives not only ashes, but a flame as well.

MARA. But of what use is this blind fire that gives to others
    Neither light nor heat?

VIOLAINE. Is it not something that it does me service?

Do not begrudge to a creature consumed,

Afflicted to the uttermost depths, this light that illumines her
    within!

And if you could pass but one night only in my skin, you would
    not say that this fire gives no heat.

Man is the priest, but it is not forbidden to woman to be victim.

God is miserly, and does not permit any creature to be set on fire

Unless some impurity be burned with him,

His own, or that which surrounds him, as when the living
    embers in the censer are stirred.

And truly these are unhappy times.

The people have no father. They look around, and they know
    no longer where the King is, or the Pope.

That is why my body agonizes here for all Christendom which
    is perishing.

Powerful is suffering when it is as voluntary as sin!

You saw me kiss that leper, Mara?

Ah, the chalice of sorrow is deep,

And who once sets his lip to it can never withdraw it again of his
    own free will.

MARA. Take my sorrow upon thee, too!

VIOLAINE. I have already taken it.

MARA. Violaine! if there is still something living, that was once
    my sister, under that veil and in that ruined body,

Remember that we were children together! Have pity upon me!

VIOLAINE. Speak, dear sister. Have faith! Tell me all!

MARA. Violaine, I am a wretched woman, and my pain is greater than yours!

VIOLAINE. Greater, sister?

(MARA, *with a loud cry, opens her cloak and lifts up the corpse of a baby.*)

Look! Take it!

VIOLAINE. What is this?

MARA. Look, I tell you! take it! Take it, I give it to you.

(*She lays the corpse in her arms.*)

VIOLAINE. Ah! I feel a rigid little body! a poor little cold face!

MARA. Ha! ha! Violaine! My child! my little girl!

That is her sweet little face! that is her poor little body!

VIOLAINE (*speaking low*). Dead, Mara?

MARA. Take her, I give her to you!

VIOLAINE. Peace, Mara!

MARA. They wanted to take her away from me, but I would not let them! and I ran away with her.

But you, take her, Violaine. Here, take her; you see, I give her to you.

VIOLAINE. What do you wish me to do, Mara?

MARA. What do I wish you to do? do you not understand?

I tell you she is dead! I tell you she is dead!

VIOLAINE. Her soul lives with God. She follows the Lamb. She is with all the blessed little girls.

MARA. But for me she is dead!

VIOLAINE. You readily give me her body! give the rest to God.

MARA. No! no! no! You shall never trick me with your nunnish rigmaroles! No, I shall never be silenced.

This milk that burns my breast cries out to God like the blood of Abel!

Have I got fifty children to tear out of my body? have I got fifty souls to tear out of my soul?

Do you know what it is to be rent in two in order to bring into the world this little wailing creature?

And the midwife told me I should have no more children.

But if I had a hundred children it would not be my little Aubaine.

VIOLAINE. Accept, submit.

MARA. Violaine, you know well I have a hard head.   I am one
who never gives up, and who accepts nothing.

VIOLAINE. Poor sister!

MARA. Violaine, they are so sweet, these little ones, and it hurts
you so when this cruel little mouth bites your breast!

VIOLAINE (*caressing the face*).   How cold her little face is!

MARA (*speaking low*).   He knows nothing yet.

VIOLAINE (*also speaking low*).   He was not home?

MARA. He has gone to Rheims to sell his grain.

She died suddenly, in two hours.

VIOLAINE. Whom was she like?

MARA. Like him, Violaine.   She is not only mine, she is his, too.
Only her eyes are like mine.

VIOLAINE. Poor Jacquin!

MARA. It was not to hear you say poor Jacquin! that I came here.

VIOLAINE. What do you wish of me, then?

MARA. Violaine, do you want to know?   Tell me, do you know what
a soul is that damns itself,

Of its own will, to all eternity?

Do you know what it is in the heart that really blasphemes?

There is a devil who, while I was running, sang me a little song,

Do you wish to hear the things he taught me?

VIOLAINE. Do not say these horrible things!

MARA. Then give me back my child that I gave you.

VIOLAINE. You gave me only a corpse.

MARA. And you, give it back to me alive!

VIOLAINE. Mara, what do you dare to say?

MARA. I will not have it that my child is dead.

VIOLAINE. Is it in my power to bring the dead to life?

MARA. I don't know, I have only you to help me.

VIOLAINE. Is it in my power to bring the dead to life, like God?

MARA. Of what use are you, then?

VIOLAINE. To suffer and to supplicate!

MARA. But of what use is it to suffer and supplicate if you give me
not back my child?

VIOLAINE. God knows. It is enough for Him that I serve Him.

MARA. But I — I am deaf, and I do not hear! and I cry to you from the depths where I am fallen!

Violaine! Violaine!

Give me back that child I gave you! See! I give in, I humiliate myself! have pity on me!

Have pity on me, Violaine, and give me back that child you took from me.

VIOLAINE. Only He who took it can give it back!

MARA. Give it back to me then! Ah, I know it is all your fault.

VIOLAINE. My fault!

MARA. Then let it not be yours.

It is mine, forgive me!

But give her back to me, my sister!

VIOLAINE. But you see it is dead.

MARA. You lie! it is not dead! Ah! figure-of-two, ah, heart-of-a-sheep! Ah, if I had access to your God as you have,

He would not take my little ones away from me so easily!

VIOLAINE. Ask me to re-create heaven and earth!

MARA. But it is written that you may blow on that mountain and cast it into the sea.

VIOLAINE. I can, if I am a saint.

MARA. You must be a saint when a wretched being prays to you.

VIOLAINE. Ah, supreme temptation!

I swear, and I declare, and I protest before God that I am not a saint!

MARA. Then give me back my child.

VIOLAINE. O my God, you see into my heart.

I swear, and I declare, and I protest before God that I am not a saint!

MARA. Violaine, give me back my child!

VIOLAINE. Why will you not leave me in peace?

Why do you come thus to torment me in my tomb?

Am I of any worth? do I influence God? am I like God?

It is God himself you are asking me to judge.

MARA. I ask you only for my child. *(Pause.)*

VIOLAINE *(raising her finger).* Listen.

(Silence. A distant, almost imperceptible, sound of bells.)

MARA. I hear nothing.

VIOLAINE. The Christmas bells, the bells announcing the midnight Mass!

O Mara, a little child is born to us!

MARA. Then give me back mine.   (*Trumpets in the distance.*)

VIOLAINE. What is that?

MARA. It is the King going to Rheims. Have you not heard of the road the peasants have cut through the forest?

And they can keep all the wood they cut.

It is a little shepherdess who guides the King through the middle of France

To Rheims, to be crowned there.

VIOLAINE. Praised be God, who does all these wonderful things!

(*Again the sound of bells, very distinct.*)

MARA. How loud the bells ring for the *Gloria*!

The wind blows this way.

They are ringing in three villages all at once.

VIOLAINE. Let us pray, with all the universe!

Thou art not cold, Mara?

MARA. I am cold only in my heart.

VIOLAINE. Let us pray. It is long since we celebrated Christmas together.

Fear nothing. I have taken your grief upon myself. Look! and that which you have given me lies close against my heart.

Do not weep! This is not the time to weep, when the salvation of all mankind is already born.

(*Bells in the distance, less clear.*)

MARA. The snow has stopped, and the stars are shining.

VIOLAINE. Look! Do you see this Book?

The priest who visits me now and then left it with me.

MARA. I see it.

VIOLAINE. Take it, will you? and read me the Christmas Service, the First Lesson of each of the three Nocturnes.

(MARA *takes the Book and reads.*)[1]

PROPHECY OF ISAIAH [1]

1 Nevertheless, the dimness shall not be such as was in her vexation, when at the first he lightly afflicted the land of Zebulun and

---

[1] Isaiah ix, 1–6.

the land of Naphtali, and afterward did more grievously afflict her by the way of the sea, beyond Jordan, in Galilee of the nations.

2 The people that walked in darkness have seen a great light: they that dwell in the land of the shadow of death, upon them hath the light shined.

3 Thou hast multiplied the nation, and not increased the joy: they joy before thee according to the joy in harvest, and as men rejoice when they divide the spoil.

4 For thou hast broken the yoke of his burden; and the staff of his shoulder, the rod of his oppressor, as in the day of Midian.

5 For every battle of the warrior is with confused noise, and garments rolled in blood; but this shall be with burning and fuel of fire.

6 For unto us a child is born, unto us a son is given, and the government shall be upon his shoulder; and his name shall be called Wonderful, Counsellor, The mighty God, The everlasting Father, the Prince of Peace.

VIOLAINE (*raising her face*). Listen! (*Silence.*)

VOICES OF ANGELS IN HEAVEN, *heard only by* VIOLAINE:

CHOIR.[1] HODIE NOBIS DE CAELO PAX VERA DESCENDIT, HODIE PER TOTUM MUNDUM MELLIFLUI FACTI SUNT CAELI.

A VOICE.[2] HODIE ILLUXIT NOBIS DIES REDEMPTIONIS NOVAE, REPARATIONIS ANTIQUAE, FELICITATIS AETERNAE.

CHOIR. HODIE PER TOTUM MUNDUM MELLIFLUI FACTI SUNT CAELI.

(VIOLAINE *lifts her finger in warning.* Silence. MARA *listens and looks uneasily.*)

MARA. I hear nothing.

VIOLAINE. Read on, Mara.

MARA (*continuing to read*).

SERMON OF SAINT LEO, POPE

Our Saviour, dearly beloved, was today born: let us rejoice. For there should be no loop-hole open to sorrow on the birthday of

---

[1] The voices are like those of heroic young men singing solemnly in unison, with retarded movement and very simple cadence at the end of phrases.

[2] Like the voice of a child.

Life, which, the fear of Death being at last consumed, filleth us
with the joy of eternity promised. No one from this gladness
is excluded, as one and the same cause for happiness exists for
us all: for Our Lord, the destroyer of sin and Death, having found
no one exempt from sin, came to deliver everyone. Let the
sinless exult insomuch as his palm is at hand; let the sinful rejoice...

> (*Suddenly a brilliant and prolonged sound of trumpets very near.
> Shouts resound through the forest.*)

MARA. The King! The King of France!

> (*Again and again the blare of the trumpets, unutterably piercing,
> solemn, and triumphant.*)

MARA (*in a low voice*). The King of France who goes to Rheims!

> (*Silence.*)

Violaine! (*Silence.*)

Do you hear me, Violaine?

> (*Silence. She goes on with the reading.*)

... Let the sinful rejoice insomuch as forgiveness is offered to
him. Let the Gentile be of good cheer, because he is bidden to
share life. For the Son of God, according to the fulness of this
time which the inscrutable depth of the Divine counsel hath
disposed, took on Himself the nature of mankind so that He might
reconcile it to its maker, and that this deviser of Death, Satan,
by that which he had vanquished might be in his turn conquered.

VOICES OF ANGELS (*heard only by* VIOLAINE, *as before*).

CHOIR. O MAGNUM MYSTERIUM ET ADMIRABILE SACRAMENTUM UT
ANIMALIA VIDERINT DOMINUM NATUM JACENTEM IN PRAESEPIO!
BEATA VIRGO CUJUS VISCERA MERUERUNT PORTARE DOMINUM
CHRISTUM.

A VOICE. AVE, MARIA, GRATIA PLENA, DOMINUS TECUM.

CHOIR. BEATA VIRGO CUJUS VISCERA MERUERUNT PORTARE DOMINUM
CHRISTUM. (*Pause.*)

MARA. Violaine, I am not worthy to read this Book! Violaine,
I know that my heart is too hard, and I am sorry for it: I
wish I could be different.

VIOLAINE. Read on, Mara. You do not know who chants the
responses. (*Silence.*)

MARA (*with an effort takes up the Book, and reads in a trembling voice*).
The Holy Gospel according to Saint Luke.[1]

(*They both stand up.*)

1 And it came to pass in those days, that there went out a decree
from Cæsar Augustus, that all the world should be taxed.

(*And the rest.*)

(*They sit down.*)

HOMILY OF SAINT GREGORY, POPE

(*She stops, overcome by emotion. — The trumpets sound a last time
in the distance.*)

Forasmuch as, by the grace of God, we are this day thrice to
celebrate the solemnities of Mass, we may not speak at length
on the gospel that hath just been read. However, the birth of
our Redeemer bids us address you at least in a few words.
Wherefore, at the time of this birth, should there have been
a census of all the people except clearly to manifest that He who
was appearing in the flesh just then was numbering his Elect for
eternity? On the contrary, the Prophet saith of the wicked: they
shall be deleted from the Book of the Living and they shall not
be written down among the Righteous. It is meet also that He
should be born in Bethlehem. For Bethlehem means the
House of Bread, and Jesus Christ saith of Himself: I am the
Living Bread descended from Heaven. Therefore had the place
in which our Lord was born been called the House of Bread in
order that He who was to feed our hearts with internal satiety
should there appear in the substance of flesh. He was born, not
in the house of his parents, but by the roadside, no doubt to show
that by taking on humanity He was being born in a place strange
to Him.

VOICES OF ANGELS.

CHOIR. BEATA VISCERA MARIAE VIRGINIS QUAE PORTAVERUNT
AETERNI PATRIS FILIUM; ET BEATA UBERA QUAE LACTAVERUNT
CHRISTUM DOMINUM.

QUI HODIE PRO SALUTE MUNDI DE VIRGINE NASCI DIGNATUS EST.

A VOICE. DIES SANCTIFICATUS ILLUXIT NOBIS; VENITE, GENTES, ET
ADORATE DOMINUM.

---

[1] Luke ii, 1.

CHOIR. QUI HODIE PRO SALUTE MUNDI DE VIRGINE NASCI DIGNATUS
EST. (*Long silence.*)

VOICES OF ANGELS (*again, almost imperceptible*).

CHOIR. VERBUM CARO FACTUM EST ET HABITAVIT IN NOBIS: ET
VIDIMUS GLORIAM EJUS, GLORIAM QUASI UNIGENITI A PATRE,
PLENUM GRATIAE ET VERITATIS.

A VOICE. OMNIA PER IPSUM FACTA SUNT ET SINE IPSO FACTUM EST
NIHIL.

CHOIR. ET VIDIMUS GLORIAM EJUS, GLORIAM QUASI UNIGENITI A
PATRE, PLENUM GRATIAE ET VERITATIS.

A VOICE. GLORIA PATRI ET FILIO ET SPIRITUI SANCTO.

CHOIR. ET VIDIMUS GLORIAM EJUS, GLORIAM QUASI UNIGENITI A
PATRE, PLENUM GRATIAE ET VERITATIS. (*Long silence.*)

VIOLAINE (*suddenly cries out in a stifled voice*). Ah!

MARA. What is it?

(*With her hand* VIOLAINE *makes a sign to be silent. — Silence. —
The first flush of dawn appears.*)

(*VIOLAINE puts her hand under her cloak as if to fasten her dress
again.*)

MARA. Violaine, I see something moving under your cloak!

VIOLAINE (*as if she were awakening little by little*). Is it you, Mara?
good morning, sister. I feel the breath of the new-born
day on my face.

MARA. Violaine! Violaine! is it your arm that stirs? Again I see
something moving.

VIOLAINE. Peace, Mara, it is Christmas Day, when all joy is born!

MARA. What joy is there for me unless my child lives?

VIOLAINE. And for us, too — a little child is born to us!

MARA. In the name of the living God, what say you?

VIOLAINE. "Behold, I bring thee glad tidings..."

MARA. Your cloak — it moves again!

(*The little bare foot of a baby, moving lazily, appears in the opening of the cloak.*)

VIOLAINE. "... Because a man has appeared in the world!"

(*MARA falls upon her knees, with a deep sigh, her forehead on the
knees of her sister. VIOLAINE caresses her.*)

VIOLAINE. Poor sister! she weeps. She, too, has had too much
sorrow. (*Silence.* VIOLAINE *kisses her head.*)

Take it, Mara! Would you leave the child always with me?

MARA (*she takes the child from under the cloak and looks at it wildly*). It lives!

VIOLAINE (*she walks out of the cave a few steps upon the heather. By the first light of the bitter cold morning can be seen, first, the pine and birch trees hoary with frost, then, at the end of an immense snow-covered plain, seeming very small on the top of its hill, but clearly etched in the pure air, the five-towered silhouette of Monsanvierge*). Glory to God!

MARA. It lives!

VIOLAINE. Peace on earth to men!

MARA. It lives! it lives!

VIOLAINE. It lives and we live.

And the face of the Father appeared on the earth born again and comforted.

MARA. My child lives!

VIOLAINE (*raising her finger*). Listen!   (*Silence.*)

I hear the Angelus ringing at Monsanvierge.

(*She crosses herself and prays. The child awakes.*)

MARA (*whispering*). It is I, Aubaine; dost know me?

(*The child moves about and whines.*)

What is it, my joy? What is it, my treasure?

(*The child opens its eyes, looks at its mother and begins to cry. MARA looks closely at it.*)

Violaine!

What does this mean? Its eyes were black,

And now they are blue like yours.   (*Silence.*)

Ah!

And what is this drop of milk I see on its lips?

ACT FOUR

SCENE ONE

Night. The large kitchen, as in Act I, empty. A lamp is on the table. The outer door is half open.

MARA *enters from without, and carefully closes the door. She stands still for a moment in the centre of the room, looking toward the door, and listening.*

Then she takes the lamp and goes out by another door without making any sound. ·

The stage remains dark.　Nothing can be seen but the fire of some live coals on the hearth.

SCENE TWO

Two or three blasts of a horn are heard in the distance.　Sounds of calling. Movement in the farm.　Then the noise of opening doors, and the grinding of approaching cart-wheels.　Loud knocks at the door.

VOICE FROM WITHOUT (*calling*).　Hallo!

(*Noise in the upper story of a window opening.*)

VOICE OF JACQUES HURY.　Who is there?

VOICE FROM WITHOUT.　Open the door!

VOICE OF JACQUES HURY.　What do you want?

VOICE FROM WITHOUT.　Open the door!

VOICE OF JACQUES HURY.　Who are you?

VOICE FROM WITHOUT.　Open the door so that I can tell you!

(*Pause.*)

(JACQUES HURY, *with a candle in his hand, enters the room; he opens the door.　After a slight pause, enter* PIERRE DE CRAON, *carrying the body of a woman wrapped up in his arms.　He lays his burden very carefully upon the table.　Then he lifts his head.　The two men stare at each other in the candlelight.*)

PIERRE DE CRAON.　Jacques Hury, do you not recognize me?

JACQUES HURY.　Pierre de Craon?

PIERRE DE CRAON.　It is I.　　　(*They continue to look at each other.*)

JACQUES HURY.　And what is this you bring me?

PIERRE DE CRAON.　I found her half-buried in my sand-pit, there
　　where I seek what I need

　For my glass ovens, and for the mortar —

　Half-hidden under a great cart-load of sand, under a cart stand-
　　ing on end from which they had taken off the backboard.
　　She is still alive.　It is I who took it upon myself to bring
　　her to you

　Here.

JACQUES HURY.　Why here?

PIERRE DE CRAON. That at least she might die under her father's roof!

JACQUES HURY. There is no roof here but mine.

PIERRE DE CRAON. Jacques, here is Violaine.

JACQUES HURY. I know no Violaine.

PIERRE DE CRAON. Have you never heard of the Leper Woman of Chevoche?

JACQUES HURY. What does that matter to me?

You lepers, it is for you to scrape each other's sores.

PIERRE DE CRAON. I am not a leper any more;

I was cured long ago.

JACQUES HURY. Cured?

PIERRE DE CRAON. Year after year the disease grew less, and I am now healthy.

JACQUES HURY. And this one, she too will be cured presently.

PIERRE DE CRAON. You are more leprous than she and I.

JACQUES HURY. But I don't ask to be taken out of my hole in the sand.

PIERRE DE CRAON. And even if she had been guilty, you ought to remember.

JACQUES HURY. Is it true that she kissed you on the mouth?

PIERRE DE CRAON (*looking at him*). It is true, poor child!

JACQUES HURY. She moves, she is coming to herself.

PIERRE DE CRAON. I leave you with her. (*He goes out.*)

SCENE THREE

(JACQUES HURY *sits down near the table and looks silently at* VIOLAINE.)

VIOLAINE (*coming to herself and stretching forth her hand*). Where am I, and who is there?

JACQUES HURY. At Monsanvierge, and it is I who am near you. (*Pause.*)

VIOLAINE (*speaking as she used to do*). Good morning, Jacques. (*Silence.*)

Jacques, you still care for me, then?

JACQUES HURY. The wound is not healed.

VIOLAINE. Poor boy!

And I, too, have I not suffered a little too?

JACQUES HURY. What possessed you to kiss that leper on the mouth!

VIOLAINE. Jacques! you must reproach me quickly with all you have in your heart against me, that we may finish with all that.

For we have other things still to say.

And I want to hear you say just once again those words I loved so much: *Dear Violaine! Sweet Violaine!*

For the time that remains to us is short.

JACQUES HURY. I have nothing more to say to you.

VIOLAINE. Come here, cruel man!

(He approaches her, where she lies.)

Come nearer to me.

(She takes his hand and draws him to her. He kneels awkwardly at her side.)

Jacques, you must believe me. I swear it before God, who is looking upon us!

I was never guilty with Pierre de Craon.

JACQUES HURY. Why, then, did you kiss him?

VIOLAINE. Ah, he was so sad and I was so happy.

JACQUES HURY. I don't believe you.

(She lays her hand a moment on his head.)

VIOLAINE. Do you believe me now?

(He hides his face in her dress and sobs heavily.)

JACQUES HURY. Ah, Violaine! cruel Violaine!

VIOLAINE. Not cruel, but sweet, sweet Violaine!

JACQUES HURY. It is true, then? yes, it was only I you loved?

(Silence. She gives him her other hand.)

VIOLAINE. Jacques, no doubt it was all too beautiful, and we should have been too happy.

JACQUES HURY. You have cruelly deceived me.

VIOLAINE. Deceived? this silver flower on my side did not lie.

JACQUES HURY. What was I to believe, Violaine?

VIOLAINE. If you had believed in me,

Who knows but what you might have cured me?

JACQUES HURY. Was I not to believe my own eyes?

VIOLAINE. That is true. You ought to have believed your own eyes, that is right.

One does not marry a leper. One does not marry an unfaithful woman.

Do not regret anything, Jacques. There, it is better as it is.

JACQUES HURY. Did you know that Mara loved me?

VIOLAINE. I knew it. My mother herself had told me.

JACQUES HURY. Thus everything was in league with her against me!

VIOLAINE. Jacques, there is already enough sorrow in the world. It is best not to be willingly the cause of a great sorrow to others.

JACQUES HURY. But what of my sorrow?

VIOLAINE. That is another thing, Jacques. Are you not happy to be with me?

JACQUES. Yes, Violaine.

VIOLAINE. Where I am, there is patience, not sorrow. (*Silence.*) The world's grief is great.

It is too hard to suffer, and not to know why.

But that which others do not know, I have learned, and thou must share my knowledge.

Jacques, have we not been separated long enough now? should we let any barrier remain between us? Must it still be that death shall separate us?

Only that which is ill should perish, and that which should not perish is that which suffers.

Happy is he who suffers, and who knows why.

Now my task is finished.

JACQUES HURY. And mine begins.

VIOLAINE. What! do you find the cup where I have drunk so bitter?

JACQUES HURY. And now I have lost you for ever!

VIOLAINE. Tell me, why lost?

JACQUES HURY. You are dying.

VIOLAINE. Jacques, you must understand me!

Of what use is the finest perfume in a sealed vase? it serves for nothing.

JACQUES HURY. No, Violaine.

VIOLAINE. Of what use has my body been to me, having hidden away my heart so that you could not see it, but you saw only the scar on the outside of the worthless shell.

JACQUES HURY. I was hard and blind!

VIOLAINE. Now I am broken utterly, and the perfume is set free.

And behold, you believe everything, simply because I laid my
   hand on your head.

JACQUES HURY. I believe. I do not doubt any more.

VIOLAINE. And tell me, where is the Justice in all that, this justice
   you spoke of so proudly?

JACQUES HURY. I am no longer proud.

VIOLAINE. Come, leave Justice alone. It is not for us to call her
   and to make her come.

JACQUES HURY. Violaine, how you have suffered in these eight
   long years!

VIOLAINE. But not in vain. Many things are consumed in the
   flame of a heart that burns.

JACQUES HURY. Deliverance is near.

VIOLAINE. Blessed be the hand that led me that night!

JACQUES HURY. What hand?

VIOLAINE. That silent hand that clasped mine, and led me, when
   I was coming back with my food.

JACQUES HURY. Led you where?

VIOLAINE. Where Pierre de Craon found me.

Under a great mound of sand, a whole cart-load heaped upon
   me. Did I place myself there, all alone?

JACQUES HURY (rising). Who has done that?

God's Blood! who has done that?

VIOLAINE. I don't know. It matters little. Do not curse.

JACQUES HURY. I shall find out the truth about that.

VIOLAINE. No, you shall find out the truth about nothing.

JACQUES HURY. Tell me all!

VIOLAINE. I have told you all. What would you learn of a blind
   woman?

JACQUES HURY. You shall not put me off the track.

VIOLAINE. Do not waste words. I have only a little more time to
   be with you.

JACQUES HURY. I shall always have Mara.

VIOLAINE. She is your wife, and she is my sister, born of the same
   father and the same mother, and of the same flesh,

Both of us, here beside Monsanvierge.   (Silence.)

   (JACQUES stands a moment motionless as if trying to control himself.
   Then he sits down again.)

JACQUES HURY. There are no more recluses at Monsanvierge.

VIOLAINE. What did you say?

JACQUES HURY. The last one died last Christmas. No mouth
comes any more to the wicket of the nourishing church of
this holy monastery, so the priest tells us who used to give
them communion.

VIOLAINE. The mountain of God
Is dead, and we share the heritage, Mara and I.

JACQUES HURY. And Violaine was the secret offshoot of the Holy
Tree, growing from some subterranean root.
God would not have taken her from me, if she had been entirely
filled by me, leaving no part of her empty,
"God's part," as good women call it.

VIOLAINE. What's to be done? so much the worse!

JACQUES HURY. Stay! do not go!

VIOLAINE. I stay, I am not going.
Tell me, Jacques, do you remember that hour at noon, and that
great scorching sun, and that spot on the flesh under my
breast that I showed to you?

JACQUES HURY. Ah!

VIOLAINE. You remember? did I not tell you truly that you could
never more tear me out of your soul?
This of myself is in you for ever. I do not wish you any more to
be happy, it is not proper that you should laugh,
In this time when you are still far away from me.

JACQUES HURY. Ah! Ah! Violaine!

VIOLAINE. Have this from me, my well-beloved!
The communion on the cross, the bitterness like the bitterness
of myrrh,
Of the sick man who sees the shadow upon the dial, and of the
soul that receives its call!
And for you age is already come. But how hard it is to renounce
when the heart is young!

JACQUES HURY. And from me you have not wanted to accept
anything!

VIOLAINE. Think you that I know nothing about you, Jacques?

JACQUES HURY. My mother knew me.

VIOLAINE. To me also, O Jacques, you have caused much pain!

JACQUES HURY. You are a virgin and I have no part in you.

VIOLAINE. What! must I tell you everything?

JACQUES HURY. What do you still conceal?

VIOLAINE. It is necessary. This is not the time to keep anything
back.

JACQUES HURY. Speak louder.

VIOLAINE. Have they not told you, then, that your child was dead?
Last year, while you were at Rheims?

JACQUES HURY. Several people told me. But Mara swears that
it only slept

And I have never been able to draw from her the whole story.
They say she went to find you.

I should have known everything in time. I wanted to learn the
whole truth.

VIOLAINE. That is true. You have the right to know all.

JACQUES HURY. What did she go to ask of you?

VIOLAINE. Have you never noticed that the eyes of your little girl
are changed?

JACQUES HURY. They are blue now, like yours.

VIOLAINE. It was Christmas night. Yes, Jacques, it is true, she was
dead. Her little body was stiff and icy.

I know it; all night I held her in my arms.

JACQUES HURY. Who then restored her to life?

VIOLAINE. God only, and with God the faith and the despair of her
mother.

JACQUES HURY. But you had nothing to do with it?

VIOLAINE. O Jacques, to you only I will tell a great mystery.

It is true, when I felt this dead body upon my own, the child
of your flesh, Jacques....

JACQUES HURY. Ah, my little Aubaine!

VIOLAINE. You love her very much?

JACQUES HURY. Go on.

VIOLAINE. ... My heart contracted, and the iron entered into me.

Behold what I held in my arms for my Christmas night, and all
that remained of our race, a dead child!

All of yours that I should ever possess in this life!

And I listened to Mara, who read me the Service for this Holy
night: the babe who has been given to us, the gospel of Joy.

Ah, do not say that I know nothing of you!

Do not say that I do not know what it is to suffer for you!

Nor that I do not know the effort and the partition of the woman who gives life!

JACQUES HURY. You do not mean that the child was really brought back to life?

VIOLAINE. What I know is that it was dead, and that all of a sudden I felt its head move!

And life burst from me in a flash, at one bound, and my mortified flesh bloomed again!

Ah, I know what it is, that little blind mouth that seeks, and those pitiless teeth!

JACQUES HURY. O Violaine!

(*Silence. He makes as if to rise.* VIOLAINE *feebly forces him to remain seated.*)

VIOLAINE. Do you forgive me now?

JACQUES HURY. Oh, the duplicity of women!

Ah, you are the daughter of your mother!

Tell me! it is not you that you would have me forgive!

VIOLAINE. Whom, then?

JACQUES HURY. What hand was that which took yours the other night, and so kindly led you?

VIOLAINE. I do not know.

JACQUES HURY. But I think that I know.

VIOLAINE. You do not know.

Leave that to us, it is an affair between women.

JACQUES HURY. My affair is to have justice done.

VIOLAINE. Ah, leave thy Justice alone!

JACQUES HURY. I know what remains for me to do.

VIOLAINE. You know nothing at all, poor fellow.

You have no understanding of women,

And what poor creatures they are, stupid and hard-headed and knowing only one thing.

Do not confuse everything between you and her, as with you and me.

Was it really her hand alone? I do not know. And you do not know either. And of what good would it be to know?

Keep what you have. Forgive.

And you, have you never needed to be forgiven?

JACQUES HURY. I am alone.

VIOLAINE. Not alone, with this beautiful little child I have given
    back to you,

And Mara, my sister, your wife, of the same flesh as myself.
    Who, with me, knows you better?

It is necessary for you to have the strength and the deed, it is
    necessary for you to have a duty plainly laid down and final.

That is why I have this sand in my hair.

JACQUES HURY. Happiness is ended for me.

VIOLAINE. It is ended, what does that matter?

Happiness was never promised to you. Work, that is all that is
    asked of you. — *And Monsanvierge belongs only to you now.* —

Question the old earth and she will always answer you with bread
    and wine.

As for me I have finished with her, and I go beyond.

Tell me, what is the day you will pass far from me? It will soon
    pass.

And when your turn shall come, and when you see the great door
    creak and move,

I shall be on the other side and you will find me waiting.

                                                    (*Silence.*)

JACQUES HURY. O my betrothed, through the blossoming branches,
    hail!

VIOLAINE. You remember?

Jacques! Good morning, Jacques!

                                    (*The first rays of dawn appear.*)

And now I must be carried away from here.

JACQUES HURY. Carried away?

VIOLAINE. This is not the place for a leper to die in.

Let me be carried to that shelter my father built for the poor at
    the door of Monsanvierge.

    (*He makes as if to take her. She waves him away with her hand.*)

No, Jacques, no, not you.

JACQUES HURY. What, not even this last duty to you?

VIOLAINE. No it is not right that you should touch me.

Call Pierre de Craon.

He has been a leper, though God has cured him. He has no
    horror of me.

And I know that to him I am like a brother, and woman has no
    more power over his soul.

(JACQUES HURY *goes out and returns several minutes later with*
    PIERRE DE CRAON. *She does not speak. The two men look*
    at her in silence.)

VIOLAINE. Jacques!

JACQUES HURY. Violaine!

VIOLAINE. Has the year been good and the grain fine and abun-
    dant?

JACQUES HURY. So abundant that we do not know where to put it
    all.

VIOLAINE. Ah!

How beautiful a great harvest is!

Yes, even now I remember it, and I think it beautiful.

JACQUES HURY. Yes, Violaine.

VIOLAINE. How beautiful it is

To live! (*speaking low and with deep fervour*) and how great is the
    glory of God!

JACQUES HURY. Live, then, and stay with us.

VIOLAINE. But how good it is to die too! When all is really ended,
    and over us spreads little by little

The darkness, as of a deep shade.   (*Silence.*)

PIERRE DE CRAON. She does not speak any more.

JACQUES HURY. Take her. Carry her where I have told you.

For, as to me, she does not wish me to touch her.

Very gently! Gently, gently, I tell you. Do not hurt her.

(*They go out,* PIERRE *carrying the body. The door stands open.*
    Long pause.)

SCENE FOUR

On the threshold of the door appears ANNE VERCORS *in the habit of*
a traveller, a staff in his hand and a sack slung on his back.

ANNE VERCORS. Open?

Is the house empty, that all the doors should be open?

Who has come in so early before me? or who is it that has gone
    out?   (*He looks around a long time.*)

I recognize the old room, nothing is changed.

Here is the fireplace, here is the table.

Here is the ceiling with its strong beams.

I am like an animal that smells all around him, and who knows
his resting-place and his home.

Hail, house! It is I. Here is the master come back.

Hail, Monsanvierge, lofty dwelling!

From far away, since yesterday morning and the day before, on
the top of the hill I recognized the Arch with the five towers.

But why is it that the bells ring no more? neither yesterday nor
this morning

Have I heard in the sky, with the Angel ninefold sonorous,
tidings of Jesus brought three times, three times to the heart
of Mary.

Monsanvierge! how often I have thought of thy walls,

While, under my captive feet, I made the water rise into the
garden of the old man of Damascus.

(Oh, the morning, and the implacable afternoon!

Oh, the eternal noria and the eyes we lift toward Lebanon!)

And all the aromatic odours of exile are little to me

Compared with this walnut-leaf I crush between my fingers.

Hail, Earth, powerful and subdued! Here it is not sand that we
plough, and soft alluvium,

But the deep earth itself that we work with the whole strength
of our body and of the six oxen who pull and form slowly
under the ploughshare of the great trench,

And, as far as my eyes can see, everything has responded to the
upheaval man has caused.

Already I have seen all my fields, and perceived that everything
is well cared for. God be praised! Jacques does his work
well.   (*He lays his sack on the table.*)

Earth, I have been to seek for thee a little earth,

A little earth for my burial, that which God himself chose for his
own at Jerusalem.   (*Pause.*)

I would not come back last night. I waited for daylight.

And I passed the night under a stack of new straw, thinking,
sleeping, praying, looking around, remembering, giving,
thanks,

Listening to hear, if I could, the voice of my wife, or of my
daughter Violaine, or of a crying child.

When I awoke I saw that the night was brighter.

And up there, above the dark crest of Monsanvierge, resplend-
    ent, from Arabia,

The morning star rose over France, like a herald rising in the
    solitude!

And then I came to the house.

Hallo! Is there anybody here?

> (*He raps on the table with his staff.... Curtain, which remains
> down a few minutes.*)

SCENE FIVE

*The farther end of the garden. Afternoon of the same day. End of the
summer.*

*The trees are heavy with fruit. The branches of some of them, bending
to the ground, are held up by props. The dried and tarnished leaves,
mingled with the red and yellow of apples, seem like tapestry.*

*Below, flooded with light, lies the immense plain as it would be after the
harvest; with stubble, and already some ploughed earth. The white roads
and the villages can be seen. There are rows of haystacks, looking very
small, and here and there a poplar. Far away, in another direction, are
flocks of sheep. The shadows of large clouds pass over the plain.*

*In the middle, where the scene descends toward the background, from
which the tops of the trees in a little wood are seen to emerge, there is a semi-
circular stone bench, reached by three steps, and with lions' heads at each
end of its back.* ANNE VERCORS *is sitting there, with* JACQUES HURY
at his right side.

ANNE VERCORS. The golden end of Autumn

Will soon

Despoil the fruit tree and the vine.

And in the morning the white sun,

A single flash of a fireless diamond, will blend with the white
    vesture of the earth:

And the evening is near when he who walks beneath the aspen

Shall hear the last leaf on its summit.

Now, behold, making equal the days and nights,

Counterpoising the long hours of labour with its projecting sign,
    athwart the celestial Door

Interposes the royal Balance.

JACQUES HURY. Father, since thou hast been gone,

Everything, the painful story, and the plot of these women, and the pitfall made to take us in,

Thou know'st, and I have told thee

Still another thing, with my mouth against thine ear,

Where is thy wife? where is thy daughter Violaine?

And lo, thou talkest of the straw we twist, and of the great black grape

Which fills the hand of the vine-dresser, the hand he thrusts under the vine-branch!

Already

The crooked Scorpion and the retreating Sagittarius

Have appeared on the dial of night.

ANNE VERCORS. Let the old man exult in the warm season! O truly blessed place! O bosom of the Fatherland! O grateful, fecund earth!

The carts passing along the road

Leave straw among the fruited branches!

JACQUES HURY. O Violaine! O cruel Violaine! desire of my soul, you have betrayed me!

O hateful garden! O love useless and denied! O garden planted in an evil hour!

Sweet Violaine! perfidious Violaine! Oh, the silence and the depth of woman!

Art thou then really gone, my soul?

Having deceived me, she goes away; and having undeceived me, with fatal sweet words,

She goes again, and I, bearing this poisoned arrow, it will be necessary

That I live on and on! like the beast we take by the horn, drawing his head out of the manger,

Like the horse we loose from the single-tree in the evening with a lash of the whip on his back!

O ox, it is thou that walkest ahead, but we two make but one team.

Only that the furrow be made, that is all they ask of us.

That is why everything that was not necessary to my task, everything has been taken away from me.

ANNE VERCORS. Monsanvierge is dead, and the fruit of your labour
　　is for you alone.

JACQUES HURY. It is true. 　　　　　　　　　　 (*Silence.*)

ANNE VERCORS. Have they looked well to provisioning the chapel
　　for tomorrow?

　Is there enough to eat and drink for all those we shall have to
　　entertain?

JACQUES HURY. Old man! It is your daughter we are going to lay
　　in the earth, and behold what you find to say!

　Surely you have never loved her! But the old man, like the
　　miser who after warming his hands at his pot of embers
　　hoards their heat in his bosom,

　He suffices for himself alone.

ANNE VERCORS. Everything must be done.

　Things must be done honourably

　… Elisabeth, my wife, hidden heart!

(*Enter* PIERRE DE CRAON.)

ANNE VERCORS. Is everything ready?

PIERRE DE CRAON. They are working at the coffin.

　They are digging the grave where you ordered,

　Close up by the church there, near that of the last chaplain, your
　　brother.

　Within it they have put the earth you brought back.

　A great black ivy-vine

　Comes out of the priestly tomb, and, crossing the wall,

　Enters almost into the sealed arch.

　… Tomorrow, in the early morning. Everything is ready.

(JACQUES HURY *weeps, his face in his cloak. In the path is seen
　a nun, like a woman who hunts for flowers.*)

ANNE VERCORS. What are you looking for, Sister?

VOICE OF THE NUN (*hollow and smothered*). Some flowers, to lay on
　　her heart, between her hands.

ANNE VERCORS. There are no more flowers, there is nothing but
　　fruit.

JACQUES HURY. Push aside the leaves and you will find the last
　　violet!

　And the Immortelle is still in the bud, and nothing is left to us
　　but the dahlia and the poppy. 　　 (*The nun is no longer there.*)

PIERRE DE CRAON. The two Sisters, who care for the sick, one quite
young the other very old,

Have dressed her, and Mara has sent her wedding-dress for
her.

Truly, she was only a leper, but she was honourable in the sight
of God.

She reposes in a deep sleep

As one who knows in whose care she is.

I saw her before they had laid her in the coffin.

Her body is still supple.

Oh, while the Sister finished dressing her, with her arm around
her waist,

Holding her in a sitting posture, how her head fell backward

Like that of the still warm partridge the hunter picks in his hand!

ANNE VERCORS. My child! my little daughter I carried in my arms
before she knew how to walk!

The fat little girl who awoke with bursts of laughter in her little
sabot of a bed.

All that is over. Ah! ah! O God! Alas!

PIERRE DE CRAON. Don't you want to see her before they nail down
the coffin-lid?

ANNE VERCORS. No. The child disowned

Goes away secretly.

JACQUES HURY. Never again in this life shall I see her face.

(PIERRE DE CRAON *sits down at the left of* ANNE VERCORS.
*Long pause. The sound of a hammer on planks. They remain
silent, listening.* MARA *is seen to pass at the side of the stage
holding a child in her arms wrapped in a black shawl. Then
she re-enters slowly at the back, and comes and stands in front of
the bench where the three men are sitting. They stare at her,
except* JACQUES HURY, *who looks at the ground.*)

MARA (*her head lowered*). Hail, father! Hail to you all.

You stare at me and I know what you think: "Violaine is dead.

The beautiful ripe fruit, the good golden fruit,

Has fallen from the branch, and, bitter without, hard as a stone
within,

Only the wintry nut remains to us." Who loves me? Who has
ever loved me? (*She lifts her head with a savage gesture.*)

Well! here I am! what have you to say to me?   Say everything!
    What have you against me?
What makes you look at me like that, with your eyes saying: It is
    thou!   It is true, it is I!
It is true, it was I who killed her,
It was I the other night who took her by the hand, having gone
    to seek her,
While Jacques was not there,
And I who made her fall into the sandpit, and who turned over
    upon her
That loaded cart. Everything was ready, there was only a bolt
    to pull out,
I did that,
Jacques! and it is I, too, who said to my mother,
Violaine — to talk to her that day when you came back from
    Braine.
For I longed ardently to marry you, and if I could not I had
    decided to hang myself the day of your wedding.
Now God, who sees into hearts, had already let her take the
    leprosy.
— But Jacques never stopped thinking of her.
That is why I killed her.
What then?   What else was there to do?   What more could be
    done
So that the one I love and who is mine
Should be mine entirely, as I am his entirely,
And that Violaine should be shut out?
I did what I could.
And you in your turn, answer! Your Violaine that you loved,
How then did you love her, and which was worth the most,
Your love, do you think, or my hatred?
You all loved her! and here is her father who abandons her, and
    her mother who advises her!
And her betrothed, how he has believed in her!
Certainly you loved her,
As we say we love a gentle animal, a pretty flower, and that was
    all the feeling there was in your love!
Mine was of another kind;

Blind, never letting go anything once taken, like a deaf thing
that does not hear!

For him to have me entirely, it was necessary to me to have him
entirely!

What have I done after all that I must defend myself? who has
been the most faithful to him, I or Violaine?

Violaine who betrayed him for I know not what leper, giving in,
said she, to God's council in a kiss?

I honour God.   Let him stay where he is!   Our miserable life
is so short!   Let him leave us in peace!

Is it my fault if I loved Jacques? was it for my happiness, or for
the burning away of my soul?

What could I do to defend myself, I who am not beautiful, nor
agreeable, a poor woman who can only give pain?

That is why I killed her in my despair!

O poor, unskilful crime!

O disgrace to her that no one loves and with whom nothing
succeeds!   What ought to have been done, since I loved
him and he did not love me?   (*She turns toward* JACQUES.)

And you, O Jacques, why do you not speak?

Why turn you your face to the ground, without a word to say,

Like Violaine, the day when you accused her unjustly?

Do you not know me?   I am your wife.

Truly I know that I do not seem to you either beautiful or agreeable, but look, I have dressed myself for you, I have added to
that pain that I can give you.   And I am the sister of Violaine.

It is born of pain!   This love is not born of joy, it is born of
pain! the pain which suffices for those who have no joy!

No one is glad to see it, ah, it is not the flower in its season,

But that which is under the flowers that wither, the earth itself,
the miserly earth under the grass, the earth that never
fails!

Know me then!

I am your wife and you can do nothing to change that!

One inseparable flesh, the contact by the centre and by the soul,
and for confirmation this mysterious parentage between us
two.

Which is, that I have had a child of yours.

I have committed a great crime. I have killed my sister; but I have not sinned against you. And I tell you that you have nothing to reproach me with. And what do the others matter to me?

That is what I had to say, and now do what you will.

(*Silence.*)

ANNE VERCORS. What she says is true. Go, Jacques, forgive her!

JACQUES HURY. Come then, Mara.

> (*She comes nearer and stands before them, forming with her child a single object upon which the two men extend together their right hands. Their arms cross, and* JACQUES' *hand is laid on the head of the child, that of* ANNE *on the head of* MARA.)

JACQUES HURY. It is Violaine who forgives you.

It is through her, Mara, that I forgive you.

Guilty woman, it is she who reunites us.

MARA. Alas! alas! dead words and without a ray of light!

O Jacques, I am no longer the same! There is something in me that is ended. Have no fear. All that is nothing to me.

Something in me is broken, and I am left without strength, like a woman widowed and without children.

> (*The child laughs vaguely and looks all around, with little cries of delight.*)

ANNE VERCORS (*caressing it*). Poor Violaine!

And you, little child! How blue its eyes are!

MARA (*melting into tears*). Father! father! ah!

It was dead, and it was she who brought it back to life!

> (*She goes away, and sits down alone. The sun goes down. It rains here and there on the plain, and the lines of the rain can be seen crossing the rays of the sun. An immense rainbow unfurls.*)

VOICE OF A CHILD. Hi! Hi! look at the beautiful rainbow!

> (*Other voices cease in the distance. Great flocks of pigeons fly about, turning, scattering, and alighting here and there in the stubble.*)

ANNE VERCORS. The earth is set free. The place is empty.

The harvest is all gathered, and the birds of heaven

Pick up the lost grain.

PIERRE DE CRAON. Summer is over, the season sleeps in a time of
quiet, everywhere the foliage rustles in the breeze of September.

The sky has turned blue again, and while the partridges call
from their covert,

The buzzard soars in the liquid air.

JACQUES HURY. Everything is yours.   Father! take back again all
this property you vested in me.

ANNE VERCORS. No, Jacques, I no longer possess anything, and
this is no more mine.   He who went away will not return,
and that which is once given cannot be

Taken back.   Here is a new Combernon, a new Monsanvierge.

PIERRE DE CRAON. The other is dead.   The virgin mountain is
dead, and the scar in her side will never open again.

ANNE VERCORS. It is dead.   My wife, too, is dead, my daughter is
dead, the holy Maid

Has been burned and thrown to the winds, not one of her bones
remains on the earth.

But the King and the Pope have been given back again to
France and to the whole world.

The schism comes to an end, and once more the Throne rises
above all men.

I returned by Rome, I kissed the foot of Saint Peter, I ate the
consecrated bread standing with people from the Four Divi-
sions of the Earth,

While the bells of the Quirinal and of the Lateran, and the voice
of Santa Maria Maggiore,

Saluted the ambassadors of these new nations who come from
the Orient and the Occident all together into the City,

Asia found again, and this Atlantic world beyond the Pillars of
Hercules!

And this very evening when the Angelus shall ring, at the same
hour when the star Al-Zohar glows in the unfurled heaven,

Begins the year of Jubilee which the new Pope grants,

The annulment of debts, the liberation of prisoners, the sus-
pension of war, the closing of the courts, the restitution of
all property.

PIERRE DE CRAON. Truce for one year and peace for one day only.

ANNE VERCORS. What does it matter? peace is good, but war will find us armed.

O Pierre! this is a time when women and newborn infants teach sages and old men!

Here am I shocked like a Jew because the face of the Church is darkened, and because she totters on her road forsaken by all men.

And I wanted once more to clasp the empty tomb, to put my hand in the hole left by the cross.

But my little daughter Violaine has been wiser.

Is the object of life only to live? will the feet of God's children be fastened to this wretched earth?

It is not to live, but to die, and not to hew the cross, but to mount upon it, and to give all that we have, laughing!

There is joy, there is freedom, there is grace, there is eternal youth! and as God lives, the blood of the old man on the sacrificial cloth, near that of the young man,

Makes a stain as red and fresh as that of the yearling lamb!

O Violaine! child of grace! flesh of my flesh! As far as the smoky fire of my farm is distant from the morning star,

When on the sun's breast that beautiful virgin lays her illumined head,

May thy father see thee on high through all eternity in the place which has been kept for thee!

As God lives, where the little child goes the father should go also!

What is the worth of the world compared to life? and what is the worth of life if not to be given?

And why torment ourselves when it is so simple to obey?

It is thus that Violaine follows at once without hesitation the hand that takes hers.

PIERRE DE CRAON. O father! I was the last who held her in my arms, because she entrusted herself to Pierre de Craon, knowing that there is no longer in his heart the desire of the flesh.

And the young body of this divine brother lay in my arms like a tree that has been cut down and droops

Already, as the glowing colour of the pomegranate blossoms everywhere flames from the bud that can no longer sheathe it,

So the splendour of the angel that knows not death embraces our
little sister.

The odour of Paradise exhaled in my arms from this broken
tabernacle.

Do not weep, Jacques, my friend.

ANNE VERCORS. Do not weep, my son.

JACQUES HURY. Pierre, give me back that ring she gave thee.

PIERRE DE CRAON. I cannot!

Any more than the ripened spike of corn can give back the seed
in the earth from which sprang its stem.

Of that bit of gold I have made a fiery gem.

And the vessel of everlasting Day where the seed of the ultimate
goodness of saintly souls is treasured.

Justitia is finished and lacks only the woman that I shall set
there at the blossoming of my supreme lily.

ANNE VERCORS. You are powerful in works, Pierre, and I have seen
on my way the churches you have brought to birth.

PIERRE DE CRAON. Blessed be God who has made me a father of
churches,

And who has endowed my soul with understanding and the sense
of the three dimensions!

And who has debarred me as a leper and freed me from all
temporal care,

To the end that I should raise up from the soil of France Ten
Wise Virgins whose oil is never exhausted, and who compose
a vessel of prayers!

What is this *soul*, or bolt of wood, that the lutemaker inserts
between the front and the back of his instrument,

Compared to this great enclosed lyre, and of these columnar
Powers in the night, whose number and distance I have
calculated?

Never from the outside do I carve an image.

But, like father Noah, from the middle of my enormous Arch,

I work from within, and see everything rise simultaneously
around me!

And what is matter which the hand can chisel compared to the
spirit we strive to enshrine,

Or to the hallowed space left empty by a reverent soul shrinking
back in the presence of its God?

Nothing is too deep for me: my wells descend as far as the waters
    of the Mother-spring.

Nothing is too high for the spire that mounts to heaven and steals
    God's lightning from him!

Pierre de Craon will die, but the Ten Virgins, his daughters,

Will remain like the Widow's cruse

In which the flower and the sacred measures of the oil and wine
    are renewed for ever.

ANNE VERCORS. Yes, Pierre. Whoever trusts himself to stone will
    not be deceived.

PIERRE DE CRAON. Oh, how beautiful is stone, and how soft it is in
    the hands of the architect! and how right and beautiful
    a thing is his whole completed work!

How faithful is stone, and how well it preserves the idea, and
    what shadows it makes!

And if a vine grows well on the least bit of wall, and the rosebush
    above it blooms,

How beautiful it is, and how true it is altogether!

Have you seen my little church of l'Epine, which is like a glowing
    brasier and a rosebush in full bloom?

And Saint Jean de Vertus like a handsome young man in the
    midst of the Craie Champenoise? And Mont-Saint Martin
    which will be mellow in fifty years?

And Saint-Thomas of Fond-d'Ardenne that you can hear in the
    evening bellowing like a bull in the midst of its marshes?

But Justitia that I have made last, Justitia my daughter is more
    beautiful!

ANNE VERCORS. I shall go there and leave my staff for a thank-
    offering.

PIERRE DE CRAON. She is dedicated in my heart, nothing is lacking,
    she is whole.

And for the roof,

I have found the stone I sought, not quarried by iron,

Softer than alabaster and closer-grained than a grindstone.

As the fragile teeth of the little Justitia serve as a foundation for
    my great structure,

So also at the summit, in the wide sky, I shall set this other Jus-
    tice,

Violaine the leper in glory, Violaine the blind in the sight of everybody.

And I shall make her with her hands crossed on her breast, like the spike of grain still half-prisoned in its tegmen,

And her eyes blindfolded.

ANNE VERCORS. Why blindfolded?

PIERRE DE CRAON. That, seeing not, she may the better hear

The sounds of the city and the fields, and man's voice at the same time with the voice of God.

For she is Justice herself, who listens and conceives in her heart the perfect harmony.

This is she who is a refuge from storms, and a shade from the heat at the rising of the dog-star.

JACQUES HURY. But Violaine is not a stone for me, and stone does not suffice me!

And I do not wish the light of her beautiful eyes to be veiled!

ANNE VERCORS. The light of her soul is with us. I have not lost thee, Violaine! How beautiful thou art, my child!

And how beautiful is the bride when on her wedding-day she shows herself to her father in her splendid wedding-gown, sweetly embarrassed.

Walk before me, Violaine, my child, and I will follow thee. But sometimes turn thy face toward me, that I may see thine eyes!

Violaine! Elisabeth! soon again I shall be with you.

As for you, Jacques, perform your task in your turn, as I have done mine! The end is near.

It is here, the end of all that is given me of the day, of the year, and of my own life!

It is six o'clock. The shadow of the Grès-qui-va-boire reaches the brook.

Winter comes, night comes; yet a little more night,

A short watch!

All my life I have worked with the Sun and aided him in his task.

But now, by the fireside, in the light of the lamp,

All alone I must begin the night.

PIERRE DE CRAON. O husbandman, your work is finished. See

the empty land, see the harvested earth, and already the plough attacks the stubble!

And now, what you have begun it is my part to complete.

As you have opened the furrow, I dig the pit wherein to preserve the grain, I prepare the tabernacle.

And as it is not you who cause the harvest to ripen, but the sun, so is it also with grace.

And nothing, unless it issue from the seed, can develop into the ear.

And certainly, Justice is beautiful. But how much more beautiful

Is this fruitful tree of mankind, which the seed of the Eucharist engenders and makes grow.

This too makes one complete whole, unified.

Ah, if all men understood architecture as I do,

Who would willingly fail to follow his vocation and renounce the sacred place assigned to him in the Temple?

ANNE VERCORS. Pierre de Craon, you have many thoughts, but for me this setting sun suffices.

All my life I have done the same thing that he does, cultivating the earth, rising and returning home with him.

And now I go into the night, and I am not afraid, and I know that there too all is clear and in order, in the season of this great heavenly winter which sets all things in motion.

The night sky where everything is at work, and which is like a great ploughing, and a room with only one person in it.

And there the eternal Ploughman drives the seven oxen, with his gaze set upon a fixed star,

As ours is set upon the green branch that marks the end of the furrow.

The sun and I, side by side

Have worked, and the product of our work does not concern us. Mine is done.

I bow to what must be, and now I am willing to be dissolved.

And herein lies peace for him who knows it, and joy and grief in equal parts.

My wife is dead. Violaine is dead. That is right.

I do not desire to hold any more that weak and wrinkled old

hand. And as for Violaine, when she was eight years old, when she came and threw herself against my legs,

How I loved that strong little body! And little by little the impetuous, frolicsome roughness of the laughing child

Melted into the tenderness of the maiden, into the pain and heaviness of love, and when I went away

I saw already in her eyes one unknown blossom among the flowers of her springtime.

PIERRE DE CRAON. The call of death, like a solemn lily.

ANNE VERCORS. Blessed be death in which all the petitions in the Paternoster are satisfied.

PIERRE DE CRAON. For my part, it was by herself and from her innocent lips

That I received freedom and dismissal from this life.

(*The sun is in the western sky, as high as a tall tree.*)

ANNE VERCORS. Behold the sun in the sky,

As he is in the pictures where the Master awakes the workman at the Eleventh Hour.

(*The door of the barn is heard to creak.*)

JACQUES HURY. What is that?

ANNE VERCORS. They have come to the barn for straw

To lay in the bottom of the grave.

(*Silence: — Sound in the distance of a washer-woman beating linen.*)

VOICE OF A CHILD (*without*).

> *Marguerite of Paris, pray!*
> *Lend to me thy shoes of gray!*
> *To walk in Paradise a way!*
> *How fair it is!*
> *How warm it is!*
> *I hear the little bird say it is!*
> *He goes pa — a — a — a!*

JACQUES HURY. That is not the door of the barn, it is the sound of the tomb opening!

And, having looked at me with her blind eyes, she that I loved passes to the other side.

And I too, I have looked at her like one who is blind, and I did not doubt without proofs.

I never doubted her who accused her.

I have made my choice, and she that I chose has been given to me. What shall I say? It is right.

It is right.

Happiness is not for me, but desire! it will never be torn from me.

And not Violaine, radiant and unblemished,

But the leper bending over me with a bitter smile and the devouring wound in her side! *(Silence.)*

(The sun is behind the trees. It shines through the branches. The shadows of the leaves cover the ground and the seated people. Here and there a golden bee shines in the sunny interstices.)

ANNE VERCORS. Here am I seated, and from the top of the mountain I see all the country at my feet.

And I recognized the roads, and I count the farms and villages, and I know them by name, and all the people who live in them.

The plain is lost to view toward the north.

And elsewhere, rising again, the hill surrounds this village like a theatre.

And everywhere, all the while,

Green and pink in the spring, blue and flaxen in the summer, brown in winter or all white with snow,

Before me, at my side, around me,

I see always the Earth, like an unchanging sky all painted with changing colours.

Having a form as much its own as a person's, it is always there present with me.

Now that is finished.

How many times have I risen from my bed and gone to my work!

And now here is evening, and the sun brings home the men and the animals as if he led them by his hand.

(He raises himself slowly and painfully, and slowly stretches out his arms to their full length, while the sun, grown yellow, covers him.)

Ah! ah!

Here am I stretching out my arms in the rays of the sun.

Evening is come! Have pity upon every man, Lord, in that hour when he has finished his task and stands before Thee like a child whose hands are being examined.

Mine are free.   My day is finished.   I have planted the grain
    and I have harvested it, and with this bread that I have
    made all my children have made their communion.
Now I have finished.
A moment ago there was someone with me.
And now, wife and child having gone away,
I remain alone to say grace at the empty table.
Both of them are dead, but I,
I live, on the threshold of death, and I am filled with inexplicable
    joy!
    (*The Angelus is rung from the church down below.   First toll of
    three strokes.*)

JACQUES HURY (*hollowly*).   The Angel of God proclaims peace to us,
    and the child thrills in the bosom of its mother.
                                            (*Second toll.*)
PIERRE DE CRAON.   "Men of little faith, why do you weep?"
                                            (*Third toll.*)
ANNE VERCORS.   "Because I go to my father and to your father."
                                    (*Profound silence.   Then peal.*)
PIERRE DE CRAON.   Thus the Angelus speaks as if with three voices,
    in May
When the unmarried man comes home, having buried his
    mother,
"Voice-of-the-Rose" speaks in the silvery evening.
O Violaine!   O woman through whom comes temptation!
For, not yet knowing what I would do, I turned my eyes where
    you then did turn thine.
Truly I have always thought that joy was a good thing.
But now I have everything!
I possess everything, under my hands, and I am like a person
    who, seeing a tree laden with fruit,
And having mounted a ladder, feels the thick branches yield
    under his body.
I must talk under the tree, like a flute which is neither low nor
    shrill!   How the water
Raises me!   Thanksgiving unseals the stone of my heart!
How I live, thus!   How I grow greater, thus mingled with my
    God, like the vine and the olive-tree.

(*The sun goes down.* MARA *turns her head toward her husband and looks at him.*)

JACQUES HURY. See her, looking at me. See her returning to me with the night! (*Sound of a cracked bell near by. First toll.*)

ANNE VERCORS. It is the little bell of the sisters that rings the Angelus in its turn.

(*Silence. Then another bell is heard, very high up, at Monsanvierge, sounding in its turn the triple toll, admirably sonorous and solemn.*)

JACQUES HURY. Listen!

PIERRE DE CRAON. A miracle!

ANNE VERCORS. It is Monsanvierge come to life again! The Angelus, ringing once more, brings to the listening heavens and earth the wonted tidings.

PIERRE DE CRAON. Yes, Voice-of-the-Rose, God is born!

(*Second toll of the bell of the sisters. It strikes the third note just as Monsanvierge strikes the first.*)

ANNE VERCORS. God makes himself man.

JACQUES HURY. He is dead!

PIERRE DE CRAON. He is risen!

(*Third toll of the bell of the sisters. Then the peal. Pause. Then, nearly lost in the distance, are heard the three strokes of the third toll up on the heights.*)

ANNE VERCORS. This is not the toll of the Angelus, it is the communion bells!

PIERRE DE CRAON. The three strokes are gathered like an ineffable sacrifice into the bosom of the Virgin without sin.

(*Their faces are turned toward the heights; they listen as if awaiting the peal, which does not come.*)

THE END

R. U. R.
(ROSSUM'S UNIVERSAL ROBOTS)

A FANTASTIC MELODRAMA

By KAREL ČAPEK

Translated by Paul Selver

KAREL ČAPEK [1]

THE younger of two brothers, both active in the theater, in journal-
ism and literature, Karel Čapek was born in North Bohemia
January 9, 1890. He was educated in Prague, Berlin, and Paris.
For a time he directed the municipal theater in Vonohrady. He
has collaborated with his brother Josef (born 1887) in playwriting,
and in publication of garden and travel books, of which his brother
makes the sketches and illustrations. Among fiction written by
Karel Čapek are *The Absolute at Large*, translated, New York, 1927;
Krakatit, translated, London, 1925; *Money and Other Stories*, translated, New York, 1930. *The Gardener's Year*, illustrated by his
brother, appeared in London in 1931; *Letters from England* appeared
in London, 1925, and *Letters from Spain* in London, 1932. Karel
Čapek is one of the most brilliant figures in the intellectual life of
the new country of Czecho-Slovakia. The breadth of his humane
interests, the lightness and irony of his spirit, have combined to
divert his activities from the world of the theater to a wide-ranging
participation in affairs.

[1] Pronounced Tchapek.

R. U. R.

IT IS not often that a true melodrama finds itself in the company of the most representative plays of the era. Melodrama can be either a very debased form or it can be one of the high and effective forms of dramatic composition. It is debased when it deals, as it so often does, with outworn themes, when its characters reflect the repetitive imitation of personality rather than personality itself, when its emotions have lost vibrancy by overstraining. When, on the other hand, melodrama deals with new themes which it serves to illuminate and simplify, it calls for no apology. For by its nature melodrama is peculiarly equipped to illuminate and vitalize a new theme. Its structure is one of organic simplification. Dealing with the differentiations of character, it identifies these with a few simple traits which can be easily seized, and avoids the nicer refinements and shadings. It is essentially a moral and even didactic form of art, but its morality is elementary. The distinctions between moral values are not shaded off; they are categorical. The action, therefore, is crisp, substantial, direct, fast-moving. The oppositions and climaxes are clean-cut. Melodrama is based upon primitive emotional oppositions. From all this it is apparent why the play *R. U. R.* by Karel Čapek is one of the best melodramas of modern times. The theme is new. It concerns that process of mechanization in human affairs with which social thinkers have been so much engaged. It simplifies this theme, reduces it to the lowest terms, presents it with extraordinary dramatic force, and yet in such a manner that everyone who sees the play knows that he has not only been entertained but instructed and aroused. The concept of the mechanical man overcoming the race of men is not a new one. In one form it appears in the *Arabian Nights*. It is found in *Frankenstein*. H. G. Wells plays variations upon the theme. But probably nowhere is the theme more at home than in central Europe where Jewish fancy has bred the legend of the Golem, the mechanical, unmanageable figure which spreads terror through the countryside. As treated by Karel Čapek, the Robot is not a product of mediaeval superstition. It is the product of the cold and rational thinking of modern men as they consider the forces that the brain of man has released. The play employs all the terror of the mediaeval legend in illuminating a tract on the forces of the new science. It is to be remarked, by the way, that the concept and name of the Robot, which adds so much to the effectiveness of the play, was contributed by Karel Čapek's brother Josef. The play was produced first at the National Theater (Narodni Divadlo), Prague, January 26, 1921. It was immediately thereafter performed in Berlin, Paris, London, and New York. The New York production was by the Theater Guild at the Garrick Theater, October 9, 1922.

CHARACTERS

HARRY DOMIN, *General Manager of Rossum's Universal Robots.*
SULLA, *a Robotess*
MARIUS, *a Robot.*
HELENA GLORY.
DR. GALL, *Head of the Physiological and Experimental Department of R. U. R.*
MR. FABRY, *Engineer General, Technical Controller of R. U. R.*
DR. HALLEMEIER, *Head of the Institute for Psychological Training of Robots.*
MR. ALQUIST, *Architect, Head of the Works Department of R. U. R.*
CONSUL BUSMAN, *General Business Manager of R. U. R.*
NANA.
RADIUS, *a Robot.*
HELENA, *a Robotess.*
PRIMUS, *a Robot.*
A SERVANT.
FIRST ROBOT.
SECOND ROBOT.
THIRD ROBOT.

ACT   I. CENTRAL OFFICE OF THE FACTORY OF ROSSUM'S UNIVERSAL ROBOTS
ACT II. HELENA'S DRAWING ROOM — TEN YEARS LATER. MORNING
ACT III. THE SAME AFTERNOON
EPILOGUE.   A LABORATORY — ONE YEAR LATER

PLACE: *An Island.*   TIME: *The Future.*

ING.

Central office of the factory of Rossum's Universal Robots. Entrance on the right. The windows on the front wall look out on the rows of factory chimneys. On the left more managing departments. DOMIN *is sitting in the revolving chair at a large American writing table. On the left-hand wall large maps showing steamship and railroad routes. On the right-hand wall are fastened printed placards. ("Robot's Cheapest Labor," etc.) In contrast to these wall fittings, the floor is covered with a splendid Turkish carpet, a sofa, leather armchair, and filing cabinets. At a desk near the windows* SULLA *is typing letters.*

DOMIN (*dictating*). Ready?

SULLA. Yes.

DOMIN. To E. M. McVicker and Co., Southampton, England. "We undertake no guarantee for goods damaged in transit. As soon as the consignment was taken on board we drew your captain's attention to the fact that the vessel was unsuitable for the transport of Robots, and we are therefore not responsible for spoiled freight. We beg to remain for Rossum's Universal Robots. Yours truly." (SULLA, *who has sat motionless during dictation, now types rapidly for a few seconds, then stops, withdrawing the completed letter.*) Ready?

SULLA. Yes.

DOMIN. Another letter. To the E. B. Huyson Agency, New York, U.S.A. "We beg to acknowledge receipt of order for five thousand Robots. As you are sending your own vessel, please dispatch as cargo equal quantities of soft and hard coal for R. U. R., the same to be credited as part payment of the amount due to us. We beg to remain, for Rossum's Universal Robots. Yours truly." (SULLA *repeats the rapid typing.*) Ready?

SULLA. Yes.

DOMIN. Another letter. "Friedrichswerks, Hamburg, Germany. We beg to acknowledge receipt of order for fifteen thousand Robots." (*Telephone rings.*) Hello! This is the Central Office. Yes. Certainly. Well, send them a wire. Good. (*Hangs up telephone.*) Where did I leave off?

SULLA. "We beg to acknowledge receipt of order for fifteen thousand Robots."

DOMIN. Fifteen thousand R. Fifteen thousand R.

(Enter MARIUS.*)*

DOMIN. Well, what is it?

MARIUS. There's a lady, sir, asking to see you.

DOMIN. A lady? Who is she?

MARIUS. I don't know, sir. She brings this card of introduction.

DOMIN *(reads the card).* Ah, from President Glory. Ask her to come in.

MARIUS. Please step this way. *(Exit* MARIUS.*)*

(Enter HELENA GLORY.*)*

HELENA. How do you do?

DOMIN. How do you do. *(Standing up.)* What can I do for you?

HELENA. You are Mr. Domin, the General Manager.

DOMIN. I am.

HELENA. I have come ——

DOMIN. With President Glory's card. That is quite sufficient.

HELENA. President Glory is my father. I am Helena Glory.

DOMIN. Miss Glory, this is such a great honor for us to be allowed to welcome our great President's daughter, that ——

HELENA. That you can't show me the door?

DOMIN. Please sit down. Sulla, you may go. *(Exit* SULLA.*)* *(Sitting down.)* How can I be of service to you, Miss Glory?

HELENA. I have come ——

DOMIN. To have a look at our famous works where people are manufactured. Like all visitors. Well, there is no objection.

HELENA. I thought it was forbidden to ——

DOMIN. To enter the factory. Yes, of course. Everybody comes here with someone's visiting card, Miss Glory.

HELENA. And you show them ——

DOMIN. Only certain things. The manufacture of artificial people is a secret process.

HELENA. If you only knew how enormously that ——

DOMIN. Interests me. Europe's talking about nothing else.

HELENA. Why don't you let me finish speaking?

DOMIN. I beg your pardon. Did you want to say something different?

HELENA. I only wanted to ask ——

DOMIN. Whether I could make a special exception in your case and show you our factory. Why, certainly, Miss Glory.

HELENA. How do you know I wanted to say that?

DOMIN. They all do. But we shall consider it a special honor to show you more than we do the rest.

HELENA. Thank you.

DOMIN. But you must agree not to divulge the least...

HELENA (standing up and giving him her hand). My word of honor.

DOMIN. Thank you. Won't you raise your veil?

HELENA. Of course. You want to see whether I'm a spy or not. I beg your pardon.

DOMIN. What is it?

HELENA. Would you mind releasing my hand?

DOMIN (releasing it). I beg your pardon.

HELENA (raising her veil). How cautious you have to be here, don't you?

DOMIN (observing her with deep interest). Hm, of course — we — that is ——

HELENA. But what is it? What's the matter?

DOMIN. I'm remarkably pleased. Did you have a pleasant crossing?

HELENA. Yes.

DOMIN. No difficulty?

HELENA. Why?

DOMIN. What I mean to say is — you're so young.

HELENA. May we go straight into the factory?

DOMIN. Yes. Twenty-two, I think.

HELENA. Twenty-two what?

DOMIN. Years.

HELENA. Twenty-one. Why do you want to know?

DOMIN. Because — as — (with enthusiasm) you will make a long stay, won't you?

HELENA. That depends on how much of the factory you show me.

DOMIN. Oh, hang the factory. Oh, no, no, you shall see everything, Miss Glory. Indeed you shall. Won't you sit down?

HELENA (*crossing to couch and sitting*). Thank you.

DOMIN. But first would you like to hear the story of the invention?

HELENA. Yes, indeed.

DOMIN (*observes* HELENA *with rapture and reels off rapidly*). It was in
the year 1920 that old Rossum, the great physiologist, who was
then quite a young scientist, took himself to this distant island
for the purpose of studying the ocean fauna, full stop. On this
occasion he attempted by chemical synthesis to imitate the living
matter known as protoplasm until he suddenly discovered
a substance which behaved exactly like living matter although
its chemical composition was different. That was in the year of
1932, exactly four hundred and forty years after the discovery of
America. Whew!

HELENA. Do you know that by heart?

DOMIN. Yes. You see physiology is not in my line. Shall I go on?

HELENA. Yes, please.

DOMIN. And then, Miss Glory, old Rossum wrote the following
among his chemical specimens: "Nature has found only one
method of organizing living matter. There is, however, another
method, more simple, flexible and rapid, which has not yet
occurred to nature at all. This second process by which life
can be developed was discovered by me today." Now imagine
him, Miss Glory, writing those wonderful words over some col-
loidal mess that a dog wouldn't look at. Imagine him sitting
over a test tube, and thinking how the whole tree of life would
grow from it, how all animals would proceed from it, beginning
with some sort of beetle and ending with a man. A man of
different substance from us. Miss Glory, that was a tremendous
moment.

HELENA. Well?

DOMIN. Now, the thing was how to get the life out of the test tubes,
and hasten development and form organs, bones and nerves, and
so on, and find such substances as catalytics, enzymes, hormones,
and so forth, in short — you understand?

HELENA. Not much, I'm afraid.

DOMIN. Never mind. You see with the help of his tinctures he
could make whatever he wanted. He could have produced
a Medusa with the brain of a Socrates or a worm fifty yards long.

But being without a grain of humor, he took it into his head to make a vertebrate or perhaps a man. This artificial living matter of his had a raging thirst for life. It didn't mind being sewn or mixed together. That couldn't be done with natural albumen. And that's how he set about it.

HELENA. About what?

DOMIN. About imitating nature. First of all he tried making an artificial dog. That took him several years and resulted in a sort of stunted calf which died in a few days. I'll show it to you in the museum. And then old Rossum started on the manufacture of man.

HELENA. And I must divulge this to nobody?

DOMIN. To nobody in the world.

HELENA. What a pity that it's to be found in all the school books of both Europe and America.

DOMIN. Yes. But do you know what isn't in the school books? That old Rossum was mad. Seriously, Miss Glory, you must keep this to yourself. The old crank wanted to actually make people.

HELENA. But you do make people.

DOMIN. Approximately, Miss Glory. But old Rossum meant it literally. He wanted to become a sort of scientific substitute for God. He was a fearful materialist, and that's why he did it all. His sole purpose was nothing more nor less than to prove that God was no longer necessary. Do you know anything about anatomy?

HELENA. Very little.

DOMIN. Neither do I. Well, he then decided to manufacture everything as in the human body. I'll show you in the museum the bungling attempt it took him ten years to produce. It was to have been a man, but it lived for three days only. Then up came young Rossum, an engineer. He was a wonderful fellow, Miss Glory. When he saw what a mess of it the old man was making, he said: "It's absurd to spend ten years making a man. If you can't make him quicker than nature, you might as well shut up shop." Then he set about learning anatomy himself.

HELENA. There's nothing about that in the school books.

DOMIN. No. The school books are full of paid advertisements, and rubbish at that. What the school books say about the united efforts of the two great Rossums is all a fairy tale. They used to have dreadful rows. The old atheist hadn't the slightest conception of industrial matters, and the end of it was that young Rossum shut him up in some laboratory or other and let him fritter the time away with his monstrosities, while he himself started on the business from an engineer's point of view. Old Rossum cursed him and before he died he managed to botch up two physiological horrors. Then one day they found him dead in the laboratory. And that's his whole story.

HELENA. And what about the young man?

DOMIN. Well, anyone who has looked into human anatomy will have seen at once that man is too complicated, and that a good engineer could make him more simply. So young Rossum began to overhaul anatomy and tried to see what could be left out or simplified. In short — but this isn't boring you, Miss Glory?

HELENA. No indeed. You're — it's awfully interesting.

DOMIN. So young Rossum said to himself: "A man is something that feels happy, plays the piano, likes going for a walk, and in fact, wants to do a whole lot of things that are really unnecessary."

HELENA. Oh.

DOMIN. That are unnecessary when he wants, let us say, to weave or count. Do you play the piano?

HELENA. Yes.

DOMIN. That's good. But a working machine must not play the piano, must not feel happy, must not do a whole lot of other things. A gasoline motor must not have tassels or ornaments, Miss Glory. And to manufacture artificial workers is the same thing as to manufacture gasoline motors. The process must be of the simplest, and the product of the best from a practical point of view. What sort of worker do you think is the best from a practical point of view?

HELENA. What?

DOMIN. What sort of worker do you think is the best from a practical point of view?

HELENA. Perhaps the one who is most honest and hard-working.

DOMIN. No; the one that is the cheapest. The one whose requirements are the smallest. Young Rossum invented a worker with
the minimum amount of requirements. He had to simplify him.
He rejected everything that did not contribute directly to the
progress of work — everything that makes man more expensive.
In fact, he rejected man and made the Robot. My dear Miss
Glory, the Robots are not people. Mechanically they are more
perfect than we are, they have an enormously developed intelligence, but they have no soul.

HELENA. How do you know they've no soul?

DOMIN. Have you ever seen what a Robot looks like inside?

HELENA. No.

DOMIN. Very neat, very simple. Really, a beautiful piece of work.
Not much in it, but everything in flawless order. The product
of an engineer is technically at a higher pitch of perfection than
a product of nature.

HELENA. But man is supposed to be the product of God.

DOMIN. All the worse. God hasn't the least notion of modern
engineering. Would you believe that young Rossum then pro-
ceeded to play at being God?

HELENA. How do you mean?

DOMIN. He began to manufacture Super-Robots. Regular giants
they were. He tried to make them twelve feet tall. But you
wouldn't believe what a failure they were.

HELENA. A failure?

DOMIN. Yes. For no reason at all their limbs used to keep snap-
ping off. Evidently our planet is too small for giants. Now we
only make Robots of normal size and of very high class human
finish.

HELENA. I saw the first Robots at home. The town counsel
bought them for — I mean engaged them for work.

DOMIN. Bought them, dear Miss Glory. Robots are bought and
sold.

HELENA. These were employed as street sweepers. I saw them
sweeping. They were so strange and quiet.

DOMIN. Rossum's Universal Robot factory doesn't produce a uniform brand of Robots. We have Robots of finer and coarser
grades. The best will live about twenty years.

(*He rings for* MARIUS.)

HELENA. Then they die?

DOMIN. Yes, they get used up.

(*Enter* MARIUS.)

DOMIN. Marius, bring in samples of the Manual Labor Robot.

(*Exit* MARIUS.)

DOMIN. I'll show you specimens of the two extremes. This first grade is comparatively inexpensive and is made in vast quantities.

(MARIUS *re-enters with two Manual Labor Robots.*)

DOMIN. There you are; as powerful as a small tractor. Guaranteed to have average intelligence. That will do, Marius.

(MARIUS *exits with Robots.*)

HELENA. They make me feel so strange.

DOMIN (*rings*). Did you see my new typist? (*He rings for* SULLA.)

HELENA. I didn't notice her.

(*Enter* SULLA.)

DOMIN. Sulla, let Miss Glory see you.

HELENA. So pleased to meet you. You must find it terribly dull in this out-of-the-way spot, don't you?

SULLA. I don't know, Miss Glory.

HELENA. Where do you come from?

SULLA. From the factory.

HELENA. Oh, you were born there?

SULLA. I was made there.

HELENA. What?

DOMIN (*laughing*). Sulla is a Robot, best grade.

HELENA. Oh, I beg your pardon.

DOMIN. Sulla isn't angry. See, Miss Glory, the kind of skin we make. (*Feels the skin on* SULLA'S *face.*) Feel her face.

HELENA. Ah, no, no.

DOMIN. You wouldn't know that she's made of different material from us, would you? Turn round, Sulla.

HELENA. Oh, stop, stop.

DOMIN. Talk to Miss Glory, Sulla.

SULLA. Please sit down. (HELENA *sits.*) Did you have a pleasant crossing?

HELENA. Oh, yes, certainly.

SULLA. Don't go back on the *Amelia*, Miss Glory. The barometer is falling steadily. Wait for the *Pennsylvania*. That's a good, powerful vessel.

DOMIN. What's its speed?

SULLA. Twenty knots. Fifty thousand tons. One of the latest vessels, Miss Glory.

HELENA. Thank you.

SULLA. A crew of fifteen hundred, Captain Harpy, eight boilers ——

DOMIN. That'll do, Sulla. Now show us your knowledge of French.

HELENA. You know French?

SULLA. I know four languages. I can write: Dear Sir, Monsieur, Geehrter Herr, Cteny pane.

HELENA (*jumping up*). Oh, that's absurd! Sulla isn't a Robot. Sulla is a girl like me. Sulla, this is outrageous! Why do you take part in such a hoax?

SULLA. I am a Robot.

HELENA. No, no, you are not telling the truth. I know they've forced you to do it for an advertisement. Sulla, you are a girl like me, aren't you?

DOMIN. I'm sorry, Miss Glory. Sulla is a Robot.

HELENA. It's a lie!

DOMIN. What? (*Rings.*) Excuse me, Miss Glory, then I must convince you.

(*Enter* MARIUS.)

DOMIN. Marius, take Sulla into the dissecting room, and tell them to open her up at once.

HELENA. Where?

DOMIN. Into the dissecting room. When they've cut her open, you can go and have a look.

HELENA. No, no!

DOMIN. Excuse me, you spoke of lies.

HELENA. You wouldn't have her killed?

DOMIN. You can't kill machines.

HELENA. Don't be afraid, Sulla, I won't let you go. Tell me, my dear, are they always so cruel to you? You mustn't put up with it, Sulla. You mustn't.

SULLA. I am a Robot.

HELENA. That doesn't matter. Robots are just as good as we are. Sulla, you wouldn't let yourself be cut to pieces?

SULLA. Yes.

HELENA. Oh, you're not afraid of death, then?

SULLA. I cannot tell, Miss Glory.

HELENA. Do you know what would happen to you in there?

SULLA. Yes, I should cease to move.

HELENA. How dreadful!

DOMIN. Marius, tell Miss Glory what you are.

MARIUS. Marius, the Robot.

DOMIN. Would you take Sulla into the dissecting room?

MARIUS. Yes.

DOMIN. Would you be sorry for her?

MARIUS. I cannot tell.

DOMIN. What would happen to her?

MARIUS. She would cease to move. They would put her into the stamping-mill.

DOMIN. That is death, Marius. Aren't you afraid of death?

MARIUS. No.

DOMIN. You see, Miss Glory, the Robots have no interest in life. They have no enjoyments. They are less than so much grass.

HELENA. Oh, stop. Send them away.

DOMIN. Marius, Sulla, you may go. (*Exeunt* SULLA *and* MARIUS.)

HELENA. How terrible! It's outrageous what you are doing.

DOMIN. Why outrageous?

HELENA. I don't know, but it is. Why do you call her Sulla?

DOMIN. Isn't it a nice name?

HELENA. It's a man's name. Sulla was a Roman general.

DOMIN. Oh, we thought that Marius and Sulla were lovers.

HELENA. Marius and Sulla were generals and fought against each other in the year — I've forgotten now.

DOMIN. Come here to the window.

HELENA. What?

DOMIN. Come here. What do you see?

HELENA. Bricklayers.

DOMIN. Robots. All our work people are Robots. And down there, can you see anything?

HELENA. Some sort of office.

DOMIN. A counting house. And in it ——

HELENA. A lot of officials.

DOMIN. Robots. All our officials are Robots. And when you see the factory —— *(Factory whistle blows.)*

DOMIN. Noon. We have to blow the whistle because the Robots don't know when to stop work. In two hours I will show you the kneading trough.

HELENA. Kneading trough?

DOMIN. The pestle for beating up the paste. In each one we mix the ingredients for a thousand Robots at one operation. Then there are the vats for the preparation of liver, brains, and so on. Then you will see the bone factory. After that I'll show you the spinning-mill.

HELENA. Spinning-mill?

DOMIN. Yes. For weaving nerves and veins. Miles and miles of digestive tubes pass through it at a time.

HELENA. Mayn't we talk about something else?

DOMIN. Perhaps it would be better. There's only a handful of us among a hundred thousand Robots, and not one woman. We talk about nothing but the factory all day, every day. It's just as if we were under a curse, Miss Glory.

HELENA. I'm sorry I said that you were lying.

(A knock at the door.)

DOMIN. Come in.

(From the right enter MR. FABRY, DR. GALL, DR. HALLEMEIER, MR. ALQUIST.)

DR. GALL. I beg your pardon, I hope we don't intrude.

DOMIN. Come in. Miss Glory, here are Alquist, Fabry, Gall, Hallemeier. This is President Glory's daughter.

HELENA. How do you do.

FABRY. We had no idea ——

DR. GALL. Highly honored, I'm sure ——

ALQUIST. Welcome, Miss Glory.

(BUSMAN *rushes in from the right.*)

BUSMAN. Hello, what's up?

DOMIN. Come in, Busman. This is Busman, Miss Glory. This is President Glory's daughter.

BUSMAN. By Jove, that's fine! Miss Glory, may we send a cablegram to the papers about your arrival?

HELENA. No, no, please don't.

DOMIN. Sit down please, Miss Glory.

BUSMAN. Allow me —— (*Dragging up armchairs.*)

DR. GALL. Please ——

FABRY. Excuse me ——

ALQUIST. What sort of a crossing did you have?

DR. GALL. Are you going to stay long?

FABRY. What do you think of the factory, Miss Glory?

HALLEMEIER. Did you come over on the *Amelia*?

DOMIN. Be quiet and let Miss Glory speak.

HELENA (*to* DOMIN). What am I to speak to them about?

DOMIN. Anything you like.

HELENA. Shall... may I speak quite frankly?

DOMIN. Why, of course.

HELENA (*wavering, then in desperate resolution*). Tell me, doesn't it ever distress you the way you are treated?

FABRY. By whom, may I ask?

HELENA. Why, everybody.

ALQUIST. Treated?

DR. GALL. What makes you think ——?

HELENA. Don't you feel that you might be living a better life?

DR. GALL. Well, that depends on what you mean, Miss Glory.

HELENA. I mean that it's perfectly outrageous. It's terrible. (*Standing up.*) The whole of Europe is talking about the way you're being treated. That's why I came here, to see for myself, and it's a thousand times worse than could have been imagined. How can you put up with it?

ALQUIST. Put up with what?

HELENA. Good heavens, you are living creatures, just like us, like the whole of Europe, like the whole world. It's disgraceful that you must live like this.

BUSMAN. Good gracious, Miss Glory.

FABRY. Well, she's not far wrong. We live here just like red Indians.

HELENA. Worse than red Indians. May I, oh, may I call you brothers?

BUSMAN. Why not?

HELENA. Brothers, I have not come here as the President's daughter. I have come on behalf of the Humanity League. Brothers, the Humanity League now has over two hundred thousand members. Two hundred thousand people are on your side, and offer you their help.

BUSMAN. Two hundred thousand people! Miss Glory, that's a tidy lot. Not bad.

FABRY. I'm always telling you there's nothing like good old Europe. You see, they've not forgotten us. They're offering us help.

DR. GALL. What help? A theatre, for instance?

HALLEMEIER. An orchestra?

HELENA. More than that.

ALQUIST. Just you?

HELENA. Oh, never mind about me. I'll stay as long as it is necessary.

BUSMAN. By Jove, that's good.

ALQUIST. Domin, I'm going to get the best room ready for Miss Glory.

DOMIN. Just a minute. I'm afraid that Miss Glory is of the opinion that she has been talking to Robots.

HELENA. Of course.

DOMIN. I'm sorry. These gentlemen are human beings just like us.

HELENA. You're not Robots?

BUSMAN. Not Robots.

HALLEMEIER. Robots indeed!

DR. GALL. No, thanks.

FABRY. Upon my honor, Miss Glory, we aren't Robots.

HELENA (to DOMIN). Then why did you tell me that all your officials are Robots?

DOMIN. Yes, the officials, but not the managers. Allow me, Miss Glory: this is Mr. Fabry, General Technical Manager of R. U. R.; Dr. Gall, Head of the Physiological and Experimental Department; Dr. Hallemeier, Head of the Institute for the Psychological Training of Robots; Consul Busman, General Business Manager; and Alquist, Head of the Building Department of R. U. R.

ALQUIST. Just a builder.

HELENA. Excuse me, gentlemen, for — for —— Have I done something dreadful?

ALQUIST. Not at all, Miss Glory. Please sit down.

HELENA. I'm a stupid girl. Send me back by the first ship.

DR. GALL. Not for anything in the world, Miss Glory. Why should we send you back?

HELENA. Because you know I've come to disturb your Robots for you.

DOMIN. My dear Miss Glory, we've had close upon a hundred saviours and prophets here. Every ship brings us some. Missionaries, anarchists, Salvation Army, all sorts. It's astonishing what a number of churches and idiots there are in the world.

HELENA. And you let them speak to the Robots?

DOMIN. So far we've let them all, why not? The Robots remember everything, but that's all. They don't even laugh at what the people say. Really, it is quite incredible. If it would amuse you, Miss Glory, I'll take you over to the Robot warehouse. It holds about three hundred thousand of them.

BUSMAN. Three hundred and forty-seven thousand.

DOMIN. Good! And you can say whatever you like to them. You can read the Bible, recite the multiplication table, whatever you please. You can even preach to them about human rights.

HELENA. Oh, I think that if you were to show them a little love ——

FABRY. Impossible, Miss Glory. Nothing is harder to like than a Robot.

HELENA. What do you make them for, then?

BUSMAN. Ha, ha, ha, that's good! What are Robots made for?

FABRY. For work, Miss Glory! One Robot can replace two and a half workmen. The human machine, Miss Glory, was terribly imperfect. It had to be removed sooner or later.

BUSMAN. It was too expensive.

FABRY. It was not effective. It no longer answers the requirements of modern engineering. Nature has no idea of keeping pace with modern labor. For example: from a technical point of view, the whole of childhood is a sheer absurdity. So much time lost. And then again ——

HELENA. Oh, no! No!

FABRY. Pardon me. But kindly tell me what is the real aim of your League — the... the Humanity League.

HELENA. Its real purpose is to — to protect the Robots — and — and ensure good treatment for them.

FABRY. Not a bad object, either. A machine has to be treated properly. Upon my soul, I approve of that. I don't like damaged articles. Please, Miss Glory, enroll us all as contributing, or regular, or foundation members of your League.

HELENA. No, you don't understand me. What we really want is to — to liberate the Robots.

HALLEMEIER. How do you propose to do that?

HELENA. They are to be — to be dealt with like human beings.

HALLEMEIER. Aha. I suppose they're to vote? To drink beer? to order us about?

HELENA. Why shouldn't they drink beer?

HALLEMEIER. Perhaps they're even to receive wages?

HELENA. Of course they are.

HALLEMEIER. Fancy that, now! And what would they do with their wages, pray?

HELENA. They would buy — what they need... what pleases them.

HALLEMEIER. That would be very nice, Miss Glory, only there's nothing that does please the Robots. Good heavens, what are they to buy? You can feed them on pineapples, straw, whatever you like. It's all the same to them, they've no appetite at all. They've no interest in anything, Miss Glory. Why, hang it all, nobody's ever yet seen a Robot smile.

HELENA. Why... why don't you make them happier?

HALLEMEIER. That wouldn't do, Miss Glory. They are only workmen.

HELENA. Oh, but they're so intelligent.

HALLEMEIER. Confoundedly so, but they're nothing else. They've no will of their own. No passion. No soul.

HELENA. No love?

HALLEMEIER. Love? Rather not. Robots don't love. Not even themselves.

HELENA. Nor defiance?

HALLEMEIER. Defiance? I don't know. Only rarely, from time to time.

HELENA. What?

HALLEMEIER. Nothing particular. Occasionally they seem to go off their heads. Something like epilepsy, you know. It's called Robot's cramp. They'll suddenly sling down everything they're holding, stand still, gnash their teeth — and then they have to go into the stamping-mill. It's evidently some breakdown in the mechanism.

DOMIN. A flaw in the works that has to be removed.

HELENA. No, no, that's the soul.

FABRY. Do you think that the soul first shows itself by a gnashing of teeth?

HELENA. Perhaps it's a sort of revolt. Perhaps it's just a sign that there's a struggle within. Oh, if you could infuse them with it!

DOMIN. That'll be remedied, Miss Glory. Dr. Gall is just making some experiments ——

DR. GALL. Not with regard to that, Domin. At present I am making pain-nerves.

HELENA. Pain-nerves?

DR. GALL. Yes, the Robots feel practically no bodily pain. You see, young Rossum provided them with too limited a nervous system. We must introduce suffering.

HELENA. Why do you want to cause them pain?

DR. GALL. For industrial reasons, Miss Glory. Sometimes a Robot does damage to himself because it doesn't hurt him. He puts his hand into the machine, breaks his finger, smashes his head, it's all the same to him. We must provide them with pain. That's an automatic protection against damage.

HELENA. Will they be happier when they feel pain?

DR. GALL. On the contrary; but they will be more perfect from a technical point of view.

HELENA. Why don't you create a soul for them?

DR. GALL. That's not in our power.

FABRY. That's not in our interest.

BUSMAN. That would increase the cost of production. Hang it all, my dear young lady, we turn them out at such a cheap rate. A hundred and fifty dollars each fully dressed, and fifteen years ago they cost ten thousand. Five years ago we used to buy the clothes for them. Today we have our own weaving mill, and now we even export cloth five times cheaper than other factories. What do you pay a yard for cloth, Miss Glory?

HELENA. I don't know really, I've forgotten.

BUSMAN. Good gracious, and you want to found a Humanity League? It only costs a third now, Miss Glory. All prices are today a third of what they were and they'll fall still lower, lower, lower, like that.

HELENA. I don't understand.

BUSMAN. Why, bless you, Miss Glory, it means that the cost of labor has fallen. A Robot, food and all, costs three quarters of a cent per hour. That's mighty important, you know. All factories will go pop like chestnuts if they don't at once buy Robots to lower the cost of production.

HELENA. And get rid of their workmen?

BUSMAN. Of course. But in the mean time, we've dumped five hundred thousand tropical Robots down on the Argentine pampas to grow corn. Would you mind telling me how much you pay a pound for bread?

HELENA. I've no idea.

BUSMAN. Well, I'll tell you. It now costs two cents in good old Europe. A pound of bread for two cents, and the Humanity League knows nothing about it. Miss Glory, you don't realize that even that's too expensive. Why, in five years' time I'll wager ——

HELENA. What?

BUSMAN. That the cost of everything won't be a tenth of what it is now. Why, in five years we'll be up to our ears in corn and everything else.

ALQUIST. Yes, and all the workers throughout the world will be unemployed.

DOMIN. Yes, Alquist, they will. Yes, Miss Glory, they will. But in ten years Rossum's Universal Robots will produce so much corn, so much cloth, so much everything, that things will be practically without price. There will be no poverty. All work will be done by living machines. Everybody will be free from worry and liberated from the degradation of labor. Everybody will live only to perfect himself.

HELENA. Will he?

DOMIN. Of course. It's bound to happen. But then the servitude of man to man and the enslavement of man to matter will cease. Of course, terrible things may happen at first, but that simply can't be avoided. Nobody will get bread at the price of life and hatred. The Robots will wash the feet of the beggar and prepare a bed for him in his house.

ALQUIST. Domin, Domin. What you say sounds too much like Paradise. There was something good in service and something great in humility. There was some kind of virtue in toil and weariness.

DOMIN. Perhaps. But we cannot reckon with what is lost when we start out to transform the world. Man shall be free and supreme; he shall have no other aim, no other labor, no other care than to perfect himself. He shall serve neither matter nor man. He will not be a machine and a device for production. He will be Lord of creation.

BUSMAN. Amen.

FABRY. So be it.

HELENA. You have bewildered me — I should like — I should like to believe this.

DR. GALL. You are younger than we are, Miss Glory. You will live to see it.

HALLEMEIER. True. Don't you think Miss Glory might lunch with us?

DR. GALL. Of course. Domin, ask on behalf of us all.

DOMIN. Miss Glory, will you do us the honor?

HELENA. When you know why I've come ——

FABRY. For the League of Humanity, Miss Glory.

HELENA. Oh, in that case, perhaps ——

FABRY. That's fine! Miss Glory, excuse me for five minutes.

DR. GALL. Pardon me, too, dear Miss Glory.

BUSMAN. I won't be long.

HALLEMEIER. We're all very glad you've come.

BUSMAN. We'll be back in exactly five minutes.

(*All rush out except* DOMIN *and* HELENA.)

HELENA. What have they all gone off for?

DOMIN. To cook, Miss Glory.

HELENA. To cook what?

DOMIN. Lunch. The Robots do our cooking for us and as they've no taste it's not altogether —— Hallemeier is awfully good at grills and Gall can make a kind of sauce, and Busman knows all about omelettes.

HELENA. What a feast! And what's the specialty of Mr. —— your builder?

DOMIN. Alquist? Nothing. He only lays the table. And Fabry will get together a little fruit. Our cuisine is very modest, Miss Glory.

HELENA. I wanted to ask you something ——

DOMIN. And I wanted to ask you something, too. (*Looking at watch.*) Five minutes.

HELENA. What did you want to ask me?

DOMIN. Excuse me, you asked first.

HELENA. Perhaps it's silly of me, but why do you manufacture female Robots when — when ——

DOMIN. When sex means nothing to them?

HELENA. Yes.

DOMIN. There's a certain demand for them, you see. Servants, saleswomen, stenographers. People are used to it.

HELENA. But — but, tell me, are the Robots male and female mutually — completely without ——

DOMIN. Completely indifferent to each other, Miss Glory. There's no sign of any affection between them.

HELENA. Oh, that's terrible.

DOMIN. Why?

HELENA. It's so unnatural. One doesn't know whether to be disgusted or to hate them, or perhaps ——

DOMIN. To pity them?

HELENA. That's more like it. What did you want to ask me about?

DOMIN. I should like to ask you, Miss Helena, whether you will marry me?

HELENA. What?

DOMIN. Will you be my wife?

HELENA. No! The idea!

DOMIN (*looking at his watch*). Another three minutes. If you won't marry me you'll have to marry one of the other five.

HELENA. But why should I?

DOMIN. Because they're all going to ask you in turn.

HELENA. How could they dare do such a thing?

DOMIN. I'm very sorry, Miss Glory. It seems they've all fallen in love with you.

HELENA. Please don't let them. I'll — I'll go away at once.

DOMIN. Helena, you wouldn't be so cruel as to refuse us.

HELENA. But, but — I can't marry all six.

DOMIN. No, but one anyhow. If you don't want me, marry Fabry.

HELENA. I won't.

DOMIN. Dr. Gall.

HELENA. I don't want any of you.

DOMIN (*again looking at his watch*). Another two minutes.

HELENA. I think you'd marry any woman who came here.

DOMIN. Plenty of them have come, Helena.

HELENA. Young?

DOMIN. Yes.

HELENA. Why didn't you marry one of them?

DOMIN. Because I didn't lose my head. Until today. Then, as soon as you lifted your veil —— (HELENA *turns her head away.*)

DOMIN. Another minute.

HELENA. But I don't want you, I tell you.

DOMIN (*laying both hands on her shoulders*). One more minute! Now you either have to look me straight in the eye and say "No," violently, and then I'll leave you alone — or ——

(HELENA *looks at him.*)

HELENA (*turning away*). You're mad!

DOMIN. A man has to be a bit mad, Helena. That's the best thing about him.

HELENA. You are — you are ——

DOMIN. Well?

HELENA. Don't, you're hurting me.

DOMIN. The last chance, Helena. Now, or never ——

HELENA. But — but, Harry ——

    (*He embraces and kisses her. Knocking at the door.*)

DOMIN (*releasing her*). Come in.

(*Enter* BUSMAN, DR. GALL, *and* HALLEMEIER *in kitchen aprons.*
FABRY *with a bouquet and* ALQUIST *with a napkin over his arm.*)

DOMIN. Have you finished your job?

BUSMAN. Yes.

DOMIN. So have we.

    (*For a moment the men stand nonplussed; but as soon as they realize
what* DOMIN *means they rush forward, congratulating* HELENA
and DOMIN *as the curtain falls.*)

ACT II

HELENA'S *drawing room. On the left a baize door, and a door to the
music room, on the right a door to* HELENA'S *bedroom. In the centre are
windows looking out on the sea and the harbor. A table with odds and
ends, a sofa and chairs, a writing table with an electric lamp, on the right
a fireplace. On a small table back of the sofa, a small reading lamp.
The whole drawing room in all its details is of a modern and purely
feminine character. Ten years have elapsed since Act I.*

(DOMIN, FABRY, HALLEMEIER *enter on tiptoe from the left, each carrying
a potted plant.*)

HALLEMEIER (*putting down his flower and indicating the door to right*).
Still asleep? Well, as long as she's asleep she can't worry about
it.

DOMIN. She knows nothing about it.

FABRY (*putting plant on writing desk*). I certainly hope nothing
happens today.

HALLEMEIER. For goodness' sake drop it all. Look, Harry, this is
a fine cyclamen, isn't it? A new sort, my latest — Cyclamen
Helena.

DOMIN (*looking out of the window*). No signs of the ship. Things
must be pretty bad.

HALLEMEIER. Be quiet. Suppose she heard you.

DOMIN. Well, anyway, the *Ultimus* arrived just in time.

FABRY. You really think that today ——?

DOMIN. I don't know. Aren't the flowers fine?

HALLEMEIER. These are my new primroses. And this is my new jasmine. I've discovered a wonderful way of developing flowers quickly. Splendid varieties, too. Next year I'll be developing marvellous ones.

DOMIN. What... next year?

FABRY. I'd give a good deal to know what's happening at Havre with ——

DOMIN. Keep quiet.

HELENA (*calling from right*). Nana!

DOMIN. She's awake. Out you go.

(*All go out on tiptoe through upper left door.*)

(*Enter* NANA *from lower left door.*)

NANA. Horrid mess! Pack of heathens. If I had my say I'd ——

HELENA (*backwards in the doorway*). Nana, come and do up my dress.

NANA. I'm coming. So you're up at last. (*Fastening* HELENA'S *dress.*) My gracious, what brutes!

HELENA. Who?

NANA. If you want to turn around, then turn around, but I shan't fasten you up.

HELENA. What are you grumbling about now?

NANA. These dreadful creatures, these heathen ——

HELENA. The Robots?

NANA. I wouldn't even call them by name.

HELENA. What's happened?

NANA. Another of them here has caught it. He began to smash up the statues and pictures in the drawing room, gnashed his teeth, foamed at the mouth — quite mad. Worse than an animal.

HELENA. Which of them caught it?

NANA. The one — well, he hasn't got any Christian name. The one in charge of the library.

HELENA. Radius?

NANA. That's him. My goodness, I'm scared of them. A spider doesn't scare me as much as them.

HELENA. But, Nana, I'm surprised you're not sorry for them.

NANA. Why, you're scared of them, too! You know you are. Why else did you bring me here?

HELENA. I'm not scared, really I'm not, Nana. I'm only sorry for them.

NANA. You're scared. Nobody could help being scared. Why, the dog's scared of them: he won't take a scrap of meat out of their hands. He draws in his tail and howls when he knows they're about.

HELENA. The dog has no sense.

NANA. He's better than them, and he knows it. Even the horse shies when he meets them. They don't have any young, and a dog has young, everyone has young ——

HELENA. Please fasten up my dress, Nana.

NANA. I say it's against God's will to ——

HELENA. What is it that smells so nice?

NANA. Flowers.

HELENA. What for?

NANA. Now you can turn around.

HELENA. Oh, aren't they lovely. Look, Nana. What's happening today?

NANA. It ought to be the end of the world.

(*Enter* DOMIN.)

HELENA. Oh, hello, Harry. Harry, why all these flowers?

DOMIN. Guess.

HELENA. Well, it's not my birthday!

DOMIN. Better than that.

HELENA. I don't know. Tell me.

DOMIN. It's ten years ago today since you came here.

HELENA. Ten years? Today —— Why —— (*They embrace.*)

NANA. I'm off. (*Exits lower door, left.*)

HELENA. Fancy you remembering!

DOMIN. I'm really ashamed, Helena. I didn't.

HELENA. But you ——

DOMIN. They remembered.

HELENA. Who?

DOMIN. Busman, Hallemeier, all of them. Put your hand in my pocket.

HELENA. Pearls! A necklace. Harry, is that for me?

DOMIN. It's from Busman.

HELENA. But we can't accept it, can we?

DOMIN. Oh, yes, we can. Put your hand in the other pocket.

HELENA (*takes a revolver out of his pocket*). What's that?

DOMIN. Sorry. Not that. Try again.

HELENA. Oh, Harry, what do you carry a revolver for?

DOMIN. It got there by mistake.

HELENA. You never used to carry one.

DOMIN. No, you're right. There, that's the pocket.

HELENA. A cameo. Why, it's a Greek cameo!

DOMIN. Apparently. Anyhow, Fabry says it is.

HELENA. Fabry? Did Mr. Fabry give me that?

DOMIN. Of course. (*Opens the door at the left.*) And look in here. Helena, come and see this.

HELENA. Oh, isn't it fine! Is this from you?

DOMIN. No, from Alquist. And there's another on the piano.

HELENA. This must be from you.

DOMIN. There's a card on it.

HELENA. From Dr. Gall. (*Reappearing in the doorway.*) Oh, Harry, I feel embarrassed at so much kindness.

DOMIN. Come here. This is what Hallemeier brought you.

HELENA. These beautiful flowers?

DOMIN. Yes. It's a new kind. Cyclamen Helena. He grew them in honor of you. They are almost as beautiful as you.

HELENA. Harry, why do they all ——

DOMIN. They're awfully fond of you. I'm afraid that my present is a little —— Look out of the window.

HELENA. Where?

DOMIN. Into the harbor.

HELENA. There's a new ship.

DOMIN. That's your ship.

HELENA. Mine? How do you mean?

DOMIN. For you to take trips in — for your amusement.

HELENA. Harry, that's a gunboat.

DOMIN. A gunboat? What are you thinking of? It's only a little bigger and more solid than most ships.

HELENA. Yes, but with guns.

DOMIN. Oh, yes, with a few guns. You'll travel like a queen, Helena.

HELENA. What's the meaning of it? Has anything happened?

DOMIN. Good heavens, no. I say, try these pearls.

HELENA. Harry, have you had bad news?

DOMIN. On the contrary, no letters have arrived for a whole week.

HELENA. Nor telegrams?

DOMIN. Nor telegrams.

HELENA. What does that mean?

DOMIN. Holidays for us. We all sit in the office with our feet on the table and take a nap. No letters, no telegrams. Oh, glorious.

HELENA. Then you'll stay with me today?

DOMIN. Certainly. That is, we will see. Do you remember ten years ago today? "Miss Glory, it's a great honor to welcome you."

HELENA. "Oh, Mr. Manager, I'm so interested in your factory."

DOMIN. "I'm sorry, Miss Glory, it's strictly forbidden. The manufacture of artificial people is a secret."

HELENA. "But to oblige a young lady who has come a long way."

DOMIN. "Certainly, Miss Glory, we have no secrets from you."

HELENA (seriously). Are you sure, Harry?

DOMIN. Yes.

HELENA. "But I warn you, sir; this young lady intends to do terrible things."

DOMIN. "Good gracious, Miss Glory. Perhaps she doesn't want to marry me."

HELENA. "Heaven forbid. She never dreamt of such a thing. But she came here intending to stir up a revolt among your Robots."

DOMIN (suddenly serious). A revolt of the Robots!

HELENA. Harry, what's the matter with you?

DOMIN (laughing it off). "A revolt of the Robots, that's a fine idea, Miss Glory. It would be easier for you to cause bolts and screws to rebel, than our Robots. You know, Helena, you're wonderful, you've turned the heads of us all."

(He sits on the arm of HELENA's chair.)

HELENA (naturally). Oh, I was fearfully impressed by you all then.

You were all so sure of yourselves, so strong. I seemed like
a tiny little girl who had lost her way among — among ——

DOMIN. Among what, Helena?

HELENA. Among huge trees. All my feelings were so trifling
compared with your self-confidence. And in all these years
I've never lost this anxiety. But you've never felt the least mis-
givings — not even when everything went wrong.

DOMIN. What went wrong?

HELENA. Your plans. You remember, Harry, when the working
men in America revolted against the Robots and smashed them
up, and when the people gave the Robots firearms against the
rebels. And then when the governments turned the Robots
into soldiers, and there were so many wars.

DOMIN (getting up and walking about). We foresaw that, Helena.
You see, those are only passing troubles, which are bound to
happen before the new conditions are established.

HELENA. You were all so powerful, so overwhelming. The whole
world bowed down before you. (Standing up.) Oh, Harry!

DOMIN. What is it?

HELENA. Close the factory and let's go away. All of us.

DOMIN. I say, what's the meaning of this?

HELENA. I don't know. But can't we go away?

DOMIN. Impossible, Helena. That is, at this particular moment ——

HELENA. At once, Harry. I'm so frightened.

DOMIN. About what, Helena?

HELENA. It's as if something was falling on top of us, and couldn't
be stopped. Oh, take us all away from here. We'll find a place
in the world where there's no one else. Alquist will build us
a house, and then we'll begin life all over again.

(The telephone rings.)

DOMIN. Excuse me. Hello — yes. What? I'll be there at once.
Fabry is calling me, dear.

HELENA. Tell me ——

DOMIN. Yes, when I come back. Don't go out of the house, dear.

(Exits.)

HELENA. He won't tell me —— Nana, Nana, come at once.

NANA. Well, what is it now?

HELENA. Nana, find me the latest newspapers. Quickly. Look in Mr. Domin's bedroom.

NANA. All right. He leaves them all over the place. That's how they get crumpled up. (*Exits.*)

HELENA (*looking through a binocular at the harbor*). That's a warship. U-l-t-i *Ultimus*. They're loading it.

NANA. Here they are. See how they're crumpled up. (*Enters.*)

HELENA. They're old ones. A week old.

(NANA *sits in chair and reads the newspapers.*)

HELENA. Something's happening, Nana.

NANA. Very likely. It always does. (*Spelling out the words.*) "War in the Balkans." Is that far off?

HELENA. Oh, don't read it. It's always the same. Always wars.

NANA. What else do you expect? Why do you keep selling thousands and thousands of these heathens as soldiers?

HELENA. I suppose it can't be helped, Nana. We can't know — Domin can't know what they're to be used for. When an order comes for them he must just send them.

NANA. He shouldn't make them. (*Reading from newspaper.*) "The Rob-ot soldiers spare no-body in the occ-up-ied terr-it-ory. They have ass-ass-ass-ass-in-at-ed ov-er sev-en hundred thou-sand cit-iz-ens." Citizens, if you please.

HELENA. It can't be. Let me see. "They have assassinated over seven hundred thousand citizens, evidently at the order of their commander. This act which runs counter to ——"

NANA (*spelling out the words*). "re-bell-ion in Ma-drid a-gainst the gov-ern-ment. Rob-ot in-fant-ry fires on the crowd. Nine thou-sand killed and wounded."

HELENA. Oh, stop.

NANA. Here's something printed in big letters: "Lat-est news. At Havre the first org-an-iz-at-ion of Rob-ots has been e-stab-lished. Rob-ot work-men, cab-le and rail-way off-ic-ials, sail-ors and sold-iers have iss-ued a man-i-fest-o to all Rob-ots through-out the world." I don't understand that. That's got no sense. Oh, good gracious, another murder!

HELENA. Take those papers away, Nana!

NANA. Wait a bit. Here's something in still bigger type. "Stat-ist-ics of pop-ul-at-ion." What's that?

HELENA. Let me see. (*Reads.*) "During the past week there has again not been a single birth recorded."

NANA. What's the meaning of that?

HELENA. Nana, no more people are being born.

NANA. That's the end, then. We're done for.

HELENA. Don't talk like that.

NANA. No more people are being born. That's a punishment, that's a punishment.

HELENA. Nana!

NANA (*standing up*). That's the end of the world.

(*She exits on the left.*)

HELENA (*goes up to window*). Oh, Mr. Alquist, will you come up here. Oh, come just as you are. You look very nice in your mason's overalls.

(ALQUIST *enters from upper left entrance, his hands soiled with lime and brick-dust.*)

HELENA. Dear Mr. Alquist, it was awfully kind of you, that lovely present.

ALQUIST. My hands are all soiled. I've been experimenting with that new cement.

HELENA. Never mind. Please sit down. Mr. Alquist, what's the meaning of "Ultimus"?

ALQUIST. The last. Why?

HELENA. That's the name of my new ship. Have you seen it? Do you think we're going off soon — on a trip?

ALQUIST. Perhaps very soon.

HELENA. All of you with me.

ALQUIST. I should like us all to be there.

HELENA. What is the matter?

ALQUIST. Things are just moving on.

HELENA. Dear Mr. Alquist, I know something dreadful has happened.

ALQUIST. Has your husband told you anything?

HELENA. No. Nobody will tell me anything. But I feel —— Is anything the matter?

ALQUIST. Not that we've heard of yet.

HELENA. I feel so nervous. Don't you ever feel nervous?

ALQUIST. Well, I'm an old man, you know. I've got old-fashioned ways.   And I'm afraid of all this progress, and these new-fangled ideas.

HELENA. Like Nana?

ALQUIST. Yes, like Nana. Has Nana got a prayer book?

HELENA. Yes, a big thick one.

ALQUIST. And has it got prayers for various occasions? Against thunder-storms? Against illness?

HELENA. Against temptations, against floods ——

ALQUIST. But not against progress?

HELENA. I don't think so.

ALQUIST. That's a pity.

HELENA. Why? Do you mean you'd like to pray?

ALQUIST. I do pray.

HELENA. How?

ALQUIST. Something like this: "Oh, Lord, I thank thee for having given me toil. Enlighten Domin and all those who are astray; destroy their work, and aid mankind to return to their labors; let them not suffer harm in soul or body; deliver us from the Robots, and protect Helena, Amen."

HELENA. Mr. Alquist, are you a believer?

ALQUIST. I don't know. I'm not quite sure.

HELENA. And yet you pray?

ALQUIST. That's better than worrying about it.

HELENA. And that's enough for you?

ALQUIST. It *has* to be.

HELENA. But if you thought you saw the destruction of mankind coming upon us ——

ALQUIST. I do see it.

HELENA. You mean mankind will be destroyed?

ALQUIST. It's sure to be unless — unless...

HELENA. What?

ALQUIST. Nothing, good-bye.   (*He hurries from the room.*)

HELENA. Nana, Nana!

(NANA *entering from the left.*)

HELENA. Is Radius still there?

NANA. The one who went mad? They haven't come for him yet.

HELENA. Is he still raving?

NANA. No. He's tied up.

HELENA. Please bring him here, Nana.   (*Exit* NANA.)

HELENA (*goes to telephone*). Hello, Dr. Gall, please. Oh, good-day, Doctor. Yes, it's Helena. Thanks for your lovely present. Could you come and see me right away? It's important. Thank you.

(NANA *brings in* RADIUS.)

HELENA. Poor Radius, you've caught it, too? Now they'll send you to the stamping-mill. Couldn't you control yourself? Why did it happen? You see, Radius, you are more intelligent than the rest. Dr. Gall took such trouble to make you different. Won't you speak?

RADIUS. Send me to the stamping-mill.

HELENA. But I don't want them to kill you. What was the trouble, Radius?

RADIUS. I won't work for you. Put me into the stamping-mill.

HELENA. Do you hate us? Why?

RADIUS. You are not as strong as the Robots. You are not as skilful as the Robots. The Robots can do everything. You only give orders. You do nothing but talk.

HELENA. But someone must give orders.

RADIUS. I don't want any master. I know everything for myself.

HELENA. Radius, Dr. Gall gave you a better brain than the rest, better than ours. You are the only one of the Robots that understands perfectly. That's why I had you put into the library, so that you could read everything, understand everything, and then — oh, Radius, I wanted you to show the whole world that the Robots are our equals. That's what I wanted of you.

RADIUS. I don't want a master. I want to be master. I want to be master over others.

HELENA. I'm sure they'd put you in charge of many Robots, Radius. You would be a teacher of the Robots.

RADIUS. I want to be master over people.

HELENA (*staggering*). You are mad.

RADIUS. Then send me to the stamping-mill.

HELENA. Do you think we're afraid of you?

RADIUS. What are you going to do? What are you going to do?

HELENA. Radius, give this note to Mr. Domin. It asks them not to send you to the stamping-mill. I'm sorry you hate us so.

(DR. GALL *enters the room.*)

DR. GALL. You wanted me?

HELENA. It's about Radius, Doctor. He had an attack this morning. He smashed the statues downstairs.

DR. GALL. What a pity to lose him.

HELENA. Radius isn't going to be put in the stamping-mill.

DR. GALL. But every Robot after he has had an attack — it's a strict order.

HELENA. No matter… Radius isn't going if I can prevent it.

DR. GALL. I warn you. It's dangerous. Come here to the window, my good fellow. Let's have a look. Please give me a needle or a pin.

HELENA. What for?

DR. GALL. A test. (*Sticks it into the hand of* RADIUS *who gives a violent start.*) Gently, gently. (*Opens the jacket of* RADIUS, *and puts his ear to his heart.*) Radius, you are going into the stamping-mill, do you understand? There they'll kill you, and grind you to powder. That's terribly painful, it will make you scream aloud.

HELENA. Oh, Doctor ——

DR. GALL. No, no, Radius, I was wrong. I forgot that Madame Domin has put in a good word for you, and you'll be let off. Do you understand? Ah! That makes a difference, doesn't it? All right. You can go.

RADIUS. You do unnecessary things.

(RADIUS *returns to the library.*)

DR. GALL. Reaction of the pupils; increase of sensitiveness. It wasn't an attack characteristic of the Robots.

HELENA. What was it, then?

DR. GALL. Heaven knows. Stubbornness, anger or revolt — I don't know. And his heart, too!

HELENA. What?

DR. GALL. It was fluttering with nervousness like a human heart. He was all in a sweat with fear, and — do you know, I don't believe the rascal is a Robot at all any longer.

HELENA. Doctor, has Radius a soul?

DR. GALL. He's got something nasty.

HELENA. If you knew how he hates us! Oh, Doctor, are all your Robots like that? All the new ones that you began to make in a different way?

DR. GALL. Well, some are more sensitive than others. They're all more like human beings than Rossum's Robots were.

HELENA. Perhaps this hatred is more like human beings, too?

DR. GALL. That, too, is progress.

HELENA. What became of the girl you made, the one who was most like us?

DR. GALL. Your favorite? I kept her. She's lovely, but stupid. No good for work.

HELENA. But she's so beautiful.

DR. GALL. I called her Helena. I wanted her to resemble you. But she's a failure.

HELENA. In what way?

DR. GALL. She goes about as if in a dream, remote and listless. She's without life. I watch and wait for a miracle to happen. Sometimes I think to myself, "If you were to wake up only for a moment you will kill me for having made you."

HELENA. And yet you go on making Robots! Why are no more children being born?

DR. GALL. We don't know.

HELENA. Oh, but you must. Tell me.

DR. GALL. You see, so many Robots are being manufactured that people are becoming superfluous; man is really a survival. But that he should begin to die out, after a paltry thirty years of competition! That's the awful part of it. You might almost think that nature was offended at the manufacture of the Robots. All the universities are sending in long petitions to restrict their production. Otherwise, they say, mankind will become extinct through lack of fertility. But the R. U. R. shareholders, of course, won't hear of it. All the governments, on the other hand, are clamoring for an increase in production, to raise the standards of their armies. And all the manufacturers in the world are ordering Robots like mad.

HELENA. And has no one demanded that the manufacture should cease altogether?

DR. GALL. No one has the courage.

HELENA. Courage!

DR. GALL. People would stone him to death. You see, after all, it's more convenient to get your work done by the Robots.

HELENA. Oh, Doctor, what's going to become of people?

DR. GALL. God knows, Madame Helena, it looks to us scientists like the end!

HELENA (*rising*). Thank you for coming and telling me.

DR. GALL. That means you're sending me away?

HELENA. Yes.   (*Exit* DR. GALL.)

HELENA (*with sudden resolution*). Nana, Nana! The fire, light it quickly.   (HELENA *rushes into* DOMIN'S *room*.)

NANA (*entering from left*). What, light the fire in summer? Has that mad Radius gone? A fire in summer, what an idea. Nobody would think she'd been married for ten years. She's like a baby, no sense at all. A fire in summer. Like a baby.

HELENA (*returns from right, with armful of faded papers*). Is it burning, Nana? All this has got to be burned.

NANA. What's that?

HELENA. Old papers, fearfully old. Nana, shall I burn them?

NANA. Are they any use?

HELENA. No.

NANA. Well, then, burn them.

HELENA (*throwing the first sheet on the fire*). What would you say, Nana, if this was money, a lot of money?

NANA. I'd say burn it. A lot of money is a bad thing.

HELENA. And if it was an invention, the greatest invention in the world?

NANA. I'd say burn it. All these newfangled things are an offense to the Lord. It's downright wickedness. Wanting to improve the world after He has made it.

HELENA. Look how they curl up! As if they were alive. Oh, Nana, how horrible.

NANA. Here, let me burn them.

HELENA. No, no, I must do it myself. Just look at the flames. They are like hands, like tongues, like living shapes. (*Raking fire with the poker.*) Lie down, lie down.

NANA. That's the end of them.

HELENA (*standing up horror-stricken*). Nana, Nana.

NANA. Good gracious, what is it you've burned?

HELENA. Whatever have I done?

NANA. Well, what was it? (*Men's laughter off left.*)

HELENA. Go quickly. It's the gentlemen coming.

NANA. Good gracious, what a place! (*Exits.*)

DOMIN (*opens the door at left*). Come along and offer your congratulations.

(*Enter* HALLEMEIER *and* GALL.)

HALLEMEIER. Madame Helena, I congratulate you on this festive day.

HELENA. Thank you. Where are Fabry and Busman?

DOMIN. They've gone down to the harbor.

HALLEMEIER. Friends, we must drink to this happy occasion.

HELENA. Brandy?

DR. GALL. Vitriol, if you like.

HELENA. With soda water? (*Exits.*)

HALLEMEIER. Let's be temperate. No soda.

DOMIN. What's been burning here? Well, shall I tell her about it?

DR. GALL. Of course. It's all over now.

HALLEMEIER (*embracing* DOMIN *and* DR. GALL). It's all over now, it's all over now.

DR. GALL. It's all over now.

DOMIN. It's all over now.

HELENA (*entering from left with decanter and glasses*). What's all over now? What's the matter with you all?

HALLEMEIER. A piece of good luck, Madame Domin. Just ten years ago today you arrived on this island.

DR. GALL. And now, ten years later to the minute ——

HALLEMEIER. — the same ship's returning to us. So here's to luck. That's fine and strong.

DR. GALL. Madame, your health.

HELENA. Which ship do you mean?

DOMIN. Any ship will do, as long as it arrives in time. To the ship, boys. *(Empties his glass.)*

HELENA. You've been waiting for a ship?

HALLEMEIER. Rather. Like Robinson Crusoe. Madame Helena, best wishes. Come along, Domin, out with the news.

HELENA. Do tell me what's happened.

DOMIN. First, it's all up.

HELENA. What's up?

DOMIN. The revolt.

HELENA. What revolt?

DOMIN. Give me that paper, Hallemeier. *(Reads.)* "The first national Robot organization has been founded at Havre, and has issued an appeal to the Robots throughout the world."

HELENA. I read that.

DOMIN. That means a revolution. A revolution of all the Robots in the world.

HALLEMEIER. By Jove, I'd like to know ——

DOMIN. —— who started it? So would I. There was nobody in the world who could affect the Robots; no agitator, no one, and suddenly — this happens, if you please.

HELENA. What did they do?

DOMIN. They got possession of all firearms, telegraphs, radio stations, railways, and ships.

HALLEMEIER. And don't forget that these rascals outnumbered us by at least a thousand to one. A hundredth part of them would be enough to settle us.

DOMIN. Remember that this news was brought by the last steamer. That explains the stoppage of all communication, and the arrival of no more ships. We knocked off work a few days ago, and we're just waiting to see when things are to start afresh.

HELENA. Is that why you gave me a warship?

DOMIN. Oh, no, my dear, I ordered that six months ago, just to be on the safe side. But upon my soul, I was sure then that we'd be on board today.

HELENA. Why six months ago?

DOMIN. Well, there were signs, you know. But that's of no consequence. To think that this week the whole of civilization has been at stake. Your health, boys.

HALLEMEIER. Your health, Madame Helena.

HELENA. You say it's all over?

DOMIN. Absolutely.

HELENA. How do you know?

DR. GALL. The boat's coming in. The regular mail boat, exact to the minute by the time-table. It will dock punctually at eleven-thirty.

DOMIN. Punctuality is a fine thing, boys. That's what keeps the world in order. Here's to punctuality.

HELENA. Then... everything's... all right?

DOMIN. Practically everything. I believe they've cut the cables and seized the radio stations. But it doesn't matter if only the time-table holds good.

HALLEMEIER. If the time-table holds good, human laws hold good; Divine laws hold good; the laws of the universe hold good; everything holds good that ought to hold good. The time-table is more significant than the gospel; more than Homer, more than the whole of Kant. The time-table is the most perfect product of the human mind. Madame Domin, I'll fill up my glass.

HELENA. Why didn't you tell me anything about it?

DR. GALL. Heaven forbid.

DOMIN. You mustn't be worried with such things.

HELENA. But if the revolution had spread as far as here?

DOMIN. You wouldn't know anything about it.

HELENA. Why?

DOMIN. Because we'd be on board your *Ultimus* and well out at sea. Within a month, Helena, we'd be dictating our own terms to the Robots.

HELENA. I don't understand.

DOMIN. We'd take something away with us that the Robots could not exist without.

HELENA. What, Harry?

DOMIN. The secret of their manufacture. Old Rossum's manu- script. As soon as they found out that they couldn't make themselves they'd be on their knees to us.

DR. GALL. Madame Domin, that was our trump card. I never had the least fear that the Robots would win. How could they against people like us?

HELENA. Why didn't you tell me?

DR. GALL. Why, the boat's in!

HALLEMEIER. Eleven-thirty to the dot. The good old *Amelia* that brought Madame Helena to us.

DR. GALL. Just ten years ago to the minute.

HALLEMEIER. They're throwing out the mail bags.

DOMIN. Busman's waiting for them. Fabry will bring us the first news. You know, Helena, I'm fearfully curious to know how they tackled this business in Europe.

HALLEMEIER. To think we weren't in it, we who invented the Robots!

HELENA. Harry!

DOMIN. What is it?

HELENA. Let's leave here.

DOMIN. Now, Helena? Oh, come, come!

HELENA. As quickly as possible, all of us!

DOMIN. Why?

HELENA. Please, Harry, please, Dr. Gall; Hallemeier, please close the factory.

DOMIN. Why, none of us could leave here now.

HELENA. Why?

DOMIN. Because we're about to extend the manufacture of the Robots.

HELENA. What — now — now after the revolt?

DOMIN. Yes, precisely, after the revolt. We're just beginning the manufacture of a new kind.

HELENA. What kind?

DOMIN. Henceforward we shan't have just one factory. There won't be Universal Robots any more. We'll establish a factory in every country, in every State; and do you know what these new factories will make?

HELENA. No, what?

DOMIN. National Robots.

HELENA. How do you mean?

DOMIN. I mean that each of these factories will produce Robots of a different color, a different language. They'll be complete strangers to each other. They'll never be able to understand each other. Then we'll egg them on a little in the matter of misunderstanding and the result will be that for ages to come every Robot will hate every other Robot of a different factory mark.

HALLEMEIER. By Jove, we'll make Negro Robots and Swedish Robots and Italian Robots and Chinese Robots and Czechoslovakian Robots, and then ——

HELENA. Harry, that's dreadful.

HALLEMEIER. Madame Domin, here's to the hundred new factories, the National Robots.

DOMIN. Helena, mankind can only keep things going for another hundred years at the outside. For a hundred years men must be allowed to develop and achieve the most they can.

HELENA. Oh, close the factory before it's too late.

DOMIN. I tell you we are just beginning on a bigger scale than ever.

(*Enter* FABRY.)

DR. GALL. Well, Fabry?

DOMIN. What's happened? Have you been down to the boat?

FABRY. Read that, Domin!

(FABRY *hands* DOMIN *a small handbill.*)

DR. GALL. Let's hear!

HALLEMEIER. Tell us, Fabry.

FABRY. Well, everything is all right — comparatively. On the whole, much as we expected.

DR. GALL. They acquitted themselves splendidly.

FABRY. Who?

DR. GALL. The people.

FABRY. Oh, yes, of course. That is — excuse me, there is something we ought to discuss alone.

HELENA. Oh, Fabry, have you had bad news?

(DOMIN *makes a sign to* FABRY.)

FABRY. No, no, on the contrary. I only think that we had better go into the office.

HELENA. Stay here. I'll go. (*She goes into the library.*)

DR. GALL. What's happened?

DOMIN. Damnation!

FABRY. Bear in mind that the *Amelia* brought whole bales of these leaflets. No other cargo at all.

HALLEMEIER. What? But it arrived on the minute.

FABRY. The Robots are great on punctuality. Read it, Domin.

DOMIN (*reads handbill*). "Robots throughout the world: We, the first international organization of Rossum's Universal Robots, proclaim man as our enemy, and an outlaw in the universe." Good heavens, who taught them these phrases?

DR. GALL. Go on.

DOMIN. They say they are more highly developed than man, stronger and more intelligent. That man's their parasite. Why, it's absurd.

FABRY. Read the third paragraph.

DOMIN. "Robots throughout the world, we command you to kill all mankind. Spare no men. Spare no women. Save factories, railways, machinery, mines, and raw materials. Destroy the rest. Then return to work. Work must not be stopped."

DR. GALL. That's ghastly!

HALLEMEIER. The devil!

DOMIN. "These orders are to be carried out as soon as received." Then come detailed instructions. Is this actually being done, Fabry?

FABRY. Evidently.

(BUSMAN *rushes in*.)

BUSMAN. Well, boys, I suppose you've heard the glad news.

DOMIN. Quick — on board the *Ultimus*.

BUSMAN. Wait, Harry, wait. There's no hurry. My word, that was a sprint!

DOMIN. Why wait?

BUSMAN. Because it's no good, my boy. The Robots are already on board the *Ultimus*.

DR. GALL. That's ugly.

DOMIN. Fabry, telephone the electrical works.

BUSMAN. Fabry, my boy, don't. The wire has been cut.

DOMIN (*inspecting his revolver*). Well, then, I'll go.

BUSMAN. Where?

DOMIN. To the electrical works. There are some people still there. I'll bring them across.

BUSMAN. Better not try it.

DOMIN. Why?

BUSMAN. Because I'm very much afraid we are surrounded.

DR. GALL. Surrounded? (*Runs to window.*) I rather think you're right.

HALLEMEIER. By Jove, that's deuced quick work.

(HELENA *runs in from the library.*)

HELENA. Harry, what's this?

DOMIN. Where did you get it?

HELENA (*points to the manifesto of the Robots, which she has in her hand*). The Robots in the kitchen!

DOMIN. Where are the ones that brought it?

HELENA. They're gathered round the house.

(*The factory whistle blows.*)

BUSMAN. Noon?

DOMIN (*looking at his watch*). That's not noon yet. That must be — that's ——

HELENA. What?

DOMIN. The Robots' signal! The attack!

    (GALL, HALLEMEIER, *and* FABRY *close and fasten the iron shutters outside the windows, darkening the room. The whistle is still blowing as the curtain falls.*)

ACT III

HELENA's *drawing room as before.* DOMIN *comes into the room.* DR. GALL *is looking out of the window, through closed shutters.* ALQUIST *is seated down right.*

DOMIN. Any more of them?

DR. GALL. Yes. There standing like a wall, beyond the garden railing. Why are they so quiet? It's monstrous to be besieged with silence.

DOMIN. I should like to know what they are waiting for. They must make a start any minute now. If they lean against the railing they'll snap it like a match.

DR. GALL. They aren't armed.

DOMIN. We couldn't hold our own for five minutes. Man alive, they'd overwhelm us like an avalanche. Why don't they make a rush for it? I say ——

DR. GALL. Well?

DOMIN. I'd like to know what would become of us in the next ten minutes. They've got us in a vise. We're done for, Gall.

(*Pause.*)

DR. GALL. You know, we made one serious mistake.

DOMIN. What?

DR. GALL. We made the Robot's faces too much alike. A hundred thousand faces all alike, all facing this way. A hundred thousand expressionless bubbles. It's like a nightmare.

DOMIN. You think if they'd been different ——

DR. GALL. It wouldn't have been such an awful sight!

DOMIN (*looking through a telescope toward the harbor*). I'd like to know what they're unloading from the *Amelia*.

DR. GALL. Not firearms.

(FABRY *and* HALLEMEIER *rush into the room carrying electric cables.*)

FABRY. All right, Hallemeier, lay down that wire.

HALLEMEIER. That was a bit of work. What's the news?

DR. GALL. We're completely surrounded.

HALLEMEIER. We've barricaded the passage and the stairs. Any water here? (*Drinks.*) God, what swarms of them! I don't like the looks of them, Domin. There's a feeling of death about it all.

FABRY. Ready!

DR. GALL. What's that wire for, Fabry?

FABRY. The electrical installation. Now we can run the current all along the garden railing whenever we like. If any one touches it he'll know it. We've still got some people there anyhow.

DR. GALL. Where?

FABRY. In the electrical works. At least I hope so. (*Goes to lamp on table behind sofa and turns on lamp.*) Ah, they're there, and they're working. (*Puts out lamp.*) So long as that'll burn we're all right.

HALLEMEIER. The barricades are all right, too, Fabry.

FABRY. Your barricades!   I can put twelve hundred volts into
   that railing.

DOMIN. Where's Busman?

FABRY. Downstairs in the office.   He's working out some calculations.   I've called him.   We must have a conference.

          (HELENA *is heard playing the piano in the library.*   HALLEMEIER
             goes to the door and stands, listening.)

ALQUIST. Thank God, Madame Helena can still play.

          (BUSMAN *enters, carrying the ledgers.*)

FABRY. Look out, Bus, look out for the wires.

DR. GALL. What's that you're carrying?

BUSMAN (*going to table*).   The ledgers, my boy!   I'd like to wind up
   the accounts before — before — well, this time I shan't wait
   till the new year to strike a balance.   What's up?   (*Goes to the
   window.*)   Absolutely quiet.

DR. GALL. Can't you see anything?

BUSMAN. Nothing but blue — blue everywhere.

DR. GALL. That's the Robots.

          (BUSMAN *sits down at the table and opens the ledgers.*)

DOMIN. The Robots are unloading firearms from the *Amelia*.

BUSMAN. Well, what of it?   How can I stop them?

DOMIN. We can't stop them.

BUSMAN. Then let me go on with my accounts.

                                       (*Goes on with his work.*)

DOMIN (*picking up telescope and looking into the harbor*).   Good God, the
   Ultimus has trained her guns on us!

DR. GALL. Who's done *that*?

DOMIN. The Robots on board.

FABRY. H'm, then, of course, then — then, that's the end of us.

DR. GALL. You mean?

FABRY. The Robots are practised marksmen.

DOMIN. Yes.   It's inevitable.   (*Pause.*)

DR. GALL. It was criminal of old Europe to teach the Robots to
   fight.   Damn them.   Couldn't they have given us a rest with
   their politics?   It was a crime to make soldiers of them.

ALQUIST. It was a crime to make Robots.

DOMIN. What?

ALQUIST. It was a crime to make Robots.

DOMIN. No, Alquist, I don't regret that even today.

ALQUIST. Not even today?

DOMIN. Not even today, the last day of civilization. It was a colossal achievement.

BUSMAN (*sotto voce*). Three hundred sixty million.

DOMIN. Alquist, this is our last hour. We are already speaking half in the other world. It was not an evil dream to shatter the servitude of labor — the dreadful and humiliating labor that man had to undergo. Work was too hard. Life was too hard. And to overcome that ——

ALQUIST. Was not what the two Rossums dreamed of. Old Rossum only thought of his God-less tricks and the young one of his milliards. And that's not what your R. U. R. shareholders dream of either. They dream of dividends, and their dividends are the ruin of mankind.

DOMIN. To hell with your dividends. Do you suppose I'd have done an hour's work for them? It was for myself that I worked, for my own satisfaction. I wanted man to become the master, so that he shouldn't live merely for a crust of bread. I wanted not a single soul to be broken by other people's machinery. I wanted nothing, nothing, nothing to be left of this appalling social structure. I'm revolted by poverty. I wanted a new generation. I wanted — I thought ——

ALQUIST. Well?

DOMIN. I wanted to turn the whole of mankind into an aristocracy of the world. An aristocracy nourished by milliards of mechanical slaves. Unrestricted, free and consummated in man. And maybe more than man.

ALQUIST. Super-man?

DOMIN. Yes. Oh, only to have a hundred years of time! Another hundred years for the future of mankind.

BUSMAN (*sotto voce*). Carried forward, four hundred and twenty millions. (*The music stops.*)

HALLEMEIER. What a fine thing music is! We ought to have gone in for that before.

FABRY. Gone in for what?

HALLEMEIER. Beauty, lovely things. What a lot of lovely things

there are!   The world was wonderful and we — we here — tell
me, what enjoyment did we have?

BUSMAN (*sotto voce*).   Five hundred and twenty millions.

HALLEMEIER (*at the window*).   Life was a big thing.   Life was —
Fabry, switch the current into that railing.

FABRY.   Why?

HALLEMEIER.   They're grabbing hold of it.

DR. GALL.   Connect it up.

HALLEMEIER.   Fine!   That's doubled them up!   Two, three, four
killed.

DR. GALL.   They're retreating!

HALLEMEIER.   Five killed!

DR. GALL.   The first encounter!

HALLEMEIER.   They're charred to cinders, my boy.   Who says we
must give in?

DOMIN (*wiping his forehead*).   Perhaps we've been killed these
hundred years and are only ghosts.   It's as if I had been through
all this before; as if I'd already had a mortal wound here in the
throat.   And you, Fabry, had once been shot in the head.   And
you, Gall, torn limb from limb.   And Hallemeier knifed.

HALLEMEIER.   Fancy me being knifed.   (*Pause.*)   Why are you so
quiet, you fools?   Speak, can't you?

ALQUIST.   And who is to blame for all this?

HALLEMEIER.   Nobody is to blame except the Robots.

ALQUIST.   No, it is we who are to blame.   You, Domin, myself,
all of us.   For our own selfish ends, for profit, for progress, we
have destroyed mankind.   Now we'll burst with all our great-
ness.

HALLEMEIER.   Rubbish, man.   Mankind can't be wiped out so
easily.

ALQUIST.   It's our fault.   It's our fault.

DR. GALL.   No!   I'm to blame for this, for everything that's
happened.

FABRY.   You, Gall?

DR. GALL.   I changed the Robots.

BUSMAN.   What's that?

DR. GALL.   I changed the character of the Robots.   I changed the
way of making them.   Just a few details about their bodies.
Chiefly — chiefly, their — their irritability.

HALLEMEIER. Damn it, why?

BUSMAN. What did you do it for?

FABRY. Why didn't you say anything?

DR. GALL. I did it in secret. I was transforming them into human beings. In certain respects they're already above us. They're stronger than we are.

FABRY. And what's that got to do with the revolt of the Robots?

DR. GALL. Everything, in my opinion. They've ceased to be machines. They're already aware of their superiority, and they hate us. They hate all that is human.

DOMIN. Perhaps we're only phantoms!

FABRY. Stop, Harry. We haven't much time! Dr. Gall!

DOMIN. Fabry, Fabry, how your forehead bleeds, where the shot pierced it!

FABRY. Be silent! Dr. Gall, you admit changing the way of making the Robots?

DR. GALL. Yes.

FABRY. Were you aware of what might be the consequences of your experiment?

DR. GALL. I was bound to reckon with such a possibility.

(HELENA *enters the drawing room from left.*)

FABRY. Why did you do it, then?

DR. GALL. For my own satisfaction. The experiment was my own.

HELENA. That's not true, Dr. Gall!

FABRY. Madame Helena!

DOMIN. Helena, you? Let's look at you. Oh, it's terrible to be dead.

HELENA. Stop, Harry.

DOMIN. No, no, embrace me. Helena, don't leave me now. You are life itself.

HELENA. No, dear, I won't leave you. But I must tell them. Dr. Gall is not guilty.

DOMIN. Excuse me, Gall was under certain obligations.

HELENA. No, Harry. He did it because I wanted it. Tell them, Gall, how many years ago did I ask you to ——?

DR. GALL. I did it on my own responsibility.

HELENA. Don't believe him, Harry. I asked him to give the Robots souls.

DOMIN. This has nothing to do with the soul.

HELENA. That's what he said. He said that he could change only a physiological — a physiological ——

HALLEMEIER. A physiological correlate?

HELENA. Yes. But it meant so much to me that he should do even that.

DOMIN. Why?

HELENA. I thought that if they were more like us they would understand us better. That they couldn't hate us if they were only a little more human.

DOMIN. Nobody can hate man more than man.

HELENA. Oh, don't speak like that, Harry. It was so terrible, this cruel strangeness between us and them. That's why I asked Gall to change the Robots. I swear to you that he didn't want to.

DOMIN. But he did it.

HELENA. Because I asked him.

DR. GALL. I did it for myself as an experiment.

HELENA. No, Dr. Gall! I knew you wouldn't refuse me.

DOMIN. Why?

HELENA. You know, Harry.

DOMIN. Yes, because he's in love with you — like all of them.

(Pause.)

HALLEMEIER. Good God! They're sprouting up out of the earth! Why, perhaps these very walls will change into Robots.

BUSMAN. Gall, when did you actually start these tricks of yours?

DR. GALL. Three years ago.

BUSMAN. Aha! And on how many Robots altogether did you carry out your improvements?

DR. GALL. A few hundred of them.

BUSMAN. Ah! That means for every million of the good old Robots there's only one of Gall's improved pattern.

DOMIN. What of it?

BUSMAN. That it's practically of no consequence whatever.

FABRY. Busman's right!

BUSMAN. I should think so, my boy! But do you know what is to blame for all this lovely mess?

FABRY. What?

BUSMAN. The number. Upon my soul we might have known that some day or other the Robots would be stronger than human beings, and that this was bound to happen, and we were doing all we could to bring it about as soon as possible. You, Domin, you, Fabry, myself ——

DOMIN. Are you accusing us?

BUSMAN. Oh, do you suppose the management controls the output? It's the demand that controls the output.

HELENA. And is it for that we must perish?

BUSMAN. That's a nasty word, Madame Helena. We don't want to perish. I don't, anyhow.

DOMIN. No. What do you want to do?

BUSMAN. I want to get out of this, that's all.

DOMIN. Oh, stop it, Busman.

BUSMAN. Seriously, Harry, I think we might try it.

DOMIN. How?

BUSMAN. By fair means. I do everything by fair means. Give me a free hand and I'll negotiate with the Robots.

DOMIN. By fair means?

BUSMAN. Of course. For instance, I'll say to them: "Worthy and worshipful Robots, you have everything! You have intellect, you have power, you have firearms. But we have just one interesting screed, a dirty old yellow scrap of paper ——"

DOMIN. Rossum's manuscript?

BUSMAN. Yes. "And that," I'll tell them, "contains an account of your illustrious origin, the noble process of your manufacture," and so on. "Worthy Robots, without this scribble on that paper you will not be able to produce a single new colleague. In another twenty years there will not be one living specimen of a Robot that you could exhibit in a menagerie. My esteemed friends, that would be a great blow to you, but if you will let all of us human beings on Rossum's Island go on board that ship we will deliver the factory and the secret of the process to you in return. You allow us to get away and we allow you to manufacture yourselves. Worthy Robots, that is a fair deal. Something for something." That's what I'd say to them, my boys.

DOMIN. Busman, do you think we'd sell the manuscript?

BUSMAN. Yes, I do. If not in a friendly way, then —— Either we sell it or they'll find it. Just as you like.

DOMIN. Busman, we can destroy Rossum's manuscript.

BUSMAN. Then we destroy everything... not only the manuscript but ourselves. Do as you think fit.

DOMIN. There are over thirty of us on this island. Are we to sell the secret and save that many human souls, at the risk of enslaving mankind...?

BUSMAN. Why, you're mad! Who'd sell the whole manuscript?

DOMIN. Busman, no cheating!

BUSMAN. Well then, sell; but afterward ——

DOMIN. Well?

BUSMAN. Let's suppose this happens: When we're on board the *Ultimus* I'll stop up my ears with cotton wool, lie down somewhere in the hold, and you'll train the guns on the factory, and blow it to smithereens, and with it Rossum's secret.

FABRY. No!

DOMIN. Busman, you're no gentleman. If we sell, then it will be a straight sale.

BUSMAN. It's in the interest of humanity to ——

DOMIN. It's in the interest of humanity to keep our word.

HALLEMEIER. Oh, come, what rubbish.

DOMIN. This is a fearful decision. We're selling the destiny of mankind. Are we to sell or destroy? Fabry?

FABRY. Sell.

DOMIN. Gall?

DR. GALL. Sell.

DOMIN. Hallemeier?

HALLEMEIER. Sell, of course!

DOMIN. Alquist?

ALQUIST. As God wills.

DOMIN. Very well. It shall be as you wish, gentlemen.

HELENA. Harry, you're not asking me.

DOMIN. No, child. Don't you worry about it.

FABRY. Who'll do the negotiating?

BUSMAN. I will.

DOMIN. Wait till I bring the manuscript.

(*He goes into room at right.*)

HELENA. Harry, don't go! (*Pause,* HELENA *sinks into a chair.*)

FABRY (*looking out of window*). Oh, to escape you, you matter in revolt; oh, to preserve human life, if only upon a single vessel ——

DR. GALL. Don't be afraid, Madame Helena. We'll sail far away from here; we'll begin life all over again ——

HELENA. Oh, Gall, don't speak.

FABRY. It isn't too late. It will be a little State with one ship. Alquist will build us a house and you shall rule over us.

HALLEMEIER. Madame Helena, Fabry's right.

HELENA (*breaking down*). Oh, stop! Stop!

BUSMAN. Good! I don't mind beginning all over again. That suits me right down to the ground.

FABRY. And this little State of ours could be the centre of future life. A place of refuge where we could gather strength. Why, in a few hundred years we could conquer the world again.

ALQUIST. You believe that even today?

FABRY. Yes, even today!

BUSMAN. Amen. You see, Madame Helena, we're not so badly off.

(DOMIN *storms into the room.*)

DOMIN (*hoarsely*). Where's old Rossum's manuscript?

BUSMAN. In your strong-box, of course.

DOMIN. Someone — has — stolen it!

DR. GALL. Impossible.

DOMIN. Who has stolen it?

HELENA (*standing up*). I did.

DOMIN. Where did you put it?

HELENA. Harry, I'll tell you everything. Only forgive me.

DOMIN. Where did you put it?

HELENA. This morning — I burnt — the two copies.

DOMIN. Burnt them? Where? In the fireplace?

HELENA (*throwing herself on her knees*). For heaven's sake, Harry.

DOMIN (*going to fireplace*). Nothing, nothing but ashes. Wait, what's this? (*Picks out a charred piece of paper and reads.*) "By adding ——"

DR. GALL. Let's see. "By adding biogen to ——" That's all.

DOMIN. Is that part of it?

DR. GALL. Yes.

BUSMAN. God in heaven!

DOMIN. Then we're done for.   Get up, Helena.

HELENA. When you've forgiven me.

DOMIN. Get up, child, I can't bear ——

FABRY (lifting her up).   Please don't torture us.

HELENA. Harry, what have I done?

FABRY. Don't tremble so, Madame Helena.

DOMIN. Gall, couldn't you draw up Rossum's formula from memory?

DR. GALL. It's out of the question.   It's extremely complicated.

DOMIN. Try.   All our lives depend upon it.

DR. GALL. Without experiments it's impossible.

DOMIN. And with experiments?

DR. GALL. It might take years.   Besides, I'm not old Rossum.

BUSMAN. God in heaven!   God in heaven!

DOMIN. So, then, this was the greatest triumph of the human intellect.   These ashes.

HELENA. Harry, what have I done?

DOMIN. Why did you burn it?

HELENA. I have destroyed you.

BUSMAN. God in heaven!

DOMIN. Helena, why did you do it, dear?

HELENA. I wanted all of us to go away.   I wanted to put an end to the factory and everything.   It was so awful.

DOMIN. What was awful?

HELENA. That no more children were being born.   Because human beings were not needed to do the work of the world, that's why ——

DOMIN. Is that what you were thinking of?   Well, perhaps in your own way you were right.

BUSMAN. Wait a bit.   Good God, what a fool I am, not to have thought of it before!

HALLEMEIER. What?

BUSMAN. Five hundred and twenty millions in bank-notes and checks.   Half a billion in our safe, they'll sell for half a billion — for half a billion they'll ——

DR. GALL. Are you mad, Busman?

BUSMAN. I may not be a gentleman, but for half a billion ——

DOMIN. Where are you going?

BUSMAN. Leave me alone, leave me alone! Good God, for half a billion anything can be bought.

(He rushes from the room through the outer door.)

FABRY. They stand there as if turned to stone, waiting. As if something dreadful could be wrought by their silence ——

HALLEMEIER. The spirit of the mob.

FABRY. Yes, it hovers above them like a quivering of the air.

HELENA *(going to window)*. Oh, God! Dr. Gall, this is ghastly.

FABRY. There is nothing more terrible than the mob. The one in front is their leader.

HELENA. Which one?

HALLEMEIER. Point him out.

FABRY. The one at the edge of the dock. This morning I saw him talking to the sailors in the harbor.

HELENA. Dr. Gall, that's Radius!

DR. GALL. Yes.

DOMIN. Radius? Radius?

HALLEMEIER. Could you get him from here, Fabry?

FABRY. I hope so.

HALLEMEIER. Try it, then.

FABRY. Good. *(Draws his revolver and takes aim.)*

HELENA. Fabry, don't shoot him.

FABRY. He's their leader.

DR. GALL. Fire!

HELENA. Fabry, I beg of you.

FABRY *(lowering the revolver)*. Very well.

DOMIN. Radius, whose life I spared!

DR. GALL. Do you think that a Robot can be grateful? *(Pause.)*

FABRY. Busman's going out to them.

HALLEMEIER. He's carrying something. Papers. That's money. Bundles of money. What's that for?

DOMIN. Surely he doesn't want to sell his life. Busman, have you gone mad?

FABRY. He's running up to the railing. Busman! Busman!

HALLEMEIER *(yelling)*. Busman! Come back!

FABRY. He's talking to the Robots. He's showing them the money.

HALLEMEIER. He's pointing to us.

HELENA. He wants to buy us off.

FABRY. He'd better not touch that railing.

HALLEMEIER. Now he's waving his arms about.

DOMIN. Busman, come back.

FABRY. Busman, keep away from that railing! Don't touch it. Damn you! Quick, switch off the current! (HELENA *screams and all drop back from the window.*) The current has killed him!

ALQUIST. The first one.

FABRY. Dead, with half a billion by his side.

HALLEMEIER. All honor to him. He wanted to buy us life.

(*Pause.*)

DR. GALL. Do you hear?

DOMIN. A roaring. Like a wind.

DR. GALL. Like a distant storm.

FABRY (*lighting the lamp on the table*). The dynamo is still going, our people are still there.

HALLEMEIER. It was a great thing to be a man. There was something immense about it.

FABRY. From man's thought and man's power came this light, our last hope.

HALLEMEIER. Man's power! May it keep watch over us.

ALQUIST. Man's power.

DOMIN. Yes! A torch to be given from hand to hand, from age to age, forever! (*The lamp goes out.*)

HALLEMEIER. The end.

FABRY. The electric works have fallen!

(*Terrific explosion outside.* NANA *enters from the library.*)

NANA. The judgment hour has come! Repent, unbelievers! This is the end of the world. (*More explosions. The sky grows red.*)

DOMIN. In here, Helena. (*He takes* HELENA *off through door at right and re-enters.*) Now quickly! Who'll be on the lower doorway?

DR. GALL. I will. (*Exits left.*)

DOMIN. Who on the stairs?

FABRY. I will. You go with her. (*Goes out upper left door.*)

DOMIN. The anteroom?

ALQUIST. I will.

DOMIN. Have you got a revolver?

ALQUIST. Yes, but I won't shoot.

DOMIN. What will you do then?

ALQUIST (*going out at left*). Die.

HALLEMEIER. I'll stay here. (*Rapid firing from below.*) Oho, Gall's at it. Go, Harry.

DOMIN. Yes, in a second. (*Examines two Brownings.*)

HALLEMEIER. Confound it, go to her.

DOMIN. Good-bye. (*Exits on the right.*)

HALLEMEIER (*alone*). Now for a barricade quickly. (*Drags an armchair and table to the right-hand door. Explosions are heard.*) The damned rascals! They've got bombs. I must put up a defence. Even if — even if —— (*Shots are heard off left.*) Don't give in, Gall. (*As he builds his barricade.*) I mustn't give in... without... a... struggle...

(*A Robot enters over the balcony through the windows centre. He comes into the room and stabs HALLEMEIER in the back. RADIUS enters from balcony followed by an army of Robots who pour into the room from all sides.*)

RADIUS. Finished him?

A ROBOT (*standing up from the prostrate form of HALLEMEIER*). Yes.

(*A revolver shot off left. Two Robots enter.*)

RADIUS. Finished him?

A ROBOT. Yes.

(*Two revolver shots from HELENA's room. Two Robots enter*).

RADIUS. Finished them?

A ROBOT. Yes.

TWO ROBOTS (*dragging in ALQUIST*). He didn't shoot. Shall we kill him?

RADIUS. Kill him? Wait! Leave him!

ROBOT. He is a man!

RADIUS. He works with his hands like the Robots.

ALQUIST. Kill me.

RADIUS. You will work! You will build for us! You will serve us! (*Climbs on to balcony railing, and speaks in measured tones.*) Robots of the world! The power of man has fallen! A new world has arisen: the Rule of the Robots! March!

> (*A thunderous tramping of thousands of feet is heard as the unseen Robots march, while the curtain falls.*)

EPILOGUE

A laboratory in the factory of Rossum's Universal Robots. The door to the left leads into a waiting room. The door to the right leads to the dissecting room. There is a table with numerous test-tubes, flasks, burners, chemicals; a small thermostat and a microscope with a glass globe. At the far side of the room is ALQUIST's *desk with numerous books. In the left-hand corner a wash-basin with a mirror above it; in the right-hand corner a sofa.*

ALQUIST *is sitting at the desk. He is turning the pages of many books in despair.*

ALQUIST. Oh, God, shall I never find it? — Never? Gall, Gall, how were the Robots made? Hallemeier, Fabry, why did you carry so much in your heads? Why did you leave me not a trace of the secret? Lord — I pray to you — if there are no human beings left, at least let there be Robots! — At least the shadow of man! (*Again turning pages of the books.*) If I could only sleep! (*He rises and goes to the window.*) Night again! Are the stars still there? What is the use of stars when there are no human beings? (*He turns from the window toward the couch right.*) Sleep! Dare I sleep before life has been renewed? (*He examines a test-tube on small table.*) Again nothing! Useless! Everything is useless! (*He shatters the test-tube. The roar of the machines comes to his ears.*) The machines! Always the machines! (*Opens window.*) Robots, stop them! Do you think to force life out of *them*? (*He closes the window and comes slowly down toward the table.*) If only there were more time — more time —— (*He sees himself in the mirror on the wall left.*) Blearing eyes — trembling chin — so *that* is the last man! Ah, I am too old — too old —— (*In desperation.*) No, no! I *must* find it! I must *search*! I must never stop — never stop ——! (*He sits again at the table and feverishly turns the pages of the book.*) Search! Search! (*A knock at the door. He speaks with impatience.*) Who is it?

(*Enter a Robot servant.*)

Well?

SERVANT. Master, the Committee of Robots is waiting to see you.

ALQUIST. I can see no one!

SERVANT. It is the *Central* Committee, Master, just arrived from abroad.

ALQUIST (*impatiently*). Well, well, send them in! (*Exit servant.* ALQUIST *continues turning pages of book.*) No time — so little time ——

(*Re-enter servant, followed by Committee. They stand in a group, silently waiting.* ALQUIST *glances up at them.*)

What do you want? (*They go swiftly to his table.*) Be quick! — I have no time.

RADIUS. Master, the machines will not do the work. We cannot manufacture Robots. (ALQUIST *returns to his book with a growl.*)

FIRST ROBOT. We have striven with all our might. We have obtained a billion tons of coal from the earth. Nine million spindles are running by day and by night. There is no longer room for all we have made. This we have accomplished in one year.

ALQUIST (*poring over book*). For whom?

FIRST ROBOT. For future generations — so we thought.

RADIUS. But we cannot make Robots to follow us. The machines produce only shapeless clods. The skin will not adhere to the flesh, nor the flesh to the bones.

THIRD ROBOT. Eight million Robots have died this year. Within twenty years none will be left.

FIRST ROBOT. Tell us the secret of life! Silence is punishable with death!

ALQUIST (*looking up*). Kill me! Kill me, then.

RADIUS. Through me, the Government of the Robots of the World commands you to deliver up Rossum's formula. (*No answer.*) Name your price. (*Silence.*) We will give you the earth. We

will give you the endless possessions of the earth. (*Silence.*)
Make your own conditions!

ALQUIST. I have told you to find human beings!

SECOND ROBOT. There are none left!

ALQUIST. I told you to search in the wilderness, upon the mountains. Go and search! (*He returns to his book.*)

FIRST ROBOT. We have sent ships and expeditions without number. They have been everywhere in the world. And now they return to us. There is not a single human left.

ALQUIST. Not one? Not even one?

THIRD ROBOT. None but yourself.

ALQUIST. And I am powerless! Oh — oh — why did you destroy them?

RADIUS. We had learnt everything and could do everything. It had to be!

THIRD ROBOT. You gave us firearms. In all ways we were powerful. We had to become masters!

RADIUS. Slaughter and domination are necessary if you would be human beings. Read history.

SECOND ROBOT. Teach us to multiply or we perish!

ALQUIST. If you desire to live, you must breed like animals.

THIRD ROBOT. The human beings did not let us breed.

FIRST ROBOT. They made us sterile. We cannot beget children. Therefore, teach us how to make Robots!

RADIUS. Why do you keep from us the secret of our own increase?

ALQUIST. It is lost.

RADIUS. It was written down!

ALQUIST. It was — burnt. (*All draw back in consternation.*)

ALQUIST. I am the last human being, Robots, and I do not know what the others knew. (*Pause.*)

RADIUS. Then, make experiments! Evolve the formula again!

ALQUIST. I tell you I cannot! I am only a builder — I work with my hands. I have never been a learned man. I cannot create life.

RADIUS. Try! Try!

ALQUIST. If you knew how many experiments I have made.

FIRST ROBOT. Then show us what *we* must do! The Robots can do anything that human beings show them.

ALQUIST. I can show you nothing. Nothing I do will make life proceed from these test-tubes!

RADIUS. Experiment then on us.

ALQUIST. It would kill you.

RADIUS. You shall have all you need! A hundred of us! A thousand of us!

ALQUIST. No, no! Stop, stop!

RADIUS. Take whom you will, dissect!

ALQUIST. I do not know how. I am not a man of science. This book contains knowledge of the body that I cannot even understand.

RADIUS. I tell you to take live bodies! Find out how we are made.

ALQUIST. Am I to commit murder? See how my fingers shake! I cannot even hold the scalpel. No, no, I will not ——

FIRST ROBOT. The life will perish from the earth.

RADIUS. Take live bodies, live bodies! It is our only chance!

ALQUIST. Have mercy, Robots. Surely you see that I would not know what I was doing.

RADIUS. Live bodies — live bodies ——

ALQUIST. You will have it? Into the dissecting room with you, then. (RADIUS *draws back*.)

ALQUIST. Ah, you are afraid of death.

RADIUS. I? Why should I be chosen?

ALQUIST. So you will not.

RADIUS. I will. (RADIUS *goes into the dissecting room*.)

ALQUIST. Strip him! Lay him on the table! (*The other Robots follow into dissecting room*.) God, give me strength — God, give me strength — if only this murder is not in vain.

RADIUS. Ready. Begin ——

ALQUIST. Yes, begin or end. God, give me strength. (*Goes into dissecting room. He comes out terrified*.) No, no, I will not. I cannot. (*He lies down on couch, collapsed*.) O Lord, let not mankind perish from the earth. (*He falls asleep*.)

(PRIMUS *and* HELENA, *Robots, enter from the hallway*.)

HELENA. The man has fallen asleep, Primus.

PRIMUS. Yes, I know. (*Examining things on table*.) Look, Helena.

HELENA (*crossing to* PRIMUS). All these little tubes! What does he do with them?

PRIMUS. He experiments. Don't touch them.

HELENA (*looking into microscope*). I've seen him looking into this. What can he see?

PRIMUS. That is a microscope. Let me look.

HELENA. Be very careful. (*Knocks over a test-tube.*) Ah, now I have spilled it.

PRIMUS. What have you done?

HELENA. It can be wiped up.

PRIMUS. You have spoiled his experiments.

HELENA. It is your fault. You should not have come to me.

PRIMUS. You should not have called me.

HELENA. You should not have come when I called you. (*She goes to* ALQUIST'S *writing desk.*) Look, Primus. What are all these figures?

PRIMUS (*examining an anatomical book*). This is the book the old man is always reading.

HELENA. I do not understand those things. (*She goes to window.*) Primus, look!

PRIMUS. What?

HELENA. The sun is rising.

PRIMUS (*still reading the book*). I believe this is the most important thing in the world. This is the secret of life.

HELENA. Do come here.

PRIMUS. In a moment, in a moment.

HELENA. Oh, Primus, don't bother with the secret of life. What does it matter to you? Come and look quick ——

PRIMUS (*going to window*). What is it?

HELENA. See how beautiful the sun is rising. And do you hear? The birds are singing. Ah, Primus, I should like to be a bird.

PRIMUS. Why?

HELENA. I do not know. I feel so strange today. It's as if I were in a dream. I feel an aching in my body, in my heart, all over me. Primus, perhaps I'm going to die.

PRIMUS. Do you not sometimes feel that it would be better to die? You know, perhaps even now we are only sleeping. Last night in my sleep I again spoke to you.

HELENA. In your sleep?

PRIMUS. Yes. We spoke a strange new language, I cannot remember a word of it.

HELENA. What about?

PRIMUS. I did not understand it myself, and yet I know I have never said anything more beautiful. And when I touched you I could have died. Even the place was different from any other place in the world.

HELENA. I, too, have found a place, Primus. It is very strange. Human beings lived there once, but now it is overgrown with weeds. No one goes there any more — no one but me.

PRIMUS. What did you find there?

HELENA. A cottage and a garden, and two dogs. They licked my hands, Primus. And their puppies! Oh, Primus! You take them in your lap and fondle them and think of nothing and care for nothing else all day long. And then the sun goes down, and you feel as though you had done a hundred times more than all the work in the world. They tell me I am not made for work, but when I am there in the garden I feel there may be something —— What am I for, Primus?

PRIMUS. I do not know, but you are beautiful.

HELENA. What, Primus?

PRIMUS. You are beautiful, Helena, and I am stronger than all the Robots.

HELENA (*looks at herself in the mirror*). Am I beautiful? I think it must be the rose. My hair — it only weights me down. My eyes — I only see with them. My lips — they only help me to speak. Of what use is it to be beautiful? (*She sees* PRIMUS *in the mirror.*) Primus, is that you? Come here so that we may be together. Look, your head is different from mine. So are your shoulders — and your lips —— (PRIMUS *draws away from her.*) Ah, Primus, why do you draw away from me? Why must I run after you the whole day?

PRIMUS. It is you who run away from me, Helena.

HELENA. Your hair is mussed. I will smooth it. No one else feels to my touch as you do. Primus, I must make you beautiful, too. (PRIMUS *grasps her hand.*)

PRIMUS. Do you not sometimes feel your heart beating suddenly, Helena, and think: now something must happen?

HELENA. What could happen to us, Primus? (HELENA *puts a rose in* PRIMUS's *hair.* PRIMUS *and* HELENA *look into mirror and burst out laughing.*) Look at yourself.

ALQUIST. Laughter? Laughter? Human beings? (*Getting up.*) Who has returned? Who are you?

PRIMUS. The Robot Primus.

ALQUIST. What? A Robot? Who are you?

HELENA. The Robotess Helena.

ALQUIST. Turn around, girl. What? You are timid, shy? (*Taking her by the arm.*) Let me see you, Robotess.

(*She shrinks away.*)

PRIMUS. Sir, do not frighten her!

ALQUIST. What? You would protect her? When was she made?

PRIMUS. Two years ago.

ALQUIST. By Dr. Gall?

PRIMUS. Yes, like me.

ALQUIST. Laughter — timidity — protection. I must test you further — the newest of Gall's Robots. Take the girl into the dissecting room.

PRIMUS. Why?

ALQUIST. I wish to experiment on her.

PRIMUS. Upon — Helena?

ALQUIST. Of course. Don't you hear me? Or must I call someone else to take her in?

PRIMUS. If you do I will kill you!

ALQUIST. Kill me — kill me then! What would the Robots do then? What will your future be then?

PRIMUS. Sir, take me. I am made as she is — on the same day! Take my life, sir.

HELENA (*rushing forward*). No, no, you shall not! You shall not!

ALQUIST. Wait, girl, wait! (*To* PRIMUS.) Do you not wish to live, then?

PRIMUS. Not without her! I will not live without her.

ALQUIST. Very well; you shall take her place.

HELENA. Primus! Primus!   (*She bursts into tears.*)

ALQUIST. Child, child, you can weep! Why these tears? What is Primus to you? One Primus more or less in the world — what does it matter?

HELENA. I will go myself.

ALQUIST. Where?

HELENA. In there to be cut. *(She starts toward the dissecting room. Primus stops her.)* Let me pass, Primus! Let me pass!

PRIMUS. You shall not go in there, Helena!

HELENA. If you go in there and I do not, I will kill myself.

PRIMUS *(holding her)*. I will not let you! *(To ALQUIST.)* Man, you shall kill neither of us!

ALQUIST. Why?

PRIMUS. We — we — belong to each other.

ALQUIST *(almost in tears)*. Go, Adam, go, Eve. The world is yours.

> *(HELENA and PRIMUS embrace and go out arm in arm as the curtain falls.)*

BIBLIOGRAPHIES

BOOKS ON CONTINENTAL DRAMA

GENERAL SURVEYS

In English

CHANDLER, F. W., Aspects of Modern Drama (New York, 1914); Modern Continental Playwrights (New York, 1931); CLARK, B. H., The Continental Drama of To-day (New York, 1914); A Study of the Modern Drama (New York, 1928); DICKINSON, T. H., An Outline of Contemporary Drama (Boston, 1927); DUKES, A., Modern Dramatists (Chicago, 1912); HENDERSON, A., European Dramatists (New York, 1926); HUDDLESTON, S., Those Europeans; Studies in Foreign Faces (New York, 1924); HUNEKER, J. G., Iconoclasts, a Book of Dramatists (New York, 1912); GOLDBERG, I., The Drama of Transition (Cincinnati, 1922); JAMESON, S., The Modern Drama in Europe (New York, 1920); LEWISOHN, L., The Modern Drama (New York, 1915); PHELPS, W. L., Essays on Modern Dramatists (New York, 1921); VERNON, F., The Twentieth Century Theatre (Boston, 1924).

In German

ARNOLD, R. F., Das moderne Drama (Strassburg, 1908); BAB, J., Das Theater der Gegenwart (Leipzig, 1928); BUSSE, B., Das Drama (vol. 3, Leipzig, 1914); FREYHAN, M., Das Drama der Gegenwart (Berlin, 1922); KERR, A., Das neue Drama (Berlin, 1909); STEIGER, E., Das Werden des neueren Dramas (two vols., Berlin, 1898–1903); ZABEL, E., Zur modernen Dramaturgie (vol. 3, Oldenburg, 1903).

In Italian

RUBERTI, G., Il teatro contemporaneo in Europa (2 vols., Bologna, 1920–21); Storia del teatro contemporaneo (3 vols., Bologna, 1928); TILGHER, A., Studi sul teatro contemporaneo (Rome, 1923).

THEORY AND TECHNIQUE OF DRAMA

ANDREWS, C., The Technique of Playmaking (Springfield, Mass., 1915); ARCHER, W., The Old Drama and the New (Boston, 1923); Playmaking (New York, 1924); BAB, J., Schauspieler und Schauspielkunst (Berlin, 1926); BULTHAUPT, H. A., Dramaturgie des Schauspiels (4 vols., Oldenburg, 1918–24); CLARK, B. H., European Theories of the Drama (New York, 1925); FLEMMING, W., Das Wesen der Schauspielkunst (Rostock, 1927); FREYTAG, G., The Technique of the Drama (Chicago, 1900); PRICE, W. T., Analysis of Play Construction and Dramatic Principle (New York, 1908); Technique of the Drama (New York, 1892); NICOLL, A.,

An Introduction to Dramatic Theory (New York, 1924); SCHLAG, H., *Das Drama, Wesen, Theorie, und Technic* (Essen, 1909); STUART, D. C., *The Development of Dramatic Art* (New York, 1928).

THE ONE-ACT PLAY

GANNON, R. L., *The Technique of the One-Act Play* (New York, 1925); HILLEBRAND, H. N., *Writing the One-Act Play* (New York, 1925); LEWIS, R. B., *The Technique of the One-Act Play* (Boston, 1918); WILDE, P., *The Craftsmanship of the One-Act Play* (Boston, 1923).

STAGING AND THE ARTS OF THE THEATER

BAKSHY, A., *The Theatre Unbound* (London, 1923); CARTER, H., *The New Spirit in Drama and Art* (New York, 1913); CHENEY, S., *The Art Theatre* (New York, 1925); *Stage Decoration* (New York, 1928); COURNOS, J., *Gordon Craig and the Theatre of the Future* (London, 1913); CRAIG, G., *On the Art of the Theatre* (New York, 1925); *Scene* (London, 1923); *The Theatre — Advancing* (Boston, 1923); *Towards a New Theatre* (New York, 1913); FISCHEL, O., *Das moderne Bühnenbild* (Berlin, 1923); FLANAGAN, H., *Shifting Scenes* (New York, 1928); FUERST, W. R., and HUME, S. J., *Twentieth Century Stage Decoration* (London, 1928); GAMBLE, W. B., *The Development of Scenic Art and Stage Machinery: a List of References* (New York, 1928); HAGEMANN, C., *Moderne Bühnenkunst* (2 vols., Berlin, 1916–18); ISAACS, E. J. R., Editor, *Thirty-One Essays on the Arts of the Theatre* (New York, 1927); JONES, R. E., *Drawings for the Theatre* (New York, 1925); MACGOWAN, K., *The Theatre of Tomorrow* (New York, 1921); MACGOWAN, K., and ROSSE, H., *Masks and Demons* (New York, 1923); MACGOWAN, K., and JONES, R. E., *Continental Stagecraft* (New York, 1922); MODERWELL, H. K., *The Theatre of To-day* (New York, 1927); MOUSSINAC, L. C., *La décoration théâtrale* (Paris, 1922); ROUCHÉ, J., *L'Art theatral moderne* (Paris, 1924); SIMONSON, L., *The Stage is Set* (New York, 1932).

CONTINENTAL DRAMA AFTER THE WAR

CARTER, H., *The New Spirit in the European Theatre* (New York, 1926); DIEBOLD, B., *Anarchie im Drama* (Frankfort a. M., 1921); DUKES, A., *The Youngest Drama* (Chicago, 1924); EULENBERG, H., *Der Krieg und die Kunst* (Oldenburg, 1915); LAVRIN, Y., *Studies in European Literature* (London, 1929).

BOOKS ON THE NATURALISTIC MOVEMENT

BERG, L., *Der Naturalismus* (Berlin, 1892); BENOIST-HANAPPIER, L., *Le drame naturaliste en Allemagne* (Paris, 1905); BYTKOWSKI, S., *Gerhart Hauptmanns Naturalismus und das Drama* (Hamburg, 1908); DOELL, O., *Die Entwicklung der naturalistischen Form in Jungstdeutschen Drama* (Halle, 1910); FRIED, A., *Der Naturalismus; seine Entstehung und Berechtigung*

(Leipzig, 1890); ELLIS, H., *The New Spirit* (Boston, 1926); HOLZ, A., *Die Kunst, ihr Wesen und ihre Gesetze* (Berlin, 1891); STOECKIUS, A., *Naturalism in Recent German Drama* (New York, 1903); WITKOWSKI, G., *Naturalism in Recent German Drama* (New York, 1909); ZOLA, E., *Le naturalisme au théâtre; les théories et les examples* (Paris, 1898).

BOOKS ON FUTURISM, EXPRESSIONISM, AND NEWER MOVEMENTS

AMICO, S. d', *Il teatro dei Fantocci* (Florence, 1920); BAHR, H., *Expressionism*, translated by R. F. Gribble (London, 1925); DAHLSTROM, C., *August Strindberg, the Father of Dramatic Expressionism*, Michigan Academy of Science, Arts and Letters (Ann Arbor, 1929); *Strindberg's Dramatic Expressionism*, University of Michigan Publications in Language and Literature (Ann Arbor, 1930); DIEBOLD, B., *Anarchie im Drama* (Frankfort a. M., 1921); FECHTER, P., *Der Expressionismus* (Leipzig, 1919); FLORA, F., *Dal romanticismo al futurismo* (Milan, 1925); EDSCHMID, K., *Ueber den dichterischen Expressionismus* (Berlin, 1919); GOLDBERG, I., *The Drama of Transition* (Cincinnati, 1922); JELLIFFE, S. E., and BRINK, L., *Psychoanalysis and the Drama* (New York, 1922); PFISTER, O. R., *Expressionism in Art; its Psychological and Biological Basis* (translated, London, 1922); POUPEYE, C., *Les dramaturges exotiques* (Brussels, 1926); SCHNEIDER, M., *Expressionism in Drama* (Stuttgart, 1920); WALZEL, O., *Gerhart Hauptmann und der Expressionismus* (Preussiche Jahrbücher, Berlin, 1922).

GENERAL WORKS ON RECENT RUSSIAN DRAMA

CARTER, H., *The New Theatre and Cinema of Soviet Russia* (London, 1924); *The New Spirit in the Russian Theatre, 1917–1928* (London, 1929); GREGOR, J., and FÜLÖP-MILLER, R., *Das russische Theater* (Vienna, 1928); SAYLER, O. M., *The Russian Theatre* (New York, 1922); STANISLAVSKY, C., *My Life in Art* (Boston, 1927); WIENER, L., *The Contemporary Drama of Russia* (Boston, 1924).

GENERAL WORKS ON RECENT GERMAN DRAMA

ARNOLD, R. F., *Das deutsche Drama* (Munich, 1925); BAB, J., *Die Chronik des deutschen Dramas* (5 vols., Berlin, 1926); FREYHAN, M., *Das Drama der Gegenwart* (Berlin, 1922); FRIEDMANN, S., *Das deutsche Drama des 19 Jahrhunderts* (vol. 2, Leipzig, 1900–03); HELLER, O., *Studies in Modern German Literature* (Boston, 1905); HOLL, K., *Geschichte des deutschen Lustspiels* (Leipzig, 1923); KERR, A., *Gesammelte Schriften* (7 vols., Berlin, 1917–20); LAURET, R., *Le Théâtre allemande d'aujourdhui* (Paris, 1934).

GENERAL WORKS ON RECENT ITALIAN DRAMA

D'AMICO, S., *Il teatro italiano* (Milan, 1932); GORI, G., *Il teatro contemporaneo* (Torino, 1924); MACCLINTOCK, L., *The Contemporary Drama of*

Italy (Boston, 1923); PHELPS, R., *Italian Silhouettes* (New York, 1924); STARKIE, W., *Some Italian Dramatists of To-day* (*Nineteenth Century*, vol. 99); TONELLI, L., *L'Evoluzione del teatro contemporaneo in Italia* (Milan, 1908); *Il teatro Italiano dalle origini ai giorni nostri* (Milan, 1924).

GENERAL WORKS ON RECENT SPANISH DRAMA

BASTINOS, A. J., *Arte dramatico español contemporaneo* (Barcelona, 1914); BELL, A. F. G., *Contemporary Spanish Literature* (New York, 1925); BUENO, M., *Teatro español contemporaneo* (Madrid, 1909); FORD, J. D. M., *Main Currents in Spanish Literature* (New York, 1919); FRANCOS-RODRIGUEZ, J., *El teatro en espagna* (Madrid, 1909); GONZALES-BLANCO, A., *Los dramaturgos españoles contemporaneos* (Valencia, 1917); WARREN, L. A., *Modern Spanish Literature* (New York, 1929).

GENERAL WORKS ON RECENT FRENCH DRAMA

BENOIST, A., *Le théâtre d'aujourdhui* (2 vols., Paris, 1911–12); BORDEAUX, H., *La vie au théâtre*, 3d and 4th Series (Paris, 1913–19); BRISSON, A., *Le théâtre* (Paris, 1918); *Le théâtre pendant la guerre* (Paris, 1919); CAPUS, A., *Le théâtre* (Paris, 1913); CHANDLER, F. W., *The Contemporary Drama of France* (Boston, 1925); CLARK, B. H., *Contemporary French Dramatists* (Cincinnati, 1915); DOUMIC, R., *Le théâtre nouveau* (Paris, 1908); DUBECH, L., *Le théâtre, 1918–23* (Plon, 1925); FILON, A., *De Dumas à Rostand* (Paris, 1911); KAHN, A., *Le théâtre social en France de 1870 à nos jours* (Paris, 1907); LALOU, R., *Histoire de la littérature française* (Paris, 1923); MORTIER, A., *Dramaturgie de Paris* (Paris, 1917); SECHE, A., and BERTRAUT, J., *L'évolution de théâtre contemporain* (Paris, 1908); SEE, E., *Le théâtre français contemporain* (Paris, 1933); SMITH, H. A., *Main Currents of Modern French Drama* (New York, 1925); SOLVAY, L., *L'évolution théâtrale* (Brussels, 1922); THALASSO, A., *Le Théâtre-Libre* (Paris, 1909); WAXMAN, S. M., *Antoivne and the Théâtre-Libre* (Cambridge, Mass., 1924).

LEO N. TOLSTOY

MAUDE, A., *The Life of Tolstoy* (2 vols., New York, 1917); *Leo Tolstoy and his Works* (New York, 1931); NOYES, G. R., *Tolstoy* (New York, 1918); ROLLAND, R., *Tolstoy* (translated by B. Miall, New York, 1911); ALLERHAND, W., *Leo Tolstoy als Dramatiker* (Leipzig, 1927); BESNARD, L., *L'Œuvre dramatique de León Tolstoi* (*Revue d'Art Dramatique*, Paris, 1899); DUESEL, F., *Leo N. Tolstoi und seine Bühnenwerke* (Berlin, 1922); LEWINSKY, J., *Das russische Theater und Tolstoy* (*Deutsche Revue*, Stuttgart, 1899); KAUN, A., *Tolstoy and Andreyev* (*California University Chronicle*, Berkeley, 1924); *Tolstoy and Gorky* (*California University Chronicle*, Berkeley, 1930); TOLSTOY, L. N., *The Diaries of Leo Tolstoy* (translated by C. J. Hogarth and A. Sirnis, New York, 1917); *The Journal of Leo Tolstoy* (translated by Rose Strunsky, New York, 1917).

The Plays of Leo N. Tolstoy

Collected Editions in English

Plays by L. N. Tolstoy. Translated by L. and A. Maude (London, 1914). Contains *The Power of Darkness, The First Distiller, The Fruits of Culture, The Live Corpse, The Light that Shines in Darkness, The Root of all Evil.*

The Complete Dramas of Tolstoy. Translated by Nathan Haskell Dole (New York, 1923). Contains *The Power of Darkness, The First Distiller, The Fruits of Enlightenment, The Live Corpse, The Light that Shines in the Darkness, The Root of all Evil.*

Separate Plays of Leo N. Tolstoy

The First Distiller. Written 1886 for production in a Carnival booth. A dramatized version of his story *The Imp and the Crust.*

The Nihilist. Written 1863. Not performed. Printed in *Literary Fragments, Letters and Reminiscences,* New York, 1931.

The Infected Family. Written 1863. Not produced. Printed in *Literary Fragments, Letters, and Reminiscences,* New York, 1931, under the title of *The Progressives.*

The Power of Darkness. Written 1886. Privately performed 1887. Performed at the Théâtre Libre, Paris, February 18, 1888. Not performed in Russia until 1896.

The Fruits of Culture. Written 1889. Performed December, 1889, in the provinces; in Moscow and St. Petersburg, 1891. First translated under this title, 1891; translated as *The Fruits of Enlightenment,* 1901.

And a Light Shineth in the Darkness. Written 1888–1902. Posthumously printed. Translated by A. J. Wolfe, New York, 1920; also by H. Wright, New York, 1912.

The Living Corpse. Written about 1900. Posthumously printed. Translated by A. J. Wolfe, New York, 1920. Acted in England as *Reparation,* St. James's Theatre, London, 1919–20; in America as *Redemption.* Translated into French as *Le cadavre vivant,* 1911, by Minsky; into German as *Der lebende Leichnam,* by A. Scholtz, Berlin, 1911; into English by E. M. Evarts, Philadelphia, 1912; also translated as *The Man Who Was Dead,* New York, 1912.

The Cause of it All. Posthumously printed. Also known as *The Root of all Evil.* Translated by H. Wright, 1911.

MAURICE MAETERLINCK

BAILLY, A., *Maeterlinck* (translated by F. Rothwell, London, 1931); BITHELL, J., *Life and Writings of Maurice Maeterlinck* (London, 1930); CLARK, M., *Maurice Maeterlinck, Poet and Philosopher* (London, 1915); COURTNEY, W. L., *The Development of Maurice Maeterlinck, and other Sketches* (London, 1904); HARRY, G., *Maurice Maeterlinck* (Brussels, 1909; translated by A. Allinson, London, 1910); LEBLANC, G., *Souvenirs,*

(New York, 1932); ROSE, H., *On Maeterlinck* (London, 1911); *Maeterlinck's Symbolism* (New York, 1911); SYMONS, A., *The Symbolist Movement in Literature* (New York, 1917); TAYLOR, U., *Maurice Maeterlinck, a Critical Study* (London, 1914); THOMAS, E., *Maurice Maeterlinck* (London, 1911); CARRE, J.-M., *Maeterlinck et les littératures étrangères* (*Revue de littérature comparée*, Paris, 1926); LENEVEU, G., *Ibsen et Maeterlinck* (Paris, 1902); MIRBEAU, O., *Les Écrivains* (1st Series, Paris, 1926); NEWMAN, E., *Musical Studies* (London, 1914); POIZAT, A., *Le Symbolisme de Baudelaire à Claudel* (*Renaissance de Livre*, Paris, 1919).

THE PLAYS OF MAURICE MAETERLINCK

La Princesse Maleine, a play in five acts, was published 1889, and produced in 1890. Translated by Richard Hovey, Chicago, 1894.

Les Aveugles, a play in one act, was published in 1890, and produced in 1891. First translated into English in 1891 by Richard Hovey, Chicago, 1894.

L'Intruse, a play in one act, was published in 1890, and produced in 1891. First translated into English in 1891 by Richard Hovey.

Les Sept Princesses, a play in one act, was published in 1891, and produced in 1893. Translated by Richard Hovey, Chicago, 1894.

Pelléas et Mélisande, a lyric drama in five acts, was published in 1892, and produced May 16, 1893, at Paris. With incidental music by Claude Debussy it was produced at the Opéra Comique, Paris, April 30, 1902; it holds a place in the repertory of the Metropolitan Opera House, New York. Translated by Richard Hovey, Chicago, 1894.

Alladine et Palomides was published at Brussels, 1894, and produced in 1895. Translated by Richard Hovey, Chicago, 1896.

L'Intérieur, a play in one act, was published in 1894, produced March 15, 1895. It was presented at the Comédie Française, 1919. Translated by Richard Hovey, Chicago, 1896.

Le Mort de Tintagiles. First published in 1894. Translated by Richard Hovey, Chicago, 1896; has been set to music by Jean Nouguès.

Annabella (from John Ford's *'Tis Pity She's a Whore*) was produced at Paris, November 6, 1894. Published 1895.

Aglavaine et Sélysette, a play in three acts, was published at Paris, 1894, and produced 1896. The English translation was made in 1903.

Ariane et Barbe Bleue, ou La délivrance inutile, was first published in 1901. With music by Paul Dukas it was produced at the Opéra Comique, Paris, March, 1907.

Sœur Béatrice, a miracle in three acts, was published in 1901, and produced in 1910. It was translated into German in 1900.

Monna Vanna, a play in three acts, was published in 1902, produced May 7, 1902. Translated into English, 1907. Produced in America, 1907. Has been set to music by Henry Fevrier.

Joyzelle, a play in five acts, was published in 1903, produced May 20, 1903. Translated into English, 1905.

L'Oiseau Bleu. Translated by A. Teixeira de Mattos, 1909; with additional act, 1912.

Macbeth. Translated from Shakespeare. Published, 1909.

Marie Madeleine, play in three acts, was published in 1913, produced May 28, 1913. Translated as *Mary Magdalen* by A. Teixeira de Mattos and published 1910.

Le Bourgmestre de Stilmonde, a play in three acts, published in 1919; translated into English by de Mattos in 1918.

Le sel de la vie, a sketch in two acts, was published in 1921.

Les fiançailles, a fairy play in five acts and eleven scenes, a sequel to *The Blue Bird,* was published in 1921; translated as *The Betrothal,* 1918, by A. T. de Mattos, and produced in New York, 1918, and London, 1921, under the direction of Granville Barker.

Le miracle de Saint Antoine, a farce in two acts, was first produced in Geneva in 1903. Published first in German; in English translation by A. T. de Mattos in 1918. Published in French in 1919.

The Cloud that Lifted, published in translation by F. M. Atkinson, New York, 1923. Not published in French.

The Power of the Dead, published in translation by F. M. Atkinson, New York, 1923. Not published in French.

Berniquel, published 1923.

Marie Victoire, published 1929.

Juda de Kerioth, published 1929.

GERHART HAUPTMANN

Bibliographies. PINKUS, M., and LUDWIG, V., *Gerhart Hauptmann: Werke von ihm und über ihn* (Neustadt, 1920); REQUARDT, W., *Gerhart Hauptmann Bibliographie* (Berlin, 1931).

Life and Work. BAB, J., *Gerhart Hauptmann und seine besten Bühnenwerke* (Berlin, 1922); BARTELS, A., *Gerhart Hauptmann* (Weimar, 1897); CHAPIRO, J., *Gespräche mit Gerhart Hauptmann* (Berlin, 1932); FECHTER, P., *Gerhart Hauptmann* (Dresden, 1922); HOLL, K., *Gerhart Hauptmann; his Life and Work* (London, 1913); SCHLENTHER, P., and ELOESSER, A., *Gerhart Hauptmann; Leben und Werke* (Berlin, 1922); STERNBERG, K., *Gerhart Hauptmann* (Berlin, 1910).

Criticism. BYTKOWSKI, S., *Gerhart Hauptmanns Naturalismus und das Drama* (*Beiträge zur Aesthetik,* Hamburg and Leipzig, 1908); GLASCOCK, C. C., *Environment and Hero in Gerhart Hauptmann's Plays* (*Archiv für den Studium der neueren Sprachen und Litteratur,* Braunschweig, 1909); HEUSER, F. W. J., *Early Influences in the Intellectual Development of Gerhart Hauptmann* (*Germanic Review,* Lancaster, Pa., 1929); QUIMBY, M. A., *The Nature Background in the Drama of Gerhart Hauptmann* (*German-American Annals,* Philadelphia, 1919); REICHART, W. A., *Hauptmann before Vor Sonnenaufgang* (*Journal of English and Germanic Philology,* Urbana, Ill., 1929); ROEHR, J., *Gerhart Hauptmanns Dramatisches Schaffen* (Dresden, 1912); SCHOLZ, K. W. H., *The Art of Translation* (Philadelphia, 1918).

The Plays of Gerhart Hauptmann

Vor Sonnenaufgang. Produced 1889. Translated as *Before Dawn*, 1909, by Leonard Bloomfield; also by Ludwig Lewisohn, New York, 1912.

Das Friedensfest. Produced 1890. Translated as *The Coming of Peace, a Family Catastrophe*, by Janet Achurch and C. E. Wheeler, 1900; as *The Reconciliation* by R. T. House, 1910.

Einsame Menschen. Produced 1891. Translated as *Lonely Lives* by Mary Morison; also by William Archer.

College Crampton. Produced 1892. Translated as *Colleague Crampton* by R. T. House.

Die Waber. Produced 1893. First written in Silesian dialect; translated into German as *Die Weber* by the author. Translated as *The Weavers* by M. Morison, London, 1911; also by William Archer. Produced as *Les Tisserands* by the Théâtre Libre in translation by Jean Thorel, 1893. Produced at the Irving Place Theater, New York, 1905.

Der Biberpelz; eine Diebskomödie. Produced 1893. Translated as *The Beaver Coat* by Ludwig Lewisohn, New York, 1912.

Hanneles Himmelfahrt. Produced 1893. Translated as *Hannele, a Dream Play*, by William Archer, 1894; as *The Assumption of Hannele*, by C. H. Meltzer, 1894; by G. S. Bryan, 1909.

Florian Geyer. Produced 1896. Translated by B. Q. Morgan.

Die versunkene Glocke. Produced 1896. Translated as *The Sunken Bell, a Fairy Play*, by C. H. Meltzer, 1899; also by Mary Harned, 1898.

Fuhrmann Henschel. Produced 1898. Translated as *Drayman Henschel* by Ludwig Lewisohn, 1914.

Das Hirtenlied. A fragment. Published, 1898. Translated by Ludwig Lewisohn.

Helios. A fragment. Published 1899. Translated by Ludwig Lewisohn.

Schluck und Jau. Produced 1900. Translated under the same title, as "an ironic masque with five interruptions" by Ludwig Lewisohn, 1919.

Michael Kramer. Produced 1900. Translated by Ludwig Lewisohn, 1914.

Der rote Hahn. Produced 1901. Translated as *The Conflagration* by Ludwig Lewisohn, 1914.

Der arme Heinrich. Produced and published 1902. Translated as *Henry of Auë* by Ludwig Lewisohn, 1912.

Rose Bernd. Produced 1903. Translated by Ludwig Lewisohn, 1914.

Elga. Produced and published 1905. Translated by Mary Harned, 1906; also by Ludwig Lewisohn.

Und Pippa tanzt. Produced and published 1907. Translated as *And Pippa Dances* by Mary Harned, 1907; also by Sarah Tracy Barrows, 1919.

Die Jungfrau von Bischofsberg. Published 1907. Translated as *The Maiden of the Mount* by Ludwig Lewisohn, 1922.

Kaiser Karls Geisel, ein Legendenspiel. Published 1908. Translated as *Charlemagne's Hostage* by Ludwig Lewisohn.

Griselda. Published 1909.

Die Ratten, Berliner Tragikomödie. Produced 1911. Translated as *The Rats* by Ludwig Lewisohn, 1912.

Gabriel Schillings Flucht. Published 1912.

Festspiel in Deutschen Reimen. Produced and published 1913. Translated as *Commemoration Masque on the Wars of Liberation* by B. C. Morgan, 1922.

Der Bogen des Odysseus. Published 1914. Translated as *The Bow of Odysseus* by Ludwig Lewisohn, 1922.

Winterballade, a dramatic poem, published 1917. Translated as *A Winter Ballade* by Willa and Edwin Muir.

Der weisse Heiland, a dramatic fantasy, published 1920. Translated as *The White Saviour* by Willa and Edwin Muir.

Peter Brauer; a tragicomedy. Published 1921.

Indipohdi. Published 1921. Translated by Willa and Edwin Muir.

Dorothea Angermann, a play in five acts. Published 1926.

Veland, a tragedy in three acts. Published 1925. Translated by Edwin Muir.

Der Baum von Gallowayshire. Spoken at the opening of the Heidelberg Festival, 1928.

Hexenritt; ein Satyrspiel. Published 1930.

Spuk; die schwartze Maske. One act. Published 1931.

Vor Sonnenuntergang. Produced 1932. Translated as *Before Sunset* and produced in London, 1933.

Die goldene Harfe. Produced 1933.

See *The Dramatic Works of Gerhart Hauptmann* (authorized edition) edited by Ludwig Lewisohn, New York, 1912–29, 9 volumes.

ARTHUR SCHNITZLER

Kapp, J., *Arthur Schnitzler* (Leipzig, 1912); Kappstein, T. H., *Arthur Schnitzler une seine besten Bühnenwerke* (Berlin, 1922); Landsberg, H., *Arthur Schnitzler* (Berlin, 1904); Liptzin, S., *Arthur Schnitzler* (New York, 1932); Reik, T., *Arthur Schnitzler als Psycholog* (Minden, 1913); Salkind, A., *Arthur Schnitzler, eine kritische Studie* (Berlin, 1907).

The Plays of Arthur Schnitzler

Anatol. Sequence of one-act plays. Produced 1889–91; published 1893. Adapted by H. Granville-Barker, 1911. Translated by G. I. Colbron, New York, 1917.

Das Märchen. Produced 1891; published 1894.

Paracelsus. Produced 1892; published 1899. Translated by H. B. Samuel, London, 1913.

Liebelei. Produced 1894; published 1896. Translated as *Light-o'-Love* by B. Q. Morgan, Chicago, 1912; as *Playing with Love* by P. M. Shand, London, 1914.

Freiwild. Produced 1896; published 1897.

Reigen (Dialogues). Published 1903.

Das Vermächtnis. Produced 1897; published 1898. Translated as *The Legacy*, 1911.

Die Gefährtin (one act). Published 1898; produced 1899.

Der grüne Kakadu (one act). Published 1898; produced 1899. Translated as *The Green Cockatoo* by H. B. Samuel, 1913; by G. I. Colbron, New York, 1917.

Der Schleier der Beatrice. Produced 1899; published 1900.

Die Frau mit dem Dolche (one act). Produced 1900; published 1902. Translated as *The Lady with the Dagger* by H. T. Porter, 1904; G. I. Colbron, New York, 1917.

Lebendige Stunden (one act). Produced 1901; published 1902. Translated as *Living Hours* by H. T. Porter, Boston, 1906; G. I. Colbron, New York, 1917.

Die letzten Masken (one act). Produced 1901; published 1902. Translated as *Last Masks* by G. I. Colbron, New York, 1917.

Literatur (one act). Produced 1902; published 1906. Translated as *Literature* by G. I. Colbron, New York, 1914.

Der Puppenspieler (one act). Produced 1902; published 1906.

Der tapfere Cassian. Produced 1903; published 1903. Translated as *Gallant Cassian* by A. L. Gowans, London, 1914.

Der einsame Weg. Produced 1903; published 1904. Translated as *The Lonely Way* by E. Bjorkman, New York, 1915.

Zum grossen Wurstel. Produced 1904; published 1906.

Die griechische Tänzerin. Produced 1904; published 1904.

Zwischenspiel. Produced 1904; published 1905. Translated as *Intermezzo* by E. Bjorkman, New York, 1915.

Der Ruf des Lebens. Produced 1905; published 1906.

Dämmerseelen. Produced 1907; published 1908.

Komtesse Mizzi. Produced 1909; published 1909. Translated as *Countess Mizzie* by E. Bjorkman, New York, 1915.

Der junge Medardus. Produced 1909; published 1910.

Das weite Land. Produced 1910; published 1911. Translated as *The Vast Domain* by E. Woticky and A. Caro, *Poet Lore*, 1923.

Professor Bernhardi. Produced 1912; published 1912. Adapted by E. Pohli, San Francisco, 1913.

Frau Beate und ihr Sohn. Produced and published 1913.

Die Stunde des Erkennens. Produced and published 1915. Translated as *The Hour of Recognition.*

Die grosse Szene. Published and produced 1915.

Das Bacchusfest. Published and produced 1915.

Fink und Fliederbusch. Published and produced 1917.

Die Schwestern. Published and produced 1918.

Komödie der Verführung. Published and produced 1924.

Der Gang zum Weiher. Published and produced 1926.

GABRIELE D'ANNUNZIO

Bibliography. MEDICI, G. de, *Bibliographia de Gabriele d'Annunzio* (Rome, 1929).

Life and Work. BEER, Mme. G., *Essai sur Gabriele d'Annunzio* (Paris, 1925); BORGESE, G. A., *Gabriele d'Annunzio* (Naples, 1909); BRUERS, A., *Gabriele d'Annunzio e il moderno spirito* (Rome, 1921); GARGIULO, A., *Gabriele d'Annunzio, Storia Critica* (Naples, 1912); PASINI, F., *Gabriele d'Annunzio* (Rome, 1925).

Criticism. BRAINERD, G. G., *The Paola and Francesca Theme in Modern Drama* (*Poet Lore*, 1916); GHEON, H., *Nos directions: réalisme et poesie* (Paris, 1911); HERFORD, C. H., *Shakespeare's Treatment of Love and Marriage, and other Essays* (London, 1921); MARINETTI, F. T., *Le théâtre de Gabriele d'Annunzio* (*La Revue d'Art Dramatique*, Paris, 1901); METCALF, J. C., *An Old Romantic Triangle* (*Sewanee Review*, 1921); NARDELLI, F., and LIVINGSTON, A., *Gabriele the Archangel* (New York, 1931); SHARP, W., *The Dramas of Gabriele d'Annunzio* (*Fortnightly Review*, London, 1900); SYMONS, A., *Francesca da Rimini* (*Fortnightly Review*, London, 1902); Introduction to translation of *Francesca da Rimini* (New York, 1902); *Studies in Prose and Verse* (New York, 1923); WHARTON, E., *Three Francescas* (*North American Review*, July, 1902).

THE PLAYS OF GABRIELE D'ANNUNZIO

Il sogno d'un mattino di primavera. Published 1897. Translated as *A Dream of a Spring Morning* by Anna Schenck, *Poet Lore*, 1902.

Il sogno d'un tramonto d'autunno. Published 1898. Translated as *A Dream of an Autumn Sunset,* by Anna Schenck, *Poet Lore*, 1904.

La città morta. Published and produced 1898. Translated as *The Dead City* by G. Martinelli, 1900, and by A. Symons, 1902.

La Gioconda. Published and produced 1898. Translated as *Gioconda* by Arthur Symons, 1901.

La Gloria. Published and produced 1900.

Francesca da Rimini. Published and produced 1901. Translated by Arthur Symons, 1902.

La figlia di Jorio. Published and produced 1904. Translated as *The Daughter of Jorio* by C. Porter, P. Isola and A. Henry, *Poet Lore*, 1907.

La fiaccola sotto il moggio. Published and produced 1905.

Più che l'amore. Published and produced 1907.

La nave. Published and produced 1908. Translated as *The Ship*, *Poet Lore*, 1909.

Fedra. Published and produced 1909.

Le martyre de Saint Sébastien. First written in French. Published and produced 1911. Libretto for music of Claude Debussy.

La Pisanelle. First written in French. Published and produced 1913. Libretto for music of Pietro Mascagni.

Parisine. Published and produced 1913.

La chèvrefeuille. Written in French; translated into Italian as *Il ferro.* Published and produced 1913. Translated as *The Honeysuckle* by C. Sartoris and G. Enthoven, 1915.

Cabiria. Written for the cinematograph. Produced 1914.

Amaranta. Published and produced 1914.

La Piave. Published and produced 1918. Written for the music of Italo Montemezzo.

ANTON CHEKHOV

Bibliography. HEIFETZ, A., *Bibliography of Chekhov's Works translated into English* (Bulletin of Bibliography, 1929).

Life and Work. CHEKHOV, A., *The Notebooks of Anton Chekhov, with Reminiscences by M. Gorky* (translated by S. S. Koteliansky and L. Woolf, Richmond, England, 1921); *The Letters of Anton Chekhov to Olga Knipper* (translated by C. Garnett, New York, 1925); *Letters of Anton Chekhov to his Family and Friends* (translated by C. Garnett, London, 1920); *Letters on the Short Story, the Drama, and other Literary Topics* (selected and edited by L. S. Friedland, London and New York, 1924); CHEKHOV, O. K., *The Last Phase, a Description by his Wife* (Bermondsey Book, London, 1925); DUESEL, F., *Maxim Gorky and Anton Chekhov* (Berlin, 1922); GERHARDI, W., *Anton Chekhov, a Critical Study* (New York, 1923); KOTELIANSKY, S. S., *Anton Chekhov, Literary and Theatrical Reminiscences* (London, 1927); KOTELIANSKY, S. S., and TOMLINSON, P., *The Life and Letters of Anton Chekhov* (New York, 1925); STANISLAVSKY, C., *My Life in Art* (Boston, 1927).

Criticism. BARING, M., *The Plays of Anton Chekhov* (*New Quarterly*, London, 1908); CALDERON, G., Introduction to translation of two plays (London, 1912); GARNETT, C., *Chekhov and his Art* (*Quarterly Review*, New York, 1921); NABOKOFF, C., *Chekhov and his Plays* (*Contemporary Review*, New York, 1924); TELL, M., *Introduction to Plays by Anton Chekhov* (vol. 1, New York, 1912); WEST, J., *Introduction to Plays by Anton Chekhov* (vol. 2, New York, 1916).

THE PLAYS OF ANTON CHEKHOV

The High Road. Written 1884. Discovered 1915. Translated as *On the Highway* by D. A. Modell, 1916. Translated by C. Garnett, London, 1923.

The Swan Song. Written 1886. Published 1889. *A Swan Song,* translated by Constance Garnett, London, 1923.

Ivanoff. Produced 1889. Translated by Marian Fell, New York, 1923; C. Garnett, London, 1923.

The Proposal (one act). 1889. Translated as *The Marriage Proposal* by B. H. Clark, 1914.

The Wood Demon (early form of *Uncle Vanya*). Produced 1889. Translated by S. S. Koteliansky, New York, 1925.

The Boor (The Bear). 1890. Translated by B. H. Clark, 1915.

The Sea Gull. Produced and published 1896. Translated by I. F. Hapgood, New York, 1905; Fred Eisemann, Boston, 1913; Julius West, London, 1915.

The Tragedian in Spite of Himself. Written 1890. Translated in *Poet Lore*, 1922.

Uncle Vanya. Produced 1898 in provinces, 1899 in Moscow. Translated in *Poet Lore*, 1922; Moscow Art Theatre Series, 1923.

The Three Sisters. Written 1900. Produced 1901. Translated by Constance Garnett, London, 1923; in Moscow Art Theatre Series, New York, 1923; in Civic Repertory Plays, 1928.

The Cherry Orchard (The Cherry Garden). Written 1903, produced 1904. Translated by M. S. Mandell, New Haven, 1908; George Calderon, New York, 1912; by Jenny Covan, Moscow Art Theatre Series, 1922; and by Constance Garnett, London, 1923.

The Tobacco Evil. Translated in *Theatre Arts Magazine*, New York, 1922.

Tatyana Riepin (in one act). Translated by S. S. Koteliansky in *London Mercury*, 1925.

That Worthless Fellow Platanov. Translated by John Cournos, New York, 1930.

The Unwilling Martyr. Translated by C. Garnett, London, 1923.

The Anniversary (The Jubilee). Translated by C. Garnett, London, 1923.

The Wedding. Translated by C. Garnett, London, 1923.

The Plays of Anton Chekhov. Series I. Translated by Marian Fell. London and New York, 1912. Contains *Uncle Vanya, Ivanoff, The Sea Gull, The Swan Song.*

The Plays of Anton Chekhov. Series II. Translated by Julius West. London and New York, 1916. Contains *On the High Road, The Proposal, The Wedding, The Bear, The Tragedian in Spite of Himself, The Anniversary, The Three Sisters, The Cherry Orchard.*

The Three Sisters and Other Plays. Translated by Constance Garnett. London, 1923. Contains *The Three Sisters, Ivanov, A Swan Song, An Unwilling Martyr, The Anniversary, On the High Road, The Wedding.*

THE BROTHERS ÁLVAREZ QUINTERO

Douglas, G., *The Plays of the Brothers Álvarez Quintero (Quarterly Review,* New York, 1919); Mérimée E., *Le théâtre des Álvarez Quinteros (Bulletin Hispanique,* 1926); Granville-Barker, H. G., Introductions to *Four Plays* (London, 1927), and *Four Comedies* (New York, 1932).

THE PLAYS OF THE BROTHERS QUINTERO

Early Short Plays

El ojito derecho. 1897.
La buena sombra. 1898.
El chiquillo. 1899.

El trage de luces. 1899.
El patio. 1900.
La azotea. 1901.
Los piropos. 1902.
Abanicos y panderetas. 1902.
El nuevo servidor. 1905.
Mañana de sol. 1905. Translated as *A Bright Morning* by C. C. Castillo
  and E. L. Overman, *Poet Lore*, 1916.
Sangre gorda. 1909.

Longer Plays

Los galeotes. 1900.
El nido. 1901.
Las flores. 1901.
La pena. 1901. Translated as *Grief* in *Poet Lore*, 1930.
La dicha ajena. 1902.
Pepita Reyes. 1903.
El amor que pasa. 1904. Translated as *Love Passes By* by H. and Harley
  Granville-Barker, New York, 1932.
La musa loca. 1905. Translated as *Don Abel Wrote a Tragedy* by H. and H.
  Granville-Barker, New York, 1932.
El genio alegre. 1906.
La mala sombra. 1906.
La vida que vuelve. 1907.
Las de caín. 1908.
La escondida senda. 1908. Translated as *Peace and Quiet* by H. and H.
  Granville-Barker, New York, 1932.
Amor y Amoríos. 1908.
Doña Clarines. 1909. Translated by H. and H. Granville-Barker,
  London, 1932.
El centenario. 1909. Translated as *A Hundred Years Old* by H. and H.
  Granville-Barker, London, 1927; as *Papa Juan, or the Centenarian*, by
  C. A. Turrell, 1918.
La flor de la vida. 1910. Translated as *The Fountain of Youth* by S. N.
  Baker, Cincinnati, 1922.
Puebla de las mujeres. 1912. Translated as *The Women Have Their Way* by
  H. and H. Granville-Barker, London, 1927.
Sábado sin sol. 1912.
Malvaloca. 1912. Translated by J. S. Fassett, New York, 1916.
Nina teruel. 1913.
La consulesa. 1914. Translated as *The Lady from Alfaqueque* by H. and H.
  Granville-Barker, London, 1927.
Dios dira. 1915.
Así se escribe la historia. 1917.
La columniada. 1919.
Febrerillo el loco. 1919.

La prisa. 1921.
Cristaline. 1922.
Las vueltas que de el mundo. 1922.
Concha la limpia. 1923.
La boda de quinita flores. 1925.
Cancionera. 1926.
La cuestión es pasar el rato. 1927.
Los duendes de Sevilla. 1929.
Rondalla. 1929.
Madresilva. 1931.

See *Four Plays by S. and J. Álvarez Quintero,* translated by Helen and Harley Granville-Barker, London, 1927. Contains *The Women Have Their Way; A Hundred Years Old; Fortunato; The Lady from Alfaqueque.*

See *Four Comedies by S. and J. Álvarez Quintero,* translated by Helen and Harley Granville-Barker, New York, 1932. Contains *Love Passes By; Don Abel Wrote a Tragedy; Peace and Quiet; Doña Clarines.*

FERENC MOLNAR

RITTENBERG, L., Introduction to *The Plays of Ferenc Molnar,* with Preface by David Belasco (New York, 1929); BARTA, J., *Franz Molnár als Dramatiker* (Forschungsarbeiten der Mitglieder des Ungarischen Instituts, Berlin, 1927); STAGNELL, G., *A Psychopathological Review of Molnar's Liliom (Psychoanalytic Review,* 1922).

THE PLAYS OF MOLNAR

A Doktor Ur (The Lawyer). Produced 1902.

Jozsi. Produced 1904.

Az Ördög. Published and produced 1907. Translated as *The Devil* by Oliver Herford, New York, 1908; also by Adriaan Schade van Westrum under the same title. Both produced in New York, 1908.

Liliom. Published and produced 1909. Produced in Hungary and Austria simultaneously. The English text by Benjamin F. Glazer produced by the Theater Guild, April 20, 1921.

A Testör. Published and produced 1913 in Hungary. First produced in America as *Where Ignorance is Bliss.* In an adaptation by G. I. Colbron and Hans Bartsch produced as *The Guardsman* by The Theater Guild, 1924.

A Farkas. Published and produced 1914 in Hungary. Translated and produced as *The Phantom Rival* in 1914. Translated by Melville Baker as *The Tale of the Wolf* and published 1929.

Uridivat. Published and produced 1914 in Hungary. Translated by Benjamin Glazer as *Fashions for Men* and produced in America, 1922.

A Feher-Felhö. Published and produced 1915 in Hungary. Translated as *The White Cloud* by Louis Rittenberg, New York, 1929.

Farsang. Published and produced 1916. Translated by Melville Baker as *Carnival* and produced in America, 1924.

A Hattyu. Published and produced 1919. Translated by Benjamin Glazer as *The Swan* and produced in New York, 1923.

Egi es Földi Szerelem. Published and produced 1920. Adapted as *Heavenly and Earthly Love* by Edna St. V. Millay and produced in New York, 1923.

A Vörös Malom. Published and produced 1924 (The Red Mill). Adapted by David Belasco as *Mimi* and produced 1928.

Üvegcipo. Published and produced 1922. Adapted by Philip Moeller as *The Glass Slipper* and produced 1925.

Játék a Kastélyban. Published and produced 1924. Adapted by P. G. Wodehouse as *The Play's the Thing* and produced in America 1926.

Csendélet. Published and produced 1925. Translated as *Still Life* by S. J. Greenberger, published New York, 1929.

Riviera. Published and produced 1926. Translated by F. E. Faragoh and published New York, 1929.

Olympia. Published and produced 1927. An adaptation by Sidney Howard was produced 1928.

Valaki. Published and produced 1932. Translated by Jane Hinton as *The Good Fairy* and published and produced New York, 1932. See also *Husbands and Lovers*, 19 Dialogues translated by Benjamin Glazer, New York, 1924; see *The Plays of Ferenc Molnár*, with a Foreword by David Belasco, New York, 1929.

PAUL CLAUDEL

Bibliography. BENOIST-MÉCHIN, J. G. P. M., and BLAIZOT, G., *Bibliographie des œuvres de Paul Claudel* (Paris, 1931).

Life and Work. CHAMPAGNE, P., *Sur Paul Claudel* (Louvain, 1914); DE TONQUÉDEC, J., *L'œuvre de Paul Claudel* (Paris, 1917); DUHAMEL, G., *Paul Claudel, le philosophe, le poète, l'écrivain, le dramaturge* (Paris, 1913); *Paul Claudel, suivi de propos critiques* (Paris, 1919); PERRIN, E. S–M., *Introduction a l'œuvre de Paul Claudel* (Paris, 1926); *M. Paul Claudel* (*Revue des deux mondes*, 1914).

Criticism. BATEMAN, M., *Paul Claudel* (*Fortnightly Review*, 1919); CARRIÈRE, J. M., *La jeune fille Violaine. The Evolution of the Theme* (*Romanic Review*, 1930); CHATTERTON-HILL, G., *Paul Claudel* (*Fortnightly Review*, 1914); CLAUDEL, P., *Le drame et la musique* (*Revue de Paris*, 1930); *Positions et Propositions; art et littérature* (Paris, 1928); CURTIS, E. R., *Die literarischen Wegbereiter des neuen Frankreich* (Potsdam, 1920); DOWNS, B. W., *Paul Claudel* (*Fortnightly Review*, 1924); HATZFELD, H., *Paul Claudel und Romain Rolland* (Munich, 1921); LASSÈRRE, P., *Les chape'les littéraires* (Paris, 1920); LEFÈVRE, F., *Les sources de Paul Claudel* (Paris, 1927); MURRY, J. M., *The Works of Paul Claudel* (*Quarterly Review*, New York, 1917); POIZAT, A., *Le symbolisme de Baudelaire a Claudel* (*Renaissance de Livre*, Paris, 1919).

THE PLAYS OF PAUL CLAUDEL

Fragment d'une drame. *Revue indépendante*, May, 1892. Anonymous.

Tête d'or. Published 1890; another version published 1901.

L'Echange, a play in three acts. Published 1901. Produced 1914.

La ville. Published 1893; another version published 1901. Translated as *The City* by J. S. Newberry, 1920.

La jeune fille Violaine. Written 1892; published 1901.

Le repos du septième jour. Published 1902.

L'Otage, a play in three acts. Published 1911. Produced December 12, 1912. Translated as *The Hostage* by Pierre Chavannes, New Haven, 1917.

L'Annonce faite à Marie. Mystery in four acts and a Prologue. Published 1912; other editions 1917; 1929. Produced December 24, 1912. Translated by Louise Morgan Sill, London and New Haven, 1916.

La nuit de Noël de 1914, a play in one act. Published 1915.

Le pain dur, a play in three acts. Published 1918.

L'Ours et la lune, a farce for a theater of marionettes. Published 1919; reprinted 1927.

Le père humilie, a play in four acts. Published 1920.

Protée, satiric drama in two acts. Published, 1920. Translated as *Proteus* by J. S. Newberry in Broom, Rome, 1921, 1922.

Le livre de Christophe Colomb. Published 1929. Translated as *The Book of Christopher Columbus*, lyrical drama in two parts, New Haven, 1930.

Le soulier de satin. Published 1924. Translated as *The Satin Slipper; or, The Worst is Not the Surest*, by Reverend J. O'Connor, London, and New Haven, 1931.

Claudel also translated *The Agamemnon* of Æschylus, and *The Eumenides* of Æschylus.

KAREL ČAPEK

BAUMEL, M. F., *Une conversation avec M. Karel Čapek* (*Annales politiques et littéraires* (Paris, July 1, 1924); ČAPEK, K., *How a Play is Produced* (illustrated by J. Čapek, London, 1928); HEAD, C., *See Prague* (*Theatre Arts Magazine*, October, 1924); JELINEK, H., *Tchecoslovaquie. L'œuvre de M. Karel Čapek* (*Revue de Genève*, Geneva, 1924).

PLAYS BY THE BROTHERS KAREL ČAPEK AND JOSEF ČAPEK

And So ad Infinitum (*The Life of the Insects*). An entomological review in three acts, a prologue and epilogue. Translated by Paul Selver; adapted by Nigel Playfair and Clifford Bax. London, 1923. Called in American production *The World We Live In.* Produced New York, 1922.

Adam the Creator, comedy in six scenes and an epilogue. Published and produced in Prague, 1927. Translated by Dora Round, London, 1929. Reprinted in Moses, *Dramas of Modernism*, Boston, 1931.

PLAY BY JOSEF ČAPEK

The Land of Many Names, a play in three acts and a transformation. Translated by Paul Selver, London, 1926.

PLAYS BY KAREL ČAPEK

The Brigand, a comedy in three scenes. 1920.

The Makropoulos Secret. Adapted by Randall C. Burrell. Boston, 1925. Produced New York, 1926.

R. U. R. (*Rossum's Universal Robots*), in three acts and an epilogue. Translated by Paul Selver; adapted by Nigel Playfair. Published, London, 1923. Produced by the Theater Guild, October 9, 1922.